PLANE IMAGE

PLANE IMAGE

A Brice Marden Retrospective

Gary Garrels

THE MUSEUM OF MODERN ART, NEW YORK

Published in conjunction with the exhibition *Brice Marden: A Retrospective of Paintings and Drawings*, organized by Gary Garrels at The Museum of Modern Art, New York, October 29, 2006–January 15, 2007. The exhibition travels to the San Francisco Museum of Modern Art, February 17–May 13, 2007, and the Nationalgalerie im Hamburger Bahnhof–Museum für Gegenwart–Berlin, Staatliche Museen zu Berlin, June 12–October 7, 2007

The exhibition is made possible by Lehman Brothers.

Major support is provided by the Mimi and Peter Haas Fund.

Additional generous funding is provided by The Henry Luce Foundation and by Jerry and Emily Spiegel.

Produced by the Department of Publications,
The Museum of Modern Art, New York

Edited by David Frankel
Designed by The Grenfell Press
Production by Marc Sapir
Printed and bound by Trifolio S.R.L., Verona, Italy

This book is typeset in Minion and Frutiger.
The paper is 150 gsm Perigord

Published by The Museum of Modern Art
11 W. 53 Street, New York, New York 10019

Distributed in the United States and Canada by D.A.P./
Distributed Art Publishers, Inc., New York
Distributed outside the United States and Canada by
Thames & Hudson Ltd, London

Library of Congress Control Number: 2006930572
ISBN: 978-0-87070-446-8

Cover: *Bear Print*. 1997–98/2000
Oil on linen, 7' x 60" (213.4 x 152.4 cm)
Collection Peter Morton, Los Angeles
See plate 160

Back cover: *4 and 3 Drawing* (detail). 1979–81
Ink on paper, 30½ x 40½" (77.5 x 102.9 cm)
Collection Phil Schrager, Omaha
See plate 89

Printed in Italy

CONTENTS

Lehman Brothers has a strong commitment to contemporary and modern art.

At Lehman Brothers we believe that we all need to be inspired. The arts not only enrich our lives, they challenge our thinking, broaden our perspective, and spark our creativity. The contemporary and modern visual arts in particular encourage us to always stay current, to embrace the ever changing, and to see the world in new and different ways.

Brice Marden: A Retrospective of Paintings and Drawings at The Museum of Modern Art represents a rare and exciting opportunity for all of us to view more than 100 paintings and drawings spanning forty years of this celebrated artist's career.

Lehman Brothers is proud to support this unprecedented presentation of Marden's works, including two new pieces being exhibited for the first time. We salute The Museum of Modern Art's initiative in bringing this collection of works together, affording so many the opportunity to study, contemplate, or simply admire Marden's genius.

LEHMAN BROTHERS

FOREWORD

Although Brice Marden's work has been the subject of museum exhibitions for over thirty years, this show is the first full retrospective of his paintings and drawings. The Museum of Modern Art is honored to organize this unprecedented overview of the development of Marden's art through more than four decades. Works have been gathered from public and private collections throughout Europe and the United States, and the exhibition ends with two new monumental paintings here shown publicly for the first time.

The exhibition has been organized by Gary Garrels, former Robert Lehman Foundation Chief Curator of Drawings and Curator of Painting and Sculpture at The Museum of Modern Art and now Senior Curator at the Hammer Museum at the University of California, Los Angeles. Gary proposed this exhibition in the spring of 2000, when he joined the curatorial staff at MoMA. His commitment to Marden's work and his understanding and knowledge of it have developed over almost twenty years, and it was he who initiated the landmark exhibition of Marden's Cold Mountain series of paintings, drawings, and prints at the Dia Center for the Arts, New York, in 1991. Gary worked closely with Marden on every aspect of the exhibition and its accompanying publication. He has assembled a group of outstanding scholars to contribute essays to this book. It has been a delight to work with Gary on this complex and ambitious project.

Such a large undertaking would not have been possible without exceptionally generous financial support. Lehman Brothers early on stepped forward to underwrite the project, giving us confidence that the exhibition and book could achieve the high level deserved by the artist and his work. We also are enormously grateful for the support of the Mimi and Peter Haas Fund, The Henry Luce Foundation, Inc., and Jerry and Emily Spiegel. Marden's works are highly prized by their collectors, and we are extremely grateful to all of the lenders, both public and private, who have supported this exhibition by allowing us to share their Marden works with the public. We are also delighted that the exhibition will travel, to the San Francisco Museum of Modern Art and the Hamburger Bahnhof in Berlin.

Finally I want to thank Brice Marden for being such a full partner with the Museum in this project. The exhibition and book have benefited enormously from his gracious and generous care and attention, and have made a tremendously complicated venture a pleasure for the Museum and its staff.

— Glenn D. Lowry
Director, The Museum of Modern Art

ACKNOWLEDGMENTS

For many years I dreamed of organizing a retrospective of the work of Brice Marden. In joining The Museum of Modern Art in May 2000, I knew the institution could make that dream possible. So first I must thank Glenn D. Lowry, Director, who has supported this project with unwavering enthusiasm. I also thank the late Kirk Varnedoe, who, as Chief Curator of Painting and Sculpture, enabled me to go forward with the exhibition.

Brice first invited me into his studio almost twenty years ago and I have visited many times since. The better I have come to know the artist and his work, the more I have admired both. I cannot thank Brice enough for allowing me the pleasure and responsibility of organizing this show. He has been unstintingly responsive and gracious through the project's innumerable demands.

I also thank the people closest to Brice—his wife, Helen, and daughters, Mirabelle and Melia, who have lent works they value and been generous with counsel and patience.

The project is indebted to the extraordinary people around Marden. Matthew Marks has made his knowledge and insight utterly available—no inquiry too small, no request too daunting. The staff of the Matthew Marks Gallery has been equally generous, especially Director Jeffrey Peabody, Associate Jacqueline Tran, and Archivist Philip Tan. In assembling the catalogue of Marden's paintings and drawings, Eileen Costello laid crucial groundwork for this book. Doris Ammann of Thomas Ammann Fine Art, Zurich, and Georg Frei, Director, have been wonderful colleagues. The staff of Marden's office and studio, especially Tina Hejtmanek, have assisted in countless critical ways. Dana Cranmer of Cranmer Art Conservation is Marden's conservator of choice; her knowledge of and delight in his work have deepened my understanding.

The essayists in this book have likewise advanced my thinking. I am deeply grateful to Richard Shiff, Brenda Richardson, and Carol Mancusi-Ungaro for both their work and their friendship.

The MoMA staff combines professionalism with enthusiasm and commitment, and the success of this project rests in large part on their shoulders. First here is Jennifer Russell, Senior Deputy Director for Exhibitions, Programs, and Collection Support. Never losing sight of either the final goal or the myriad details along the way to it, Jennifer works with verve and élan. Susanna Kise, former Assistant to the Senior Deputy Director, kept us on track. Maria DeMarco Beardsley, Coordinator of Exhibitions, Randolph Black, Associate Coordinator of Exhibitions, and Deborah Straussman, Assistant to the Coordinator of Exhibitions, tuned the project's mechanisms. Ramona Bannayan, Director of Collections Management and Exhibition Registration; Susan Palamara, Registrar, Exhibitions; Allison Needle, Assistant Registrar; Pete Omlor, Manager, Art Handling and Preparation; Rob Jung, Assistant Manager; and Mark Williams, Harvey Tulcensky, and the preparator staff handled the works beautifully. Gael LeLamer, Susanna Ivy, and Eliza Sparacino in Collections and Exhibition Management all brought their skills to bear.

Marden's works are often fragile in their materials, but Jim Coddington, Agnes Gund Chief Conservator; Karl Buchberg, Senior Conservator; and Scott Gerson, Assistant Conservator, have cared for them impeccably. Besides attending to Marden's paintings, Michael Duffy, Paintings Conservator, contributed to this book an interview with the artist on materials and techniques. The safety of art both so enticing and often so delicate brought special concerns; Ron Simoncini, Director of Security, Managers Louis Bedard, Fimbar Byam, and Joanne Hughes, and all of the Museum guards have my heartfelt thanks for their attention to the works' safekeeping.

The extraordinarily talented staff of the Museum's Department of Exhibition Design and Production gave me the utmost confidence in the balance between the art and the exhibition's visual character. My grateful thanks to Jerome Neuner, Director, Betty Fisher, Manager, Peter Perez, Conservation Framer, and Hope Cullinan, former Assistant. On this front thanks also go to Ed Pusz, Director, Claire Corey, Production Manager, and Jill Weidman, Senior Graphic Designer, in the Department of Graphic Design.

This book is both a serious contribution to Marden scholarship and a pleasure. Leslie Miller of The Grenfell Press brought her keen eye and intelligence to its design, giving it both clarity and warmth. In MoMA's Department of Publications, Christopher Hudson, Publisher; Kara Kirk, Associate Publisher; Marc Sapir, Production Director; Bryan Stauss, Assistant Business Manager; and Rebecca Zimmerman, Promotions/Marketing Coordinator, all exercised their remarkable skills. David Frankel, Managing Editor, simply sets the standard as an editor. Erik Landsberg, Head of Collections Imaging; Robert Kastler, Production Manager; David Allison and Thomas Griesel, Collections Photographers; Rosa Laster-Smith, Senior Archiving Technician; and Roberto Rivera, Production Assistant, Imaging Services, all contributed to the wonderful quality of the book's reproductions.

Large financial resources were mustered for this ambitious project. It would be hard to imagine a match for the MoMA team: Michael Margitich, Senior Deputy Director, External Affairs; Nicole Goldberg, Assistant Director, Government and Foundation Support; Todd Bishop, Director, Exhibition Funding; and Mary Hannah, Assistant Director, Exhibition Funding. Their work allowed me to dream and to see those dreams realized.

The fruition of an exhibition lies in its reaching its audience. Here I am indebted to Ruth Kaplan, Deputy Director for Marketing and Communications; Peter Foley, Director of Marketing; Mark Swartz, Writer/Editor, Marketing and Development; Kim Mitchell, Director of Communications; Daniel Stigh, Manager of Communications; and Kim Donica, Research Assistant, Communications. Nicholas Apps, Director, Elizabeth Pizzo, Senior Events Coordinator, and Robert Basinger, Event Coordinator, Special Programming and Events, have helped us to celebrate the exhibition.

For their work on MoMA's public programs and outreach, I especially thank David Little, Director, Adult and Academic Programs; Laura Beiles, Associate Educator; and Sara Bodinson, Associate Educator, Department of Education. For their help in research, and in engaging the exhibition with the Museum's ongoing history, I thank Milan Hughston, Director, Library and Museum Archives; Jennifer Tobias, Librarian; Philip Parente, Senior Library Assistant; Karan Rinaldo, Library Assistant; Michelle Elligott, Museum Archivist, and Michelle Harvey, Associate Archivist.

No project of this scale could advance without key people in the Museum's administration. My heartfelt thanks to James Gara, Chief Operating Officer; Karen Davidson, Deputy Director of Policy, Planning, and Administration; Patty Lipshutz, General Counsel; Stephen Clark, Deputy General Counsel; and Nancy Adelson, Associate General Counsel. I also bow to two adept and gracious individuals: Diana Pulling, Senior Manager, Director's Office, and Maria Martin, Senior Receptionist, navigator and friend of every visitor to MoMA's Ronald S. and Jo Carole Lauder Building.

On the Museum's curatorial staff I especially want to thank Peter Reed, Senior Deputy Director for Curatorial Affairs, whose judgment, insight, and intelligence are a constant blessing. John Elderfield, The Marie-Josée and Henry Kravis Chief Curator of Painting and Sculpture; Cora Rosevear, Associate Curator; and Avril Peck, Curatorial Assistant, facilitated loans from the Museum's collection. The staff of the Department of Drawings has contributed in countless ways, and their expertise, thoughtfulness, and friendship continue to sustain me: Jodi Hauptman, Associate Curator; Luis Enrique Pérez-Oramas, Adjunct Curator; Kathleen Curry, Assistant Curator; Geaninne Gutiérrez-Guimarães and Tricia Paik, Curatorial Assistants; Carrie Elliott, Research Assistant; John Prochilo, Department Manager; Maura Lynch, Assistant to the Chief Curator; and David Moreno and Eleanor White, Preparators. Interns addressing crucial tasks include Anna Field Kallop, Jenna Moss, Tovah Moss, Adam Rothschild, Emily Schuchardt, and Elisabeth Sherman. Connie Butler, my successor as The Robert Lehman Foundation Chief Curator of Drawings, has maintained a warm welcome for me in the Department.

The two critical contributors in the Department of Drawings have been Esther Adler, Curatorial Assistant, and Francesca Pietropaolo, former Curatorial Assistant. Francesca led the research effort and prepared the book's excellent Chronology. Her sensitive engagement with the work, her love of art and life, have brought a subtle richness to the project. Esther has coordinated between the curatorial team and other departments and has been the liaison with everyone involved in the exhibition outside the Museum. Her energy, enthusiasm, and attention to detail have never wavered and her wry wit, patience, and warmth have eased the crossing of all thresholds.

I am deeply grateful for the generosity of the lenders, whom I thank on behalf of the artist and all of the exhibition's host museums. Their names appear later in this book. I also want to mention some who facilitated loans at particular institutions. At The Art Institute of Chicago: President and Director James Cuno; Curators Douglas Druick, James Rondeau, and Suzanne Folds McCullagh; and Associate Curator Mark Pascale. At The Blanton Museum of Art, The University of Texas at Austin: Director Jessie Otto Hite and Curator Annette Carlozzi. At Daros Services A.G., Zurich: Director Walter Soppelsa and Curator Hans-Michael Herzog. At the Solomon R. Guggenheim Museum, New York: Director Lisa Dennison, Curator Susan Davidson, and Associate Conservator Julie Barten. At the Hirshhorn Museum and Sculpture Garden, Smithsonian Institution, Washington, D.C.: Smithsonian Under Secretary for Art Ned Rifkin, Director Olga Viso, and Associate Curator Anne Ellegood. At the Kunstmuseum, Basel: Director Bernhard M. Bürgi and Head of the Department of Prints and Drawings Christian Müller. At The Menil Collection, Houston: Director Josef Helfenstein. At the Musée national d'art moderne, Centre Georges Pompidou, Paris: Director Alfred Pacquement and Isabelle Monod-Fontaine. At the Museum of Contemporary Art, Chicago: Director Robert Fitzpatrick and Chief Curator and Deputy Director for Programs Elizabeth Smith. At the Museum of Contemporary Art, Los Angeles: Director Jeremy Strick and Chief Curator Paul Schimmel. At the National Gallery of Canada, Ottawa: Director Pierre Théberge and Deputy Director and Chief Curator David Franklin. At the San Francisco Museum of Modern Art: Director Neal Benezra and Senior Curator Madeleine Grynsztejn. At the Stedelijk Museum, Amsterdam: Director Gijs van Tuyl and Curator Geurt Imanse. And at the Whitney Museum of American Art, New York: Director Adam Weinberg and Chief Curator Donna De Salvo.

Others who assisted in different ways include Associate Registrar Meredith Sutton, The Blanton Museum of Art; Joanna Cook, Rights and Reproductions, Clare Elliott, Assistant Curator, and Judy Kwon, Assistant Registrar, The Menil Collection; Associate Registrar Jude Palmese, Museum of Contemporary Art, Chicago; Andrea Dixon, Copyright Division, and Anne Grace, Curatorial Assistant, National Gallery of Canada; Abigail Hoover, Darlene Oden, and Barbi Spieler, Registration, Whitney Museum of American Art; Director John R. Lane and Curator Charles Wylie, Dallas Museum of Art; Director Jeff Fleming and Curator Patty Hickson, Des Moines Art Center; Director Peter C. Marzio and Curator Barry Walker, Houston Museum of Fine Arts; Curator John Ravenal, Virginia Museum of Fine Arts; Barbara Annis, Barbara Annis Fine Art; Jessica Sullum, Neal Meltzer Fine Art; Lauren Jaeger and Mary Zlot, Mary Zlot & Associates; and Carola Amsinck, Syd Bae, Sandra Berlin, Thomas Buehler, Maria Brassel, Ginger Burenin, David Carney, Kristen Donaldson, Debbie Jaffe, Elizabeth Kujawski, Arabella Makari, Ann Marcus, Guillermo Ovalle, Jinnine Pak, Jeanette Preston, Maureen Pskowski, Luc Racine, Margery Reich, Katie Salvi, Jackie Sanchez, Laura Satersmoen, Lisa Schiff, Susanna Singer, Ileen Kohn Sosa, Joan Staas, Colleen Thorne, Katherine Thorpe, Emily Wei, David White, Saralyn Whitney, and Robyn Wiley.

Some works demanded new photography and here I especially thank Bill Jacobson, as well as Benjamin Blackwell, Mark Gulezian, Ralf Höffner, Ian Reeves, Michael Tropea, and Joshua White. Providers of images for essays, as well as research support, include Sylvan Barnet and William Burto, Stan Dart, Frances Dittmer, Eskenazi Ltd., David Geffen, Kemin Hu, Charles Jencks, the Mugrabi Collection, Andrea Feldman of the Ovitz Family Collection, Pierre Rambach, Steve Rothenberger, and Muffie Dunn and Edgar B. Howard of Checkerboard Films.

Choosing complementary works for each gallery in each museum involved visits to many collections to see works that I finally did not include despite their quality. I want to thank everyone who nevertheless welcomed me in. In keeping their works to themselves for the period of the exhibition, they may be the lucky ones.

I am delighted that the exhibition will appear in San Francisco and Berlin. For their enthusiastic commitment I thank, at the San Francisco Museum of Modern Art: Neal Benezra and Madeleine Grynsztejn; Ruth Berson, Deputy Director, Exhibitions and Collections; Tara McDowell, former Curatorial Assistant; Olga Charyshyn, Registrar, Exhibitions; and Kent Roberts, Exhibition Design Manager and Chief Preparator. At the Hamburger Bahnhof, Museum für Gegenwart, and the Staatliche Museen zu Berlin: Peter-Klaus Schuster, General Director, Staatliche Museen zu Berlin; Peter Raue, Chairman of the Friends of the Nationalgalerie; Joachim Jaeger, Curator, Nationalgalerie; Angela Schneider, Deputy Director, Nationalgalerie; and André Odier, Project Manager, Brice Marden.

When I left MoMA, in June 2005, to join the Hammer Museum, Los Angeles, as Senior Curator, the Hammer's Director, Ann Philbin, knew I would remain involved with this show. I am profoundly grateful for her support. Emily Gonzalez, Administrative Assistant at the Hammer, has been swept up with the exhibition on many occasions as well.

This exhibition would be impossible without substantial funding, and I want to join my thanks with Glenn Lowry's to Lehman Brothers, the Mimi and Peter Haas Fund, The Henry Luce Foundation, and Jerry and Emily Spiegel. Their generous underwriting is a gift to both the Museum and the public.

Finally I thank Richard Hoblock, the most considerate of critics and the most committed forgiver of lapses in life to art.

— Gary Garrels

Gary Garrels

Beholding Light and Experience: The Art of Brice Marden

Brice Marden has sustained exceptional intensity and continuous invention in his art for more than forty years. As early as 1962–63, while he was still a graduate student at Yale University's School of Art and Architecture, he developed a style and way of painting and drawing that were distinctly his own. His first public recognition came in 1966, with a one-person exhibition of paintings at the Bykert Gallery in New York. Almost immediately, artists and critics acknowledged his work as singular, powerful, and important in the art of the time.[1] Within a few years, curators and collectors followed, and in 1975, when he was thirty-six years old, the Solomon R. Guggenheim Museum, New York, organized an early survey of paintings and drawings. Today more than ever, Marden is an artist whom other artists, writers, art historians, curators, and collectors hold in the deepest respect.

Brice Marden: A Retrospective of Paintings and Drawings is the first overview of the entirety of Marden's career. Organized chronologically, it reveals the development of Marden's work as astonishingly coherent and consistent without ever settling into simple reiteration or repetition. Marden has never ceased to challenge himself with the same intensity with which he began his career. The daunting uncertainty that a blank canvas or sheet of paper may assert has never lost its power for him, and he has always maintained that the confrontation posed by any new body of work is laden with risk. What art historian Yve-Alain Bois has described as Marden's "doubt" haunts the artist's mind.[2] The studio process—the working through of the issues of a work or series, the handling of the materials, the constant back-and-forth of examination, reflection, and action, sometimes over years—eventually distills a painting or drawing into a resolved, finished work. Only then is it allowed to leave the studio, into public scrutiny and shared experience.

For Marden, art wrests out of life an essence of experience and memory, thought and feeling, that attains its own autonomy. Human reason and emotion take their place in the world through the experience of art, both as it is made and as it is viewed. Marden's work, like that of many artists, is deeply influenced by the places he has lived and worked, the people in his life, and the cultures in which he has immersed himself, not the least of them the art of the past, both ancient and recent. From his sharp syntheses and distillations of his experiences an art is made that in turn gives viewers an incisive means to reflect more deeply on their own perceptions, knowledge, and experience.

Marden's work is fundamentally linked to light, the ultimate means by which we have vision. Light is absorbed or reflected by surfaces and fractures into color. Observation is mediated by light, essentially unstable and changing, just as our ability to hold an experience is fleeting and subjective. As Marden stated in 1980, "Color is a way of arriving at light. The illusion of light is one of the things that a painter works with, I mean, that's how you get an image. Without light there is no visible image."[3]

Light is held by the plane of a canvas or sheet of paper—a geometric construct, one of the simplest, purest, and most profound products of the rational mind. For Marden the plane becomes the stage on which to create a honed rendering of life, not a representation or shadow of observed experience but a springboard for experience itself. Color, surface, gesture, and mark transform the plane; edges and internal divisions are its armature; and the result is an image, albeit an abstract one. That image opens up a reflective experience—retinal and cognitive, emotional and spiritual. As Marden has said of Vermeer's *Kitchen Maid* (fig. 1), "It's just this great painting—the experience of looking at it is just very exciting. You're seeing a whole. One person looked at reality and put it on a two-dimensional plane."[4] In a set of notes from 1966, Marden confessed, "I seem to worry about realism. Art as a real thing. There can be, for me, all sorts of illusionism but the painting must rise above the illusions created and be able to stand as a real thing or solid fact. The best paintings do this."[5]

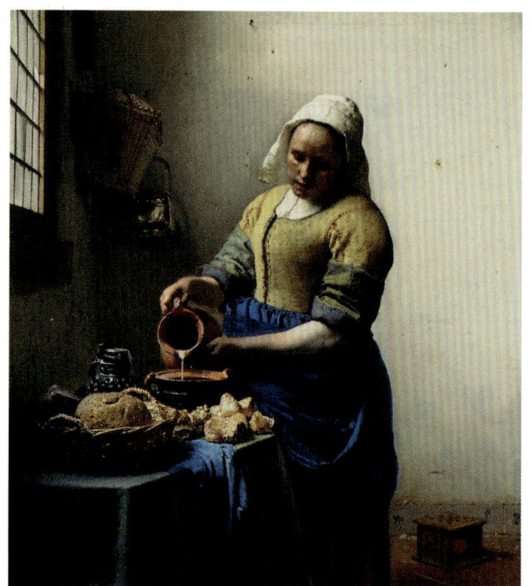

> *Nebraska* (1966)
> *I had been to Nebraska that summer, drove across the country. And I just loved Nebraska. . . . It was the kind of landscape that looked as though it was supposed to be very boring, but it wasn't. There were these subtle changes in the landscape—you'd be driving along and then you'd suddenly go over a little rise, and there was this incredible gorge or something—not a big, huge thing, but with little trees in it. I thought it was a very surprising landscape—the green I saw was exquisite.*
> —Brice Marden, 1980

> *D'après la Marquise de la Solana* (1969)
> *Painted in Paris about some aspects of a Goya in the Louvre. A portrait of a severe woman standing in an awesome landscape on dainty feet with a big pink bow in her hair, not fooling a soul. It has to do with Goya's color. A black, a green, and a pink. A full panel of pink. I remember a funkiness to the drawing.*
> —Brice Marden, 1972

A tracing of the development of Marden's work up through his breakthrough exhibition in 1966 provides the underpinnings for understanding his career. As an undergraduate at Boston University's School of Fine and Applied Art, from 1958 to 1961, Marden had thorough and traditional training, including drawing classes, printmaking, design, lettering, and the study of

1. Johannes Vermeer. *The Kitchen Maid.* c. 1658
Oil on canvas, 18 x 16 1/8" (45.5 x 41 cm)
Rijksmuseum, Amsterdam

anatomy and perspective. The faculty generally practiced and promoted a style of figurative expressionism, but two newer members, the painter Arthur Hoener and the sculptor Hugh Townley, pursued abstraction, and Marden has said that he learned from them a lot about art at a philosophical level, "what it's all about."[6] The syllabus included a course on color based on Josef Albers's famous course at Yale University, but Marden said that "using these little tricks" made no sense to him.[7] His way into understanding color instead came from faculty member Reed Kay, who he said "would talk more about old master paintings and color . . . you could discuss a Matisse color painting or something like that . . . and the idea of seeing a dark against a dark, what kind of color came that way."[8]

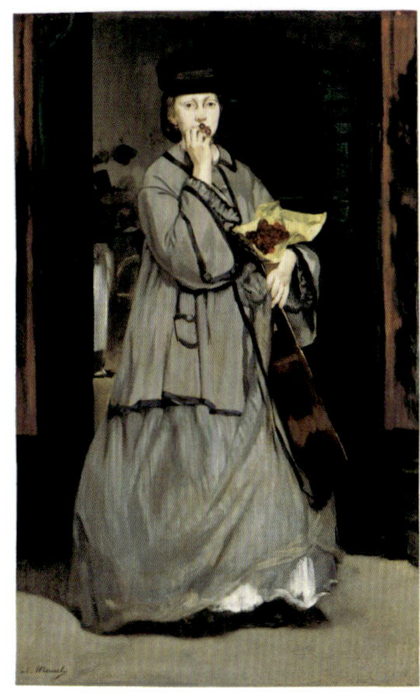

Marden spent time outside school going to galleries and museums in Boston and New York, and having continuous discussions about art. He remembers looking at art and then asking teachers "what am I supposed to be looking for, and they said you look at things that help you solve problems. It's not easy and it wasn't easy; it took a long time to really begin to be able to look."[9] At Boston's Museum of Fine Arts, two paintings by Edouard Manet, *Street Singer* (c. 1862; fig. 2) and *Execution of the Emperor Maximilian* (1867), were favorites for Marden, both of them distinguished by close contrasts of dark tones. Marden later remarked that *Street Singer* was "the painting I was looking at when I really started learning about color."[10] Meanwhile his keenness of observation was reinforced by his response to the Spanish painter Francisco de Zurbarán (fig. 3): "He was looking so hard at what he was looking at. In his paintings he went . . . beyond and transformed [the subject] into something else. It's like this mystical painting stage."[11] The paintings of Paul Cézanne also had a strong impact: "Cézanne had loosened up a lot of things about how to structure. The subject matter really became irrelevant. . . . What he was really doing was making the painting. The painting was much more important than the picture of the mountain."[12] He also studied the early paintings of Henri Matisse: "I've thought of Matisse's surface as a work surface. He leaves changes, he shows you how to make the painting."[13] Marden's paintings from these student years underline these influences (fig. 4).

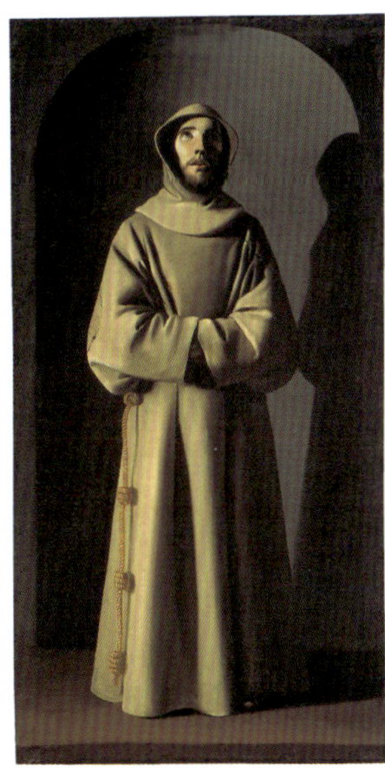

Upon graduating from Boston University, in the spring of 1961, Marden was recommended by the faculty for study at the Yale Summer School of Music and Art, in Norfolk, Connecticut. From there he was selected to attend the Yale University School of Art and Architecture, which he entered that fall. At Yale, Jeremy Lewison writes, he discovered that his "training had been much more academic than that of most of his fellow students. . . . He had appreciated his own Boston training for its immediacy: 'We had a model and you painted your painting and it was talked about in relation to the model,' whereas students at other universities had been taught 'the look of art and it

2. Edouard Manet. *Street Singer*. c. 1862
Oil on canvas, 67 3/8 x 41 5/8" (171.1 x 105.8 cm)
Museum of Fine Arts, Boston
Bequest of Sarah Choate Sears in memory of her husband, Joshua Montgomery Sears

3. Francisco de Zurbarán. *Saint Francis*. c. 1640–45
Oil on canvas, 6' 9 1/2" x 42" (207 x 106.7 cm)
Museum of Fine Arts, Boston. Herbert James Pratt Fund

was all very secondhand.'"[14] A thesis statement Marden wrote in 1963 reinforces this idea: "Constant painting and drawing from nature developed a sense of the real, that which was correct and had form. It left no room for arbitraries [*sic*], and one learned to see when something was wrong."[15] Even so, it was during his time at Yale that Marden stopped making figurative paintings and began to paint abstractions only. He had discovered the work of Willem de Kooning and Franz Kline before he got there, and both now became inspirations for his work (fig. 5)—to the point where two of his teachers, Jack Tworkov and Alex Katz, challenged him to break away from their precedents. As Marden would say of this period later, "I thought that's really what it's about, you've got to learn to paint like yourself."[16]

By the end of Marden's first year at Yale, he had begun to organize paintings and drawings around a four-part grid (plates 2–4), which by 1963 had been submerged into two flanking planes of gray (plate 5). He describes these works in his Yale thesis statement of 1963:

> The paintings are made in a highly subjective state within Spartan limitations. Within these strict confines, confines which I have painted myself into and intend to explore with no regrets, I try to give the viewer something to which he will react subjectively. I believe these are highly emotional paintings not to be admired for any technical or intellectual reason but to be felt.[17]

In his drawings of this period the grid is broken down into rectangular segments of graphite, charcoal, or both (plates 9–11). Speaking many years later of these drawings, he noted,

> I've always thought of the grid as a measure or a way of measuring a space and each different grid makes a completely different space, but they're all very similar spaces. Like I think of these drawings as, say, details of that space. I see space as infinite—an infinity with lots of changes, permutations, shifts, plays, happening in it. And lots of tension. Lots of tension. And I try to get that into the work.[18]

In 1960, while Marden was still an undergraduate in Boston and immersed in his studio and in a social world built around art, he had married Pauline Baez, sister of the singer Joan Baez. They had decided to start a family and in 1961 they had a son, Nicholas. In the fall of 1963 they moved together to New York, taking up residence in a railroad flat on Avenue C on the Lower East Side. Marden found a job as a part-time guard at The Jewish Museum, which in the winter of 1964 would present the first retrospective of

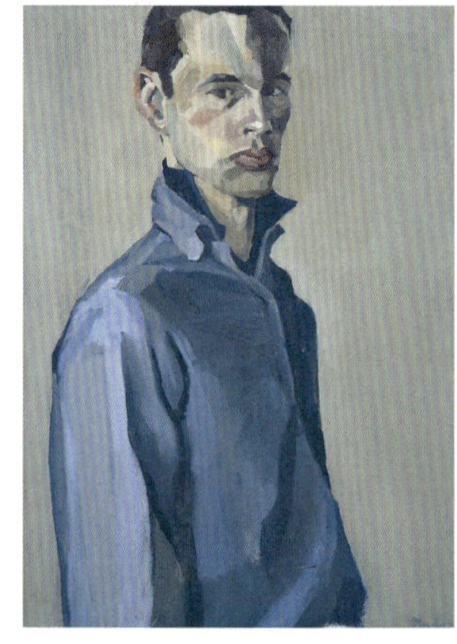

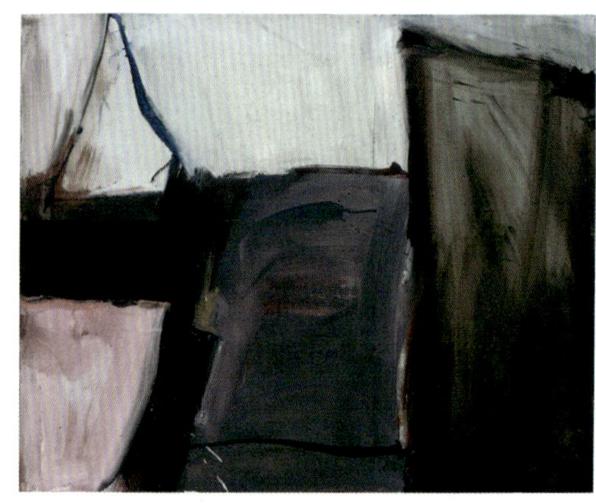

4. Brice Marden. *Self-Portrait*. 1959
Oil on canvas, 34 x 24" (88.3 x 61 cm)
Collection the artist

5. Brice Marden. *Norfolk*. 1961
Oil on canvas
Location unknown

the work of Jasper Johns. Marden was "forcefully struck by Johns' ability to create such a physically convincing unity of shape and painted subject," Klaus Kertess writes; "The prominence of gray in Johns' production at this time further encouraged Marden's own commitment to gray" (fig. 6).[19] Most important in Marden's experience of these paintings, though, was the affirmation of his own attitude about the subject of painting. "With Johns," he would write two years later,

> there was an advance in illusionistic realism, or the depiction of things, because he made the thing himself. Other pop artists painted pictures of pictures but Johns' paintings are actually the real thing elevated, through the use of traditional plastic means, to a higher, or aesthetic state. He has imbued his objects or things, his subject matter with a new mystery. (Painting is also a main part of his subject matter, paint and painting.) The flag remains a flag yet becomes art, capable of awakening the spirit in a more moving way than flags ordinarily do. . . . My paintings are blatantly simple color shape statements, but then go very confusing, as do the simple Johns flag paintings, and the object becomes a playground of contents, mysteries and questions. Because there are no answers.[20]

In the spring and summer of 1964, Marden and his family moved to Paris, staying with his in-laws. There he saw a retrospective of the painter Jean Fautrier and had the opportunity to look closely at the paintings and sculptures of Alberto Giacometti (fig. 7). He was affected by the physicality and space in the paintings of both artists; in Giacometti's portraits, for example, he discovered a "spatial exactness within the frame."[21] At the end of the summer Marden separated from his wife, returned to New York, and began to reconsider the work in his studio. He had deeply absorbed the effects of his four months in France, and not just in response to its art: during his time in Paris, André Malraux, then the French minister of culture, was overseeing a dramatic cleanup of the city's buildings, and Marden would later write, "They were re-plastering or stuccoing a lot of the walls. And I would just spend an afternoon watching them work down these walls. And then when I got back to New York—there were paintings that I had started at Yale, and then I just sort of reworked them, and they became more . . . field-like" (plate 13; p. 113, figs. 2, 3).[22]

By the fall of 1966, Marden had completed the paintings and drawings that he would exhibit beginning that November in a one-person exhibition at the Bykert Gallery, his first exhibition in New York. These works fully distilled the lessons and experience of the prior eight years. For most of the paintings

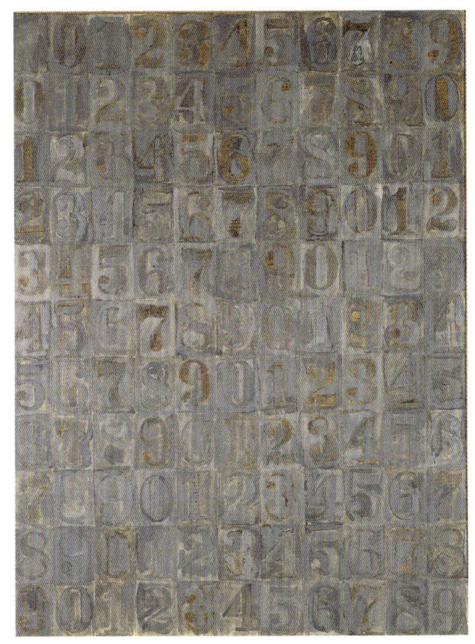

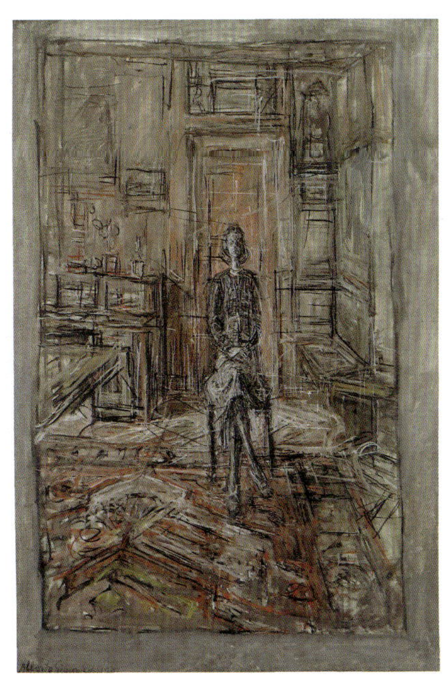

6. Jasper Johns. *Gray Numbers.* 1958
Encaustic and collage on canvas, 67 x 49 1/2" (170.2 x 125.7 cm)
Collection David Geffen, Los Angeles

7. Alberto Giacometti. *The Artist's Mother.* 1950
Oil on canvas, 35 3/8 x 24" (89.9 x 61 cm)
The Museum of Modern Art, New York
Acquired through the Lillie P. Bliss Bequest

Marden used a new technique, mixing paint, turpentine, and melted beeswax in an effort to tone down the shine of the oil. He worked the surfaces with a combination of spatula, knife, and brush, leaving irregularities, breaks, and marks as the material of the painting flowed and shifted before hardening. The shape and proportion of each painting were distinct. Although generally akin to gray, the color of each work was unique and almost impossible to describe. The titles alluded to people and places: *The Dylan Painting* (plate 17), in a bruised purple, was named in homage to Bob Dylan; *Nico* (plate 16) was a tawny evocation of the singer in the rock band the Velvet Underground, and of her "blondness and light tan pants suits"; *Nebraska* (plate 15) honored "the mysterious greens of Nebraska," seen in a drive across the country that summer.[23] The paintings have a maturity and confidence as well as a sense of grandeur and ambition, without any hint of hesitancy or tentativeness. These prodigious works stand as fundamental touchstones for the time. Marden was now fully launched as a painter to be reckoned with.

> *A Mediterranean Painting* (retitled *For Pearl*), 1970
> *It started out to be painting from notes I'd taken when I was in France. . . . This was going to be the blue, the Mediterranean, the red, the earth, and the green—a very specific blue, red, and green that runs all the way down the coast as you drive along the Mediterranean in France. I was going to do a painting about that. The painting was made in about three days, and in the process Janis Joplin died, and the whole thing just kind of turned into a dirge for her.*
>
> —Brice Marden, 1971

> *Summer Table* (1972–73)
> *The painting was started from a note to myself that said "a table of glasses of lemonade and Coca-Cola. Interesting color." The painting started with colors that approached those colors from memory. As it progressed that idea became less important than the formal aspects which dealt with creating a strong tension and pull between the outside panels. I also wanted to push the color to a stronger intensity than that to which I had been accustomed. After a summer in Greece I felt the light should be intenser, clearer and less shrouded. . . . In Greece I stayed on an island overlooking the sea. I worked in a garden, drawing. I studied light changes and the movements of the sea. I watched light changes change edges. . . . the painting deals with a lot of those moments. . . . I did not consciously put that into the painting. It happened.*
>
> —Brice Marden, 1973

Once Marden's work leaves the studio and is given over to the public, what is his expectation of the viewer? As early as his Yale thesis of 1963, he addressed the issue explicitly: "Emotional participation (sympathy) is desired on the part of the viewer as is physical participation (empathy)."[24] In 1976, when an interviewer asked him "who do you paint for?" Marden answered,

> I paint because it's my work. And I paint because I believe it's the best way that I can pass my time as a human being. I paint for myself. I paint for my wife. And I paint for anybody that's willing to look at it. Really at heart, for anybody who wants to see it. And when I say see it, I mean see it. I don't mean just look at it. Well, I do everything I can in terms of what I put out for people to look at. I mean I supply them with all of the information I possibly can. And they just have to take care of it from there on in. As in anything, you know, like the more responsive, the more open, the more imaginative you are when you deal with something, the much better experience it will be. . . . It's hard to look at paintings. It's really difficult, a very strenuous kind of activity but very, very rewarding. I mean just like it's strenuous to listen to a great piece of music. Very complicated. You have to think a lot. You have to be able to bring all sorts of things together in your mind, your imagination, in your whole body. Really get off on it. It's a very high experience. . . . It's something very deep and felt.[25]

So how might Marden's work be better understood? Landscape, the human figure, art: these are his primary references. Memory and process, the immediacy of drawing from nature and the extended time of drawing and painting in the studio, are his means of transforming experiences and references into art. These subjects and this attitude toward artmaking have been constants through Marden's career, even as the work shifted from overall fields of primarily single colors to translucent grounds embedded with undulating ribbons. The beginnings, sources, and allusions in any of Marden's paintings and drawings cannot necessarily be known by looking at the pictures themselves. As the artist intends, the work has become autonomous. He has said, "The painting is based on reality, a reality. And the painting itself becomes an addition to the reality, if it's a successful painting."[26] At the same time, and just as much, for Marden a painting cannot be truly known: "The idea of painting is just sort of this grand idea that's undefinable. . . . one of the nice things about painting is that there aren't answers. It's all questions that there are no answers for; it's that whole thing about mystery."[27]

The shifts in Marden's sources and inspirations over time help to explain the changes in the form and style of the finished work. In the 1960s, when Marden was living in New York, his primary influences came from life in the city, its streets, buildings, and architecture. Marden has commented,

> Living in the city, it's all verticals and horizontals. It's all grids. You walk down the street and look at the ground and you pass, you know, how many horizontals. This is by your eyes, just looking at the cracks in the concrete. Each one of those is a different line. Each line is made by two shapes meeting. It's all out there.[28]

The light that is specific to New York is also crucial to the work, and Marden has often spoken about it:

> It's a really beautiful light in New York, which is very important for painters. [Barnett] Newman used to say that Matisse had to come to New York in order to discover what light was about. This is after living in Paris, the supposed City of Light. There's a beautiful, silvery kind of light here. And that's very exciting, just working in that light because that's going to affect your color.[29]

The culture of the city is equally reflected in Marden's work of the time. The art in museums and galleries—the European painting of the past (Vermeer, Zurbarán, Goya, Manet, Cézanne, Matisse)—and the painting Marden was absorbing as he became a painter himself (de Kooning, Kline, and Johns) are all present. But just as present is an expanding bohemian culture—bars, clubs, pop culture, and most of all music, specifically the troubadours of the time: Dylan, Otis Redding, Janis Joplin, and later Patti Smith. Paintings are dedicated and homages made to each of these singers. The social and political upheaval that was pervasive in the 1960s also worked its way into Marden's early paintings:

> These paintings were done when war was a major issue. It was like the call of death. Your country is making death. There is going to be a reflection of that in the art of the time. It's not that people are going to make paintings about death. . . . You could say that I was showing some of the bleaker aspects. In this sense I was making a political statement. One likes to think that art is on the side of truth.[30]

In addition to these external elements, personal influences also had their effect. Throughout Marden's career, family, friends, and lovers would prove important sources of both inspiration and reflection; love, emotional tension, ecstasy, and loneliness all abide under the surfaces of his works. A key painting made after the Bykert Gallery exhibition is the two-panel *For Helen* (1967; plate 19), dedicated to Helen Harrington, whom Marden would marry in 1968. Each panel was the height of her body and the width of her shoulders, but the artist decided to double the panels, leaving a small space between them, since he felt that a single panel was just too thin. As strong as their relationship would prove to be, at one point Helen and Marden were estranged.[31] It was after this time that Marden made the Back Series, seven single panels dating from 1967–68, of the same height as *For Helen* (plates 22, 23).[32]

In 1971, after years of working almost exclusively in New York, Marden visited Hydra, a Greek island in the Aegean Sea, off the east coast of the Peloponessus. He and his wife decided to buy a small property there for a house and studio. Since then the Mardens have returned to the island almost every summer, and a subsequent shift in his work is palpable—colors intensify, surfaces become lusher, canvases grander and bolder. Allusions to the Mediterranean landscape—the olive groves, the sea, the simple ancient structures of Hydra, the grand remains of classical Greek civilization—underlie many paintings and drawings beginning at this time, and remain primary through the early 1980s. Both the myths of the Greek gods and the drama of early Christianity—both Hera and the Annunciation—make appearances (plates 68, 70, 71), and the cycles of nature—the seasons, the phases of the moon, the daytime intensity of the sun and of light and shadow, twilight enfolding the sea in evening—can all be seen and felt (plates 40, 64, 69, 73). Post-and-lintel architecture, common to both the ordinary structures of Hydra and the fragments of Greek monuments (fig. 8), specifically inflect the composition and structure of his work of the late 1970s, early '80s, and into the '90s. These sources underlie one of Marden's most ambitious paintings, *Thira* (1979–80; plate 83). The title is the Greek word for "door" but also the name of a Cycladic island near Crete, an important archaeological site.[33]

Throughout this period Marden was also reconsidering the development of abstract painting in New York. In 1971, the critic Thomas Hess organized a retrospective of the work of Barnett Newman at The Museum of Modern Art, after the artist's death the year before. Newman's stately and grand planes of paint seemed to force open the space of Marden's own paintings, which expanded in scale. Newman's great series of four large works titled "Who's Afraid of Red, Yellow, and Blue" (fig. 9), executed between 1966 and his final year of 1970, had a significant impact. Three years later Marden would begin his own series of works dealing with red, yellow, and blue, the primary colors (plates 62, 63). As much as the influence of Newman, these paintings also reflect his long-held admiration for Piet Mondrian, who in 1940, as an émigré from the Europe of World War II, had carried European geometric abstraction

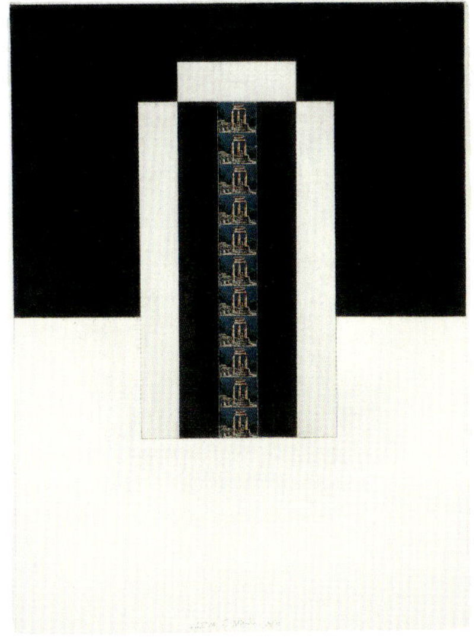

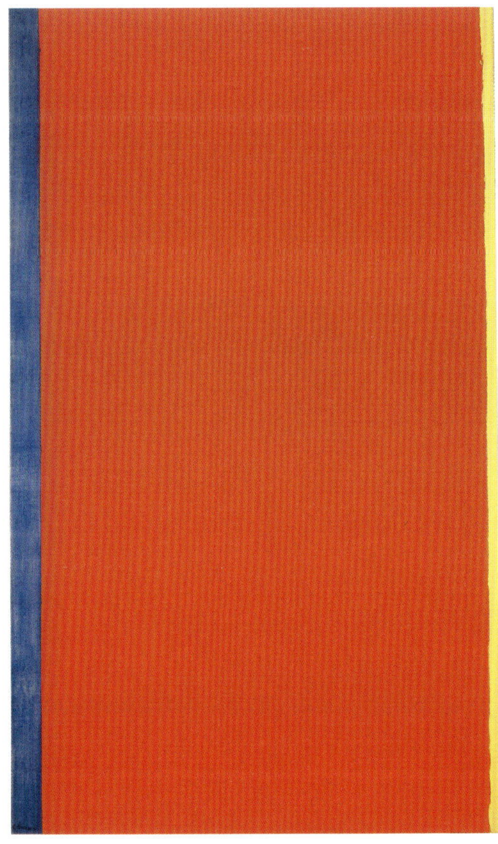

8. Brice Marden. *Souvenir de Grèce 16.* 1974/1996
Graphite, beeswax, and collage on paper
29¾ x 22½" (75.6 x 57.2 cm)
Courtesy Locksley Shea Gallery, Minneapolis

9. Barnett Newman. *Who's Afraid of Red, Yellow and Blue I.* 1966
Oil on canvas, 6' 3" x 48" (190.5 x 121.9 cm)
Private collection

across the Atlantic to New York. Mondrian's painting, like Marden's, was transformed by the grid of the city, its insistent rhythm and palpable energy (fig. 10). The year of 1971 also saw the dedication of the Rothko Chapel in Houston, commissioned by Dominique and John de Menil to house the great mural cycle painted for it by Mark Rothko between 1964 and 1967, now visible publicly for the first time. As Carol Mancusi-Ungaro notes in her essay here, Marden visited the chapel in 1972 and was profoundly affected.[34]

The late 1970s through the mid-1980s were a period of transition for Marden. Three significant facets of this transition aligned to influence his work. First, in 1978 Marden was commissioned to design new stained glass windows for the Basel Münster, the city's great Protestant cathedral. Work on this project absorbed Marden through 1985, until the project was canceled because of political disagreements in the city.[35] Then, in 1981, Marden abandoned the use of wax, because of the fragility of the surfaces of the wax paintings, and developed a new technique using terpineol, a medium he mixed with oil to produce a pigment that dries to a flat surface. Finally, Marden was beginning to question his work's potential for development. As he would later recall, "I . . . came to feel that my work had reached a point where it was too preoccupied with the refining of a concept."[36] And, "I got to a point where I could go on making 'Brice Marden paintings' and suffer that silent creative death. . . . You get to this point where you just have to make a decision to change things."[37]

As in the past, changes and upheavals in Marden's personal life also affected his art. The Mardens had children for the first time, two daughters—Mirabelle, born in 1978, and Melia, born two years later. Marden dedicated important series of drawings to each of his daughters when they were born (plates 77–82, 90–98). In the early 1980s, soon after Melia was born, strains developed between Marden and Helen and they separated for a period. By 1983, however, Marden had reconciled with his wife and returned to his family. Helen, who loves to travel (it was she who had led the couple to their first visit to Hydra), now suggested and planned a trip to Thailand, Sri Lanka, and India.

This trip marked the beginning of Marden's interest in Asian culture, art, and landscape, an interest that would develop rapidly and passionately, profoundly affecting his work over the next two decades. In Thailand he began collecting seashells, particularly volutes, and began making sketches inspired by them (fig. 11): "I would pick them for the graphic quality of their markings. . . . It was purely visual. . . . You hold the shell, and there would be a little mark and then you would just draw it as if you were doing a portrait of something."[38] He considered the patterns of the shells as "patterns of growth sort of petrified."[39] The next year, at Helen's suggestion, Marden visited the exhibition

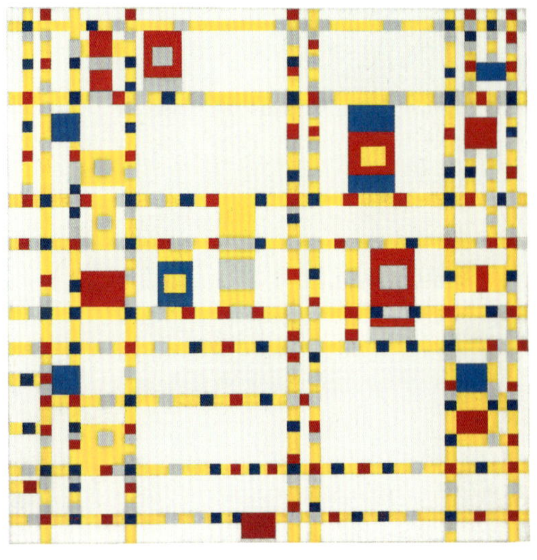

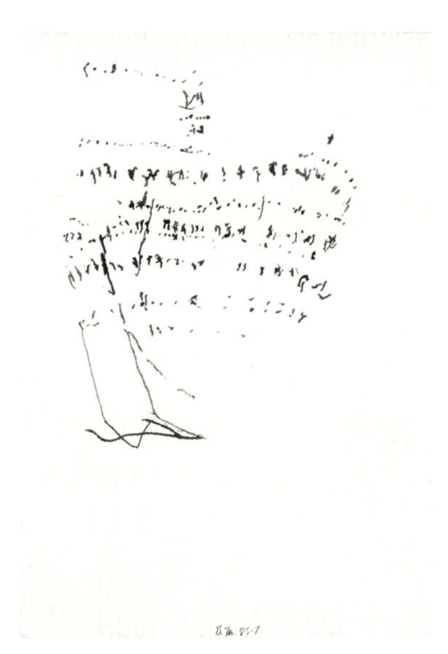

10. Piet Mondrian. *Broadway Boogie Woogie.* 1942–43
Oil on canvas, 50 x 50" (127 x 127 cm)
The Museum of Modern Art, New York. Given anonymously

11. Brice Marden. *Shell Drawing #1.* 1985–87
Ink on paper, 11³/₈ x 8" (29 x 20 cm)
Collection the artist

Masters of Japanese Calligraphy, 8th–19th Century, at the Asia Society and the Japan House Gallery in New York, and immersed himself in the study of calligraphy, looking carefully and repeatedly at the exhibition's catalogue. Asian calligraphy would soon become a predominant influence in his work. Discussing his interest in calligraphy, Marden has said,

> Calligraphy is very personal because it is very physical. It's not a technique or an ideology; it's a form of pure expression. Each time a calligrapher makes a mark, it will be distinctive because he has a particular physicality. Great artists exploit this; their thinking and their physicality become one. Paintings are physical. So is the act of creating them. This physicality should be emphasized. If you're not working with preconceived forms and thinking, then you can concentrate on expression. It is possible, I think, to make art on this instinctive level, out of deeply felt response. The longer I paint, the more I think this is true.[40]

All of these influences came together in a dramatic shift in Marden's work, developed first in his drawings and etchings and later in new paintings, first shown publicly in 1987 (plates 111–13).

While calligraphy was the major influence in the transition in Marden's work of the mid-1980s, drawing has always been crucial to him. He draws both in the studio and directly from nature, making works of a number of different types: "Drawings for me take a number of stages. Little notebook drawings, then a little bit more elaborate ones, and then the point where I'm familiar enough so that I work it on a major scale."[41] The medium has often been Marden's method of working through problems before attempting a painting that would deal with the same issues. The relationship runs in both directions; while drawings may inform paintings, paintings may also affect drawings. Marden has called drawing

> an intimate medium. It's very direct, it's very close. There is less between the artist and the art. There is real closeness, direct contact. A painting is about refinement of image. And drawing isn't. Drawing is not refinement. I don't think drawing is less than painting. . . . I find that painting doesn't have the fluidity that drawing has. And that's always, to me, the battle, to get fluidity into the painting.[42]

Just as the first years in Hydra inspired the extraordinary Grove Group works, five drawings and five paintings made between 1972 and 1976 (plates 41–49), Marden's interest in Asia and his attention to calligraphy would be synthesized in the Cold Mountain group. This series of numerous drawings (plates 129, 130), three suites of etchings, and six monumental paintings made between 1988 and 1991 (plates 123–25) were shown together at the Dia Center for the Arts, New York, in 1991.[43] Critical reaction to the new work from 1986 to 1988 had been mixed, but the Cold Mountain group again consolidated Marden's reputation as one of the most important abstract artists of his generation, his work again a touchstone for contemporary art.[44]

Indeed, the paintings and drawings from the twenty years since the mid-1980s equal in stature, consistency, and invention the works from the first half of Marden's career. Critics and historians of art often relate those earlier works to the pared-back Minimal art of the 1960s and '70s, but the work from the mid-1980s forward is more resolutely singular—and Marden is now at a level of maturity that places him without an immediate peer. Painters such as the German artist Sigmar Polke, who exhibited very little in New York before the early 1980s, and who worked in a variety of figurative styles (fig. 12), opened up arguments and possibilities for contemporary painting that had an impact on Marden's reassessment of his own work. But Marden draws on myriad influences in his later art, and among the strongest of these is Matisse. In 1975, discussing the two mural-sized paintings *Music* (1909–10) and *Dance (II)* (1909–10; fig. 13) in the Hermitage, Marden had said, "Those are unbelievable paintings. They go right to cave painting. . . . One thing about Matisse is the sort of richness and life that he can incorporate into a painting, to have a painting mean more than it actually looks like." Continuing with a consideration of *Portrait of Mme. Matisse* (1913), Marden noted, "Beautifully drawn, beautiful structure. That torsion, just that movement. That gesture. It's so specific, so beautiful, like a great moment of dancing caught forever."[45]

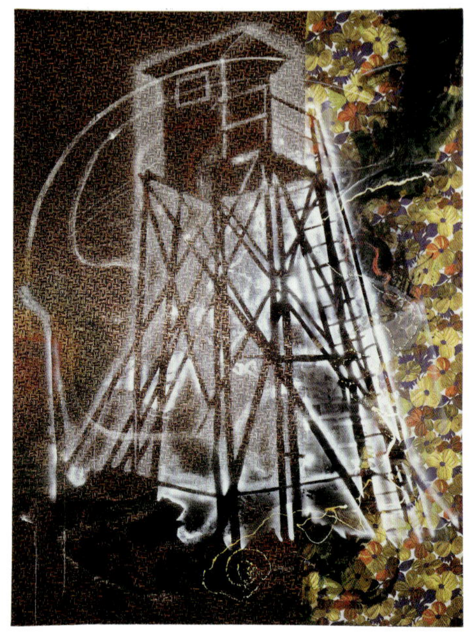

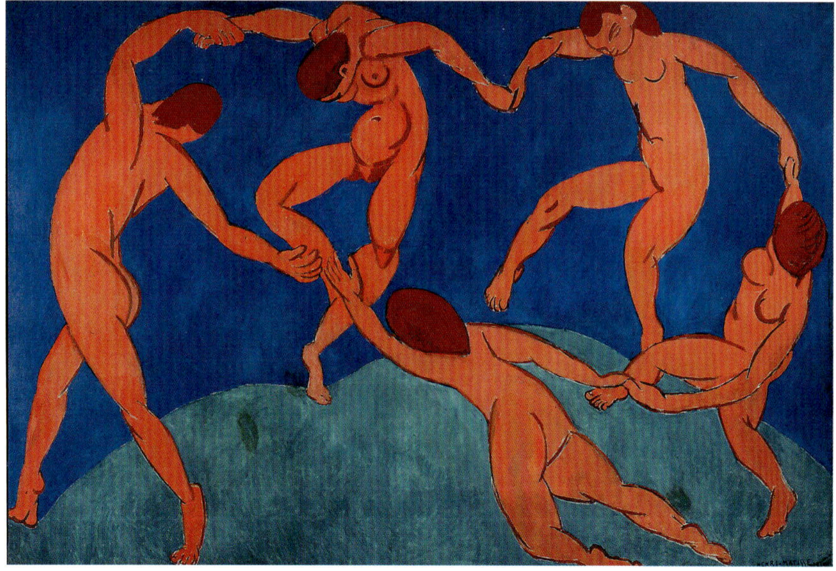

12. Sigmar Polke. *Watchtower.* 1984
Synthetic polymer paints and dry pigment on fabric, 9' 10" x 7' 4½" (300 x 224.8 cm)
The Museum of Modern Art, New York
Fractional and Promised gift of Jo Carole and Ronald S. Lauder

13. Henri Matisse. *Dance (II).* 1909–10
Oil on canvas, 8' 5⅝" x 12' 9½" (260 x 391 cm)
The State Hermitage Museum, Saint Petersburg

The description is clearly apt for the works Marden would start to produce ten years later. Another master Marden had long admired would also reassert a presence: de Kooning's paintings from the 1980s, the so-called "ribbon paintings," were first exhibited in 1984 at the Xavier Fourcade Gallery in New York (fig. 14). They were much discussed by artists at the time, and Marden's admiration of them is well known. Two years after seeing them Marden began his own calligraphic paintings.

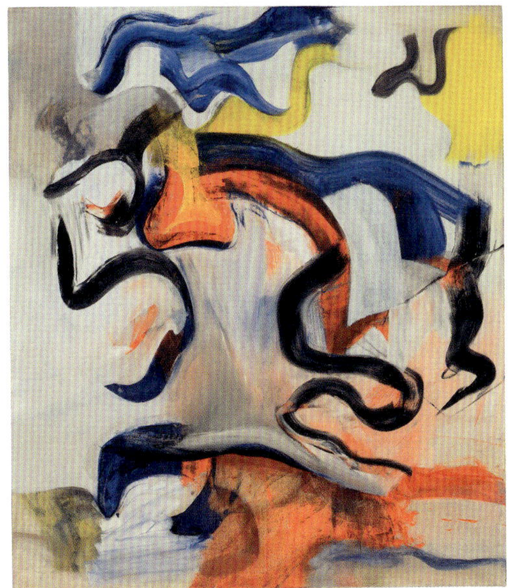

Certainly Jackson Pollock looms largest as the twentieth-century artist most clearly echoed in the Cold Mountain works (fig. 15). As Brenda Richardson emphasized in her comprehensive and insightful essay of 1991 on the Cold Mountain series, "Pollock is a very real presence in Marden's Cold Mountain work."[46] The influence was one not simply of look and style but also of spirit. Richardson embeds in her text a transcription of a lecture on Pollock that Marden delivered at The Museum of Modern Art on November 16, 1989, just when he was beginning the Cold Mountain paintings. Here Marden asserted, "To maintain any kind of life as an artist is to make change. Yet for most observers change in an artist's work is the most difficult thing to grasp." He continued,

> There's a great deal of confusion about what an artist does in the studio as opposed to what happens outside the studio and what effect each of these environments and circumstances has on the artist. The great thing about Pollock—and something that since his death seems to have been forgotton about art—was his conviction that each work is part of a continuing quest. To be an artist is not about making individual works. To be an artist is to do your work and let your work express the evolution of a vision.[47]

In his work since the Cold Mountain group, Marden has returned continually to Asian art and culture for inspiration, just as in the 1970s he was consistently influenced by the ancient cultures of the Mediterranean. His paintings evidence the impact of not only calligraphy but Chinese landscape painting and Han- and Tang-dynasty sculpture (plates 152, 153, 156–58), gravestones (plates 161, 163), and "scholar's rocks" (plates 166–68), direct sources absorbed and transformed into a personal style that is constantly evolving and shifting. Perhaps most extraordinarily, in the series of works from the late 1980s and early '90s titled The Muses (plates 131, 135, 137, 138, 145), Marden melds Greek and Asian influences with New York School abstract painting in a seamless synthesis. But here again his muses are not only abstract or cultural but also specific and real, for the Muses paintings are inspired by his two daughters, Mirabelle and Melia, as are the related paintings *Virgins* (1991–93; plate

14. Willem de Kooning. *Untitled V.* 1982.
Oil on canvas, 6' 8" x 70" (203.2 x 177.8 cm)
The Museum of Modern Art, New York.
Gift of Philip Johnson

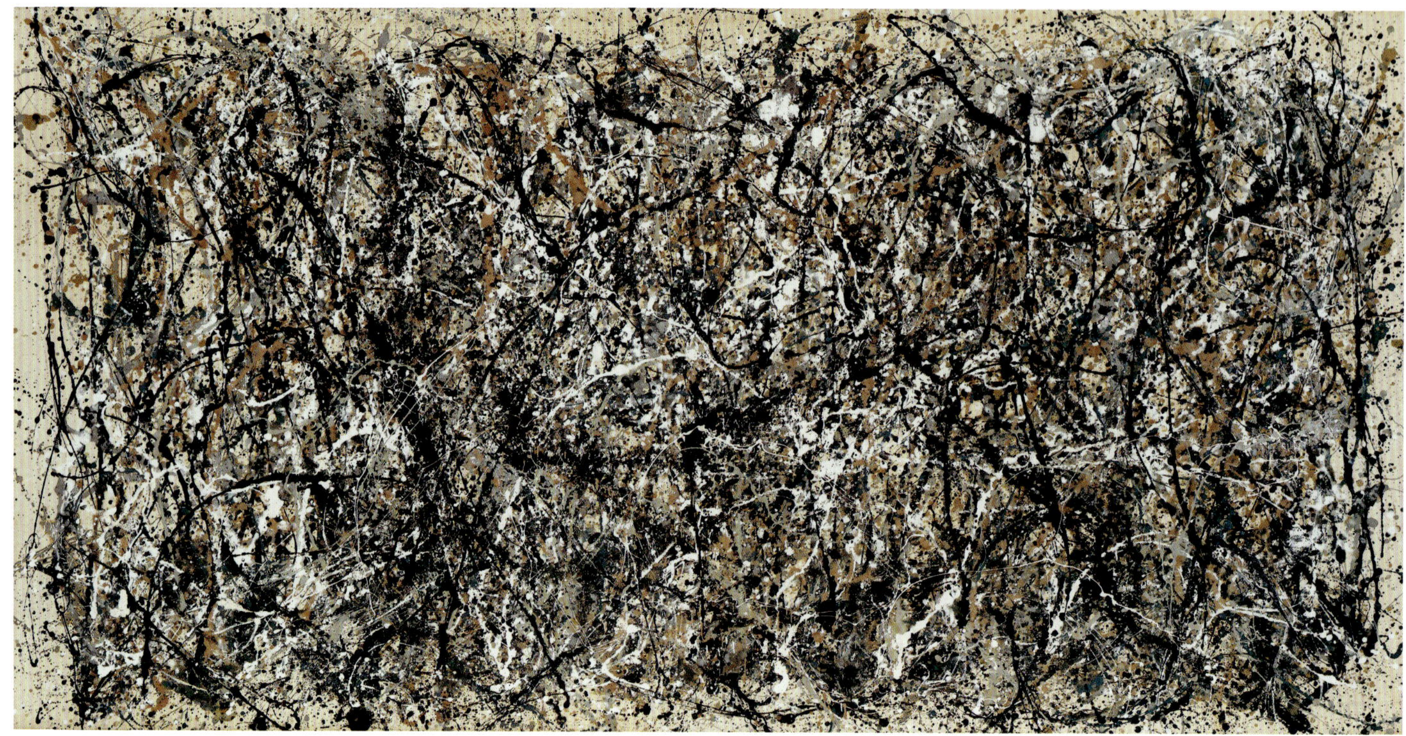

139) and *The Sisters* (1991–93; plate 136). As Richardson notes, when Marden painted *The Muses* (1991–93; plate 137) he also had in mind his father, and the memory of the experience of "nature and the outdoors through his father's eyes."[48] Thus this painting, which is among Marden's most monumental and important works, conjoins past and future, culture and family, a unity of aspects of Marden's life and work across decades.

Over the past fifteen years, the Mardens have acquired two rural properties—one in Eagles Mere, Pennsylvania, not far from the home of Helen's mother, and most recently a house and land outside Tivoli on the Hudson River, near where the nineteenth-century Hudson Valley painters Frederic Edwin Church and Thomas Cole lived and worked. In Eagles Mere, a barn on the property was renovated for a studio, and yet another set of influences began to take hold: the softer rural light, the colors of the landscape, the forests, rock formations, and animal life of the Pennsylvania countryside would all make themselves felt (plate 160). At Tivoli Marden has returned to his own roots, to the life and landscape he knew before leaving home to become an artist, and to memories of the Hudson from his youth.

In the Tivoli studio Marden has embarked on two of the most ambitious paintings of his career. Each is twenty-four feet in length and is composed of six panels explicitly exploring the spectrum of six colors—red, orange, yellow, green, blue, violet. Titled *The Propitious Garden of Plane Image, Second Version* and . . . *Third Version* (plates 171, 172), the paintings refer back in

15. Jackson Pollock. *One: Number 31, 1950.* 1950
Oil and enamel on unprimed canvas,
8' 10" x 17' 5⅝" (269.5 x 530.8 cm)
The Museum of Modern Art, New York.
Sidney and Harriet Janis Collection Fund (by exchange)

their horizontal formats to two works from the late 1970s and early '80s, *Frieze* and *Frieze II* (p. 101, fig. 28), which allude to classical Greek compositions; an added reference in the new works is to Chinese handscrolls. The potential associations of the color spectrum are many, whether to classical, Biblical, or popular culture or to the history of art, from the Renaissance through the Hudson Valley painters to the unfolding prismatics of Marcel Duchamp and Johns. The word "propitious" in the title, meaning "favorable" or "giving promise of success," is joined in the dictionary with classical references, such as "the fates were propitious" or "propitious omens,"[49] and the garden is an ancient motif for constant change, growth, and renewal. Marden has used the phrase "plane image" for decades; he has often said and written that his work is a synthesis of the plane and the image. For years the front-door buzzer of his studio on the Bowery was labeled "Plane Image," and his office and archives are organized under the same title.

At the time of this writing, Marden continues to work on these two most recent paintings. They will certainly provide the conclusion to *Brice Marden: A Retrospective of Paintings and Drawings*, but there is a chance they may return to the studio at the exhibition's close, for Marden, in examining paintings he has already released to the world, has occasionally decided that he wants to continue to work on them.[50] The continuing evolution of a single painting can often parallel the challenge Marden has set himself throughout his career. For the conclusion offered by "finishing" is only temporary: "When the painting really lives, has a right to exist on its own strengths and weaknesses, I consider it finished. When I have put all I can into it and it really breathes, I stop. There are times when a work has pulled ahead of me and goes on to become something new to me, something that I have never seen before; that is finishing in an exhilarating way."[51]

NOTES

1. See, e.g., Carl Andre, "Brice Marden Paintings Bykert Gallery, 15 W 57 NYC Nov 15 Two Part Review," *57th Street Review*, November 15, 1966, n.p.; Lucy R. Lippard, "The Silent Art," *Art in America* 55, no. 1 (January–February 1967): 58–63; Harris Rosenstein, "Total and Complex," *Artnews* 66, no. 5 (May 1967): 52–54, 67–68; and Lippard, "Rebelliously Romantic," *New York Times*, June 4, 1967, p. D25.

2. Yve-Alain Bois, "Marden's Doubt," in Ulrich Loock and Bois, *Brice Marden: Paintings, 1985–1993* (Bern: Kunsthalle, 1993), pp. 12–67.

3. Brice Marden, in "Interview by Robin White at Crown Point Press, Oakland, California, 1980," *View* 3, no. 2 (June 1980): 3.

4. Ibid., p. 14.

5. Marden, notes, November 20, 1966, typescript, courtesy Marden.

6. Marden, in "Interview with Brice Marden conducted by Paul Cummings, October 3, 1972," Archives of American Art, Smithsonian Institution, Washington, D.C., p. 8.

7. Ibid., p. 11.

8. Ibid.

9. Ibid., p. 8.

10. Marden, lecture, Skowhegan School of Painting and Sculpture, summer 1971, transcript, p. 7. In Skowhegan Lecture Archive, Brice Marden, The Museum of Modern Art Archives, New York.

11. Ibid.

12. Ibid., p. 8.

13. Marden, statement, in Jean-Claude Lebensztejn, "Eight Statements," *Art in America* 63, no. 4 (July–August 1975): 72.

14. Jeremy Lewison, *Brice Marden Prints, 1961–1991: A Catalogue Raisonné* (London: Tate Gallery Publications, 1992), p. 12.

15. Marden, "Statements and Photographs submitted in partial fulfillment of the requirements for Master of Fine Arts degree," Yale University, May 1, 1963, p. 1.

16. Marden, in Alan Moore, Edit deAk, and Mike Robinson, "Conversation with Brice Marden," *Art-Rite* no. 9, special issue on painting (Spring 1975): 42.

17. Marden, "Statements and Photographs," pp. 3–4.

18. Marden, in the transcript of an interview with Edgar B. Howard, December 11, 1976, p. 3. Selections from this interview form much of the sound track for the film *Brice Marden* (New York: Tuckernuck Productions, 1977), produced and directed by Howard and Theodore R. Haimes and available through the Checkerboard Film Foundation, New York. All quotations from the interview are courtesy Edgar B. Howard, Checkerboard Film Foundation, New York.

19. Klaus Kertess, *Brice Marden Paintings and Drawings* (New York: Harry N. Abrams, 1992), p. 13.

20. Marden, notes, November 20, 1966.

21. Marden, in an interview with Sol Ostrow, "Brice Marden," *Bomb* no. 22 (Winter 1988): 16.

22. Marden, in conversation with Gary Garrels in the series "Dialogues in Contemporary Art," Museum of Contemporary Art, Los Angeles, April 3, 2004, in conjunction with the exhibition *A Minimal Future*.

23. Marden, notes, November 20, 1966.

24. Marden, "Statements and Photographs," p. 5.

25. Marden, in the transcript of the interview with Howard, pp. 30, 31.

26. Ibid., pp. 8–9.

27. Marden, in Moore, deAk, and Robinson, "Conversation with Brice Marden," p. 39.

28. Marden in the transcript of the interview with Howard, pp. 12–13.

29. Ibid., p. 34.

30. Marden, statement, in Maurice Poirier and Jane Necol, "The '60s in Abstract: 13 Statements and an Essay," *Art in America* 71, no. 9 (October 1983): 122.

31. See Kertess, *Brice Marden Paintings and Drawings*, pp. 20–21.
32. Only six of these paintings are now extant. One painting was completely reworked in 1971 and eventually destroyed.
33. As Brenda Richardson wrote in an early version of her essay "Even a Stone Knows You" in the present volume, "Thera, or Thira, is also the name of a Cycladic island (called by the Venetians Santorini) that lies about 125 miles southeast of Hydra and is one of the most important archaeological sites in the Aegean. Although the architectural ruins there are echoed in the post-and-lintel configuration of Marden's *Thira*, the island's name did not figure in the artist's choice of title. The Mardens visited Thera for the first time only around 2000, although they had long known of it as a landmark archaeological site."
34. See also Marden, in Moore, deAk, and Robinson, "Conversation with Brice Marden," p. 41, and in "Brice Marden: Interview by Mark Rosenthal, September 19, 1997," in Jeffrey Weiss et al., *Mark Rothko* (Washington, D.C.: National Gallery of Art, 1998), pp. 358–62.
35. See *Brice Marden, Samuel Buri, Ernst Messerli: Projekte für das Basler Münster* (Liestal: Kunsthalle Palazzo, 1990), and Kathy L. Maschke, "The Revelation of Brice Marden: Designs for the Stained Glass Windows of the Basel Cathedral," *Glass Magazine* no. 44 (1991): 28–35.
36. Marden, in Lilly Wei, "Talking Abstract, Part One," *Art in America* 76, no. 7 (July 1987): p. 83.
37. Marden, in Robert Mahoney, "Brice Marden: This Is What Things Are About," *Flash Art* 23, no. 155 (November–December 1990): 118.
38. Marden, in Janie C. Lee, "Interview with Brice Marden," *Brice Marden Drawings: The Whitney Museum of American Art Collection* (New York: Whitney Museum of American Art, 1998), p. 19.
39. Marden, in "Brice Marden in conversation with William Furlong," *Art Monthly* no. 117 (June 1988): 4.
40. Marden, in Wei, "Talking Abstract, Part One," p. 83.
41. Marden, in Pat Steir, "Brice Marden, an Interview," *Brice Marden: Recent Drawings and Etchings* (New York: Matthew Marks Gallery, 1991), n.p.
42. Ibid, n.p.
43. Organized by the author, then Director of Programs at Dia, the exhibition was on view from October 17, 1991, to May 31, 1992, before traveling to Minneapolis, Houston, Madrid, and Bonn. See Richardson, *Brice Marden Cold Mountain* (Houston: Houston Fine Art Press, 1991).
44. See ibid.; Kay Larson, "Different Strokes," *New York*, October 21, 1991, pp. 74–83; Robert Hughes, "Lines That Go for a Walk," *Time*, November 4, 1991, pp. 96–97; John Yau, "Brice Marden's Cold Mountain: Drawing from Jackson Pollock," *Artspace* 16, nos. 1 and 2 (January–April 1992): 48–51; and Mahoney, "Brice Marden, DIA Center for the Arts," *Flash Art* 25, no. 162 (January–February 1992): 129–30, among others.
45. Marden, statement, in Lebensztejn, "Eight Statements," pp. 72, 73.
46. Richardson, *Brice Marden Cold Mountain*, p. 45.
47. Marden, quoted in ibid, pp. 40, 41.
48. Richardson, "Even a Stone Knows You," p. 91.
49. *The New Lexicon Webster's Dictionary of the English Language*, p. 801.
50. Marden has reworked several major paintings after they were publicly exhibited. On *The Seasons* (1974–75) see Mancusi-Ungaro, "Marden's Materiality: The Monochromes," in the present volume, pp. 115–16; on *Study for the Muses (Eaglesmere Version)* (1991–94/1997–99) see Charles Wylie, *Brice Marden, Work of the 1990s: Paintings, Drawings, and Prints* (Dallas: Dallas Museum of Art, 1998), p. 25.
51. Marden, "Statements and Photographs," p. 8.

Richard Shiff

Force of Myself Looking

When I sit here looking at [my finished paintings], I am incapable of identifying with them personally. I don't see these as myself. One of the things about being a painter is that you're trying to make things that you want to see. . . . It's more like knowing yourself by forgetting about yourself, learning not to be so involved with yourself.

—Brice Marden, 1991[1]

About his work and about all of life, Brice Marden speaks with the plainest language. His straightforward manner has not dulled his philosophical edge. Some years ago Brenda Richardson aptly characterized the effect: "Marden has a disarming way of crystallizing issues." When Richardson challenged him to explain his purpose, he returned with a question for himself and everyone else: "What are you going to strive for?" He is a dreamer, but also realistic, and answered himself candidly: "It's not that you're going to get there. If I was concerned about getting there, I would choose a likely method—whether Zen study or something else—and I would do it. I guess in a way I have chosen my method, and my method is painting."[2]

Painting is unlikely to "get there"; instead, it keeps going. "I carry on with my studies," Paul Cézanne, terminally ill, confided, "and I think I'm making some slow progress"—progress, not resolution.[3] "The first step toward finding out," argued Charles Sanders Peirce, Cézanne's exact contemporary, "is to acknowledge you do not satisfactorily know already."[4] Neither Cézanne nor Peirce was seduced by certainty. Conducting his philosophical study, Peirce became an inventive artist, investigating possibilities, accepting chance and doubt. He confessed that his "modes of thought and of expression [were] peculiar and gauche"; his was a left-handed style of reasoning.[5] Contrary to type, artists sometimes speak like proper philosophers, as when Piet Mondrian declared a principle to be applied to himself, just as we might now apply it to Marden (principles generalize): "The more the natural is abstracted, the more pronounced is the relationship."[6] Later, regarding his quest as an abstract artist, Mondrian admitted, "I don't want pictures; I just want to find things out."[7]

In this pragmatic spirit of "finding out"—like his "hero" Cézanne, or like Mondrian, to whom he dedicated a drawing, or like Peirce, modernity's wayward logician—Marden expects no perfection.[8] A sense of progress suffices. Not necessarily progress, even: merely an openness to movement, change, and fortunate occurrence. Marden strives. Toward what? Perhaps toward a beneficial state of alienation, letting go of the social identity to which his culture confines him as an individual—"forgetting about yourself, learning not to be so involved with yourself."

Romantic

Must it be the self that becomes the target of an artist's deepest resistance? Around the time Marden stressed the notion of "forgetting about yourself," he was remembering his past. In an interview of 1990, he reflected on earlier moments of his career and his penchant for making bold pronouncements, such as "An artist's life is an intense search for truth. . . . The rectangle, the plane, the picture, the structure, is but a trampoline to bounce on spirituality" (fig. 1).[9] Truth and spirituality were as central to his thinking as color and shape, since "the artist is the necromancer, the priest."[10] Above all, Marden's work would be guided by emotions and appeal to emotions: "Emotion is the lasting thing in art."[11] In 1963, on completing his graduate study at Yale University, he described his accomplishment: "These are highly emotional paintings not to be admired for any technical or intellectual reason but to be felt."[12]

From the perspective of 1990—more established, older and perhaps wiser—Marden acknowledged that during the 1960s and into the '70s he had indulged in "a very romantic attitude. . . . The things I was saying were really embarrassing."[13] But here he is too hard on himself. Committed to painting as an emotional and moral cause, he had, and continues to have, a right to his "romantic" opinions. He tends to use this term in a colloquial, not a literary or academic sense: "My reasons for studying painting were very romantic. . . . All those bohemians and Greenwich Village and stuff like that. But then you get involved in it. . . . I mean we [painters] represent our tradition."[14]

During Marden's undergraduate years, art provided him with the route to a romantic, bohemian life-style and quickly became much more. Among his fellow students, he was the enterprising one—volunteering for special assignments from his Boston University instructors, hanging a show of Edwin Dickinson in the university gallery in 1959 (fig. 2), seeking out Henry Geldzahler, later a well-known New York curator, then a graduate student across the river at Harvard and known as an insider. Beyond his bohemianism (never rejected), Marden assumed more than one person's share of the collective responsibility to maintain "the painter's tradition [which] dates back 30,000 years."[15] He was the traditionalist among his equally ambitious contemporaries, differing from them in considering the history of painting, from the walls of the caves to Abstract Expressionism, as "one big thing."[16] He felt no need to break off from history in aesthetic defiance: "There's something very basic, very human about art."[17] He meant all art of all ages.

With a certain irony, this uncompromising abstractionist acknowledges the conservatism of his lifelong interest in the past. Classically trained in drawing the human figure, instructed in color by the masterpieces of the

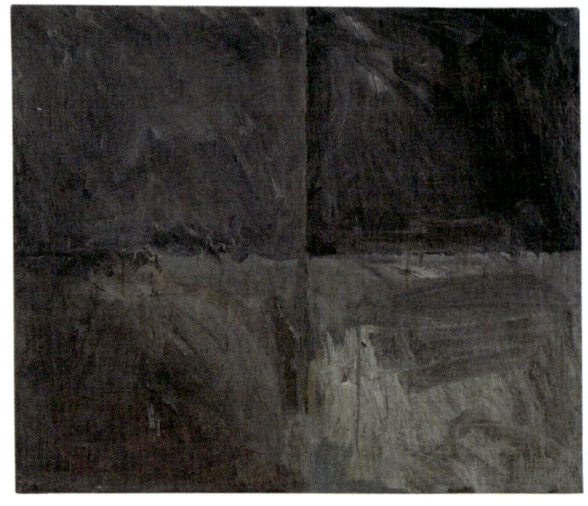

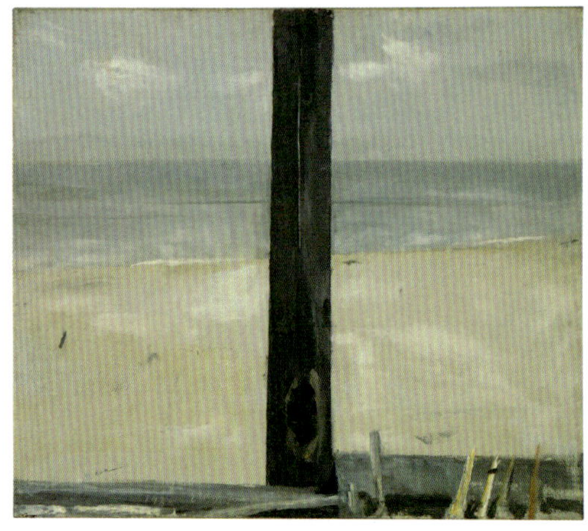

1. Brice Marden. Untitled. 1963
Oil on canvas
20 x 24" (50.8 x 61 cm)
Private collection, Los Angeles

2. Edwin Dickinson. *Cottage Porch, Peaked Hill*. 1932
Oil on canvas, 26⅛ x 30⅛" (66.4 x 76.3 cm).
The Museum of Modern Art, New York.
Grace Rainey Rogers Fund

museums, Marden may feel embarrassed about the way he once articulated his romantic notions, but he continues to engage in romantic hero-worship. Examples set by the likes of Cézanne, Manet, Courbet, and above all Zurbarán, a master of grays, still guide his understanding, which has been expanded through study of ancient Mediterranean art as well as Asian traditions. As a developing artist, Marden "painted more through old master influence than through contemporary influence."[18] Yet from a very early stage, he had his particular way of converting complex imagery into a set of direct strokes and deceptively simple forms—totally contemporary. He concentrated so much visual experience within his abstractions that the complexity of classical representation returned and may even have increased. During the 1960s, his manner was already distinct. It was also oddly without a category. Despite the romantic aura his comments contributed, his art failed to fit the prevailing sense of individual self-expression (an interpretive extension on my part, requiring explanation). To compound the classification problem, his abstract geometry lacked the degree of structural regularity perceived in much of the art it resembled.

The history of art is "one big thing," Marden said. As a late-modern abstract painter, he belongs to the 200-year "Romantic" end of this 30,000-year, Stone Age tradition. "Romanticism," Charles Baudelaire wrote in 1846, "does not consist in a perfected execution, but in a conception analogous to the ethical character of the era."[19] A century later, Willem de Kooning, a traditionalist at heart, agreed: "Painting is a way of living today, a style of living."[20] When he began to be received with enthusiasm, de Kooning reminded his public that he was "still working out of doubt."[21] Whether indulging in bohemianism or getting serious about painting, at a romantic's core is an ethic, not a professional strategy: how you conduct yourself, what you look at, how you feel about it, what you come to know, your degree of disquiet over it all. "I like painters where there seems to be a lot of doubt involved," Marden confesses.[22] He acts on the romantic desire for fresh experience, accepting the emotional risk that follows from his openness to sensation.

If at every moment a certain psychosomatic state of equilibrium constitutes the individual—stabilized, you are "involved with yourself," as Marden might put it—then what we call experience is everything this selfsame individual is not. Experience takes you out of yourself. Peirce, like twentieth-century theorists to follow, defined experience by acknowledging its inherent negativity and disruptiveness: "Breaking of the silence by noise [is] an experience. . . . Consciousness of the action of a new feeling in destroying the old feeling is what I call an experience. Experience generally is what the course of life has compelled me to think."[23] Experience compels. Altering the mental and physical state you call "yourself," experience becomes disorienting, requiring adjustments to perceptual habit. This is the condition toward which Marden strives in painting.

Romanticism divides. On the one hand, the experience that a romantic artist seeks entails a degree of psychic insecurity. On the other hand, because Romanticism has a theory, a set of principles, it affords solid ground. Early Romanticism established the solitary act of painting as an effective means of self-expression, a way to know the entity a person could be most certain of knowing: the self, secure even in its disorientation. While jolted by sensation, the self molded sensation. Acts of artistic representation projected the self as embodied in the created object, so that a person became self-aware, as well as a transparent image for others (you are what you make). Akin to lyric poetry, Romantic painting—in principle, *any* painting—spoke of the sensibility and sensitivity of an individual. In this respect Marden's thesis statement of 1963 ("paintings . . . to be felt") was hardly unreasonable or extreme. The arrangement of a representational subject, the constellation of abstract shapes, and, most of all, the figured touch visible in a vectored stroke or textured bit of impasto: these features revealed the temper of the painter and did so with or against the individual's conscious will. Artistic representation manifested secret movements of the soul. Those who valued painting more for its individuality than for its establishment of a collective standard (though the two can be compatible) believed that its practice isolated the qualities and capacities of a particular hand and eye, certain characteristic gestures and tones revealing a regulative "temperament," a physiological type subject to idiosyncratic variation—a self fully in possession of itself.[24]

About this aspect of art there seems to have been little doubt among nineteenth-century Romantics. What distinguished one critical viewer from another was the degree of appreciation (or tolerance) for deviant variation. Early modern critics observed that even in cases of direct, seemingly objective representation, a factor of subjectivity would "slip in. . . . This element is the personality of the artist."[25] *Temperament* and *personality* were often interchangeable terms; when distinguished, temperament was the more corporeal feature and personality the more emotional. In its expressive capacity, pictorial representation operated reciprocally, feeding upon itself. By setting external appearances into a form consistent with the individual artist's physical capacities, emotional disposition, and imaginative fantasies, representation reconfirmed and strengthened the very mentality that brought it to life.[26] Like modern artists before him, Marden acknowledges an element of reciprocity in his painting, and does so with his usual disarming directness: "It works on me and I work on it. Give and take."[27] Mind (the painter's emotions) and matter (the substance of painting) are not separate entities but evolve as a relation.

Mythic

With regard to personality, or the artist's characteristic range of emotion, a complication arises. What is a personality? How malleable or flexible is it? Where do we locate it? It may be inborn and natural, truly one's own. But it may also be the product of a social and cultural environment over which an individual has little if any control. The former, "natural" possibility is a cornerstone of mainline bourgeois culture and as such, paradoxically, likely to be a historical, cultural construct rather than natural and timeless. Critics dissatisfied with the drift of their modern society tend to challenge beliefs fundamental to it; they regard untainted self-expression as a mythological fiction. If a culture promotes a certain art as a model of free expression because of its naturalness and spontaneity, then it falls on criticism to question the "natural" and the "spontaneous." "What appears as spontaneity," T. W. Adorno famously wrote of American jazz performance, "is in fact carefully planned out in advance with machinelike precision." The "spontaneous" form that jazz assumed was like a fashion statement, incapable of accommodating variation freely: "The range of the permissible in jazz is as narrowly circumscribed as in any particular cut of clothes."[28]

Any attribute that common sense attaches to an object or a practice, Roland Barthes warned in 1961, "risks being mythical," for everyone accepts it without question—and acceptance without question is a defining feature of myth or ideological belief.[29] Barthes was a member of a new generation of cultural critics concerned with ideological pressures on postwar European life. In 1961, he was addressing new generations of readers; in America, the generation of Marden and those still younger formed a potential audience.[30] To the extent that Barthes and other European theorists eventually spawned the American postmodernism of the 1980s, Marden grew wary that this form of critique had degenerated, encouraging political and cultural defeatism: "I always considered postmodernism to be a political idea, it wasn't really about aesthetics. [It gives] up on certain ideals, the belief that you can always make it better."[31] Colloquially, Marden speaks here as a romantic. He has ideals; he ventures new works; he strives: all the while unsure of success.

What of the alternative? The new critics argued that a flow of structured information (language, signs of all kinds) directs and limits human perception and behavior. As the likes of Adorno and Barthes knew, the belief that individuals realize their desires through cultural practices often works against individual interests: most acts passing for self-expression and self-fulfillment do little more than restate the ideological values of the culture. The time for pursuing moments of childlike wonder—once encouraged by the notion that what is natural to a person is best perceived in a state of innocence—had long passed for Marden's generation.[32] During the 1960s, a new critical message (exemplified by Adorno and Barthes, as different as they were) reached socially concerned Americans, many of them culturally disenchanted in reaction to the politics of the Cold War and the war in Vietnam. As artists, some, not all, would nevertheless maintain faith in the redeeming human value of the material, sensory experience that the traditional visual arts afforded. "Paintings are physical," Marden has insisted; "So is the act of creating them. This physicality should be emphasized."[33] There was a politics to his materialized romanticism: "I think any artist striving to make art is making a political act."[34] Speaking to the situation in 1990, Marden called for something definitively human, "more basic, about the earth, and about the reality of how we live."[35] He was distinguishing political action as an ideological gesture (which compromised art, shaping it into sound-bites and slogans) from a politically beneficial attitude toward human behavior—a sustaining ethic ("more basic") as opposed to a series of responses to contingencies.

Certain sources of imagery were less freely human than others—dematerialized yet controlling. "Television delivers people to an advertiser," Richard Serra announced in a short film of 1973: "You are the product of TV."[36] He was arguing that the viewers are the viewed, that the cultural practice known as commercial television was determining personal desires and expressions of choice in advance of each individual's experience of those feelings. What jazz and other cultural commodities were to Adorno, television was to Serra.[37] In response to this world of pervasive commodification—its false spontaneity, its pretense to free choice—artists would use materials to counter rather than confirm prevailing orders of experiential resolution. Works of art could stimulate an excess of experience, exceeding the holding capacity of ideological concepts.

Leaving the language of personal expression to debunkers, letting therapists take responsibility for psychoanalysis, many cultural critics of Marden's time—that is, now—regard the self as ideologically determined at its core, if it even has a core, an essence.[38] We have become inured to thinking that the self is constructed rather than experientially self-forming—or, if self-forming, that social institutions filter all experience and frame the process. If the individual is a product of social forces, an "expression" of the patterns of behavior and emotional states those forces induce, then self-expression will have been compromised from the start. It can operate only within boundaries established by the social discourse. Each individual becomes a type, a social identity, an image for someone else's eye.

What can artists do when the working of the system thoroughly dismays them, when, as Marden says, ordinary political life and its image of the world have become "horrendous"?[39] Can another self be felt within or beyond the social self—a self to be known after "forgetting about yourself"?[40] This is one way to conceive of the question of art and life as Marden's generation confronted it. The old "romantic" forms of visual self-expression had produced modern icons but their continuing use was suspect. Like Adorno's improvisational jazz, they offered little in the way of aesthetic provocation—Peircean experience—to late-twentieth-century artists. Marden seems to have moved outside the cultural limitations of expression in a way that his romanticized language only vaguely intimated. He had little trust in the inherited forms of self-expression, yet remained unconvinced that social forces predetermine what can be done with the material basis of those and other artistic devices. From within his romanticism, he pursued a third possibility.

Art Shield

The modern, Romantic practice of painting includes a counter-tradition. Sometimes it assumes the name *realism*, which Marden himself might favor: "The paper is an integral part of the drawing. The wax . . . everything's a real part of the drawing. It becomes very real." He was referring (in 1976) to drawings worked heavily in wax and graphite on weighty, high-quality paper, with even the irregular deckled edge receiving a coating of the applied material (*Study for the N Drawing*, 1975; plate 72): "A piece of paper practically becomes an object. And I always show drawings full sheet."[41] Similarly, Marden insists that a painting must occupy the entirety of its canvas. Its figuration (the applied color itself) sits neither within the field nor upon it, but becomes the field. Marden's paint bonds with the surface and edges as if it were finding its natural limit, like water in surface tension. Paint passes around the edge of a stretcher bar only so far as the physical process of brushing, scraping, and spreading dictates. When a work consists of two panels abutting along a common boundary (*Fave*, 1968–69; plate 28), the contrast of color, and the relative buildup of paint along the doubled edge, enhance its physicality. The edge makes a material distinction, not merely an optical one.

According to Marden's sense of the real, "There's no optical play . . . no optical illusions in a painting."[42] This statement requires qualification, as Marden understood. Paintings do entail illusion, but of a kind removed from the conventional aims of illusionistic rendering: "You deal with illusion. But it's not illusion about things that you see. It's an illusion of an abstraction of things that you see."[43] Here he was referring to the fact that a surface might appear visually thick when it was materially thin, or monochromatic when it was multicolored: Marden's "real" illusory features relate to physical qualities of the planar surface itself, as opposed to evoking something external to which the plane might allude through color or shape. In his oil-and-wax panels, the actual weave of the underlying canvas often shows; yet it remains unclear to the eye whether this should be understood as a tactile effect (minor variation in the surface plane transferred upward by the buildup of layers of paint) or as an optical effect (the same variation visible underneath the surface plane because it is translucent). Both causes might obtain: Marden's paint is like a fluid body of water in which any isolated element may appear located near the surface or in the depths. Most of his paintings have little actual layering because he scrapes down surfaces between successive applications of color. The complex result is more a matter of an optics of hue and value than of a textured physicality. His drawing sheets nevertheless display the physical reality of buckling and tearing, caused by the stress of his pressing, rubbing, and grinding graphite and wax into the fibers.

Works consisting of multiple panels, whether abutted or spaced at intervals (fig. 3; *The Seasons*, 1974–75, plate 64), have an especially Mardenesque feature of the real: "If each panel is the same size, I want them all to look the same size. That's realism." He struggled to fit each shape with a suitable color so that no panel seems nearer or farther from the viewer than its neighbors, for otherwise the apparent size of the containing shape would be affected and the integrity of the plane violated; the colored rectangle would no longer be itself. All the while, Marden enjoined his panels corporeally, as if setting his own body into them. Their reality was never far removed from his: "You are always aware that you can reach so high and you can reach so wide."[44] This reality has no correlative visual signs in the way that the "reality" of self-expression does, whether through marks that index a telling gesture or a perspective that reveals the character of a person's vision. Marden's kind of reality belongs to an immediate order of experience—oddly depersonalized experience. In 1976, he commented: "The sizes usually relate closely to the human size. I mean they're usually around six feet or so. I'm human size."[45] Of course he is. And so is everyone else.

Marden's allusion to his "human" size—disarming in its directness—ought to bring a smile of human recognition, even as it may cause a pretentious critic to wince. Realism amounts to more than matching an artist's body to the dimensions of a canvas, often just a practical consideration of studio manufacture. The term *realism* does little to suggest how objects might function as a solution to a culturally disenchanted artist's impasse. Marden nevertheless offers an intriguing notion. An intuition comes to him in the course of explaining himself: his drawings, with their heavy layering of wax and graphite, their imposing physicality (see Untitled, 1970, plate 32; *Study for the N Drawing*; *Inside Outside*, 1977, plate 73), are actually quite solid and potentially protective; each becomes a guard against external dangers, an "art

3. Brice Marden. Untitled. 1968
Oil and beeswax on canvas
Two panels, overall: 69" x 7' 6" (175.3 x 228.6 cm)
Private collection, San Francisco

shield." "Shield" is Marden's metaphor, accompanied, in a film from 1976, by a gesture of holding forth the imaginary object, backed by handles. As quickly as the thought arises, he realizes its absurdity and laughs at his own conceit.[46] But the notion has substance. It demonstrates that in the hands of an artist—actually or imaginatively—a drawing shifts instantaneously from image to object, from fiction to the truth of fact.

Self-expression, one would think, ought to be an internal matter. When institutionalized in the culture, however, it presents an external danger, a temptation to artists, because it remains available to be exploited mythologically. It allows artists to grow certain of themselves, providing the general form of a self-image for individuals who can repeat it, with variation, in order to be true to themselves (true to the cultural, ideological self). Removing doubt, the mythic forms of self-expression solve all professional problems. Expressive surfaces—say, a flurry of marks in a distinctive style, or a characteristic representational distortion—threaten to seduce artists into believing that they have found their true image, original to the individual. It is telling that Marden hardly, if ever, speaks of originality. To the contrary, his art brings attention back to materiality and weightiness, the status of the image in its capacity as a physical object like others.[47] Any one of his drawings might serve as an "art shield," transformed by the artist's act of physical imagination, supplemented by the movement of his hands (as if to grasp a shield by handles).

In 1976, performing his "art shield" gesture before a filmmaker's camera, Marden acted out the realist counter-tradition within Romanticism—not an antiromanticism but a corrective tendency within the lyrical, self-expressive tradition he was engaging. Some form of depersonalized realist technique has probably appeared just as often in the past of modern art as have the various modes of self-expression. Material realism may seem less prominent simply because it is less commonly theorized, whether by critics or historians. Donald Judd was an exception. Labeled a Minimalist as Marden sometimes was and is, he converted his critical description of material fact into a pragmatist's theory of human understanding. Barnett Newman's art, Judd wrote, "doesn't suggest a great scheme of knowledge; it doesn't claim more than anyone can know."[48] Within the counter-tradition of romantic-realist practice, painting provides escape from the prison of the constructed self, from a person's cultural pretense to self-formation. *Materially*, painting shields artists from themselves, their mythologies, their grandiose illusions. Colloquially, we would say that art of this sort—the very art that Marden regarded as a springboard to "spirituality"—brings us down to earth.[49] (I imply no contradiction.)

During the nineteenth century, a realist could find protection in becoming a nature painter of an almost naïve sort. Naturalism served as a shielding reservoir of the real. In 1847, the French critic Paul Mantz asked his readers to imagine passing along an isolated forest path, disposed (as they must be) in a certain mood. Whether you are "exhilarated or depressed," he observed, "it seems that something of yourself remains suspended in the hushed thickets and in the branches of the mute trees. . . . According to whether your heart is sanguine or somber, nature celebrates with you or consoles. . . . You see nature agitated or at ease, according to what is happening within yourself."[50] A living, feeling person leaves a mark on nature just by being there, nature having the magical power to assimilate human emotion spontaneously. By this reasoning, the impressionable natural environment is itself passionate, unlike the cultural environment, which is more rigid, less forgiving, unsympathetic. Artists leave an impression on nature, just as nature impresses artists and everyone else. The latter direction (nature impresses us) seems to be the natural one, because we are sentient and nature is not. We assume a certain distance and view nature objectively as if it were a picture, something to look at, to be affected by; yet Mantz implied that the material world may equal the human world in its capacity to receive feeling. Nature and its materials share feelings with the artist, who joins with their world in a "school of reality."[51]

Adopting a self-conscious intent to be expressive, an artist would have been tempted to follow cultural protocols, making the brushstroke showy, projecting it as self-expressive. The art-shield trick to the emerging realist account was reciprocity: because nature adjusted itself automatically to the emotional state of the painter, no compositional or stylistic devices were required as aids to faithful expression. A painter needed only to represent things as they appeared by whatever means were at hand, the more directly and physically felt the better. In this regard Mantz found that he could appreciate the work of landscape painters who had little to recommend them other than the straightforwardness of their rendering: "Less able in execution than most others, barely initiated into the subtleties of their craft, they copy like grown-up children, [yet] their painstaking incapacity is not without a strange seductiveness"—art with no expertise, no style.[52]

Marden is hardly without technical subtlety, but he coordinates his technique with his directness. "I'm human size," he says; and although he has painted "monochrome" panels larger than himself, he does not extend them beyond a size he can cover in its entirety before the paint surface dries.[53] He intends to color the planar surface, not trace out his gestures, even though the paint may faintly record them. For his oil-and-wax panels of the late 1960s and '70s, he would apply an initial layer with a brush, then "erase the brush strokes with a cooking spatula," shielding himself from the dangers of commonplace displays of manual facility.[54] The result has a "strange seductiveness." It seems fitting that during his tenure as an assistant to Robert Rauschenberg he produced a number of white panels for an exhibition at the Leo Castelli

Gallery, New York, in 1968, refabrications of versions of Rauschenberg's *White Painting* of 1951. His specific instruction was to "do it so no brushstroke shows"—an exercise in romantic realism of a twentieth-century type.[55]

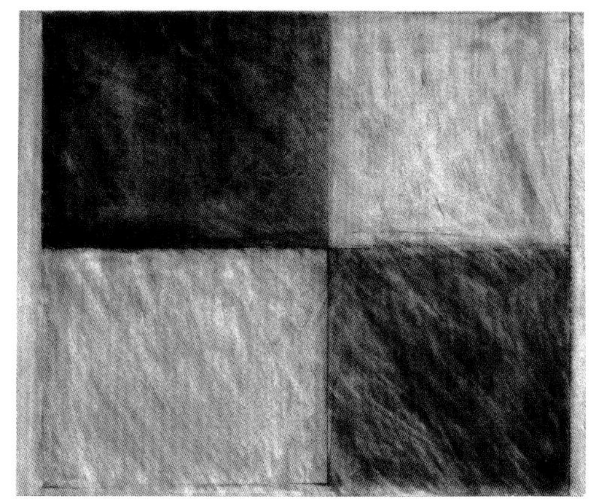

There are strokes that show, but show nothing. For a number of drawings of the early 1960s, organized into quadrants (fig. 4), Marden developed a broad range of grays by stroking the paper with sticks of compressed charcoal at various levels of pressure and removing or smudging some of the strokes with a kneaded eraser (Untitled, 1962; fig. 5). The strokes typically arc from upper left to lower right, as befits a left-handed draftsman. They are fluid, agile, sensitively varied; and yet, by the standards of the medium, they lack personality. Like Jasper Johns, Marden succeeded in keeping his surfaces semiologically anonymous and relatively neutral—not in the sense that we would be unable to identify the artist (with familiarity, this is easy enough to do) but in the sense that we would find it difficult to attribute these specific marks to either *this* personality (Marden's) or *any* specific personality. We sense a human presence and even, with the varying of the marks, a passing set of emotions, yet no specific person.

Conversing with Richardson, Marden referred to "trying to make things that you want to see." This is to create actively what nature offered passively to romantics of a previous era—the things you want to see, the things that are in natural sympathy with who you are, not in some essential sense but in the flow of life's transience. The "things that you want to see" are not fantasy images now becoming visualized in material form, but material forms that come into being only as paintings, things worthy of a person's sustained visual attention, things neither imagined nor visualized at any other moment. The Romantic analogy would be this: the experience of a state of nature as it appears in accordance with the emotional state of the individual within it. Without *this* person, *this* state of nature would never appear. This is not self-expression in the conventional sense, because no "self" guides such an operation.

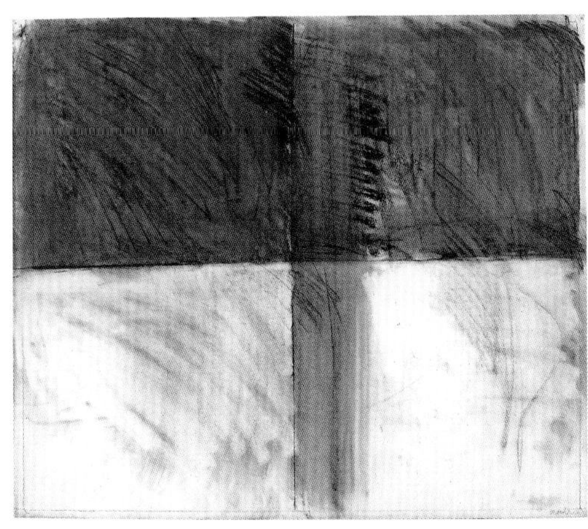

Elemental Painting

Behind Marden's plain language and self-criticism lurks another disarming aspect to his manner: he qualifies his achievements with a Cézannean sigh of resignation, as if it could hardly have been any other way. "I'm a really repressed guy," he says; "that's what this stuff is all about."[56] For better or worse, he cannot but paint, even if the kind of realist abstraction he creates conveys little meaning to the uninitiated. "It's hard to look at paintings. You have to be able to bring all sorts of things together in your mind, your imagination, in your whole body."[57] Simultaneously mental and physical, painting resembles conscious perception itself, intensifying its immediacy and integrity. Marden

4. Brice Marden. Untitled. 1962
Charcoal on paper
14⅜ x 17½" (36.5 x 44.5 cm)
Collection the artist

5. Brice Marden. Untitled. 1962
Charcoal on paper, 14 x 18" (35.5 x 45.7 cm)
Collection Sarah-Ann and Werner H. Kramarsky

would never attempt to encompass his art by intellectual order alone. Nor would it be contained within a reiterative system: "You aren't making what you [already] know."[58]

He shares this notion of working beyond the point of understanding with the generation that preceded him. In 1958, the year Marden entered Boston University, Franz Kline (also a Boston graduate) presented his account of art: "It has nothing to do with knowing, it has to do with giving. . . . When you've finished giving, the look surprises you as well as anyone else."[59] A model for Marden, Kline was committed not so much to knowing as to finding out. As a matter of practice more than principle, Marden had to diverge from Kline to let painting lead beyond himself, beyond his knowledge and self-knowledge. Nineteenth-century artists with similar beliefs immersed themselves in external, alien nature; Abstract Expressionists like Kline concentrated on the force of gesture, its origin internal. In Marden's time, however, gesture did little more than substitute for earlier forms of naturalism. Judd made the relevant argument: "The work of Kline, [Philip] Guston and de Kooning is . . . a continuation of [early-twentieth-century] expressionism . . . which is the old [nineteenth-century] picture of nature distorted by the artists' feelings."[60] Kline, from this viewpoint, might as well have been a nineteenth-century naturalist.

Marden observed his surroundings intently and developed skills of the hand, but he used neither nature nor gesture as an expressive engine. Rather, he confronted sensation through the material values of painting. He gave his surface of marks the prominence Kline gave his, while forgoing allusions to self-expression. This caused painting, a cultural form, to perform like external nature, itself in need of being rescued from culture. The process delivered Marden outside the cultural form he knew most intimately: the social construction that was himself ("yourself" in his statement about "knowing yourself by forgetting yourself"). His aesthetic deliverance amounted to a self-forgetting. It was as if—*as if*—painting were no longer instructed by the general culture of the painter. Instead, it established its address through its persistent materiality. This is how art gives an artist something to see, never before seen or imagined.

If I have adequately characterized the Marden effect, I may also have argued counter-intuitively (hence the need for "as if"). It is strange that a person would require isolation creating paintings in a studio in order to have a form of the elemental experience of being immersed in nature—experience that involves no making, just looking and perceiving. What do painting, drawing, and other modes of figuration add to what ordinary perception provides? In 1972, when asked if his color "comes from observation of something," Marden answered that he "travels around and looks at things."[61] "We look for form in nature," he stated in a note to himself around 1974.[62] Concerning his painting *Nebraska* (1966; plate 15) he elaborated for an interviewer, "I paint nature. I mean, I refer to nature. I accept nature as a reality; it's the best reference; it's what the painting's about."[63] And later, with his disarming doubt, he added, "I could never figure out if [the representational factor] was cheating or not [that is, cheating on the principle of abstraction]. . . . It's just references. I'm always working out of some kind of naturalistic reference" (fig. 6).[64] If painting and drawing add to what the direct perception of nature provides, why would this figuration depart from the painter's self when he himself was creating it? Perhaps the naturalistic reference in Marden's abstract art parallels the function that nature assumed for representational painters of the nineteenth century, just as Mantz had theorized it: "Something of yourself remains suspended in the hushed thickets and in the branches of the mute trees." This is to say, nature takes something of yourself outside yourself where you can see it, but not in a form that you fully control. Like Cézanne and Mondrian, and Kline too, you "find out," though what you discover eludes resolution, completeness, and perfection. There is more to find out.

These notions are puzzling in relation to the spare art of Marden's earlier career, whereas the irregular bands of shifting color typical of his later career readily connote organic nature. Marden once said, however, that his "one-color painting could be considered a detail of a [Jackson] Pollock line in space," as if it were a close-up or a blow-up, retaining all the energy associated with the sweep of Pollock's linearity as well as its potential to evoke nature. This reference to Pollock appeared in 1976 in the context of a description of "grid drawings . . . showing different things that could be happening . . . on the plane simultaneously"—happenstance incidents, conceivably analogous to Pollock's tangled irregularities.[65] Marden's rectangle forms a diversified grid of "different things," even when lacking subdivision. But if the rectangle and its grid are Pollock-like and linked to nature, they are also the opposite: "The rectangle becomes the beginning of the separation from nature, it's an abstraction. I have always worked from a given rectangle."[66] So Marden, who "always [works] out of some kind of naturalistic reference," "always" works from the rectangle. This makes his romantic realism a double-sided project and potentially contradictory. Art sometimes asserts for the senses and emotions what reason would deny.

A rectangle has the abstract, structural form of a single grid unit and can generate any number of units by a self-less process of bisection—"self-less" because personal taste takes no bearing on symmetrical division. Brought to its extreme, a rectilinear grid can become so dense and concentrated that it displaces conceptions of matter and space as their equivalent in reality.[67] At a fully materialized level (a grid of countless internal divisions marked by a

6. Brice Marden. *Adriatic Study.* 1972
Graphite and beeswax on paper
21 3/4 x 30" (55.2 x 76.2 cm)
Private collection, St. Louis

corresponding quantity of pigment), it would no longer be meaningful to regard the image as an abstraction by way of reduction. The substance of the marks configuring the grid, their specific materiality, would obscure the sense of a conceptualized order. This degree of materiality would make the pictorial configuration as "real" as it was "abstract" (just as Pollock's acceptance of the material flow and viscosity of his various types of paint made him a realist—or a romantic realist like Marden).

Untitled #1 (fig. 7), an ink drawing of 1973 made with a Mont Blanc pen, represents a situation in which Marden seems to suspend his process midway, as if he might be moving in either of two directions, or perhaps both. Here the orthogonals of the grid appear unevenly articulated; the elements may be precipitating and solidifying or they may be dissolving. *Untitled #1* can be interpreted as magnifying a single rectilinear unit to reveal its internal, reticular idiosyncrasies—difference within uniformity. Or it can be interpreted as averaging up an endlessly varied structure, isolating certain features by creating a grid limited in the number of units, "different things that could be happening . . . on the plane simultaneously." In either case the image is unstable. Marden points out that *Untitled #1* divides vertically along the first bisection he made, with its eight rows of units to the left of center being darker on average than the eight rows to the right. As a result, the drawing breaks down to a grid of only two units, like *Fave* or any of Marden's two-panel "monochrome" paintings. For an exhibition he curated at the Boston Museum of Fine Arts in 1991, he took two Zurbarán figure paintings out of their frames and hung them between works of his own, each Zurbarán becoming a grid of one unit (fig. 8). Each is an endlessly varied representational image that also becomes a single "gray," its totality.

As cultural forms, the rectangle and the grid usually lack specific expressive intent.[68] Rather than acting, they establish a ground for action. But Marden works these basic forms so intensely that they become the action. "My grid comes from the outside shape [the stretcher bars or chassis]. I start with the outside shape and then the grid comes as a result of that shape, breaking down that shape."[69] For many years Marden had a reproduction of a Conté-crayon drawing by Seurat pinned to his studio wall, a study for *Petit Homme au parapet* or *L'Invalide* (c. 1881; fig. 9). Seurat had marked his drawing with a prominent grid to transfer its image to a painting.[70] Within certain units of the grid, sets of parallel strokes with an anonymous look are quite similar to those of Marden, who remembers Seurat's order as containing everything from "a soft curve to a right angle."[71] For him, Seurat's representational image was a formal abstraction, or, more to the point, an array of differential sensory qualities that could be averaged up to an integral plane or averaged down to granularity.

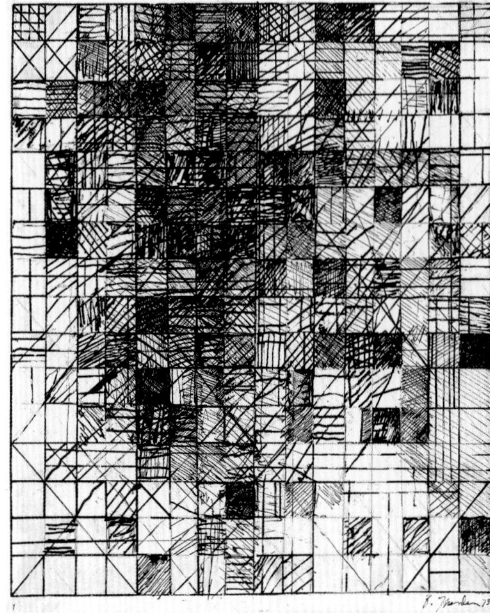

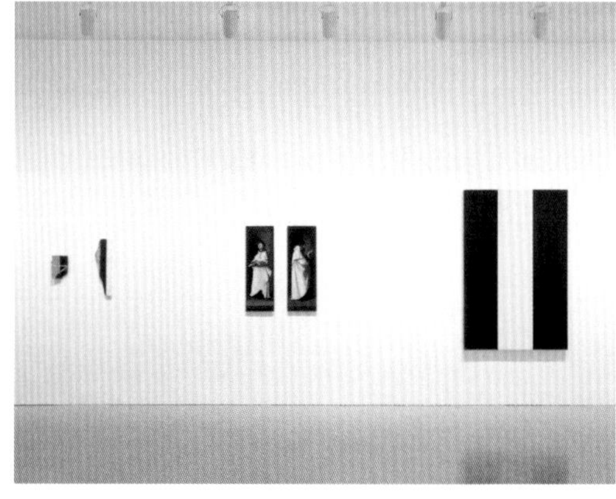

7. Brice Marden. *Untitled #1.* 1973
Ink on paper, 14½ x 12" (37 x 29 cm)
Collection the artist

8. *Connections: Brice Marden.* Installation view of exhibition curated by Marden, Museum of Fine Arts, Boston, March 23–July 21, 1991, showing two paintings by Zurbarán and three by Marden

During his short career, Seurat was known for his knowledge of materials and the intensity of his labor; he liked to attribute his impressive results to the exercise of his empirical method, as opposed to the poetic genius some admirers claimed he possessed. Marden, too, commits himself to long hours in the studio, drawing from his traditional artist's materials oddly new qualities of performance. Like Seurat, he demystifies his endeavor by invoking standards of craft and a familiar work ethic: "My father . . . used to build beautiful dry stone walls. I used to try to explain my paintings to him by saying 'You build dry stone walls and everything has to fit together right in order for it to stand, and I make paintings and everything has to fit together right in order for it to stand.'" This wry analogy—part structural, part ethical—led nowhere: "[My father] never quite got the comparison."[72] Seurat had encountered the same problem when explaining his dot, reduced to insisting, "I apply my method and that's all."[73]

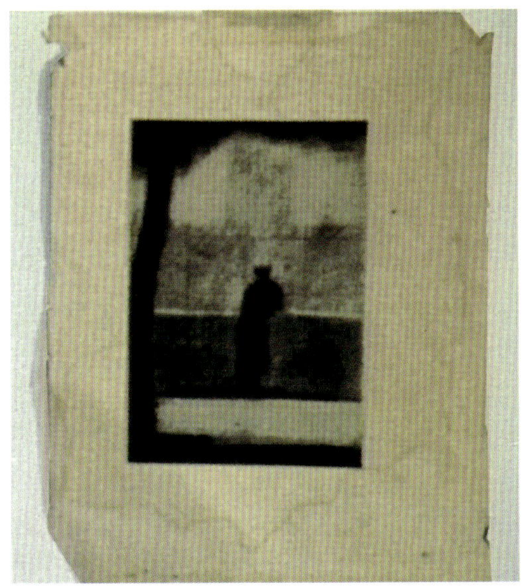

Ultimately it may not matter. More of an issue for Marden than explanation and acceptance is the benefit to be associated with the physicality of a handmade product. Here opinion within his generation divides: where he has been particularly reluctant to abandon labor-intensive handicraft, many distinguished contemporaries have adopted photomechanical and electronic means, or have employed assistants to realize their images by whatever process may be efficient. For some, the lesson of Seurat is not mark-making but digitization. If there is a divide between hand-workers and machine-workers (so to speak), in the past the hand-workers splintered among themselves. Some developed distinctive brush techniques as either representational or expressive devices (Delacroix, Munch); this is the side of the Romantic tradition that prevails in the history books under that rubric. Others preferred to establish concrete, structural relationships through the physical nature of their marks (Pissarro, Picasso)—Romanticism's internal alternative, which often receives other designations. Relative to the autographic quality perceived in the "personal" styles of the former group, the latter group have developed various looks of anonymity. (Anonymity has no argument with individuality, established by other means.) When a painter's mark achieves anonymity, its physical "fit," like that of stones in a wall, dominates the sense of its style.

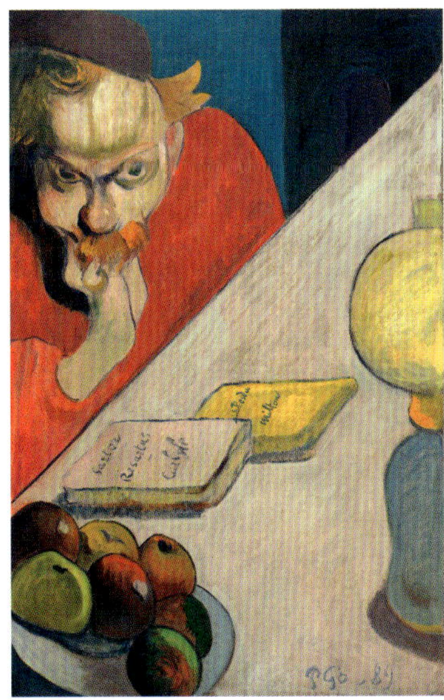

If these distinctions have themselves become all too structural and abstract, consider the historical case of Paul Gauguin. His symbolist imagery—its emotive thematics and simplified, evocative forms—seemed to him adequate for expressive purposes (fig. 10). He provoked his excitable colleague Vincent van Gogh by maligning superficial flourishes, "messing around with brushwork."[74] Yet Gauguin had a remarkable hand, adept at linear arabesque and subtle coloristic modeling. By his own standard he had nevertheless reduced his means to eliminate artful distractions. With no need to

9. Reproduction of Georges Seurat's study for *Petit Homme au parapet* or *L'Invalide* (c. 1881), pinned to the wall of Marden's studio. Still from Edgar B. Howard and Theodore R. Haimes, *Brice Marden*, New York: Tuckernuck Productions, 1977

10. Paul Gauguin. *Portrait of Jacob Meyer de Haan*. 1889
Oil on wood, 31⅜ x 20⅜" (79.6 x 51.7 cm)
The Museum of Modern Art, New York.
Fractional and promised gift from a private collection

personalize his handling of materials, he joined the side of structure and fit. When he visited Paris galleries in 1884, he complained of Claude Monet's excessively stylish technique, his all-too-evident virtuosity. Cézanne became the anti-Monet, praised for his "purity," seen especially in the blunt physicality of his brushstrokes, which Gauguin took to imitating.[75] To better or worse effect, critics of the time perceived in Cézanne's mark less representational rigor and restraint than was customary. The mark assumed an independent materiality, whether or not this was what the artist intended. Cézanne, a nature painter, seemed to have treated his rectangle and his repetitive block-like stroke as "the beginning of the separation from nature . . . an abstraction" (Marden's words about his own rectangle).

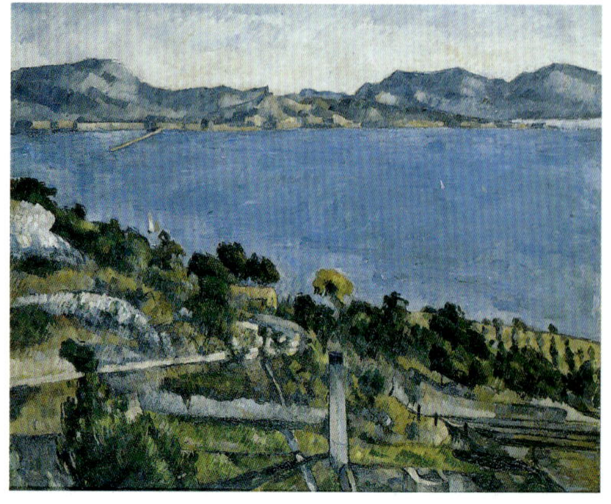

Such judgments are entirely relative and unstable. For every viewer who saw in Cézanne's repetitive marking a determination to impose an abstract order on pictorial naturalism, there was another who saw it as an unmediated expression of anxiety or agitation.[76] In any event, the association of Cézanne's stroke with pictorial structure stuck. As Marden himself put it, "There's a big difference between being realistic and depicting realistic subject matter . . . I think Cézanne was painting, and not painting anything, just painting."[77] On a visit to Paris he noted the "weightiness" of the gridlike plane in *L'Estaque—View of the Gulf of Marseille* (c. 1878–79; fig. 11). In response, he sketched a two-unit, two-tone grid to "represent" sea and sky.[78] Consistent with his understanding of Cézanne, Marden's representational factor operates at a remove from nature, processed through the material fundamentals of painting. What we call realistic subject matter is no more than a painter's fantasy, or perhaps a critic's. The painting becomes the reality.

Despite their strong egos, many artists closer to Marden's time acted on an antiegoist platform: no inflation of the self, no thematic fantasy. Like Gauguin and Cézanne, Barnett Newman refused to indulge in "fancy tricks with the paint." Willing to risk extremes, he proposed to make art "with nothing," that is, no form recognized by the culture as an expressive means (fig. 12).[79] Others shared his interest in exploiting a look of anonymity. To broaden the perspective, this very diverse group would include Clyfford Still as well as Ad Reinhardt, Robert Rauschenberg as well Robert Ryman, Josef Albers as well as Frank Stella, Andy Warhol as well as Roy Lichtenstein—not to mention a variety of those labeled photorealist and Minimalist. None of their art lacks an emotional charge; rather, it eliminates emotional histrionics in order to enhance a base of sensation, of feeling. Here phenomenology displaces psychoanalysis, self-analysis, and a fixation on personal identity. This was the sense in which the alternative Romantic tradition might be called antiexpressionist: it was indeed that, but it never eliminated emotion. It was an adjustment more of the expressive means than of the traditional Romantic ends of art.

11. Paul Cézanne. *L'Estaque—View of the Gulf of Marseille.* c. 1878–79
Oil on canvas, 21⅞ x 28¾" (55.5 x 73 cm)
Musée d'Orsay, Paris

12. Barnett Newman. *The Third.* 1962
Oil on canvas, 8' 5½" x 10' ¼" (257.8 x 305.4 cm)
Walker Art Center, Minneapolis.
Gift of Judy and Kenneth Dayton

Sensitivity to this issue may have peaked during the 1960s, just as Marden was settling into his mature aesthetic (his period of graduate study was 1961 to 1963). In 1962, Newman offered a reason not to feign gestures of spontaneous self-expression: "It is an endless search for a personality that never happens. . . . I do not work . . . to express myself, to tell the story of my life, or to act out in painting a personality by acting out some character."[80] Like a character on Serra's TV, "character" in Newman's sense could be no more personal than one of the personality types that the prevailing commercial culture fostered and in turn recognized—an artificial and institutionalized stand-in for the mythical "natural" self.

Unlike his Yale classmates Serra, Robert Mangold, Chuck Close, and others who soon emerged as significant new figures in modern art, Marden paid little attention to Newman during the 1960s. With respect to expressive anonymity, however, he joined his generation, who were at various stages of adopting Newman's attitude.[81] Mangold eliminated brushwork by using sprayers and rollers to apply his color. He would later describe the surface effect he sought as "matter-of-fact": "I wanted to paint the surface [as if I were] painting a real wall in a loft or apartment, no more or less artful than this."[82] While avoiding artfulness, Mangold made certain not to fetishize its antithesis; rather, he eliminated the issue from consideration. Like Marden, he reduced factors of illusion, stressing the integrity of the plane: "The edges are simply edges of a surface. The thickness is the thickness of the material chosen to work upon."[83] Close for his part disciplined himself to suppress "virtuoso flourishes that were signs of a painter's touch."[84] And Serra, who adopted dense strokes of oily Paintstik as his drawing medium, wanted his marks "as anonymous as possible"; it was blackness that mattered, not personality.[85]

At least one critic, Lucy Lippard, perceived the depersonalizing aspect of Marden's work right away. On viewing his *Return II* (1964–65; fig. 13) in a group show in 1966, she explained that here "'expressionist' techniques (thick paint, drips) are used non-expressionistically."[86] She isolated the word *expressionist* to identify it as a cultural convention—an indication on her part that the fiction of self-expression had faded. Either its artificiality had been unmasked by the prevailing critical discourse or the culture at large had lost interest in this particular fantasy (perhaps only to replace it with another: ideological control). This tacit acceptance that the expressionist game was over may account for Lippard's having chosen the better term to describe Marden's contrary position: he was a *non*-expressionist, not an antiexpressionist. Though still treated with irony by the generation of Rauschenberg and Warhol, expressionism for Marden ceased to be an issue altogether, if it ever had been one. A year later, however, Lippard's commentary lost some of its precision. Specifying that Marden had "stripped the impasto of its gestural,

13. Brice Marden. *Return II*. 1964–65
Oil on canvas, 50 x 68" (127 x 173 cm)
Mugrabi Collection

emotional connotations," she concluded that he "seems to exclude emotion entirely."[87] It would have been more accurate to say that he was excluding the indirect *signs* of emotion, those "expressionist techniques" that Newman had eliminated, as others had also, even Gauguin and Cézanne. Marden and his contemporaries were unloading the indicators of expression as quickly as they could. But emotional expression remained—its manifestation strengthened for having no sign. Another of Marden's early commentators, John Ashbery, put it this way in 1972: "Marden's surfaces . . . aren't, like so much of today's art, allusions or comments, however oblique, on ideas that are elsewhere: they are themselves what is happening."[88]

Like the colors of an organized color chart, there are emotions we can name: they have signs. The figures that illustrate these emotions are formulas for recognition. There are still other emotions, feelings of the moment that find neither a common vocabulary nor a cultural symbolism. They fall across the lines of the cultural grid. By self-forgetfulness, Marden strives to feel what remains uncharted. "Feeling," Peirce contended, is "nothing but sensation minus the attribution of it to any particular subject."[89] If feeling is an indefinite, self-less quality to be distinguished from sensation, then sensation is an emotionally charged fact. The full force of sensation returns to Marden when he engages a canvas as if it were the nature beyond him, entering into its forest, its water, its light—feeling his art of emotion arise out of painting's elements.

Saltus

First, feeling, the consciousness which can be included with an instant of time, passive consciousness of quality, without recognition or analysis. Second, consciousness of an interruption . . . I have a sense of a saltus, of there being two sides to that instant.

—Charles Sanders Peirce, c. 1890[90]

Color losing identities, becoming color.

—Brice Marden, 1967[91]

Peirce's rare word *saltus* refers to a jump or disruption that affects the inertia of consciousness. The derivation is Latin, *saltus*, leap; and the concept bears connotations of risk, because when jumping people cannot be certain where they will land. Every leap goes into a void. In the statement quoted, Peirce was referring to a condition, essential to human experience, in which attention shifts from sensing a quality to the perception of sensing *this* quality. For example, you see greenish color without situating it or identifying the object bearing it; then you notice green grass. Being struck by a quality that follows on another, even if both are indistinct and unidentifiable, may be enough to force consciousness to attach to *something*, not only becoming aware of specific externals but also becoming self-aware. Possibly, a distinction between these two states of consciousness, or any two, stabilizes only in theory, since the "two sides to that [perceptual] instant" comprise . . . an instant. And instants are indivisible. With his saltus, Peirce was describing the indescribable, setting his own description at risk.

Peirce alluded to a saltus when, on occasion, he distinguished "percepts" from "perceptual judgments." On the one hand, you sense; on the other hand, you know that you are sensing. "If one *sees*, one cannot avoid the percept"—the sensory feeling, greenish; "and if one *looks*, one cannot avoid the perceptual judgment"—the intuition that something significant is being sensed, green grass.[92] As already noted, Peirce tended to consider "sensation" as sensation-of-something, whereas "feeling" was an indeterminate psychic state.[93] "Feeling" resembles an emotion somehow lacking both a subject and an object: imagine that you sense a tension, but without understanding either the origin of this feeling or its target.

"Peculiar and gauche" was Peirce's characterization of his own thinking, and he must have found the confusing logic of his saltus amusing. Saltus: in the passage from one psychic state to another, a break occurs, as in a jump or leap; this is the gap leapt over. But—not to remain solely in the realm of metaphor—there must also be an experience of continuity: the actual physical movement or trajectory of the leap. Spatially and temporally, a break has a near side and a far side, a before and after. Perhaps Peirce would locate pure quality or "feeling" on one side and perceptual judgment or "sensation" on the other side—between them, a metaphoric gap.[94] What of the continuity? Here Marden's painting becomes a paradigm case, itself a saltus: his art passes freely between feeling and sensation, sensation and feeling, without the absolute division of a before and after. He may have referred to "color losing identities, becoming color"—odd syntax, to be sure—because he was directing his color to leave its cultural order. He was ignoring its assigned identity so it might appear just as it is, no longer a regulated factor in art ("color losing identities"). It would become indefinite like feeling ("becoming color"). On his part, Peirce located this type of feeling in no-man's-land and no-man's-time: "At the instant a sensation stops there is a second sensation. Between them there is a state of feeling."[95] Marden's color occupies such a state—a two-sided, instantaneous saltus. The immediate color-feeling he creates hovers between any number of more determined sensations, which may offer themselves as its surrogates but cannot be its doubles.

If Marden ever turned from a stabilizing art of personal identity to one of depersonalized, unhinged feeling, the conversion does not seem to have been dramatic. His response to Kline, one of his expressionist heroes, nevertheless indicates a degree of transformation. "I used to love Klines," he said in 1972, implying that any engagement with Abstract Expressionism, whatever it was, had passed.[96] In the summer of 1961 Marden painted *Quaquaversals*, constituted of broad strokes on the diagonal, with a range of dark gray tones set against a heavily brushed, dirty white ground, all Kline-like. A perceptive young artist like Marden could grasp what Kline was doing, even though Kline himself was hardly straightforward, as a witness account indicates: "He does countless drawings, quickly in broad strokes. . . . Later he goes through these and may find a theme that has been unconsciously working its way into the open. . . . He may then select one drawing . . . and work directly from it onto the canvas."[97] In *Quaquaversals* Marden engineered his individual brushstrokes to coalesce into proportionately large forms—not the most direct way of painting but rather Kline-like.

In December 1961, Marden visited an exhibition of Kline's new work at the Sidney Janis Gallery, New York, where *Zinc Door* (1961; fig. 14) especially impressed him.[98] Despite its bold graphic strokes, Marden seems to have focused on its range and distribution of tonal values, developed primarily in blacks and grays. As a protracted response, during 1962 and 1963 he made a series of five charcoal studies after Kline. For the first four he arranged rectangles asymmetrically, as (it could be argued) *Zinc Door* did as well, except that its geometry flowed freely, like that of an oversized sketch. Esteban Vicente, himself an Abstract Expressionist and one of Marden's Yale professors, had recommended that his student refrain from using symmetrical grids. "You're working yourself into a corner; there are too many restrictions on yourself. And why don't you try and open it up," Vicente had urged.[99] The problem with being told to open up—how? by what method?—is that it may counter a person's habitual, therefore "open," inclinations. Vicente imposed a Kline-like aesthetic of irregularity on Marden, who had never developed either an expressive or a theoretical need for it. (Adorno might have found in this enforced improvisation a confirmation of his dark view of culture in America.)

Following Vicente's instruction, Marden designed paintings and drawings in the form of asymmetrically quartered rectangles. They are neither open nor restricted. For his painting *Arizona* (1962) he combined a number of chromatic colors, moving the mixture toward a unifying grayish, brownish tone. It remains unclear whether the point of this effort was to generate these subtle grays and browns (color becoming neutralized, as at twilight) or to render the chromatic range all the more complex and full, since each component hue insistently reemerges from the neutralizing mix. *Arizona* foretells the greater ambiguities that would follow.

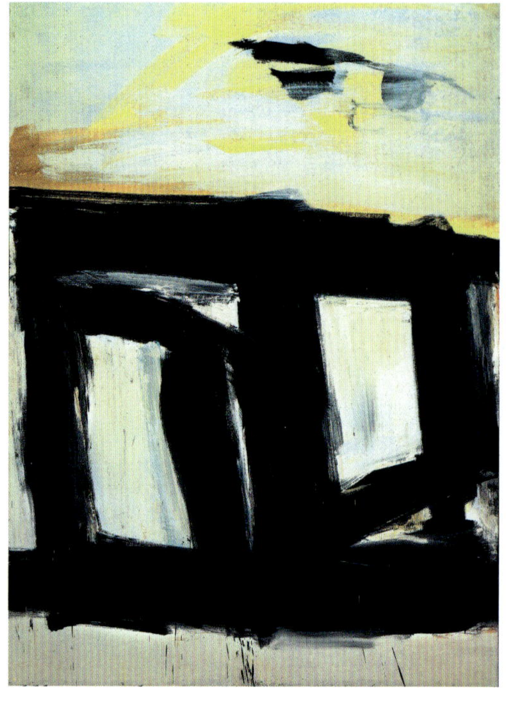

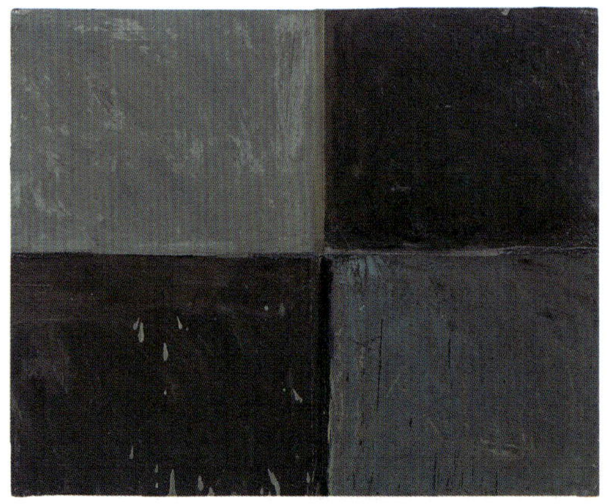

14. Franz Kline. *Zinc Door.* 1961
Oil on canvas, 7' 8 1/2" x 67 3/4" (235 x 172.1 cm)
Private collection

15. Brice Marden. *Number 1.* 1962
Oil and beeswax on canvas, 18 x 22 1/2" (46 x 57 cm)
Collection the artist

The effect of color and line in Marden's early drawings and paintings tends to be restrained, as if he were taking a passive-aggressive stance toward the compositional dynamism that Vicente and others recommended, not to mention what the example of Kline advised from a distance. In many instances Marden's compositional divisions are only barely off-center and his colors seem to sit on the edge of the divide between chromatics and neutrals (*Number 1*, 1962; fig. 15). All this leaves a viewer in doubt as to which principle is at work, and therefore forced to look ever more closely. In analogous charcoal drawings that display grids of a greater number of units (more than four quarters), Marden allowed each unit its discernible difference; but such differences appear to occur by happenstance, with the artist judging intuitively how loose or how dense to let the surface become (Untitled, 1964, plate 10; Untitled, 1964–65, plate 12). His various marks appear more "natural" to the process than "expressive" of the artist who directs the process. From one unit to another and even within a single unit, movement occurs but is curiously suspended, as if lacking a final coordinated purpose. Lippard's characterization—expressionist techniques used nonexpressionistically—is apt. Even as a student, Marden followed nonexpressive lines. He may have been a romantic but he resisted the pretensions of a lyric, Romantic self.

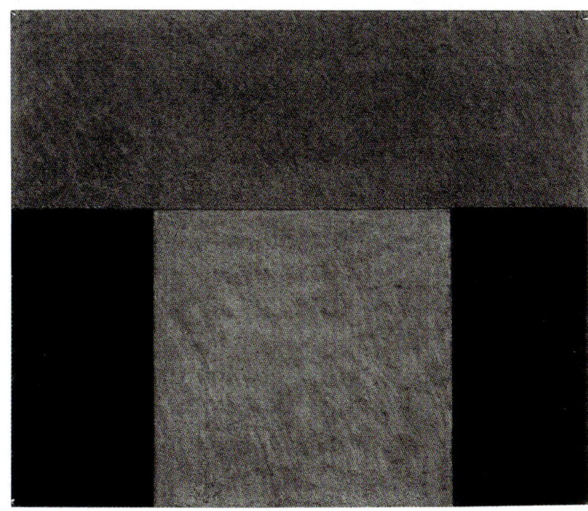

For the final member of his Kline Study series, *Kline Study #5* (1962–63; fig. 16), Marden returned to symmetry. He removed the dynamic of Kline's expressionism, its casual but forceful irregularity. By introducing left-right symmetry into a Kline-derived art, Marden believed that he had succeeded in "getting from Kline to myself."[100] Having displaced asymmetry by symmetry, his drawing became more Marden-like than Kline-like, but this did not mean that Marden's "myself" was the self of self-expression. All symmetrical arrangements are balanced by the same means: mirroring around an axis. Symmetry hardly leaves room for idiosyncrasy. "Getting from Kline to myself" entailed manipulating Kline into the position of Marden's self-forgetfulness.

Despite the precision of grids and symmetry, or perhaps on account of it, Marden has long been concerned that his art look handmade, if only because this is its reality. He enhanced this look in his early "monochrome" panels by leaving a narrow strip of drips and smears along the bottom, representing successive applications of component pigments—"an index or history of the painting," as he once put it.[101] The practice began around 1965 with works like *Decorative Painting* (1964; plate 8); it appears more definitively with *Teddy's Drawing* (1964–65; plate 14), *Return I* (1964–65; plate 13), and *Pair* (1965; fig. 17). Typically, the residual markings appear below a thin line incised with a hard pencil parallel to the bottom edge. This establishes a zone of "process"—less than an inch, often about half an inch, in a canvas that

16. Brice Marden. *Kline Study #5*. 1962–63
Charcoal on paper, 18 x 21¾" (45.7 x 55.2 cm)
Collection the artist

17. Brice Marden. *Pair*. 1965
Oil and charcoal on canvas, two panels, overall: 18 x 38" (45.5 x 96.5 cm)
Collection Helen Harrington Marden

might reach a height of sixty-nine inches (as in the Back series of 1967–68). "The dripped edge keeps the painting from looking mechanical," Marden explained: "When you see it, you know the work was done by hand, with a brush. And the scratches [from a spatula or knife], they keep the painting coarse. Also more complicated. . . . I exercise little or no control over what happens below the drawn edge."[102] Rather than leaving a look of spontaneity, this studied lack of control corresponds to a material effect belonging to the labor-intensive process; it ensures that the panel not be mistaken for a machine-tooled object.[103] Robert Pincus-Witten commented appropriately in 1972, "The spotting [at the bottom margin] denotes that the monochrome was arrived at *slowly*."[104]

Beyond the handmade quality, its coarseness, and the added factor of preserving an index to the painting's internal history, Marden wanted to acknowledge the play of gravity: "You could tell the top from the bottom. The work had a gravitational pull."[105] In a number of grid drawings he offset a directionally neutral, symmetrical order with a narrow strip at the bottom of the sheet: Untitled (1964–65; plate 12) is an example. It was never his understanding that a grid implies idealization or conceptualization. By introducing an anomalous, asymmetrical feature within a symmetrical design, he reinforced its physical, gravitational order. To Marden, the pull of gravity "seemed visceral."[106] In this respect he related his practice to Johns, who in his own compositions left an analogous area free to reveal a material layering and a gravitational bottom. Johns also sometimes stretched his canvas so that a dark blue selvage thread would line up with the bottom edge (*White Target*, 1957; p. 115, fig. 7). He could then set the reality of his encaustic paint against the reality of the canvas, materially accentuated by the blue thread, which acts as an optical sign of a physical limit. When the painter reaches this blue barrier, he knows he has reached bottom. Marden developed his bottom-edge technique independently but was encouraged by Johns's example, which he studied while employed as a guard during the 1964 Johns retrospective at New York's Jewish Museum.[107] He felt an affinity for this art; from it, he received a confirmation.

In works like *Nebraska* and *The Dylan Painting* (1966/1986; plate 17), the narrow bottom zone adds a distinctive set of irregularities to what, by comparison at least, appears to be a relatively polished surface. Under scrutiny, however, little about Marden's work remains regular. He has occasionally described a drawing or painting as "funky," meaning that, despite the rigor of his methods, the surface plane came to incorporate more than the usual amount of physical features not specifically intended.[108] Many happenstance features are nevertheless acceptable to Marden once they appear. Specifically, he suggested that a certain coarseness is desirable ("scratches . . . keep the painting coarse"). Funkiness has a similar appeal. In a sense, all of Marden's works are funky—loaded with incidental features, so much imperfection. Bits of foreign matter (hairs, fibers, mere dirt) become embedded in the layers of beeswax he applies to large sheets of drawing paper. Abrasions, sometimes small holes, appear due to the force of his hard graphite strokes. Using an ultrahard 8H pencil, he incises razor-thin edges with such pressure that he nearly cuts the paper (Untitled, 1964–67; plate 24). And in any of the waxy painting surfaces large enough to require him to stretch and bend with brushes and spatulas, scratches and nicks result.

Perhaps *Return I*, which predates Marden's use of beeswax, should be regarded as funky because of its general scruffiness, especially at the sides and bottom, the result of numerous manipulations of the paint surface. In a "monochrome," any developmental or corrective reworking is likely to introduce new irregularities and flaws no less noticeable than previous ones. With each application a bit of paint may dry and harden; it then adds a scratch wherever caught by a sweep of the spatula. Although Marden takes his technique to its highest level of perfection, his method is barred from perfection by its own physicality. So, as he paints, each work becomes both perfected and imperfected: the first, according to its pragmatic standards, as the artist develops them even as he proceeds; the second, according to the fundamental nature of the process. Marden's materials establish the rules, which he extends until they break.

A certain funkiness pervades his etching, too, where foul biting and other incidental irregularities appear. In the group of eight prints collectively titled *Ten Days* (1971; fig. 18), stray markings bring definition to otherwise blank, un-inked areas, granting them a physical presence.[109] Needless to say, Marden adjusts objects in which surface irregularities begin to interfere with the aesthetic qualities that concern him. Because materiality is at the core of his aesthetic, *some* material incident—dirt, a tear, a scratch—may be more desirable than none. Otherwise he would prefer screen printing to etching, photography to drawing, video to painting.

It was in 1967 that Marden spoke of "color losing identities, becoming color." He applied this notion to *Private Title* (1966; fig. 19), which he had described suggestively some months before: "Often thought of as the orange painting. . . . It is probably the strangest gray I have ever made."[110] Similarly, *Nico* (1966; plate 16) was "a soft light yellowish green [which] turns to a soft slightly threatening gray."[111] In 1969 he mentioned his interest in "putting on a gray . . . that under certain conditions shows up green, so you aren't sure about the color at all."[112] And in 1972: "[I] wanted a complicated color experience from one color—yellow-gray one day, red-gray the next."[113] And later: "What I liked about [gray] was . . . how you could make it be gray, and also be

18. Brice Marden. *Ten Days.* 1971
Etching with aquatint on paper,
print B from a portfolio of eight sheets,
plate: 21 5/8" x 10 5/8" (55 x 27 cm),
sheet: 30 x 22 1/8" x (76 x 56.3 cm)
Collection the artist

19. Brice Marden. *Private Title.* 1966
Oil and wax on canvas, 47 3/4" x 7' 11 3/4"
(121.3 x 243.2 cm)
Solomon R. Guggenheim Museum, New York.
Panza Collection

red."[114] Still later: "I saw you could make a color be ambiguous. A gray could turn itself into a green."[115] Each of these statements indicates that Marden worked to destabilize color through complex mixtures of hues—"color losing identities, becoming color."

Color in the second sense ("becoming color") is a Peircean "percept," a "quality": volatile, indeterminate, unidentifiable, yet entirely specific. In the very moment when Marden imposes a judgment on his color—this is more green than gray, this is more light than dark—he slips to one side of his perceptual instant, his saltus. And then, as the color itself slips from his identifying grasp, he passes to the other side. This is the condition he cultivates, his realist position. Life is like this: uncertain. Perhaps with so much jumping and shifting, Marden's art represents a nonposition. It demonstrates that sensory reality takes no position; only cultural constructs do.

"I'm really shocked that I can spend so much time looking at one of my paintings and really enjoying it," Marden says.[116] The time factor must be related to the instability of the work; it changes, ever new before his eyes. Once a certain threshold of complexity and density of effect has been crossed, the work releases aspects and qualities beyond those consciously set into it. Accordingly, Marden often experiences a failure of memory when he returns to a painting: "The color might be a little bit different than you remember. Sometimes it's surprising; sometimes it's very surprising."[117] Like the forest that would change in appearance in response to the mood of a nineteenth-century painter, Marden's color changes. He draws forth qualities of feeling from his painting that may be alien to the emotions with which he imbued it while making it.[118] It is expansive.

Some of Marden's paintings demonstrate the Peircean saltus with situational directness. *Fave* consists of two "monochrome" panels that become "two sides to that instant" as each regulates the view of the other. Identify the color of one side and it will suggest a color for its neighbor. Yet each panel also divides within itself (like a grid without lines), because each "monochrome" is many hues, changing with each viewing. When the left panel appears brown, the right appears gray. When the right panel turns a faded blue, the left becomes a dull yellow. When the left shifts to orange, the right appears violet. But perhaps not truly violet, because this panel—turned by the light, exposing its thin-skinned layers—must be more than one color: blue-red, then. If the left has become blue-red, the right now looks yellow-green. Marden painted each of these possibilities into *Fave*, as well as many more, more than he fully controlled. *Fave* offers "things that you want to see . . . knowing yourself by forgetting about yourself." You want to see unseen things. *Fave* becomes the vehicle for finding them out.

Around the time of *Fave* and other works of similarly nuanced color,

Marden and Mangold, always sympathetic to each other's art, agreed to exchange drawings.[119] Marden offered Mangold his Untitled of 1970, in which graphite stroked over beeswax produces the deep black of the left side while translucent beeswax alone produces the dirty yellowish white of the right side (fig. 20).[120] A ruled border of buff paper surrounds both "colors," which form a two-unit grid. The graphite unit obscures every bit of light that might escape through pinpoint holes in the waxy surface. To its right, a layering of wax "colors" the paper without added graphite pigment. The wax side is empty, a grid unit with zero value, no marks having been invested in it; but it is clearly just as full, just as physical, as what faces it in graphite. Since this waxy "white" is not quite white and may fit a concept of "white" only by association with the black opposed to it, it encourages a viewer to question the degree of blackness in the black, and to realize that every black varies even from the standard it sets for itself. Marden's black reveals its qualities only to those who look and can see its changes. Otherwise it is generic—just "black."

On occasion, Marden would juxtapose two deep black rectangles, using the same stroke and the same grade of graphite stick to render them, separating them by no more than a thin incised pencil line, intending the two areas of blackness to appear identical (*Grove Group 4*, 1972; plate 44). He nevertheless understands that, as products of hand labor, his blacks must differ. Aside from the distinction of placement, there is a temporal distinction and an emotional distinction, leading finally to an indeterminate visual distinction—each area of blackness has its history, its experiential specificity. Yet such distinctions resist meaningful definition. In the Untitled of 1970, where there is all the difference in the world between "black" and "white," a viewer cannot determine which of the two sides is positive or primary and which is negative or secondary. In Marden's art, every grade of black and white exists as a specific quality; each is positive and primary. Their relationship in Untitled is neither structural, nor conceptual, nor hierarchical. If Peirce were to declare that "there [are] two sides to that instant"—black and white—his aesthetic intuition would capture the nature of this art. There are indeed two sides at once. A moment later, however, there are two other sides, feeling different from the two of the first instant.

In their exchange, Mangold offered Marden a set of three of the twenty-one drawings comprising his Perimeter Series (1969; fig. 21). The two artists' choice of objects to exchange shows how well they either understood each other or related to each other's art without needing to understand. The differences in the three units of the Perimeter Series can be analyzed because they can easily be measured. The exterior dimensions of the first rectangle total 96 inches, of the second 100 inches, and of the third 104 inches. To arrive at these sums, Mangold increased the length of each of the four sides of a drawn

20. Brice Marden. Untitled. 1970
Graphite and beeswax on paper
26 x 40" (66 x 101.6 cm)
Collection Robert Mangold and Sylvia Plimack Mangold

21. Robert Mangold. Perimeter Series. 1969
One of a series of twenty-one drawings,
this one drawn with a perimeter pf 96",
graphite on paper, 39½ x 27½" (100 x 70 cm)
Collection Brice Marden

rectangle by one inch while keeping the paper size constant. The perceptual differences are much less stable than their numerical conceptualization would seem to predict: they can be sensed but do not compute into a recognizably meaningful order, symbolism, or expression.[121] Just as Marden's drawing denies the conceptual scheme of positive and negative, Mangold's drawing undermines the practice of measure, which in his case leads nowhere. Both artists understand that the feel of a drawing is all you need to find out.

Into the Tree

Concepts never satisfy Marden. He converts them into material form, a materiality that reverses like "black" and "white," continually activating his thinking and feeling (Peirce's definition of experience: "consciousness of the action of a new feeling in destroying the old feeling"). Pencil or pen in hand, Marden lingers over experience that he records materially in his numerous notebooks: sketches for compositions, sometimes pursued to extraordinary detail; renderings of objects and natural phenomena; collaged pictures from magazines and newspapers; diary entries; passages of poetry and prose deemed worth keeping, copied by hand. A bound hardback with pages of squared (*quadrillé*) paper bears the inscription "July 1975," presumably the date the artist began to use it. He collaged a reproduction of Pablo Picasso's *Demoiselles d'Avignon* to its cover, one of his many casual homages to the achievements of the past, the "30,000 years" of the painting tradition. The inside pages hold numerous studies for the configurations of Marden's multipanel paintings and related prints of the late 1970s and early '80s. Most of these sketches are graphite; some are ink.[122]

Marden set relatively little text into this notebook. The most significant entry is his handwritten copy of a brief but famous alchemic treatise recorded as early as the seventh or eight century A.D., purported to represent teachings of the legendary god-mortal Hermes Trismegistus; it became known through the centuries as the "Emerald Tablet" ("Whatsoever is below, is like that which is above . . ."). Several pages farther along Marden inscribed a sample of Gustave Flaubert's political vitriol. Coincidentally, the latter statement, like the former, relates what is below to what is above: "The whole dream of democracy is to raise the proletariat to the level of stupidity attained by the bourgeoisie."[123] Marden apparently perceived wisdom in both sources: the dream (presented as reality) of an alchemic correspondence between opposing forces in nature; the reality (presented as dream) of a developmental correspondence between opposing forces in society. On the one hand, he finds inspiration in individual human achievement: dirt becoming gold in art; the luminous grays of Zurbarán and Manet; the fusion of mark, space, and image in

Cézanne and Pollock.[124] On the other hand, lapses in civility depress him, and he is aware that the political order brings less light into the world than does the blackness of graphite. His romantic faith in the potential of artists to benefit society is tempered by his mordant Flaubertian wit—often self-deprecating, since Marden himself is only too human and must share at least some of the failings that defeat governance everywhere.

Taking solace in sensations of nature, Marden has an alchemist's appreciation of the spiritual potential of the four Aristotelian elements: earth, water, air, fire.[125] To sense the light of the atmosphere or the color of the land, deriving well-being from that quality of sense, requires no classificatory grasp of what kind of light or color is involved and no analysis of the cultural significance of the situation. "Earth" can be Nebraska, viewed from a passing automobile, its abrupt shifts in topography, its "mysterious greens"; "water" can be the Hudson River, viewed daily, always moving into a new color.[126] Neither need be elemental and generalized, for Marden is a pragmatic materialist even if he is also a romantic spiritualist: "Maybe I am confusing the aesthetic response with the spiritual response. But I'd just like to believe that there could be some kind of transcendence. . . . I would rather keep it open, and say that there are magical, spiritual possibilities in painting rather than be cynical about it."[127] Hence, his romanticism.

The context of this remark was the situation of the art world in the 1980s (discussed briefly above in relation to the critical legacy of postwar European theorists). It was a time when cynicism would have been better directed at politics rather than burdening art with that argumentation, emphasizing its contribution to social problems, ignoring its capacity to provide alternative actions and solutions. The postmodernist notion "that everything has been done drives me up the wall," Marden admitted in 1986. To the contrary, "nobody else can do [painting] your way [if only because] they're not your size."[128] Against rarefied theoretical arguments concerning the prefiguration of all human invention in its encompassing system of signs, Marden asked that we observe the actions of a human body, any human body, of any size—our own or another's—as a source of physical difference, not cultural difference. Or better, do not observe this but act it out: "What one is physically . . . I am 5' 8½", and I weigh this much, and I am left-handed, and I'm a certain age. That has a big effect on what the thing looks like. The kind of mark I can make physically. If everybody tried to draw the same line, they just couldn't do it."[129] Rather than a self, Marden's line expresses an experiential metrics.

Here he took a purposefully naïve view of matters; it allowed him to see that the idea of a postmodernist impasse was no more productive than faith in an Aristotelian notion of four physical elements and its alchemic implications. In the context of postmodernism, Aristotelian and Hermetic texts were inspiring. Marden's response was to continue to put trust in his experience in the physical world, especially as he intensified his sensation in the studio. In 1976, he remarked on one of the advantages of being there: "You can sit and look out the window and see nothing but the sky."[130] At certain times of the day the sky was inside the studio as well as outside, its light reflected by the dark gloss of painted floorboards, with the effect resembling the black drawings Marden was making by stroking reflective graphite into absorptive wax on paper.

Explaining details of his procedure in 1976, Marden justified his commitment to painting with a broad ethical pronouncement:

> I paint because I believe it's the best way that I can pass my time as a human being. . . . Good painting usually occurs at times of bad government, bad times; and I think we live in horrendous times. Horrendous times. And when the artists, the painters, the poets, the sculptors, the dancers, musicians, rise to those occasions, they give man a reason to believe that he's just not ordinary, that he's really great. And yet at the same time—remaining humble.[131]

Why humble? Because artists who rise above social conflict still feel diminished in relation to the material force of nature: color, light, surface, depth, the land, the firmament. These are sources of sensation with which painting competes.

Not long before, summering in Greece in 1974, Marden had recorded a note to himself that put an ancient Mediterranean spin on the social rationale for his profession: "Painters are amongst the priests—worker priests of the cult of man—searching to understand but never to know. As a painter I believe in the indisputability of the plane."[132] This is neither a theoretical statement of formalist principle nor an assertion that a fantasy world of personal creation holds more credibility than everyday sensation. "For Marden," John Yau writes, "the plane is not finally an image of the self but a way of discovering the infinite domain of the other."[133] Conceptualized doctrines of form and expression disable the priest within the worker priest. But painters are more workers than priests. The worker within the worker priest confronts reality as elemental materiality: on the plane, indisputable yet changing.

For a thematic exhibition on color in 1971, Marden was asked to state the principle of his art or to articulate a theory. In response, he offered a short but ambitious piece of writing that includes this contrary remark: "I work with no specific theories or ideas." Just before this sentence, however, he offered a number of principles important to his use of color, such as "Color and surfaces must work together." In advance of his generalities he gave a cryptic account of a particular study in color, a tripartite painting that he had shifted from one set of hues to another as it evolved from a "landscape" into a paean to Janis Joplin upon her death in October 1970 (*For Pearl*; plate 34). "The Mediterranean painting," Marden wrote, "ended up a glad day-glo dirge for a great dancing lady. A spot of deep mediterranean earth red is all that remains under an evasive flesh color that fights its way back and forth between flesh life, or death as a Daytona Beach tract house brown."[134] Both the vivid flesh color and the morbid brown were to be seen in the third of the painting's three "monochrome" panels. Marden was alluding to the surface effect he had developed in his painting throughout the 1960s. Although his color might first appear "monochrome," its identity would escape the viewer's reckoning and, as one kept looking to determine it, to isolate it, the "monochrome" would devolve into many hues—constituents that Marden had layered into the surface, as well as others optically present even if not materially. In one and the same instant, in two sides of one instant, the color would appear as "flesh" and as "tract house brown"—chromatic life and chromatic death—strangely aligned in their nature. Like *Fave*, but in a somewhat different manner, *For Pearl* enacts the Peircean saltus.

Marden's statement on the "Mediterranean painting" that eventually became *For Pearl* appears in rudimentary form in a notebook he used on his first trip to Greece, in 1971. There his observations on color sit on the page in a different sequence. An odd sentence follows his description of life color and death color, flesh and brown: "Ride away into the tree."[135] Conceivably this evocation of movement brought to a halt by accident, by fatal happenstance, reflects on Joplin's life. The final version of the text expands the phrase but dissociates it from the reference to Joplin, appending it instead to a relatively long list of things to do with color. Rather than modifying the lament for the loss of "Pearl," the ride-away image modifies the theory (or nontheory) Marden had been asked to compose. In its definitive form, the sentence reads: "A child mounts his tricycle and rides away into a tree."[136] Such misfortune does not rise to the level of tragedy and no longer suits Joplin (or possibly Pollock, for that matter). It does, however, suit Marden's theory of color—a delayed response to the chromatic logistics of Albers, which, as an undergraduate, he had found confusing and useless.

The ride-away remark deflates all that has come before, undermining the sense of self-importance projected by an artist, any artist, in a process of self-explanation. Perhaps Marden had observed the unfortunate meeting of a child's command of technology and nature's material resistance; it happens every day. Yet he may have been recalling—or indeed projecting—his analogous fall from grace. He may have appended his canard because he had been obliged to speak with an authority (no matter whether aesthetic or political) greater than what he would ever have accepted in another. It caused him to hit the tree.

Telepathy

Marden has a history of deflecting pressure to reduce his activity to a verbal proposition. His customary wryness and occasional romantic pronouncements might be considered effective deflective devices. But all in all, as Richardson observed, he is disarming in his genuineness. He worries even now that he may never have been sufficiently receptive to the full force of external conditions, that he still falls short of forgetting himself, that is, losing his acculturated inhibitions. In an interview of 2004, he stated the point through a comparison: "I have this idea about Pollock: he allowed the image to come up from the work. . . . I don't think I have really allowed the image to come up enough [to] liberate me."[137] If in fact Pollock dared to let his materials and their forms introduce imagery of the forms' own making, then in his case painter and materials had become united as a single organism. Pollock's consciousness was flexible, not rigid; it could be compelled to adjust its orientation. This was a sign not of weakness but of a sensitivity to experience.

Marden aspires to some variant of the condition he perceives in Pollock: an oceanic immersion in a process. His switch from a Kline-like (pseudo-) expressionism to the rectilinearity of *Kline Study #5* made the processing of the older artist's tonal values his own. But he needed more than this to get beyond himself. In 1974, he composed some notes in response to the landscape of Hydra, the Greek island where he keeps a studio, first visited in 1971. (I refer to the same sheet of notes quoted above, in which Marden concluded by alluding to the "indisputability of the plane.") His description assumes the perspective of a swimmer in the sea, enveloped by both water and air, looking toward the rocky, earthen shore with its scattering of trees:

> There are the rocks, Hydra rocks, the pines bending to the winds, echoing the bends the rocks have undergone for so many more years. Nature—forces. . . . I am of the stuff to be of it but only through my work which, unfortunately (but I am young), is my life. Remember immersion—water—land—sky—the all.[138]

Pollock, in Marden's view, may have become sufficiently open to experience that he united with "the all" directly, meaning that there was no longer a distinction between the life and the art, and "only through my work" would be an unnecessary qualification. In this respect Marden recalls Pollock's famous remark "I am nature." He himself is not: "I do not feel that when I paint I am nature, there is too much built in, I know too much."[139] He identifies his predecessor's late paintings, such as *Untitled (Scent)* (c. 1953–55; fig. 22), as "about forces of nature. Somehow he can make that image but it's not necessarily an image."[140] If not an image of the force, it must be the force itself—neither a pictorial nor a gestural reference to a quality or sensation, nothing *about* the thing, but instead the very thing, as if the artist were sharing in it. Following Pollock's example but as more of a naturalist than an expressionist, Marden sees "something in nature"; he "search[es] to be able to depict this energy . . . a life force."[141] Recently he stated, "I take from nature only its energy; I don't try to reproduce it. If I want to paint water, I'm going to think of its reflections, its fluidity, its energy, its temperature, but not its appearance."[142] Presumably its visual appearance would already be too conventional, too much like a culturally conditioned picture, less like a liberated Pollock line.

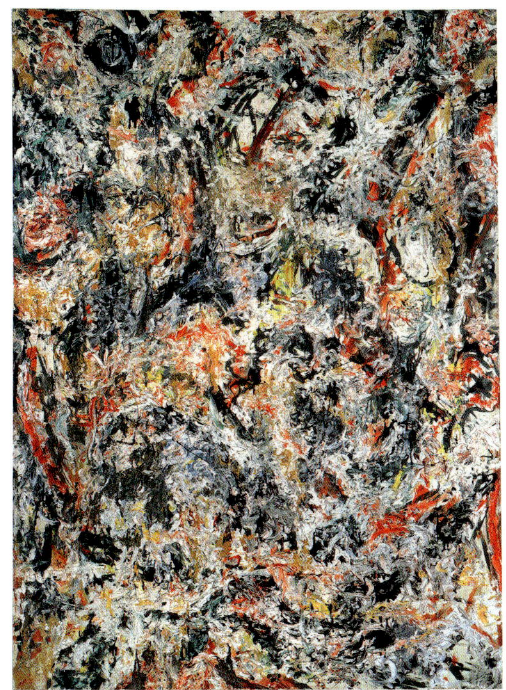

This does not mean that water lacks visual interest for Marden. In fact it challenges his vision. Exercising his dog, he likes to walk out on the Christopher Street Pier in Lower Manhattan to observe the Hudson close up, an approach to Pollock-like immersion. The river reflects changing atmospheric conditions above, complicated by its flow, which is tidal in that area and so reverses: "Every day the river is different," Marden notes.[143] He could say the same of *Fave* and *For Pearl* and other works consisting of "monochrome" elements, whether with respect to their color, their movement, or their energy. Viewing the Hudson, applying his own energy—the force of himself looking—he attempts to perceive the flow as still, to "stop the flow of sensation."[144] Why this paradoxical impulse? Peirce's saltus is again apropos. The stillness that Marden seeks is not that of photography, for which a moving river deposits its still image like a sediment. As a painter, Marden would instead capture water's flow in a still rendering without actually stilling the image of flow, that is, without losing the flowing quality of the water. Presented as the feel of a painting, movement can be captured outside of a concept, a stock figure. "Two sides to that instant" of watery flow remain in evidence in Marden's paintings and drawings.

It may be that Marden wishes his vision were as effective as his art. If it were, he could view nature all the more directly from the pier, from his Lower Manhattan studio window, or from his studio in Hydra—all positions above water. Given the quality of paintings like *Fave*, one wonders why Marden is still striving. *Fave* already produces the desired effect of a stillness that contains movement. "But only through my work," the painter might object. The fact that he relates to nature best through painting confirms his opinion of his personal limitations. Contained in the "monochrome" of *Fave* and works like it, the flow of sensation reappears in an alien register, presenting the same

22. Jackson Pollock. *Untitled (Scent)*. c. 1953–55
Oil and enamel on canvas, 6' 6" x 57½" (99 x 146 cm)
Collection David Geffen, Los Angeles

challenge to Marden in viewing it as does the flow of the Hudson. It is relevant that he usually describes observed color in an additive, nonhierarchical way. Any single color eludes him, for there are always many. The trunk of a tree is "black brown yellow cold dark." His impression of an olive grove is "evasive silver gray green, blue gray green light, black gray browns." Sky above the sea is "blue, gray, yellow, sulphur, turquoise, yellow, blue."[145]

"I like movement," Marden says.[146] As a student he made landscape drawings from a moving automobile.[147] Asked about his involvement with de Kooning's art, he replied that he preferred the "landscape" abstractions of around 1960, which his predecessor associated with moving along New York area parkways (fig. 23).[148] These also happen to be among the most anonymous images de Kooning produced with respect to brushstroke. And like Marden, he developed a pictorial interest in movement as associated with water: "I reflected upon the reflections on the water," he stated in 1972; "I do that almost every day."[149]

During the early 1970s, Marden created a type of abstraction that may strike viewers as belated naturalism; these are his water drawings. As in de Kooning's work, their instability alludes to a sensory quality just as it is a source of that quality.[150] *Houston Drawing 3* (1973; fig. 24), for example, consists of broken parallel lines that leave an impression of light reflected on water, a surface effect. For certain images of this type, Marden drew the parallel lines—waves, so to speak—vertically rather than horizontally. Here as elsewhere in his work, he focuses so intently on a specific quality derived from his visual experience that it becomes independent of its context in nature and subject to willful studio manipulation. If there is a sense of gravity, it will belong to the drawing, not its naturalistic allusion—the same syndrome long before attributed to Cézanne, who exchanged the physicality of a horizontal stroke for Mediterranean depths.

If *Houston Drawing 3* is a surface, other drawings—a suite of eight charcoals titled *Water-Hydra* (1975; fig. 25)—seem inspired by watery soundings. Their lines move without establishing a pattern. Pursuing many directions, self-canceling, Marden's line evokes a gentle agitation. It seems reasonable that *Water-Hydra* and *Fave* have been made by the same person, one who prospers in an indeterminate state of finding out, wishing to "stop the flow of sensation" but doing so "only through [his] work." Experientially, the pictures Marden makes are unstable, whether abstracted from water, from solid rock, or from a mere quality of color:

> Two Hydra paintings. [One] a landscape color of rock; it's kind of this strange gray and strange green. . . . [The other] was just a very dark and light painting which didn't have anything to do with

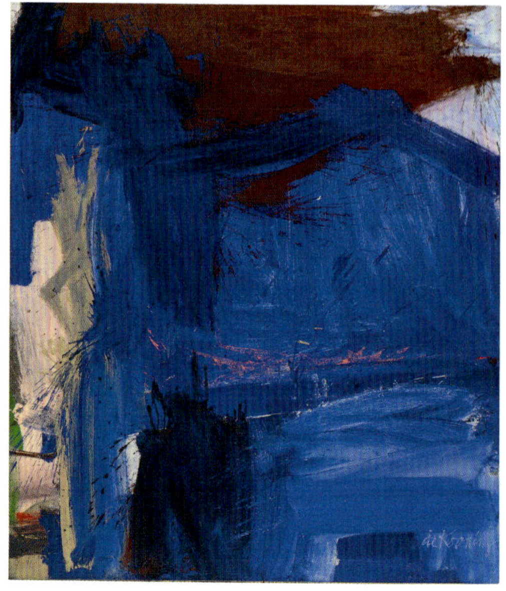

23. Willem de Kooning. *A Tree in Naples.* 1960
Oil on canvas, 6' 8¼" x 70⅛" (203.7 x 178.1 cm)
The Museum of Modern Art, New York.
The Sidney and Harriet Janis Collection

24. Brice Marden. *Houston Drawing 3.* 1973
Charcoal on paper, 41¼ x 29½" (104.8 x 74.9 cm)
The Museum of Modern Art, New York.
Gift of Sarah-Ann and Werner H. Kramarsky

anything visual. . . . You get a color memory in mind and then you try to make that color.[151]

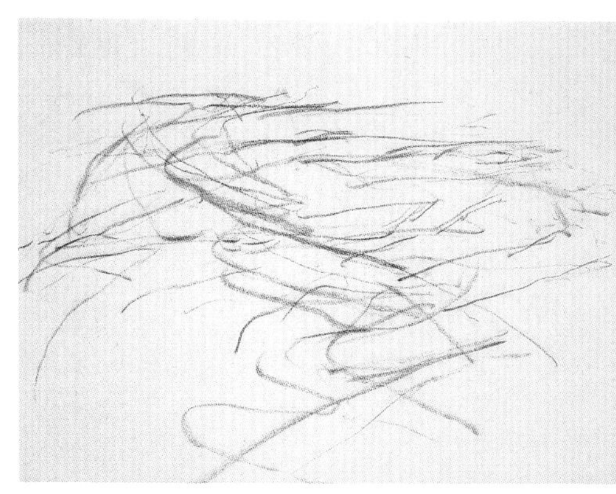

25. Brice Marden. *Water-Hydra.* 1975
Charcoal on paper, drawing six from a series of eight, 8 15/16 x 11 15/16" (22.7 x 30.3 cm)
Collection the artist

You just try to make: "If you paint your whole life," de Kooning said, "you take that for granted, and after a while all kinds of painting become just painting for you—abstract or otherwise."[152] This is a fact of Marden's understanding as well. Whether beginning from nature or not, at a certain point his painting becomes painting; it assumes a "formal aspect," its reality.[153] "When I go someplace, it's in my work." "We would be at a place and make notes. . . . Then you go into your studio and you are just trying to get the painting to work."[154]

What if someone else took responsibility for the "notes"? This was the case with the two-panel "monochrome" *For Helen* (plate 19) of 1967, the prototype for the series of Back paintings Marden would show at the Bykert Gallery in January 1968, all of them sixty-nine inches high—the height of Helen Harrington Marden, his wife.[155] He gave each member of the Back series a width of forty-five inches—an arbitrary dimension chosen because it generated rectangles in a proportion devoid of obvious associations ("just trying to get the painting to work"). In contrast, each of the two panels of *For Helen* measured 17 1/2 inches, corresponding to Helen Marden's shoulder-width. The decision to double this physical index came intuitively, once Marden decided that its inherent elegance caused the single-panel painting to appear too much like the figure it was, too decorative and diminished in visual challenge. This was an aesthetic judgment motivated by a desire to compel viewers to look at something unseen (a Peircean "experience") rather than recognize value in resemblance to a type known previously, whether classed as abstractly mimetic or as a variation on stylish, abstract form.

Marden describes the color of *For Helen* as a "warm pinkish gray," likely to have been constituted through a series of many mixtures, layerings, and enfoldings of alizarin crimson, ultramarine blue, raw umber, and silver white, along with other pigments in lesser amounts.[156] Although the color refers obliquely to Helen Marden's complexion, it is more of a memory of her many aspects than an imitation of a specific hue.[157] Curiously, it also refers to mud flats along the Cornish coast in southwestern England. In the summer of 1967, traveling through this area by rail, Helen was impressed by the pinkish color of the mud, observed when looking to sea. She telephoned Brice and described this color, necessarily only vaguely. By the time she returned to New York he had completed the painting. On viewing it, she was astonished, just as he was, to realize that the color fit her memory of the mud "exactly."[158]

When I asked about the circumstances of *For Helen*, Marden called it a case of "telepathy" (literally, feeling at a distance, long-distance feeling).[159] I do not know whether he had conceived of the situation in quite this way on a previous occasion or the word merely slipped out as fitting. The telepathic possibility should not have been other than a strange coincidence; completing the painting, Marden would have reached a stage at which he was "just trying to get [it] to work." But in this instance he had been inspired by the feeling of another (Helen) and had been approaching something never seen (the mud). Accordingly, his painting surface assumed an alien presence almost from the start. His long-distance feeling through the medium of Helen afforded an opportunity for self-forgetting. The color of the painting was for him a Peircean experience, something he had never seen and could not identify except to the extent that it corresponded to someone else's concentrated vision. From force of feeling (Helen's) to force of feeling (Brice's), an exchange of emotion: telepathy.

Compression

It seems natural that rocks which have lain under the heavens so long should be gray, as it were an intermediate color between the heavens and earth.

—Henry David Thoreau, 1852[160]

Idea. Trip down from SF. in plane. Hills. California hills. Compress them, flatten them to a flat plane. Painting with this in mind.

—Brice Marden, 1966[161]

Marden recorded these two thoughts in a notebook he used sporadically from 1966 until about 1974. He copied the statement from Thoreau under the heading "Lecture Notes" (he does not remember toward what end). The other thought came to him during a cross-country trip to northern California that began on June 1, 1966. The initial pages of the notebook document this travel in diary form. It was not Marden's first visit to the Pacific Coast but his first by automobile. Rather than a "California" notebook, I think of this as a "Nebraska" notebook, because commentary on the land in that state, viewed going west by car with four friends and returning east alone by Greyhound bus, dominates all other observations.

This type of commercial spiral-bound notebook has squared graph pages alternating with lined pages. Its design suits students of engineering: the left-hand sheets are for diagramming and calculating, the right-hand sheets for writing. Marden usually, but not always, respected this division, setting schematic drawings for "monochrome" paintings across from text matter not necessarily related to them save for the possibility that they shared a place and time.

Marden labored over several of the notebook "sketches" in a particularly painstaking manner—an odd practice given their provisional nature. But perhaps not so odd: if experience, sensation, and a selfless quality of feeling are desired ends of art, it does not do to keep this purpose actively in mind, for what counts as feeling will then become conceptualized before feeling ever arises. Unanchored, provisional drawing can be advantageous. "The quality of red," Peirce wrote, "is not thought of as belonging to you, or as attached to [something external]. It is simply a peculiar positive possibility regardless of anything else." (The skin-and-mud color of *For Helen* was a "positive possibility" for Marden but not his possession.) The antidote to the restrictiveness of conceptualization is effort—striving. An artist's effort does not liberate a color from every association. Nevertheless, it bonds a quality or feeling to one person at one moment, beneficially masking concerns that lie beyond this situation: "In sustained effort we soon let the [ulterior] purpose drop out of view."[162] In a manner with which most people are familiar, intense effort affords concentration and focus, even a self-forgetting. Marden recently recollected his technique of drawing as he practiced it in 1967, more or less the time of the notebook sketches, his two trips across Nebraska, and his painting *For Helen*: "It was almost meditative. . . . I would sand down the graphite area in the rectangle. Then I would scrape it with a razor blade, smooth it out. Then I would rub beeswax onto that surface, and then scrape the beeswax down with the razor blade . . . so that when I applied the graphite, there wouldn't be texture."[163]

26. Brice Marden. *Back Study*. n.d.
Notebook sketch, graphite on paper,
11¹/₁₆ x 9¹/₂" (28 x 24.1 cm)
Collection the artist

A notation in Marden's hand in the Nebraska notebook, not necessarily contemporaneous with the drawing it accompanies, indicates that one of his detailed sketches (fig. 26) is a "Back Study" in the height-to-width proportion of 69:50 ("Back" referring to the series of paintings previously mentioned, which have a width of forty-five inches). The sketch is actually not 69:50, but 69:51.5—Marden may have made slight adjustments to the rectangular shape as its surface gradually became denser and darker, in line with how he imagined an analogous oil-and-wax painting would appear.[164] In any event he wanted a rectangle unfamiliar as an art-rectangle. In an interview he referred to making "fat rectangles," hardly finely cut figures. Traveling cross-country, he invented "shapes to paint on . . . ugly shapes . . . kind of like fat rectangles, near squares but . . . an inelegant shape, because with just one color . . . you didn't want the shape to be making it look nice."[165] A fat rectangle approaches a square but, conflating two perceptual judgments, remains awkward in proportion, neither here nor there, like a saltus. A vertical with a ratio of 69 to 51.5—the notebook sketch—has a significant horizontal dimension that distracts from its verticality. A horizontal with a ratio of 58 to 72—the painting *Nebraska*—has a marked verticality that undermines any allusion to landscape in panoramic extension.

Marden's notebook sketch shines with a polished blackness. This distinguishes it from the usual run of artists' sketchbook pages. It might be called a study to scale, but "sketch" is a more appropriate designation, because the drawing incorporates evolutionary adjustments to its external proportions: "One of the ways I work is I'll develop an idea, it starts. It's just sort of a note in a notebook, and it's worked up through a series of drawings."[166] The density of this sketch is extreme. Filling a ruled-off section of the notebook page by applying strokes of multiple directions with a graphite stick or pencil, Marden darkened his rectangle with such pressure that the relatively strong grade of paper buckled while its heavy surface acquired a vaguely metallic sheen. The surface is both deadpan opaque and enlivened by its reflective pattern of ridges and valleys (the buckling). Marden incised the outer edges of the rectangle with a sharp, hard pencil. The reflectivity of such a line grants it visibility, one blackness against another—an opticality dependent on tactile surface variation (the incision) as much as on any other factor. Another graphite sketch in the Nebraska notebook projects a two-panel, two-color painting (fig. 27). Marden rendered its symmetrical sides with slightly different grades of graphite and slightly different patterns of stroke, articulating the central division by an incised line that nearly cuts through the paper.

By similar means, Marden demarcated a thin horizontal reserve at the bottom of the single-color composition, just as he would do in a painting at full scale. Scale is surely an issue, for the ratio of this sketch to its projected painting is 1 to 10, meaning that this tonal and textural sampling is only a hundredth the size of what it appears to call into existence. Given this differential, the sensory experience of working the materials can hardly be the same: in order to cover the surface efficiently, maintaining relative uniformity, the relationship of the artist's body to the plane of the image would shift from applying pressure with a wrist-and-elbow movement through an arc of only about half an inch (for the sketch) to gesturing broadly with the arm and shoulder through an arc of about two feet (for the painting). Even if the internal relationships were perceived to be very similar, the two works would necessarily *feel* differently in the experience of their making.

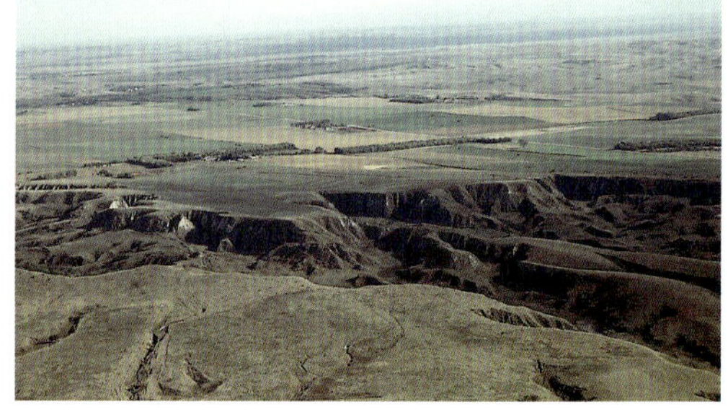

Marden thinks and feels on all scales. In Nebraska, he was impressed by the expansiveness of the land as well as the surprising ruggedness of the state's western counties—sudden shifts in elevation, gullies, fissures (fig. 28). To capture his sense of the endlessness of the American Great Plains he drew a horizontal line bounded by slightly elevated forms at either end. Above it—and curling around it, as if in a shieldlike gesture of protective holding—he extended an arc (fig. 29). He explained his figure with this notation: "On the flat country seeing the dome of sky, often filled with beautiful clouds. You see how the sky goes over the edge of the land makes you believe world is round." In Nebraska, the heavens were cupping the earth, all around. However infinite it might seem (like an endless grid, but curved), the sky suggested to Marden

27. Brice Marden. Notebook sketch. 1968
Graphite on paper, 11 1/16 x 9 1/2" (28 x 24.1 cm)
Collection the artist

28. The landscape of Custer County, Nebraska. Spring 1973

that it formed a containing shape (like one of his rectilinear planes, but spherical). This was how things appeared to him as he looked, given the force of his looking. In his diagram, the dome of the sky resembles an inverted hand-held vessel. His subsequent musing is pertinent: "I have some pots made by Southwest American Indians whose surfaces contain, for me, one of the great expressions about landscape in American drawing. Think of the pot as the landscape or as the sky over this landscape, which is identified with the 360 degrees of the horizon rather than 180 degrees."[167] Mediterranean landscape assumed an analogous quality: "In Greece you have mountains that diagonally frame the water beyond. They become vessels."[168]

More than by figures of containment, however, Marden works by compression. His containing "vessels" compress light, color, and shape itself. Looking down from the air, he imagined compressing California's elevations to a single level, in the way that a grid would show "different things that could be happening . . . on the plane simultaneously"—projected, flattened onto a plane.[169] He envisioned the Mediterranean likewise, "as a huge rolling Plane. From above."[170] Setting specific locations aside, he generalized: "I like the idea of the space being compressed up against the plane."[171] This notion—whether called compression, concentration, condensation, or projection—seems fundamental to Marden's art. He was exercising it when he rubbed graphite or beeswax into paper or spread and scraped oil paint upon canvas. His many pigments would become a gray, "an intermediate color" like Thoreau's rocks, an alchemic precipitation from mixtures of heaven and earth. In Nebraska, Marden remarked on "white green gray trees"; the colors appeared in temporal succession but spatial compression. Like rocks and grasses on the plains, the trees he observed grew from the earth while reflecting the sky. Compressed into *Nebraska*, they contributed to its "mysterious greens," growing indeterminate: "It looks quite green in relation to the other paintings [shown in 1966]. Blocking out the others it is very gray."[172]

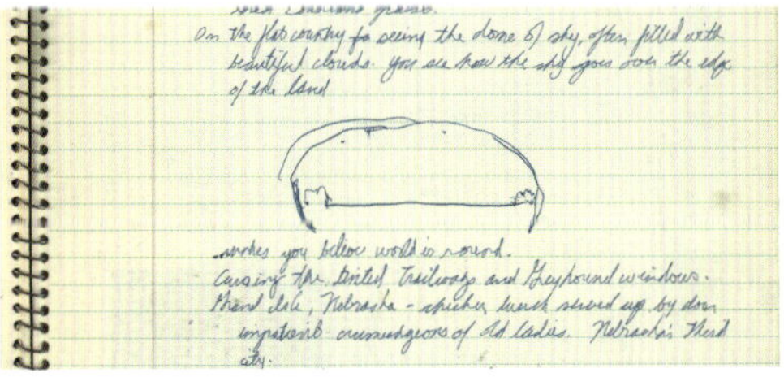

Marden's "Lecture Notes" include a second quotation from Thoreau: "Life is but the stream I go a-fishing in. I drink at it, but while I drink I see the sandy bottom and detect how shallow it is." Here he either used an inaccurate source or made an error in transcription, for Thoreau's statement refers to "time," not "life" ("Time is but the stream . . .").[173] Perhaps Marden's version is the more appropriate, since feeling and experience give life its definition whereas time is subject to mechanization. Life flows like the stream, ever changing, all the while contained within its shallow limits. Painting stills life's image in the moment but retains its movement, recovering a dimension that would never be sensed had painting not done its romantic-realist-abstract work. When an artist responds to painting and achieves the related self-forgetting, it is time for critics to dispense with their historical and cultural categories (Romantic, realist,

29. Brice Marden. Notebook page (detail). 1966
Ballpoint pen on paper, 11 1/16 x 9 1/2" (28 x 24.1 cm)
Collection the artist

abstract). With the space of nature "compressed up against the plane," art opens onto depths of unclassified feeling. Think of the complexities of the painting *Nebraska* or the drawing *Water-Hydra*: both images are at once materially flat and materially deep, with movements independent of any device of abstract or representational perspective. The best critical response may be a disarmingly naive statement of how such work feels. Go a-fishing. Drink at it.

Farther along in his "Lecture Notes" Marden wrote,

> Landscape. Today revisiting places I painted here. The change. My window tree. How different without force of myself looking at it. My time here was landscape time.

"My window tree" is not a tree you "ride away into" except in a very metaphoric sense. When I asked what tree this was, Marden replied that it must have been outside the window of his urban New York studio. Like artists of centuries past, he relates windows to picture planes: "Space [extending outward] is compressed and compacted up onto the flat surface, say, onto the window." [174]

In Marden's absence, the tree outside his window had been deepening, lifting, living. What was its "change"? Whether or not Marden had been continuously present to observe it, the tree endured its history—like the domed space of the Nebraska plains, or the reversing flow of the Hudson River, or the shallow passage of Thoreau's time. Nature lives through its changes apart from art. The force of Marden's looking nevertheless compressed the life of the tree onto the plane of the studio window, that is, onto the plane of his pictorial consciousness, his painting and drawing plane. Focusing on "my window tree," he became a naturalist attuned to the forest, lost in the romance of this specific tree, forgetting himself in his and its shared "landscape time." His painting or drawing might be no more mimetic than a rectangle or grid but he would experience it as a compression of the qualities of the tree, and an expansion of their emotional range as well as his own. Concentrating on the tree as he had on Helen's distant sensation of mud flats, Marden was "finding out." He would discover how to look with ever greater force at a tree, at mud, at water, or at any other terrestrial element.

Or how to view the heavens. As I was questioning him about Nebraska, his window tree, and the emotional feel of his related art, he turned from our talk, as well as from himself, to look at the rising moon.

NOTES

The focus of this essay is Brice Marden's early career, up to about 1975. Accordingly I give precedence to his statements of the 1960s and early '70s, though he may have offered a more elaborate account of an issue at a later date. I have questioned Marden about most of the issues raised in his early writings and interviews. His memories tend to be consistent with what the archival record indicates. My interpretation of his intentions and the cultural significance of his achievement (not necessarily the same) owes much to our conversations from September 2005 through April 2006. In the text to follow, I note the specific dates of direct quotations from these conversations; facts and opinions attributed to Marden without other citation derive from them as well. I thank him for his generosity and patience in talking through many issues about which he has been asked often in the past.

For aid essential to my research, I am grateful as well to Adrian Kohn, Eileen Costello, Tina Hejtmanek, Dana Cranmer, Esther Adler, Francesca Pietropaolo, Susan Braeuer, Clare Elliott, Paul Walter, and Kathy Fuld. I am indebted to Robert Mangold and to the Matthew Marks and PaceWildenstein galleries, New York, for quick, willing responses to requests for documentation. Throughout this essay, unless otherwise noted, translations are mine.

1. Brice Marden, quoted in Brenda Richardson, *Brice Marden Cold Mountain* (Houston: Houston Fine Art Press, 1992), p. 74. When I asked Marden (March 14, 2006) whether this statement, made in 1991, remained representative of his views, he replied without hesitation, "Sounds pretty good to *me*"—a characteristically forthright response.

2. Ibid., p. 76. Along the same lines, Marden has said, "My form of meditation is painting, looking at things." Quoted in James Reginato, "Marden's Retreat," *W* 26, no. 11 (November 1997): 251.

3. Paul Cézanne, letter to Emile Bernard, September 21, 1906, in John Rewald, ed., *Paul Cézanne, correspondance* (Paris: Bernard Grasset, 1978), pp. 326–27. The remark may involve irony and false modesty, but lack of fulfillment or realization is nevertheless a dominant theme of Cézanne's recorded discourse.

4. Charles Sanders Peirce, untitled manuscript fragment, c. 1897, in *Collected Papers*, ed. Charles Hartshorne, Paul Weiss, and Arthur W. Burks, 8 vols. (Cambridge, Mass.: Harvard University Press, 1958–60), 1.xi. An emphasis in the quotation has been eliminated.

5. Peirce, letter to William James, October 3, 1904, *Collected Papers*, 8:200.

6. Piet Mondrian, *Natural Reality and Abstract Reality: An Essay in Trialogue Form*, 1919–20, trans. Martin S. James (New York: George Braziller, 1995), p. 21.

7. Mondrian, quoted in Carl Holty, "Mondrian in New York: A Memoir," *Arts* 31 (September 1957): 21.

8. Marden called Cézanne "my hero" in his statement "Past Recent Now," in Trevor Fairbrother, *Brice Marden: Boston* (Boston: Museum of Fine Arts, 1991), p. 30. He incorporated a reproduction of Mondrian's *Broadway Boogie Woogie* (1942–43) in his *Homage to Art 9* (1973; Whitney Museum of American Art, New York).

9. These two statements are from notebooks Marden kept from 1971 to 1974; see Marden, "The Grove Group Notebook," reproduced and transcribed in Robert Pincus-Witten, *Brice Marden: The Grove Group* (New York: Gagosian Gallery, 1991), pp. 16–17, 21. Throughout this essay, in quoting from Marden's notes and writings, I have regularized his orthography; for example, his *grey* (British spelling) becomes *gray* (American spelling).

10. Marden, "Star (for Patti Smith)," in Jennifer Licht, *Some Recent American Art* (New York: The Museum of Modern Art, 1973), n.p.

11. Marden, quoted in Douglas M. Davis, "'This Is the Loose-Paint Generation': The New Painting Harks Back to Abstract Expressionism," *National Observer* (Washington), August 4, 1969, p. 20. Explaining himself on this occasion, Marden invoked the thinking of Ezra Pound.

12. Marden (signing himself Nicholas Brice Marden, Jr.), "Statements and Photographs submitted in partial fulfillment of the requirements for Master of Fine Arts degree," Yale University, May 1, 1963, p. 4.

13. Marden, in an interview with Robert Mahoney, "Brice Marden: This Is What Things Are About," *Flash Art* (Milan) 23, no. 155 (November–December 1990): 119. Marden was referring especially to his remarks in the film *Brice Marden*, produced and directed by Edgar B. Howard and Theodore R. Haimes (New York: Tuckernuck Productions, 1977) and available through the Checkerboard Film Foundation, New York. I make extensive use of the information provided by this film, since its production occurred at the end of the period of Marden's career on which this essay focuses. While encouraging me to view it (as a

videotape), Marden distanced himself from the romanticism he had expressed at that moment.

14. Marden, in the transcript of an interview with Howard, December 11, 1976, p. 29. Selections from this interview form much of the sound track for the Howard/Haimes film *Brice Marden*. All quotations from the transcript are courtesy Edgar B. Howard, Checkerboard Film Foundation, New York.

15. Ibid.

16. Marden, in "Interview with Brice Marden conducted by Paul Cummings, October 3, 1972," transcript (edited to eliminate redundancy), Archives of American Art, Smithsonian Institution, p. 35.

17. Marden, in "Interview by Robin White at Crown Point Press, Oakland, California, 1980," *View* 3, no. 2 (June 1980): 19.

18. Marden, in "Interview by Paul Cummings," p. 35. Marden had been attracted to Edwin Dickinson's work because of the older artist's enthusiasm for Zurbarán, along with his pictorial imagination and versatility. Dickinson made both large, elaborately planned compositions and small, spontaneous studies from nature.

19. Charles Baudelaire, "Salon de 1846," in *Oeuvres complètes*, ed. Claude Pichois, 2 vols. (Paris: Gallimard, 1975–76), 2:421.

20. Willem de Kooning, "What Abstract Art Means to Me," *The Museum of Modern Art Bulletin* 18 (Spring 1951): 7.

21. De Kooning, quoted in anonymous, "Willem the Walloper," *Time* 57 (April 30, 1951): 63.

22. Marden, statement, in Jean-Claude Lebensztejn, "Eight Statements," *Art in America* 63, no. 4 (July–August 1975): 73. Compare John Yau, "A Vision of the Unsayable," *Brice Marden: Recent Paintings and Drawings* (London: Anthony d'Offay Gallery, 1988), n.p.: "From the outset of his career, Marden accepted the inevitability of being continuously thwarted, of never being able to arrive at a purely spiritual realization."

23. Peirce, letter to Lady Victoria Welby, October 12, 1904, *Collected Papers*, 8:222–23 (emphasis eliminated).

24. On naturalistic painting as an expression of artistic temperament, see, for example, Champfleury (Jules Fleury), "L'Aventurier Challes," *La Revue de Paris* 21 (May 15, 1854): 574, and Emile Zola, "Proudhon et Courbet," 1866, in *Mes Haines* (Paris: Charpentier, 1879), p. 25.

25. Paul Mantz, *Salon de 1847* (Paris: Ferdinand Sartorius, 1847), p. 96.

26. Art "is nothing but the image of a fantasy reflected in an appearance it has created and which reproduces it. . . . It unites . . . material substance and immaterial thought." Gabriel Séailles, "L'Origine et les destinées de l'art," *Revue philosophique* 22 (1886): 347. "We can no longer make a true distinction between perception and the thing perceived, between quality [the self] and movement [material substance]." Henri Bergson, *Matière et mémoire*, 1896 (reprint ed. Paris: Presses Universitaires de France, 1968), p. 245.

27. Marden, "Star (for Patti Smith)," n.p.

28. Theodor W. Adorno, "Perennial Fashion—Jazz," 1936, in *Prisms*, trans. Samuel and Shierry Weber (Cambridge, Mass.: The MIT Press, 1981), p. 123.

29. Roland Barthes, "Le Message photographique," *Communications* 1 (1961): 129.

30. Susan Sontag was an early popularizer of Barthes in America; see her "Against Interpretation," 1964, in *Against Interpretation* (New York: Dell, 1969), p. 22. Marden's awareness of the emerging European social critique developed in part through his interest in the films of Jean-Luc Godard, including *Alphaville* (1965), which he appreciated not only for its message but also for its dramatic cinematography in black and white (a visual effect he mentioned several times in our conversations). On Marden's interest in Godard, see Jeremy Gilbert-Rolfe, "Brice Marden's Painting," *Artforum* 13, no. 2 (October 1974): 30.

31. Marden, in Mahoney, "This Is What Things Are About," p. 119. Adorno had already warned of critical recognition turning into critical defeatism: "[The consumer] is made to feel that he is not expected to take the idea of something special seriously, let alone believe in it. . . . The laughter we hear is familiar to us from the radio where the announcer not only laughs, but laughs at his own laughter, defrauding the listener of the very deception which is being perpetrated against him." Adorno, "Commodity Music Analyzed," 1934–40, in *Quasi una Fantasia: Essays on Modern Music*, trans. Rodney Livingstone (London: Verso, 1992), pp. 44–45.

32. On this complex of issues during the earlier twentieth century, see Richard Shiff, "From Primitivist Phylogeny to Formalist Ontogeny: Roger Fry and Children's Drawings," in Jonathan Fineberg, ed., *Discovering Child Art: Essays on Childhood, Primitivism, and*

Modernism (Princeton: at the University Press, 1998), pp. 157–200.

33. Marden, in an interview with Lilly Wei, "Talking Abstract," *Art in America* 75, no. 7 (July 1987): 83.

34. Marden, in Pat Steir, "Brice Marden: An Interview," *Brice Marden: Recent Drawings and Etchings* (New York: Matthew Marks Gallery, 1991), n.p.

35. Marden, in Mahoney, "This Is What Things Are About," p. 120.

36. Richard Serra, in Serra, *Television Delivers People*, 1973, videotape, color, sound, 5:47. Quoted in Annette Michelson, Serra, and Clara Weyergraf, "The Films of Richard Serra: An Interview," 1979, in Serra, *Writings/Interviews* (Chicago: at the University Press, 1994), p. 74.

37. Serra's commentary evokes Adorno and related late-Marxist cultural analysis: "[The consumer] belongs to the product and not the product to him." Adorno, "Commodity Music Analyzed," p. 45.

38. See Shiff, "Originality," in Robert S. Nelson and Shiff, eds., *Critical Terms for Art History* (Chicago: at the University Press, 2003), pp. 145–59.

39. Marden, in the transcript of the interview with Howard, p. 25.

40. The notion of self-forgetting is Marden's but appears also in Adorno: "The most sublime lyric works, therefore, are those in which the subject, without a trace of his material being, intones in language until the voice of language itself is heard. The subject's forgetting himself, his abandoning himself to language as if devoting himself completely to an object—this and the direct intimacy and spontaneity of his expression are the same. . . . When the speaking subject, the 'I' [of lyric poetry] forgets himself completely, he is yet entirely present." Adorno, "Lyric Poetry and Society," 1957, trans. Bruce Mayo, *Telos* 20 (Summer 1974): 62.

41. Marden, in the transcript of the interview with Howard, pp. 7, 3 (punctuation altered).

42. Ibid., p. 13.

43. Marden, in "Interview by Robin White," p. 17.

44. Marden, in an interview with Denise Green, November 1992, in Green, *Metonymy in Contemporary Art: A New Paradigm* (Minneapolis: University of Minnesota Press, 2005), p. 87.

45. Marden, on the sound track to Howard and Haimes, *Brice Marden* (not in the transcript of the interview with Howard).

46. Marden, in the transcript of the interview with Howard, pp. 7, 13. The sound track for the Howard/Haimes film *Brice Marden* includes Marden's laugh. He also says, "I think of these drawings as practically like shields. I mean, they do have a very strong physical quality to them. . . . Instead of putting frames on them, you can put little handles on the back, walk around with your art shield." Transcript of the interview with Howard, pp. 3, 7. The idea of the shield may have struck Marden because of his interest in ancient Greek sculpture, including figures of warriors with shields; see his *Souvenir de Grèce 3* (1974/1994), which incorporates four identical images of an arm grasping a shield.

47. Along these lines, Marden made a suggestive comment in a recent interview: "I think of my paintings as icons—but the icon is really open to all sorts of interpretations. It doesn't just become some physical fact that you can't read beyond. There are fourteen icons that can't be traced to human hands, acheiropoetos, meaning not made with the hand. Icons made from something other than human hands. I mean, that's to me the kind of painting you strive for." Marden, in an interview with Saul Ostrow, "Brice Marden," *Bomb* no. 22 (Winter 1988): 35. Marden's reflection on icons was spurred by conversations with David Novros.

48. Donald Judd, "Barnett Newman," 1964–70, in *Complete Writings 1959–1975* (Halifax: Nova Scotia College of Art and Design, 1975), p. 202. There are obvious parallels between Marden's often quoted principle of the "indisputability of the plane" (summer 1974; see Pincus-Witten, *The Grove Group*, p. 25) and any number of statements by Judd, for example, "If you are going to use just an optical effect, it has to be made so definite that you don't have an illusionistic surface, so that you don't somehow destroy the surface you are working on." Judd, statement at the New York University symposium "Is Easel Painting Dead?," November 1966, transcript, ed. Barbara Rose, in the Barbara Rose papers, Archives of American Art, Smithsonian Institution, p. 31. Judd recognized the inescapable presence of optical illusion, noting that certain forms of it should nevertheless be avoided. He insisted that the designation "Minimalist" was inappropriate: "I've said and written many times that the label 'minimal' is meaningless in all ways." Judd, "A long discussion not about masterpieces but why there are so few of them, Part II," 1984, in *Complete Writings 1975–1986* (Eindhoven: Van Abbemuseum, 1987), pp. 71–72. Judd had earlier elaborated, "I object to the whole reduction idea, because it's only reduction of those things someone doesn't want.

If my work is reductionist it's because it doesn't have the elements that people thought should be there. But it has other elements that I like." Judd, in an interview with Bruce Glaser, February 1964 (modified December 1965), in Lucy R. Lippard, ed., "Questions to Stella and Judd," *Artnews* 65 (September 1966): 60. When Marden was asked in 1998 whether he had been disturbed by critics classifying him as a Minimalist during his earlier career, he replied in a way that would have pleased Judd: "Minimalism is not an elimination of things. It can be the amalgamation of a lot of things, brought to a very refined state. . . . Many people thought of it as simplistic, whereas it's really a highly complex system of image-making. So, I don't mind. I didn't mind then much. I figured that's what they're going to call you." Marden, in Vincent Katz, "Curiously Determined Objects: An Interview with Brice Marden," *On Paper* 2, no. 3 (January/February 1998): 29.

49. Marden, notes, c. 1971–74, in Pincus-Witten, *The Grove Group*, p. 21.

50. Mantz, *Salon de 1847*, pp. 96–97.

51. Ibid., p. 98.

52. Ibid., pp. 102–3.

53. "Monochrome" is a misnomer here, for Marden's subtle color mixtures appear monochromatic only at a certain distance, as I will discuss below. I will continue to set this word within quotation marks as a device to maintain awareness of its ultimate inappropriateness.

54. Marden, statement, in Carl Andre, ed., "New in New York: Line Work," *Arts* 41, no. 7 (May 1967): 50. For "monochrome" panels of oil and wax on canvas, such as *The Dylan Painting* (1966/1986; plate 17), Marden had to cover the entire surface within about thirty minutes, before the melted beeswax hardened. See Roberta Pancoast Smith, "Brice Marden's Painting," *Arts* 47, no. 7 (May 1973): 37.

55. Marden, conversation with the author, November 10, 2005; Walter Hopps, *Robert Rauschenberg: The Early 1950s* (Houston: Menil Foundation, 1991), p. 80.

56. Marden, quoted in Reginato, "Marden's Retreat," p. 264.

57. Marden, in the transcript of the interview with Howard, p. 31.

58. Marden, conversation with the author, March 14, 2006.

59. Franz Kline, quoted in Frank O'Hara, "Franz Kline Talking," *Evergreen Review* 2 (Autumn 1958): 64. Clement Greenberg wrote of Barnett Newman in a similar vein, also in 1958, "The truth of art lies for him, as for any genuinely ambitious artist, somewhat beyond what he *knows* he can do": Greenberg, "Introduction to an Exhibition of Barnett Newman," 1958, in *Clement Greenberg: The Collected Essays and Criticism*, ed. John O'Brian, 4 vols. (Chicago: at the University Press, 1986–93), 4:54.

60. Judd, "Abstract Expressionism," 1983, in *Complete Writings 1975–1986*, p. 40.

61. Marden, in "Interview by Paul Cummings," p. 33.

62. Marden, note from a personal notebook in use from 1966 to around 1974, courtesy Marden. The note appears on a page containing a sketch of Marden's four-panel composition *The Seasons* (1974–75), which he painted in both a small version and a large one. The tonal values of the sketched panels (rendered in pencil hatchings) correspond best to the small version of *The Seasons*, though the proportions differ.

63. Marden, in "Interview by Robin White," pp. 12–13.

64. Marden, in Yau, "An Interview with Brice Marden," February–March 2003, in Eva Keller and Regula Malin, eds., *Brice Marden* (Zurich: Scalo, 2003), p. 50.

65. Marden, in the transcript of the interview with Howard, p. 5.

66. Marden, in Jonathan Hay, "An Interview with Brice Marden," *Brice Marden: Chinese Work* (New York: Matthew Marks Gallery, 1997), p. 20.

67. "I think the grid is an arbitrary measure to put on space; it's like a molecule next to a molecule": Marden, quoted in Lebensztejn, "From," *Brice Marden: Recent Paintings and Drawings* (New York: The Pace Gallery, 1978), n.p. See also the reference to the molecular structure of a gridded plane, accompanying a quadrant drawing, in Marden, *Suicide Notes* (Lausanne: Editions des Massons, 1974), p. 40: "form of a plane, made up of planes, planes made of planes, diminishing planes, molecular, Cézanne plane study."

68. Marden thinks of Manhattan as a grid (in the transcript of the interview with Howard, p. 7); in Paris in 1964, he took rubbings of a grid of tiles on the floor of his apartment, providing an arbitrary form from which to work.

69. Marden, in "Interview by Paul Cummings," p. 34, and quoted in Lebensztejn, "From," n.p.

70. See Henri Dorra and Rewald, *Seurat* (Paris: Les Beaux-arts, 1959), cat. nos. 9b and 9, pp. 8, 9.

71. Marden, conversation with the author, December 13, 2005.

72. Marden, on the sound track to Howard and Haimes, *Brice Marden* (not in the transcript of the interview with Howard).
73. Georges Seurat, quoted by Charles Angrand in Gustave Coquiot, *Georges Seurat* (Paris: Albin Michel, 1924), p. 41.
74. Paul Gauguin, letter to Emile Bernard, late November 1888, in *Correspondance de Paul Gauguin, 1873–1888*, ed. Victor Merlhès (Paris: Fondation Singer-Polignac, 1984), p. 284. Gauguin wrote this letter while visiting Van Gogh in Arles; its content reflects their debates.
75. Gauguin, letter to Camille Pissarro, c. July 10, 1884, in ibid., p. 65.
76. See Shiff, "Apples and Abstraction," in Eliza E. Rathbone and George T. M. Shackelford, eds., *Impressionist Still Life* (Washington, D.C.: The Phillips Collection, 2001), pp. 42–47, 227–28, and "Sensation, Movement, Cézanne," in Terence Maloon, ed., *Classic Cézanne* (Sydney: Art Gallery of New South Wales, 1998), pp. 13–27.
77. Marden, in Willoughby Sharp, "Points of View: A Taped Conversation with Four Painters," *Arts* 45, no. 3 (December 1970): 42.
78. See Marden, notes, c. 1974, in Pincus-Witten, *The Grove Group*, p. 29. On Marden and Cézanne see also Yve-Alain Bois, "Marden's Doubt," in Ulrich Loock and Bois, *Brice Marden: Paintings, 1985–1993* (Bern: Kunsthalle Bern, 1993), pp. 53–67.
79. Newman, quoted in Harold Cohen, introduction to "Barnett Newman Talks to David Sylvester," BBC radio broadcast, November 17, 1965, transcript, Barnett Newman Foundation, New York.
80. Newman, in an interview with Dorothy Gees Seckler, 1962, transcript with manuscript additions and emendations by Newman, Barnett Newman Foundation, New York.
81. "I think Newman is a fantastic painter. That show last year [Newman's posthumous retrospective at The Museum of Modern Art in 1971] was just beautiful. But I don't think I was working with those ideas." Marden, in "Interview by Paul Cummings," p. 34. On Newman's impact on younger artists during the 1960s see Shiff, "Whiteout: The Not-Influence Newman Effect," in Ann Temkin, ed., *Barnett Newman* (Philadelphia: Philadelphia Museum of Art, 2002), pp. 77–111.
82. Robert Mangold, statement to the author, August 29, 1999.
83. Mangold, "Flat Art," 1967, in Shiff et al., *Robert Mangold* (London: Phaidon, 2000), p. 162.
84. Chuck Close, quoted in Michael Kimmelman, *Portraits: Talking with Artists at the Met, the Modern, the Louvre and Elsewhere* (New York: Random House, 1998), p. 246.
85. Serra, in "Richard Serra, interviewed by Lynne Cooke, 21 May 1992," *Richard Serra Drawings* (London: Serpentine Gallery, 1992), p. 13. On Marden in relation to his immediate contemporaries see also Klaus Kertess, *Brice Marden: Paintings and Drawings* (New York: Harry N. Abrams, 1992), pp. 18–19.
86. Lippard, "Rejective Art," *Art International* 10, no. 8 (October 20, 1966): 36. Also very much to the point, Gilbert-Rolfe would later refer to Marden's "methodical suppression of gesture"; Gilbert-Rolfe, "Brice Marden's Painting," p. 32.
87. Lippard, "The Silent Art," *Art in America* 55, no. 1 (January/February 1967): 63.
88. John Ashbery, "Grey Eminence," *Artnews* 71, no. 1 (March 1972): 65.
89. Peirce, "Phaneroscopy or the Natural History of Concepts," c. 1905, *Collected Papers*, 1:167 (emphasis eliminated). See also Peirce, "Phaneroscopy," c. 1906, *Collected Papers*, 1:152: "By a feeling I mean an instance of that sort of element of consciousness which is all that it is positively, in itself, regardless of anything else."
90. Peirce, "A Guess at the Riddle," c. 1890, *Collected Papers*, 1:200–201 (punctuation altered for clarity). Peirce's "First" and "Second" do not necessarily imply sequence, but rather two categories of psychic phenomenon. First or Firstness corresponds to what he calls monadic "quality," represented as an iconic sign; Second or Secondness corresponds to dyadic "fact," represented as an indexical sign. See Peirce, "The Logic of Mathematics: An Attempt to Develop My Categories from Within," c. 1896, in ibid., 1:230–40, and "The Icon, Index, and Symbol," c. 1893–1902, in ibid., 2:156–65.
91. Marden, statement, in Andre, ed., "New in New York: Line Work," p. 49.
92. Peirce, "Telepathy and Perception," 1903, *Collected Papers*, 7:373. With regard to the experience of painting, an observation by David Reed is relevant: "When I first started working abstractly, part of me would identify with the painting, as if I were inside it working through the forms. Another part of me would stay outside and watch what was happening. I felt split in two. . . . Finally, I decided that this experience of being split apart was necessary to make a painting." Reed, in an interview with Stephen Ellis, October 29, 1989, in William S. Bartman, ed., *David Reed* (Los Angeles: A.R.T. Press, 1990), p. 5.
93. Peirce, "Phaneroscopy or the Natural History of Concepts," p. 167.

94. But conscious judgment and belief also entail a type of feeling. See, for example, Peirce, "The Probability of Induction," 1878, *Collected Papers*, 2:419, and "Phaneroscopy," p. 152.
95. Peirce, "Phaneroscopy or the Natural History of Concepts," p. 167.
96. Marden, in "Interview by Paul Cummings," p. 9.
97. Robert Goodnough, "Kline Paints a Picture," *Artnews* 51 (December 1952): 37. See also David Anfam, "Kline's Colliding Syntax: 'Black, White, and Things,'" *Franz Kline: Black & White 1950–1961* (Houston: Menil Foundation, 1994), pp. 9–31.
98. See *New Paintings by Franz Kline* (New York: Sidney Janis Gallery, 1961), n.p. *Zinc Door*, which includes a prominent area of yellow (perhaps zinc yellow was the source of its title), is cat. no. 8 in this black and white publication. See also Kertess, *Paintings and Drawings*, p. 12.
99. Esteban Vicente, c. 1962–63, as recounted by Marden in "Interview by Paul Cummings," p. 18.
100. Marden, conversation with the author, February 4, 2006.
101. Marden, on the sound track to Howard and Haimes, *Brice Marden* (not in the transcript of the interview with Howard).
102. Marden, quoted in Davis, "'This Is the Loose-Paint Generation,'" p. 20; Marden, statement, in Andre, ed., "New in New York: Line Work," p. 50. Interestingly, even critics who disparaged or were puzzled by Marden's work seem to have been drawn to see it as he wished: "An admixture of wax lends the surface a very slight unevenness, but one that is noticeable only very close to." Michael Peppiatt, "Paris," *Art International* 13, no. 9 (November 1969): 56.
103. "I paint paintings in panels. They are not color panels [mere pieces of colored material]. . . . They are *painted* panels." Marden, notes, 1971, in Pincus-Witten, *The Grove Group*, p. 18 (emphasis added).
104. Pincus-Witten, "Ryman, Marden, Manzoni: Theory, Sensibility, Mediation," *Artforum* 10, no. 10 (June 1972): 52 (emphasis added).
105. Marden, in the transcript of the interview with Howard, p. 11. On gravitational effects see also Marden's remarks on observing the pressure-cleaning of Paris walls in 1964: Marden, in "Interview by Paul Cummings," p. 22, and in Ostrow, "Brice Marden," p. 31.
106. Marden, conversation with the author, March 14, 2006.
107. See Marden, in "Interview by Paul Cummings," p. 34, and Alan R. Solomon, *Jasper Johns* (New York: The Jewish Museum, 1964). Marden became best acquainted with Johns's painting *Tango*, which hung in the gallery to which he was assigned. See also Sheldon Nodelman, *Marden, Novros, Rothko: Painting in the Age of Actuality* (Houston: Institute for the Arts, Rice University, 1978), p. 61.
108. Marden used the term *funky* in this sense on several occasions during our conversations, September 2005 through April 2006. When I asked him to elaborate, he mentioned cases where the surface may have little tears or holes in it from being stressed, or a waxy coating may have acquired specks of dirt or dried pigment as it was being worked. Marden increased his opportunities for irregularity by developing a practice of using long sticks as drawing instruments, particularly hard to control (a factor bearing primarily on works outside the chronological focus of this essay).
109. "Marden asked [the printer Kathan] Brown to put on a ground to encourage foul biting. . . . From Marden's point of view, [finger marks and other stray elements] activate the surface and ensure that 'blank' panels read as surfaces and not as voids." Jeremy Lewison, *Brice Marden Prints 1961–1991: A Catalogue Raisonné* (London: Tate Gallery, 1992), p. 94.
110. Marden, statement, in Andre, ed., "New in New York: Line Work," p. 50; Marden, notes taken while viewing his one-person exhibition at the Bykert Gallery, New York, November 20, 1966, typescript, courtesy Marden.
111. Marden, notes in the Bykert Gallery, November 20, 1966.
112. Marden, quoted in Davis, "'This Is the Loose-Paint Generation,'" p. 20.
113. Marden, quoted in Ashbery, "Grey Eminence," p. 64. See also Marden, in "Interview by Paul Cummings," p. 32: "I was working to get a color that would be like gray and yet could also be considered green or red."
114. Marden, statement, in Maurice Poirier and Jane Necol, "The '60s in Abstract: 13 Statements and an Essay," *Art in America* 71, no. 9 (October 1983): 122.
115. Marden, in Ostrow, "Brice Marden," pp. 33–34. See also Kertess, *Paintings and Drawings*, p. 12. For early commentary on Marden's unstable, ambiguous color, see Harris Rosenstein, "Brice Marden (Bykert)," *Art News* 68, no. 3 (May 1969): 69; Carter Ratcliff, "New York Letter," *Art International* 15, no. 2 (February 20, 1971): 69; Ashbery, "Grey

Eminence," p. 64; and Smith, "Brice Marden's Painting," p. 38.

116. Marden, quoted in Lebensztejn, "From," n.p. See also Marden, in "Interview by Paul Cummings," p. 36.

117. Marden, in "Interview by Paul Cummings," p. 32.

118. This may be why Marden has occasionally repainted works after exhibiting them: because each painting is many feelings, there may be a compulsion to stress or extend one feeling at one moment, another at another moment in the life of the same work. Reciprocally, as Marden explained to me (April 5, 2006), he cannot refinish a damaged painting merely by "imitating" the present appearance of the surface color. He would have to recover the complicated history of the painting, the succession of mixtures of various pigments that generated it over an extended period.

119. Mangold's best recollection is that the exchange occurred during the summer of 1969, when the two participated in the Yale program at Norfolk. Mangold, statement to the author, April 14, 2006. Marden signed and dated his drawing years later, assigning it to 1970.

120. Marden's works on (white) paper often distinguish between the paper as it comes, the paper when sanded, and the paper when covered by a layer of wax. These are different qualities of "white."

121. Mangold's Perimeter Series establishes relationships far more complex than what I have described here; see Rosenstein, "To Be Continued," *Artnews* 69 (Summer 1970): 63.

122. Two of the pencil sketches are reproduced without identification in Lebensztejn, *Recent Paintings and Drawings*, n.p. On Marden's notebooks see Dieter Schwarz and Michael Semff, *Brice Marden: Work Books 1964–1995* (Düsseldorf: Richter Verlag, 1997).

123. Marden's source for the "Emerald Tablet" was Serge Hutin, *A History of Alchemy*, trans. Tamara Alferoff (New York: Walker and Company, 1962), pp. 51–53. The same text appears along with explanatory commentary in Wayne Shumaker, *The Occult Sciences in the Renaissance* (Berkeley: University of California Press, 1972), pp. 179–80; see also pp. 201–51. For Flaubert's statement in context see his letter to George Sand of October 7, 1871, in Jean Bruneau, ed., *Flaubert: Correspondance*, 4 vols. (Paris: Gallimard, 1973–98), 4:384.

124. "A painting, you know, it's all dirty material. But it's about transformation. Taking the earth, that heavy earthen kind of thing, turning it into air and light." Marden, in Steir, "Brice Marden: An Interview," n.p.

125. William Zimmer's "Marden 1982: Hermeticism Made Visible," in *Brice Marden: Marbles, Paintings, and Drawings* (New York: The Pace Gallery, 1982), testifies to the artist's involvement with alchemic notions in a strict sense at that moment. To the contrary, I invoke Marden's interest in alchemy for what it may suggest about his attitude throughout his career, but especially in the 1960s and early '70s.

126. Marden, notes in the Bykert Gallery, November 20, 1966. Marden's experience of Nebraska topography is discussed below, as is his interest in the Hudson.

127. Marden, in "Brice Marden: Interview with Robert Storr on October 24, 1986," in Rosemarie Schwarzwälder, ed., *Abstract Painting of America and Europe* (Klagenfurt: Ritter, 1988), p. 71.

128. Ibid., p. 72.

129. Marden, in Steir, "Brice Marden: An Interview," n.p. (ellipsis original).

130. Marden, in the transcript of the interview with Howard, p. 17.

131. Ibid, pp. 25, 30. Marden established a similarly "horrendous" context for the emotional intensity of his work of the mid-1960s: "These paintings were done when war was a major issue. It was like the call of death. Your country is making death. There is going to be a reflection of that in the art of the time. It's not that people are going to make paintings about death. . . . You could say that I was showing some of the bleaker aspects. In this sense I was making a political statement. One likes to think that art is on the side of truth." Marden, in Poirier and Necol, "The '60s in Abstract," p, 122. See also his statement of 1991 during the Gulf War: "I paint, but there's a war going on. I think the events of the last year have been really upsetting, and the political situation is terrible. . . . I think any artist striving to make art is making a political act." Marden, in Steir, "Brice Marden: An Interview," n.p.

132. Marden, draft of a statement dated summer 1974, in Pincus-Witten, *The Grove Group*, p. 25.

133. Yau, "Words for and from Brice Marden," in Fairbrother, *Brice Marden: Boston*, p. 25.

134. Marden, "A Mediterranean Painting," 1971, in Marcia Tucker, ed., *The Structure of Color* (New York: Whitney Museum of American Art, 1971), p. 20 (punctuation added for clarity). Janis Joplin died on October 4, 1970; in response, Marden quickly repainted his "Mediterranean" painting, dedicating it to Joplin's memory. *For Pearl* manifests an

unusual bit of funkiness (if I can put it this way), a sign of Marden's impetuousness at that moment: he allowed a slight splash of the color of the center panel to remain visible on the right side of the left panel and allowed a comparable splash of the color of the right panel to remain visible on the right side of the center panel. This effect is "impure" in an uncharacteristic way but also reveals Marden's characteristic procedural moves as he worked the panels from left to center to right, finishing each in its turn.
135. Marden, note, 1971, in Pincus-Witten, *The Grove Group*, p. 20.
136. Marden, "A Mediterranean Painting," p. 20.
137. Marden, quoted in Bettina von Hase, "Full Beam," *Art Review* 2, no. 3 (March 2004): 68. See also Marden, in Yau, "An Interview with Brice Marden," p. 58: "With Pollock, the image grows out of the paint up to the plane."
138. Marden, draft of a statement dated summer 1974, p. 25. In its entirety Marden's statement also suggests that his swimming companion is able to establish a connection to nature without the mediation of art that he requires. The text originally appeared in Licht, *Eight Contemporary Artists* (New York: The Museum of Modern Art, 1974), p. 46. Marden recalls that when Licht requested an artist's statement for the 1974 exhibition, he submitted this one, well aware that it was not particularly suited to the purpose at hand.
139. Marden, in "Brice Marden in Conversation with William Furlong," *Art Monthly* no. 117 (June 1988): 3. See also Marden, in Steir, "Brice Marden: An Interview," n.p. On the context of Pollock's statement see Glaser, "Jackson Pollock: An Interview with Lee Krasner," *Arts* 41, no. 6 (April 1967): 38.
140. Marden, statement to Lewison, 1991, quoted in Lewison, *Brice Marden Prints 1961–1991*, p. 51.
141. Marden, in "Brice Marden in Conversation with William Furlong," p. 3.
142. Marden, in an interview with Anouchka Roggeman, "Des tremplins pour l'esprit," *L'oeil* no. 577 (February 2006): 55.
143. Marden, conversation with the author, February 20, 2006.
144. Marden, conversation with the author, February 12, 2006.
145. Marden, notes, c. 1971–74, in Pincus-Witten, *The Grove Group*, pp. 14, 31, 28.
146. Marden, in Yau, "An Interview with Brice Marden," p. 57.
147. Murray Reich, a teaching assistant at Boston University, advised Marden to draw in this manner; for an etching derived from these drawings see Untitled (1961), in Lewison, *Brice Marden Prints 1961–1991*, p. 76.
148. See de Kooning, statement, in David Sylvester, "Content Is a Glimpse . . . ," *Location* 1 (Spring 1963): 47–48. Marden's longstanding interest in de Kooning parallels his interest in Kline: "For me, as a student, de Kooning was really the master. He was the one you refer to—the supreme source." Marden, "Brice Marden in conversation with William Furlong," p. 4.
149. De Kooning, in Harold Rosenberg, "Interview with Willem de Kooning," *Artnews* 71 (September 1972): 58.
150. See Shiff, "Water and Lipstick: de Kooning in Transition," in Marla Prather, ed., *Willem de Kooning: Paintings* (Washington, D.C.: National Gallery of Art, 1994), pp. 32–73.
151. Marden, in "Interview by Paul Cummings," pp. 32–33. See also Kertess, *Paintings and Drawings*, p. 22: "Rather than describing an image, color—as light, as surface, as shape, as feeling—becomes the image."
152. De Kooning, quoted in anonymous, "Willem the Walloper," p. 63.
153. Marden, in the transcript of the interview with Howard, p. 9.
154. Marden, conversation with the author, February 1999; Marden, in Yau, "An Interview with Brice Marden," p. 48.
155. Among the thoughts that Marden associated with his Back series was rejection, turning the back, including a time when Helen rejected him (see, for example, Marden, in the transcript of the interview with Howard, p. 9); but this association does not apply to the period in which he was working on *For Helen*.
156. Marden, conversation with the author, March 14, 2006.
157. To call the color "orificial," as John Richardson does (because of its tonality), is to impute a literalness uncharacteristic of Marden; see Richardson, "Brice Marden's Abstract Heart," *Vanity Fair* no. 465 (May 1999): 201.
158. Helen Marden's initial response to the painting in 1967, as confirmed by her in conversation with Brice Marden, March 13, 2006.
159. Marden, conversation with the author, February 16, 2006. John Richardson gives Helen Marden's account: "Helen claims that the pink was inspired by a color Marden had never

seen—the color of the wet sand at low tide in Cornwall—which she had described to him." Richardson, "Brice Marden's Abstract Heart," p. 201. Among the statements from Peirce that I have enlisted for this essay—concerning perception, sensation, and feeling—some were occasioned by his involvement in debates over telepathy; see Peirce, "Telepathy and Perception," pp. 359–97. In Peirce's view, claims made by advocates of telepathy, similar to the following, were overstatements that could not be adjudicated scientifically: "Telepathy renders a purely materialistic philosophy untenable, and furnishes the prospect of a far more perfect interchange of thought than by the clumsy mechanism of speech." W. F. Barrett, *Psychical Research* (London: Williams and Norgate, 1911), p. 69. At the same time, Peirce would not have supported materialists in their blanket dismissal of the claims made for telepathy. As in other matters, he believed that there were things that remained to be found out on both sides of the question. See Peirce, "Telepathy and Perception," pp. 396–97.
160. Henry David Thoreau, journal entry, June 23, 1852, in *The Journal of Henry D. Thoreau*, ed. Bradford Torrey and Francis H. Allen, 14 vols. (Boston: Houghton Mifflin, 1949), 4:134.
161. Marden, note, June 11, 1966 (apparently written incorrectly as 1965), from a personal notebook in use from 1966 to around 1974.
162. Peirce, letter to Lady Victoria Welby, October 12, 1904, pp. 221–22.
163. Marden, in Janie C. Lee, "Interview with Brice Marden," May 21, 1998, in *Brice Marden Drawings: The Whitney Museum of American Art Collection* (New York: Whitney Museum of American Art, 1998), p. 14.
164. The lined page facing this notebook sketch is devoid of writing, but successive images from the squared sketch page appear to have been recorded on it unintentionally, in part because drawing on following squared pages put pressure on preceding squared pages, causing a transfer of graphite. The pattern of transfer seems to indicate that Marden first sketched in blue parallel lines (an unusual procedure) the proportions of a two-panel work for which each panel would be 40 by 17 1/2 inches, but he has no memory of what this may have signified.
165. Marden, in "Interview by Paul Cummings," p. 25 (typographical errors corrected).
166. Marden, in the transcript of the interview with Howard, p. 1. As an elaborate demonstration of Marden's visual thinking, see the forty-four double-sheet drawings that constitute his *Shape Book* (1973–75; Graphische Sammlung Albertina, Vienna).
167. Marden, in "Brice Marden in conversation with William Furlong," p. 3. Newman had similar thoughts during the 1960s; see Shiff, "Whiteout," pp. 100–104.
168. Marden, in Ostrow, "Brice Marden," p. 35.
169. Marden, in the transcript of the interview with Howard, p. 5.
170. Marden, notes, c. 1971–74, in Pincus Witten, *The Grove Group*, p. 24.
171. Marden, in "Interview by Robin White," p. 16.
172. Marden, note, June 1966, from a personal notebook in use from 1966 to around 1974; notes in the Bykert Gallery, November 20, 1966.
173. See Thoreau, *Walden*, 1854, in *A Week on the Concord and Merrimack Rivers; Walden, or Life in the Woods; The Maine Woods; Cape Cod*, ed. Robert F. Sayre (New York: The Library of America, 1985), p. 400. Marden also wrote *a fishing* instead of *a-fishing*. Thoreau's passage continues: "Its thin current [the current moment] slides away, but eternity remains. I would drink deeper; fish in the sky, whose bottom is pebbly with stars." Marden also copied into his "Lecture Notes" Constantine Cavafy's poem "Walls" (1896), which he associated with times of isolation in his studio.
174. Marden, in the transcript of the interview with Howard, p. 17.

Brenda Richardson

Even a Stone Knows You

Light, Water, Place

In recent years Brice Marden has spent much of his time along the Hudson River, living and working in a landscape that, nearly two centuries before him, inspired a generation of artists who painted the majestic river so often that its name became theirs, generically, as the Hudson River School (fig. 1). Marden maintains four studios, two of them sited on the Hudson. In lower Manhattan, he works in a tenth-floor space with expansive, unobstructed west and south views of the Hudson. On the days when he paints there, he walks his dog along the river. Gazing at the rhythmic movement of light on water, he is most amazed, he says, when the water seems to stop.

Lower Manhattan is built on deeply buried rock known as the Manhattan schist or gneiss—a rock composed mostly of mica and quartz, usually in delicate layers that are complexly folded, reflecting the high pressures and temperatures they were subjected to when buried. These are the core rocks of the Appalachians, buried to a depth of ten miles when the Appalachians were at their most imposing (say 450 million years ago).

Following the river northward, into Dutchess County, one comes to the village of Tivoli, which is some miles south of Olana, the home of the Hudson River School painter Frederic Edwin Church, itself situated just across the Hudson from Catskill, the home of Thomas Cole, the School's founding figure. Not far from Tivoli is Rose Hill, the Mardens' forty-acre property. (The Watts family, who first built on the site in 1840, named Rose Hill for their ancestral home in Scotland.) Somewhat up the hill from the main house, Marden's painting studio is perched on a rocky outcrop overlooking the Hudson through a scrim of old-growth oak and poplar. The river is close enough that freighters loom large as they pass the studio's ranks of seventeen-foot window walls facing west and north to the water. Prominent just beyond the studio's north window is a low cascade of nested gray boulders that Marden plans to cultivate as an Asian-style moss garden.

The rocks along the east bank of the Hudson at Tivoli are mostly dark gray shales and sandstones deposited in a deep-water marine environment in a tectonically unstable area (like southeast Asia today) with a few red and green slates, and a very few blocks of limestone. . . . Across the river to the west [are] the hills of the Catskills, made of red sandstones deposited by rivers draining the Appalachians to the west, carrying debris eroded from higher peaks to the east (say 380 million years ago).

The Hudson feels personal to Marden. It was his father's river, he says, and now it's his. In the 1950s, Marden's father serviced mortgages for a living; his assigned territories included small banks and savings-and-loan associations in towns along the Hudson in the Albany area. (The artist nostalgically remembers being allowed, as a boy, to accompany his father on a day of Hudson calls.) Marden has mythologized the awe with which his father imbued the river; the son recounts the senior Marden summarizing his impression of the Rhine after a European holiday with the comment, "It's beautiful, but it doesn't compare to the Hudson." In late 2001, when Brice and his wife Helen Marden first saw the place near Tivoli, situated as it was on his father's river, the artist said he knew that he had come home.[1]

Place defines what and how Marden paints. The places where he lives and works include Manhattan and Tivoli in New York State; Eagles Mere in Sullivan County, north-central Pennsylvania, abutting the southeastern edge of a densely wooded, mountainous state forest; and Hydra, an island southeast of the Argolid in the Peloponnese of Greece. For the last two decades the Mardens have also spent enough time on St. Barts and Nevis in the Caribbean that those

1. John Frederick Kensett. *View on the Hudson.* 1865
Oil on canvas, 28 x 45" (71.1 x 114.3 cm)
The Baltimore Museum of Art. Gift of Mrs. Paul H. Miller

islands, too, have become ad hoc studio sites for the artist, whose drawings from his travels there and elsewhere consistently generate fresh ideas.

The Mardens have spent summer months for more than three decades at their place in Hydra, which includes studios for both Brice and Helen. Geologists describe Hydra, one of the Argo-Saronic islands, as "inhospitable, waterless, and infertile."[2] The island, situated at the head of the Mirtoan Sea (which merges southward into the Sea of Crete, eastward to Athens and the Aegean beyond, and westward to the Ionian Sea), is composed of Triassic and Jurassic gray limestones.

[Hydra's] massive and thickly bedded limestones are resistant to erosion and make up the spine of the island. Permian and older sedimentary rocks occur sparsely on the south coast. Most rocks on Hydra have been tilted 20–30 degrees to the north to north-west, giving an elongation at right angles to this of the outcrops of the different rocks, the topography of the hills and indeed the island itself.

Eagles Mere is something over six thousand miles from Hydra, nearly a quarter of the way around the globe (although at proximate latitude). The landscape there is wet, dark, and overgrown with moss and hemlock. In this the place reminds Marden of the eighth-century poet Cold Mountain's descriptions of his retreat on the Chinese mountain of Tiantai, where it was cold, dark, and wet, all moss and pines and vines.[3] Where the waters of the Hudson and the Aegean conjure history and grandeur, the water on Marden's 400 acres in Eagles Mere is a lake created from a dammed stream that runs through the property. Aged stones survive in masonry ruins at water's edge; a stand of pines dominates an island in the middle of the lake. The word "mere" derives from Old English for "small lake, pond, or marsh." (Meres may not be grand but can inspire poets all the same. The *American Heritage Dictionary* looks to Tennyson—sounding rather like Cold Mountain—for its usage citation: "Sometimes on lonely mountain meres/I find a magic bark.") An archaic derivation, also from Old English, is "boundary," and Eagles Mere indeed sits at the boundary of the Loyalsock State Forest, bountiful habitat for the bald and golden eagles that flourish there.

The rocks at Eagles Mere are slightly younger [than those along the Hudson River], and represent a slightly later stage in the story of the Appalachians (say 340 million years ago). They are red and gray sandstones, much like those of the Catskills, with a few layers of shale and very minor limestone.

Marden draws and paints in all four places, and there is typically work in progress in each studio. The artist is completely clear, however, about which works were done where. For him, a painting done in Eagles Mere has an entirely different character from one done in Manhattan, just as a painting done in Hydra feels nothing like one done at Rose Hill. He recently commented about his new Propitious Garden paintings (plates 169, 171, 172), "I could *never* have painted these in Eagles Mere."[4] And he doesn't mean simply because the Rose Hill space is his only studio with walls long enough to accommodate, side by side, all six panels of the biggest of these paintings. Marden did make a smaller-scale version of the new paintings, as well as related drawings, in his Manhattan studio; both Manhattan and Rose Hill have the right light for them, that is, they have the Hudson River.

The art historian Barbara Novak, writing on the development of Luminism in American art of the nineteenth century, identifies the metaphysical impediments that confronted artists with ambitions to paint light:

> The American necessity for the ideal, for "sentiment," which needs but a touch of profundity to become "lyricism," militated against an objective, analytic dissection of God's world. Sunlight, as a divine attribute, could hardly be broken down into the light rays of the spectrum. God's rocks could not be dissolved (the conceptual integrity of form had to be maintained), nor could they really lose their local color. . . . For the American artist, atmosphere was as metaphysical as it was physical. It was natural that the artist interested in the sentiment and divinity of the atmosphere should take the only path open to him. The path that most genuinely incorporated the real with this ideal was not the coloristic analysis of Impressionism but the poetry of light in luminism.[5]

Marden has embraced luminism ("the poetry of light") from his earliest paintings. The light he sees reflected off the waters of the places where he works has become the medium of his art every bit as much as the pigments he applies.

Metamorphosed Limestone

2. Brice Marden. *Marble #8.* 1981
Oil on marble, 12¾ x 11¾ x 1⅛" (32 x 30 x 3 cm)
Collection the Honorable Ann Brown and Donald A. Brown

In Hydra in the summer of 1981, Helen Marden hired some local workmen to build a marble bench for the property's garden. (No marble is quarried on Hydra, but a local shop sells marble brought in from other Greek islands.) As stone was cut to construct the bench, leftover fragments were strewn on the ground, where the artist found them and got the idea of painting on them.[6] The hard white surface was smooth, without the subtly pebbled or woven texture of canvas or paper, and it simultaneously absorbed and reflected light. Marden quickly realized how easily he could correct his work on marble: when he wasn't satisfied with what he had done, he wiped the marks away with the acid used by the Greek workmen to clean the stone, then started over. Most significant, perhaps, was Marden's discovery that painting on the oddly shaped fragments led him away from the orthogonal framework that had always dictated his work. He was particularly taken with the irregular shapes of the triangular and trapezoidal fragments. Their angled planes moved him to the diagonal, a shift that would have a profound impact on his work of the next two decades.

But the marble fragments were not just oddly shaped, and thus challenging, diversions from the rectangular supports on which Marden had worked for decades, they were also *chunks* (fig. 2; see also plates 99–101). Marden's persistent assertion of "the indisputability of the plane" as the single most fundamental formal premise of his painting is often cited;[7] yet again, during a studio conversation in 2005, he commented wryly, "Everything is a plane—*I'm* a plane." But the marbles he salvaged—in the context of the materials characteristically used as supports for drawing and painting—are planes with an unusually distinctive inherent dimensionality. And although quite small, they also have meaningful weight. More notably, each has visible stratigraphic substance. Marden's marbles are the product of millennia of heat and weight on Mesozoic limestone; these fragments came from layer upon layer of rock thrown up from the seabed, their geologic origin evident in tracings of veining and texture and pattern. This material coincides with what interests Marden most about life and art, namely, the stratigraphy of time itself, of duration, of the layering from which meaning is constructed.

The naturalist Terry Tempest Williams writes of her attraction to the archaeology of the Great Basin, in the American West, "Artifacts alone have never interested me. It's the stratigraphy that speaks. The human stories are told within the layers of sediments. . . . The exposed geologic layers in the redrock mirror the depths within myself."[8] It is precisely this quality in marble that led the ancient Daoist Chinese to quarry, cut, and polish choice, dramatically veined fragments into "dreamstones" (fig. 3), artworks created and prominently displayed for their evocations of the "Breath Force."

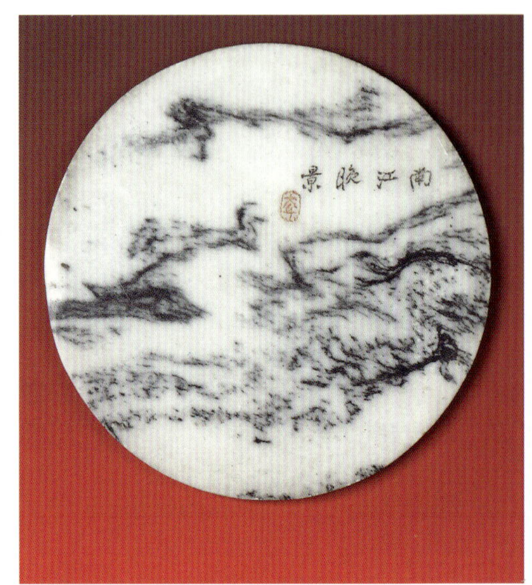

3. *Evening Scene South of the River*
Dreamstone, eighteenth century
Marble, 4¾" (12.2 cm) diam.
Collection Pierre Rambach

Marden has a reverence for the materials of art. He once memorably remarked that in creating his art he thinks in terms of its lasting for 30,000 years. But his sensitivity to the substance of an artwork is not simply a matter of preservation or even historical resonance (though both of those aspects are significant to him). When he picked up a chunk of marble with the notion of painting on it, he would have been aware of the history of marble and of the larger chunk of rock on which he stood, Hydra itself.

> The Argolid [of which Hydra is a part] . . . was settled at a very early date. The Franchthi Cave was inhabited from the Late Palaeolithic, about 8000 B.C., into the Neolithic. . . . This world came to a violent end around 2000 B.C. with the arrival of less civilised newcomers, probably the ancestors of the Greeks. They gradually settled down and by 1700 B.C. were in a position to trade with Minoan Crete, and also with Egypt, Syria and Asia Minor. Thus arose the impressive civilisation, based on Mycenae, which we call Mycenaean. This age, which ran from 1600 to 1100 B.C., was the inspiration for the legends of Classical Greece and the Homeric poems.[9]

Marble is also, of course, the quintessential building material of ancient Greece and Rome, as well as the most traditional of all sculpture materials from classical times to the present. It is the very stuff of what is universally recognized not only as eternal but as art and history rolled into one. In architecture, historically significant buildings everywhere, from classical times onward, have been constructed of marble or its limestone basis. Roman roads and viaducts were laid of marble, and survive yet. And, with their etched histories intended to echo through the centuries, gravestones are carved of marble.

The subject of architecture is apt in relation to Marden's marbles. Just the year before he began working on them, the artist had finished the eighteen-panel *Thira* (1979–80; plate 83), his largest and most complexly structured painting to that time. The painting's rich reds, greens, and browns are organized in a rhythmic progression of T shapes. (It is not much of a stretch to read the three crosses of Calvary in the hieratic composition of *Thira*, with its larger central T form raised above those to left and right.) The word "*thira*" is Greek for "door," and the post-and-lintel construction that Marden first adopted here (and used in subsequent paintings through the culminating *Coda* of 1983–84) was evocative of architectural forms—doorway, window, passage through, the view beyond. In other words, both inside and outside at once.

Marden describes his painted marbles as an "offhand summer project," a serendipitous exercise in learning. Beginning in August 1981, he worked on marble fragments, always in Hydra during the family's visits there, through the summer of 1987. The marbles are properly understood within the framework of Marden's *Souvenir de Grèce* drawings (plates 149–50), begun in 1974, and more significantly of *Thira* and the elemental body of work from 1979–83 centered on the post-and-lintel paintings. (Marden chose the title *Souvenir de Grèce* in the sense not of the tourist memento but of *souvenir* as in Matisse's 1907 *Blue Nude: Souvenir de Biskra*, that is, the memory or impression of a place.) The marbles resonate with Marden's experience of Greece, its geology and landscape, its classical culture and architecture, and of course its light and color.

During the same years that he was painting marble in Hydra, Marden was also thinking about light and color from a more literally architectural perspective. In 1978 he had been commissioned to design stained glass windows for the altar area (properly called the chevet) of the Basel Cathedral. Although Marden is not religious, he harbors a highly refined sense of the sacred. He fully understood the magnitude of the Basel commission, and its implications both architectural (the cathedral dates from the Late Gothic) and ecclesiastical. The artist had been deeply impressed by the Rothko Chapel in Houston when he visited it in 1972, although the modernist, nondenominational spirituality of that setting scarcely offered a precedent for a commission to create stained glass windows for a historical monument of Swiss Reform Protestantism.

To accommodate the transmission of light through colored glass, Marden turned to a brighter, purer palette than was his usual preference and settled on the primaries plus green for the Basel windows. In part influenced by his growing interest in alchemy, he decided to work with combinations of colors limited to three (the Trinity) for the linear components and four (the elements—earth, air, fire, water) for the monochrome panels. Devising such a "program" to generate paintings is characteristic of Marden, who typically adopts a conceptual scheme from which to work. As with the Basel concept, the programs often draw on premises derived from his readings in literature, mythology, symbolism, philosophy, and world religion. The artist would be quick to demur that he is not a scholar. But he spends time with books, trolling for information, studying images, weighing opinions and perspectives. He gravitates to knowledgeable people with stimulating views. Marden looks and listens very, very attentively, and thus learns what he needs for his work.

Mixed (and usually muted) colors may dominate Marden's work, but, like many artists, he has done his "red, yellow, and blue" paintings. Explicit primaries appear in, for example, *Fourth Figure (Red Yellow Blue)* (1973–74; plate 62) and *Red Yellow Blue I*, *II* (plate 63), and *III* (all three 1974). The Elements group (plates 103, 105), encompassing paintings and drawings created between 1979 and 1984, is also composed of the primaries plus green (like the Basel scheme). Unlike the earlier Red Yellow Blue paintings, the Elements paintings are post-and-lintel constructions, closely related to *Thira* and *Frieze II* (1982). For the Basel Cathedral Marden focused on color and line, imagining how light refracted through the glass windows would direct shafts of colored light through the church interior. In this context he was constrained by architectural considerations that were only implied in *Thira*, *Frieze II*, and the marbles.

Although Marden received the cathedral commission in 1978, his most focused work on it took place in 1983–85. This makes his Basel project concurrent not only with what he was learning from painting on marble fragments but also with his eye-opening experience of South Asia in 1983–84, when he spent nine months traveling through Thailand, Sri Lanka, and India. Marden always draws in the course of his travels, commonly generating work books identified by place and date.[10] He most often draws trees and foliage, but during his time in Thailand he began to collect seashells (particularly volutes) and developed an interest in their infinitely variform patterns and stipples (fig. 4). Also in Thailand he began to make drawings based on calligraphy, an interest that had significantly intensified by late 1984, after he visited, at Helen Marden's insistence, the New York exhibition *Masters of Japanese Calligraphy, 8th–19th Century*.[11]

In the Basel work, Marden fully exploited a potential of the diagonal that he says he discovered through his work on marble. In *First Window Painting*

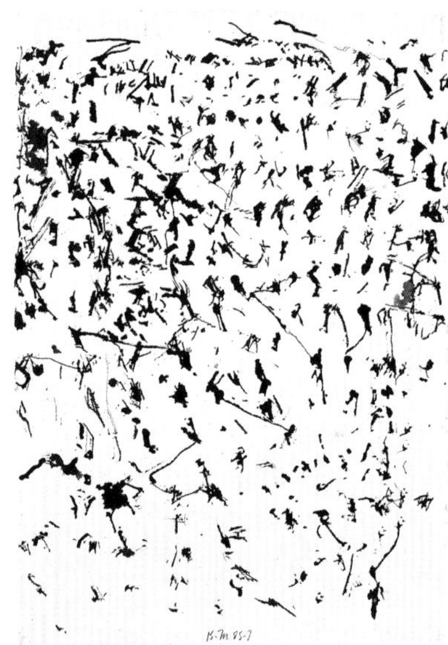

4. Brice Marden. *Shell Drawing #2*. 1985–87
Ink on paper, 11⅜ x 8" (29 x 20 cm)
Collection the artist

(1983) and *Five Part Window Study (Second Window Painting)* (1983; fig. 5), diagonal lines intersect verticals and horizontals to suggest incipient cone, star, and diamond shapes. For Marden, the diagonal served a specific formal purpose in his program for the Basel windows:

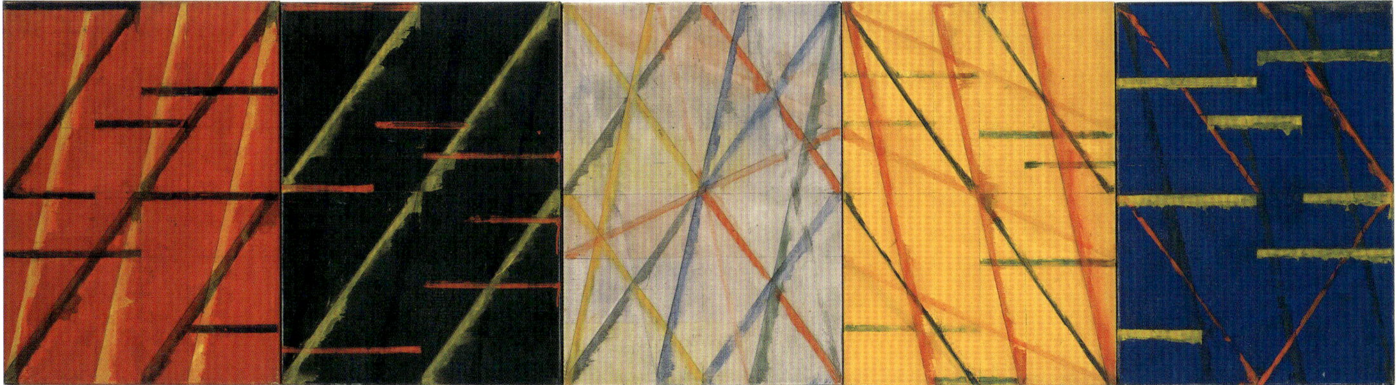

> There was also the introduction of the diagonal, which was a way of dealing with the number situation, the three colors that would be linear (red, yellow, blue) and the four monochromatic panels (red, green, yellow, blue). . . . These three, four combinations of colors—how do you combine them? You needed something to combine them and that was the diagonal, the line that continues into the adjacent painting, but in a different color. Once you had the diagonal, you were in another place. . . . When I was doing the windows, in order to have meetings between the threes and the fours, I started using diagonals. . . . Suddenly there's perspective, a completely different kind of space.[12]

As it happened, consensus failed to emerge among the several civic factions in Basel with shared authority over the cathedral commission, and the project collapsed. But although Marden's window designs were never realized in stained glass, his many drawn and painted studies for them would prove to have a sustained impact on his later art. Overall, this cluster of works from 1978 to 1985—*Frieze II* (in particular), the Basel Cathedral window designs, *Thira*, the painted marbles, and ultimately *Coda*—constitutes an essential precedent for the Propitious Garden paintings conceived nearly two decades later.

Coda n. Music. *A passage at the end of a movement or composition that brings it to a formal close. [Italian, from Latin* cauda, *tail.]*

Marden painted *Coda* in 1983–84 (fig. 6). Knowing that the painting marked the end of the kind of art with which he had heretofore been identified, he

5. Brice Marden. *Five Part Window Study (Second Window Painting).* 1983
Oil on linen, five panels, overall: 24" x 7' 6" (61 x 229 cm)
Daros Collection, Switzerland

titled it accordingly. Marden is finely attuned to the stages in which his art evolves, and consistently senses when he's coming to the end of a cycle. Even so, *Coda* reflects an unusual degree of personal and artistic conviction. The artist has acknowledged that this was not simply a point at which he segued naturally to the next stage in his work, as had happened at fairly regular intervals in the past. (A review of the work from the early 1960s to the present suggests that those moves have occurred at more or less ten-year intervals.) Marden has candidly described the awakening marked by *Coda* as a crisis, a turning point at which he determined he would recommit to a stable life-style as husband and father (his daughters were then ages six and four). He equally knew that he was at a point where he could continue to work in what for him had become a predictable and tediously familiar way of painting, or he could embark on a new path. *Coda* was Marden's latent manifesto. In its starkly frontal six-over-four configuration, with top and bottom abutted in a strike-slip fault, *Coda* is bannerlike in proclaiming scission.

Han Shan and the Muses

In the course of 1983–84—the period of *Coda* and the life transformations it marked—Marden had also visited South Asia and, back in New York, had experienced the revelation of the Japanese calligraphy exhibition. He knew what he wanted to leave behind, and at that point his view of the future must have been substantially colored by his recent Asian experiences. There was nothing superficial in Marden's intention; he was serious in his commitment and he knew what was at stake—most crucially, his marriage and family life. Marden is not a Buddhist, but he admires the moral conviction (the "striving") that is central to Buddhist tenets:

> The Buddha is a human perfection. It's not that I strive for human perfection, but it is a path. I look at Rembrandt, and that's a path. [Jackson] Pollock is a path. It comes down to a single question: what are you going to strive for? It's not that you're going to get there. If I was concerned about getting there, I would choose a likely method—whether Zen study or something else—and I would do it. I guess in a way I have chosen my method, and my method is painting. To me, one of the most compelling aspects of modernism is its commitment to constant striving, to improve on what was there before. Zen's path is a striving toward Buddhist enlightenment. I mean, the Buddha's perfect. And you [by which Marden means *he*] can become perfect.[13]

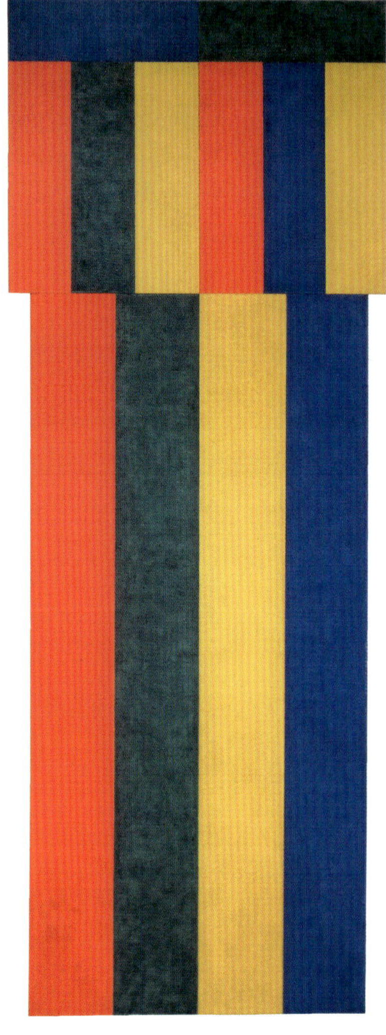

6. Brice Marden. *Coda*. 1983–84
Oil on canvas, two panels, overall: 6' 5¼" x 39" (196 x 99 cm)
Philadelphia Museum of Art.
Purchased with funds contributed by the Daniel W. Dietrich Foundation in honor of Mrs. H. Gates Lloyd, and gifts (by exchange) of Samuel S. White 3rd and Vera White and Mr. and Mrs. Charles C. G. Chaplin, 1985

At this stage Marden was still working on the Basel Cathedral window project, which, however, would come to its unexpected conclusion by 1985. In that year the artist created an etching commissioned by the Swiss art journal *Parkett* as part of its series of collaborative editions with artists (fig. 7). The etching is very much in the mode of Marden's window studies, although it was ultimately executed in subtle gradations of black rather than in the colors planned for the windows. Then in January of 1986 Marden began work on the prints for his *Etchings to Rexroth* portfolio. He had been reading Kenneth Rexroth's translations of the work of the Tang-dynasty poet Du Fu (712–770).[14] A few weeks into the *Rexroth* work, the portfolio's publisher, Peter Blum, gave Marden a first-edition copy of *Cathay*, Ezra Pound's translations of early Chinese poems, most of them written by the great Tang poet Li Bo (701–762). (Pound identifies Li Bo by his Japanese name, Rihaku.)[15] The longings associated with departure, separation, and absence dominate *Cathay*. The cover of the first edition, published in London in 1915, features a bold calligraphic imprint of Chinese characters, a design in tune with the forms Marden had devised for the *Rexroth* etchings.

Much has been made of the purportedly dramatic change in Marden's painting from *Coda* to Cold Mountain, with less attention going to the overriding continuities. It is instructive to consider precisely what it was that Marden looked to change when he reached his self-identified crisis point in 1984—and what he had neither the need nor the desire to change. Consideration of the artist's personal life should probably be set aside as being his own business, but one cannot overstate the centrality of Marden's relationship to his wife, Helen (herself a painter and the person Brice consistently describes as having the critical eye and mind he trusts more than any other to talk about his paintings in progress), and his daughters, Mirabelle and Melia. The sustained growth and passion one senses in the artist's work are reflections of his intense and heartfelt family life. Accordingly, the life-changes to which Marden committed in 1984 were clearly essential to his art as well as to his personal well-being.

And what about the art? Marden's conviction on the subject reveals both candor and humility:

> I was working on *Coda*, and I could still be working on that painting today. It was set up to be refined—*all* those paintings were set up to be refined—in almost a Libran sense in which you seek perfect balance. There was always a hypothetical state of achievement: if I got it right, I could attain true form. I could have gone on making "Brice Marden paintings" for the rest of my life.[16]

By definition, of course, Marden continued to make "Brice Marden paintings." What he stopped making were paintings that superficially *looked* like what the world had come to expect in a "Brice Marden painting." In other words, he stopped painting discrete rectangular slabs in lucent, idiosyncratic colors with skinlike, wax-infused surfaces. But Marden paintings remained Marden paintings in all of their fundamental premises. The artist stayed "out on the plane," as he himself might say. His commitment to drawing in paint remained intact, as did his conviction about obliterating the perceived distinction between figure and ground. He continued to channel the art of Cézanne and Pollock. He still painted light; he still relied on the feelings engendered by certain places he called home. He still sought to erase illusion, and to create depth by building a plane of embedded line. He was, above all, still a painter of abstraction, committed to the belief that whatever subjects and spiritual convictions he put into a painting could be conveyed intuitively to the willing viewer.

Marden moved, figuratively speaking, from *Parkett* one year to *Rexroth* the next. It is revelatory to set the 1985 *Parkett* etching next to a 1986 *Rexroth* etching (fig. 8), and to observe the shift from a closed-form grid to an open-form framework; from verticals, horizontals, and bands to loops, cones, and splashes; from the rectilinear structure of Western art and architecture to the measured naturalism of Eastern calligraphy; and from the suggestion of clenched-hand application at close range to the implication of a more sweeping shoulder/body engagement at arm's length (even though we know that's not how etchings are made). Within another two years one would also see the move from the vertical orientation and body scale of the Couplet paintings of 1988–89 to the horizontal orientation and mural scale of the Cold Mountain works of 1988–91. In short, Marden changed *how* he painted but not *what* or *why* he painted.

Throughout 1985–86 the artist was reading more Chinese poetry, notably the work of the Tang-dynasty hermit Cold Mountain, or Han Shan. The poet Gary Snyder had published his translations of Han Shan's poems in 1958, in *Evergreen Review*, and they were later republished in book form. Marden had seen the Snyder translations shortly after they first appeared, but it wasn't until a friend gave him a copy of the translations by Red Pine, published in 1983, that Cold Mountain's work struck him forcefully—a fascination derived specifically from the book's layout (fig. 9). Each left-hand page features four poems aligned from top to bottom, each poem four couplets of typeset Chinese characters. Chinese is written and read from right to left and from top to bottom. In Red Pine's book, each of Cold Mountain's poems in Chinese is eight characters across and five down—forty characters to a poem, then, and ten characters to a couplet. The right-hand page features the English translations of the poems on the facing page. For Marden, this book marked the first

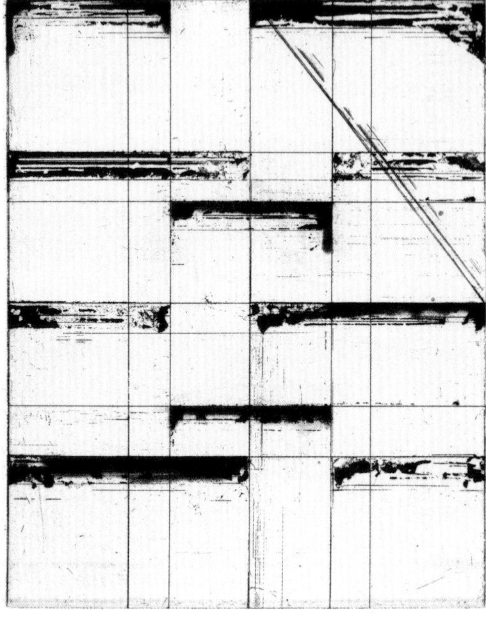

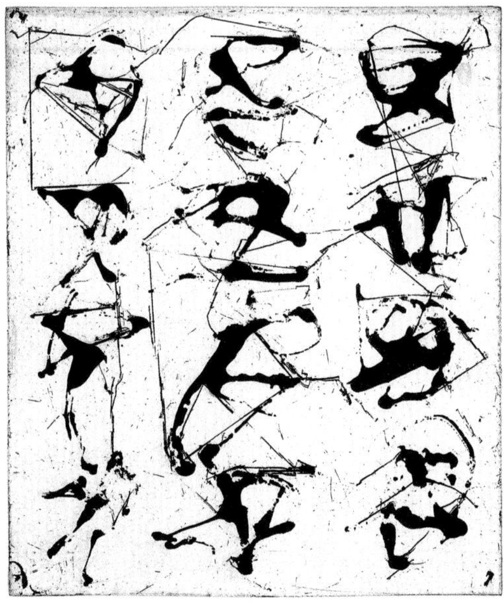

7. Brice Marden. *Etching for Parkett.* 1985
Etching and aquatint bound into the journal *Parkett* no. 7, plate: 8 1/16 x 6 1/2" (20.5 x 16.5 cm), sheet: 10 x 8 1/4" (25 x 21 cm),
The Museum of Modern Art, New York.
Riva Castleman Endowment Fund, Lily Auchincloss Fund, and Gift of Parkett

8. Brice Marden. *Untitled.* 1986
Plate 6 from the portfolio *Etchings to Rexroth*, etching and sugarlift aquatint, plate: 8 x 7" (20.3 x 17.8 cm), sheet: 19 5/8 x 16" (49.7 x 40.5 cm)
Davis Museum and Cultural Center, Wellesley College, Mass.
The Nancy Gray Sherrill, Class of 1954, Collection

time he really saw abstract Asian characters as language, i.e., as meaning. He had previously viewed them as calligraphy, which is to say, as visual art. In the case of Cold Mountain's poems, the meaning of the Chinese characters was deeply spiritual and the spirit was dominated by nature. (Marden was also excited by what he learned from Red Pine's footnotes, which appeared on the same pages as the poems.)

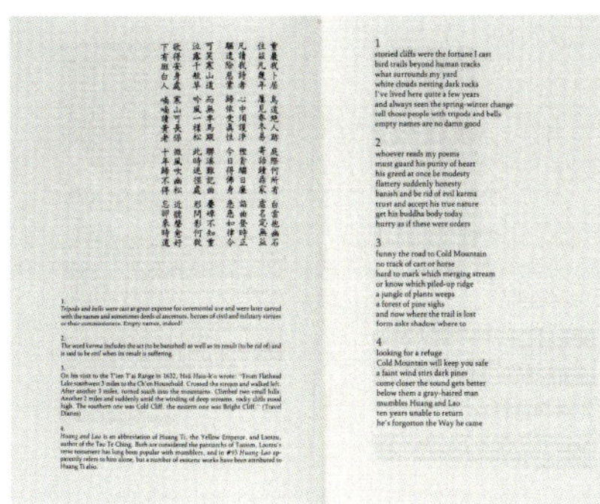

9. *The Collected Songs of Cold Mountain*, translated from the Chinese by Red Pine
Spread, n.p. Port Townsend, Wash.: Copper Canyon Press, 1983

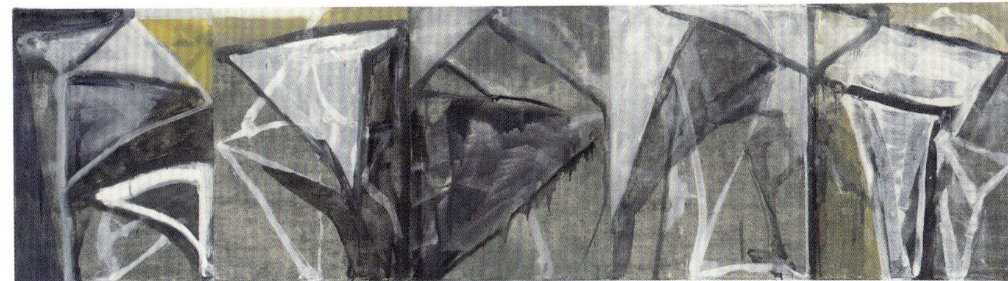

10. Brice Marden. *Mimesis*. 1985–86
Oil on linen, 24" x 7' 6" (61 x 228.5 cm)
Collection Marjorie and Louis Susman

It was during this same period of 1985–86 that Marden painted *Mimesis* (fig. 10), a five-panel painting in an attenuated horizontal format (an early intimation of the "handscroll" format that Marden would adopt in 2000 for his Propitious Garden works). Each of the five segments of the painting framed nesting triangular forms, often interpenetrating, sometimes transparent. Within a few months, these closed diamond shapes had morphed into abstract forms that the artist identified as "glyphs" in the 1986 painting of that title, his first explicit indication of the direction he was taking. There followed several larger paintings in which the glyphs were rendered in more confident, more abstract, and more open form (closer, really, to the nested triangles of *Mimesis* than to anything derived from Asian calligraphy). In these works (*Untitled #3* of 1986–87, for instance; plate 112) the strong, angular forms are linked by webs of thick lines, and transparent washes of color are used purposefully to reveal networks of pentimenti "beneath."

In a series of twelve paintings from 1987–88—works of exceptional authority and grace, all measuring seven feet high and five feet wide, including *4 (Bone)* and *11 (To Léger)* (plates 115, 116)—Marden systematically explored color issues using a set of predetermined variations. With a palette of what deceptively appear to the viewer's eye to be only two or three colors—cream, red, and black, for instance, in *11 (To Léger)*—the artist generated compositions that balance vivacity and stillness. *5 (Note to Myself)* is fundamentally a painted drawing. Lovely and deeply intimate, it presented, almost primerlike, the grammar of forms (the glyphs) from which first the Couplet paintings and then the Cold Mountain cycle would be composed in the coming years. Marden's glyphs are not Asian characters or calligraphy per se; nor are they pictographs, or volute seashells, or leaves curling into the branches of a tree, or renderings of clouds or rocks or ocean waves. What his drawings and work books reveal is that the glyphs are all of those things. Essentially cone-shaped, they sometimes open fanlike, or fold into soft tent or box shapes. Like cocoons, they emerge in curves and curls, loops and coils, line twisting into edge. Their genesis is more in nature than in art, but they do take their *alignment* from calligraphy—or, more specifically, from the way in which Asian characters are arrayed in the four-couplet poems of Han Shan.

In 1988, Marden began the paintings he called Diagrammed Couplets (fig. 11) and, simply, Couplets (plates 121, 122). The skeletal structure of each of these paintings was an array of glyphs organized in the form of a Cold Mountain couplet, that is, with two side-by-side vertical columns each composed of five forms (or "characters"). The title "Diagrammed Couplets" reflects a precise parsing: the new paintings (including the Cold Mountain work that grew out of the Couplets) interweave structure and poetry. Before the year was out, and while still working on Couplet paintings, Marden arranged to have delivered to his studio a newly stretched canvas in what were, for him, unprecedented dimensions. The new painting he planned would measure nine by twelve feet; he arrived at that size by tripling the width of *Couplet II* (1988–89), which was nine feet high by four feet wide. Imagining three of those side by side seemed right to Marden for the painting that ultimately became *Cold Mountain 1 (Path)* (1988–89).

As early as March 1988, on the sheets of his Cold Mountain Studies (1988–91), Marden explored myriad compositional options and experimented with glyphs in various formats and relationships. That same spring he did five ink drawings he called Group of Five, Cold Mountain I–V. An untitled work book from 1986 features ink drawings closely related to Cold Mountain forms and configurations (fig. 12), and similarly close in spirit to the Cold Mountain paintings is a series of drawings from 1989–91 titled St. Barts (plates 126, 127). Marden knew from the outset that the paintings would be called Cold Mountain, after Han Shan. He laid down the skeletal framework of the Cold Mountain paintings in the form of Han Shan's four-couplet poems: working right to left, top to bottom, in the Chinese manner, he painted forty glyphs (eight rows of five). He then brushed his premixed pigments onto the canvas from that basis, adding and "erasing" pigment, scraping, adding and "correcting," again and again, always accepting pentimenti as integral to the composition.

Cold Mountain 1 (Path) was finished by the spring of 1989. Marden worked on other canvases in his studio, paintings of smaller scale and with colored grounds. (One of those paintings eventually became half of the great diptych *Picasso's Skull*, finished in 1990.) Then late that year, more than six months after he had finished *Cold Mountain 1*, he brought into the studio the materials for the next five paintings in the group. (Although he had done previous drawings for the Cold Mountain sequence as units of five, he was by

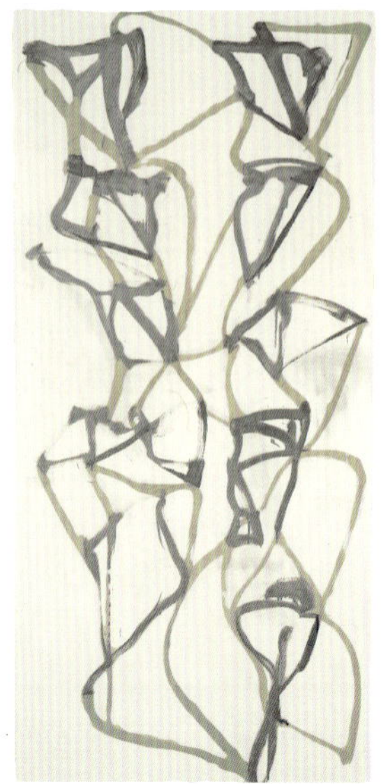

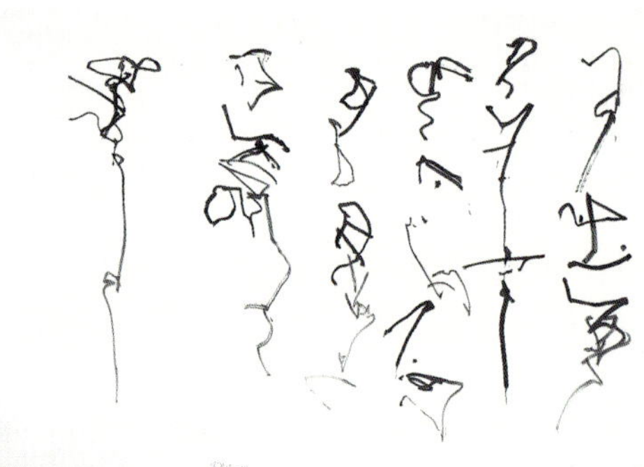

11. Brice Marden. *Diagrammed Couplet #1*. 1988–89
Oil on linen, 7' x 40" (213 x 101.5 cm)
Collection the artist

12. Brice Marden. Drawing from untitled work book. 1986
Ink on paper, $19^{3}/_{4}$ x $29^{1}/_{2}$" (50 x 75 cm)
Collection the artist

now certain that the series would consist of six paintings.) Marden's Bowery studio could accommodate five of the six Cold Mountain canvases aligned against the walls at any given time. A sixth painting typically got stacked behind another, and there was a routine of shifting and repositioning the big canvases in order to accommodate the artist's painting plans on a given day. Marden continued painting the Cold Mountain group up to the fall of 1991; he worked on the last five paintings (plates 123–25) for almost exactly two years. The Cold Mountain paintings, as well as the Couplets, share a muted palette of mixed-pigment greens, grays, whites, and blues. *Cold Mountain 1 (Path)* is essentially gray/black and white. In its final state it remains the closest of the six paintings to its original skeletal structure, that is, to Marden's limning of the four couplets of glyphs that emulate the composition of Han Shan's poems. Legend has it that those poems were mostly written on rock walls in the Tiantai (Heavenly terrace) mountain range in southeastern China, where Han Shan was a hermit in the second half of the eighth century. The monk made a rough home in a remote and wild land familiar mostly to Buddhist and Daoist monks and pilgrims. It is that land of pines and vines and mists that is evoked in the palette Marden chose for his painted Cold Mountain poems.

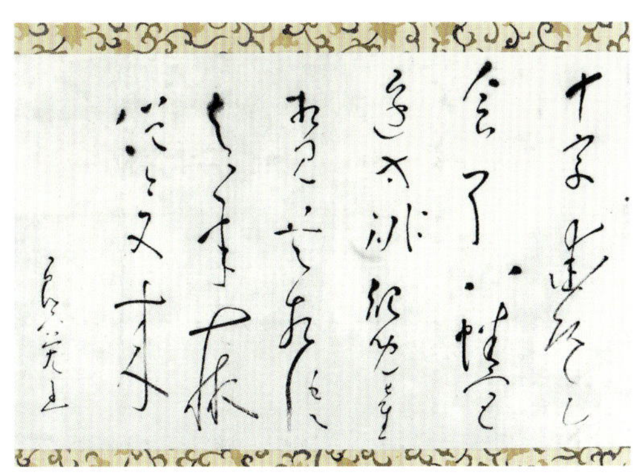

The curled-cone form of the seashell is as significant as calligraphy in Marden's glyphs. The artist had drawn from both during his time in Thailand in the early 1980s. During the same period he engaged with Japanese calligraphy (fig. 13), an interest that led him to Chinese calligraphy, then to Chinese poetry—Rexroth's Du Fu, Pound's Li Bo, and finally Red Pine's Han Shan. Inevitably, Marden developed an interest in Chinese painting, most especially the masters of landscape. It is an art form that speaks in the colors of nature cloud whites, foliage greens, mountain-rock reds and grays, tree-trunk and earth browns, sky and water blues. These colors drawn from nature are usually painted as if viewed from a great distance, through the haze and mists of time. Sometimes the paintings are so restrained in color as to be essentially monochrome.

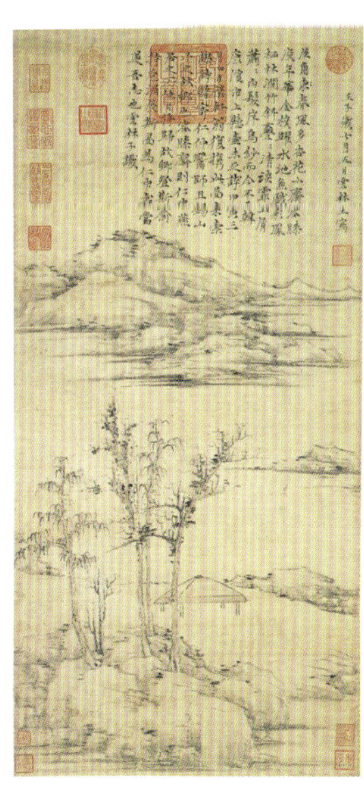

After years of looking at early Chinese landscape art, Marden has most recently focused on the work of the Yuan-dynasty painter Ni Zan (1301–1374). There's no mystery in Marden's affinity. In Ni Zan's painting (fig. 14) every brushstroke rests on the plane; there is an up-and-down orientation to the composition but no in-and-out, no perception of recession into distant space. Everything we see is as close to the surface as it can possibly be, meeting Marden's most rigorous criteria for the best modernist painting. Ni Zan's paintings demonstrate a dry restraint and a love of the void—a sensibility indelibly commemorated by one scholar as "transcendental thinness."[17] The pigment appears to have fallen vertically down the paper like rain sheeting a windowpane, or like the elusive eighth-century calligraphic script

13. Daigu Ryokan. *Poem about a Crazy Monk.*
Nineteenth century
Ink on paper, 21¾ x 35⅜" (55.3 x 89.7 cm)
Collection Sylvan Barnet and William Burto

14. Ni Zan. *The Jung-hsi Studio.* 1372
Ink on paper, 29⅜ x 14" (74.7 x 35.5 cm)
National Palace Museum, Taiwan, Republic of China

known as "wild cursive." Ni Zan's color is transparent and feels not so much applied as perfused. Zheng Yuanyou, a friend and contemporary, wrote a poem and inscribed it on a Ni Zan painting of a rock: "Master Ni makes a painting as if chopping ice,/With turbidness he cleanses, and alone achieves purity./The stream is cold, the sands lean, no trace of scum,/Rock bared, tree bark wrinkled; a feeling shared."[18]

Marden adopted the palette of Chinese landscape painting for his Cold Mountain works, though that didn't occur to him until about three-quarters of the way toward finishing the series.

> One day I thought to myself, "Isn't it interesting that they are looking like the color you find in Chinese paintings." I had not thought of that at the beginning. I just decided to limit the palette because I didn't want to run into a lot of color problems. . . . For these new paintings I wanted a complexity in terms of drawing. . . . And then this color just evolved.[19]

Marden also looked to Chinese painting for the conceptual organization of the works: in conceiving of the group as individual paintings yet as an integral work at the same time, he was emulating the form of the Chinese album, a folio of multiple leaves or sheets in which each leaf can stand equally as both a single painting and as one part of the larger whole. The album as a collection generally constitutes a narrative, not necessarily sequential, with each leaf addressing part of the "story." Marden created his six Cold Mountain paintings with these albums in mind, expecting them to be dispersed as individual works yet knowing that they would never be stronger than when seen side-by-side.

Similarly, when Marden settled on the nine-by-twelve-foot dimensions of each painting, he had Chinese art in mind: he was thinking of the format of the handscroll (albeit at enormously magnified scale). Chinese convention puts no limit on the length of a handscroll; it can be as long as the artist deems the subject to require. Handscrolls seldom exceed a foot in height, however, since that is about the limit of convenience in handling a scroll for viewing. The precedent of Pollock's many attenuated horizontals, a format he used in both painting and drawing especially from 1948 on, was also influential (fig. 15).

As central as Han Shan is to the Cold Mountain series, Pollock is equally so. If Marden looked to the Tang poet for both spiritual and formalist inspiration, he had long responded to those same values in Pollock's work. Marden reveres Pollock's paintings and drawings for their energy and originality and integrity. He equally reveres Pollock as an artist who never let up on himself, who saw painting as a matter of life and death, and whose work reveals an unwavering commitment to the picture plane. Pollock drew in paint with unerring control over how he placed line on ground. His intricate webs announced a new and far more complex modernism. Marden had always known that Pollock's achievement was one he would emulate.

The spirit of Zen represented by Han Shan and Tiantai was reinforced through Marden's reading of Peter Matthiessen's *Nine-Headed Dragon River: Zen Journals* (1986), a book he once described simply as being "helpful" to him both personally and in his work during the post-*Coda* years. He came to the Matthiessen book around the same time that he and Helen bought the Eagles Mere property, which he describes as the most "Zen-like" of his studio locations. Not long ago, the artist told a story of being asked why he is so engaged with earlier Chinese landscape painting. The questioner wanted to know what it is in Marden that generates such kinship with ancient Asian art. For the artist there was no way to answer: it just is. That word "helpful" in relation to Matthiessen's Zen journals is equally laconic, though the ninth-century Chinese painter and collector Bai Juyi, citing a contemporary's response to queries about why he loved rocks, provided a crystalline answer of curiously similar logic: "If something suits my disposition, it is very useful."[20]

The Cold Mountain paintings represent a plateau in Marden's work. The culmination of three decades of striving, they seem to be centered at T. S. Eliot's "still point of the turning world," a place where cerebration and passion commingle. Formalism and expression, structure and poetry, intersect in mindful dialogue. The paintings are open and comfortably contained at the same time; they are both austere and generous. Moving into the Cold Mountain works, one senses the full heart and questing spirit of Han Shan himself.

Before the Cold Mountain group was finished, Marden had ordered an even larger stretched canvas for his next work. He envisioned this new painting at nearly mural span: nine by fifteen feet. The Mardens had recently acquired their land in Eagles Mere (about an hour's drive from Williamsport, where Helen Marden grew up and where her late mother lived). The artist loved spending time in Eagles Mere and it was his idea from the beginning to paint the fifteen-foot canvas there. The place reminded him of his childhood, when he had experienced nature and the outdoors through his father's eyes.

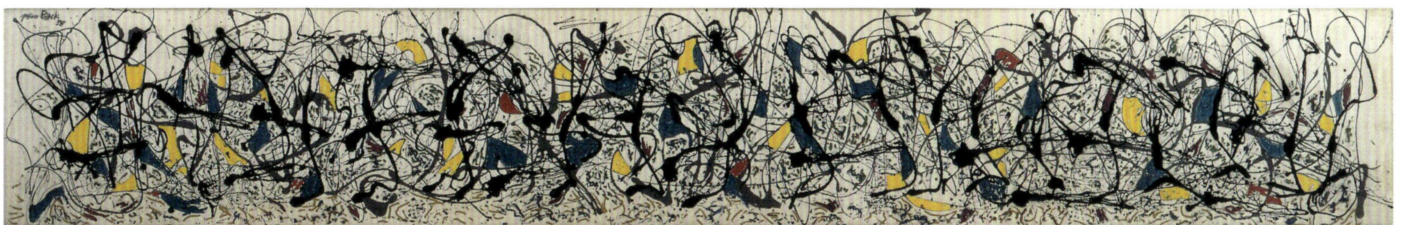

15. Jackson Pollock. *Summertime: Number 9A, 1948.* 1948
Oil, enamel, and house paint on canvas,
33¼" x 18' 2" (84.4 x 553.7 cm)
Tate Collection, London. Purchase

> My father was very much into gardening, planting trees, walking in the woods, being with nature. He used to build beautiful dry stone walls. I used to try to explain my painting to him by saying "You build dry stone walls and everything has to fit together in order for it to stand, and I make paintings, and everything has to fit together in order for it to stand."[21]

So Marden had the idea that he would make the big new painting about his father. But although this painting, which ultimately became *The Muses* (1991–93; plate 137), was indeed painted in Eagles Mere, and was initially focused on feelings about the artist's father and their shared experience of the natural world, it ultimately seems to have become a conduit for Marden's feelings not about his father, exactly, but about fatherhood itself. For Marden that meant the painting grew into a meditation on his daughters—his muses. Reinforcing that conclusion are two major paintings of the same two-year period, *Virgins* (plate 139) and *The Sisters* (plate 136), both of which share the unusually elongated loops seen in *The Muses.* Already in 1991, when asked how he was doing on the big painting and if his father was still on his mind, Marden replied, "No, I'm thinking more of wood nymphs."[22] He had been rereading Robert Graves and was enlivened with thoughts of Greek myth and magic.[23] Thus *The Muses* came by its title and its layered "subject matter."

The Muses was started with the same format of glyphs as the Cold Mountain paintings, but to accommodate its wider expanse the artist laid down fifty "characters" (five couplets of five glyphs each) rather than the forty of the previous group. As early as 1989, he had begun drawings that he later identified by title as belonging to the *Muses* work (plates 131, 135, 138). And for nearly a decade he worked on two other large *Muses* paintings, each measuring just under seven feet high by a bit over eleven feet wide. Both were begun in Greece in 1991, the same year *The Muses* was started in Pennsylvania. Though both are finished, large-scale paintings, Marden ultimately designated them "studies": *Study for The Muses (Hydra Version)* (1991–95/1997; plate 145) and *Study for The Muses (Eaglesmere Version)* (1991–94/1997–99).[24]

Through the decade of *The Muses,* Marden seems to be searching, experimenting, testing formal issues. The paintings show dense pentimenti; twisted, even contorted interlocks, nearly mazelike in places; stretched and thinning linear elements. This is a period of very hard work, of asking questions about what and how to paint. When Marden finally finished the big *Muses,* he embarked on a series of paintings very different in character from anything of the preceding decade. *Calcium, Skull with Thought* (plate 148), *Light in the Forest* (plate 147), *The Golden Pelvic,* and *Progression* all date from 1993–95 and reveal Marden at his most open and transparent. These are paintings with the ease and eloquence evident in the linear arabesques of Arshile Gorky and Willem de Kooning even more than the intensity and layering of Pollock. The surface, Marden's sacred plane, is notably assertive in all the work from *The Muses* on. The network of webbing that embraces the suppressed glyphs is ever more intricately spun.

At the same time, the artist was working on the large, exuberant *Chinese Dancing* (1994–96; fig. 16), composed within the self-imposed constraints of a red-yellow-blue palette. One has to acknowledge that something about

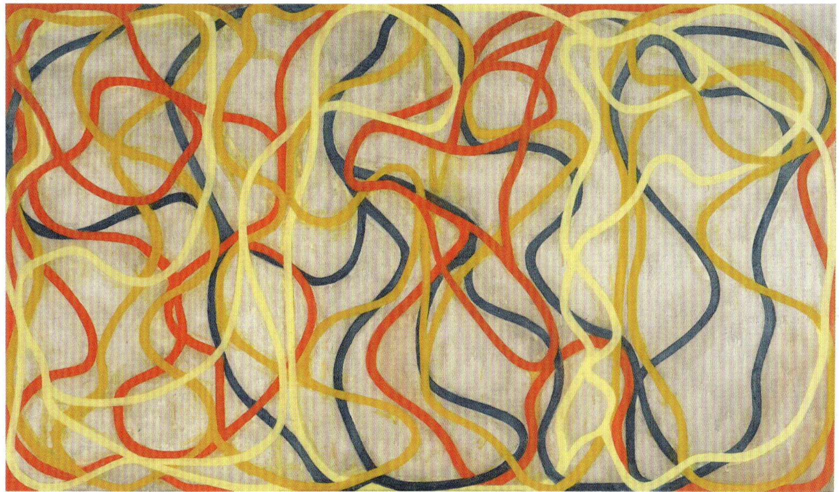

Chinese art instills the artist with confidence. The inspiration for the dancers of *Chinese Dancing* clearly came from Han-dynasty tomb figures (fig. 17), elegant earthenware pieces made to accompany the deceased into the afterlife. Dancing in the China of the period roughly the four centuries beginning in 206 B.C.—was done not only for entertainment but as an integral component of certain religious ceremonies, and it was common to include dancing figures among grave goods.

> There appear to have been two main dances in the Han period, the "long-sleeved dance" (*changxiu wu*) and the "drum dance" (*pan wu*), the latter also requiring long sleeves. . . . [In] funerary rites [the dancer] acted for the soul of the deceased as the conduit between the terrestrial and spiritual worlds. . . . [Long sleeves] were intrinsic to the performance and the effects created by their skilful manipulation were celebrated in poems of the time.[25]

The linear elements in *Chinese Dancing* are almost pictorially evocative of the dynamic curves and swirls of those long swinging sleeves. It's a resonant painting made ineffably memorable when considered in the context of its Han-dynasty iconography.

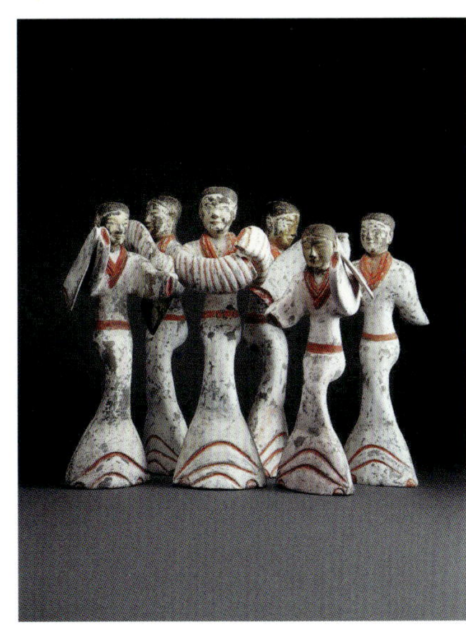

16. Brice Marden. *Chinese Dancing.* 1994–96
Oil on linen, 61" x 9' (155 x 274 cm)
The UBS Art Collection

17. Chinese dancing figures. Western Han Period, 206 B.C.–9 A.D.
Earthenware, average height 22½" (57 cm)
Courtesy Eskenazi Ltd.

Suzhou and Gongshi

In 1995 Marden traveled to Japan, China, and Hong Kong. He was moved by the asceticism, refined geometries, and meticulously framed vistas of the Japanese rock gardens, and in Kyoto he must have thought of his father, builder of dry stone walls, when he saw the dry cascade in the Saiho-ji (Kokedera) paradise garden. But it was only when he got to China and the rock gardens at Suzhou that he fully grasped the spiritual resonance and compositional authority of this ancient art form. Marden said he "got it," all at once, when Suzhou's famous "Cloud-Capped Peak" (fig. 18) came into view; it was instantly clear to him how a rock could be the subject of veneration.[26]

In China, rocks may be venerated in nature (whether as mountains or as isolated boulders), in gardens (where they are carefully sited in composed landscapes, often having been transported at great expense and effort from remote locations), or on the tabletops and in the display cases of connoisseurs. The latter objects, known as *gongshi* in China, are often called "scholar's rocks" in the West, but the term "spirit rock" comes closer to the Asian sensibility regarding these preternatural works of art. (The term *gongshi* comes from the characters for "respect" and "stone.") Marden bought his first spirit rock in 1995 and now has a number of fine examples, which he keeps in view in his studios.

Gongshi were collected by Chinese emperors and poets beginning in ancient times. Both garden rocks and *gongshi* were favored subjects for Chinese painters from the earliest periods; one artist, the seventeenth-century painter Ni Yuanlu, specialized in rocks and did countless evocative renderings. A connoisseur knows *gongshi* when he sees *gongshi*: "Gongshi are selected for their unusual and beautiful shape, good color, and material. Of prime importance are features such as holes (*tou*), channels (*lou*), thinness (*shou*) and wrinkles (*zhou*) as well as their natural forms."[27] The four essential criteria of *tou*, *lou*, *shou*, and *zhou* were first set out by Mi Fu in the eleventh century. In the mid-twelfth century, Du Wan wrote the *Yunlin Stone Catalogue*, a comprehensive, indeed exhaustive compilation of 114 different types of rock. In 1613, during the Ming dynasty, Lin Youlin compiled the *Suyuan Stone Catalogue*, documenting many of the most famous rock collections then known, including that of Mi Fu (e.g., fig. 19). Unlike the *Yunlin Stone Catalogue*, the *Suyuan Stone Catalogue* was illustrated. It became a fundamental historical resource and remains so even today. One of the most frequently scanned volumes in Marden's personal library is a facsimile edition of the book. Inspired by the double-rule black borders of its illustrations, Marden inked a black border in an extraordinary series of drawings of rocks he did in 2003–5 (fig. 20), titled *First Folio* through *Fifth Folio*. (The drawings in all but *First Folio* include the

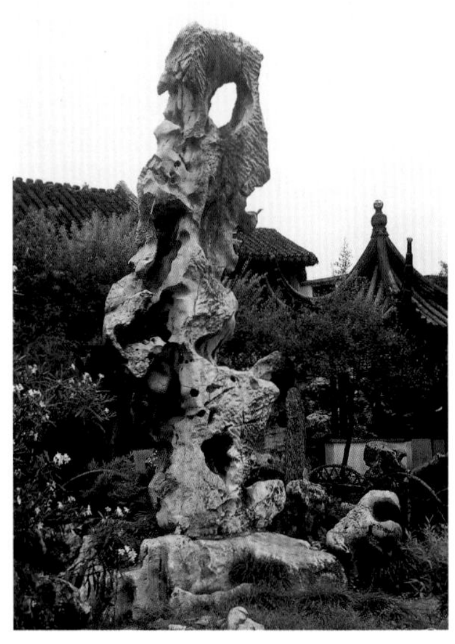

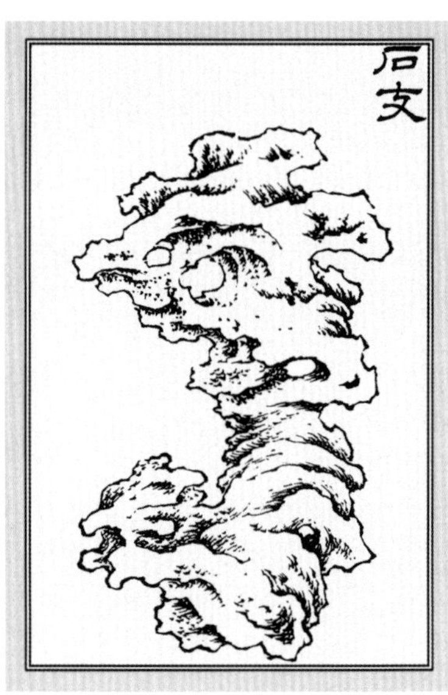

18. "Cloud-Capped Peak," Liuyuan (Garden to linger in) garden, Suzhou, China

19. Stone Elder (Shi zhang), from the *Suyuan Stone Catalogue*, vol. 2, p. 36

distinctive border.) Not long before the Folio drawings, too, Marden had come across and admired Goya's drawings for his *Black Border Album* of around 1816–20, which features a thicker, single-rule black outline.

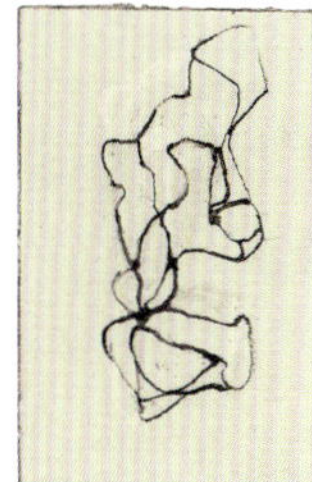
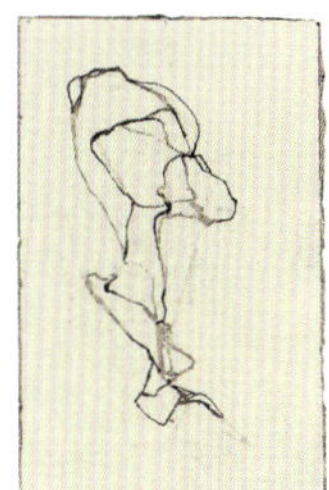
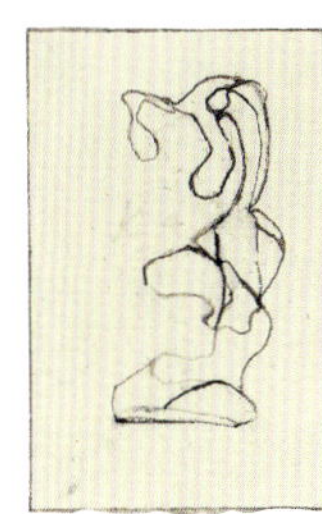
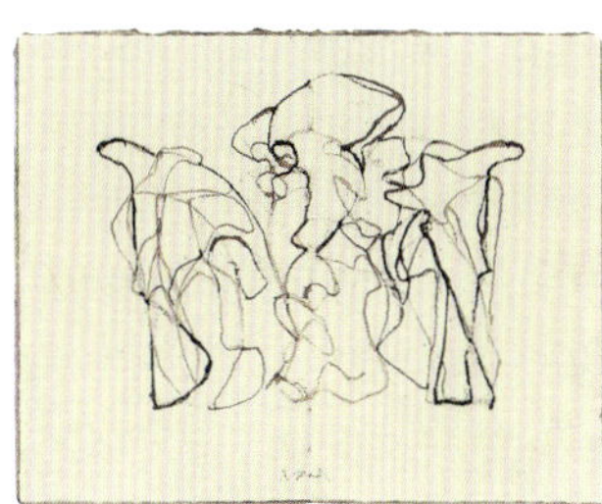
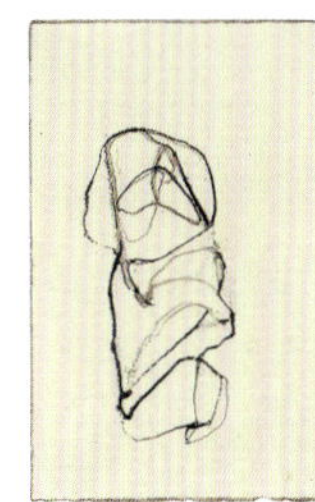
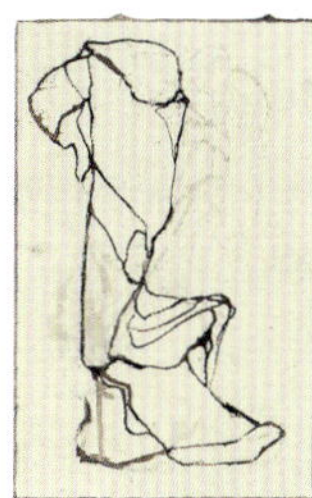
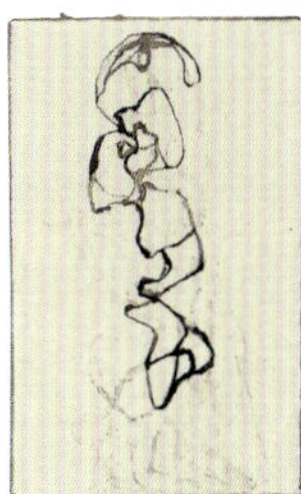

In Asian culture, the importance of rocks extends far beyond their value as inspiring landscape elements or even as objects of aesthetic admiration. Buddhists use meditation stones as a way of reaching enlightenment. For the Chinese, rocks are metaphors, carriers of spiritual values with cosmological import: "Rare stones are exemplary products of nature, the result of billions of years of pressing, scouring, eroding, melting, and distorting by water, heat, wind, sand, and movement of the earth's crust. Collecting stones is appreciating, absorbing, and melding with nature, symbolically becoming one with heaven and earth."[28] In this context it is not surprising that Suzhou was such a revelation for Marden. The artist was energized by the trip; the work he began in 1995 and continued through later years spoke directly to his experience of the Chinese gardens. There were the serene and stately paintings *Suzhou* (plate 153) and *Suzhou, Before and After* (both 1995–96), misty-moonlight toned and both in a format reminiscent of the slender towering form of Suzhou's Cloud Capped Peak. New prints inspired by the dramatic rock forms at Suzhou included an etching titled *The Fungoid Rock* (1996–97) and then a sequence of four etchings of stunningly lyrical, liquid, looping forms titled *Suzhou I–IV* (1996–98). The prints were done in shades of ivory and taupe, moss green and rock gray. Also in 1995–96 Marden painted other canvases reflecting his ongoing passion for Chinese art and culture, including *China Painting* (plate 154) and *Tang Dancer* (plate 152). During the same period, he did paintings inspired by the engraved characters on Chinese epitaph stones (plates 161,163) and also by the color patterns on Buddhist prayer flags he had first seen in Sri Lanka.

In the fall of 1998, Marden turned sixty. Over the preceding few years he had spent a good bit of time in Eagles Mere, at home in its quiet wooded isolation. Finishing the two large *Muses* "study" paintings, he essentially put a significant cycle of work behind him. Hydra summers continued to exert a powerful influence on his sensibilities as well. He was perhaps more productive now than at any time in the preceding four decades of making art, and there were rocks everywhere, from the craggy bedrock of Hydra to the miniature

Fig. 20. Brice Marden. *Fourth Folio*. 2003–5
Ink on paper, seven drawings, six 12⅝ x 8¼" (32 x 21 cm), one 12⅝ x 16⅝", (32 x 43 cm)
Private collection

mountains in Marden's growing personal collection of *gongshi*. More and more, the artist drew those rocks, sometimes from life, sometimes from memory: *gongshi* forms in *Rock Collection (1–7)* of 2000; Greek limestone in *Hydra Rock 1–5* (2002; fig. 21); Suzhou imagery in *Rockery*, drawn in Hydra over the summer of 2002 (figs. 22, 23); and what could be Chinese garden and/or *gongshi* forms in the Folio drawings of 2003–5, among others.

The fluency of line evident in Marden's work of this half-decade is striking. His rock drawings in particular are conspicuous for their easy grace and freedom. There is an apparent speed and fluidity in the forms that imbue them with raw energy. The character of line in this work is reminiscent of that in certain Chinese paintings of mountains and cliffs. James Cahill has written eloquently of one such painting (fig. 24), by the seventeenth-century artist Shitao:

> The movement of line in the drawing of rocks is too grand, too sweeping, to be limited to particular objects, and the use of multiple contours suggests the artist's refusal to fix such limits. [Shitao] is not so much depicting rocks as presenting to our senses the forces that mold and destroy rocks. . . . [His strokes] do not cling to the masses but seem to hover above them, like agitated motes of weightless matter, reducing the bulk of the underlying forms to the point where the rocks change before one's eyes from corporeal objects to insubstantial networks of line, like grasses blown in the wind.[29]

Between early 1996 and the spring of 2002 Marden had completed a substantial body of major work, both paintings and drawings. Much of that work was presented concurrently in two locations of the Matthew Marks Gallery, New York, under the exhibition title *Brice Marden: Attendants, Bears, and Rocks*. The "attendants" (plates 156–58; there was also one painting called *The Attended*), all dating from 1996–99 and all in a format of eighty-two by fifty-seven inches, take their name from Han tomb figures. Both the Han and the Tang produced tomb figures of attendants, as well as other genre figures, including musicians and dancers, along with grooms, merchants, and so forth.

Not unlike dancing figures in overall style, color, and line, attendants can be male or female (in which case they are identified as Female Attendant) while dancers are female. Male dancing figures would be identified as "Performers" or "Singers." Sometimes attendants were monks, as indicated in Marden's *Attendant 4 (Monk)*. These figures were designed to serve, assist, or entertain in the afterlife, as their human counterparts would have in life. Han attendants wore simple belted robes with long draped sleeves extending well

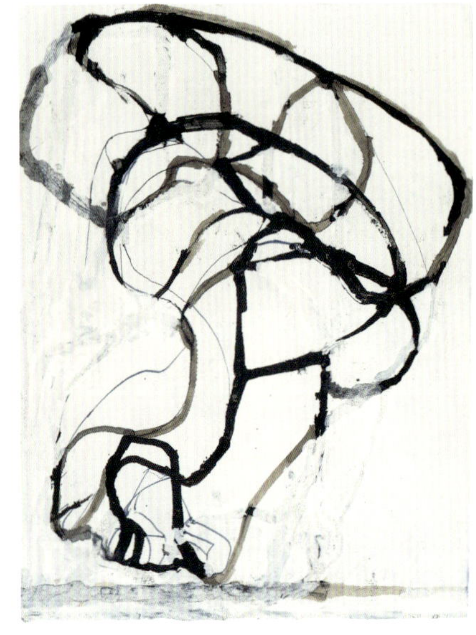

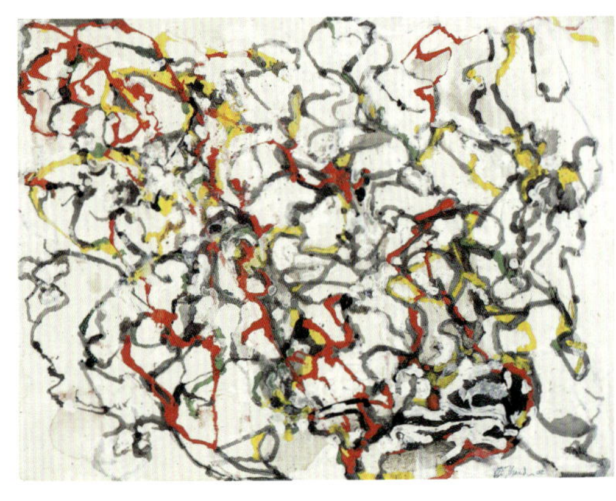

21. Brice Marden. *Hydra Rock 5*. 2002
Ink on paper, one of five drawings, 11 7/8 x 8 7/8" (39 x 23 cm)
Private collection, New York

22. Brice Marden. *Rockery*. 2002
Ink on paper, 15 x 20" (38.1 x 50.8 cm)
Collection Donald B. Marron/Lightyear Capital, New York

beyond the fingertips, though those sleeves were not of the length designed to swirl and spin like the dancers' sleeves.

The "bears" in Marden's 2002 exhibition included three extraordinary paintings: *Bear*, *About Bear* (both 1996–97), and *Bear Print* (1997–98/2000; plate 160). The subject of these paintings is *Ursus americanus*, the common black bear, resident in the lower forty-eight U.S. states. Marden encountered his bear when he was at Eagles Mere, which adjoins the deep forests of Loyalsock State Park—Edenic habitat for *Ursus americanus.* He recounts a moment of primitive recognition of the superiority of that animal's physicality. (Black bears are predatory by nature but mellow by preference. Given the option, they will retreat into forest cover rather than attack.) The artist's bear paintings contain the tense energy emanating from brute animal confrontation, magnetism derived equally from mythology and reality. The paintings are large (seven by five feet) and the linear elements of their compositions are squarely planted in space. Although one might imagine Marden's black bear surprised and very still at the edge of the forest, the exceptionally vivid color and dancing movement in these paintings suggest a bristling life force.

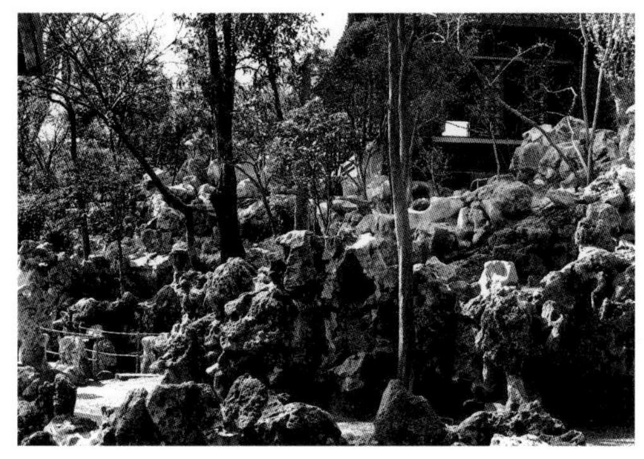

And the rocks in the Marks exhibition? Viewers who saw a seismic move in Marden's work at the time of the Cold Mountain group might more reasonably have waited for the 2000–2002 Rocks series. Familiar as the snaking, ribbonlike forms of the paintings' linear elements may have been by that point, the deep-toned intensity of the Rocks palette seemed a meaningful divergence for Marden. Color was in charge here. Indeed, the several Red Rocks paintings (plates 166–68) were named explicitly for their primary pigment color, not because the rocks of their subject were red, as many assumed. They are beautiful paintings but they are boldly powerful too. Their jewel-hued colors, sometimes layered to a glaze, are very different from the dry palette and scrubbed matte surface common to most of Marden's painting of the previous decade.

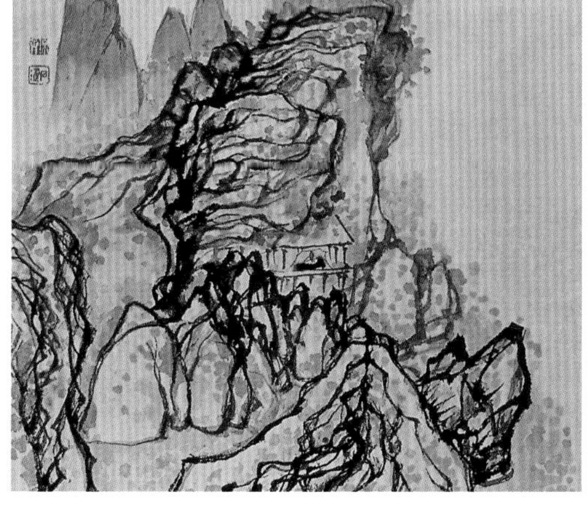

As it happens, the artist once again had color on his mind as a painting program: not just color but the spectrum, and not just the spectrum as abstraction but the spectrum as garden. A Chinese garden, a propitious garden. Since Marden is a painter of abstract art, a painter committed to holding the plane, his propitious garden would be The Propitious Garden of Plane Image.

"No Black, No White"

In the early seventeenth century, the Chinese garden scholar Wen Zhenheng wrote in his *Treatise on Water and Rocks* of the cosmological implications of garden design:

23. Shi Zi Lin (Lion Grove) rockery, Suzhou, China

24. Shitao. *A Man in a House beneath a Cliff.*
Late seventeenth century
Album leaf. Ink and light color on paper,
9½ x 11" (24.1 x 28 cm)
Private collection

> Rocks lead one to antiquity, water leads one to remoteness. In a garden grove (*yuan lin*) water and rocks are the most indispensable things. They absolutely must return and encircle, thrusting vigorously, and must be grounded in a suitable manner. One peak is the eight thousand feet of Mounts Tai and Hua, and one dipperful of water is ten thousand *li* of rivers and lakes.[30]

In Hydra in the summer of 2000 Marden laid out seven sheets of drawing paper, each measuring 6 by 11 1/2 inches (fig. 25). The first sheet is covered with notes for a new painting program. In a single line along the top of the sheet is a title with date information: "The Propitious Garden of Plane Image, Summer 2000 Hydra, first ptg started Summer 1999 (August)." The line just below that reads, "6 canvas' four images each 8-21-00." Then the next line: "ground color in a spectral progression? color left->right drawing right->left (left<-right)." Below that: "propitious Presenting favorable circumstances; auspicious. See Synonyms at favorable kindly, gracious." At middle left on the sheet are numbers apparently reflecting the artist's thoughts about dimensions for the six paintings:

6 4' x 6'

8' x 12'?

The rest of the sheet includes jottings about family matters—phone numbers, appointments, dates. It is notable, however, that Marden's personal calligraphy seal, his red ink chop, appears on the sheet, signaling both authenticity and gravity. And indeed, that "first ptg started Summer 1999" ultimately became the celestial *3 Hydra Rocks* (2001–4), a harmony in deep sea-blue.

The artist moved on to the remaining six sheets, levitating four distinct forms in ink on each one. The imagery is that of Chinese rocks, and it matters not at all whether the source is Suzhou's Cloud-Capped Peak or *gongshi*: whatever the scale of the source, the sensation of the imagery is soaring. And whatever the life dimensions of the particular rock (or rocks) that served as Marden's inspiration for these drawings, the artist has fulfilled a primary commitment of the *gongshi* connoisseur: one is to view the rock from many angles, since the finest *gongshi* have great variation in their multiple facets and reward examination from every perspective. Marden's rocks duly offer several planes to the viewer; they dance and twist across the sheet, sometimes touching, occasionally nesting.

Marden set a question mark after the phrase "a spectral progression" on sheet 1 of these seven drawings, but "spectral" turns out to be a resonant

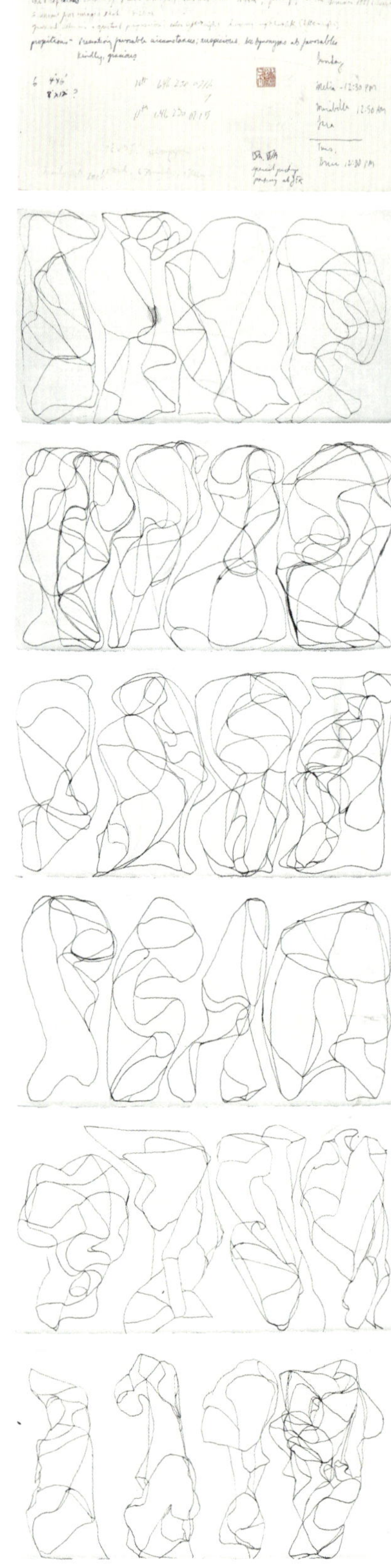

25. Brice Marden. Study for *The Propitious Garden of Plane Image*. 2000
Ink on paper, seven sheets, each: 6 x 11½" (15 x 28 cm)
Collection the artist

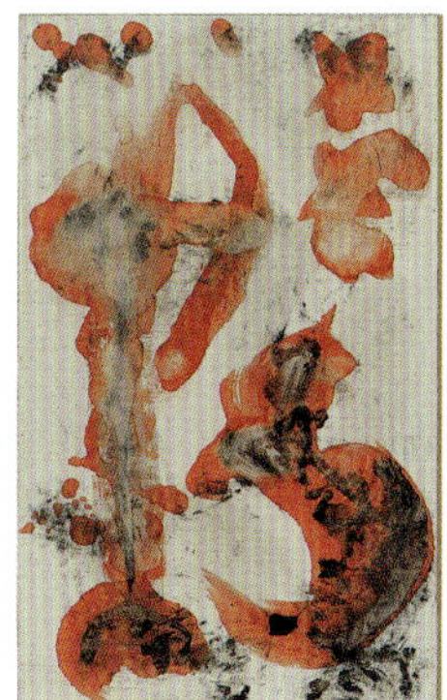 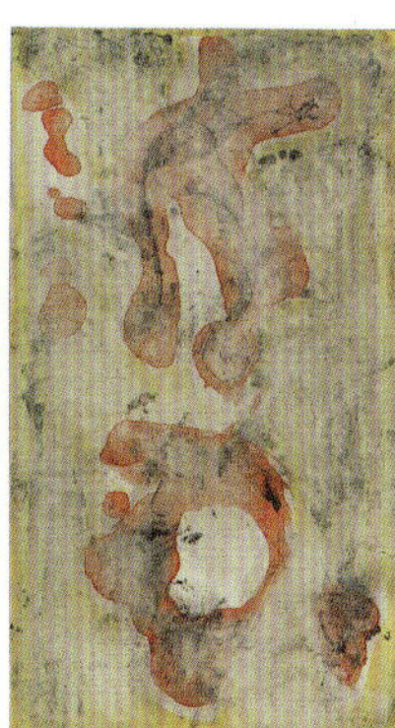 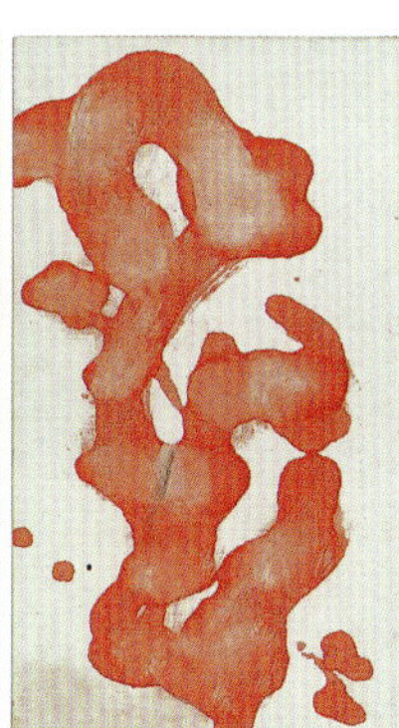 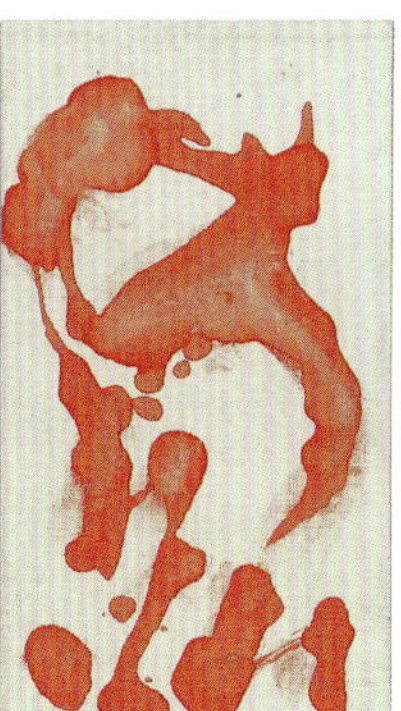 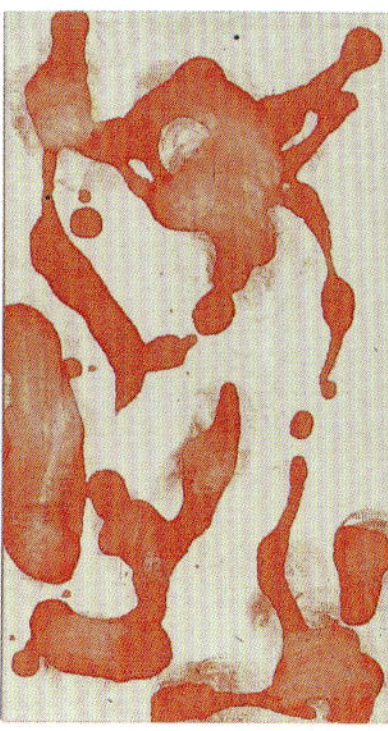 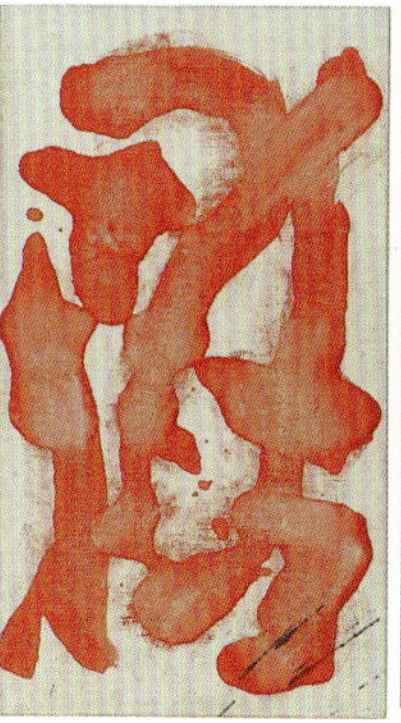 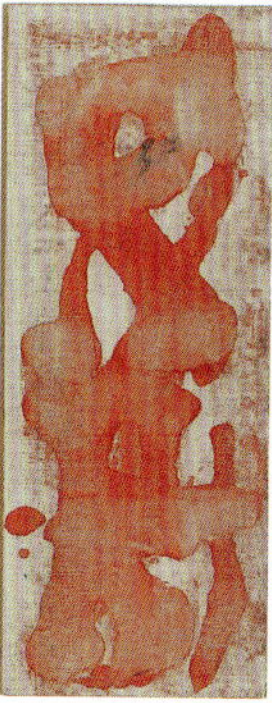

adjective for this new work: not only was the artist thinking of a color progression, that is, of *the* spectrum, but the ink forms dancing across the sheets of these formative drawings are also distinctly spectral, as in "spiritlike." It is more than simple poetry, then, to reflect on the Propitious Garden works in both senses of the word "spectral": light expressed as color, and form conveying some reverberation of past lives. In this context Marden's drawings for his Propitious Garden bear comparison with Pollock's *Untitled [Red Painting 1–7]*, of around 1950 (fig. 26). Pollock's measured sequence of primordial forms unfolds across *Red Painting*'s seven canvases in what is most plainly described as spectral progression.

A spectrum is the organization of light as separated by wavelength or frequency. "The separation of visible light into a spectrum," the encyclopedia tells us, "may be accomplished by means of a prism or a diffraction grating. Each different wavelength or frequency of visible light corresponds to a different color, so that the spectrum appears as a band of colors ranging from violet at the short-wavelength (high-frequency) end of the spectrum through indigo, blue, green, yellow, and orange, to red at the long-wavelength (low-frequency) end of the spectrum."[31] Observed in nature as the rainbow, the spectrum is white light dispersed, as by a prism, into adjacent bands of its seven color components. As color, the spectrum might be thought of as the most fundamental of all artist's tools, and indeed some artists have used it as subject—for example Ellsworth Kelly, who did a series of sparely geometric Spectrum paintings in the 1960s (fig. 27). But Marden is more interested in the spectrum for its qualities as light than as color (although this is not to suggest any absence of attention to the character of color as pigment, and vice versa).

Marden's Elements series of paintings and drawings, created between 1979 and 1984, represents important grounding for the later spectrum work. His detailed deliberations on matters of color are reflected, for example, in notes for his painting *Elements III* from 1983–84: "orig black over ptd/with terre vert/earth ptg./landscapes. . . . More red in the yellow/for the yellow in

26. Jackson Pollock. *Untitled [Red Painting 1–7]*. c. 1950
Oil on canvas, seven panels, ranging from 20 x 8" (50.8 x 20.3 cm) to 21 x 13" (53.3 x 33 cm).
Private collection

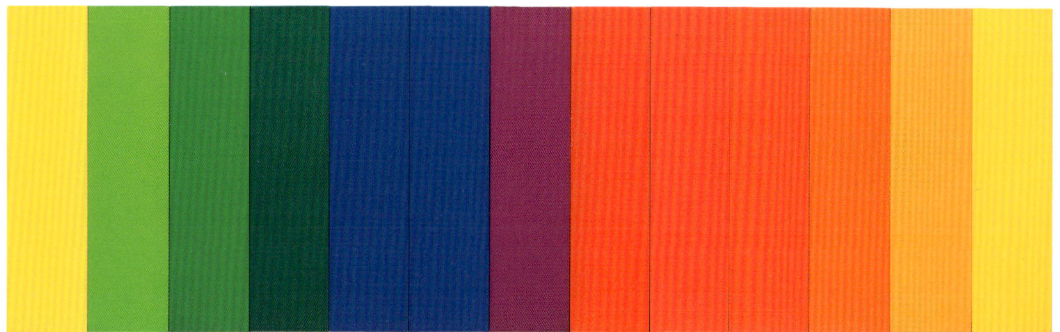

the/red." On another drawing page, this one for the painting *Green (Earth)*, also 1983–84 (plate 104), Marden writes notes on the color green: "middle color of spectrum and therefore the balanced receptacle of the totality of vibration."[32] Only an artist of consummate color sensibilities sees in terms filtered through the prisms, equally, of physics and mysticism: "More red in the yellow for the yellow in the red"—!

For the new paintings, Marden opted to limit his palette to six colors, merging blue and indigo as one. He explains that he knew he could do anything he wanted with blue, pushing it toward indigo if needed. Taught in art school to remember the spectrum through the acronym ROYGBIV (red, orange, yellow, green, blue, indigo, violet), he adopted that sequence for the Propitious Garden hexads. He explicitly chose the six-part format because of the layered and cross-cultural symbolism associated with the number six. As J. C. Cooper writes, six stands for

> equilibrium; harmony; the perfect number within the decad: 1+2+3=6. . . . It also symbolizes union of polarity, the hermaphrodite being represented by the two interlaced triangles, the upward-pointing as male, fire and the heavens, and the downward-pointing as female, the water and the earth. . . . There are six rays of the solar wheel and the interlaced triangles, the six-pointed star or Seal of Solomon, also represents perfect balance. *Chinese:* The universe takes the number six, with the four cardinal points and the Above and Below making the six directions; there are six senses (mind being the sixth); the day and night each have six periods. *Christian:* Perfection; completion; the six days of creation. *Hebrew:* The six days of creation; meditation; intelligence. In Qabalism it is creation, beauty. *Pythagorean:* Chance; luck. *Sumerian:* The six days of creation.[33]

In Buddhism, too, the number six is central. There are six segments on the Buddhist Wheel of Life, representing the six realms of existence (gods, antigods, animals, hell beings, hungry ghosts, humans). The left side of the

27. Ellsworth Kelly. *Spectrum III*. 1967
Oil on canvas, thirteen joined panels, overall: 33¼" x 9' ⅝" (84.3 x 275.7 cm)
Private collection

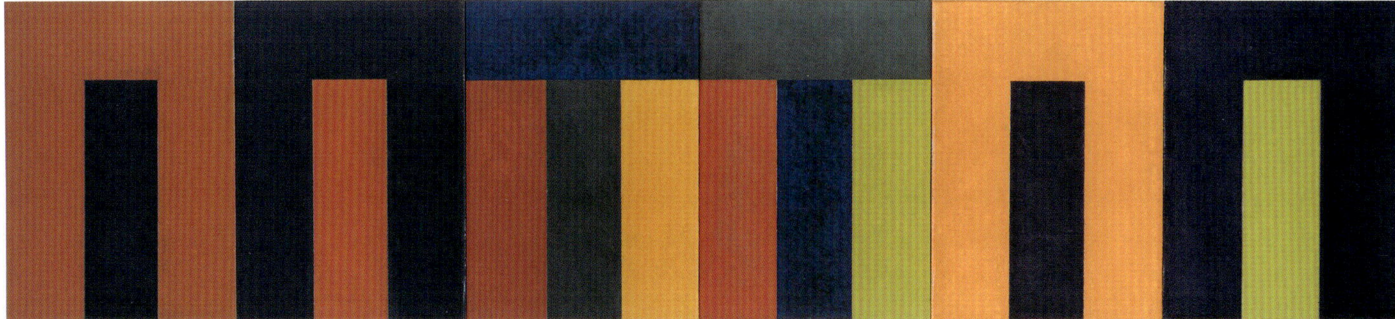

wheel is light and upward-moving to represent positive karma; the right side is dark and downward-moving to represent negative karma. (Marden's "Notes 1979–82/84," relating to the planning of his Elements paintings, includes simple diagrams of circles formed out of arrows to indicate up or down movement, and annotations referencing Buddhist meditations.)[34] The Buddhist path to enlightenment features six "perfections" or practices: generosity, ethical behavior, patience, effort, concentration, and wisdom.

There are also six Cold Mountain paintings, with which the six-part Propitious Garden works share both formal and spiritual kinship. Marden's early paintings were often composed in units of two, three, and four, but by 1980, and the eighteen-part *Thira*, multiples of six became common. *Frieze II* (1982; fig. 28), essential precedent for the Propitious Garden group, comprises six units (each in turn a three-part post-and-lintel construction). *Green (Earth)*, *Number One*, *Number Two*, and *Coda*, all from 1983–84, are each twelve-part paintings.

Accordingly, when Marden got back to New York following the Hydra summer of 2000, he had six stretched canvases brought to his Manhattan studio. Each panel measured three-and-a-half feet high by two feet wide; once joined, the six-panel painting would assume a format twelve feet wide. This painting was *The Propitious Garden of Plane Image, First Version* (plate 169). It was finished in December 2005, more than five years after it was begun.

At the same time, Marden ordered twelve stretched canvases for the Tivoli studio. These panels each measure six feet high by four feet wide, and they constitute two pendant paintings, *The Propitious Garden of Plane Image, Second Version* (plate 171) and *The Propitious Garden of Plane Image, Third Version* (plate 172). Each six-panel painting measures twenty-four feet in length. The artist from the outset envisioned the Propitious Garden works as taking the format of a Chinese handscroll. He also always thought of the paintings as pendants; they were equal "halves" of a systematic color program. Marden saw them ideally exhibited in a space where they would face one another as somewhat disquieting mirror images.

The color program is straightforward (just as the notes on the 2000

28. Brice Marden. *Frieze II*. 1982
Oil on paper mounted on shoji screens,
six panels, overall: 30" x 11' 3" (76 x 343 cm)
Ovitz Family Collection, Los Angeles

Hydra drawing specify). Both *Propitious Garden, Second Version* and *Propitious Garden, Third Version* receive the same ground colors in the same ROYGBIV sequence from left to right. Marden mixed all the colors in advance, in sufficient quantities for both paintings. In *Propitious Garden, Second Version* the linear elements are applied in a color sequence in the order of the spectrum, starting at the ground. For *Propitious Garden, Third Version*, the linear elements are applied in reverse spectrum sequence starting at the ground. Accordingly, the leftmost panel in *Propitious Garden, Second Version* is layered with "ribbons" (the artist uses the phrase "linear elements" to avoid contextual associations) starting with orange on the bottom next to the red ground, then building up through yellow, then green, then blue, and finally violet on the top. Conversely, in *Propitious Garden, Third Version*, the leftmost panel's ribbons move through a sequence beginning with violet on the bottom (next to the ground color, which remains red), then building through layers of blue, then green, then yellow, then orange on top. In other words, *Propitious Garden, Third Version* has its orange ribbon on top, farthest from its red ground, which means least synchronized with true spectrum sequence. In contrast, the layering of ribbons in *Propitious Garden, Second Version* is sequenced in accord with the actual physical properties of the spectrum. In both paintings, each color must touch all four sides of each panel. Occasionally, a ribbon is seen to loop in a continuum from one panel to the next.

What's dumbfounding about this color program (and why the paintings presented in mirror imaging can be fairly described as "disquieting") is that their six colors are precisely the same, notwithstanding appearances to the contrary. Because of the way we perceive various colors "under," "over," and adjacent to other colors, our brain adjudges that the pigments simply cannot be the same. They are. Every red, every orange, every yellow, every green, every blue/indigo, and every violet used on all twelve panels of both paintings is precisely the same color.

Yet another six-part painting with the same six colors is a part of the larger conception for The Propitious Garden of Plane Image. In his Eagles Mere studio in the summer of 2002, Marden pulled from storage three panels (each four by eight feet) that he had originally worked on for the Basel Cathedral windows. Abutting them, he made an attenuated horizontal measuring four feet high by twenty-four feet wide. This work (whose material is paper mounted on honeycomb board) was to be a monochrome variant of the Propitious Garden works. The artist describes the painting's essential premise as "finely tuned color." He had a title from the outset: *Balanced Expression*. Not yet finished in the early spring of 2006, the painting follows Marden's spectrum sequence—from left to right, red orange yellow green blue/indigo violet. The colors are bright but deep and intense. The painting is slightly textured, conveying a distinct, faintly marbled facture. For all of its conceptual simplicity, the painting embodies an elemental gravitas.

Language is an impediment to seeing the Propitious Garden paintings. Words like "under" and "over," "top" and "bottom," "up" and "down," "layering" and "building," and "figure and ground" all essentially contradict our ability to perceive a Propitious Garden as a singular plane. Indeed, that contradiction is precisely the pivot on which Marden's painterly ambitions rest. The artist insists that for this most recent body of paintings he above all wants transparency. He has long admired the complexity of the layering in Pollock's work, noting that the skeins of pigment often elude the viewer's ability to resolve what's above and what's below. Yet Marden wants his viewers to see "through" the layers of linear elements in this new work, to parse with clarity which ribbon of color lies over which other ribbon of color. He wants everything about the way the Propitious Gardens come together to be entirely legible. At the same time, and even more important, we are to see the painting as an undifferentiated plane.

In a recent conversation on the subject, Marden acknowledged that it's all very "tricky," even to him. The key is that however much pigment he applies to the canvas, in however many layers, over no matter how many years, regardless of how many tubes of paint are consumed in the process, or how much the pigment-heavy canvas may weigh in the end, the goal is to create a painting that will be perceived (seen *and* felt) as one singular, undifferentiated plane. "Modernist painting," says Marden, "has been about how the color comes up closer to the surface and how that affects the viewer. The whole evolution of modernism is about getting up, up, up to the surface, tightening the surface to the plane."[35] (Marden's most compelling signal in those comments rests with his words, "and how that affects the viewer.") The greatest challenge for the artist, apparently, is to subsume the process without concealing any aspect of it. Marden embraces the Daoist "way" in all this. He lays down one color and then its opposite in a dance of yin and yang. In the course of this back-and-forth dialogue the artist often finds he has taken a painting to a place of chaos, from which it must be retrieved.

Materially, a painting is composed of a support and a medium. For Marden, whatever medium he applies to the support composes the plane. In other words, we dispense with considerations of figure and ground; there is no illusion of depth or recession in space. There is no distinction between foreground and background. There is only the plane. The viewer must accept a certain disjunction between visual information and intellectual understanding—must see multiple layers of color on a particular ground color, and several linear elements interweaving and overlapping, yet also see that the ground and the linear elements inhabit a single plane. Marden sees "application of the linear elements as drawing and application of the ground color as painting." But he doesn't want the ultimate effect to be clearly one or the other. In the end, the drawing and the painting should be indistinguishable—what we should see is, in his words, "a drawn painting."

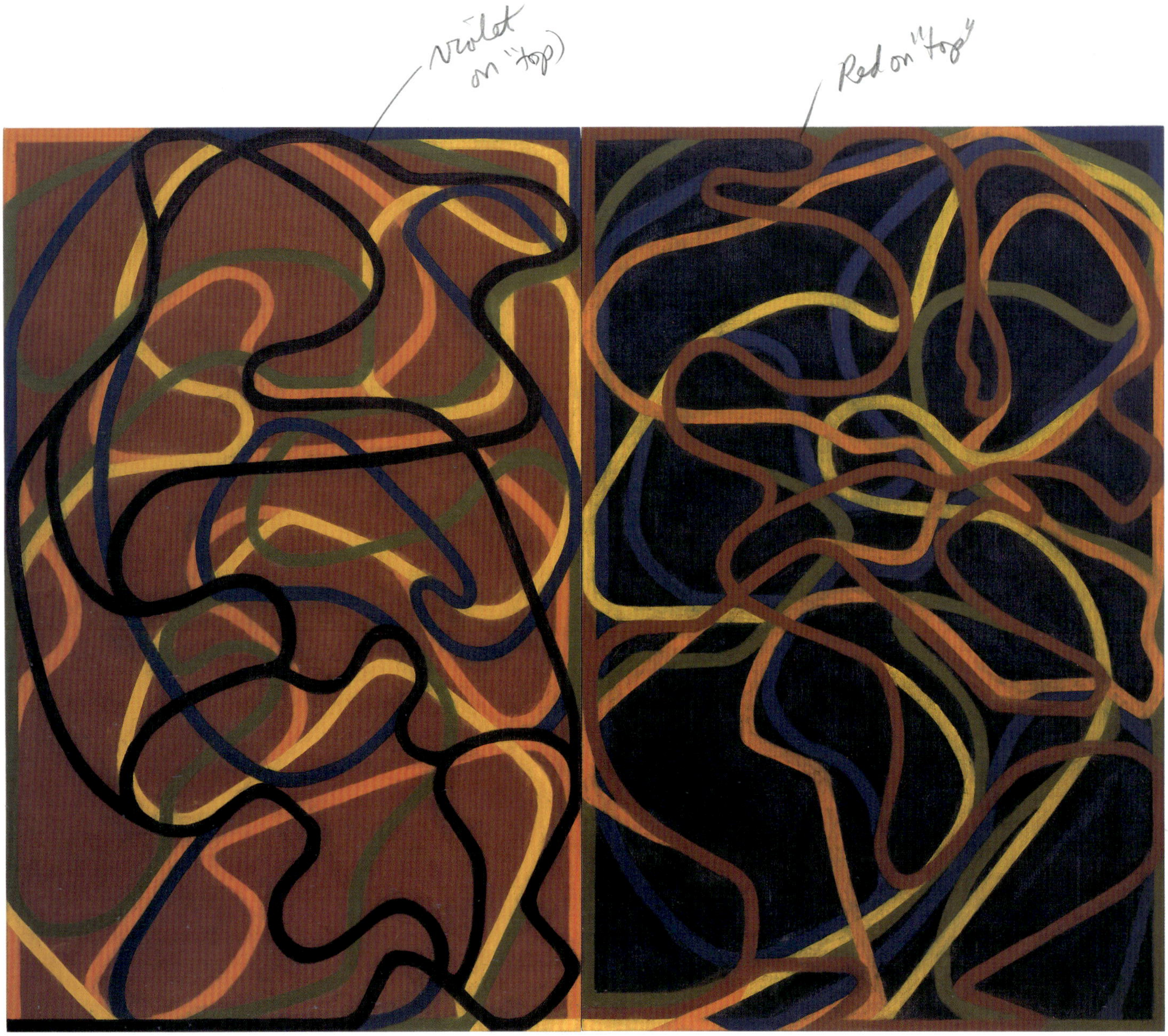

A program is not a painting. For Marden, the programs he conceives are frameworks outlining a coherent course. At the same time, he knows that since he made the rules, he can also break them. Various components of the Propitious Garden work have been underway in four studios for six years. In that time the artist has done a great deal of other work as well, including major paintings and countless drawings. Among his spectrum-generated work, for example, is *Extremes*, a diptych finished in late 2005 (fig. 29). (The artist planned to title the painting *In Extremis* until he learned that the Latin phrase meant "at the point of death.") Its two panels, of the same six-by-four-

29. Brice Marden. *Extremes*. 2004–5
Oil on linen, two panels, overall: 72" x 8' (183 x 244 cm).
Centre Pompidou, Musée national d'art moderne–Centre de création industrielle, Paris.
Gift of the Clarence-Westbury Foundation

foot dimensions as the Rose Hill Propitious Garden panels, are painted in red and violet, the extremes of the spectrum. The linear elements are sequenced in spectrum order from the ground up. (The red panel has violet on "top" and the violet panel has red on "top," resulting in an especially active dialogue on the plane across the two panels.) A second diptych featuring a pairing of yellow and green grounds is also underway in the Manhattan studio. But there is no question that Marden's self-imposed limitation to the colors of the spectrum is wearing on him. It seems he misses the shadows, the multitude of grays, the ambiguities. As he moves toward the finish of the cycle, he can't help but remark during a 2005 studio visit, "I simply cannot *wait* to use black and white again."

All of Marden's paintings, and the many drawings as well, come into being only slowly—one might even say arduously—with forward progress routinely offset by missteps only he perceives. Paint is brushed on the canvas, scraped off and erased and corrected and painted again. Not long ago the artist decided that he needed to alter the ground colors of *Propitious Garden, Second Version* and proceeded to repaint each of the six grounds over a period of weeks. As he studied the effect of the change, he began to realize he most likely would have to repaint the linear elements now as well, since the balance had been altered. As with the Attendants, Bears, and Rocks, this new work carries many, many layers of paint. The surfaces are smooth and slightly glazed, the colors dense and deep. They are intensely felt paintings, proving once again that Marden is incapable of generating a painting programmatically.

The Aegean and the Hudson. Mountain and water. Han Shan and the Muses. Ancient Greece and China. Attendants, bears, rocks. Gardens and the spectrum. Marden says that he wants his painted planes to be "something like an insect caught in amber." It is evident that we should take that to mean infinite eons of time, *transparent* geological layers of time—stratigraphies at once wholly visible to the naked eye. Marden's commitment to plane image has never wavered.

In early 2006, with the Propitious Garden paintings nearing finish, the artist is ready to move on. He says that he always knows when he's come to the end of a particular stage in his work when he begins to think about what he's going to do next (as opposed to being exclusively within whatever he's working on at the time). At Rose Hill in the summer of 2005, the artist talked about the water, about the Hudson just beyond his windows. He said he knew that whatever he would paint next, it would be about that water. In winter, when the leaves are off the trees, Marden can be nearly hypnotized by the light and movement he sees in the patterned reflections of the river water on the studio's expanse of white walls. He says that he's even considered the possibility of hanging stretched canvases on the walls to capture the water's reflections, like a projection, so that he can paint them. The reflections offer a way to begin making marks; fragments of water patterns could become the skeletal webbing of a future painting's ground layer. It is a prospect that calls to mind the first lines of "Water," Philip Larkin's 1954 poem: "If I were called in/To construct a religion/I should make use of water."

Over the last two decades Marden has come to know mountain and water. And perhaps mountain and water have come to know him, too. In his story "The Kidney-Shaped Stone That Moves Every Day," Haruki Murakami writes a character's drowsy soliloquy:

> For example, the wind has its reasons. You just don't notice it as you go about your life. Then, at some point, you are made to notice. The wind envelops you with a certain purpose in mind and shakes you up. It knows everything that's inside you. And it's not just the wind. Everything, even a stone, knows you. And all you can do is go with those things. As you take them in, you survive and deepen.[36]

NOTES

1. The artist's father, who died in 1988, was named Nicholas Brice Marden and was called Nick. The artist's full name is Nicholas Brice Marden, Jr., and he was called Brice to distinguish him from his father. Brice's son (born in 1961, when Marden was still an art student at Yale) in turn was named Nicholas Brice Marden II, and he goes by the name of Nicholas. He is a rock musician and lives in New York.

2. Michael Dennis Higgins and Reynold Higgins, *A Geological Companion to Greece and the Aegean* (Ithaca, N.Y.: Cornell University Press, 1996), p. 38.

3. For more on Han Shan and Tiantai, see Brenda Richardson, *Brice Marden Cold Mountain* (Houston: Houston Fine Art Press, 1992), especially chapter 2, "A Journey of Ghosts." This Menil monograph is the fullest study to date exclusively focused on Marden's Cold Mountain works.

4. Except when otherwise noted, quotations of Marden in the present text derive from the author's telephone conversations with him during the preparation of the essay and from studio visits in Tivoli (July 2005) and Manhattan (November 2005). The author visited the Manhattan studio again in January 2006, in the artist's absence, to view finished paintings.

5. Barbara Novak, *American Painting of the Nineteenth Century: Realism, Idealism, and the American Experience* (New York: Praeger Publishers, 1969), p. 91.

6. The first comprehensive publication on Marden's painted-marble works is Lisa Liebmann, *Brice Marden: Paintings on Marble* (Göttingen: Steidl/mm, 2006), in press at the time of this writing. I am grateful to the Matthew Marks Gallery, New York, for providing me with a typescript of Liebmann's essay and with color prints of all of the marbles. A more modest publication on the marbles accompanied the 1982 Pace Gallery exhibition *Brice Marden: Marbles, Paintings, and Drawings* (New York: Pace Gallery, 1982), featuring a text by William Zimmer, "Marden 1982: Hermeticism Made Visible."

7. The earliest publication of the phrase would seem to be that of a statement Marden

wrote for the exhibition catalogue to *Eight Contemporary Artists* (New York: The Museum of Modern Art, 1974, p. 46). In subsequent decades, Marden has reiterated the phrase, over and over, as essential to his artistic ambitions. In a 2003 interview with John Yau, for example, he definitively concluded their discussion of formalist issues by stating, "I also said that I believe in the indisputability of the plane." See Yau, "An Interview with Brice Marden," in *Brice Marden* (Zurich: Daros Services, and Zurich, Berlin, and New York: Scalo, 2003), p. 59.

8. Terry Tempest Williams, *Refuge* (New York: Vintage Books, 2001), pp. 184, 136.

9. Higgins and Higgins, *A Geological Companion to Greece and the Aegean*, p. 45.

10. Marden prefers the description "work book" to more common alternatives (sketchbook, notebook, drawing pad, etc.). His work books are central to the evolution of his art. Accordingly, one of the most valuable and revelatory publications on Marden's work is Dieter Schwarz and Michael Semff, *Brice Marden: Work Books 1964–1995* (Düsseldorf: Richter Verlag, Munich: Staatliche Graphische Sammlung, Winterthur: Kunstmuseum, and Cambridge, Mass.: Harvard University Art Museums, 1997).

11. Asia Society Galleries and Japan House Gallery, New York, October 4, 1984–January 6, 1985. The exhibition's catalogue, by Yoshiaki Shimizu and John M. Rosenfield, for a time became Marden's bible. He purchased multiple copies of the book so that he could have it at hand in each of his studios.

12. Marden, quoted in Yau, "An Interview with Brice Marden," pp. 51, 54.

13. Marden, quoted in Richardson, *Brice Marden Cold Mountain*, p. 76.

14. Kenneth Rexroth, *One Hundred Poems from the Chinese* (New York: New Directions, 1971).

15. In addition to Japanese variants such as this one, many Chinese names are spelled differently in English depending on what system of transliteration is used. "Du Fu," for example, is the Pinyin spelling of a name that has also been transliterated as "Tu Fu" in the Wade-Giles system, and that appears in this form in much of the older literature. "Li Bo," similarly, may also appear as "Li Po," and "Dao" as "Tao." The preferred system today is Pinyin.

16. Marden, quoted in Richardson, *Brice Marden Cold Mountain*, p. 75.

17. James Cahill, *Hills beyond a River: Chinese Painting of the Yüan Dynasty, 1279–1368* (New York: John Weatherhill, Inc., 1976), p. 116. I welcome this opportunity to extend my warmest gratitude to Dr. Cahill, distinguished scholar of Chinese painting, who generously shared with me both his expertise and his lively interest. I have over the years gained invaluable insights from Dr. Cahill's publications, notably *Chinese Painting* (Switzerland: Editions d'Art Albert Skira, 1960), *Fantastics and Eccentrics in Chinese Painting* (New York: The Asia Society, 1967), and *Hills beyond a River*. I am equally grateful to my friend and former colleague Frances Klapthor, Curator of the Arts of Asia, The Baltimore Museum of Art, who was my early mentor in the arena of Chinese art. Whenever my work has intersected with her field of expertise, Frances has responded to my questions with enthusiasm and sound guidance for two decades now, and I thank her for her support relative to this present work. I have also consulted the following sources on the subject of Asian art and calligraphy: Jan Fontein and Money L. Hickman, *Zen Painting & Calligraphy* (Boston: Museum of Fine Arts, 1970); *Eight Dynasties of Chinese Painting: The Collections of the Nelson Gallery–Atkins Museum, Kansas City, and The Cleveland Museum of Art* (Cleveland: The Cleveland Museum of Art, 1980); *Chinese Calligraphy* (New York and Tokyo: John Weatherhill, 1983); Shimizu and Rosenfield, *Masters of Japanese Calligraphy, 8th–19th Century* (New York: The Asia Society Galleries and Japan House Gallery, 1984); Jean François Billeter, *The Chinese Art of Writing* (Geneva: Editions d'Art Albert Skira, 1990); Kiyohiko Munakata, *Sacred Mountains in Chinese Art* (Urbana-Champaign: University of Illinois, 1991); Robert E. Harrist, Jr., and Wen C. Fong, *The Embodied Image: Chinese Calligraphy from the John B. Elliott Collection* (Princeton, N.J.: The Art Museum, Princeton University, 1999); and Robert L. Thorp and Richard Ellis Vinograd, *Chinese Art and Culture* (New York: Harry N. Abrams, 2001).

18. Zheng Yuanyou, quoted in John Hay, *Kernels of Energy, Bones of Earth: The Rock in Chinese Art* (New York: China House Gallery, 1986), p. 90.
19. Marden, quoted in Richardson, *Brice Marden Cold Mountain*, p. 65.
20. See Kemin Hu, *The Suyuan Stone Catalogue: Scholars' Rocks in Ancient China* (Trumbull, Conn.: Weatherhill, 2002), p. 146.
21. Marden, quoted in Klaus Kertess, *Brice Marden Paintings and Drawings* (New York: Harry N. Abrams, 1992), p. 11. The statement was originally made in 1976, in conjunction with a film then being made about Marden and his work.
22. Marden, quoted in Richardson, *Brice Marden Cold Mountain*, p. 54.
23. Robert Graves, *The Greek Myths*, 2 vols. (London and Baltimore: Penguin, 1955, and later editions).
24. An excellent resource for consideration of Marden's work of the 1990s is Charles Wylie, *Brice Marden. Work of the 1990s: Paintings, Drawings, and Prints* (Dallas: Dallas Museum of Art, 1999).
25. *Early Chinese Art: 8th Century BC–9th Century AD* (London: Eskenazi, 1995), p. 60.
26. On the subject of Chinese gardens, I am indebted to the following sources: Craig Clunas, *Fruitful Sites: Garden Culture in Ming Dynasty China* (Durham, N.C.: Duke University Press, 1996); Maggie Keswick, *The Chinese Garden: History, Art and Architecture* (Cambridge, Mass.: Harvard University Press, 2003); and Pierre and Susanne Rambach, *Gardens of Longevity in China and Japan: The Art of the Stone Raisers* (Geneva: Skira, and New York: Rizzoli, 1987). For Japanese gardens, and for informed guidance on all things related to Asian architecture and design, I turned, as so often, to my good friend Marc Treib (University of California, Berkeley) and to his invaluable book, cowritten with Ron Herman, *A Guide to the Gardens of Kyoto*, 1980 (rev. ed. Tokyo: Kodansha International, 2003).
27. Hu Zhaokang, quoted in Kemin Hu, *The Spirit of Gongshi: Chinese Scholar's Rocks* (Newton, Mass.: L. H., Inc., [1998?]), p. 18. In addition to *The Spirit of Gongshi* the following have been invaluable resources on this subject: Hay, *Kernels of Energy, Bones of Earth*; Kemin Hu, *The Suyuan Stone Catalogue*; and Richard Rosenblum, *Art of the Natural World: Resonances of Wild Nature in Chinese Sculptural Art* (Boston: Museum of Fine Arts, 2001).
28. Kemin Hu, *The Suyuan Stone Catalogue*, p. 139.
29. The author has conjoined two sources in which Cahill discusses the painting: *Chinese Painting*, pp. 180–81, and *Fantastics and Eccentrics in Chinese Painting*, p. 87.
30. Wen Zhenheng, quoted in Clunas, *Fruitful Sites*, p. 172.
31. Entry for "spectrum," *The Concise Columbia Encyclopedia* (New York: Columbia University Press, 1983), pp. 799–800.
32. Marden, sheet #5, dated 4/15/83 and 8/84, and sheet #3, dated 4/12/83 and 4/15–8/84, reproduced in *Brice Marden: Recent Work* (New York: The Pace Gallery, 1984), n.p.
33. J. C. Cooper, "Numbers," in *An Illustrated Encyclopaedia of Traditional Symbols*, 1978 (reprint ed. London: Thames & Hudson, 2004), pp. 116–17.
34. Reproduced in *Brice Marden: Recent Work*, n.p.
35. Marden, quoted in Yau, "An Interview with Brice Marden," p. 51.
36. Haruki Murakami, "The Kidney-Shaped Stone That Moves Every Day," *The New Yorker*, September 26, 2005.

The three sidebar comments on the geology of the U.S. locations where the Mardens maintain properties (Manhattan, Tivoli, and Eagles Mere) were provided in an e-mail communication to the author on March 3, 2006, by Dr. George W. Fisher, Professor Emeritus, Department of Earth and Planetary Sciences, Johns Hopkins University, Baltimore. I am profoundly grateful to Dr. Fisher for the seriousness with which he greeted my inquiry and for the time he dedicated to my questions. His comments are here transcribed verbatim, with all the historical weight and poetry they convey.

In his thoughtful e-mail message, Dr. Fisher added a personal reflection: "The interesting thing is that these three homes represent very different stages in the development of the Appalachians: the earliest Appalachian sediments in New York, later deeply buried, heated, and deformed; an intermediate belt of rocks formed during the tectonically active phase of the Appalachians at Tivoli; and [at Eagles Mere] a sequence of rocks formed late in the Appalachian cycle, when the mountains had been largely eroded."

The sidebar comment on the geology of Hydra is from Higgins and Higgins, *A Geological Companion to Greece and the Aegean*, p. 38.

Author's Acknowledgments

My primary acknowledgment is to Brice Marden, whose work has meant so much to me for so many years. It is a privilege to have worked with him in the context of such a significant endeavor as this retrospective exhibition undertaken by The Museum of Modern Art. I am profoundly grateful for the artist's generosity in giving me so much time with him and his work in his studios and, as always, for his candid and thoughtful articulation of painting matters. I also want to thank Tina Hejtmanek, who oversees Marden's office and studio operations. She has been efficient and responsive to my constant telephone and e-mail appeals for materials and information, and fully supportive in meeting my needs at all times.

At the Matthew Marks Gallery, New York, the staff has extended its fullest cooperation and demonstrated a model level of collegial support. I want to thank Matthew himself, who encouraged my participation from the outset, and Jacqueline Tran, who coordinated the gallery's response to my research needs with kindness and extraordinary efficiency.

I was warmly welcomed by the several professionals at The Museum of Modern Art on whom I relied to do my work. It is a pleasure to thank Gary Garrels, who invited me to write for this book. It has been both daunting and rewarding to think seriously and attempt to write meaningfully about such a rich and challenging body of work. I am grateful to Gary for his confidence. Also at MoMA I was for a time in almost daily contact with Esther Adler and Francesca Pietropaolo. Despite the enormous pressure under which they work, both were consistently responsive to my needs and generous with their support and assistance. I was deeply impressed with the evidence of their commitment to the highest standards. Finally, I very much appreciate the thorough and sensitive attention David Frankel exercised in editing my manuscript.

Bibliographic Note

I wish to acknowledge my indebtedness to several writer/scholars whose work on Marden's art has been important to me over the years and has expanded my own thinking on the subject, notably including Yve-Alain Bois, Klaus Kertess, and Roberta Smith, well as others whose names appear in notes above.

Carol Mancusi-Ungaro

Marden's Materiality: The Monochromes

Paintings are physical. So is the act of creating them. This physicality should be emphasized. If you're not working with preconceived forms and thinking, then you can concentrate on expression. It is possible, I think, to make art on this instinctive level, out of a deeply felt response. The longer I paint, the more I think this is true.

—Brice Marden, 1987[1]

The monochrome painting offers a unique vista on the relationship between an artist's intentions and their material expression in paint. The monochrome's suppression of overt narrative and drawing might be supposed to effect a corresponding suppression of all traces of the artist's process, in favor of a hands-off, affect-free surface. But as the work of the first decades of Brice Marden's career shows, a monochrome painting is nonetheless an expressive image and a vehicle of emotion. A reductive form may shift the experience of viewing but the shift is toward, not away from, an awareness of the work's physical qualities; the absence of imagery ends up giving a proportionately greater expressive significance to the more subtle aspects of facture. For Marden, who admits that his art is a "combination of intuition and formality,"[2] painting is about transformation, "taking . . . that heavy earthen kind of thing, turning it into air and light."[3] It is the achievement of that transformation, through hand and instinct, that propels Marden's process and ultimately informs his art.

Although Marden has asserted on more than one occasion that he is "no technique freak," his careful reassessments of material matters over time argue for an acute interest in formal issues.[4] He has said, for example, that he had no interest in the 1960s debate about the "objectness" of a painting, a discussion involving the issue of the depth of a painting's support, and how far a painting projected into the space it occupied.[5] Yet these were clearly questions he considered carefully, even if he responded to them more intuitively than theoretically, preferring to let the scale of the work determine the depth of the auxiliary support and often choosing a stretcher with a depth of less than two inches. He was likewise keenly aware of the physical impact of the stretchers' crossbars, and tried to prevent them from leaving an imprint on the work's surface by carefully inserting a foam rubber interleaf behind the canvas, or by otherwise holding the canvas away from the bars as he painted.[6] Even so, the skeleton of the stretcher occasionally did impose itself on the paint, and ultimately the artist came to accept "the chassis as a piece of drawing—a kind of grid that relates to the painting and thinking about the painting—an obscure thing but still a part of it."[7]

Marden used both linen and cotton as supports for his monochrome works, but he eventually eliminated cotton because he feared that its natural movement in response to climatic changes induced cracking in the paint layers. That said, when using linen he missed the resiliency of cotton to the pressure of a loaded brush. Throughout he sought a sharpness to the edge of the surface and immediately noticed when a painting that had been lined with a second canvas during a conservation treatment lost its crispness where the surface met the sides. The tacking margins of his early paintings were carefully taped and the paint along that border was steadily deposited by even pressure on the knife, all to maintain that sharp edge.

The artist customarily began by applying a lead-white and oil ground that provided a hard physical plane, as opposed, for example, to the tinted wash over the canvas favored notably by Mark Rothko. "I wanted a real surface, a paint surface," Marden has explained. "Lead-white priming was the beginning step of the painting. So, it was important that my hand be involved. Always my hand. I would prime, let dry, sand, and prime again."[8] Although, in time, he would come to allow others to prime the canvases, he carefully scrutinizes the results. Recently he noted that the grounds on two canvases, prepared at the same time as four others of a set, had inexplicably cracked. When two replacements arrived, their preparation did not match the hard and smooth surface of the originals. The resultant discrepancy in the surfaces of works intended as a series sufficiently concerned him that he considered discarding the replacements rather than trying to compensate for their greater absorbency through other means.

1. Brice Marden. *Wax I.* 1966
Oil and beeswax on canvas, 45 x 56" (114 x 142 cm)
Collection John and Mary Pappajohn

In the early 1960s in New York, Marden created monochrome paintings with a mixture of oil paint and damar, a natural resin that adds viscosity and gloss. The mixture produced a surface so reflective that he had to admit, "There were elements of hostility involved. You make a painting that people couldn't see,"[9] paintings that "were viewer resistant. They had lots of varnish and lots of oil, highly reflective surfaces. It was like a hedge."[10] Eventually the artist became interested in exploring variations of the color gray and decided that reflective surfaces impeded that inquiry. He began, with *Wax I* of 1966 (fig. 1), to add a mixture of beeswax and turpentine, rather than the damar resin, to his oil paint to create matte surfaces. He preferred Winsor & Newton oil paint because it purportedly already contained a small quantity of wax in the proprietary formula.[11] He would heat the wax-turpentine medium in a double boiler warmed by a hot plate, which was set on a refrigerator door that served as his palette. Meanwhile, using oil paint, he would mix a desired color on this temperate palette. When ready, he would dip his brush into the hot wax and turpentine, mix that solution into the paint, and apply it to the canvas. If dissatisfied, he would scrape off the waxy paint mixture and return it to the palette. This leftover solution would then add its color to the residual paint that was there, which in turn would inform the next batch he mixed. The practice produced a natural continuity of color between batches, and between the layers of paint they were used to create, an effect the artist carefully sought.

Evidence of the paint-application process remains as subtle markings on the surface of each painting (figs. 2, 3). Initially applying the paint with a brush, the artist would rework it with a palette knife or large spatula, drawing barely visible forms. "I was really drawing with the finger because the finger was pressing on the spatula. It's all coming out through the finger."[12] Rounded cusps at the top of the so-called wax paintings attest to this use of the spatula, as do other marks, including knots in the fabric accentuated by layers of paint. Referring to this type of imperfection, Marden has noted, "People thought that that was a damage, and it was actually, you know, indigenous."[13] Rather than shunning such marks, as might be expected from a minimalist seeking an impersonal effect, Marden actually courted them as reminders of his intervention: "I always thought that the hand was about making something."[14] For this reason he intentionally chose not to employ the traditional encaustic technique, which would have required reheating the final layers in order to meld them together. He did not want to diminish the definition of his strokes set in the paint, or the autonomy of each layer. "You build up these veils of feelings. It seems as though, because the early paintings were just one color, one could say one color, no feelings—but instead of no feelings they were all this feeling. Each layer was a color, was . . . a feeling that related to the feeling, the color, the layer beneath it."[15]

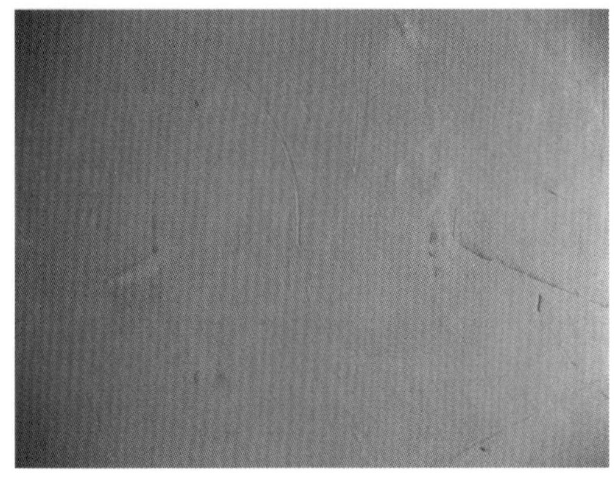

2 and 3. Brice Marden. *Return 1* (details). 1964–65
Oil on canvas, 50¼ x 68¼" (127.6 x 173.4 cm)
The Museum of Modern Art, New York.
Fractional and promised gift of
Kathy and Richard S. Fuld, Jr.

In the early 1980s, having recognized over time that the wax/oil medium was easily damaged, Marden chose to modify his paint once again and began adding terpineol (a turpentine derivative) instead of beeswax to his oil paint. The mixture, which dries perfectly flat, still serves his needs to this day, but he continues to grapple with the nature of its sheen and the properties of its natural aging. In considering his use of materials, it is worth remembering that when he was attending Boston University School of Art, from 1958 to 1961, he studied under Reed Kay, who stressed that a serious artist is well acquainted through experience with the properties of materials and that the learning curve does not end in student days. Technical changes, Kay noted in a practical guide to studio practice that he subsequently published, were made by painters "knowledgeable in their craft, who required new materials or methods to express new ideas. Naturally, since each material differs from the rest in respect to drying rate, brushing qualities, transparency and covering quality, tonal and textural range, each carries certain implications as to style and pictorial effect."[16] "It was good that I studied with him," remembers Marden, "because he gave you a sense that there is a better way to do it or that you can figure out other ways to do what you do."[17]

Although Marden's current work differs overtly in its linearity from his earlier, monochromatic work, the backbone of the method remains amidst a logical progression. Some aspects of that process may be illuminated by a discussion of *The Seasons* (fig. 4, plate 64), which Marden began in New York in 1974 and completed in Houston, Texas, in the autumn of 1975. The work was made at the invitation of Harris Rosenstein, then director of the Institute for the Arts at Rice University in Houston, who asked Marden and David Novros to create paintings that would be installed simultaneously (although at a different site) with four paintings that Rothko had made in conjunction with the commission for the Rothko Chapel but that were not included in the final installation. The Chapel itself, featuring fourteen large, alternatively painterly and hard-edged canvases, had opened in Houston in February 1971 (fig. 5); Marden visited it a year later, and in 1976 told Cecile McCann, "A good portion of my work . . . has been based on that in some way."[18] There are many comparable qualities in each artist's work. Wrought out of multiple layers of paint to create subtle variations in hue, the Chapel paintings eschew decorative color. Marked by pentimenti and deposits of extraneous material from their process, they hold a history of their making. They resonate within a space that embraces their scale and composition. Indeed Marden once claimed that the Rothko Chapel was "one of the most beautiful places in the world," although he quickly added that it was not the building "but those paintings—when you get in there and you look at the paintings, you go from one to one, you get to figuring them all out, and then you start cross referral. Plus there's a reverberation thing that happens in the paintings, that's sort of like a pulsation, that's really beautiful."[19]

In response to Rosenstein's proposal, Marden decided to paint the traditional theme of the seasons. "I had these paintings in mind for a long time. I was interested in enlivening the space in my paintings. Up to that point they were [independent] monochromatic panel paintings."[20] Working in his New York studio, he began by determining the size and proportions of four panels in a series of drawings made with consecutive layers of graphite and wax. "If I don't use the wax," he explained, "I can't get this smooth graphite surface. You'd have a furry surface without the wax. So, this gives me a surface that I want. And in effect, it makes these paintings on paper because the wax acts as a binder and the graphite becomes a pigment."[21] Rothko's preparatory studies for the Chapel paintings provide an instructive comparison: sketchy and immediate, they principally indicate the artist's evolving thoughts about the proportions of forms. Although made with relatively shiny graphite pencil on matte black paper, they focus on issues apart from materiality. Marden's drawings, on the other hand, make no such distinction. The melding of material and method was so ingrained in his thinking that even studies were finished works.

The Seasons comprises four vertical panels, each eight feet by five,

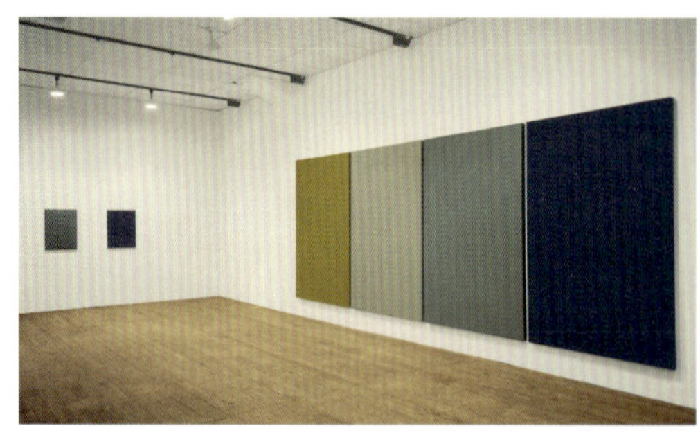

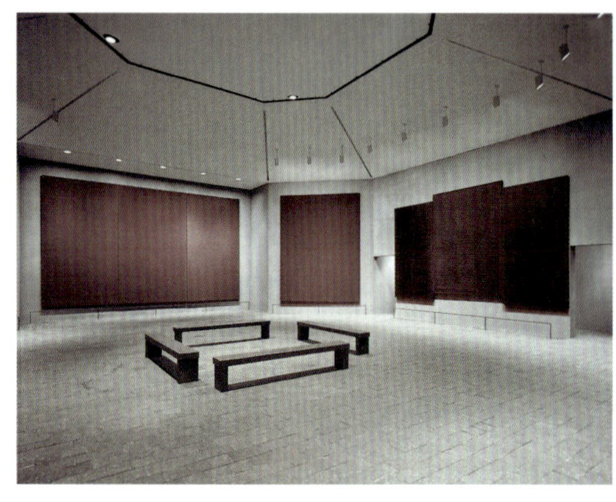

4. Brice Marden. Left: two of the four panels of *The Seasons—Small Version*. 1974–75
Oil and beeswax on paper mounted on canvas, 29¾" x 7' 5" (75.5 x 226 cm)
Right: *The Seasons*, 1974–75, prior to completion (see plate 86)
Oil and beeswax on canvas, four panels, overall: 8' x 20' 9" (243.8 x 632.5 cm)
Both The Menil Collection, Houston
Installation view at Rice University, Houston, April–June 1975

5. The Rothko Chapel, Houston, opened 1971, with north, northeast, and east paintings by Mark Rothko

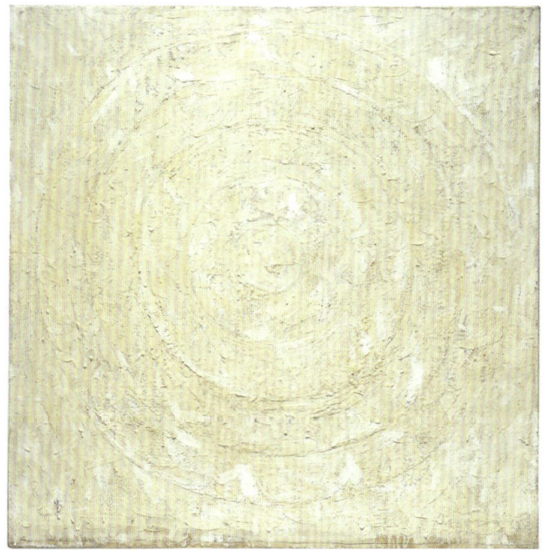

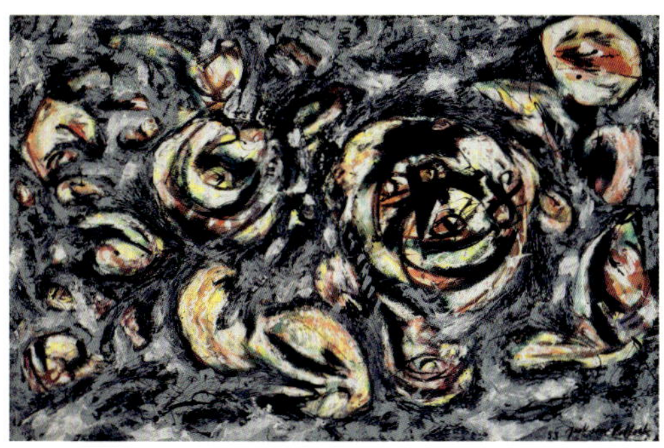

6. Brice Marden. *The Seasons* (detail). 1974–75

7. Jasper Johns, *White Target*. 1957
Wax and oil on canvas, 30 x 30" (76.2 x 76.2 cm)
Whitney Museum of American Art, New York. Purchase

8. Jackson Pollock. *Ocean Greyness*. 1953
Oil on canvas, 57³/₄" x 7' 6¹/₈" (146.7 x 229 cm)
Solomon R. Guggenheim Museum, New York

installed sequentially with an interval of three inches between them. "The interval," according to Marden, "had to do with the overall size of the piece" as opposed to the allotted exhibition space. He chose to separate the panels because "in terms of subject matter, they're each unto themselves. Yet they had to be together. I really wanted *The Seasons* to be able to stand alone."[22] He also made a small version of the painting on four small panels that he exhibited along with the larger work. He worked simultaneously on both versions, making changes and corrections on the smaller one, then using them as a reference while he adjusted the color in the larger panels. Although its canvases were exhibited with an interval between them, *The Seasons* looks ahead to later polyptychs in which a number of panels are conjoined. All feature the same carefully crafted dialogue among their individual parts. For the later works, done in the early 1980s, Marden had a custom of loosening, but not removing, the connective bolts in order to insert protective papers between the panels while painting. He described the process as a "part of this fetishistic thing . . . if I took it apart, it sort of broke the spirit of it."[23]

When Marden first visited the Rothko Chapel, he was immediately engaged by the brushwork in the paintings. His reading of Rothko's vertical strokes exerted an influence on his execution of *The Seasons*, and on his work thereafter: "I would take a knife [loaded with paint] . . . and I could guide it by running one finger down the side of the canvas. So, I got the stroke straight. Then I would align all the other strokes to that stroke."[24] In so doing he created an expressive language that bore witness to the touch of his hand. Marden worked minutely over the surfaces from top to bottom, ultimately closing out in the bottom right hand corner. He deliberately never resolved the bot tom lest the painting open up elsewhere. "It's superstition or something," he confided. "It was a working ritual."[25] The practice of reserving a reveal of the execution at the bottom edge progressed from a scoring and scraping of layers, as in *For Helen* (1967; plate 19), to an irregular accumulation, in later works, of drips emanating from the various paint layers (fig. 6). These reveals serve as a reference, a history, or even a "memento mori . . . a concentration of feelings in layers. The drips memorized the feelings, the layers, the colors. I always thought that was very expressionistic."[26] The device calls to mind the unfinished bottom edges in the work of Jasper Johns (fig. 7), and also the vortexlike eyes into the process of Jackson Pollock's *Ocean Greyness* (1953; fig. 8). These exposed histories do not simply represent discarded versions of the painting but rather are crucial stages in the dialogue of creation and response from which the work has evolved.[27]

The Seasons, Marden's largest work to date, was exhibited, along with its smaller counterpart, in the spring of 1975 at Rice's Institute for the Arts (fig. 4). But the artist did not consider it finished. "I was working with the other small paintings in the context of the exhibition, but I wanted to take *The Seasons* further. With the first set," he admits, "the color wasn't there."[28] After the exhibition closed, *The Seasons* was delivered to a loft in Houston, and Marden returned to "destroy what was there and bring it back up. . . . I didn't feel it was resolved enough. The surface wasn't any near as worked up as it is [now]. And that has something to do with the feeling of the painting."[29] Comparison of the 1975 installation photographs, the extant smaller panels, and the finished painting (figs. 6, 9) indicates that there was an addition of at least two layers of paint, as referenced on the bottom edges. The artist brought the colors into a closer relationship by forcing the panels to weigh against one another in a more measured way; yellow, for example, evolved from a harder color to a much softer, greener, and mellower hue in the final painting, just as green became cooler, then warmer. The darkest panel, *Winter*, moved from a dark blue black to a much lighter one. "The live color part becomes the dead color part. This becomes value and this becomes color. [*Winter*] would appear much bluer in another context. . . . Color is really something trying to summarize a feeling about each season. If you took them out of context, you'd not get it . . . it's a thematic thing."[30] Marden attributes this evocation of color to what he had experienced between finishing the painting in New York and returning to it after the Rice show: after a western sojourn, he was struck, seemingly without knowing it, by a "cottonwood effect on the painting" that resulted in a more subtle tonality associated with a maturity of color and value.[31] "Color is a way of arriving at light," Marden asserts, and *The Seasons*, created in two different environments, attests to the artist's expression of feeling through the transformation of matter into light.[32]

9. Brice Marden. *The Seasons* after completion, fall 1975

In earlier work, Marden had applied tape to the tacking edges of stretched canvases. When that tape, which collected random brushstrokes, was temporarily removed during a conservation treatment, he disliked the resultant white tacking edges of the canvas, which had the effect of visually flattening the picture plane. Returning to the Rothko Chapel often while finishing *The Seasons*, Marden began to appreciate the sense of volume that Rothko's painted tacking edges gave to the immense dark surfaces of his paintings. Seeking a similar dimensionality, he finished *The Seasons* by scraping paint against the hefty tacking edges. In completing the Grove Group works, begun in 1972, after his return to New York, he continued this practice with the last two paintings in the series, *Grove Group IV* and *V* (plates 48, 49).[33]

It is instructive to compare Marden's process in finishing *The Seasons* to the way he reworks paintings that have been damaged: "I have no compunction—I mean, I don't have to make them the same. I am not just restoring the painting; I'm repainting the painting," he has said.[34] He once reworked a Grove Group painting in a manner that retained the same situation of dark, light, and middle values because "those were the ideas of the painting," but the colors inevitably changed.[35] With regard to a reworking of *The Dylan Painting* (1966/1986; plate 17), he explains, "So, you have maybe four grays that are like the gray, but aren't the gray, that was finally on there."[36] A synthesized gray in a single surface application simply cannot duplicate the developed color of many layers. Marden considers a paint that has been mixed specifically to simulate a color underneath "depersonalized" and without "history." The painting "takes on a history and complicatedness that you don't get in just mixing a color," he explains.[37] Distinguishing himself from a conservator who is trained to match color, he admits that he cannot do that because each layer results from what came before and informs what comes next: "The colors would go through so many variations when you're working on the painting. I didn't know how to go right to the color."[38] He makes a similar distinction with regard to the importance of the hand: when asked if someone else could repaint his work, Marden replied emphatically, "No. It's a lot about stroke."[39] In similar fashion, when Pollock was once asked to restore *Number 5* (1948) after a small section of the painting had been damaged, he could not correct the disruption locally. Instead, Alfonso Ossorio would remember, he undertook a "thorough but subtle overpainting" that retained the original concept but was "affirmed and fulfilled by a new complexity and depth of linear interplay."[40]

Artists take risks to fight the threat of a creative death. Pollock once told the painter Peter Busa, "Go ahead, make a mess. You might find yourself by destroying yourself and by working your way out of it."[41] In part striving to avoid conventional beauty, Marden stopped using his monochromatic palette in the mid-1980s because "all I could get were chords. I wanted to be able to make something more like fugues, more complicated, back-and-forth renderings of feelings."[42] Eventually he tried to bridge the differing camps of his drawings and paintings with the Cold Mountain paintings of 1988–91. His comment on them echoes Pollock's remark to Busa: "What I'd like from these paintings is to get them to a point where I really get lost and terribly confused, and then bring them back around," he confided to Robert Mahoney in 1990.[43]

"To be an artist is not about making individual works. To be an artist is to do your work and let your work express the evolution of a vision."[44] There remains in the later work a familiar conjunction of materials. Gone is the veiling or obliteration; the history of the process is now explicit. What before was encapsulated within the substance of the paint layers and released only at the bottom edge is now made visible throughout. Yet the mark-making that Marden consistently preserves as the surface of his paintings is not just the history of that particular work but a gesture at the history of expression and the role of artists in it. These traces combine with the size of the work to reassert a human scale. Mysterious and unpredictable, the layered color presents itself inevitably as an expression of human feeling. Marden understood the constant risk-taking and thinking that went into Pollock's work, the investment of self that attests to an artist's humanity. He had to rework *The Seasons* because he intuitively knew that leaving these canvases as they were would subject them to the danger of being little more than a personal cliché.[45] The Rothko Chapel paintings provided formal devices, but ultimately what Marden admired most was the artist's heroic humanist effort.[46]

The seemingly radical formality of Marden's monochromes can be misread: these works are without image, but they are not depersonalized. They are about an artist transforming "that heavy earthen kind of thing, turning it into air and light." For in the end, as Marden has acknowledged, "Modern art is about a physical identification. It's not so much a picture anymore, it's you."[47]

NOTES

For their assistance in research, I would like to thank Julie Barton, Heather Cox, Dana Cranmer, Ian Glennie, Fredricka Hunter, Mary Kadish, Christina Rosenberger, and Paul Winkler. Bradford Epley and Christa Haiml provided valuable insight and technical information regarding *The Seasons*, and Yve-Alain Bois, Mark Flood, and William Steen offered discerning and perceptive comments on the text. My understanding of Brice Marden's materials and method results from the many hours I have spent interviewing him over the years. My thoughts have been enriched immeasurably by this engagement.

1. Brice Marden, quoted in Lilly Wei, "Talking Abstract, Part One," *Art in America* 75, no. 7 (July 1987): 83.
2. Marden, conversation with the author, December 21, 2005.
3. Marden, quoted in Pat Steir, "Brice Marden: An Interview," in *Brice Marden: Recent Drawings and Etchings* (New York: Matthew Marks Gallery, 1991), n.p.
4. Marden, interview with the author, October 1, 1992; conversation with the author, December 21, 2005. There is a videotape of the 1992 interview in the archives of the Menil Collection, Houston.
5. Marden, interview with the author, October 1, 1992.
6. Marden, interview with Gary Garrels, Dana Cranmer, Matthew Marks, and the author, Museum of Contemporary Art, Los Angeles, March 30, 2004, transcript in the Archives of The Museum of Modern Art, New York, tape one, p. 19.
7. Marden, interview with the author, October 1, 1992.
8. Ibid.
9. Ibid.
10. Marden, in Saul Ostrow, "Brice Marden," *Bomb* no. 22 (Winter 1988): 33.
11. It was the painter Harvey Quaytman who recommended that Marden use beeswax and turpentine as a medium; see Klaus Kertess, *Brice Marden: Paintings and Drawings* (New York: Harry N. Abrams, 1992), p. 15. For the precise proportions of the mixture, see Marden, "Technical Statement," in *Brice Marden* (New York: Solomon R. Guggenheim Foundation, 1975), p. 28. For the reference to Winsor & Newton oil paint, see Marden, interview with Garrels, Cranmer, et al., March 30, 2004, tape one, p. 7. Alun Foster of Winsor & Newton, ColArt Fine Arts & Graphics, has disclaimed the inclusion of wax in the formula for the paint. Conversation with the author, May 19, 2006.
12. Marden, interview with the author, October 1, 1992.

13. Marden, interview with Garrels, Cranmer, et al., March 30, 2004, tape one, p. 9.
14. Marden, in Ostrow, "Brice Marden," p. 34.
15. Ibid., pp. 32–33.
16. Reed Kay, *The Painter's Companion* (Cambridge, Mass.: Webb Books, 1961), pp. 15–16.
17. Marden, interview with the author, October 1, 1992.
18. Marden, in Cecile N. McCann, "An Interview with Brice Marden," *Artweek*, December 4, 1976, p. 16.
19. Ibid.
20. Marden, interview with the author, October 1, 1992.
21. Marden, quoted in Stephan Götz, *American Artists in Their New York Studios: Conversations about the Creation of Contemporary Art* (Cambridge, Mass.: Center for Conservation and Technical Studies, Harvard University Art Museums, and Stuttgart: Daco-Verlag Günter Bläs, 1992), p. 105.
22. Marden, interview with the author, October 1, 1992.
23. Marden, interview with Garrels, Cranmer, et al., March 30, 2004, tape two, p. 13. Marden reused the papers that had separated the panels to create the Masking Drawings of the same period.
24. Ibid., p. 12.
25. Marden, interview with the author, October 1, 1992.
26. Marden, in Ostrow, "Brice Marden," pp. 31–33.
27. For a fuller discussion of Jackson Pollock's use of this device, see Carol C. Mancusi-Ungaro, "Jackson Pollock: Response as Dialogue," in Kirk Varnedoe and Pepe Karmel, eds., *Jackson Pollock: New Approaches* (New York: The Museum of Modern Art, 1999), p. 151.
28. Marden, interview with the author, October 1, 1992.
29. Ibid.
30. Ibid.
31. Ibid., and conversation with the author, December 21, 2005.
32. Marden, 1980, in "Brice Marden: Selected Statements, Notes and Interviews," in *Brice Marden: Paintings, Drawings, and Prints 1975–80* (London: Whitechapel Art Gallery, 1981), p. 57.
33. Marden, conversation with the author, November 15, 2005.
34. Marden, in "Interview by Robin White Robin White at Crown Point Press, Oakland, California, 1980" *View* 3, no. 2 (June 1980): 7.
35. Marden, in "Interview by Ibid., p. 7.
36. Marden, interview with Garrels, Cranmer, et al., March 30, 2004, tape one, p. 29.
37. Marden, conversation with the author, December 21, 2005.
38. Marden, interview with the author, October 1, 1992.
39. Ibid.
40. Alfonso Ossorio, quoted in Mancusi-Ungaro, "Response as Dialogue," p. 145, note 13.
41. Peter Busa, quoted in Sidney Simon, "Concerning the Beginnings of the New York School: 1939–42," *Art International* 11, no. 6 (Summer 1967): 20.
42. Marden, in Steir, "Brice Marden: An Interview," n.p.
43. Marden, in Robert Mahoney, "Brice Marden: This Is What Things Are About," *Flash Art* 23, no. 155 (November/December 1990): 116.
44. Marden, quoted in Brenda Richardson, *Brice Marden Cold Mountain* (Houston: Houston Fine Art Press, 1992), p. 41.
45. Marden, interview with the author, October 1, 1992.
46. See McCann, "An Interview with Brice Marden," p.16.
47. Marden, in Paul Gardner, "Call It a Mid-Life Crisis," *Artnews* 93, no. 4 (April 1994): 143.

Michael Duffy

Two and Four Make Six:
In the Studio with Brice Marden

This interview took place on January 17, 2006, in Brice Marden's studio on West Street, Manhattan.

Michael Duffy: You've been in this studio overlooking the Hudson River for about five years, and we're surrounded here by several paintings from your most recent series. Do they have titles yet?

Brice Marden: Yes, this is a version of *The Propitious Garden of Plane Image*, a painting in three versions—the two others I have going in my studio in Tivoli, New York.

MD: It consists of six panels.

BM: Yes, and now it starts getting complicated: what is propitious is the number six. It has to do with my birth date: you get the propitious number by adding these other numbers together, and I was born on the 15th, so one plus five, that's a six. So it's six panels for six colors. And each panel has six colors on it, it's a progression: red, orange, yellow, green, blue, violet. In the larger Propitious Garden works, the panels are six by four feet; six by four is twenty-four, and two and four make six, so it all adds up to six. That's the propitious thing.

"Plane Image" is me. I consider it a synonym.

MD: Do you assign titles to the works as you're working on them or only after they're finished?

BM: They don't usually get titled until the end. This whole—I mean, "Propitious Garden of Plane Image," it's a little pretentious [LAUGHS].

MD: I see in the studio a selection of scholar's rocks, from China, that you've collected over the years—they form one influence for the paintings?

BM: Very much so. Each of these things starts out with a rock—the form is loosely based on one. It all has to do with looking at Chinese paintings, which came out of my involvement with calligraphy.

MD: Were you working with calligraphy as an art form?

BM: No, I just saw a show, *Masters of Japanese Calligraphy, 8th–19th Century*, at the Asia Society and Japan House. I was very moved by it and started looking at calligraphy, mostly Chinese, as much as I could find. And then I got much more interested in Chinese culture. One of the ways in was by reading poems; I read Ezra Pound and Kenneth Rexroth translations, and then I found a book by Han Shan, or Cold Mountain, translated by a poet named Red Pine and printing the poems in Chinese as well. I basically took the Cold Mountain paintings from that Chinese form. All the time I was making the paintings, I was reading the poems, which are very Zen influenced and nature oriented.

MD: Here in the studio we're surrounded by not only the paintings you've been working on but also the materials, brushes, palettes, the sticks you draw with, and other things you use (fig. 1). How do you start off? You choose stretchers of a certain size—do you make them yourself?

BM: Simon Liu [of Simon Liu Inc., Brooklyn] makes them, to certain specifications—there's a certain depth to the structure, and I choose the canvas, which is linen and double primed.

MD: And it's stapled only on the back.

BM: I don't like staples on the side, because I don't frame the paintings.

MD: So the edges are important. And the thickness of the stretcher is important as well?

BM: That has to do with the fact that I apply a lot of pressure to the surface. I put the paint on with a brush but then scrape and repaint it.

MD: Do you use the knife to apply more paint, or just to rework the paint already on the surface?

BM: I'm basically taking paint off. I'm trying to keep the paint close to the surface, I'm not trying to build it up. The paint is oil paint with terpineol.

MD: So you're not using wax at all anymore?

BM: No, I started using terpineol as my substitute for it.

MD: And that acts as a medium for the oil—thins it, or makes it the consistency you want?

BM: Yes, it makes it a proper consistency, and when you add it to oil it gives it a uniform flatness. That's the reason I started using wax, to get a flat surface so you could read the colors specifically. I was using wax when I was doing monochromatic panels—

MD: Like the Grove Group series?

BM: —Yes, and I wanted to switch, because wax never dries and never hardens. You can put additives in it, but I didn't want to do that, which meant the paintings didn't harden, they're soft, and you run into all kinds of technical problems.

MD: In *The Propitious Garden*, from where I'm standing, I can see areas that strike me as more glossy and areas that are matte; there's a difference in the

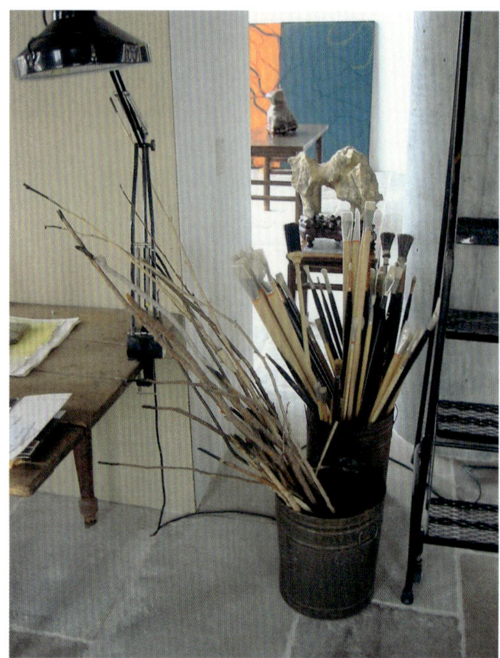

1. Brice Marden's Manhattan studio, January 2006

paint application.

BM: The more layers go on, the shinier it gets. This one has a lot of layers on it, so there are some very shiny areas.

MD: Could you estimate the number of layers of paint on that painting at this point?

BM: Probably about five. That might be an overestimate. First I put on a ground color.

MD: Depending on the panel, red on the left, running through orange, yellow, green, and blue to violet on the right.

BM: Yes, and then that violet becomes the first linear figure on the red. I consider each of the linear-painted colors a figure.

MD: Ah, so you go back to the beginning.

BM: Yes, exchanging the colors. The red of the panel at the far left becomes the first figure on the orange panel to its right, the orange becomes the first figure on the yellow panel, and so they go. And then I do the progression of figures on each panel. If this violet has become the first figure on the red ground, then the blue is painted to lie behind it, and the green behind that, and then the yellow, and then the orange. And then orange being the last color, or the farthest back, it becomes the next panel's ground color. There the red goes first, and so on through the blue, the green, then the yellow, and so on. That's the whole progression.

Of the two I'm working on in Tivoli, one uses this progression and the other reverses it. So instead of violet here, there's orange—it's just the reverse.

MD: The different linear figures make a frame around the inside of the work, in a way that leads your eye through the series.

BM: There are more layers on the linear part than on the ground. I put the ground coat on first, and then all the linear aspects; and then I went back in and repainted the ground color over everything, and then all the figures again. Then I kept repainting the linear thing rather than the ground. On some parts when I went back in, I just painted the ground between the lines.

MD: So when you're working on the panels side by side, they're in a similar state of finished quality, because you're going back and forth?

BM: I work one panel at a time. But I might go through this whole thing and do all the violet, then all the red, and so on.

MD: You can see in some places that there have been drips during the paint application, and areas where maybe you weren't satisfied with the direction of the line and you've gone in and repainted.

BM: There's a lot of correction. Some things just get painted out. See, here's a place where there's just one coat of ground color and one coat of the first color of the line. Ordinarily what I would do is, when I got all this worked out, I'd go back in and do the orange coat again, obliterating the corrections. Up until a couple of years ago I used to leave the corrections in, as a sort of counter-image. But then I didn't want that anymore, because I was putting in more figures.

MD: Yes, so in another painting here we have three figures over the orange ground.

BM: It was intended to be complementary colors: orange ground, blue figure, red ground, green figure. Everything was going to be Daoist, opposites, yin yang. That has a lot to do with the thinking when I draw the figures, which are based on rock forms.

MD: I see you've done a study for the painting, on a thick watercolor paper. And you've divided the paper into six sections, so that you have an idea of the current progression.

BM: Yes, it has the same progressions as the painting.

MD: It's in a watercolor or gouache?

BM: This is shellac ink.

MD: And here are some drawings in black ink on watercolor paper showing figures sketched on the white ground.

BM: This was the first manifestation of the idea. Then I have these notes: "This is The Propitious Garden of Plane Image, summer 2000, Hydra, first painting started summer '99 August." That's a painting that's now in the collection of the Whitney [Museum of American Art, New York]. "Six canvases of four images, ground color, spectral progression." These are notes I made, and then I made these drawings—there are four images on each, and six drawings, so twenty-four images (p. 98, fig. 25). There are twenty-four watercolor rocks.

MD: So in each drawing we have four sketched images in ink of the rocks, which then become incorporated into the painting. And the introduction of color happens spontaneously in the next step?

BM: The color progression comes out of the Red Rock paintings, which were all started with the red line. I used that same color progression except I altered it. The Propitious Garden works are more formalized than those were.

MD: Are these ink drawings done with a brush, or are you also using sticks?

BM: Sticks, chosen for being pretty slim and kind of flexible.

MD: They're ailanthus?

BM: No, this is bamboo. I find sticks wherever I go—"Build with the bricks at hand." With the drawings I make out in Pennsylvania, there's a lot of hemlock around, so I use hemlock branches. We were just in the Caribbean and I'd go out and try to find sticks there.

MD: What is it you like about applying ink or paint with a stick that you don't have when you're using a brush, say, or a palette knife?

BM: I've just been doing it for so long now that I feel I can control it the way some people can control a brush. Or rather, brushes are a more controllable kind of instrument, but the stick has the kind of control and also *lack* of control that I like. I also like to go back and forth between the two.

MD: Some of the sticks you have here are three or four feet long.

BM: Yes, which means you get a lot of accidents. But it's also a kind of extension of the body. I'll start these drawings with a longer stick, but when I narrow in, the stick gets shorter.

MD: Would the paper or canvas be on the floor while you're painting with the stick?

BM: It's usually on a board leaning against the wall. *The Propitious Garden of Plane Image, First Version* [plate 169] is really the first painting I've worked while it's directly on the wall. I worked it for a couple of years just leaning against this wall, but I'd take each panel separately and work it over there. I'd get nervous because it's so friezelike, and I felt I really should have it up on the wall to see what it looked like while I was working on it. But this is really the first painting I've worked on that way.

MD: Do you have a typical display height that you feel is best?

BM: There's no typical height, but I like to hang them lower than usual. People usually like to hang paintings at some sort of average eye level, in the middle. I like it lower than that. These things are more human-shaped, and you have a more corporal relation to them.

MD: When you're finished with a painting, or at a stage where the figures and ground are satisfactory, is there a step after that? Do you varnish the paintings or use any other kind of surface treatment?

BM: No. There have been times when, say, if a part is too shiny I'll go over it with the knife and try to dull it down. That doesn't really work too well.

MD: You're using palettes that look like baking pans or cookie sheets.

BM: Yes, I get them in the kitchen-supply places on the Bowery.

MD: You also have some coffee cans for your medium or for mixing paint.

BM: This is just terpineol. It's a little more viscous than turpentine. It was suggested to me by a technician at the Grumbacher paint company—we got into some sort of technical discussion and I said I wanted something to replace wax, something matte. He said I should try terpineol. I buy it from scent suppliers; it has a very strong pine smell. I started using it, and it seemed to work okay, so I've been using it ever since.

MD: I noticed you're using an oil paint made by Williamsburg Art Materials. Is that your preferred paint these days?

BM: Yes, though I use it in combination with Blockx and Winsor & Newton.

MD: Did you ever consider making your own paint?

BM: When I was in art school, at Boston University, I studied with a guy named Reed Kay, who wrote a book called *The Painter's Companion*. We had to take two years of technical painting and we used all kinds of media, tempera and encaustic and—

MD: I understand Kay wouldn't let you use acrylic?

BM: No, he didn't believe in acrylic. He'd say, It's unproven, it's too recent, we don't know how it's going to last. He was really traditional—you practically had to weave your own canvas—and he made us grind our own pigment. I wasn't ready to start doing that in the studio.

MD: When you're working, do you squeeze the oil out into a pan and then add the right amount of terpineol to get it to the proper consistency?

BM: I mix the color, then add the terpineol. But what I've been doing is, I'll just keep adding. I try not to change the color, which I'm keeping consistent, but I'm finding that because I have these pans out for years, so there's this evaporation, I'm not exactly sure what I'm getting. I don't know how much has evaporated, how gummy it gets. . . . I think that's why the more layers I put on, the shinier it gets.

MD: As the terpineol evaporates, you're getting more oil. It's almost like enamel, it's so shiny. It has a much more matte appearance on the canvas, but is that partly because, in the violet, it looks quite thin? Have you scraped it back with a palette knife in some places?

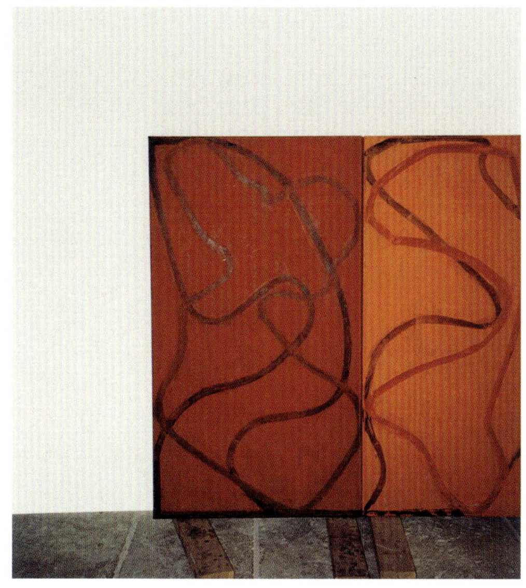

BM: Yes, I'm scraping it, though I'm also making sure it's an even surface. Then usually—well, what's happening with these ones I'm working in the country is, I've gotten all the twelve panels started, and on one painting I went back and put on a second coat of the ground color to refine the progression, or to refine the colors—I did a lot of remixing of the colors. Then I used *those* colors as the ground colors on the second painting. Then, because there were these changes between the two paintings, I went back to the first painting and I'm reapplying the ground colors again. This is the third ground coat. And when I did that, I went back in and sanded the painting down, using a medium-grade sandpaper. I also did that because one of them was cracking.

MD: So do you sometimes take paintings that you've finished and redo some cracked areas?

BM: I used to. In the beginning, paintings would get damaged and I'd take them back and say, Look, I'm not restoring it, but I'll do this: I'll repaint the thing. I'm not trying to make it the way it was. Then I ended up always having one of these in the studio. That got to be a real hindrance, and there wasn't any reason I had to do it—I mean, I wasn't injuring the paintings, and the technique was good. Sure the wax was soft, but still, you know, they weren't being properly taken care of.

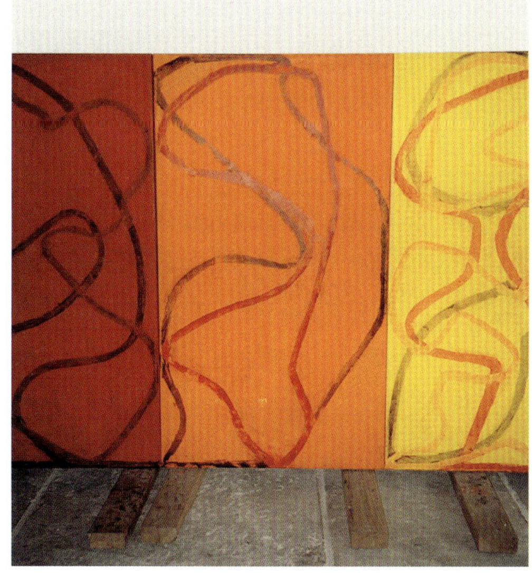

2–7. Marden's working photographs, 2000, of *The Propitious Garden of Plane Image, First Version* (2000–2005; plate 169)
Oil on linen, six panels, overall: 42" x 12' (106.7 x 365.8 cm)

MD: That's a concern, though, for paintings with wax in them: the surfaces are fragile.

BM: That's why I switched to terpineol, which I haven't had any problems with.

MD: When you see paintings that you might not have seen for five or ten years, are you ever struck by changes in their appearance?

BM: No, that doesn't happen much. If they're in good shape, they're in good shape.

MD: You have to be a little forgiving of some of the signs of aging.

BM: Oh yes. But these things are in a lot better shape than a lot of other stuff I see that was made at the same time. And my stuff is supposedly vulnerable.

MD: I know you've sometimes worked on marble, an unusual support for a painter. Those works were done at your house on Hydra?

BM: Yes, there were these marble remnants around, and I was looking at them and remembering painted buildings—the Parthenon was painted originally—and I wondered should I paint on them. Marble is a very porous surface; the paint just sucks right in.

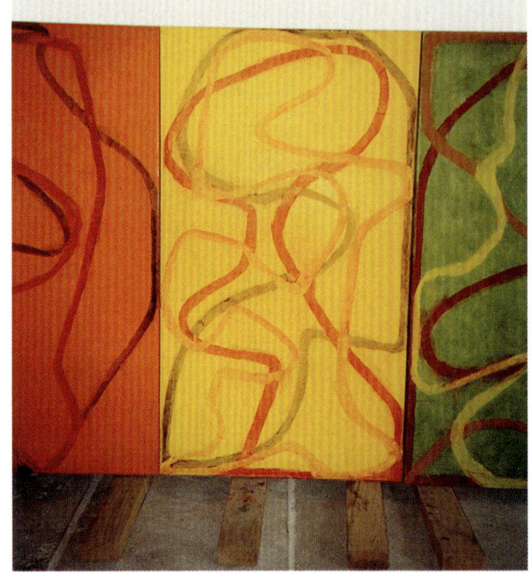

MD: What attracted you to marble? Did its whiteness remind you of canvas? Or was it the idea of using materials indigenous to the place where you were?

BM: It was just around. You're in Greece. I couldn't do those works here. But it was there, outside, and I liked the shapes. I kept looking at them and thinking, These shapes are similar to landscape shapes.

MD: What shapes were they?

BM: A lot of triangulation—rectangles with triangles cut out. These pieces were architectural; the original ones were leftovers from a bench we had made in our garden. Pieces had been cut out and they were just sitting around. And then it was Greece, and you could go to marble yards and pick out a big piece of marble, and it would have these holes in it where it was drilled out of the quarry. We had a marble floor in one room—you use marble for your floors there because it's cheaper than tile. And it's beautiful. I just love the material. And then I saw you could paint on it and it took the paint.

MD: Did you have to do anything to prepare it?

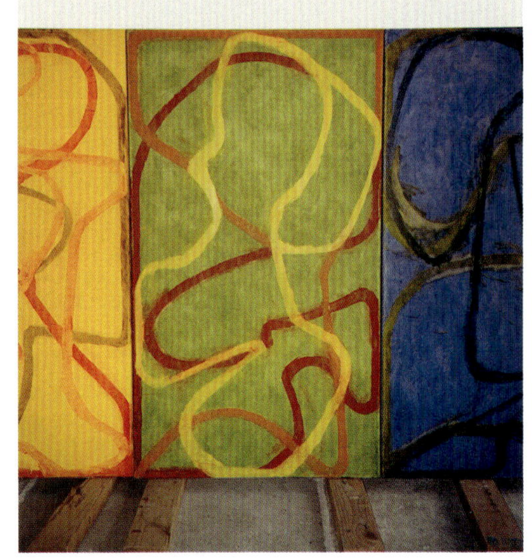

BM: I cleaned it with hydrochloric acid. People would do that in their kitchens at the time, but I was working outside, so I could use a hose to wash the marble down with water. I put the acid on and I had rubber gloves and a brush. I could start the painting, and if it wasn't right, I could make corrections, or just erase the whole thing, with the acid. That's how those got made. I redrew a lot of the edges with pencil, with a fine graphite line. Sometimes I would just use the brush and leave it that way, or else I would scrape it with a knife or with razor blades.

MD: Other works are drawn or painted on parchment [plate 142] panels. Was that decision based on your drawing technique or was it again your interest in the material?

BM: That was a material thing. The parchment came from New York Central Art Supply. They said, You should see this. It was lamb belly.

MD: *Real* parchment.

BM: Yes. That's what they used to do old manuscripts on. So I had a guy make panels, and we stretched the parchment over them, and I think we wetted it and then stretched it so it dried really tight. I put on a thin wash and then worked directly on it. I didn't rework those things a lot, but I would put the stuff on and scrape it, so they were almost like palimpsests. That's the way they read.

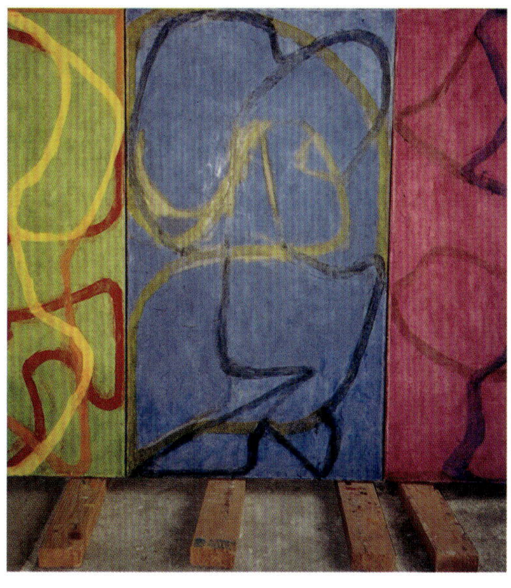

MD: It's a solid birch panel with the parchment stapled to the back. It's taut, feels kind of like a drum. How does the parchment hold the paint?

BM: You just put it on. It takes it, but with irregularities. This darker line going down the middle of the work is basically where the spine of the animal was. This green is a green that I mixed, applied very thinly, and then rubbed. This is a black put on and scraped.

MD: But it's an oil paint, like the other?

BM: Yes, with terpineol.

MD: Do you document the works while you're making them? Do you photograph them to see them in intermediate steps?

BM: Yes, I photograph them in stages (figs. 2–7). When I do something like this, I sometimes lose the image; I don't know what it was. So I use the photographs as a reference. I've only been doing that recently, I would say with the Red Rock paintings and these paintings. Maybe in the last five years or so.

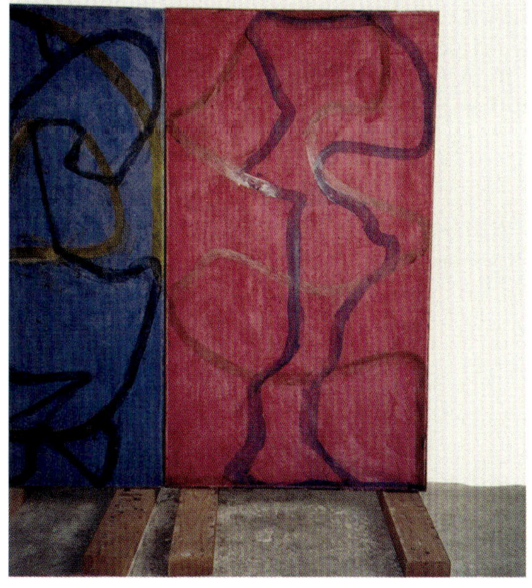

MD: In this studio in New York you have a window that's about twenty feet tall and probably about ten feet wide. That's a lot of light.

BM: Yes. My studio in Tivoli, which is also on the river, has windows based on the windows at Monticello, so they're triple-tiered—you can push the windows up two levels and have an eight-foot opening, and you look right out on the river. If I work in there at night, I turn out all the lights and stand in the middle of the room and just hear the river.

MD: You're surrounded by nature there.

BM: Yes. I paint on the east wall, and then the west wall has these unbelievable Hudson River and Catskill sunsets, like the Hudson River School. You get all these pinks and . . .

MD: Is the light much different from here?

BM: No, very similar to here. When you're painting in here in the afternoon, the light comes in and casts this grid. . . . It's blinding. But I'm sort of used to it.

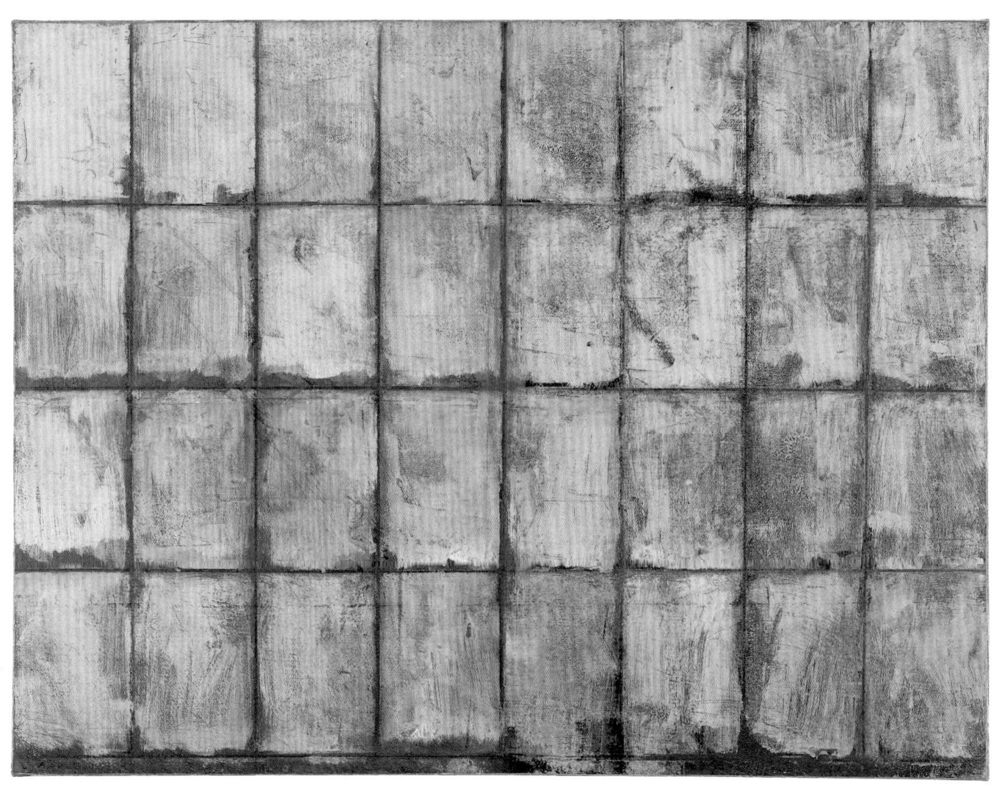

1. Untitled. 1963
Oil on paper mounted on canvas
$20^3/_4$ x $27^3/_4$" (52.7 x 70.5 cm)

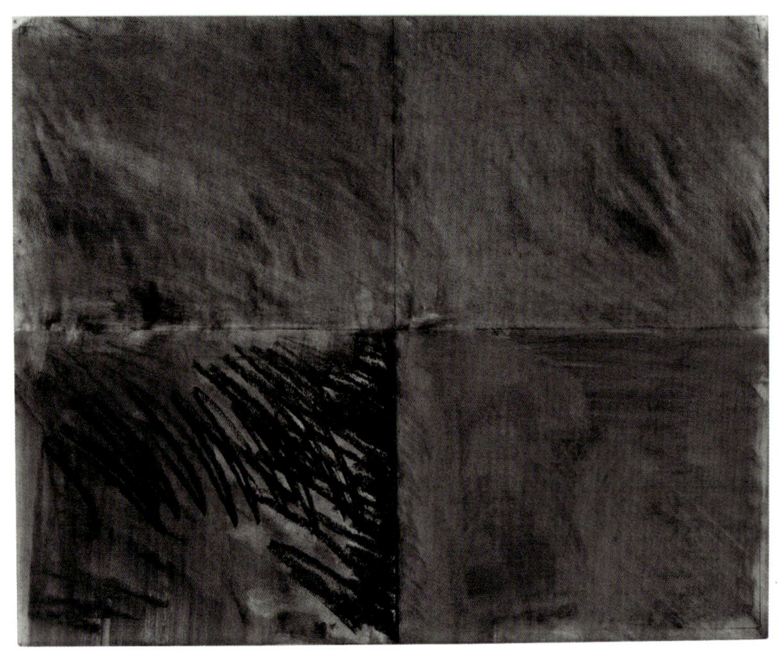

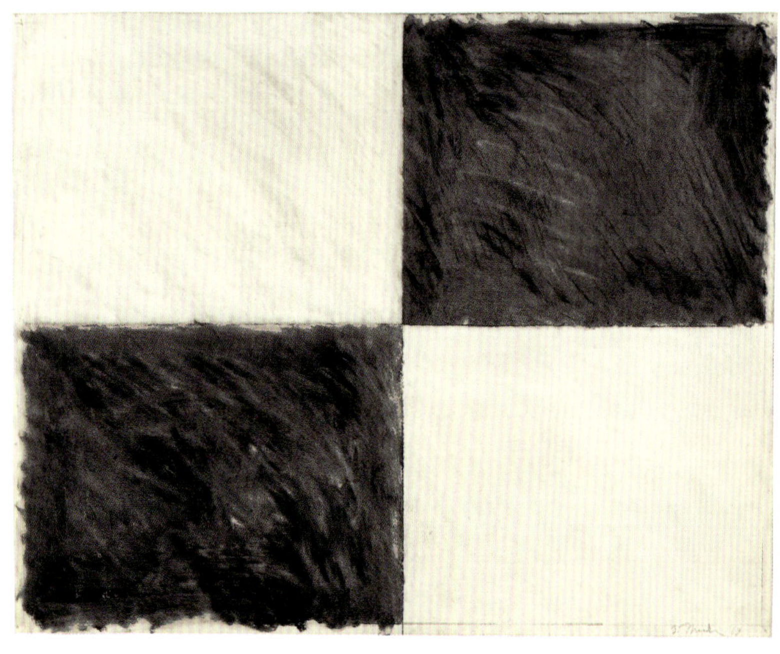

2. Untitled. 1962–63
Charcoal and graphite on paper
14½ x 18¼" (36.8 x 46.4 cm)

3. Untitled. 1963
Charcoal and graphite on paper
14¼ x 18¼" (36.2 x 46.4 cm)

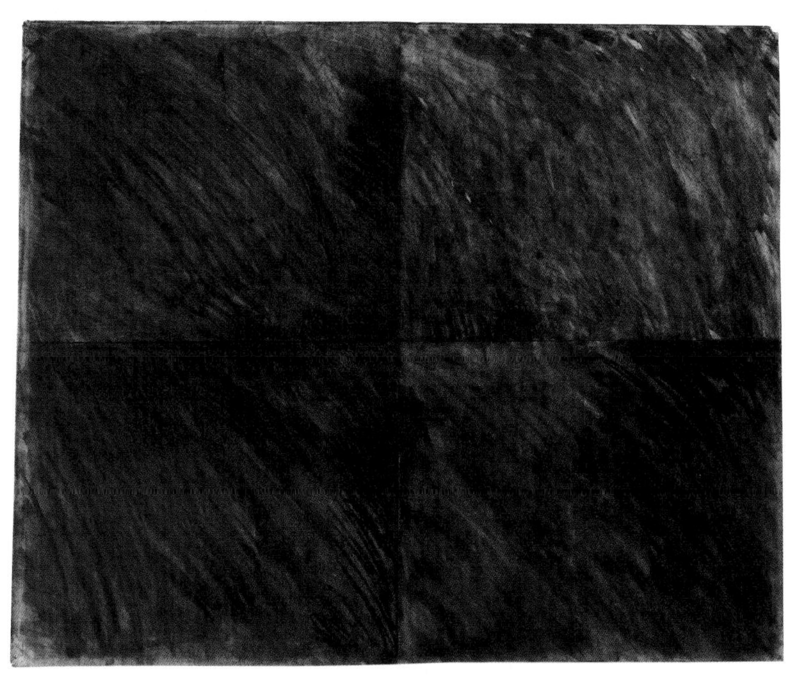

4. Untitled. 1963
Charcoal on paper
14½ x 18⅛" (36.8 x 46 cm)

5. *Dark*. 1963
Oil on canvas
48 x 46" (121.9 x 116.8 cm)

6. Untitled. 1964
Charcoal on paper
22¼ x 30⅜" (56.5 x 77.2 cm)

7. Untitled. 1964–65
Oil on canvas
20 x 39" (50.8 x 99.1 cm)

8. *Decorative Painting.* 1964
Oil on canvas
41½ x 17¾" (105.4 x 45.1 cm)

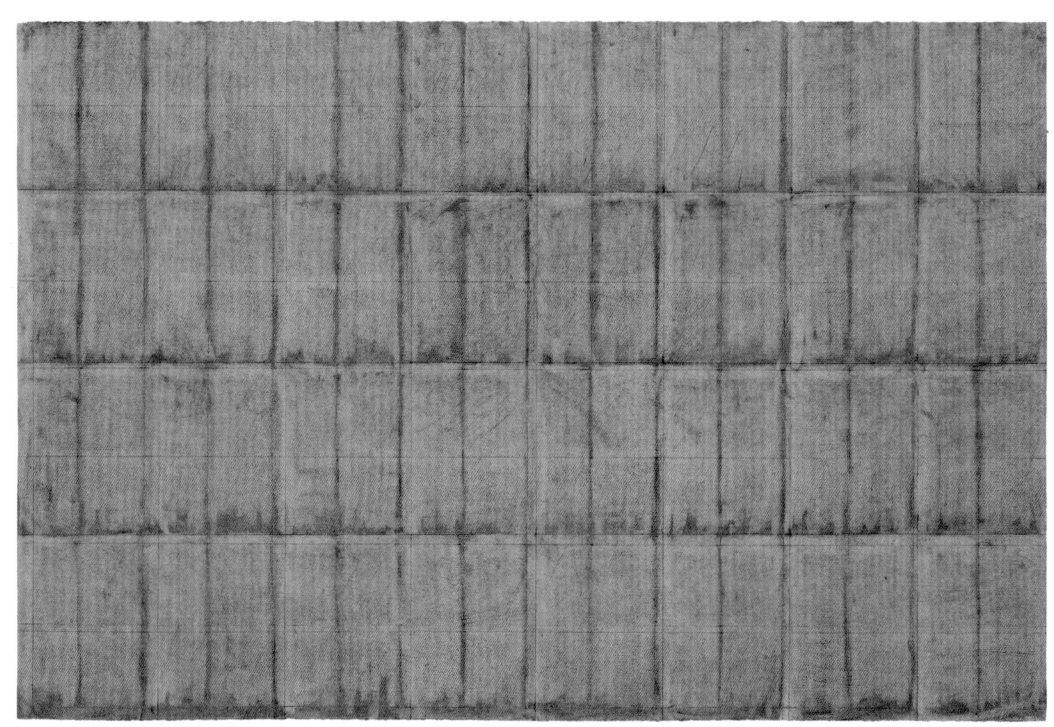

9. Untitled. 1964
Graphite and charcoal on paper
26 x 40" (66 x 101.6 cm)

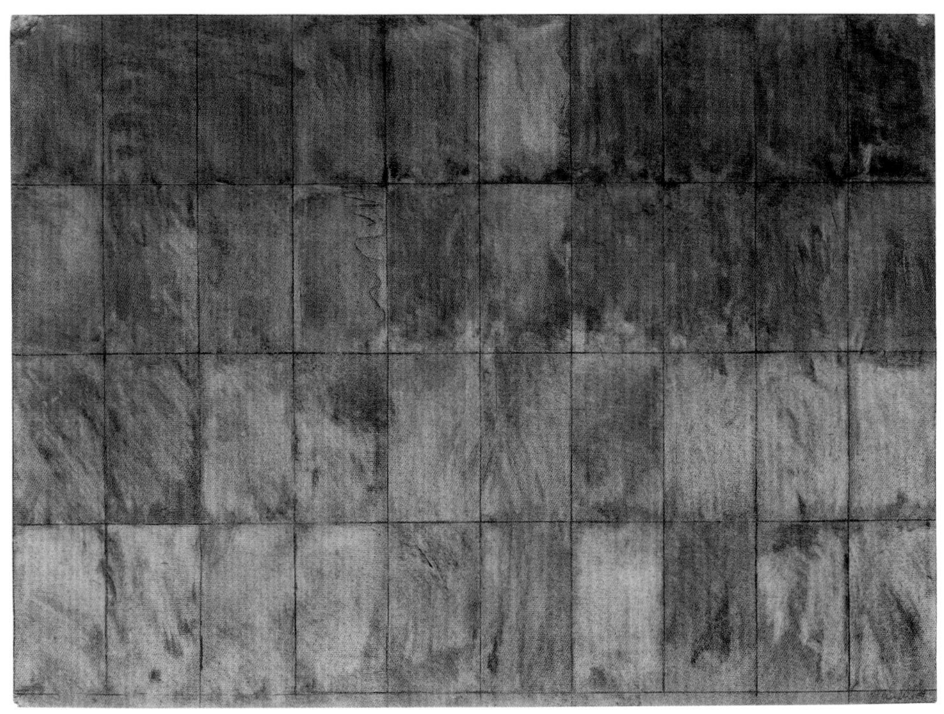

10. Untitled. 1964
Charcoal and graphite on paper
21¾ x 29½" (55.2 x 74.9 cm)

11. Untitled. 1964–65
Graphite and beeswax on paper
22 x 30" (55.9 x 76.2 cm)

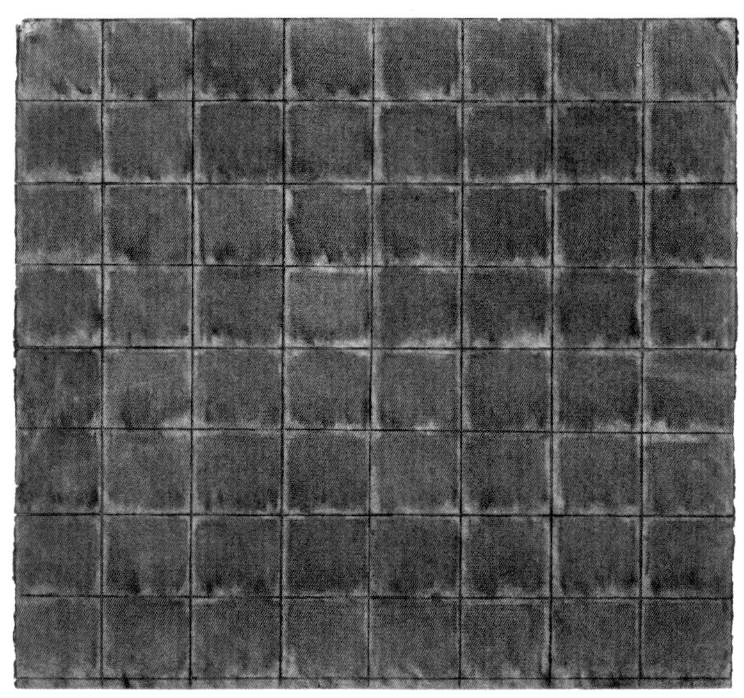

12. Untitled. 1964–65
Charcoal on paper
$19^{3}/_{4}$ x $22^{1}/_{4}$" (50.2 x 56.5 cm)

13. *Return I.* 1964–65
Oil on canvas
50¼ x 68¼" (127.6 x 173.4 cm)

14. *Teddy's Drawing*. 1964–65
Graphite and beeswax over silkscreen on paper
40 x 26" (101.6 x 66 cm)

15. *Nebraska*. 1966
Oil and beeswax on canvas
58 x 72" (147.3 x 182.9 cm)

16. *Nico.* 1966
Oil and beeswax on canvas
68" x 8' 4" (172.7 x 254 cm)

17. *The Dylan Painting.* 1966/1986
Oil and beeswax on canvas
60" x 10' (152.4 x 304.8 cm)

18. *Two Part Study*. 1966
Oil and beeswax on canvas
Two panels, overall: 26 x 30" (66 x 76 cm)

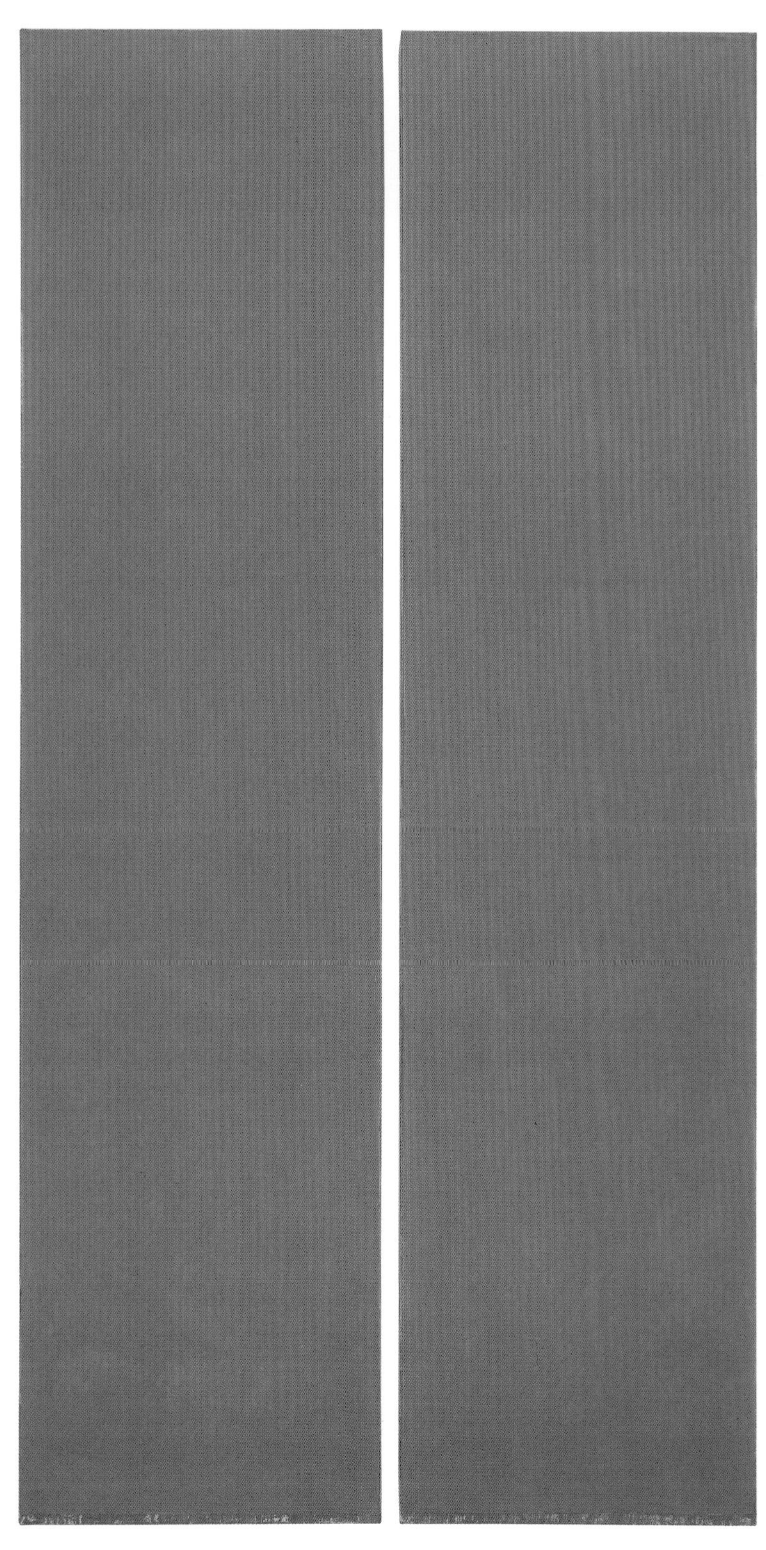

19. *For Helen*. 1967
Oil and beeswax on canvas
Two panels, overall: 69 x 36" (175 x 91 cm)

20. *Patent Leather Valentine*. 1967
Graphite and beeswax over pastel on paper
16½ x 14¾" (41.9 x 37.5 cm)

21. *Two Studies, Back Series*. 1967
Graphite over pastel on paper
23 x 31" (58.4 x 78.7 cm)

22. *For Me (Back Series)*. 1967–68
Oil and beeswax on canvas
69 x 45" (175.3 x 114.3 cm)

23. *For Otis (Back Series).* 1967–68
Oil and beeswax on canvas
69 x 45" (175.3 x 114.3 cm)

24. Untitled. 1964–67
Graphite, ink, and beeswax on paper
26 x 40" (66 x 101.6 cm)

25. Untitled. 1968
Graphite and oil pastel on paper
26 x 40" (66 x 101.6 cm)

26. Untitled. 1968
Graphite and beeswax on paper
22 x 30" (55.9 x 76.2 cm)

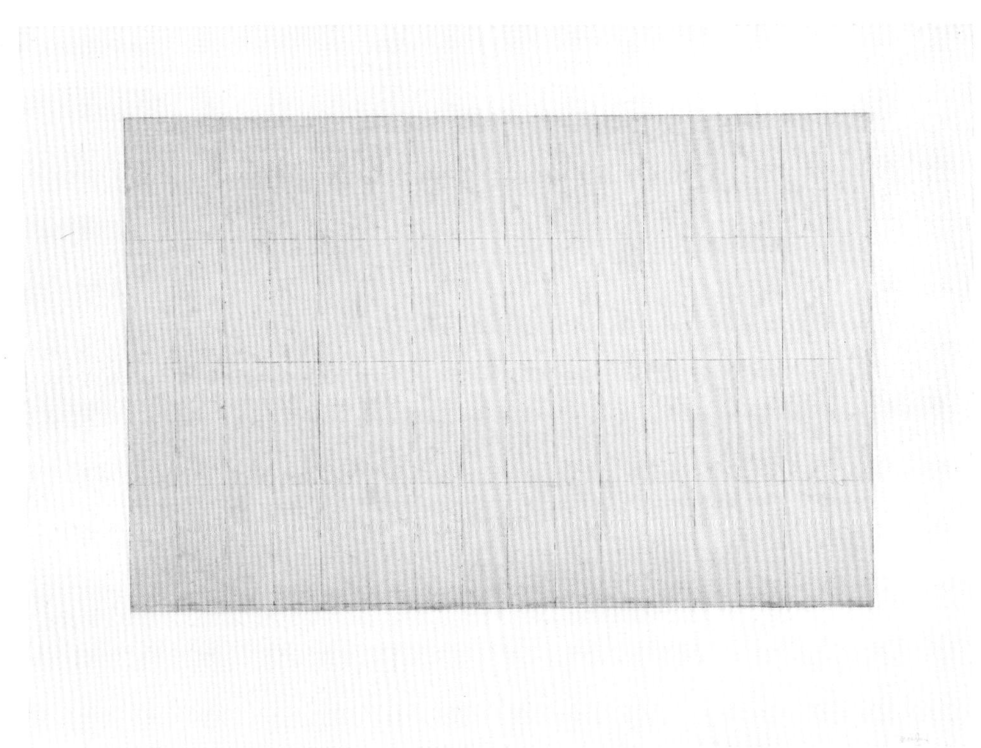

27. Untitled. 1968
Oil crayon, pastel, and graphite on paper
22½ x 30½" (57.2 x 77.5 cm)

28. *Fave*. 1968–69
Oil and beeswax on canvas
Two panels, overall: 72" x 66" (182.8 x 167.6 cm)

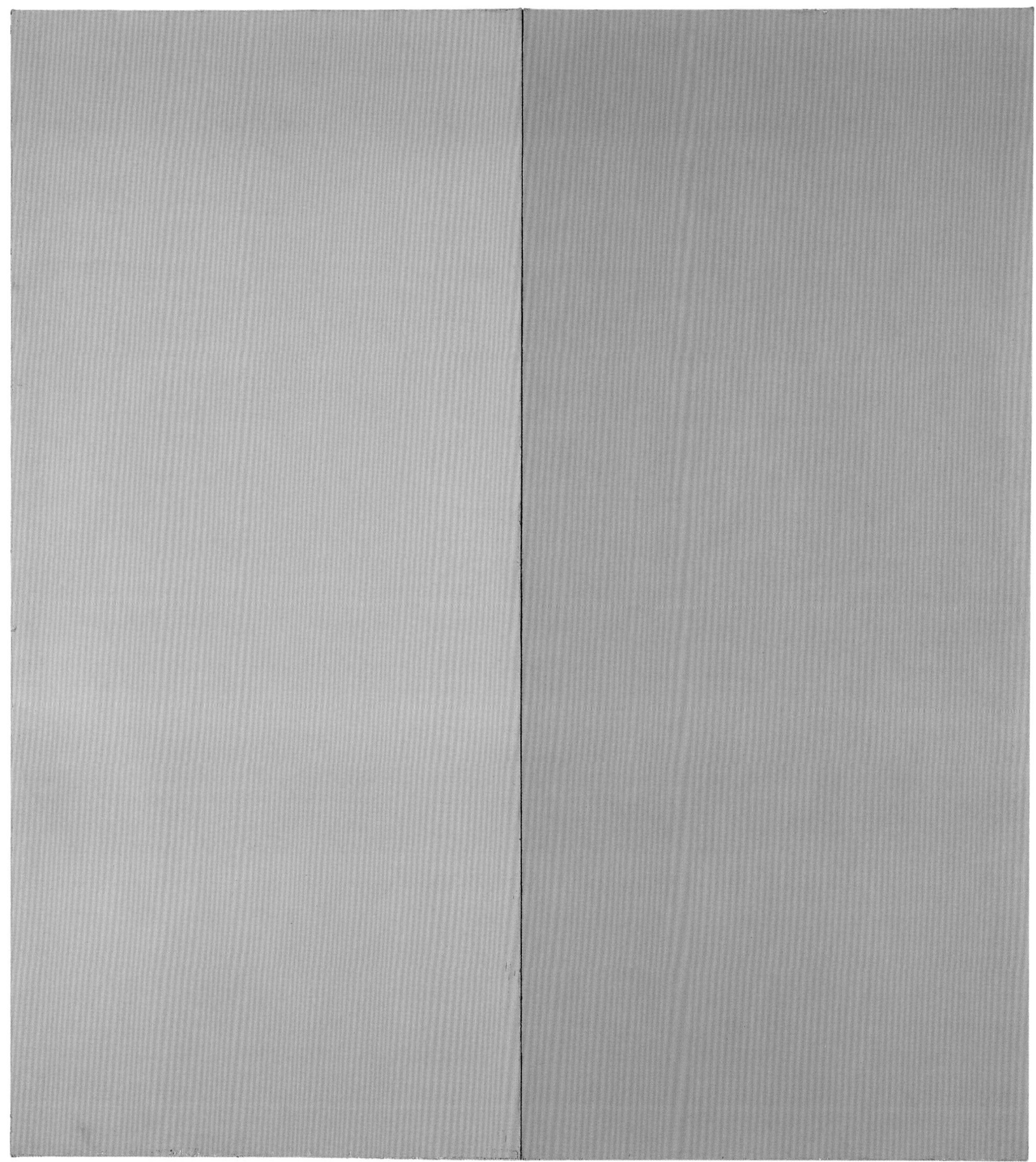

29. *Point.* 1969
Oil and beeswax on canvas
Three panels, overall: 53" x 8' 9" (134.5 x 267 cm)

30. *D'après la Marquise de la Solana*. 1969
Oil and beeswax on canvas
Three panels, overall: 6' 5 5/8" x 9' 9 3/8" (196 x 297 cm)

31. *Three Deliberate Greys for Jasper Johns.* 1970
Oil and beeswax on canvas
Three panels, overall: 72" x 12' 6" (183 x 381 cm)

32. Untitled. 1970
Graphite and beeswax on paper
Two sheets, overall: 40 x 50" (101.6 x 127 cm)

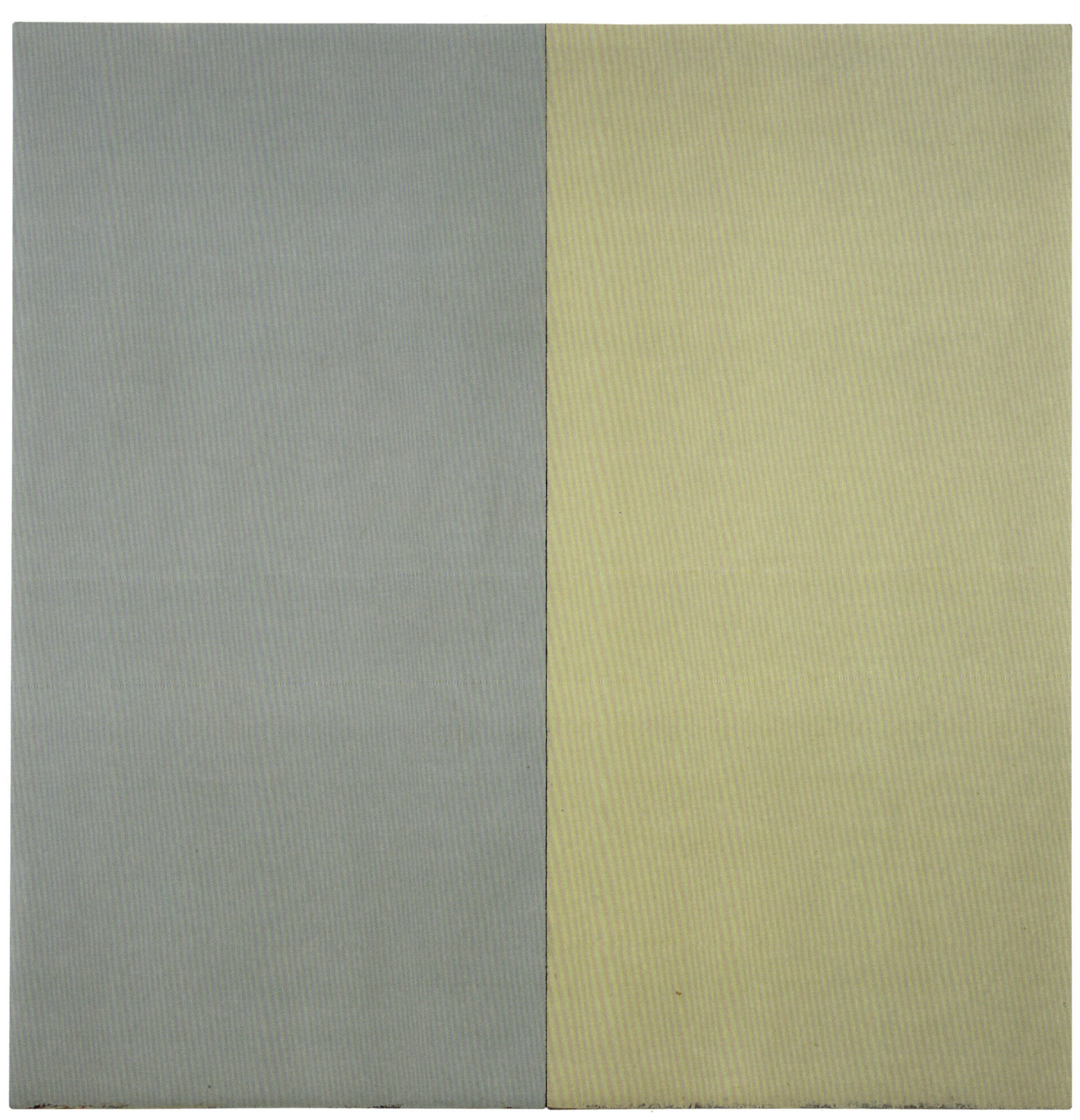

33. *Toward Brindisi.* 1972
Oil and beeswax on canvas
Two panels, overall: 72 x 72" (182.9 x 182.9 cm)

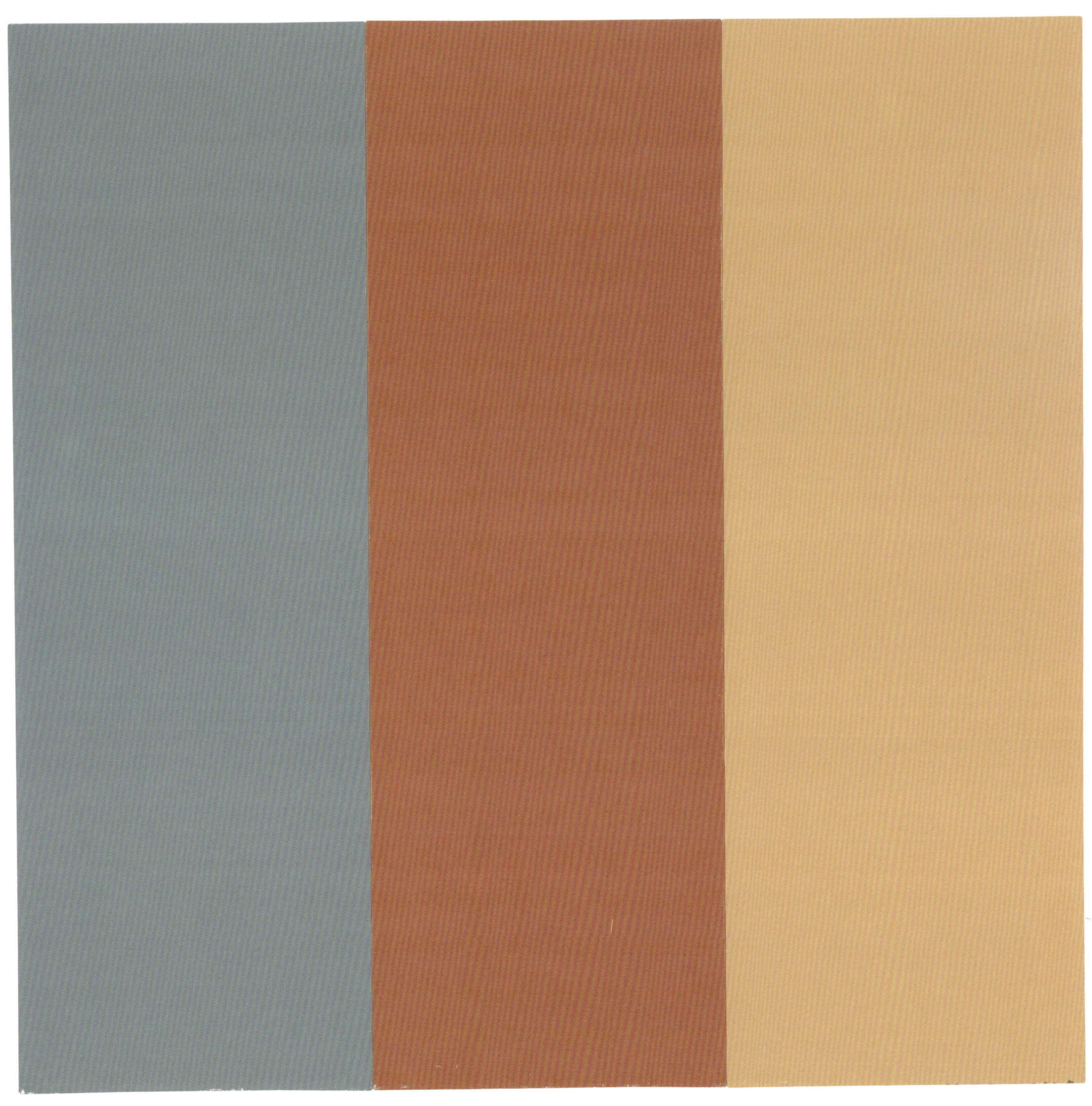

34. *For Pearl*. 1970
Oil and beeswax on canvas
Three panels, overall: 8' x 8' 2 1/4" (243.8 x 249.6 cm)

35. *Rodeo.* 1971
Oil and beeswax on canvas
Two panels, overall: 8 x 8' (243.8 x 243.8 cm)

36. *Summer Table.* 1972–73
Oil and beeswax on canvas
Three panels, overall:
60" x 8' 9¼" (152.4 x 267.3 cm)

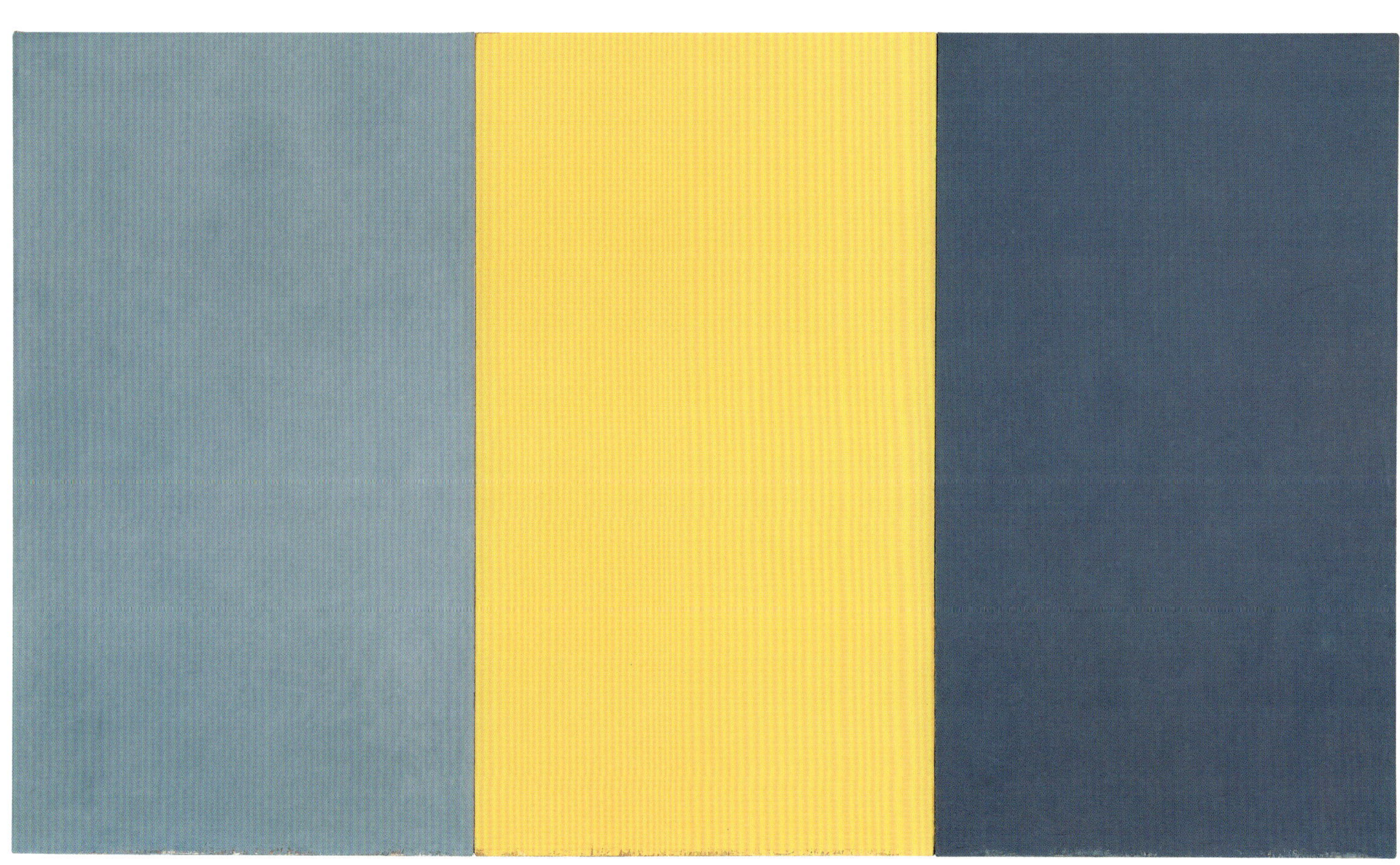

37. *Star (for Patti Smith).* 1972/1974
Oil and beeswax on canvas
Three panels, overall: 68 x 45" (173 x 114 cm)

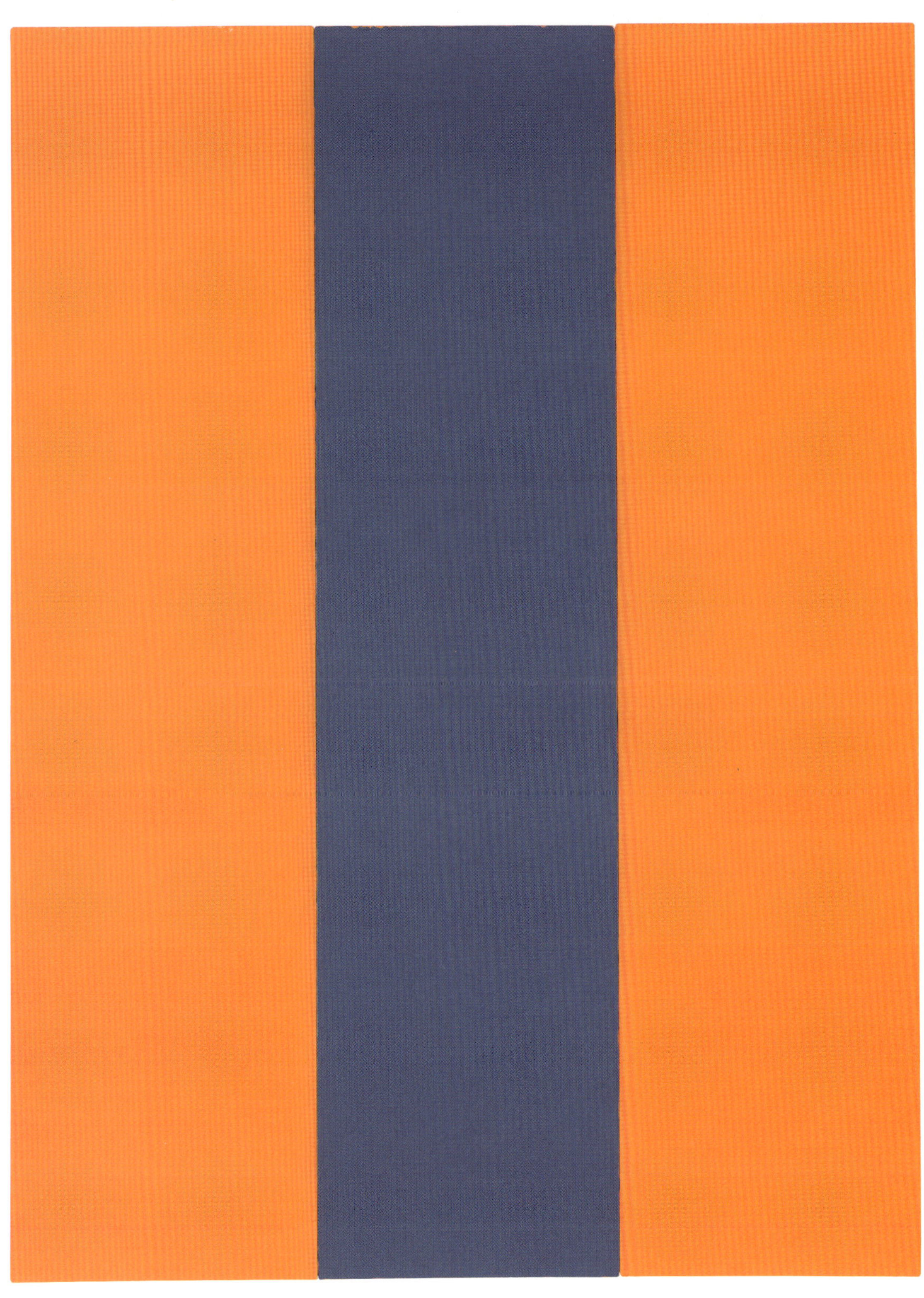

38. *Pumpkin Plumb*. 1970/1973
Oil and beeswax on canvas
Three panels, overall: 69 x 51¼" (175 x 130 cm)

39. Untitled. 1972
Graphite and beeswax on paper
22 x 30" (55.9 x 76.2 cm)

40. *Adriatic.* 1972–73
Oil and beeswax on canvas
Two panels, overall: 6' 1/16" x 9' 7/16" (183 x 275.4 cm)

44. *Grove Group 4.* 1972
Graphite and beeswax on paper
22 x 30" (55.9 x 76.2 cm)

40. *Adriatic.* 1972–73
Oil and beeswax on canvas
Two panels, overall: 6' 1/16" x 9' 7/16" (183 x 275.4 cm)

41. *Grove Group 1.* 1972
Graphite and beeswax on paper
22 x 30" (55.9 x 76.2 cm)

42. *Grove Group 2.* 1972
Graphite and beeswax on paper
22 x 30" (55.9 x 76.2 cm)

43. *Grove Group 3.* 1972
Graphite and beeswax on paper
22 x 30" (55.9 x 76.2 cm)

44. *Grove Group 4.* 1972
Graphite and beeswax on paper
22 x 30" (55.9 x 76.2 cm)

45. *Grove Group 5.* 1972
Graphite and beeswax on paper
22 x 30" (55.9 x 76.2 cm)

46. *Grove Group I.* 1972–73
Oil and beeswax on canvas
72" x 9' (182.9 x 274.3 cm)

47. *Grove Group II.* 1972–73
Oil and beeswax on canvas
Two panels, overall: 72" x 9' (182.9 x 274.3 cm)

48. *Grove Group IV*. 1976
Oil and beeswax on canvas
Two panels, overall: 72" x 9' (182.9 x 274.3 cm)

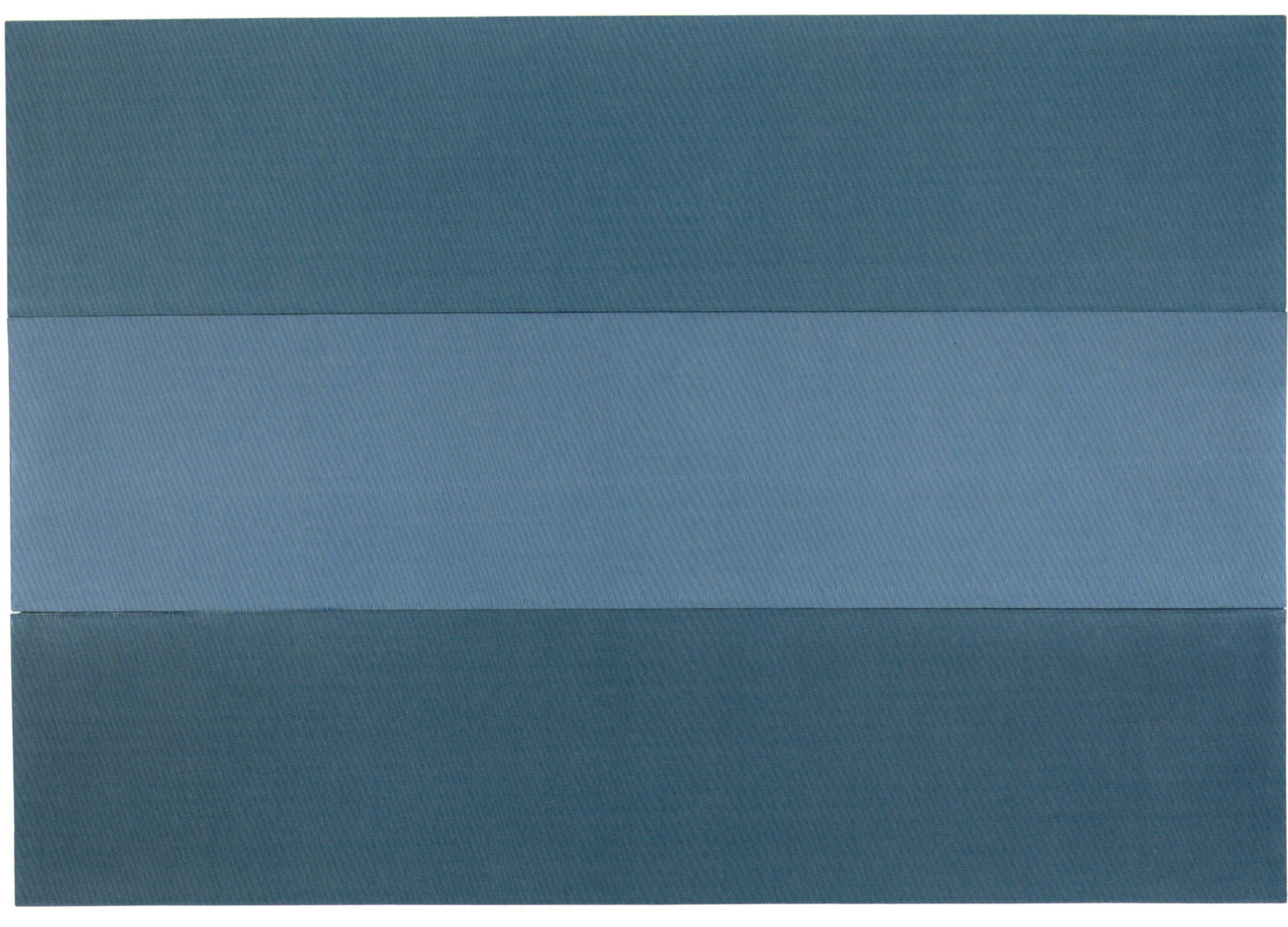

49. *Grove Group V.* 1976
Oil and beeswax on canvas
Three panels, overall: 72" x 9' (182.9 x 274.3 cm)

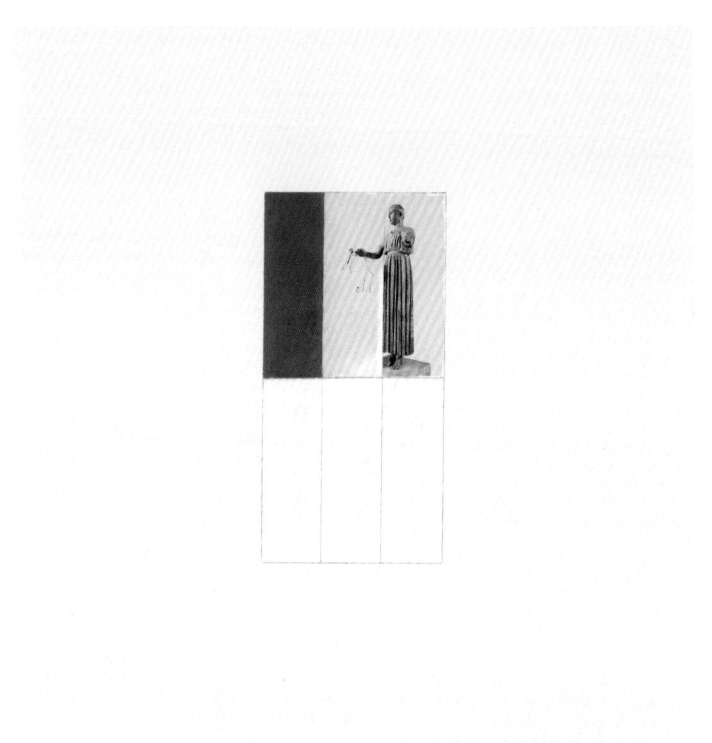

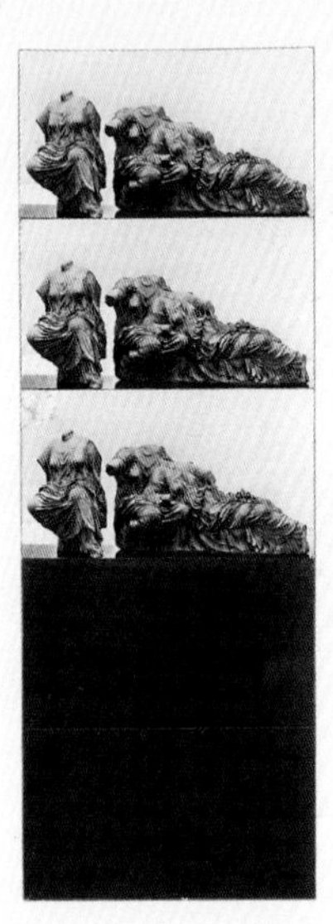

50. *Grove Addenda II.* 1973
Collage, graphite, and beeswax on paper
30 x 22" (76.2 x 55.9 cm)

51. *Grove Addenda III.* 1973–74
Collage, graphite, and beeswax on paper
30 x 22¾" (76.2 x 57.8 cm)

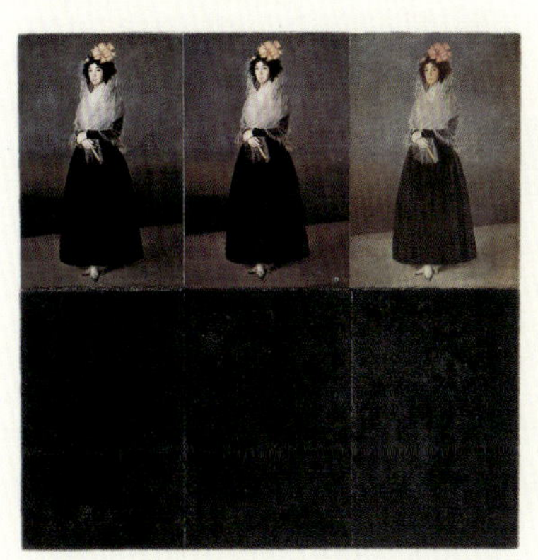

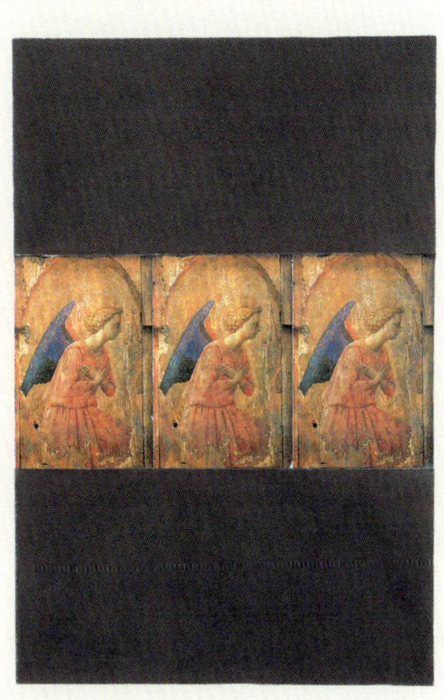

52. *Homage to Art 2 (Goya).* 1973
Graphite, beeswax, and collage on paper
30¼ x 22¾" (76.8 x 57.8 cm)

53. *Homage to Art 14 (Fra Angelico).* 1974
Graphite, beeswax, and collage on paper
30¼ x 20¾" (76.8 x 52.7 cm)

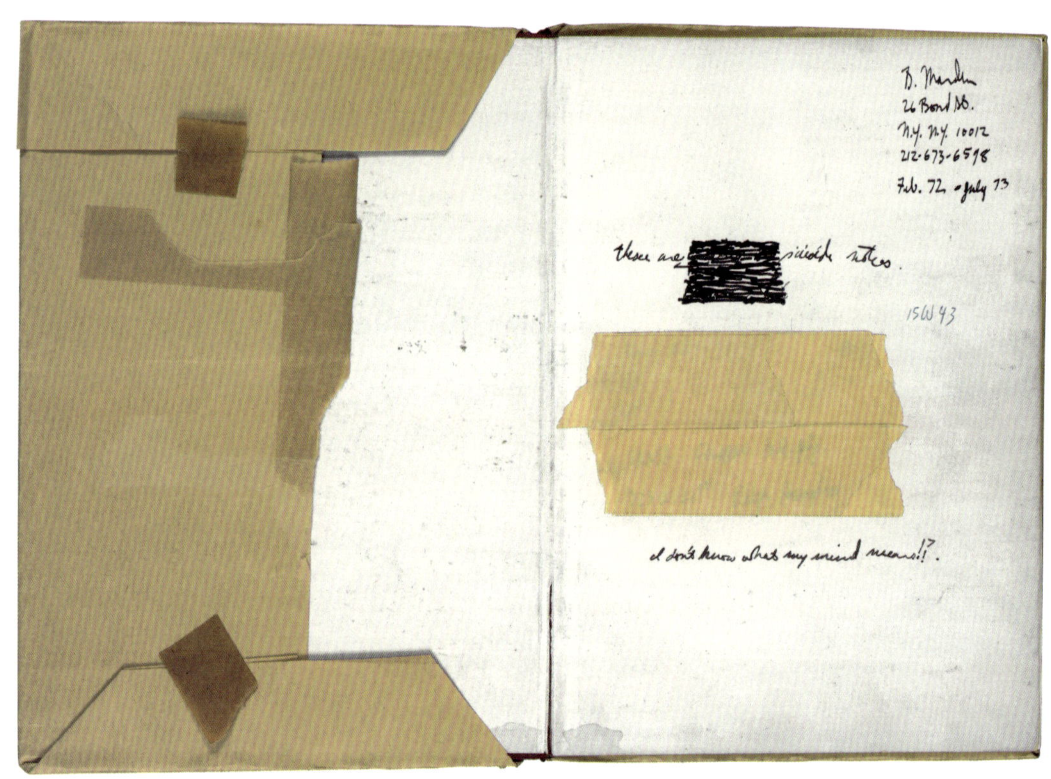

54. *Suicide Notes*. February 1972–July 1973
Brown-paper-covered notebook, ink on paper
Twenty-eight sheets, 12¼ x 8¾" (31.1 x 22.2 cm)

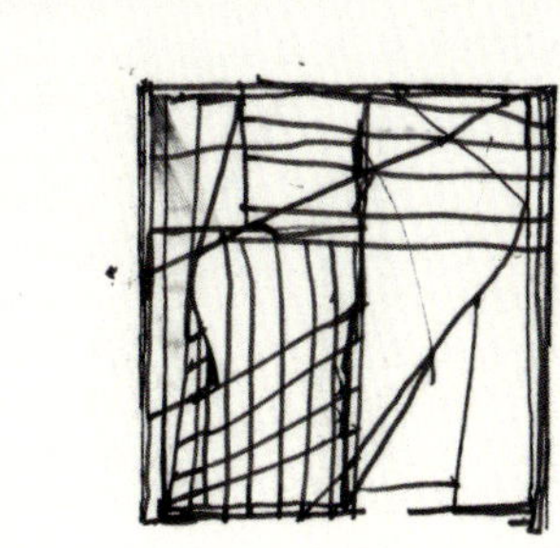

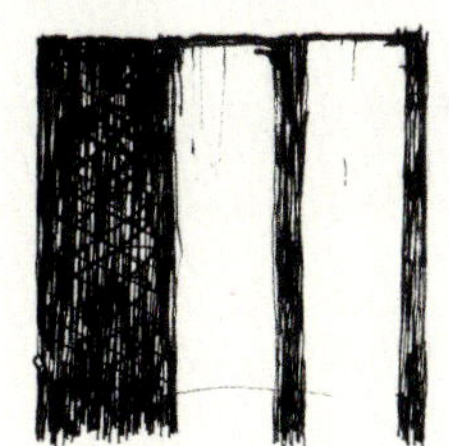

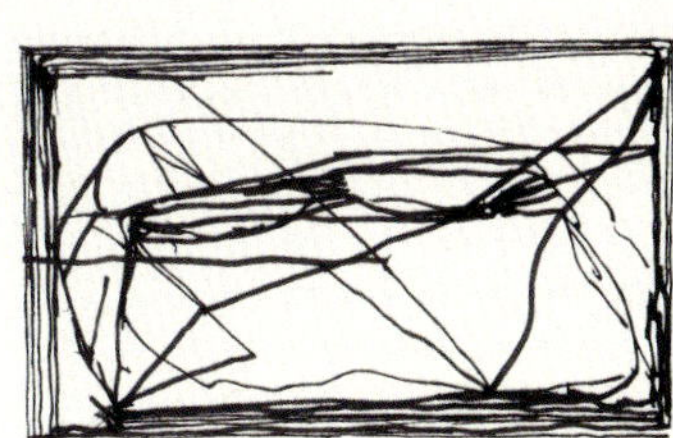

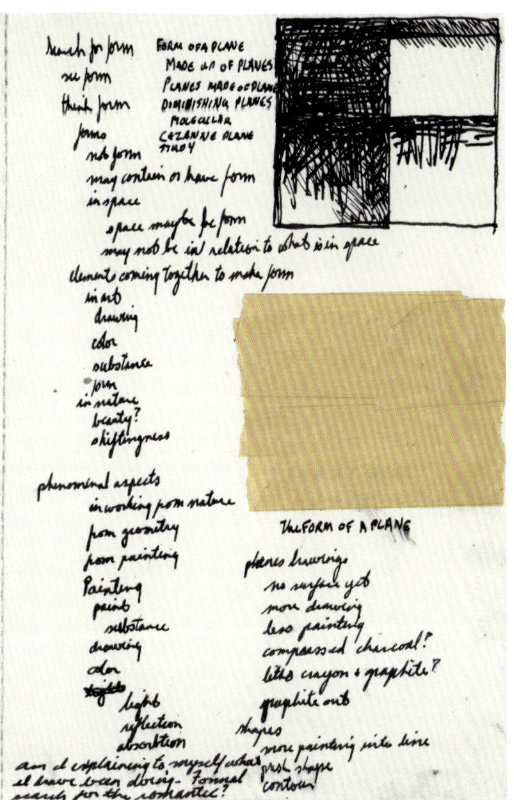

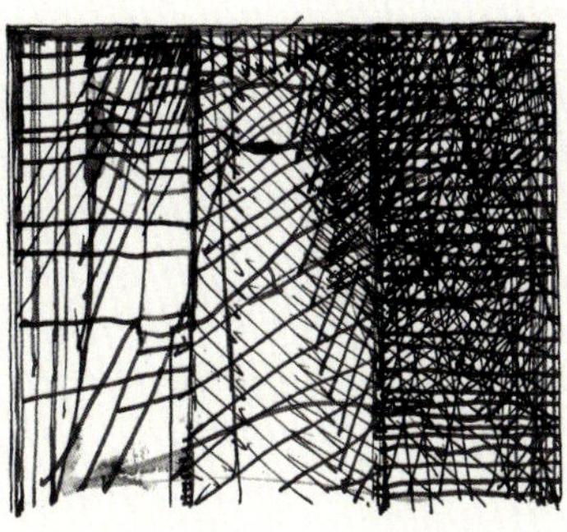

55–60. Suicide Notes. February 1972–July 1973
Sheets from notebook, ink on paper
11¾ x 7¾" (29.8 x 19.7 cm). 55, 56, 59: bound in notebook. 57, 58, 60: separated from notebook

61. *First Figure (Homage to Courbet)*. 1973–74
Oil and beeswax on canvas
Three panels, overall: 6' 3" x 30" (190.5 x 76.2 cm)

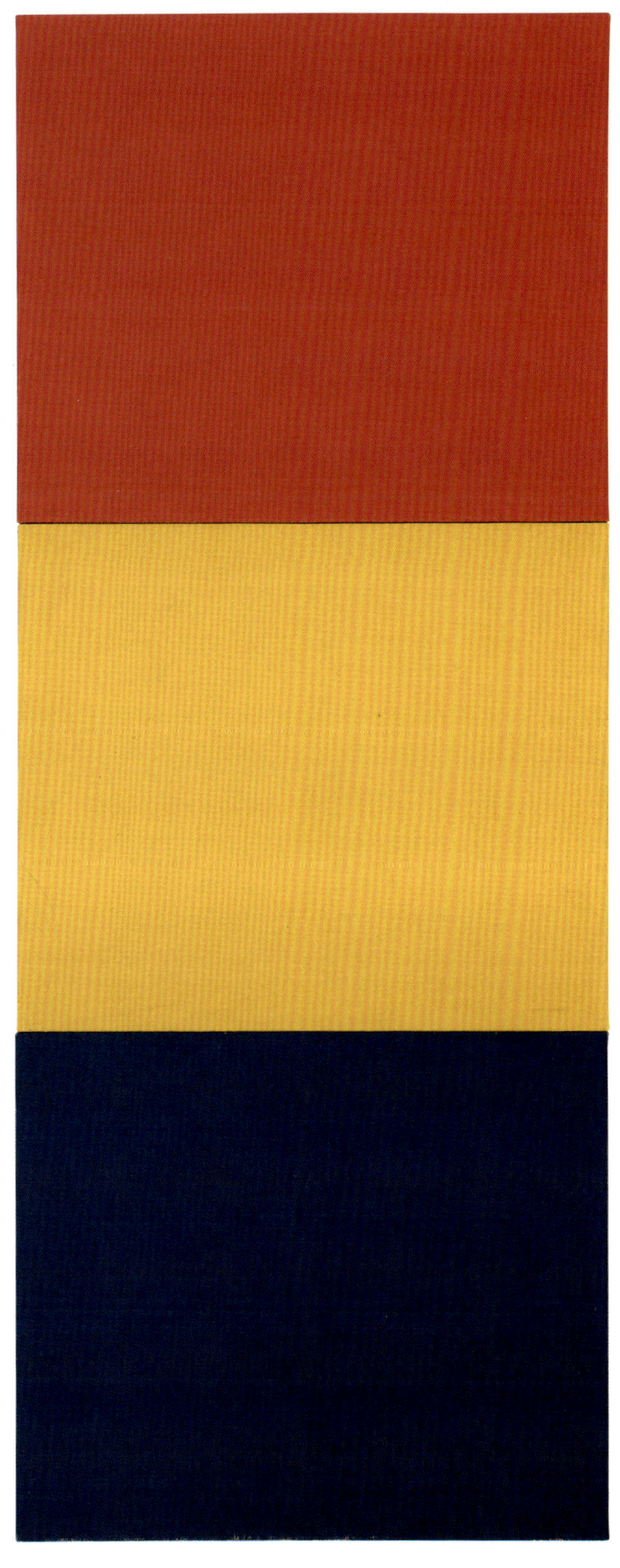

62. *Fourth Figure (Red Yellow Blue).* 1973–74
Oil and beeswax on canvas
Three panels, overall: 6' 3" x 30" (190.5 x 76.2 cm)

63. *Red Yellow Blue II.* 1974
Oil and beeswax on canvas
Three panels, overall: 6' 2" x 72" (188 x 182.9 cm)

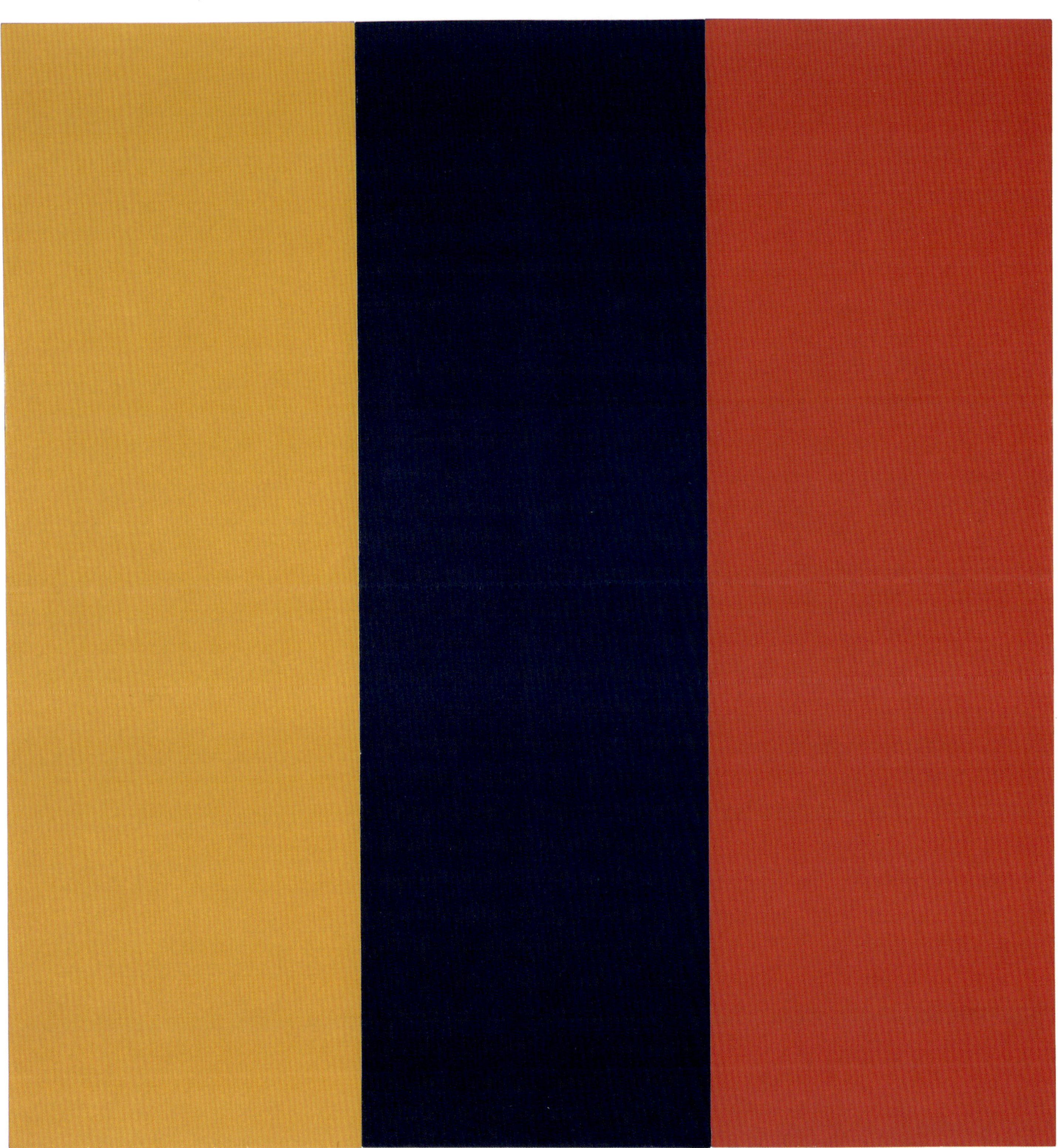

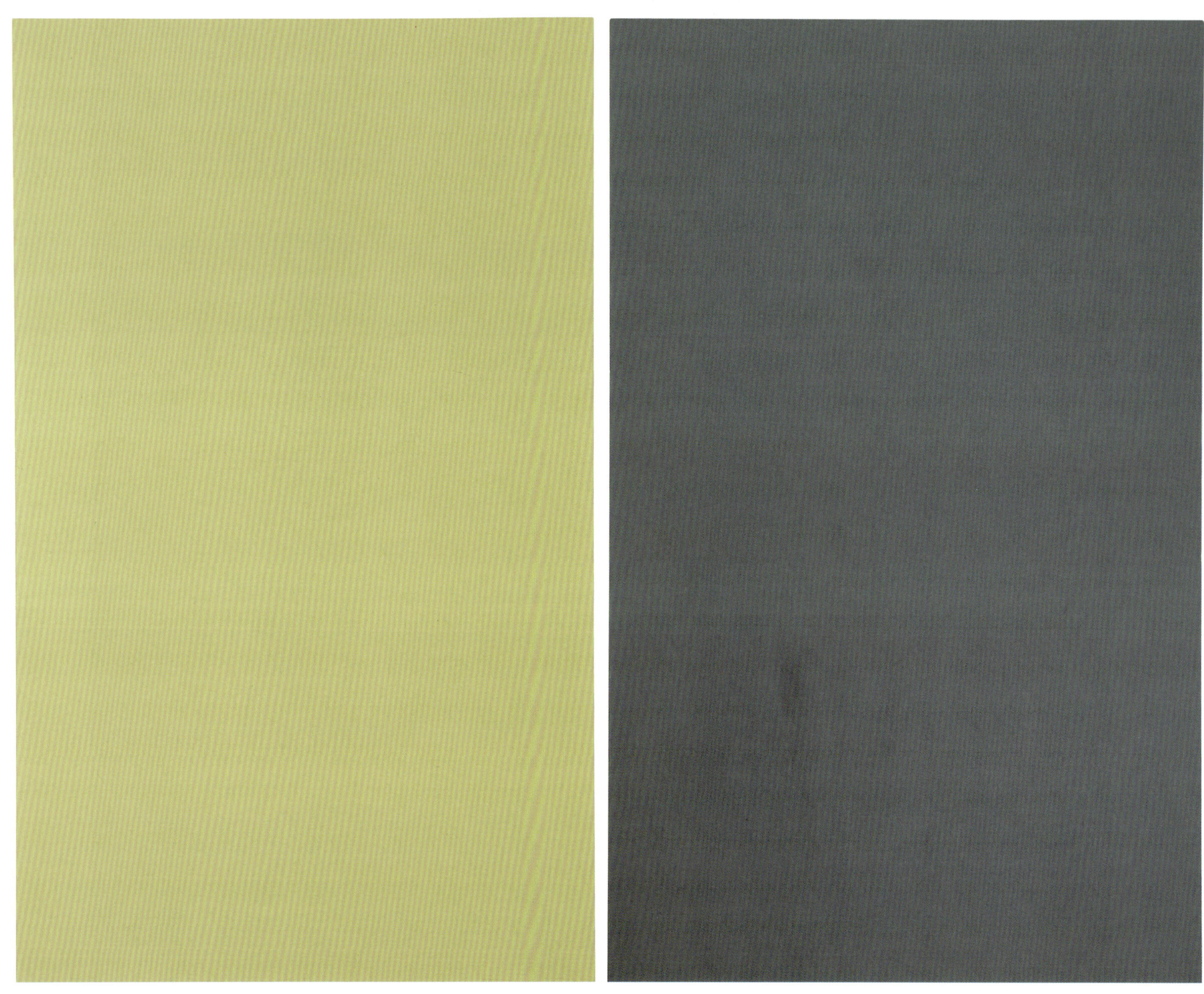

64. *The Seasons*. 1974–75
Oil and beeswax on canvas
four panels, overall: 8' x 20' 9" (243.8 x 632.5 cm)

65. *Winter Painting.* 1973–75
Oil and beeswax on canvas
Three panels, each (left to right):
72 x 60" (183 x 152 cm), 72 x 30" (183 x 76 cm),
72 x 30" (183 x 76 cm),
overall: 72" x 10' (183 x 305 cm)

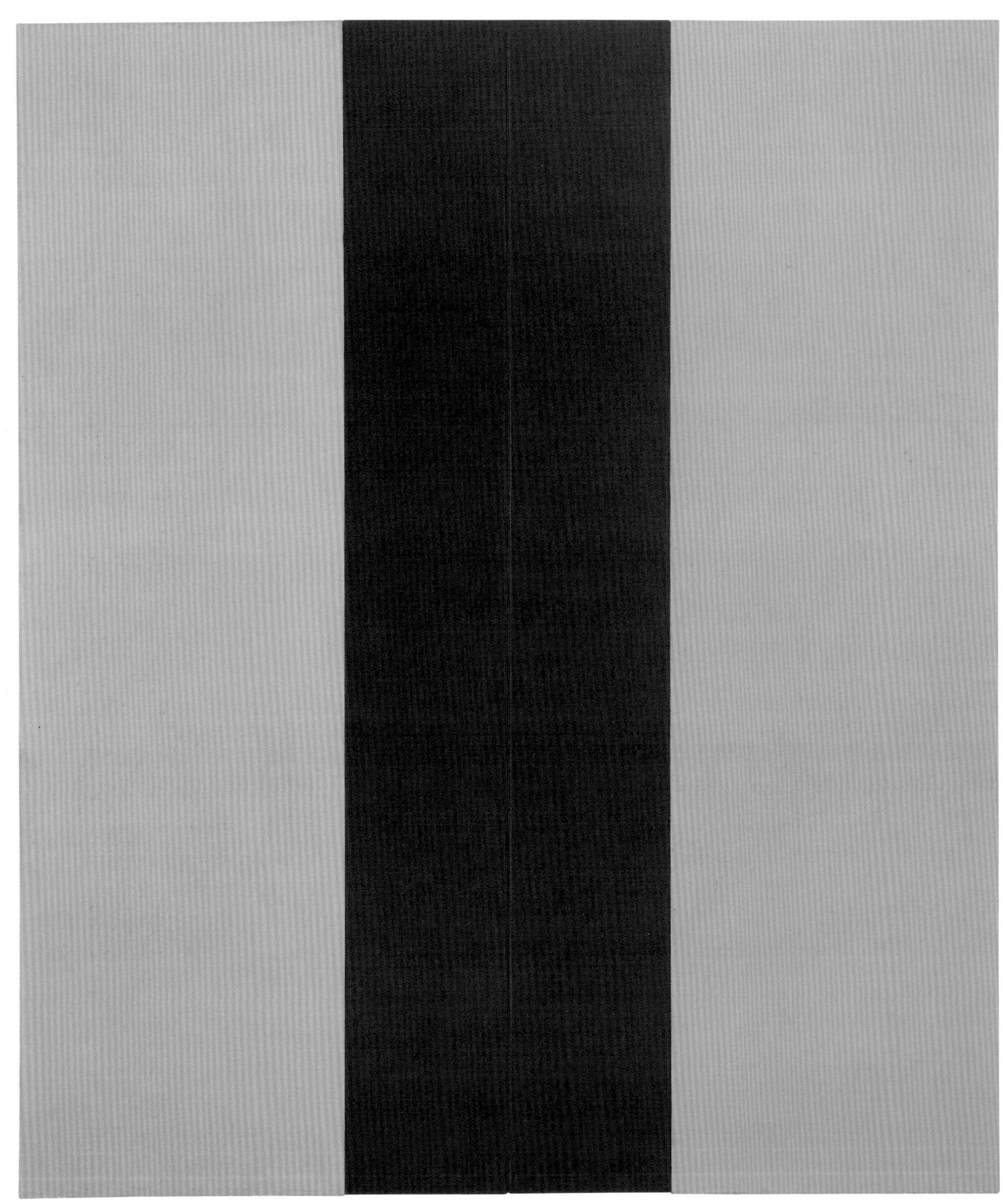

66. *Lethykos (for Tonto).* 1976
Oil and beeswax on canvas
Four panels, each (left to right):
7' x 24" (213.4 x 61 cm), 7' x 12" (213.4 x 30.5 cm),
7' x 12" (213.4 x 30.5 cm), 7' x 24" (213.4 x 61 cm),
overall: 7' x 72" (213.4 x 182.9 cm)

67. *Morada.* 1976
Oil and beeswax on canvas
Four panels, each (left to right):
7' x 24" (213 x 61 cm), 7' x 12" (213 x 30.5 cm),
7' x 12" (213 x 30.5 cm), 7' x 24" (213 x 61 cm),
overall: 7' x 72" (213.4 x 182.9 cm)

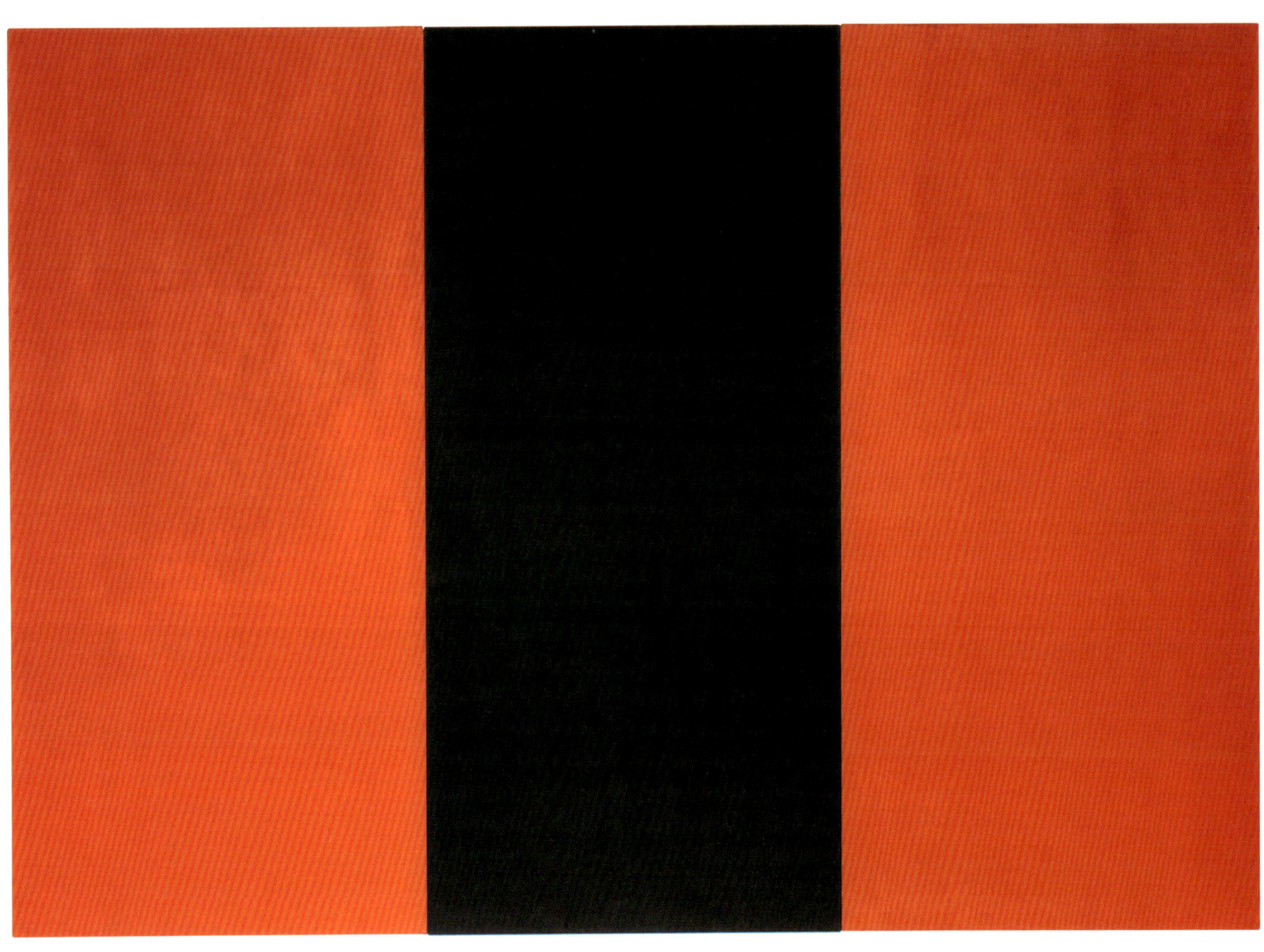

68. *For Hera.* 1977
Oil and beeswax on canvas
Three panels, overall: 7 x 10' (213.4 x 304.8 cm)

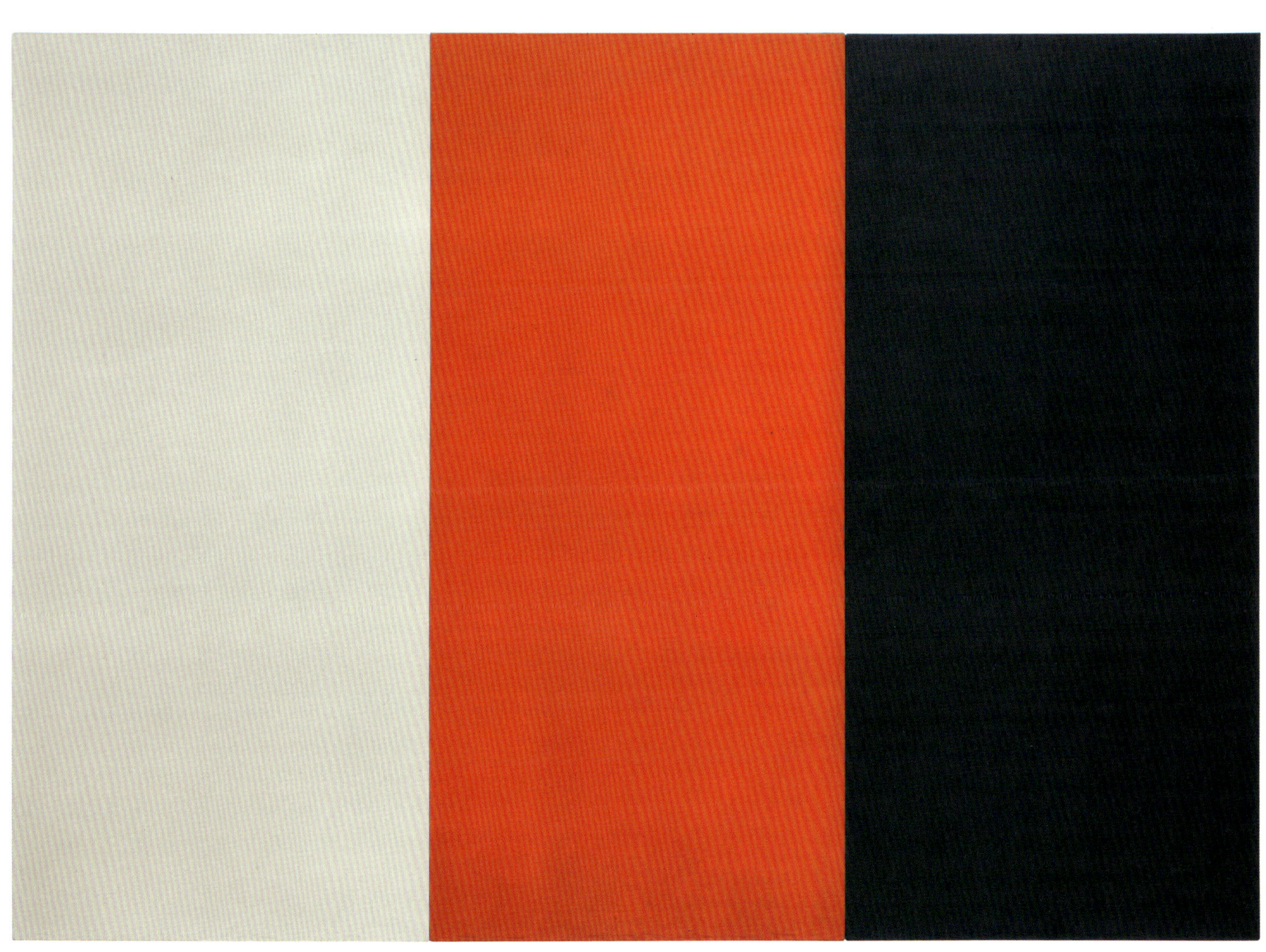

69. *Moon III.* 1977
Oil and beeswax on canvas
Three panels, overall: 7 x 10' (213.4 x 304.8 cm)

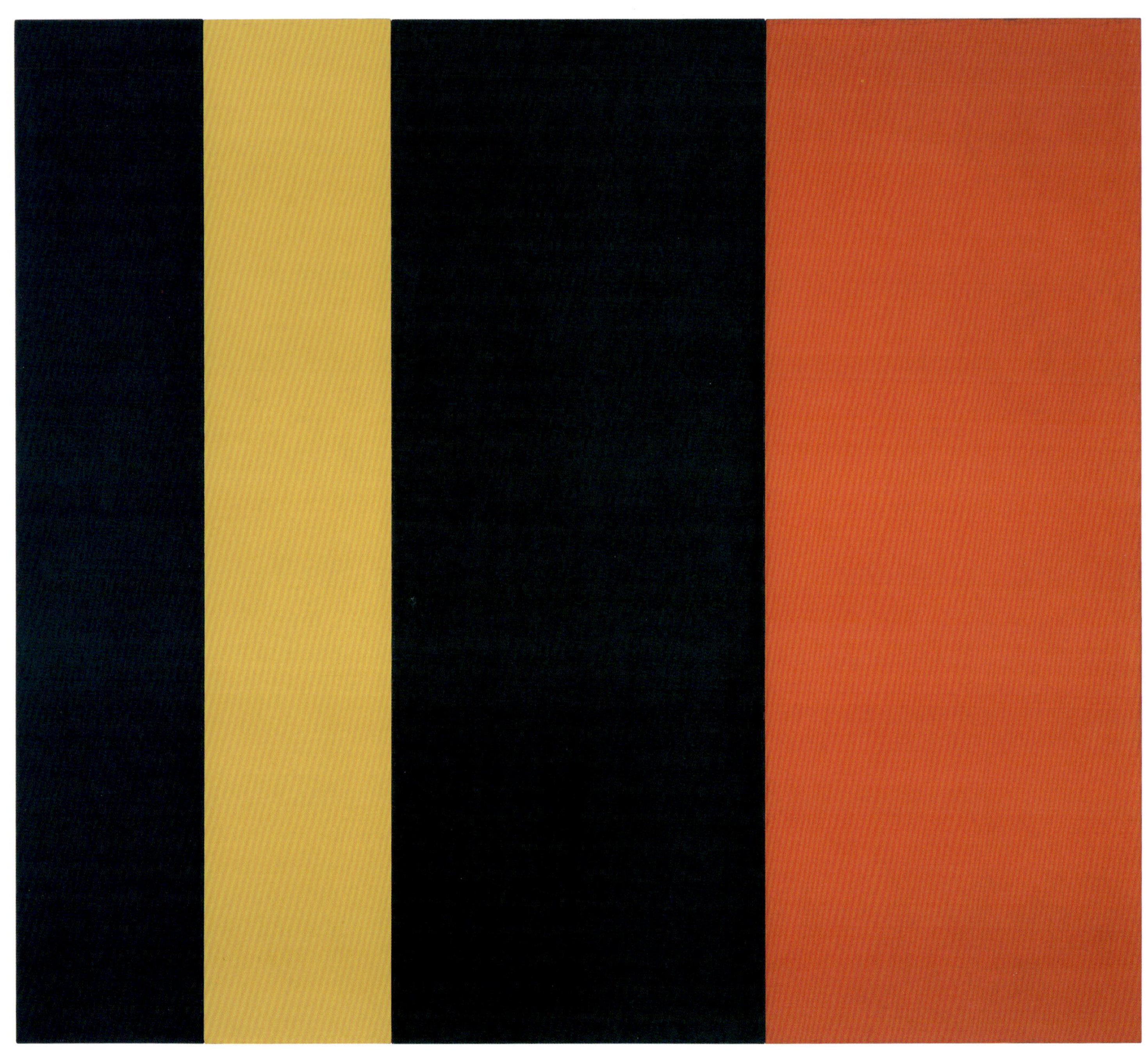

70. *Conturbatio.* 1978
Oil and beeswax on canvas
Four panels, each (left to right):
two panels 7' x 16" (213.4 x 40.6 cm),
two panels 7' x 32" (213.4 x 81.3 cm),
overall: 7' x 8' (213.4 x 243.8 cm)

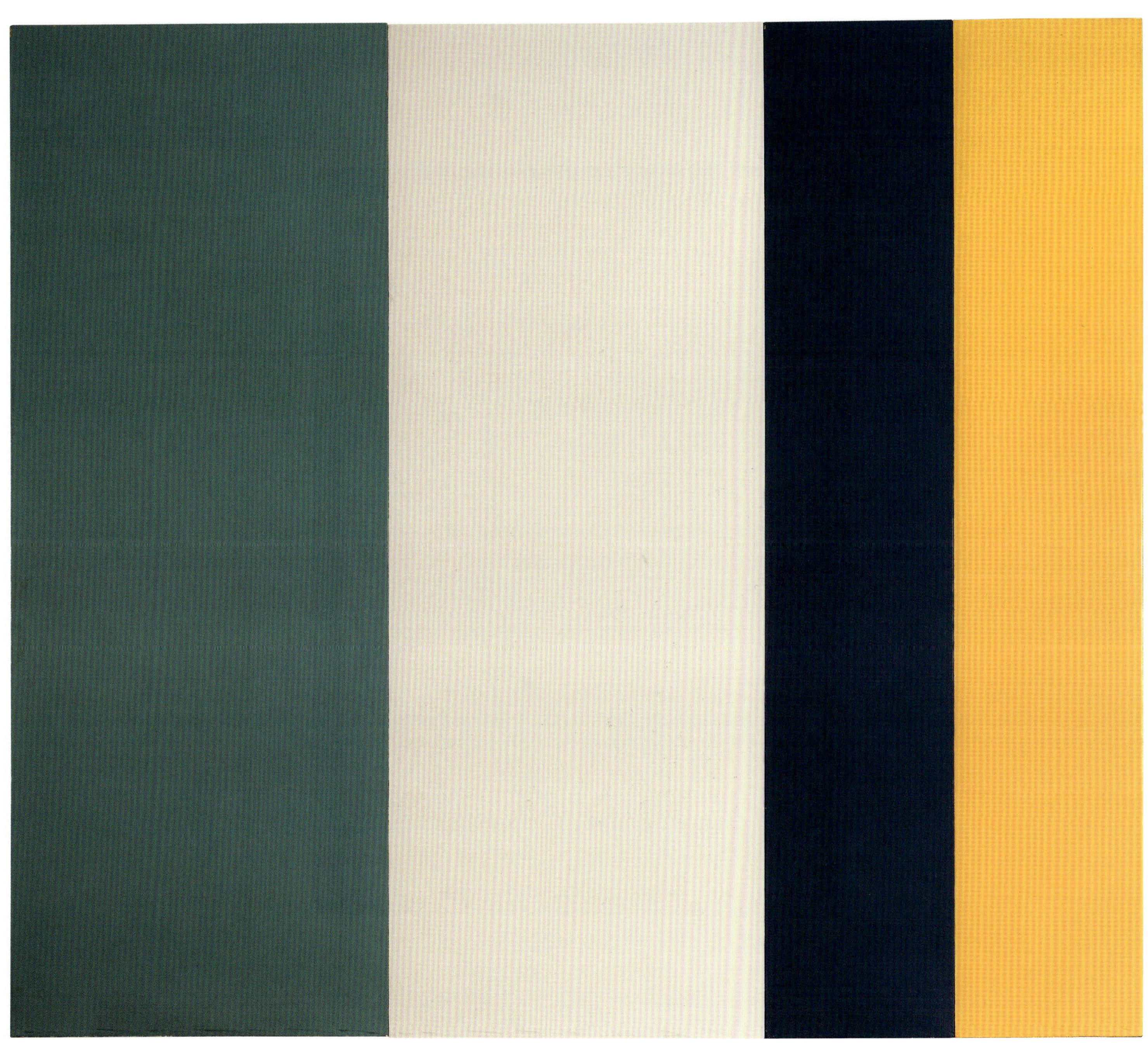

71. *Meritatio.* 1978
Oil and beeswax on canvas
Four panels, each (left to right):
two panels 7' x 32" (213.4 x 81.3 cm),
two panels 7' x 16" (213.4 x 40.6 cm),
overall: 7' x 8' (213.4 x 243.8 cm)

72. *Study for the N Drawing.* 1975
Graphite and beeswax on paper
30 3/8 x 22 1/4" (77.2 x 56.5 cm)

73. *Inside Outside*. 1977
Graphite and beeswax on paper
Two sheets, overall: 30 x 44½" (76.2 x 113 cm)

74. *Mosaic Study #3.* 1978
Graphite, oil, and beeswax on paper
30¼ x 22¼" (76.8 x 56.5 cm)

75. *Mosaic Study #4.* 1978
Graphite, oil, and beeswax on paper
30¼ x 22¼" (76.8 x 56.5 cm)

76. *Mosaic Study #5.* 1978
Graphite and beeswax on paper
30¾ x 22¼" (78.1 x 56.5 cm)

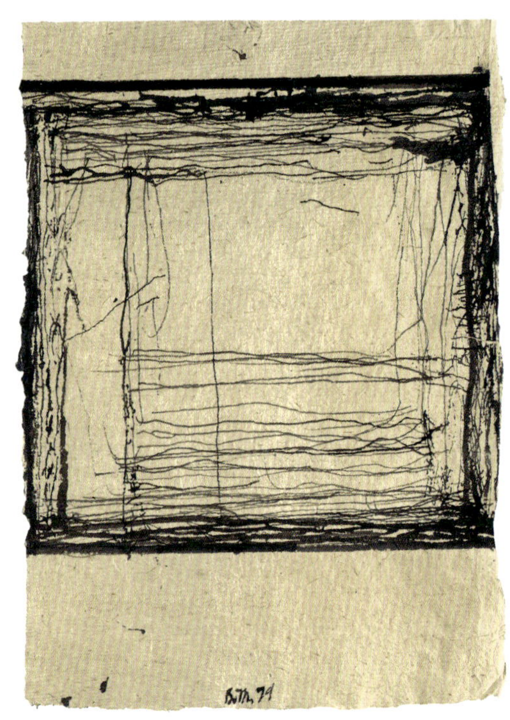

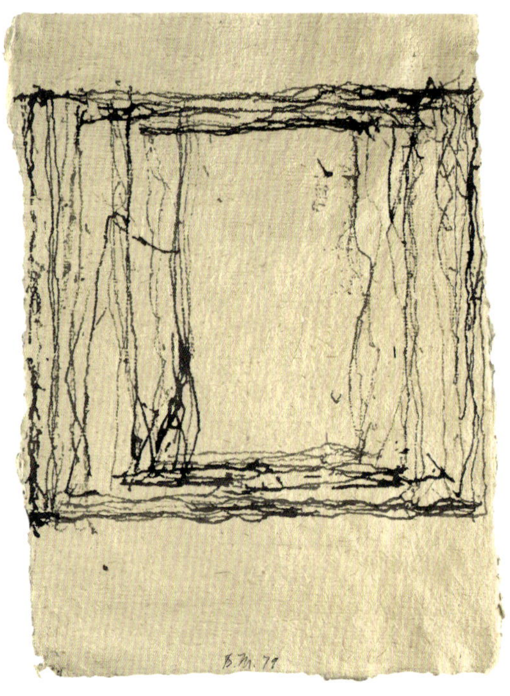

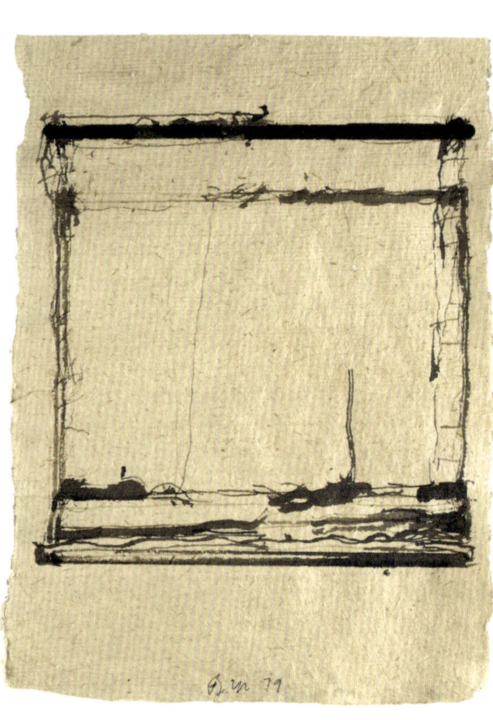

77–82. Mirabelle Addenda 1–9. 1979
All ink on paper
Nos. 3–5, 6, 7, and 9 of nine sheets,
ranging from 9³/₁₆" to 9¹/₄"
(23.3 to 23.5 cm) vertically and from
6³/₄" to 7¹/₄" (17.1 to 18.4 cm) horizontally

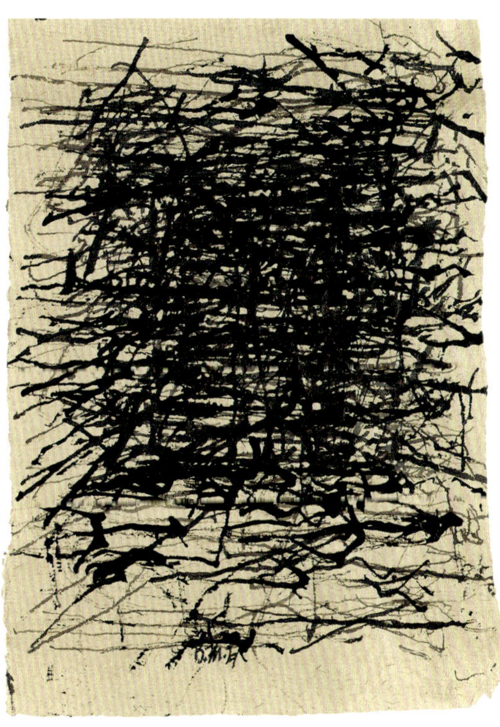

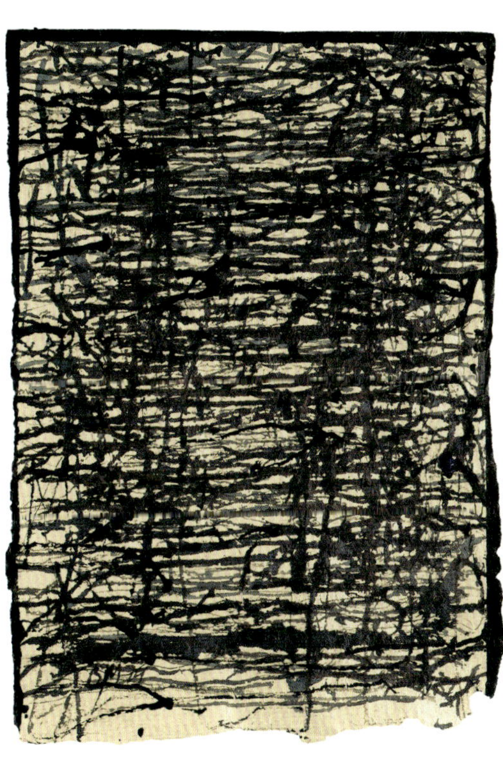

83. *Thira.* 1979–80
Oil and beeswax on canvas
Eighteen panels assembled in three parts,
overall: 8 x 15' (243.8 x 457.2 cm)

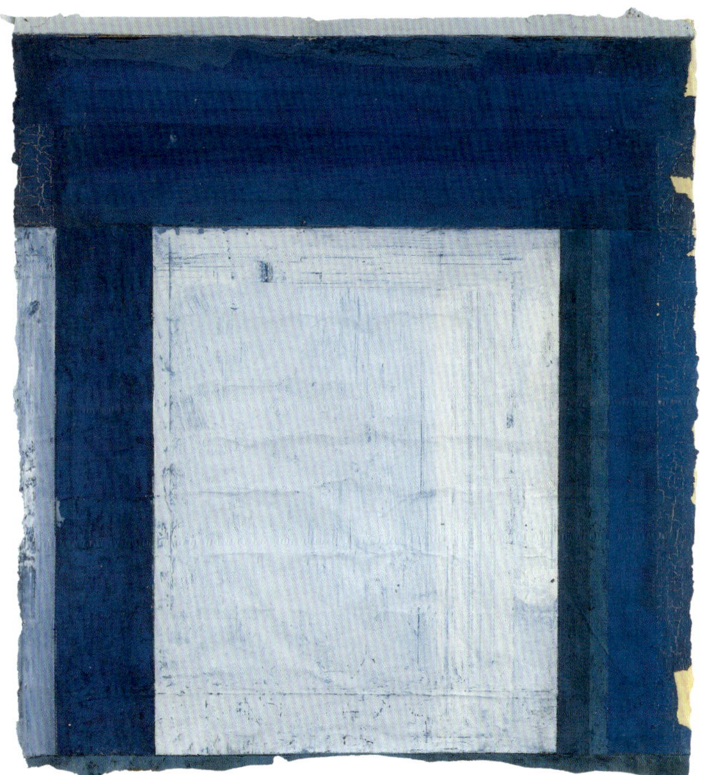

84. *Hydra Group II.* 1979–81
Oil on paper
19½ x 18¾" (49.5 x 47.6 cm)

85. *Hydra Group X.* 1979–81
Oil on paper
19½ x 18¾" (49.5 x 47.6 cm)

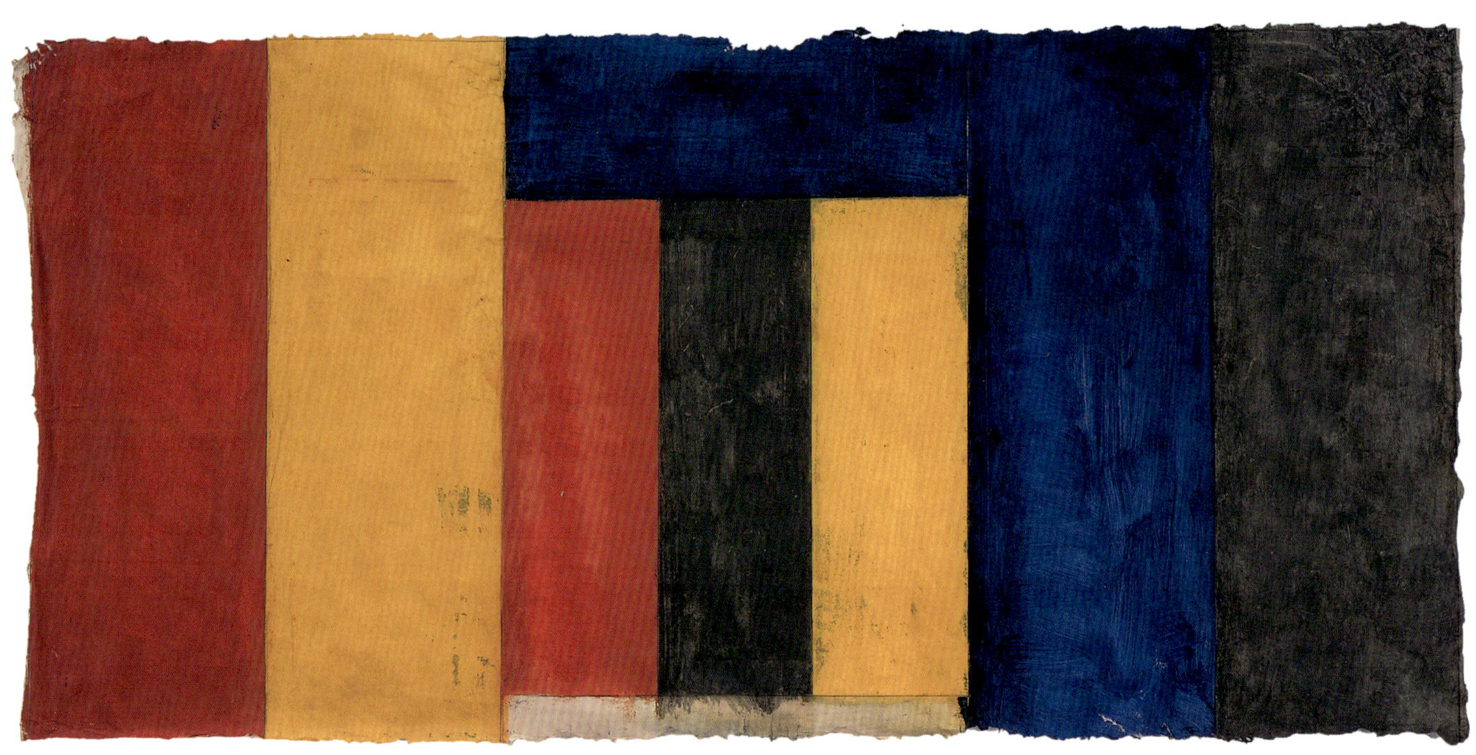

86. *Study #I.* 1981–82
Oil and graphite on paper
18½ x 39½" (47 x 100.3 cm)

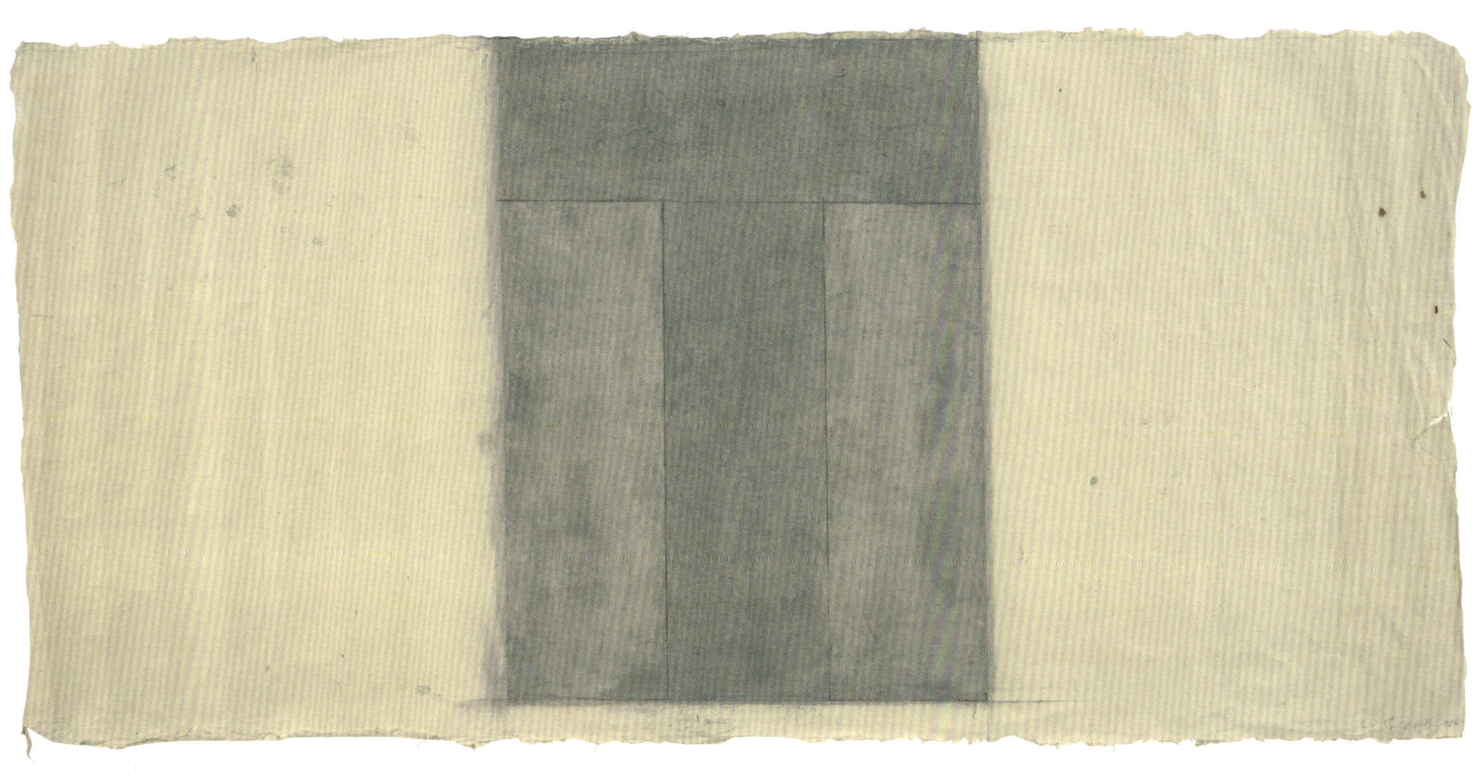

87. *2.* 1986
Oil and graphite on paper
18¼ x 39½" (46.4 x 100.3 cm)

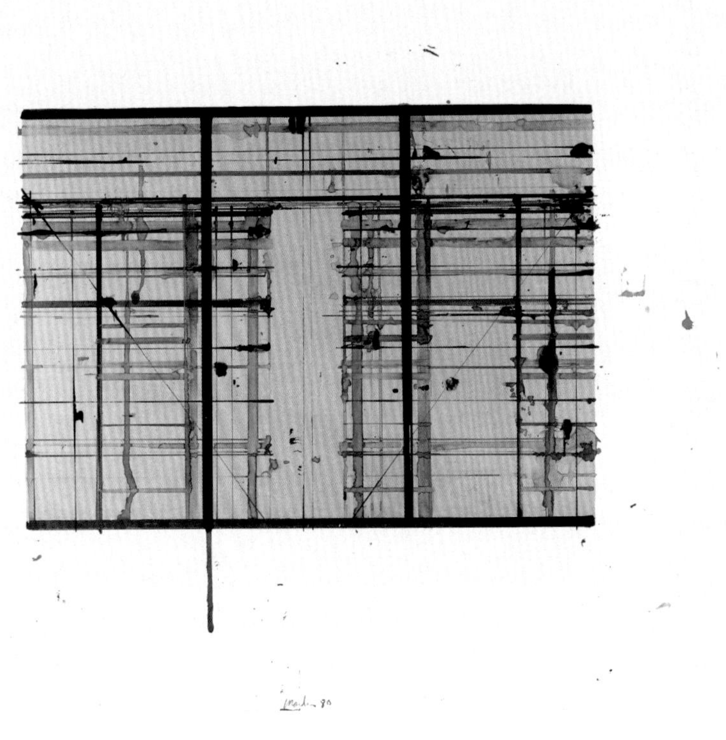

88. *Painting Study II.* 1980
Ink over screenprint on paper
20 x 24" (50.8 x 61 cm)

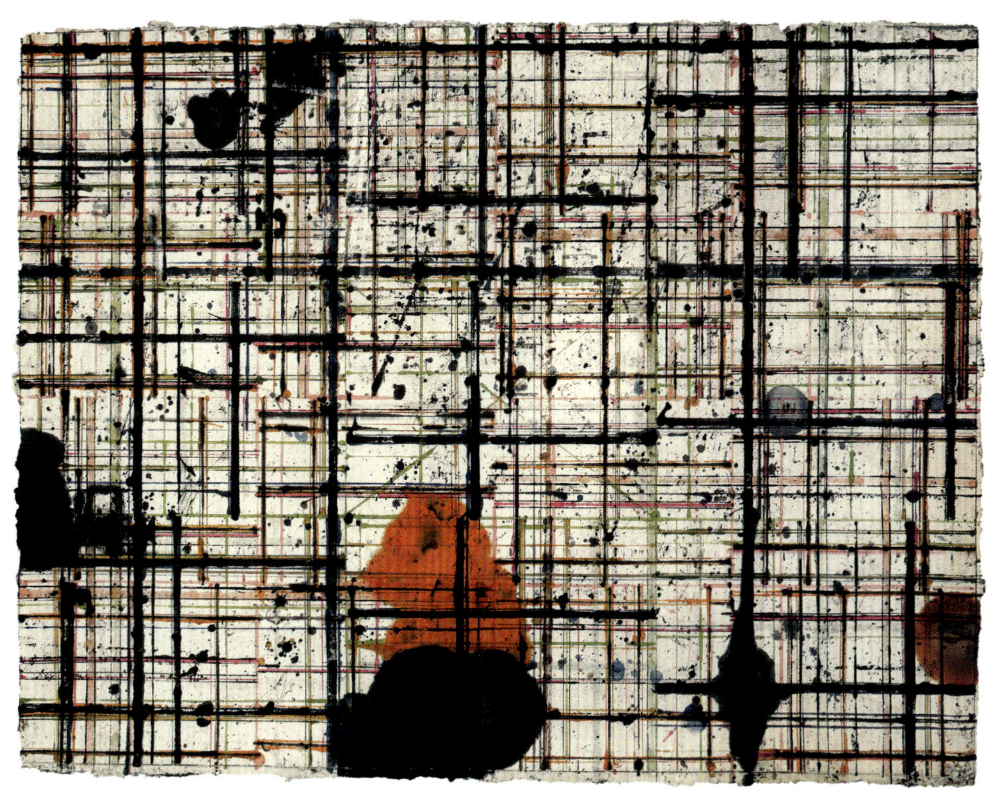

89. *4 and 3 Drawing*. 1979–81
Ink on paper
30½ x 40½" (77.5 x 102.9 cm)

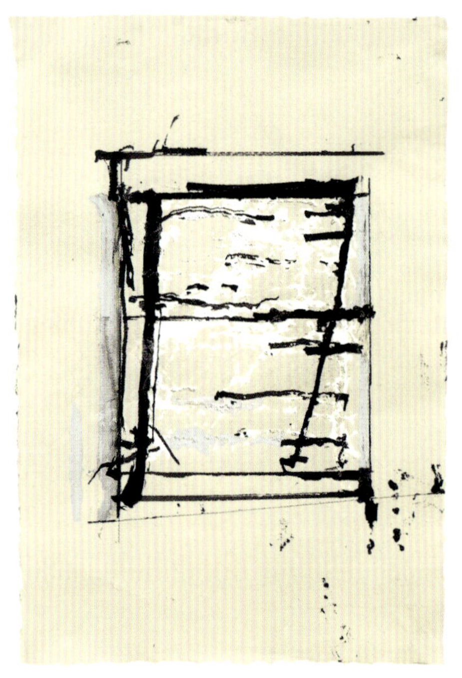

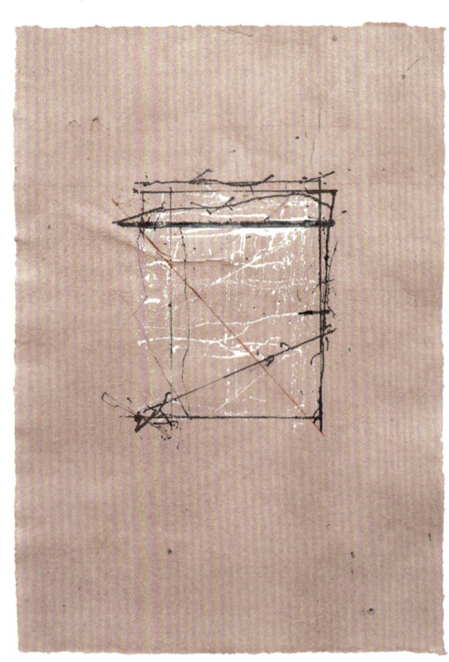

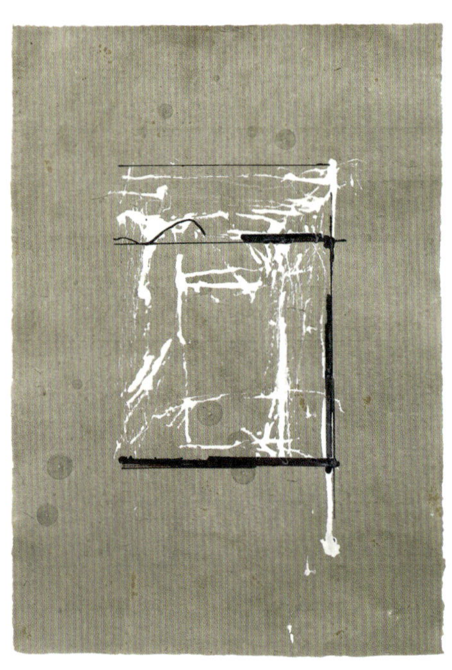

90–98. *Melia Group*. 1980–81
All ink and gouache on paper
Nine sheets, ranging from
$11\frac{1}{4}$" to $11\frac{3}{4}$" (28.6 to 29.8 cm) vertically
and from $7\frac{3}{4}$" to $8\frac{1}{2}$" (19.7 x 21.6 cm) horizontally

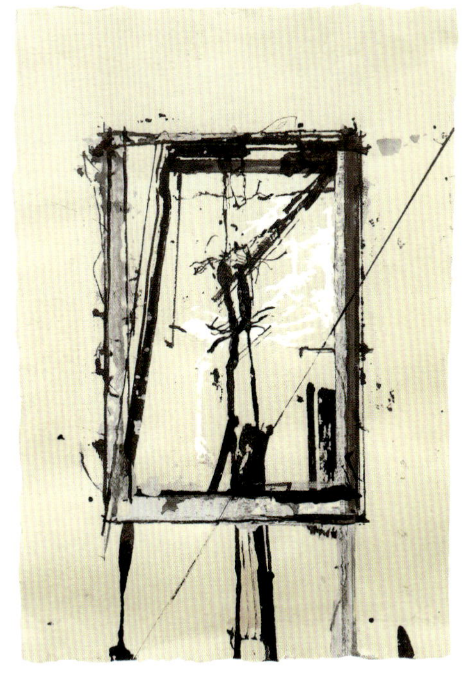
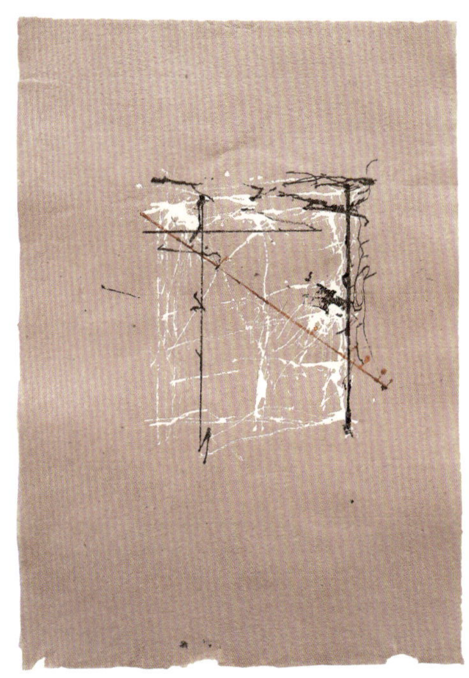
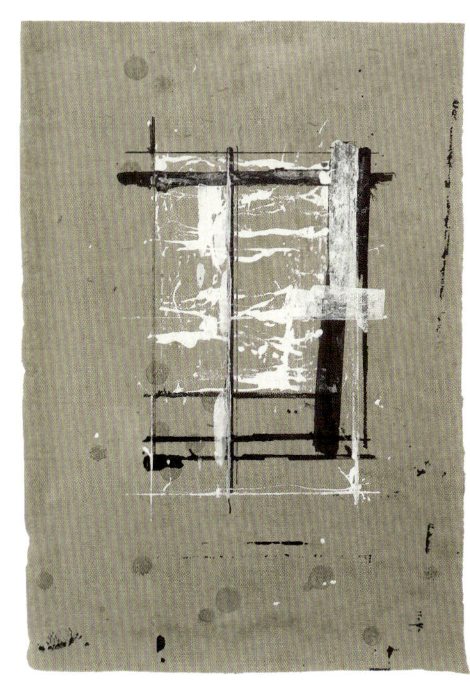
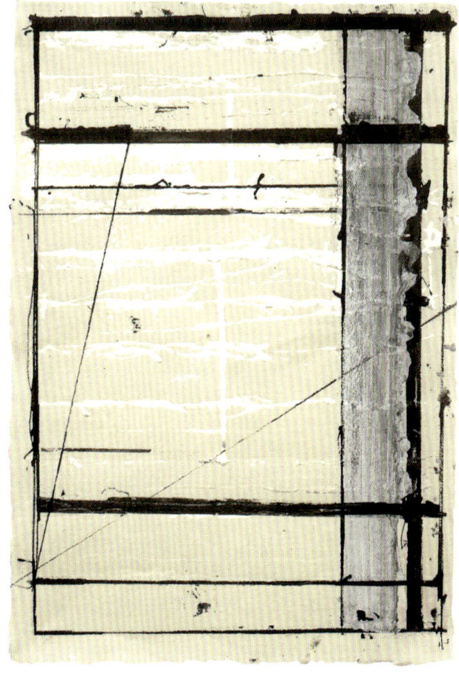
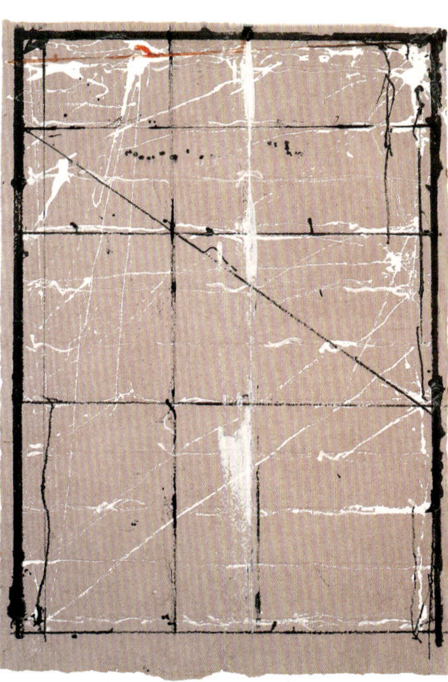
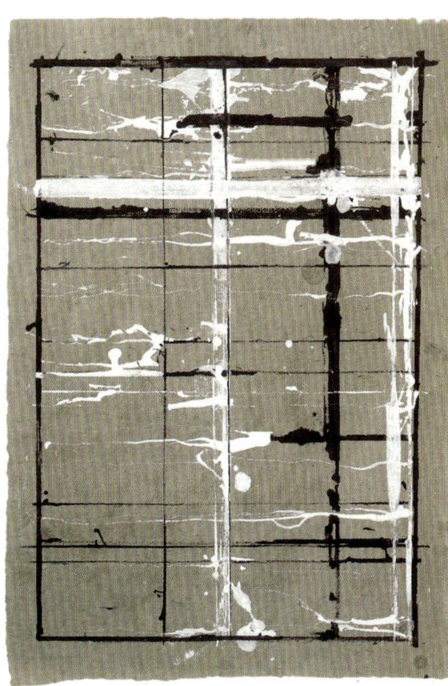

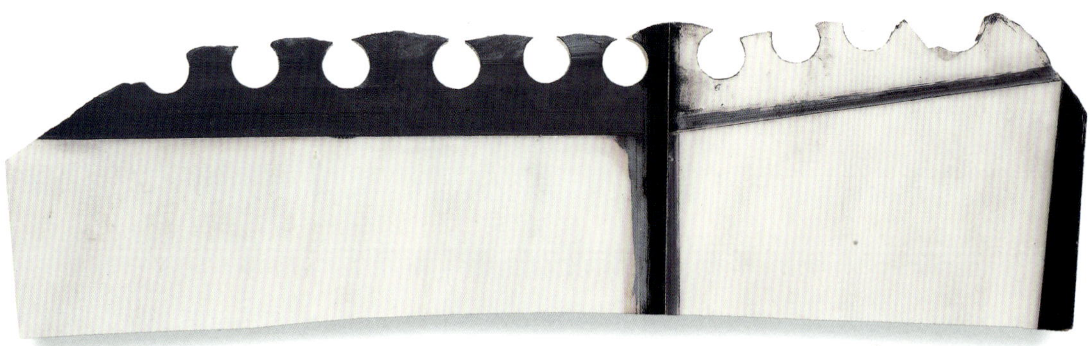

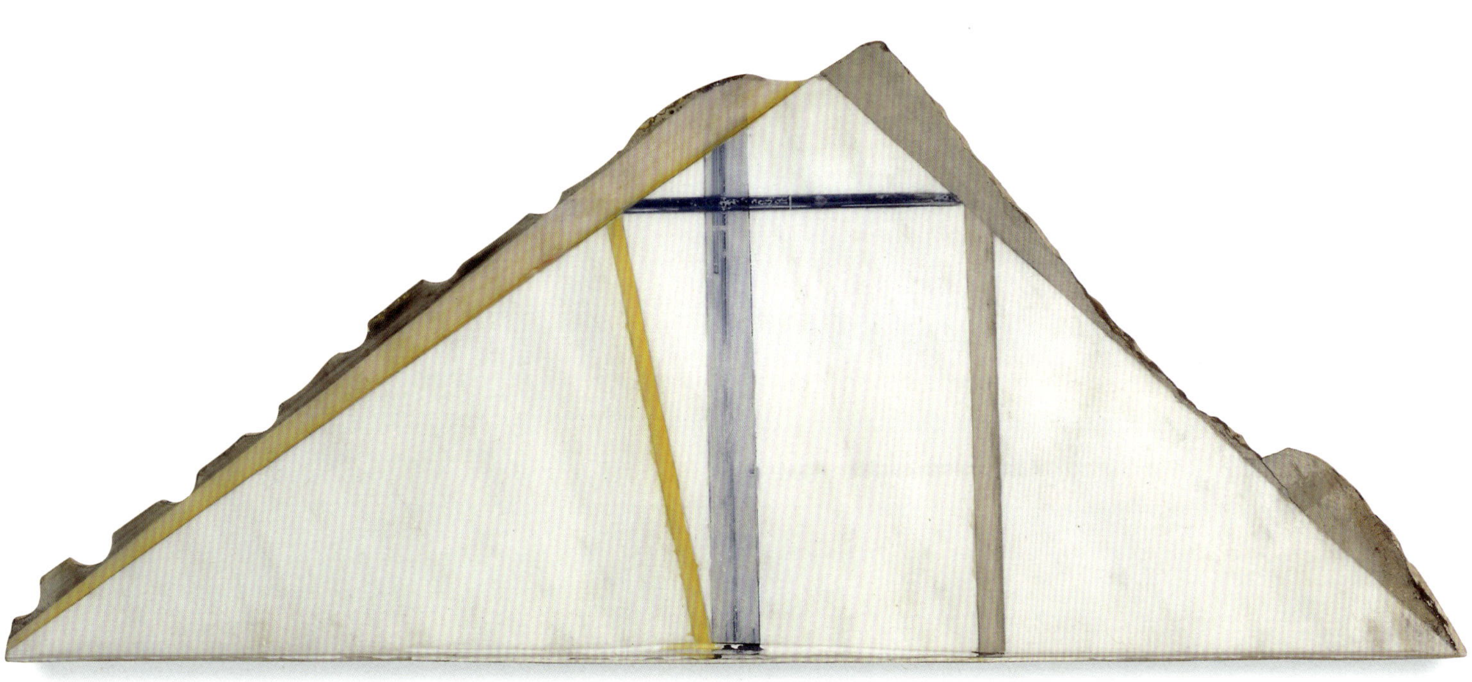

99. *Marble #4.* 1981
Oil on marble
9³/₈ x 32³/₄ x ³/₄" (23.8 x 83.2 x 1.9 cm)

100. *Marble #12.* 1981
Oil on marble
16⁵/₈ x 45³/₄ x ⁷/₈" (42.2 x 116.2 x 2.2 cm)

101. *Marble #6 (Papastratos Table).* 1981
Oil on marble
29 1/4 x 19 3/4 x 7/8" (74.3 x 50.2 x 2.2 cm)

102. *Black and White Painting.* 1982
Oil on canvas
24 x 18" (61 x 45.7 cm)

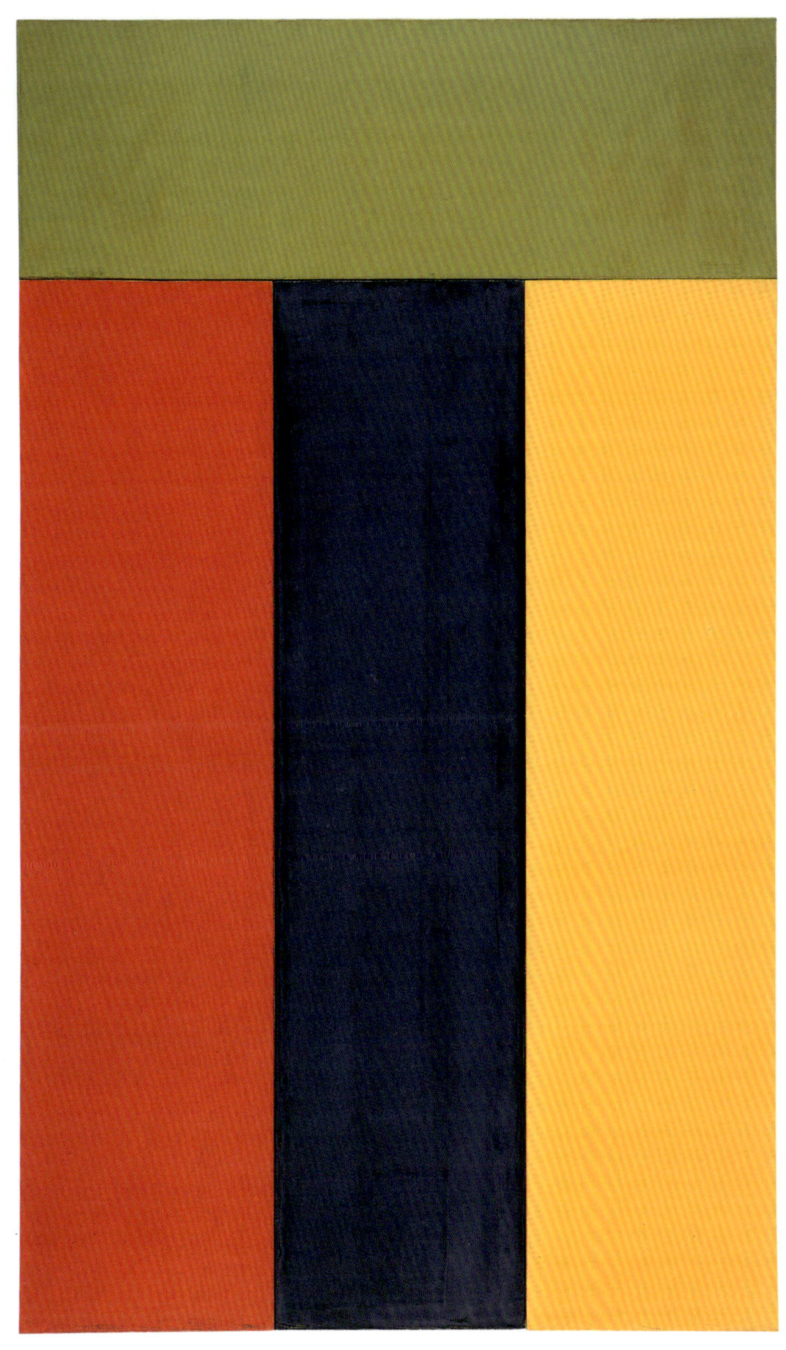

103. *Elements I*. 1981–82
Oil on canvas
Four panels, overall: 7' x 51" (213.4 x 129.5 cm)

104. *Green (Earth).* 1983–84
Oil on canvas
Twelve panels, overall:
7' x 9' 1" (213.4 x 276.9 cm)

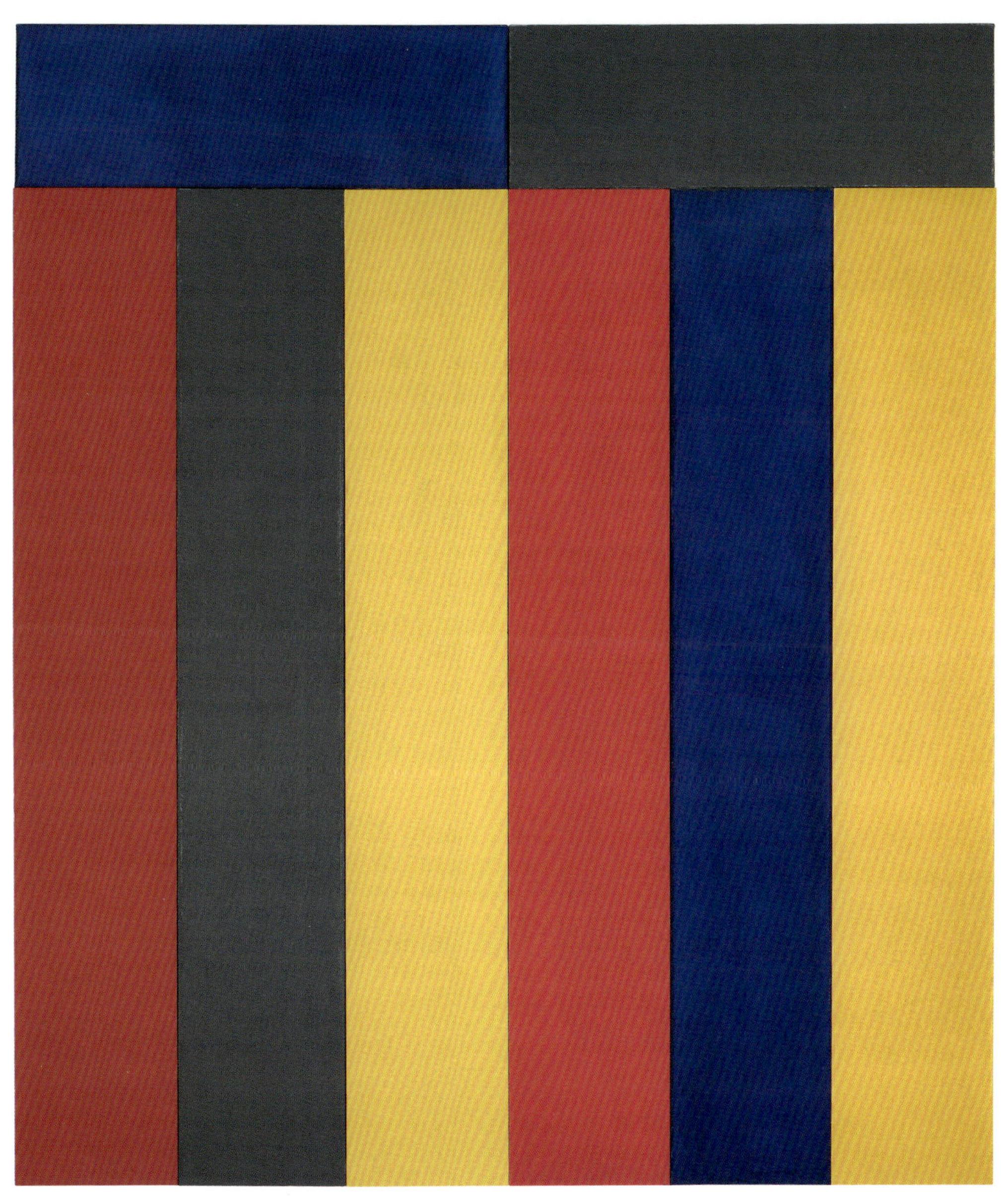

105. *Elements IV.* 1983–84
Oil on canvas
Eight panels, overall:
7' x 6' ½" (213.4 x 184.2 cm)

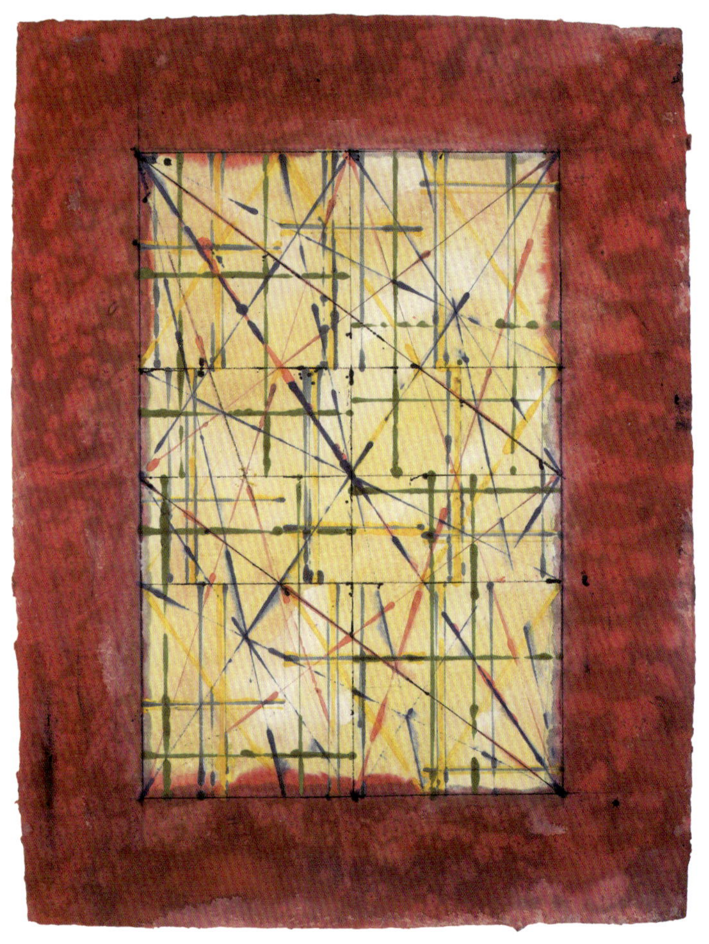

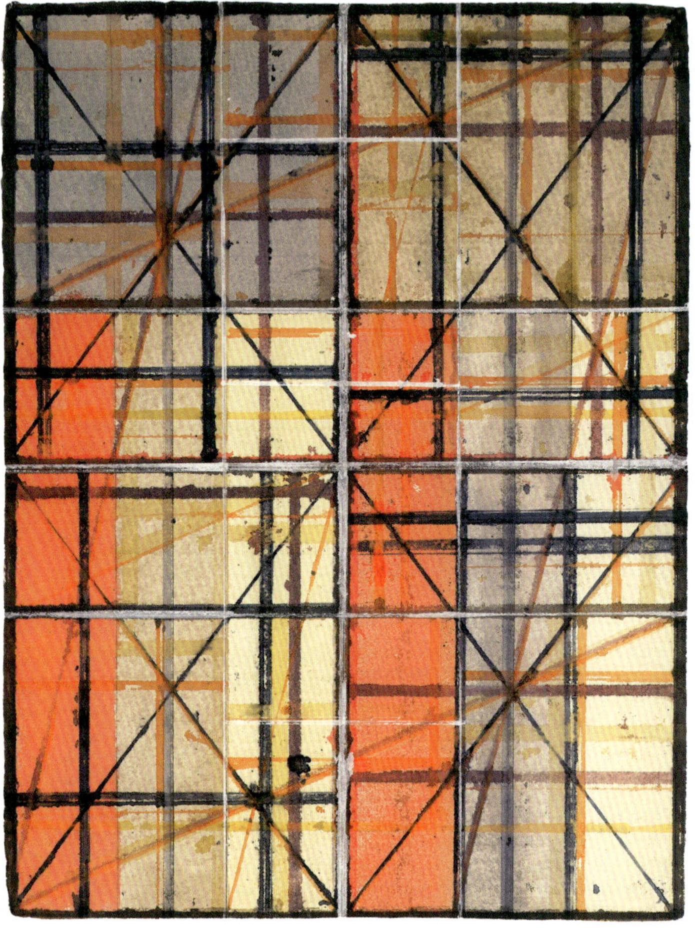

106. *Untitled (Window Study No. 1).* 1983
Ink on paper
$23^1/_4$ x 18" (59.1 x 45.7 cm)

107. *Basel Drawing.* 1983
Ink and gouache on paper
$25^1/_2$ x $19^3/_4$" (64.8 x 50.2 cm)

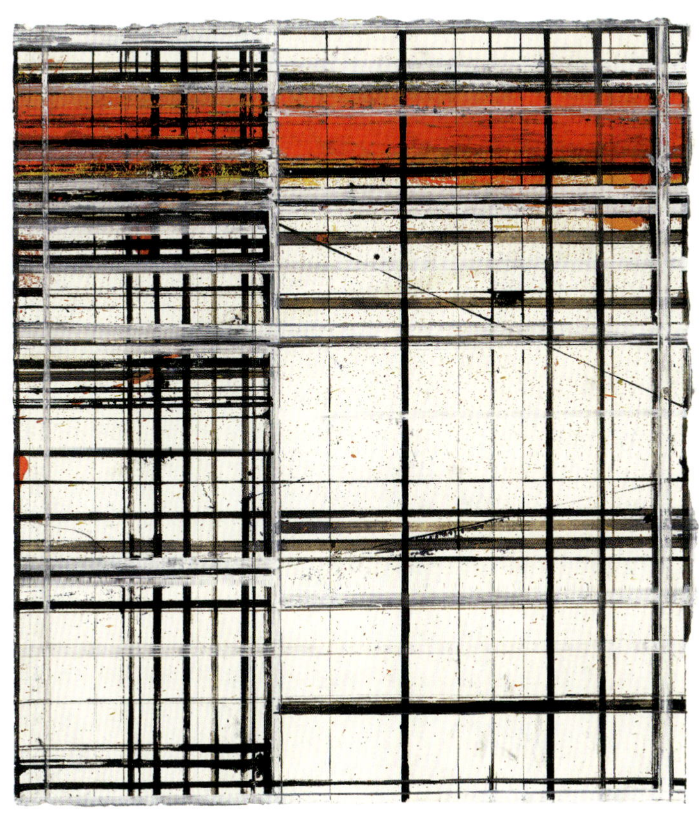

108. *Masking Drawing Five (Red Drawing Five).* 1984
Gouache, graphite, ink, and oil on paper
14 7/8 x 13 1/2" (37.8 x 34.3 cm)

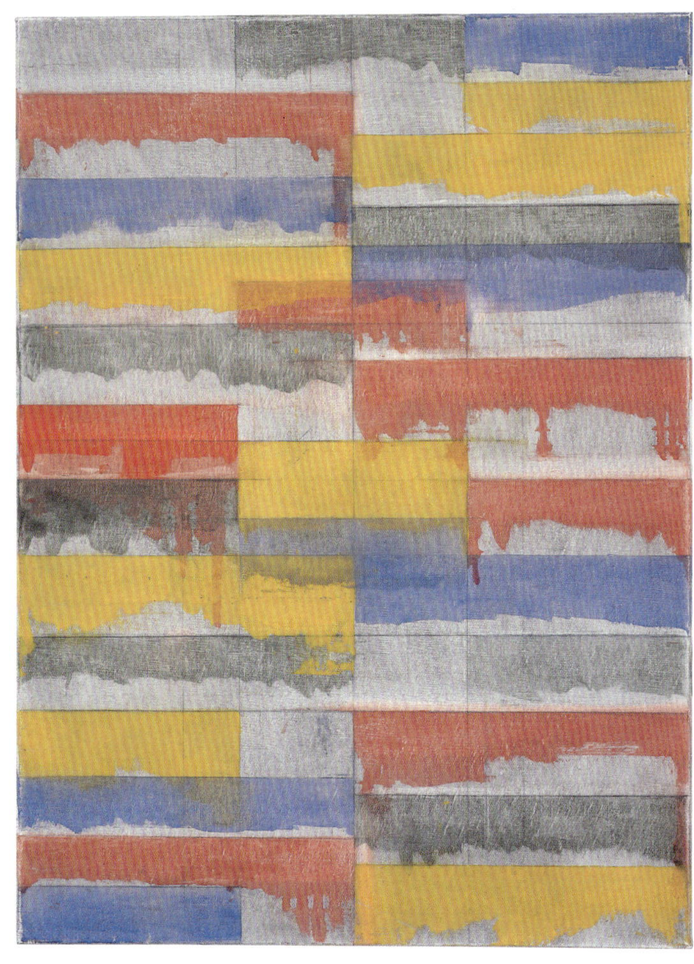

109. *Window Study #3.* 1983–85
Oil on linen
24 x 18" (61 x 45.7 cm)

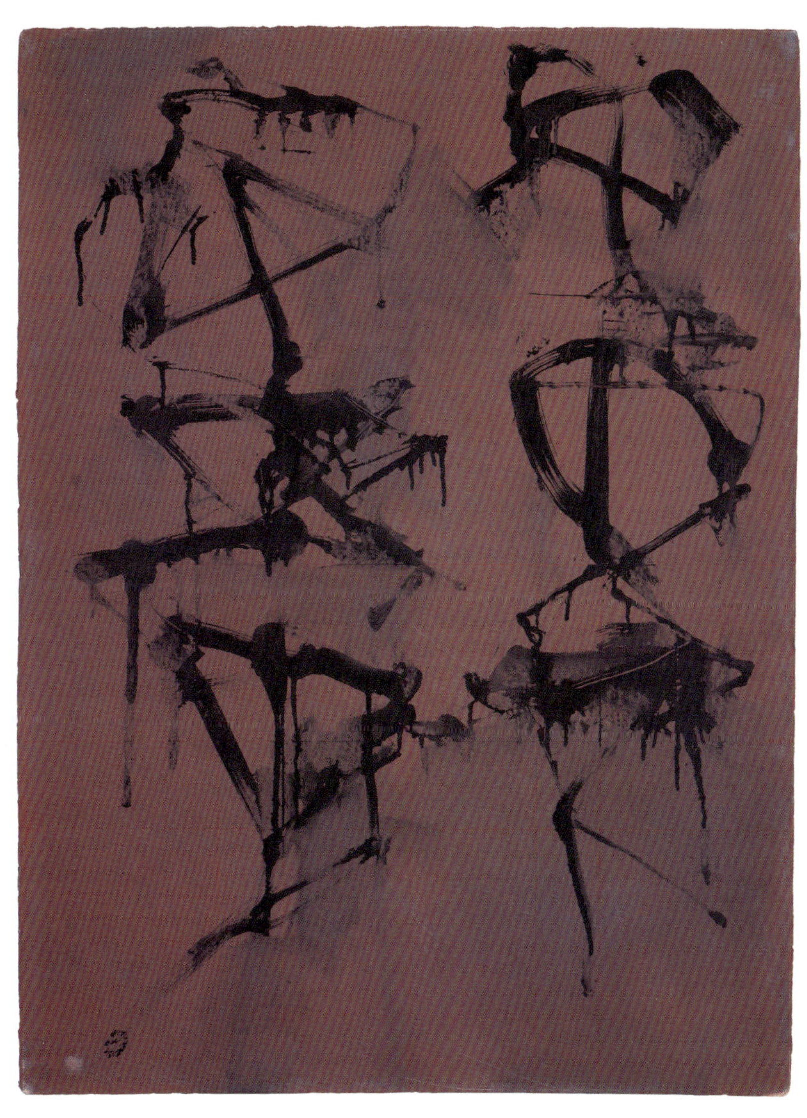

110. *#13 Helen's Valentine*. 1986
Oil on paper
30⅛ x 22½" (76.5 x 57.2 cm)

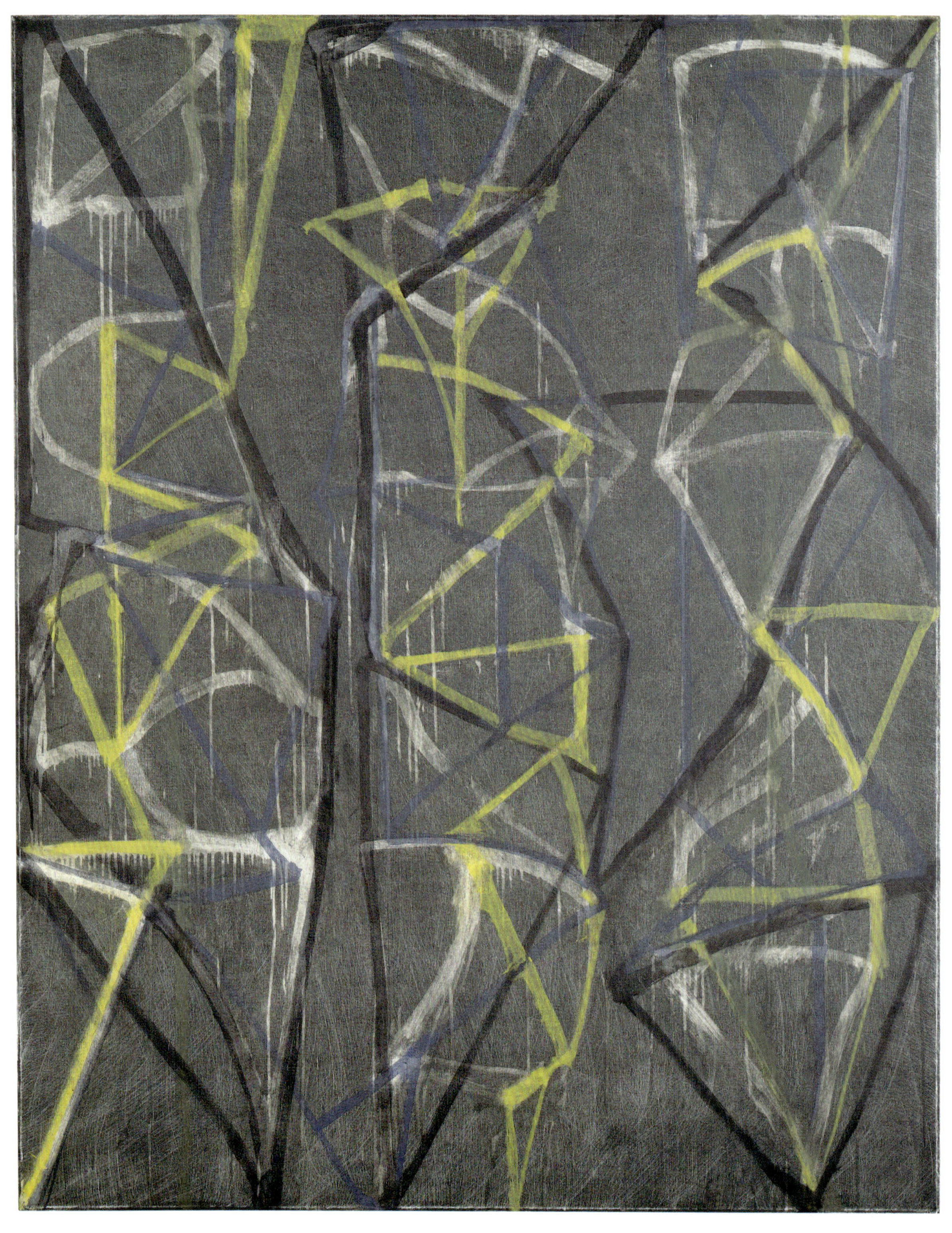

111. *Untitled #1.* 1986
Oil on linen
72 x 58" (183 x 147 cm)

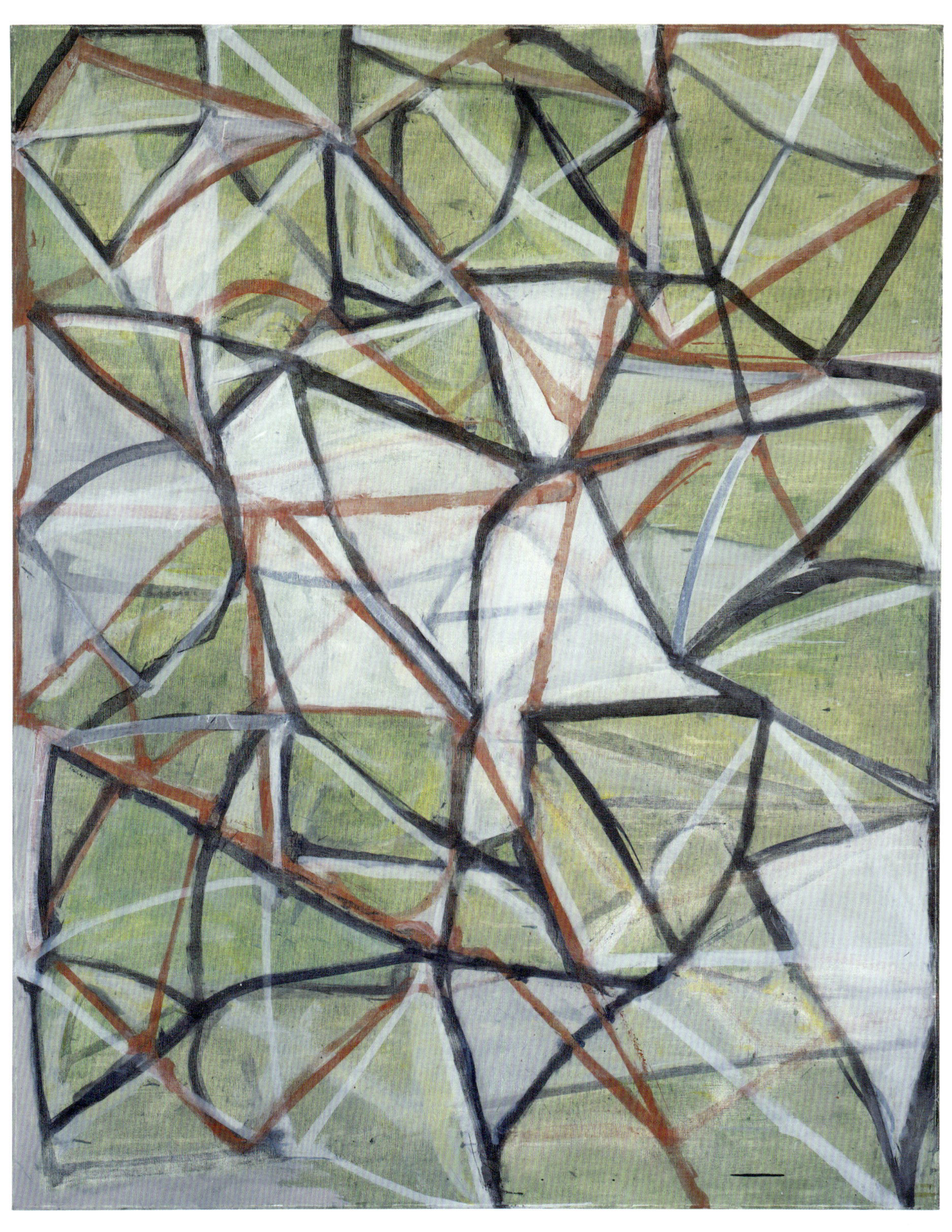

112. *Untitled #3.* 1986–87
Oil on linen
72 x 58" (182.9 x 147.3 cm)

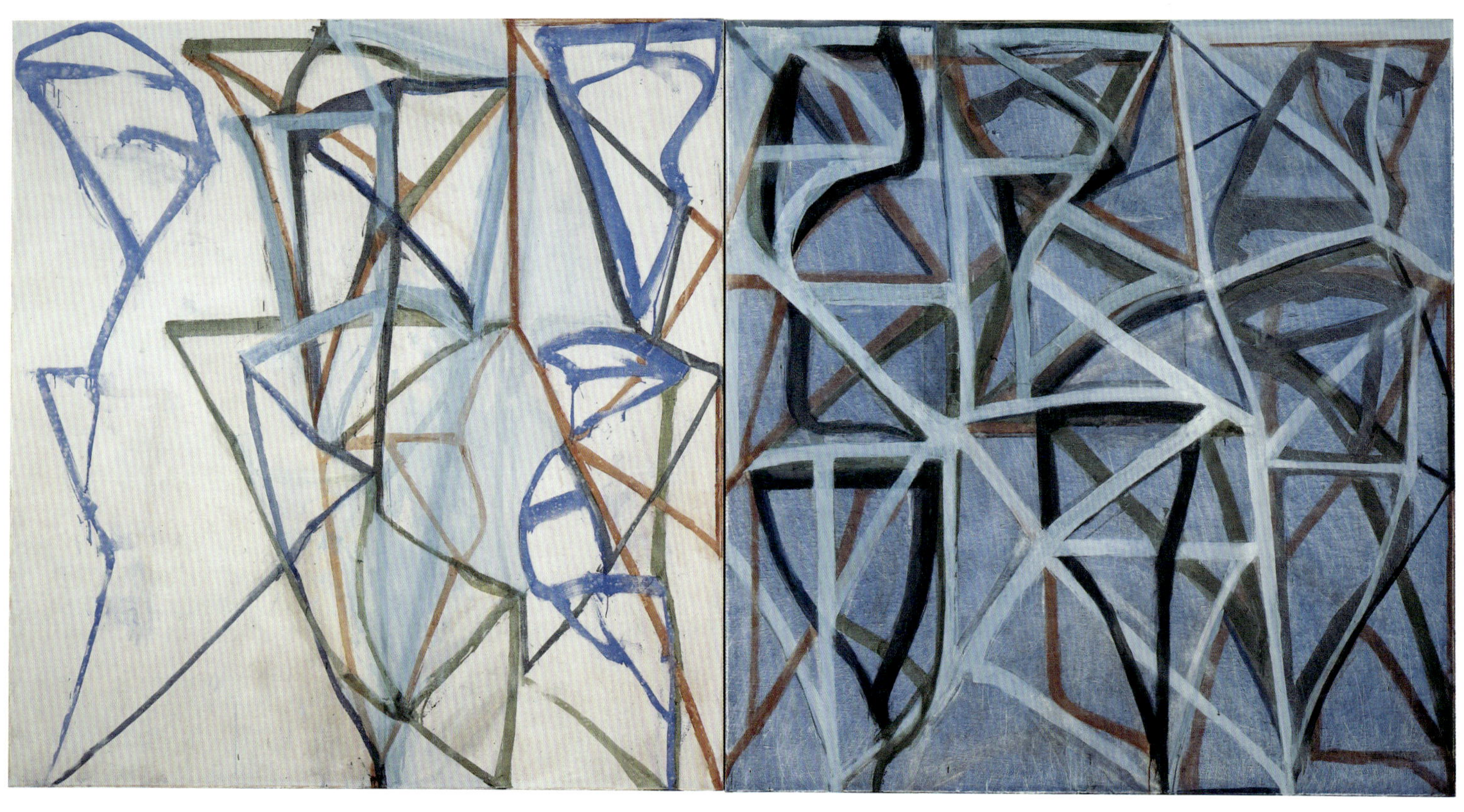

113. *Diptych.* 1986–87
Oil on linen
Two panels, overall: 6' 3" x 12' (190.5 x 366 cm)

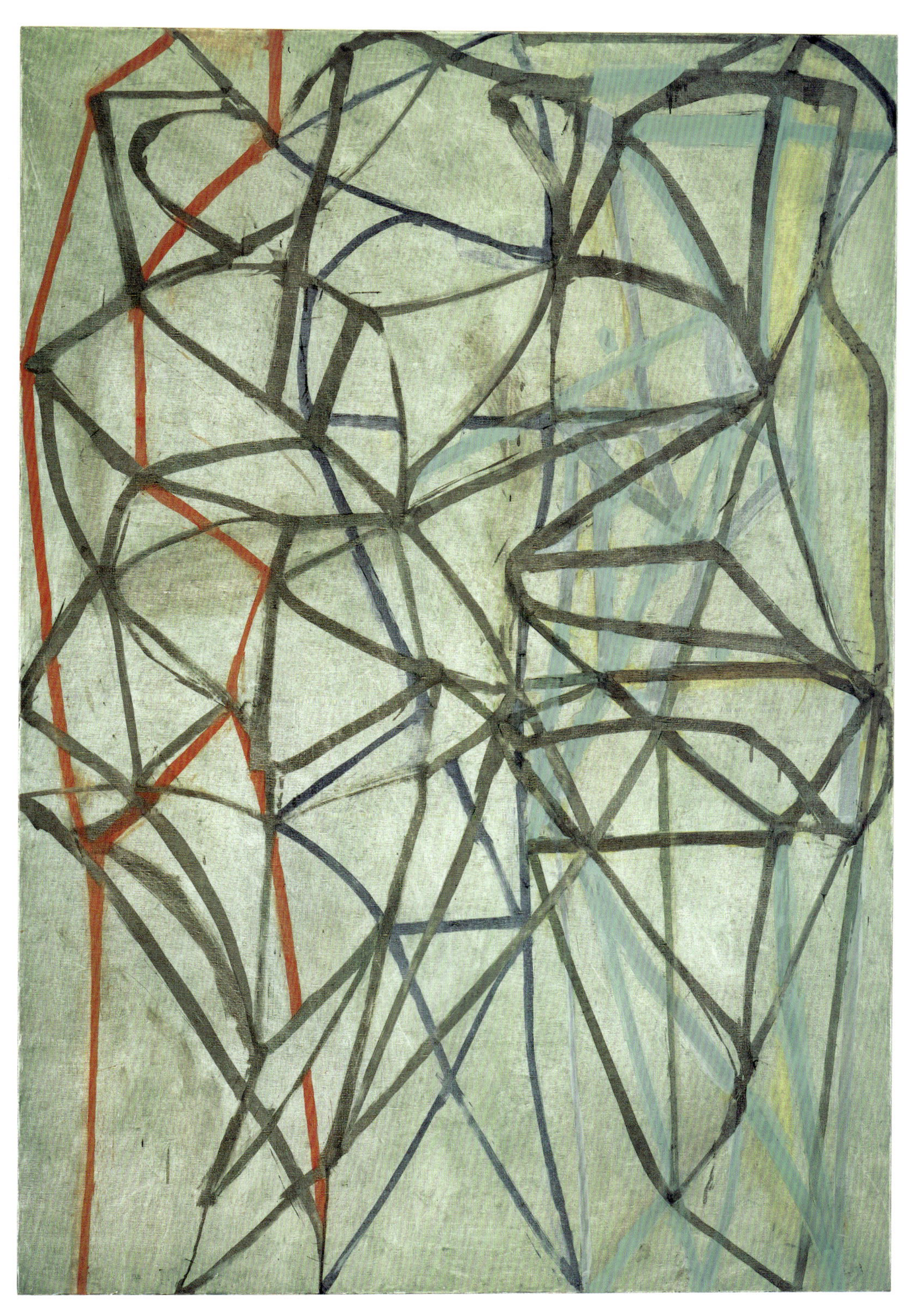

114. *2 (Dialog).* 1987–88
Oil on linen
7' x 60" (213.4 x 152.4 cm)

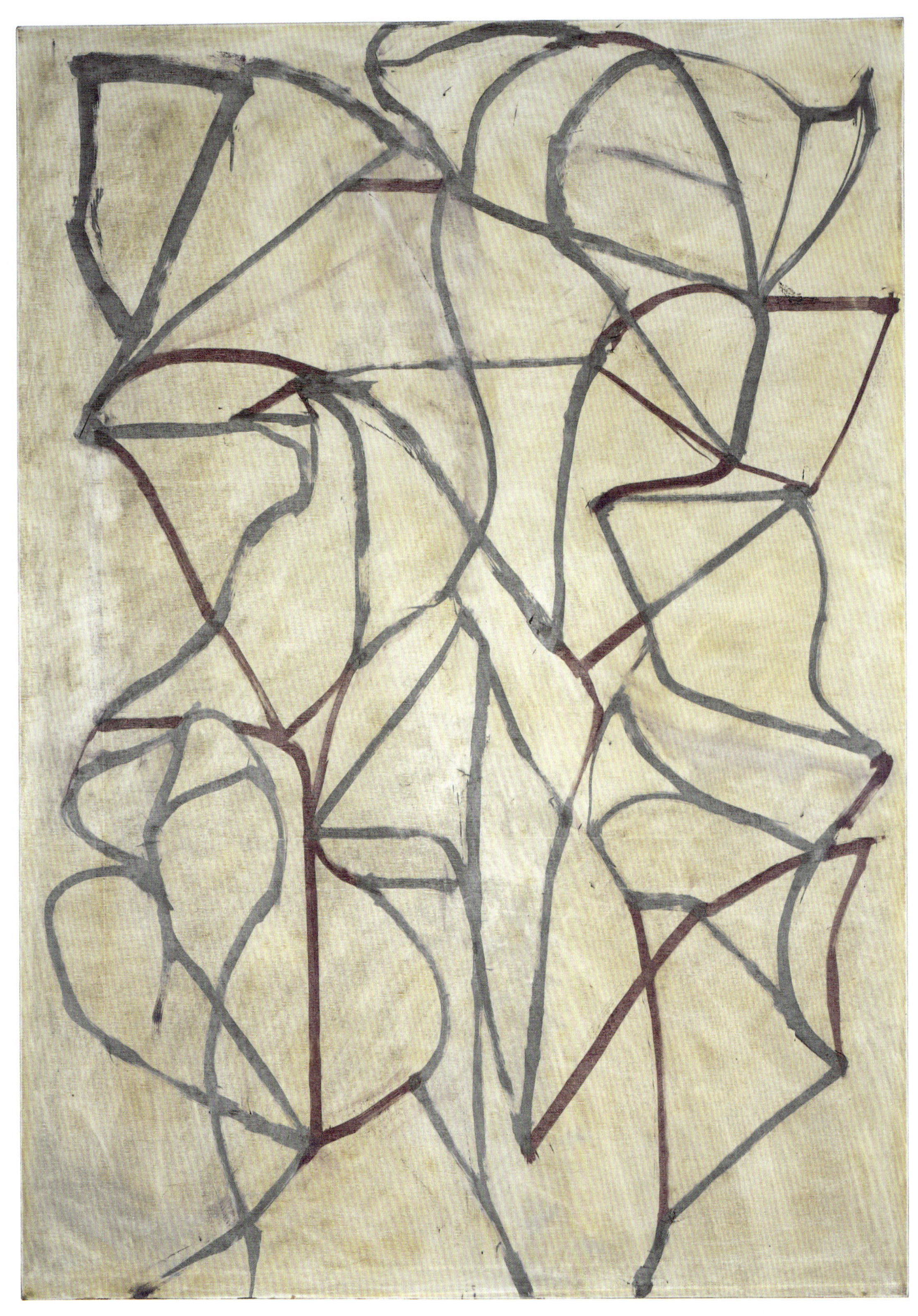

115. *4 (Bone).* 1987–88
Oil on linen
7' x 60" (213.4 x 152.4 cm)

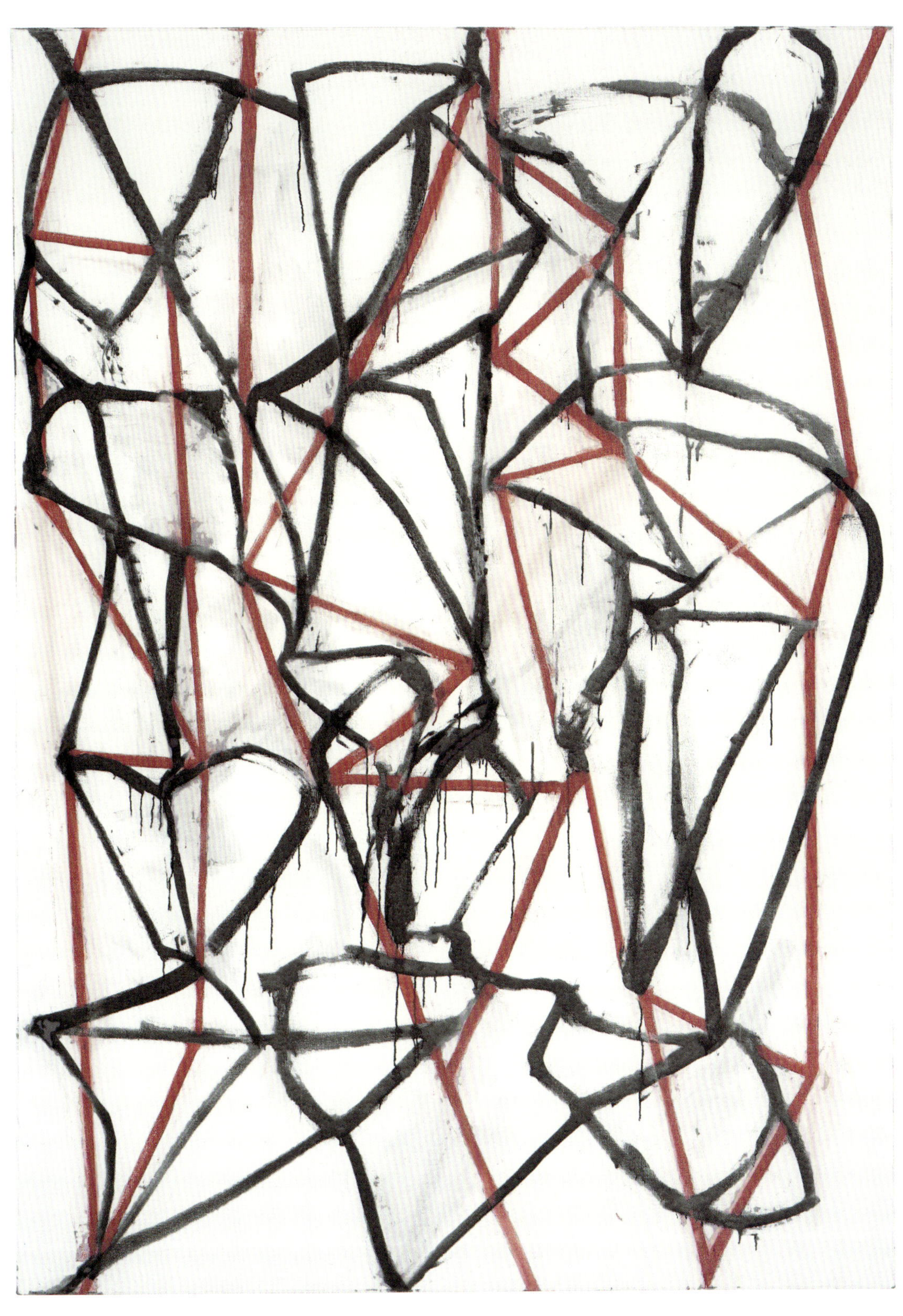

116. *11 (To Léger)*. 1987–88
Oil on linen
7' x 60" (213.4 x 152.4 cm)

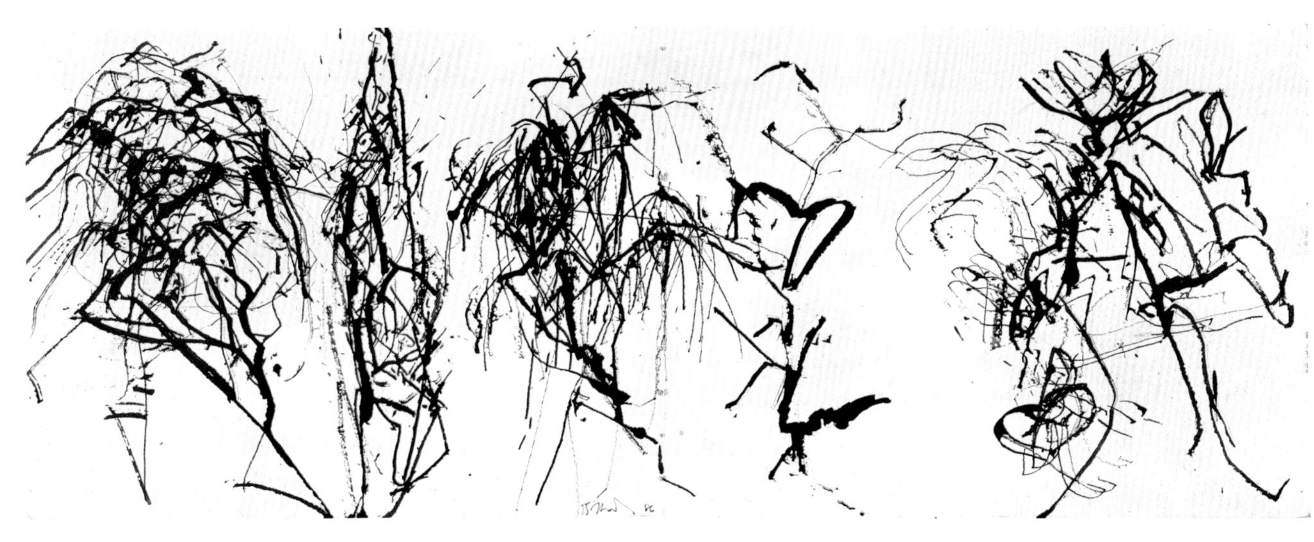

117. *Summer Scroll #8*
(Five Kinds of Hydra Trees). 1986
Ink on paper
$10^{3}/_{4}$ x $29^{1}/_{4}$" (27.3 x 74.3 cm)

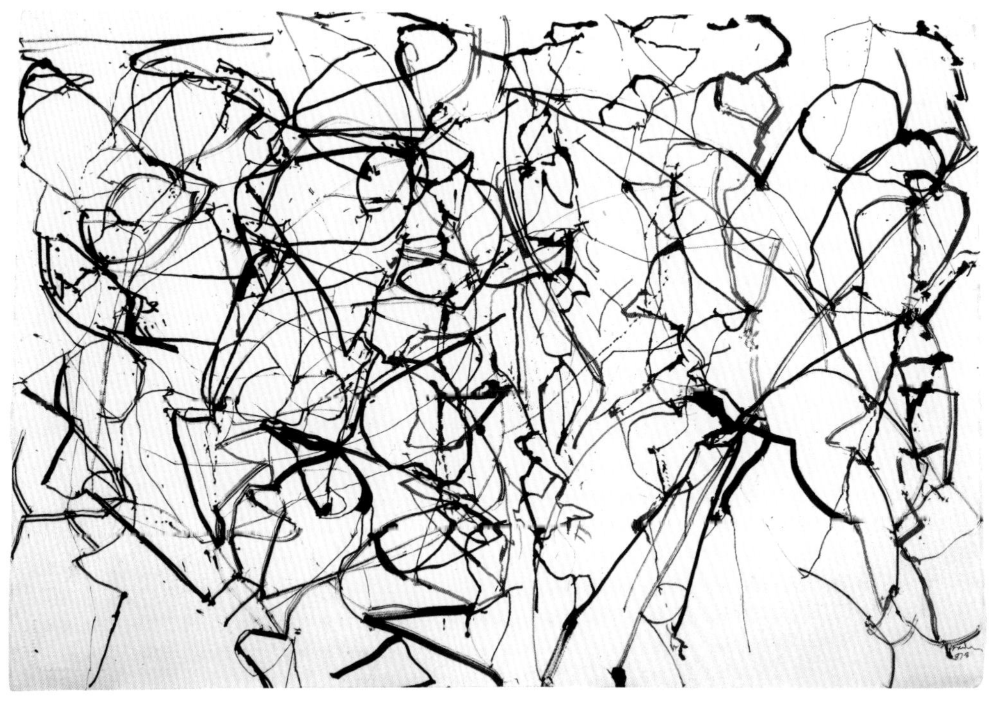

118. *In the Summer Garden II.* 1987–88
Ink on paper
15 x 22½" (38.1 x 57.2 cm)

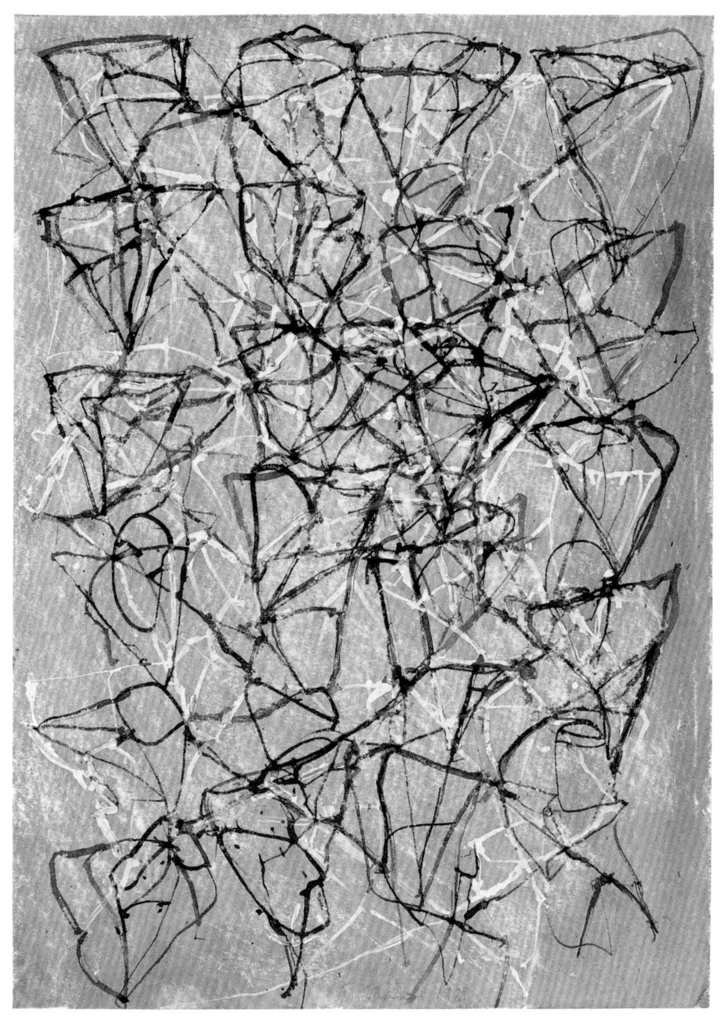

119. *Drawing for Conjunctions.* 1988–89
Ink and gouache on paper
16 x 11¾" (40.6 x 29.8 cm)

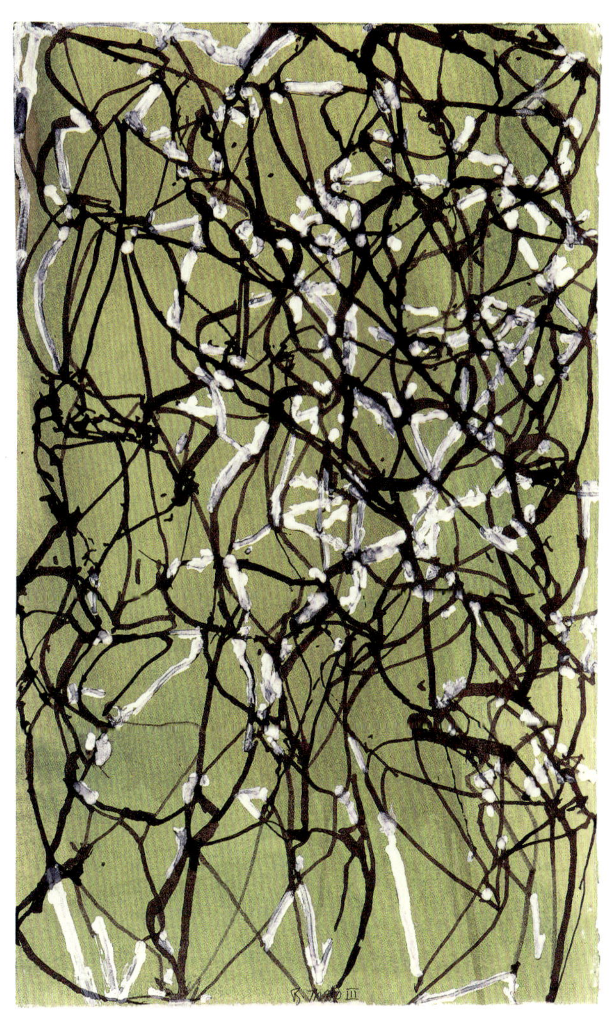

120. *Hydra Summer 1990 III.* 1990
Ink and gouache on paper
14 x 8½" (35.6 x 21.6 cm)

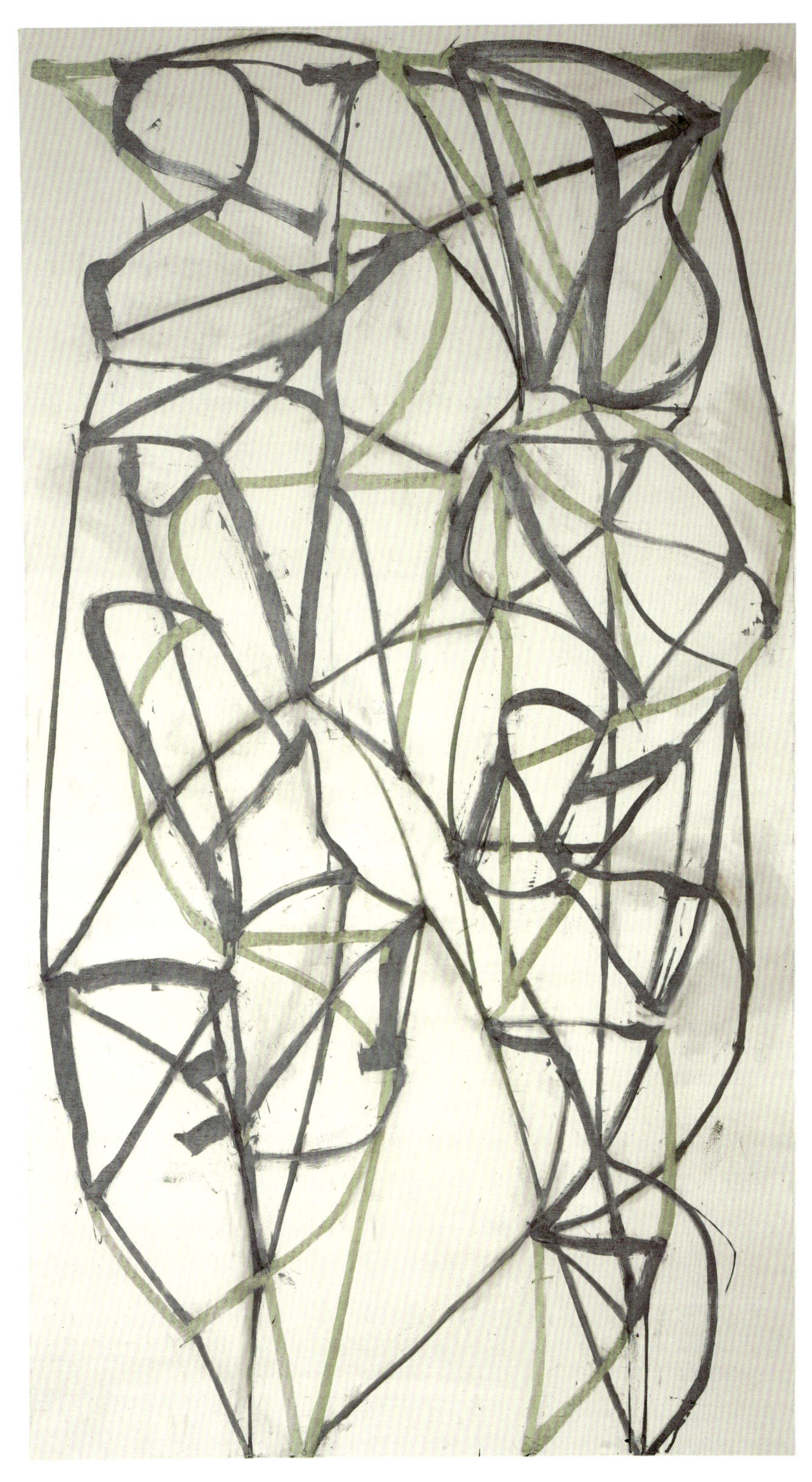

121. *Couplet I.* 1988–89
Oil on linen
9' x 60" (274.3 x 152.4 cm)

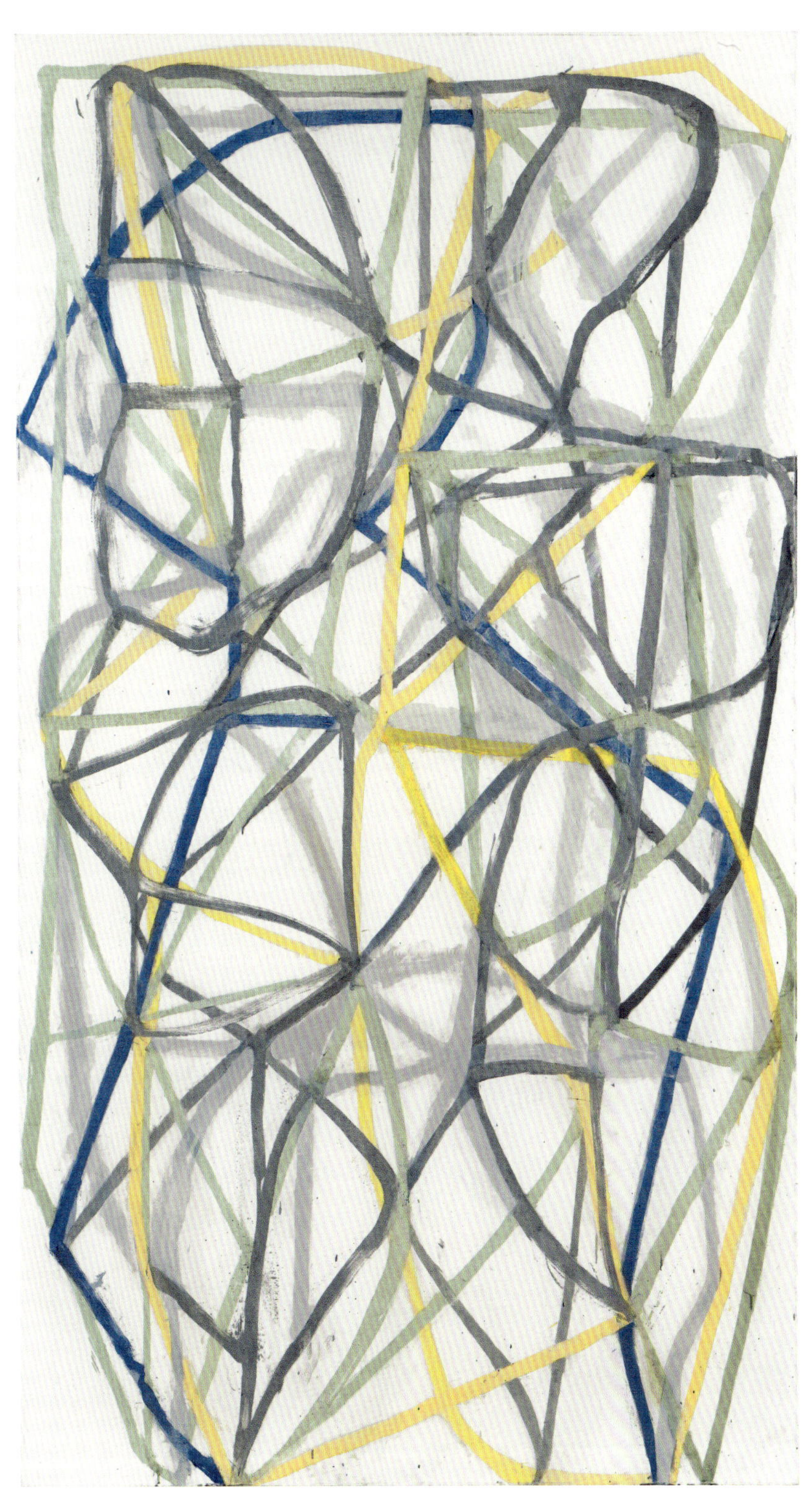

122. *Couplet IV.* 1988–89
Oil on linen
9' x 60" (274.3 x 152.4 cm)

123. *Cold Mountain 2.* 1989–91
Oil on linen
9 x 12' (274.3 x 365.8 cm)

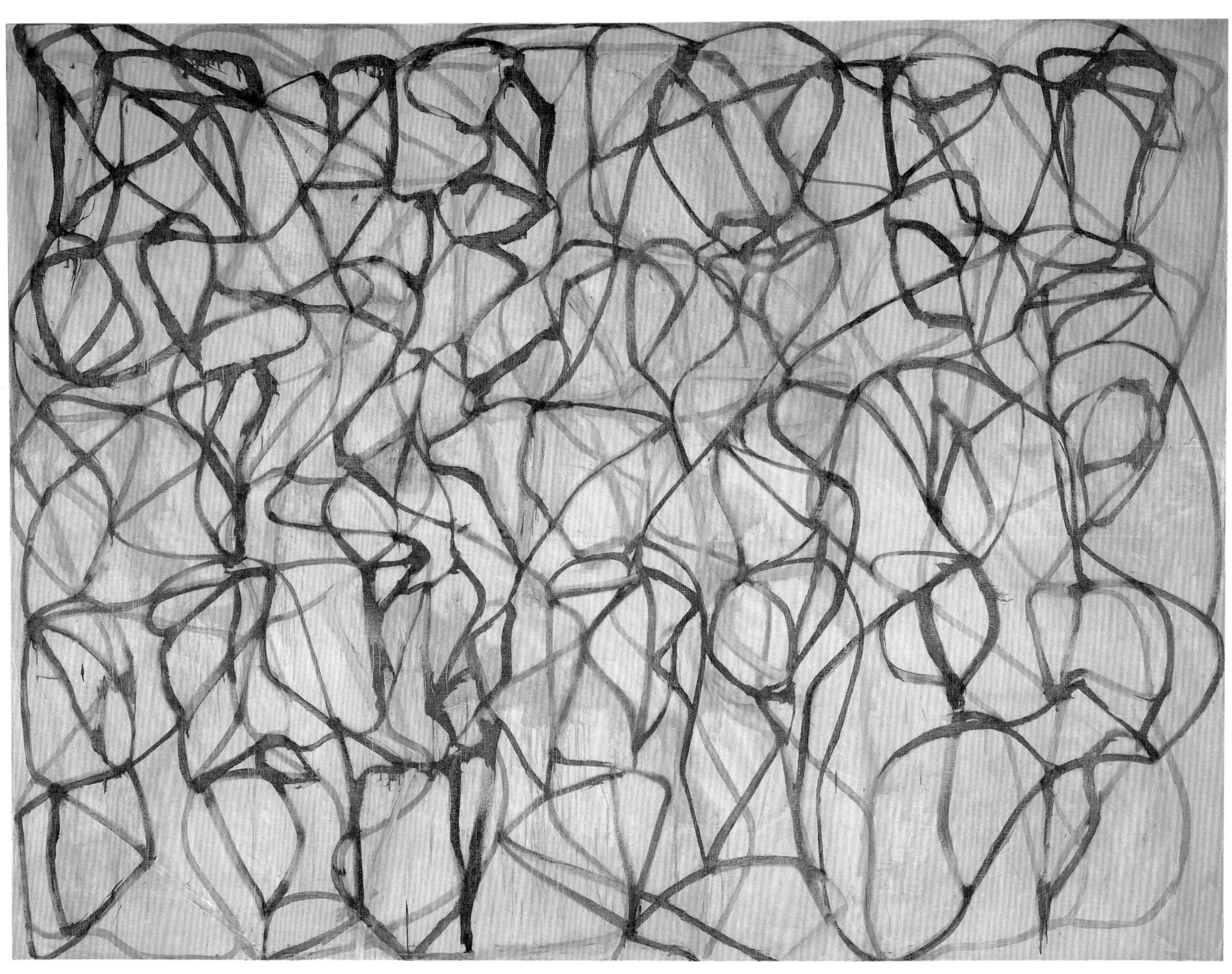

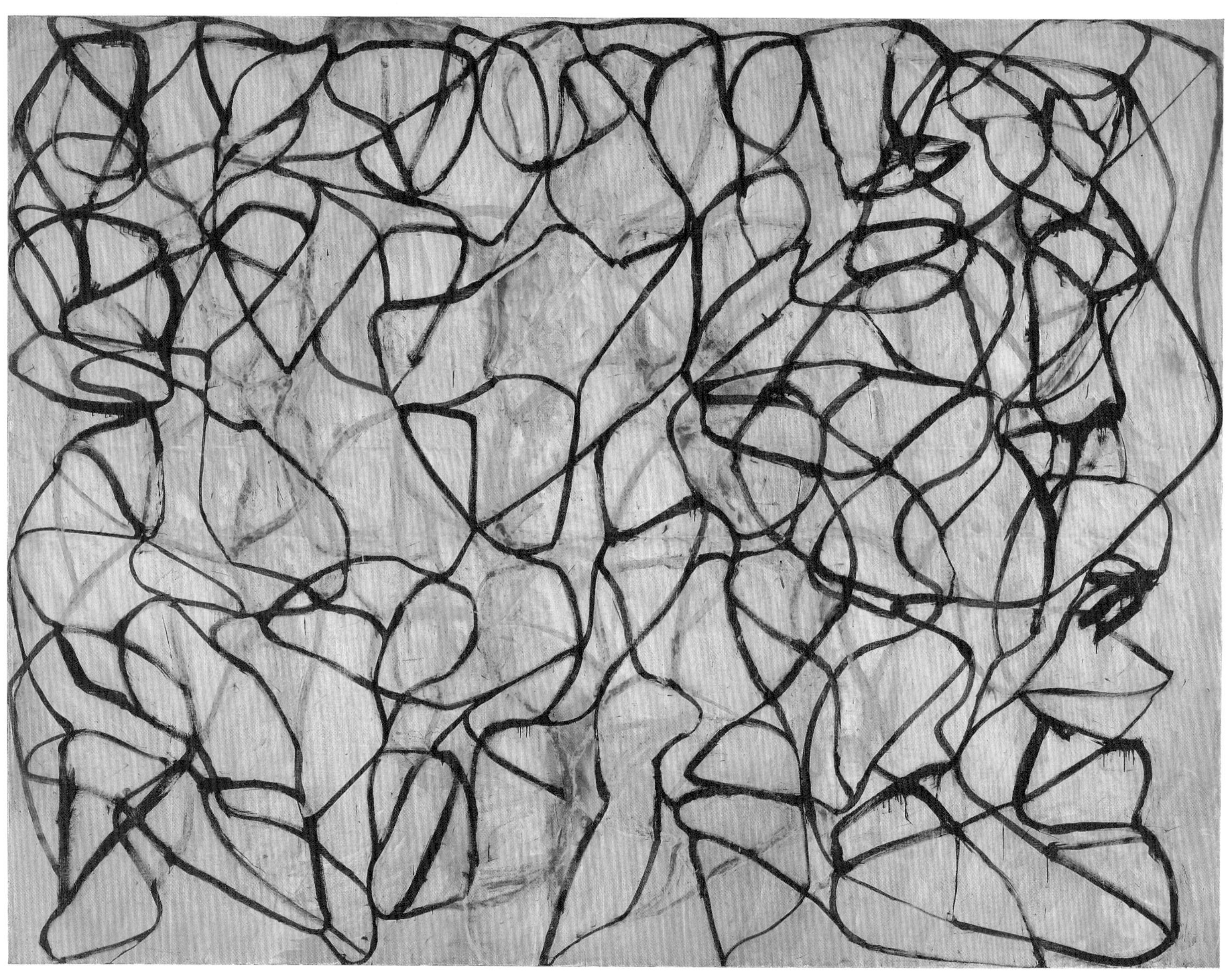

124. *Cold Mountain 5 (Open).* 1989–91
Oil on linen
9 x 12' (274.3 x 365.8 cm)

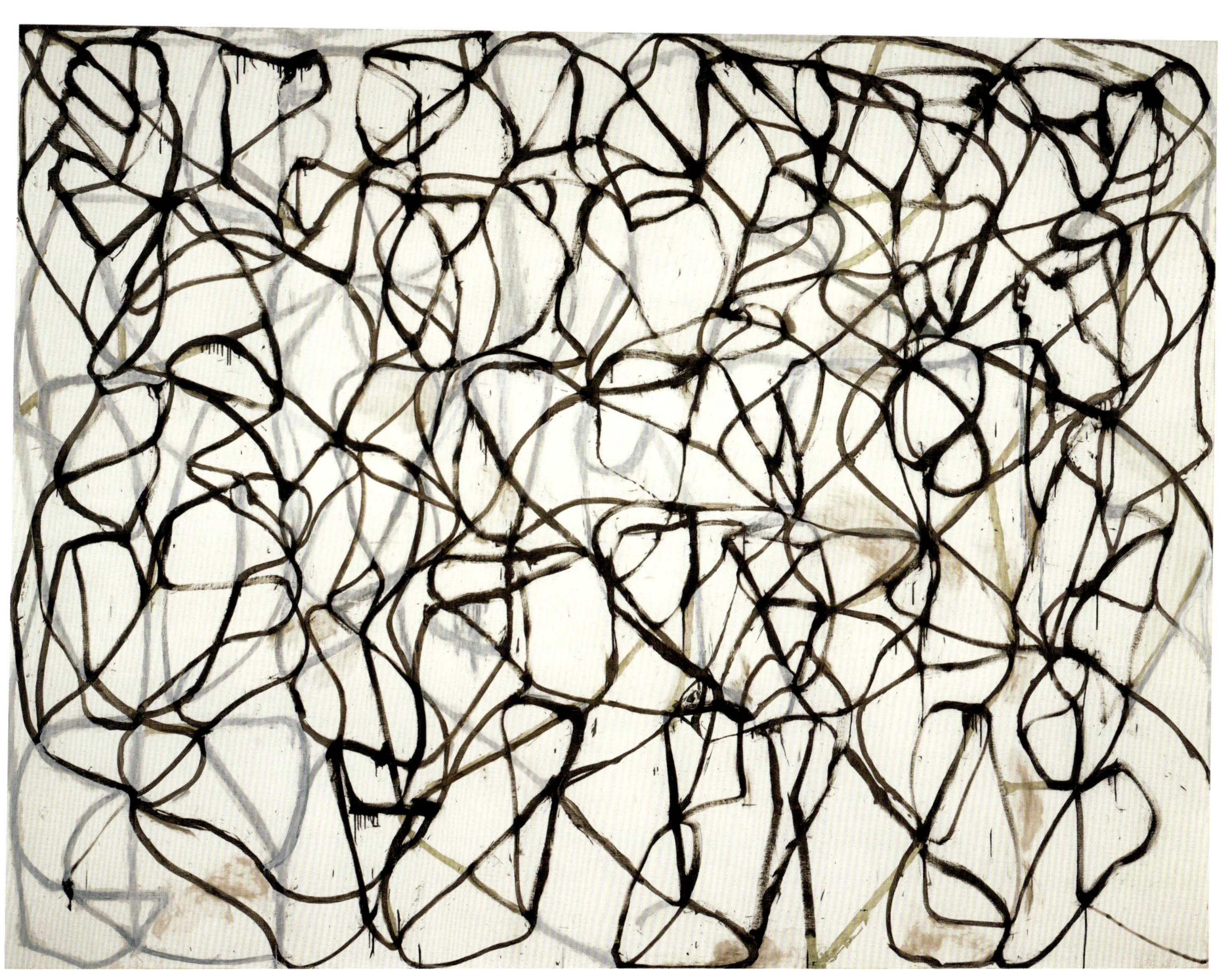

125. *Cold Mountain 6 (Bridge).* 1989–91
Oil on linen
9 x 12' (274.3 x 365.8 cm)

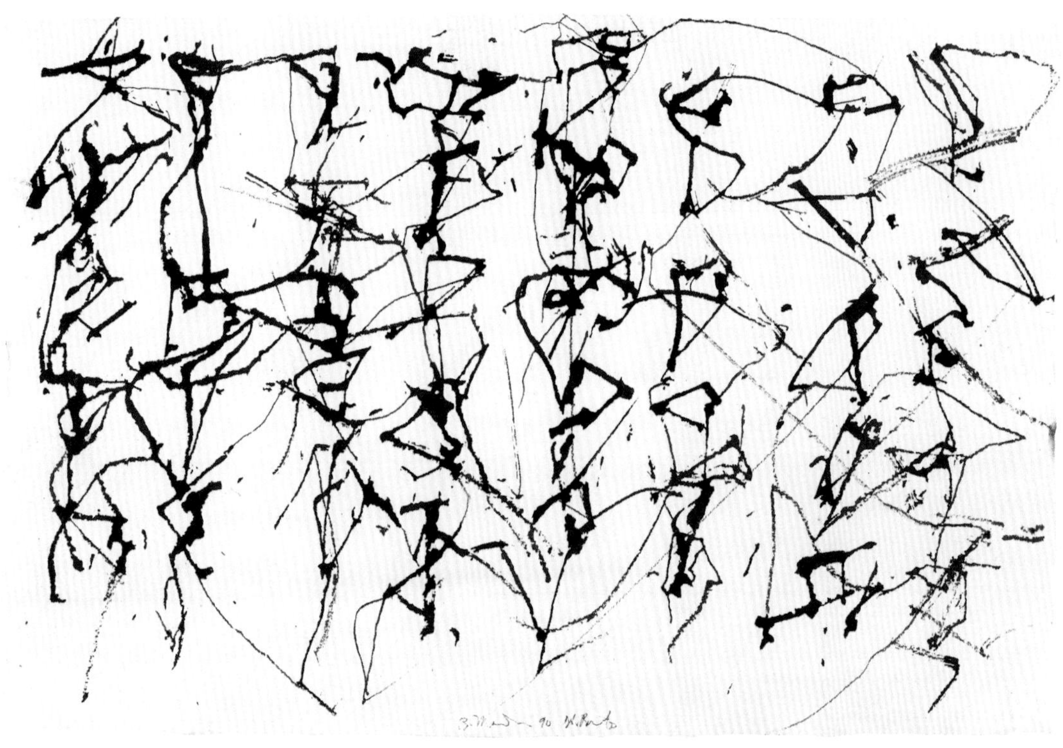

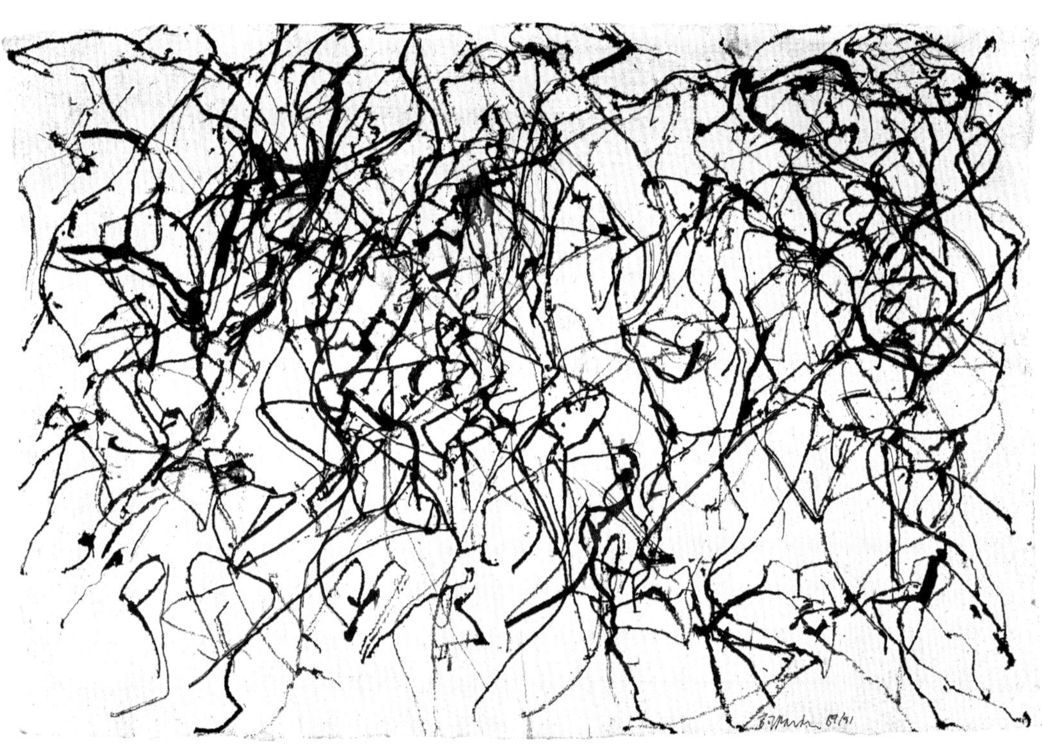

126. *St. Barts 2.* 1990
Ink on paper
10¾ x 16" (27.3 x 40.6 cm)

127. *St. Barts 10.* 1989/1991
Ink on paper
10¾ x 16" (27.3 x 40.6 cm)

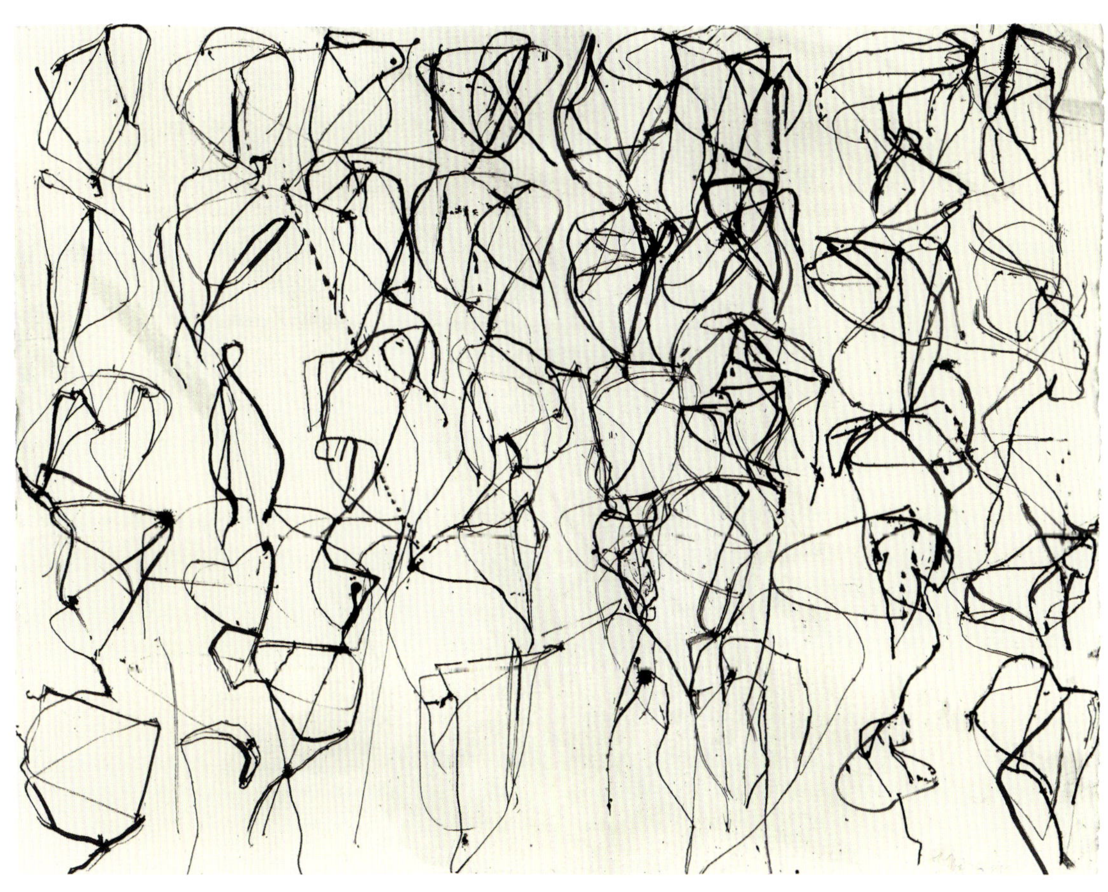

128. *Han Shan Goes to the Tropics.* 1991
Ink and ink wash on paper
25 7/8 x 34 3/8" (65.7 x 87.3 cm))

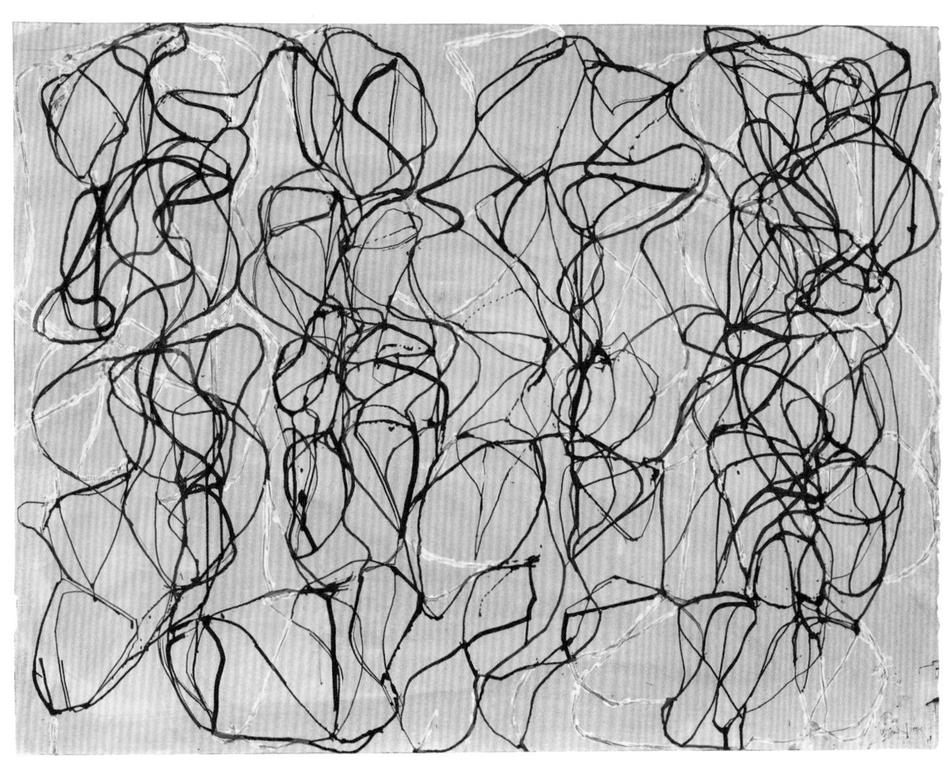

129. *Cold Mountain Addendum 1.* 1991–92
Ink, ink wash, and gouache on paper
26 x 34¼" (66 x 87 cm)

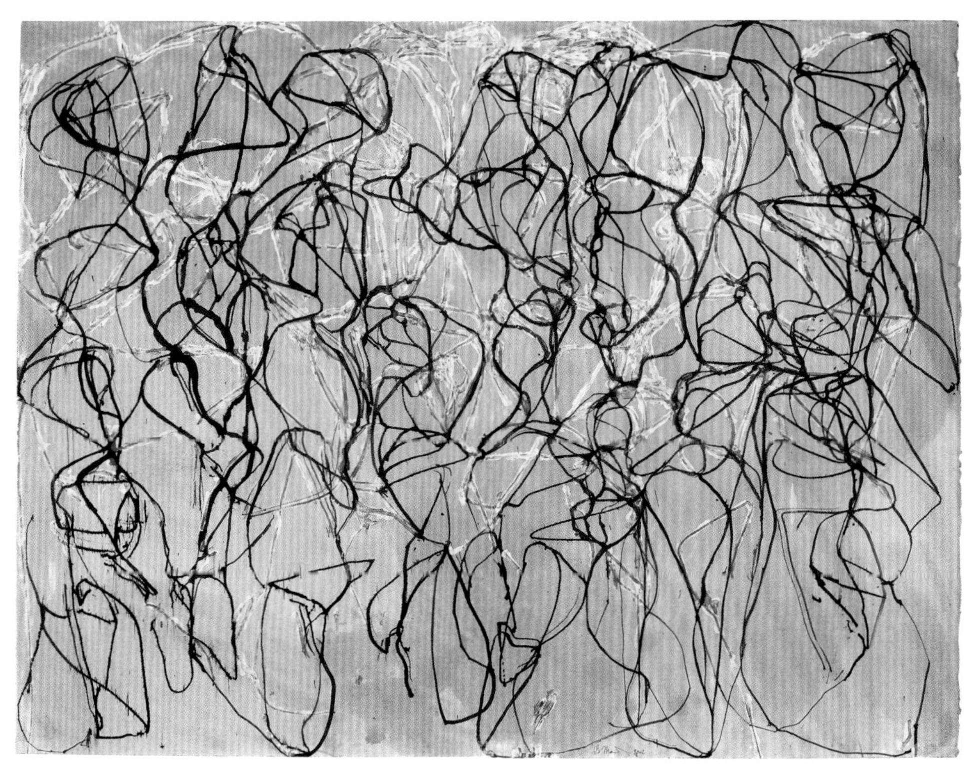

130. *Cold Mountain Addendum 2.* 1990–92
Ink, ink wash, and gouache on paper
25¾ x 34¼" (65.4 x 87 cm)

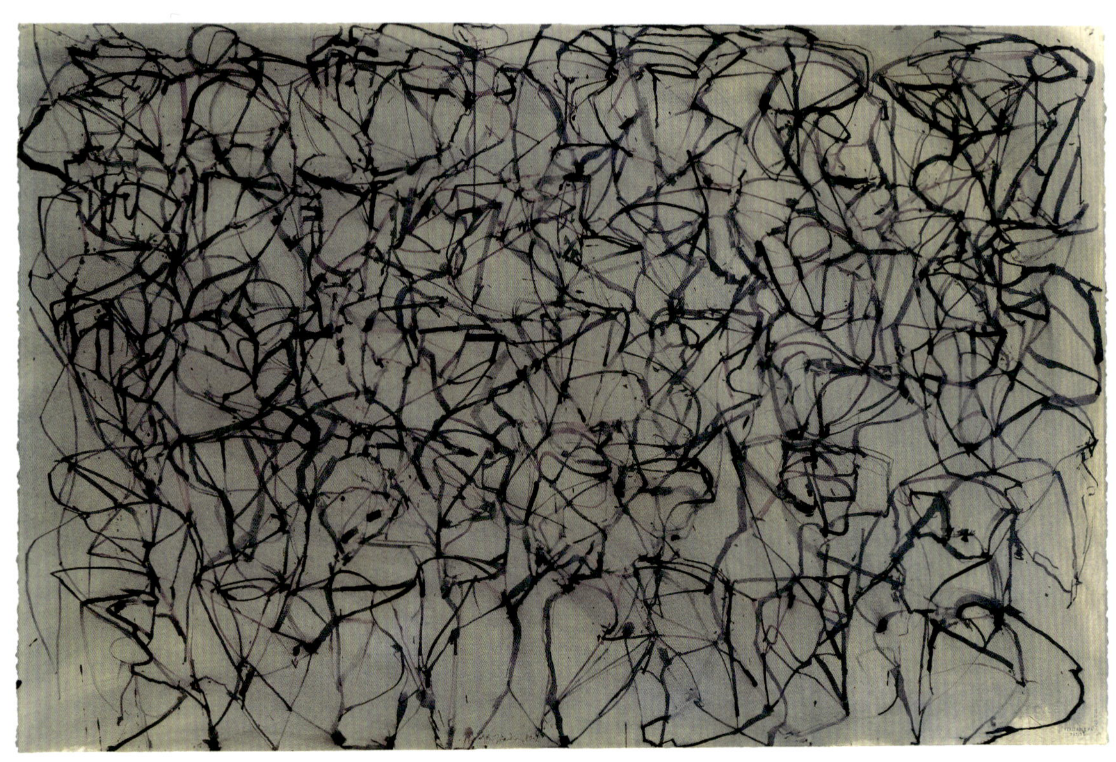

131. *Muses Drawing 5 (Mnemosyne).* 1989–91
Ink and ink wash on paper
26 x 40⅝" (66 x 103.2 cm)

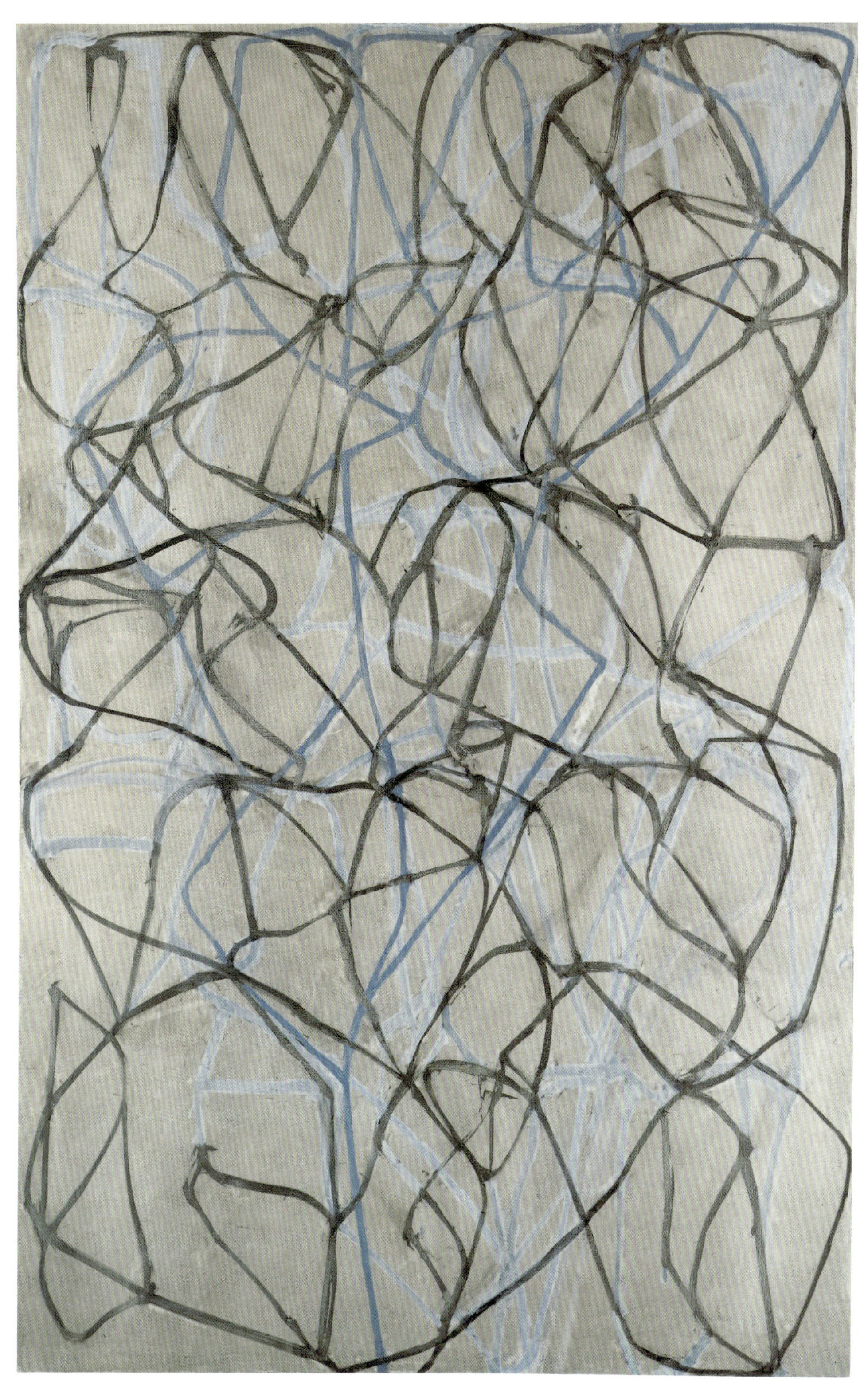

132. *The Studio.* 1990
Oil on linen
7' 8 5/8" x 59" (235.3 x 149.9 cm)

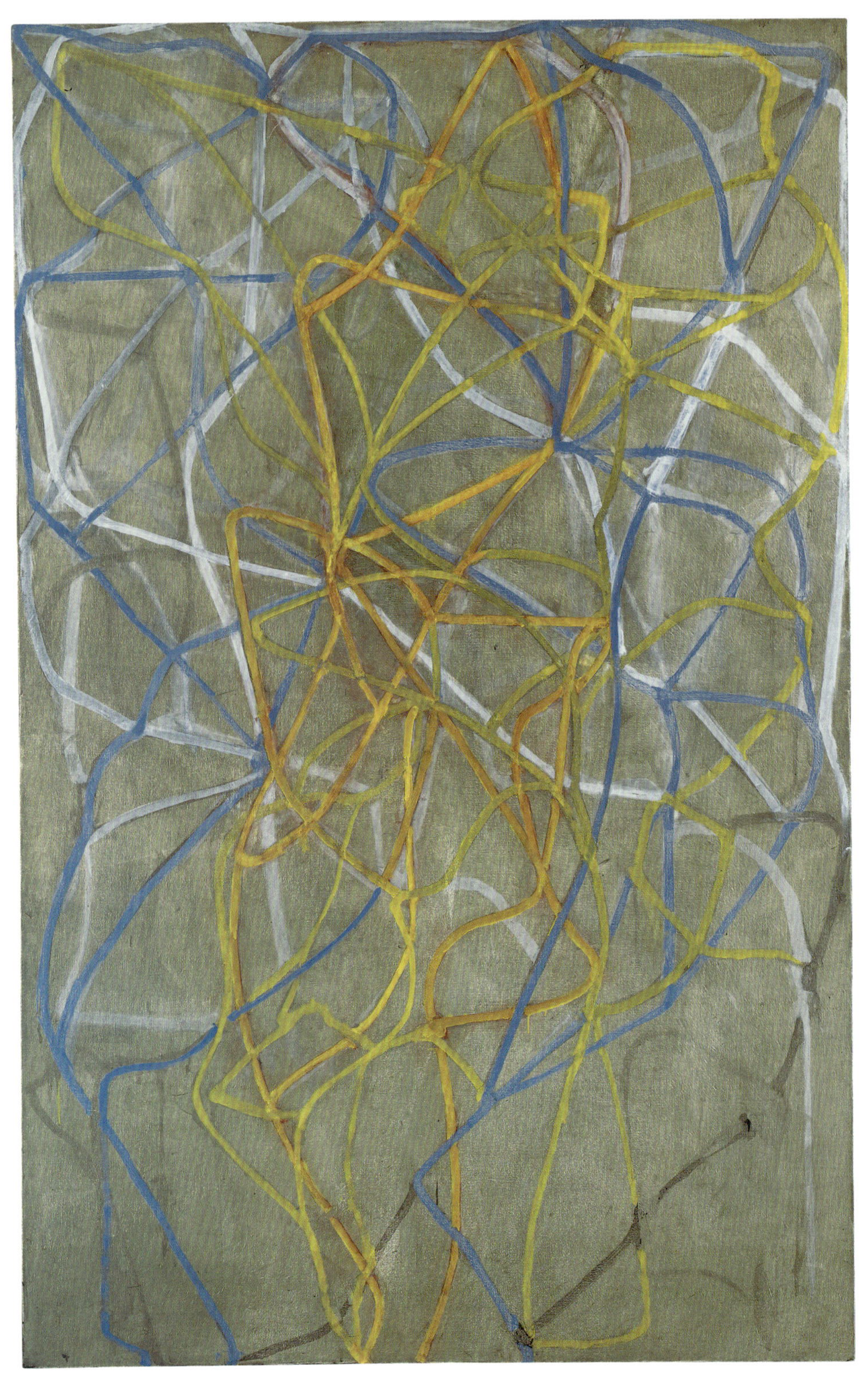

133. *Kalo Keri.* 1990
Oil on linen
7' 8⅝" x 59" (235.3 x 149.9 cm)

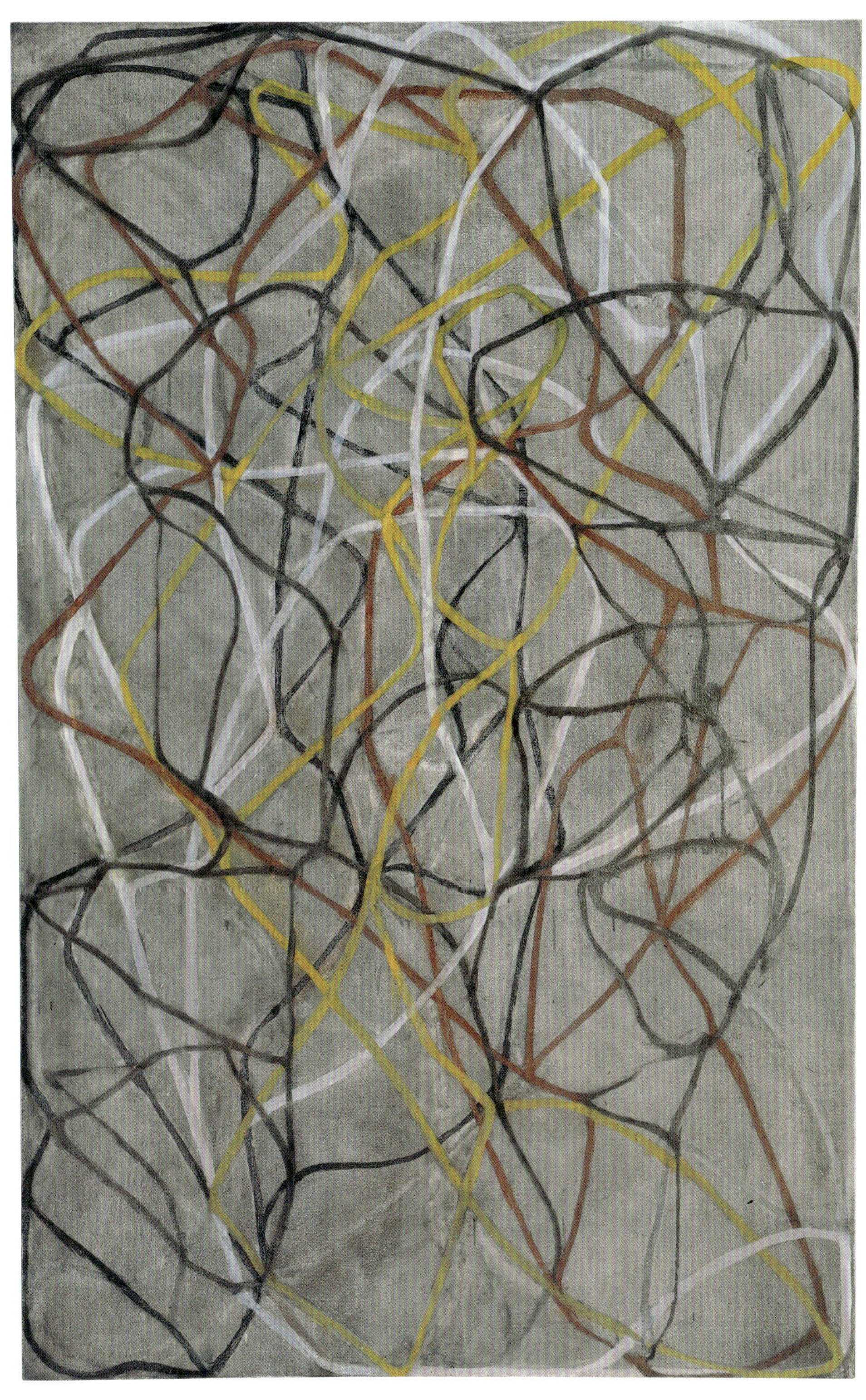

134. *Presentation*. 1990–92
Oil on linen
7' 8 3/8" x 59" (234.6 x 149.9 cm)

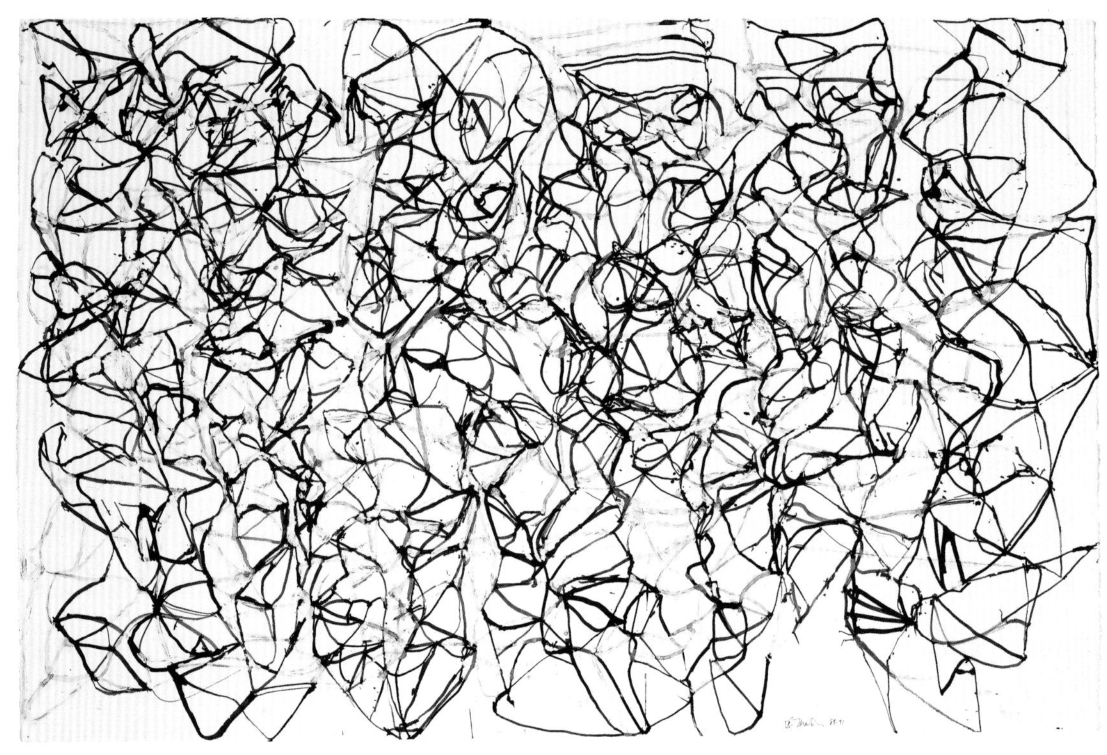

135. *Muses Drawing 4.* 1989–91
Ink and gouache on paper
26 x 40⅝" (66 x 103.2 cm)

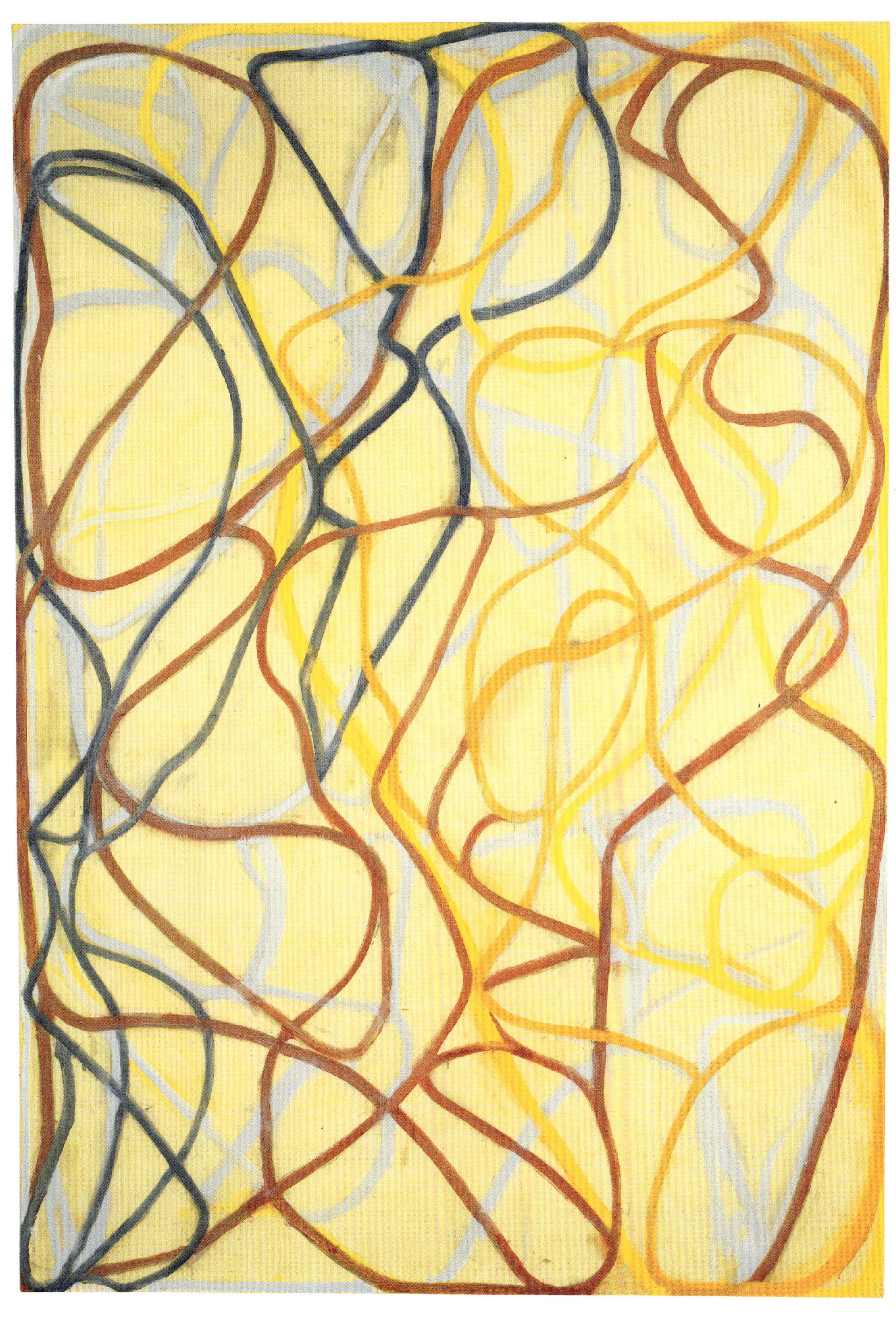

136. *The Sisters.* 1991–93
Oil on linen
7' x 59" (213.4 x 149.9 cm)

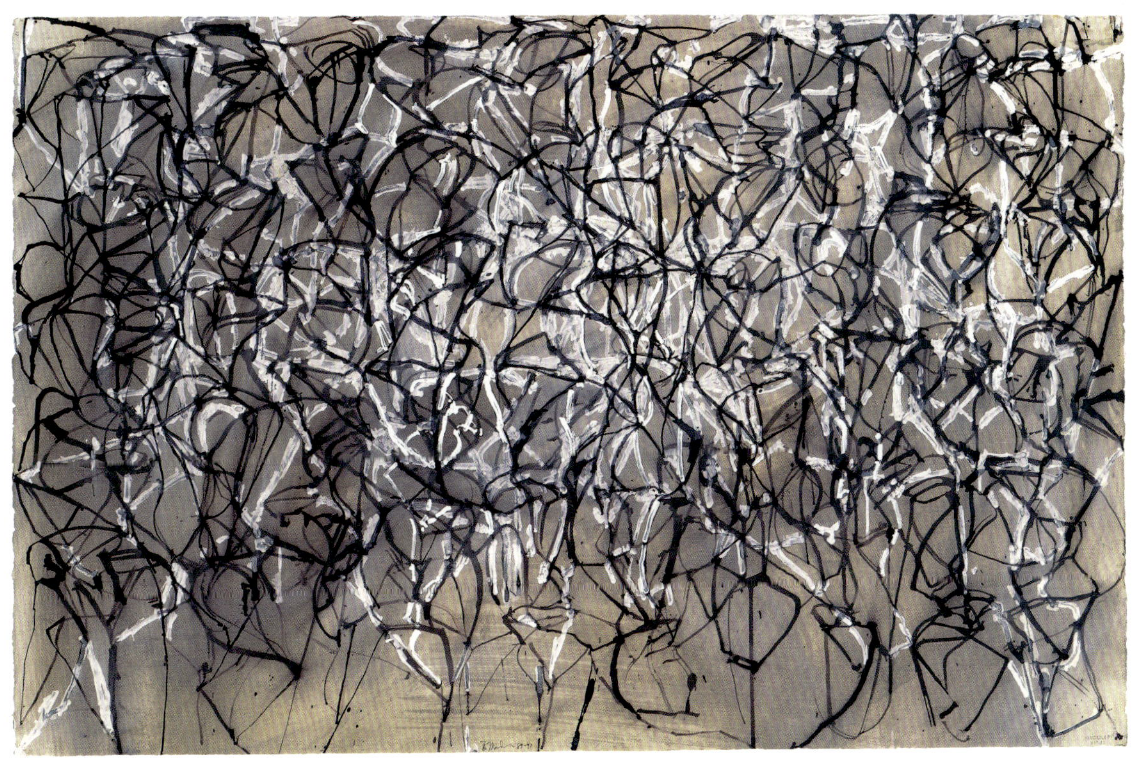

138. *Muses Drawing 2.* 1989–91
Ink, ink wash, and gouache on paper
26 x 40⅝" (66 x 103.2 cm)

139. *Virgins*. 1991–93
Oil on linen
8 x 8' 6" (243.8 x 259.1 cm)

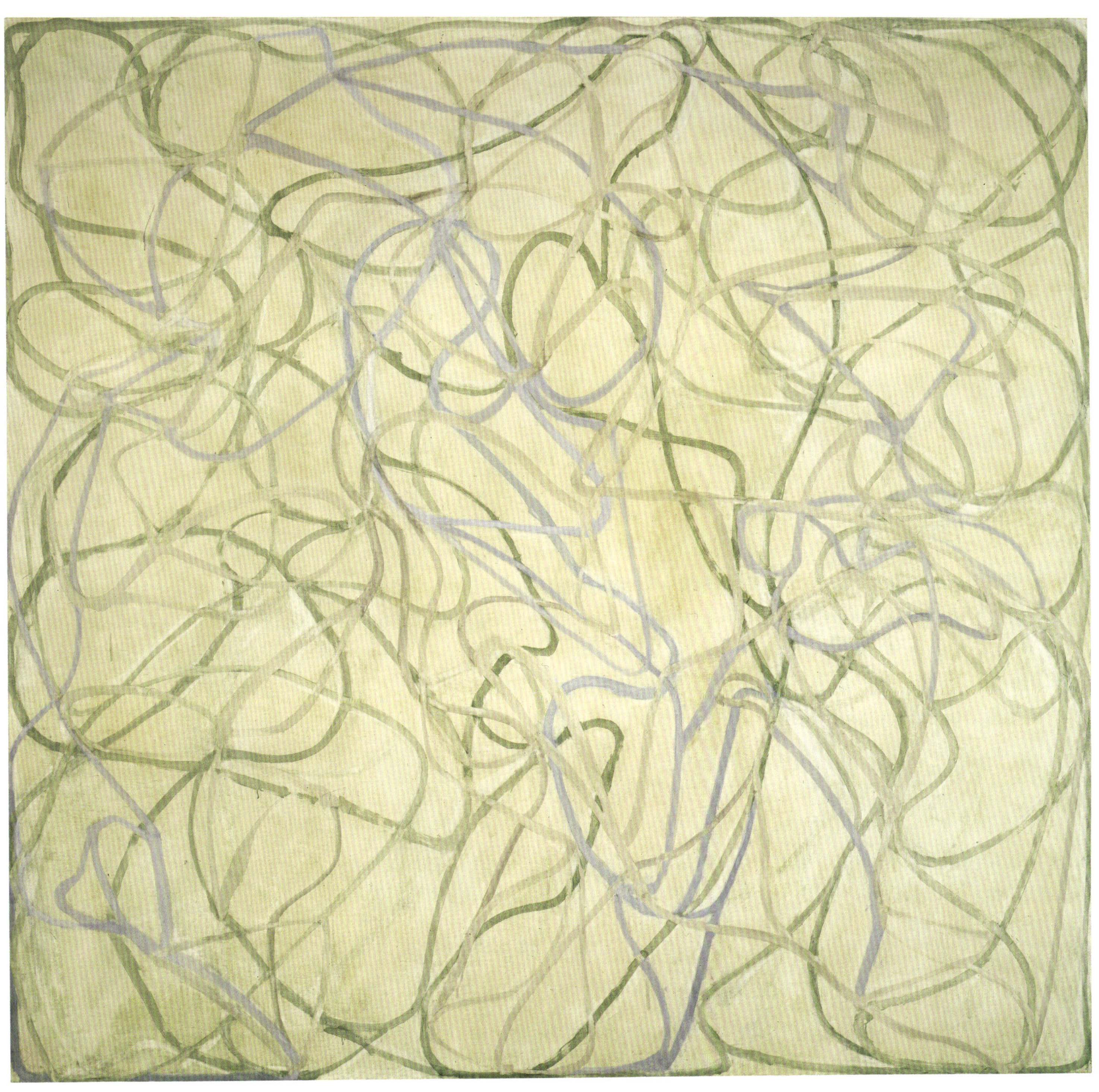

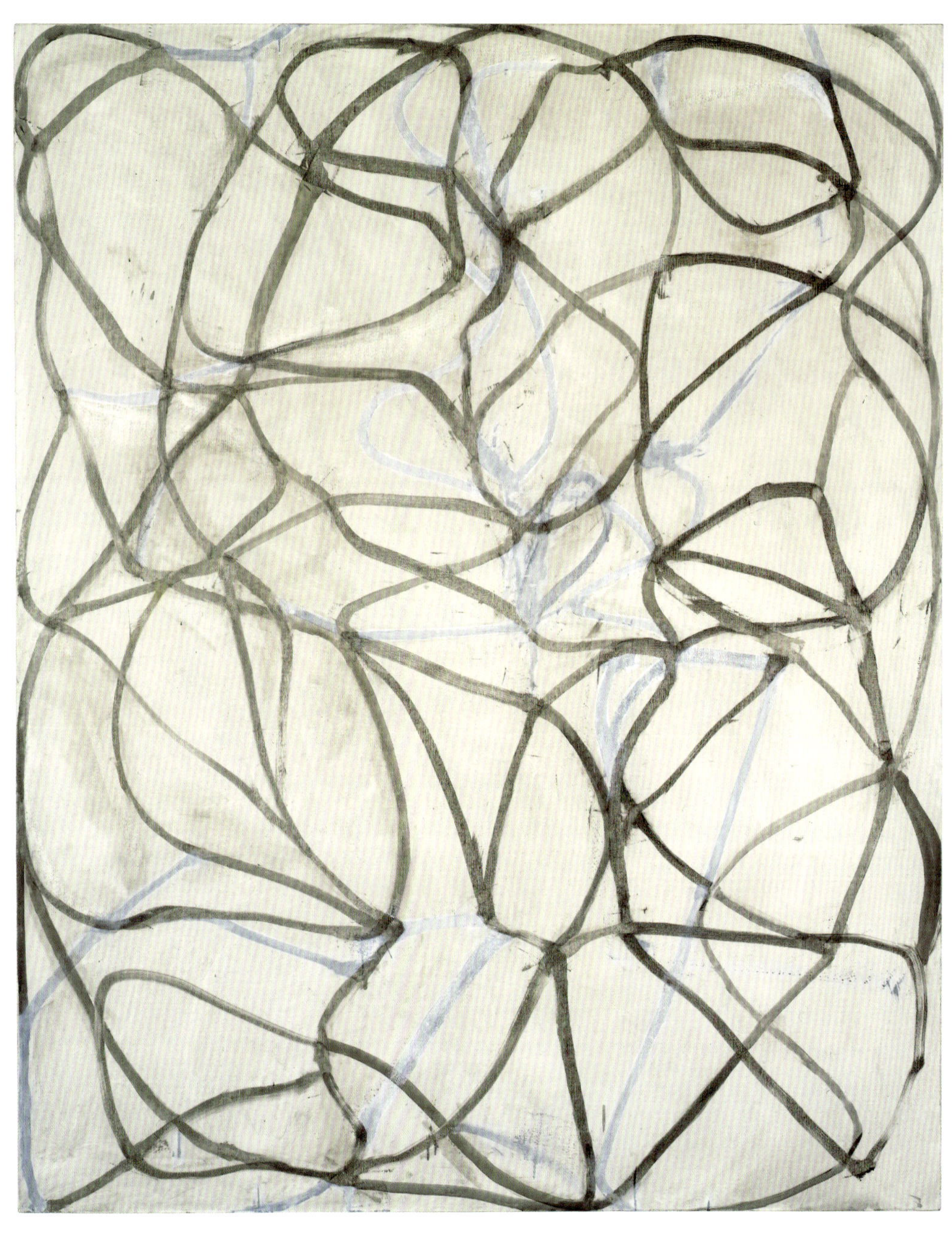

140. *Corpus*. 1991–93
Oil on linen
6' 7" x 57" (200.7 x 144.8 cm)

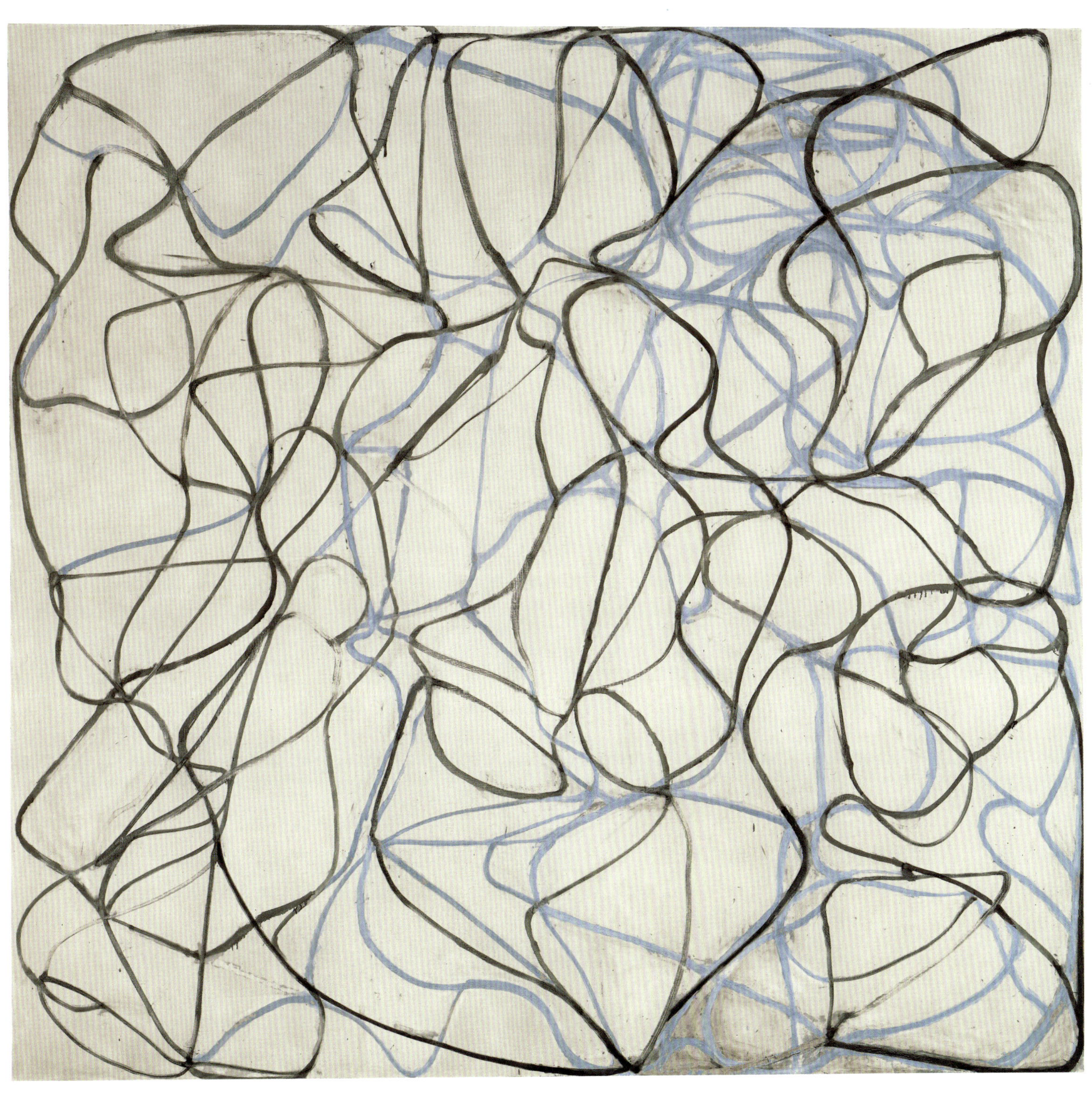

141. *Vine*. 1992–93
Oil on linen
8' x 8' 6" (243.8 x 259.1 cm)

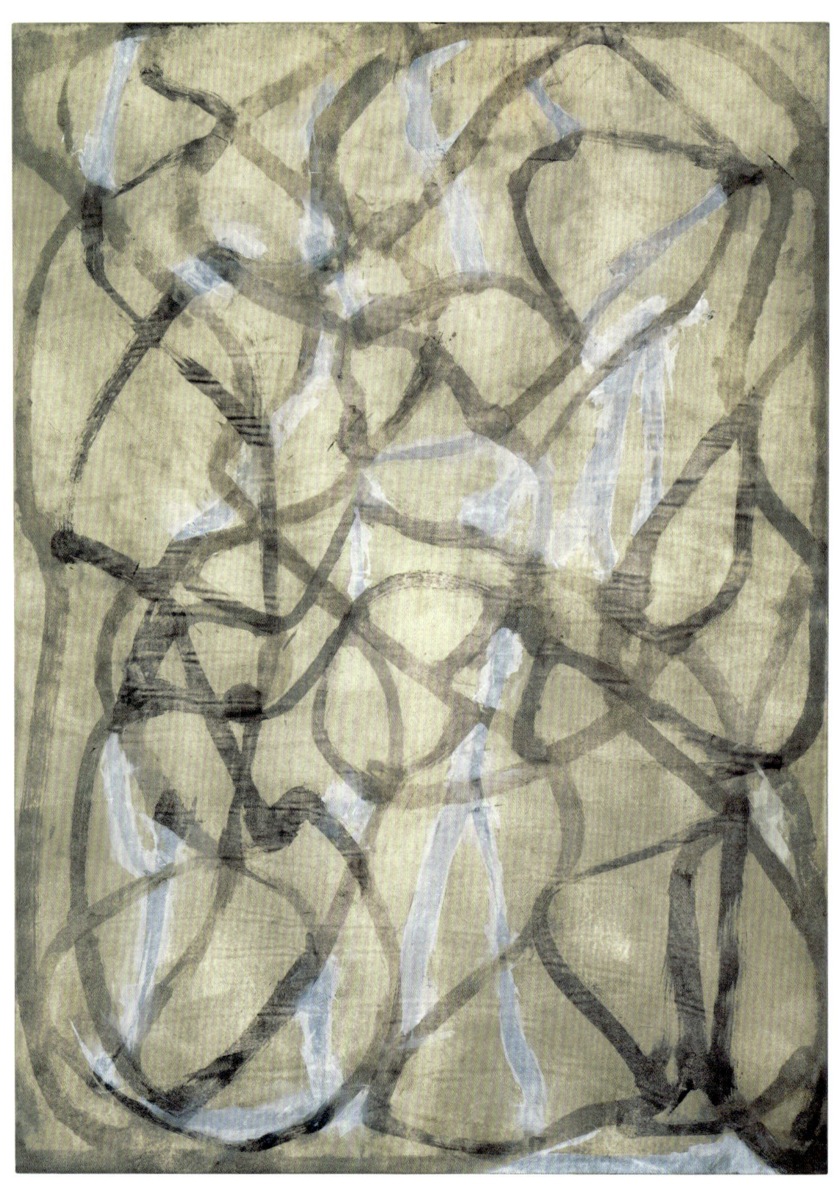

142. *Small Corpus.* 1989–94
Oil on parchment stretched over birch panel
$26^{1/2}$ x $19^{3/8}$" (67.3 x 49.2 cm)

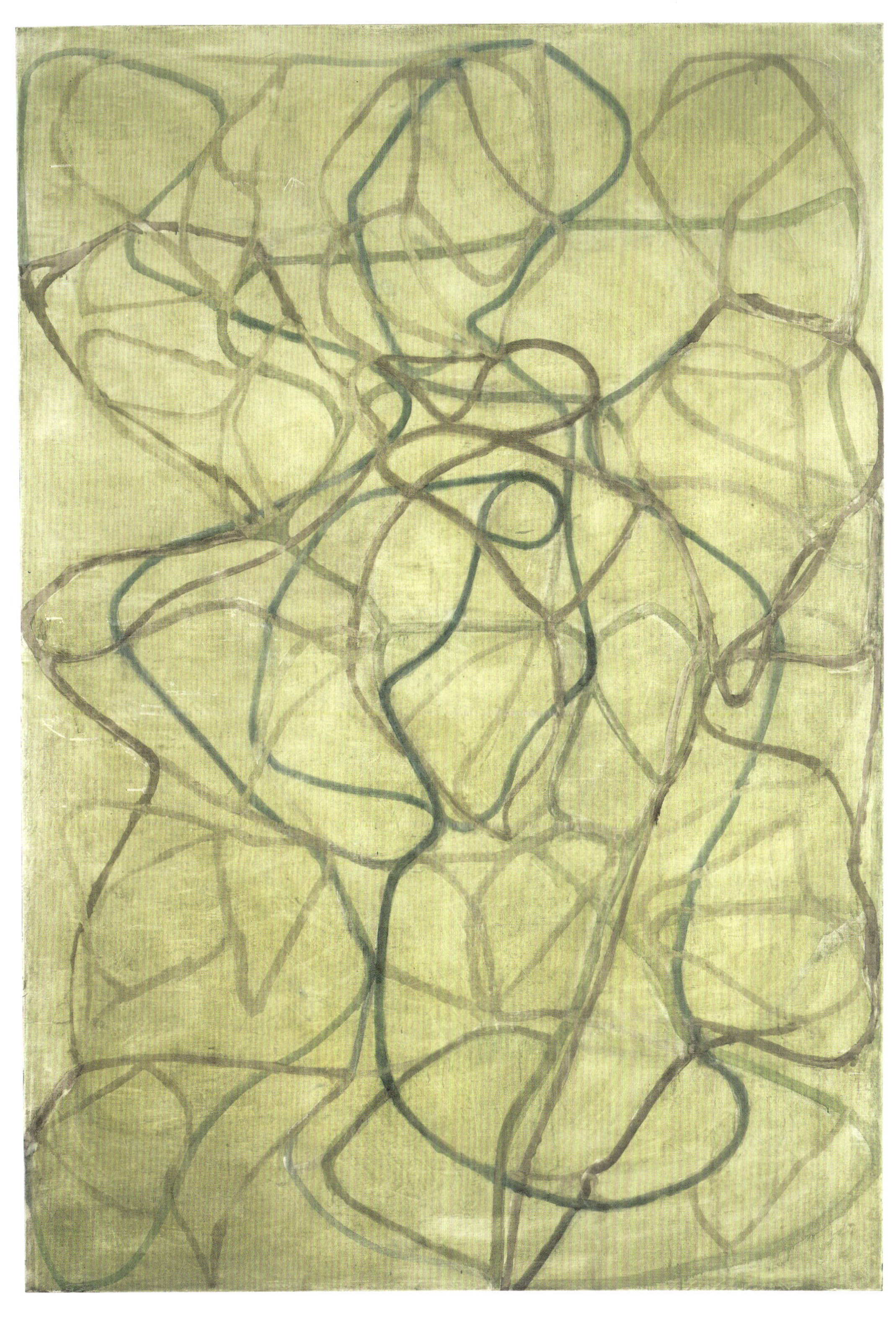

143. *Aphrodite*. 1991–93
Oil on linen
8' 4" x 70" (254 x 177.8 cm)

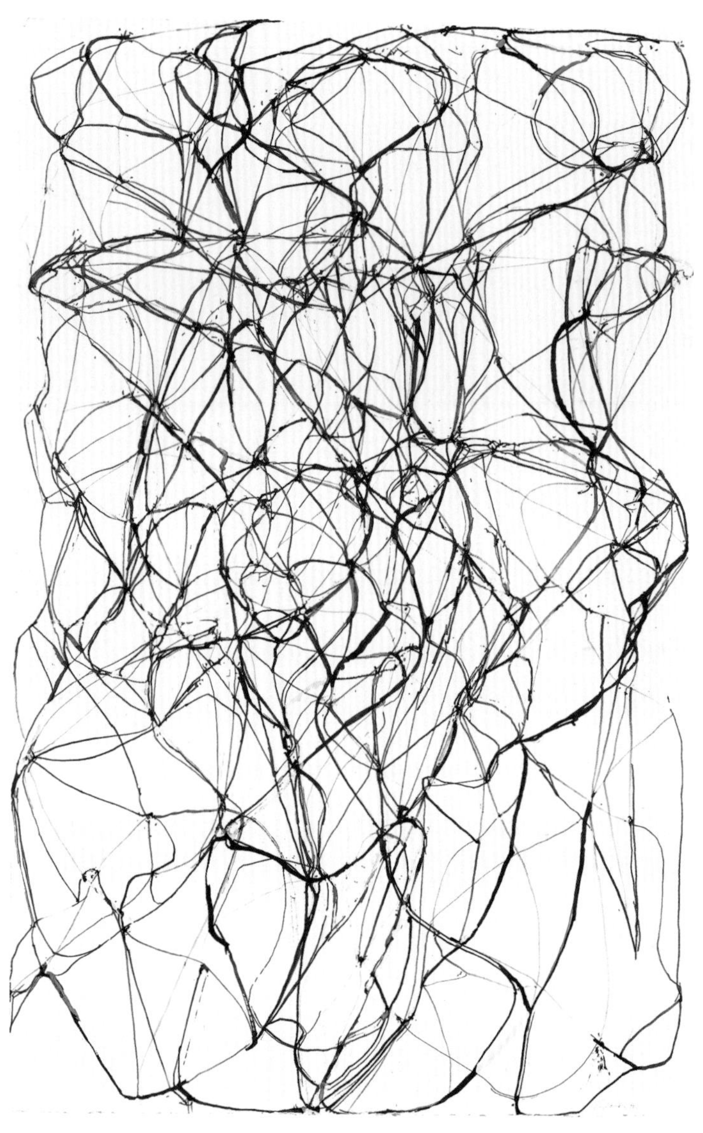

144. *Venus*. 1990–91
Ink and gouache on paper
40 x 25½" (101.6 x 64.8 cm)

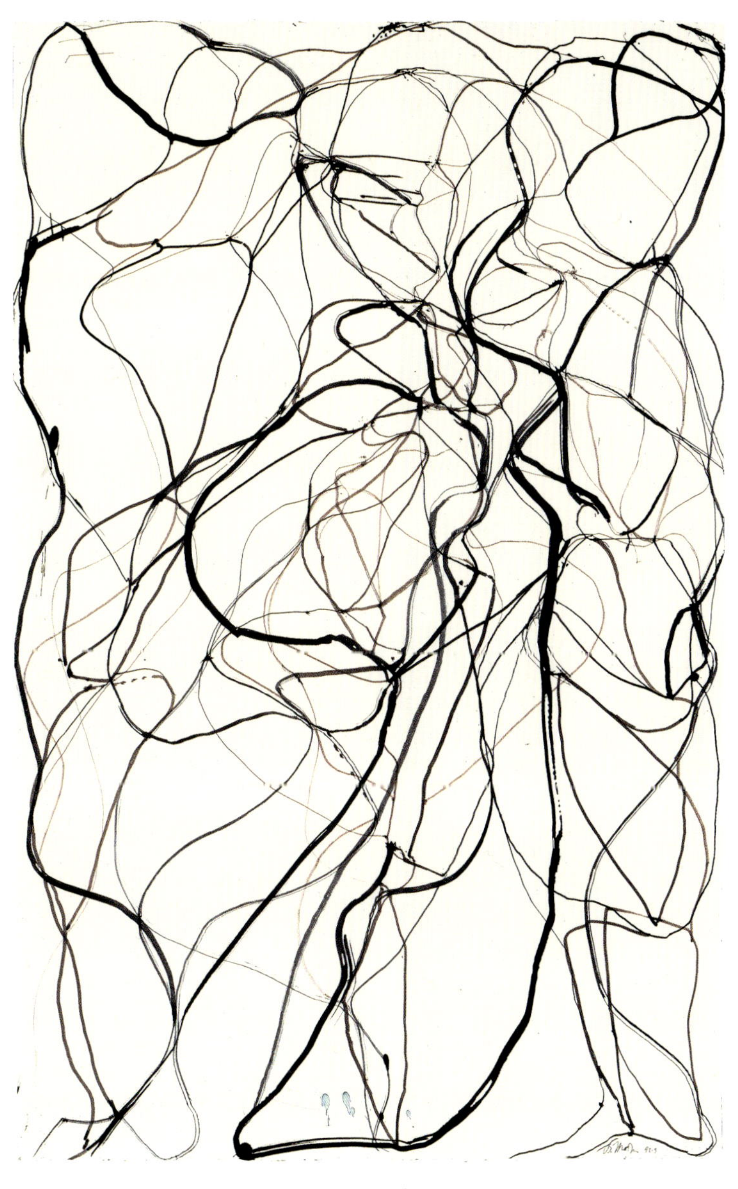

146. *Aphrodite (Negril).* 1992–93
Ink on paper
40½ x 25⅞" (102.9 x 65.7 cm)

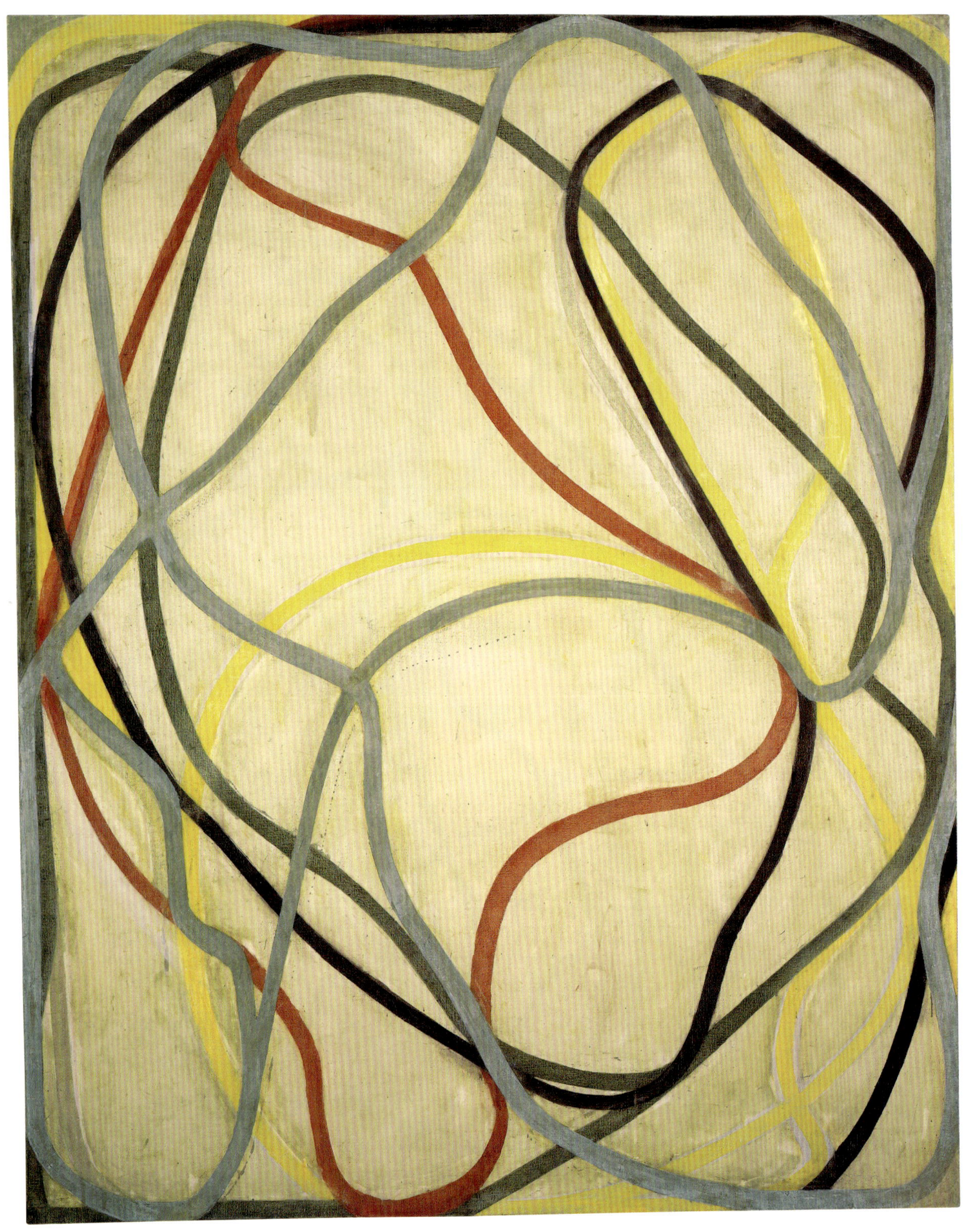

147. *Light in the Forest.* 1993–95
Oil on linen
71 x 57" (180.3 x 144.8 cm)

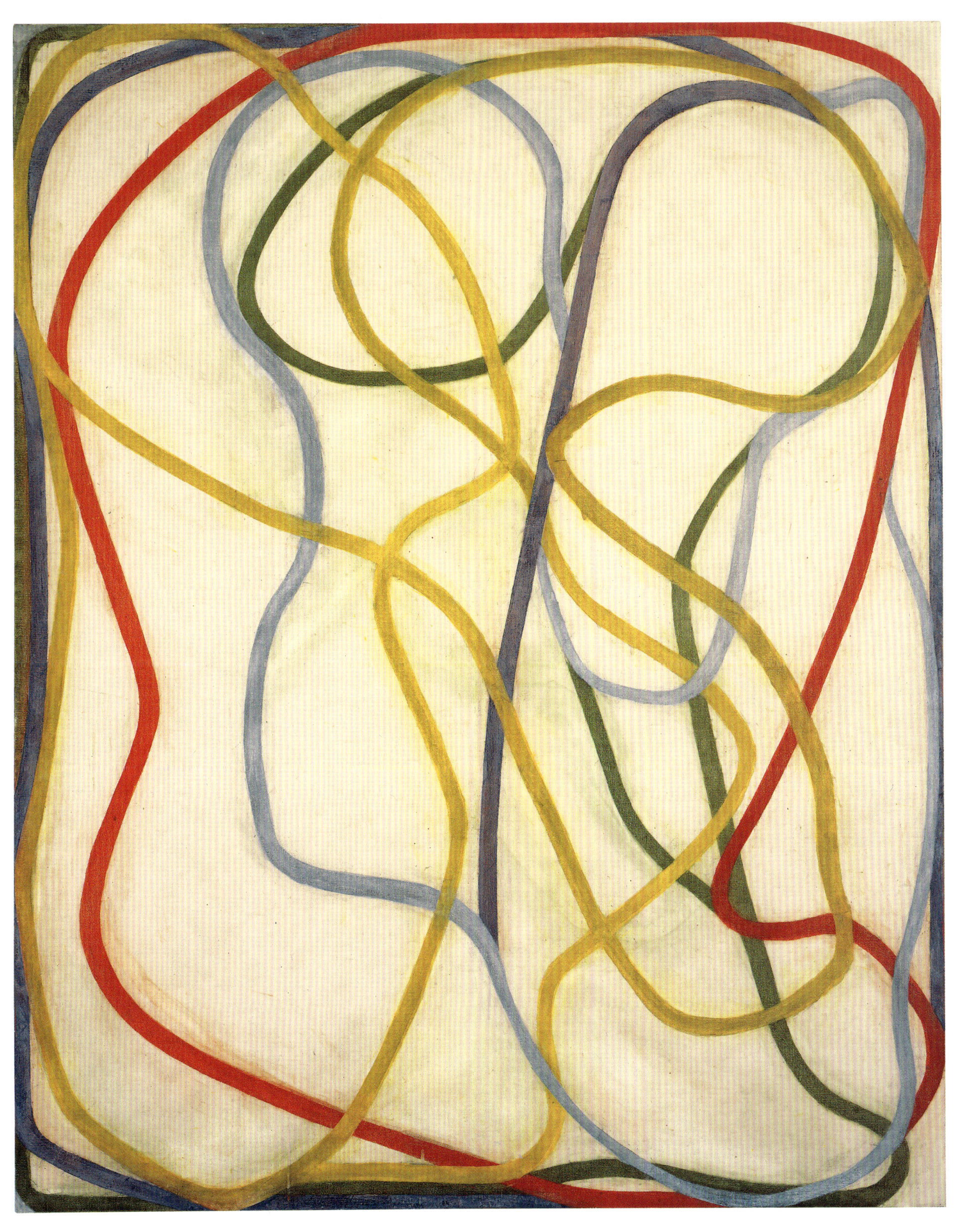

148. *Skull with Thought.* 1993–95
Oil on linen
71 x 57" (180.3 x 144.8 cm)

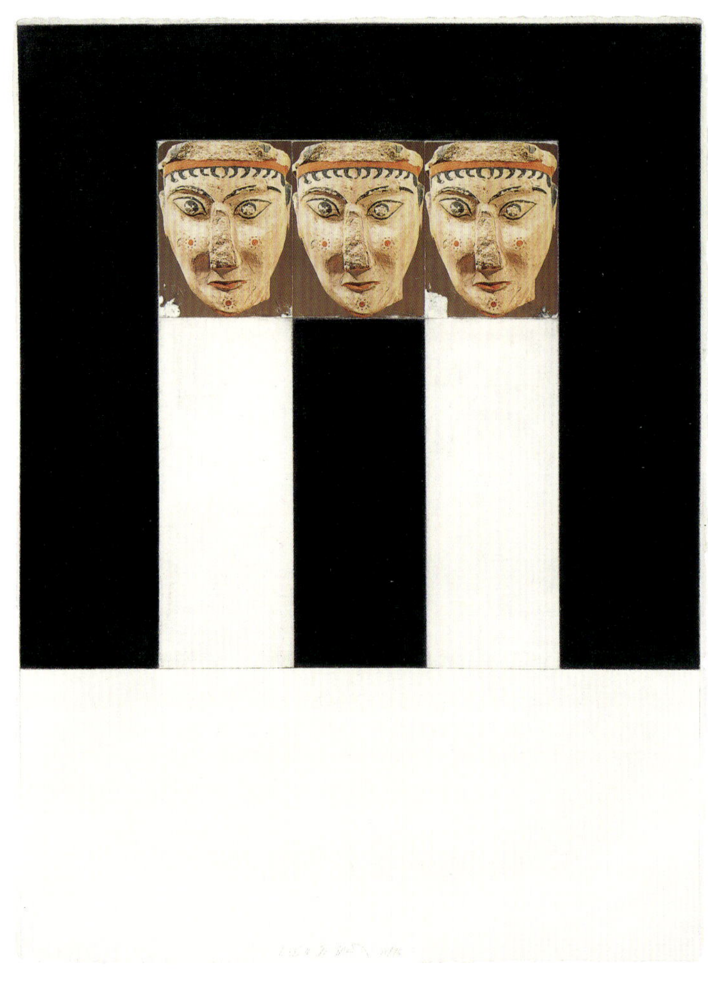

149. *Souvenir de Grèce 11.* 1974/1996
Graphite, beeswax, and collage on paper
29¾ x 22½" (75.6 x 57.2 cm)

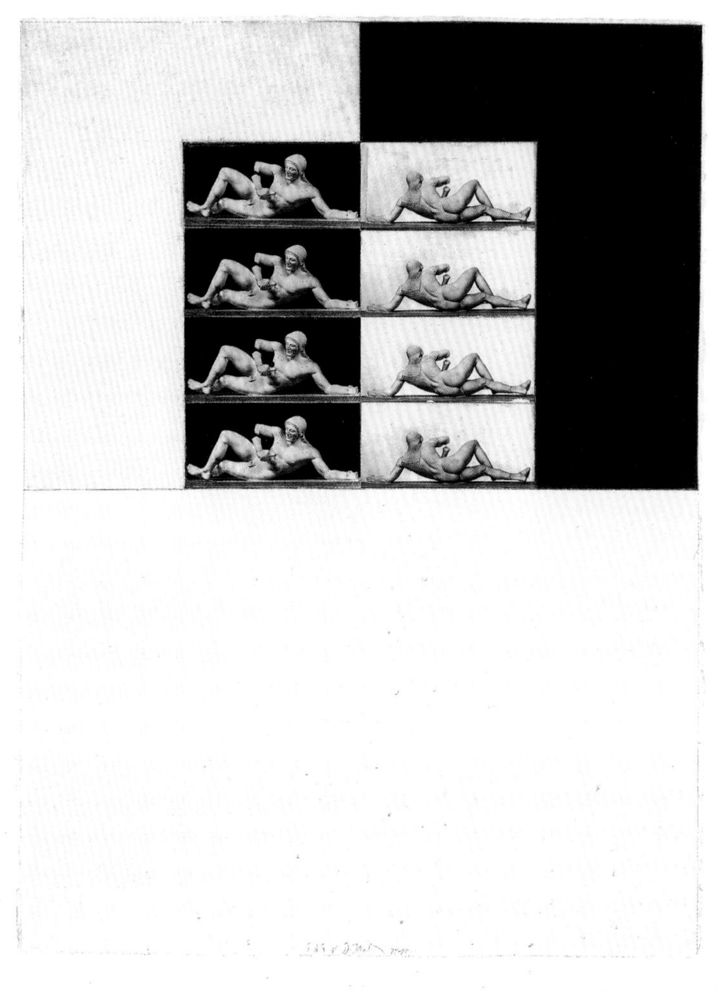

150. *Souvenir de Grèce 4.* 1974/1994
Graphite, beeswax, and collage on paper
$29^{3}/_{4}$ x $22^{1}/_{2}$" (75.6 x 57.2 cm)

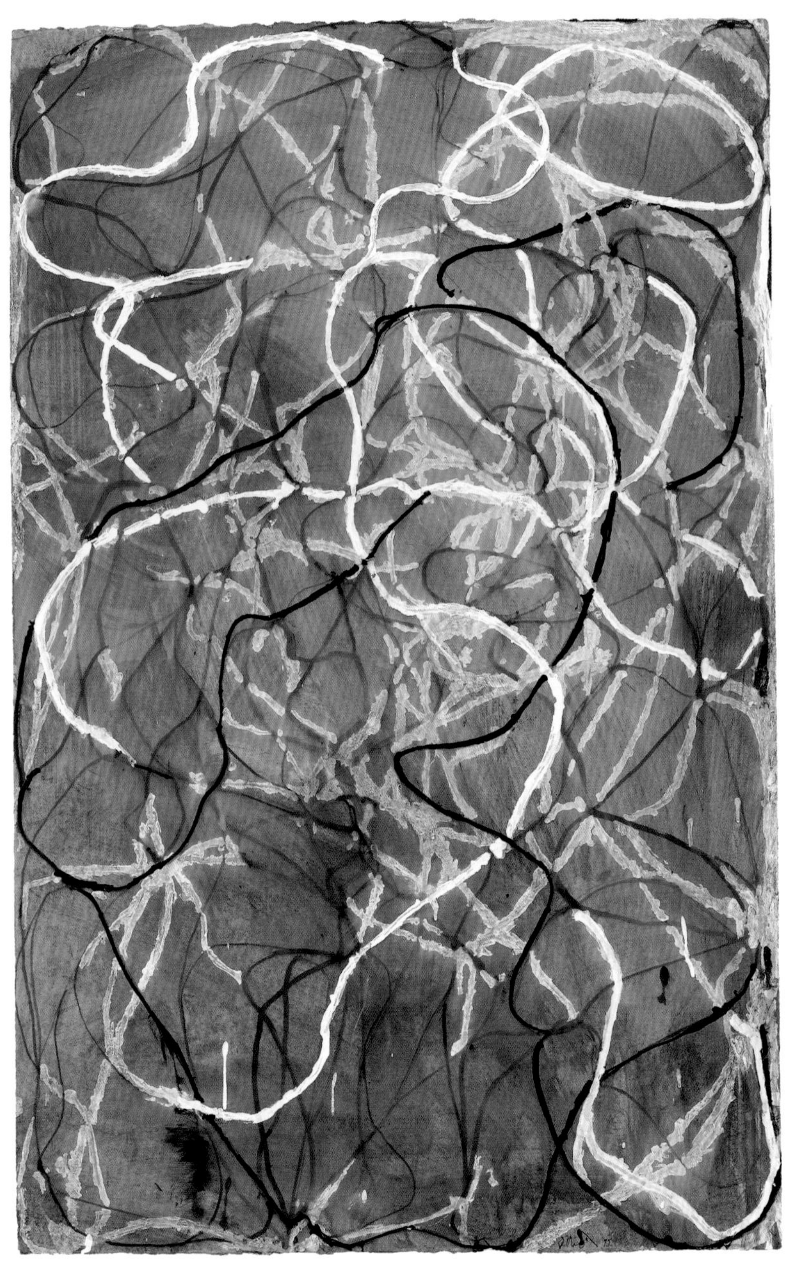

151. *Daoist Conclusion.* 1991–95
Ink and gouache on paper
40½ x 25⅞" (102.9 x 65.7 cm)

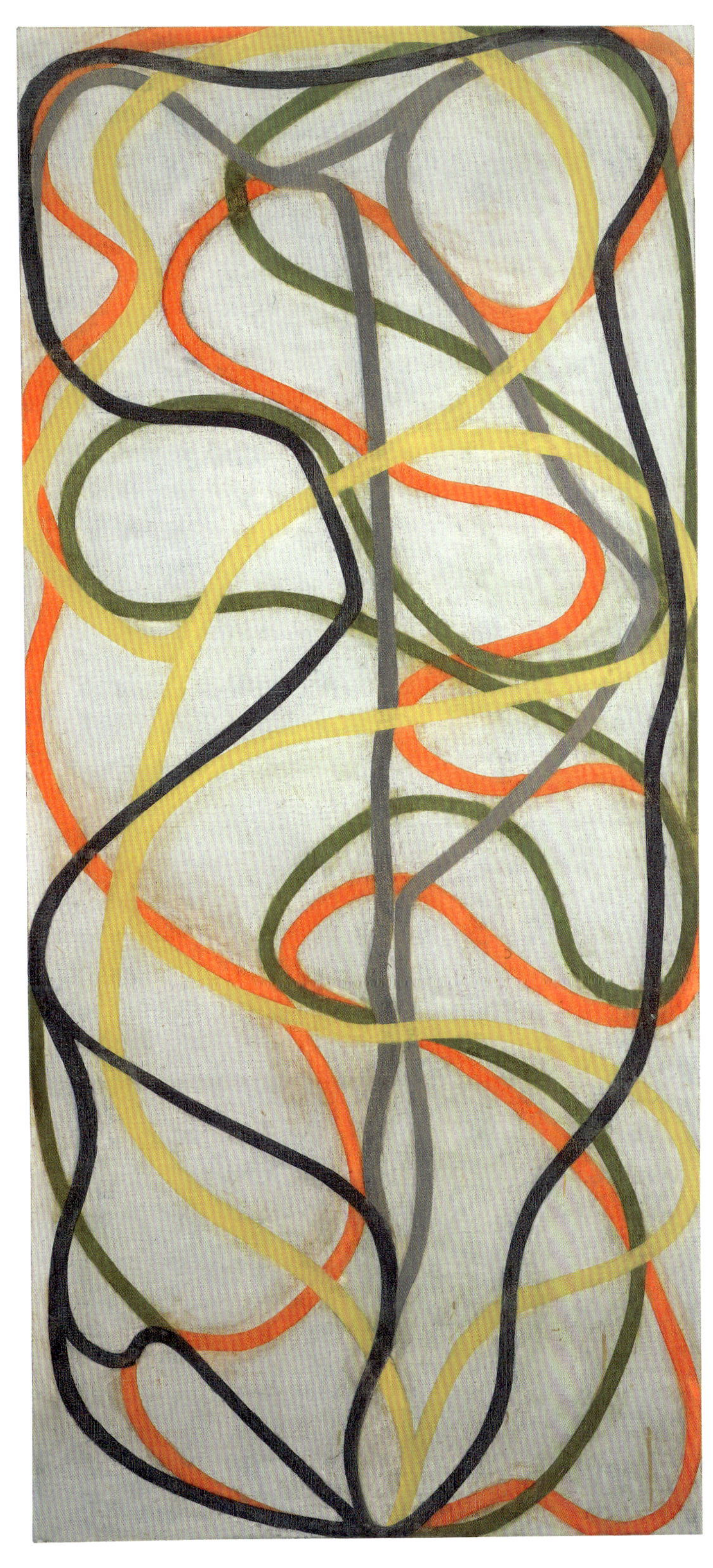

152. *Tang Dancer*. 1995–96
Oil on linen
72 x 33" (182.9 x 83.8 cm)

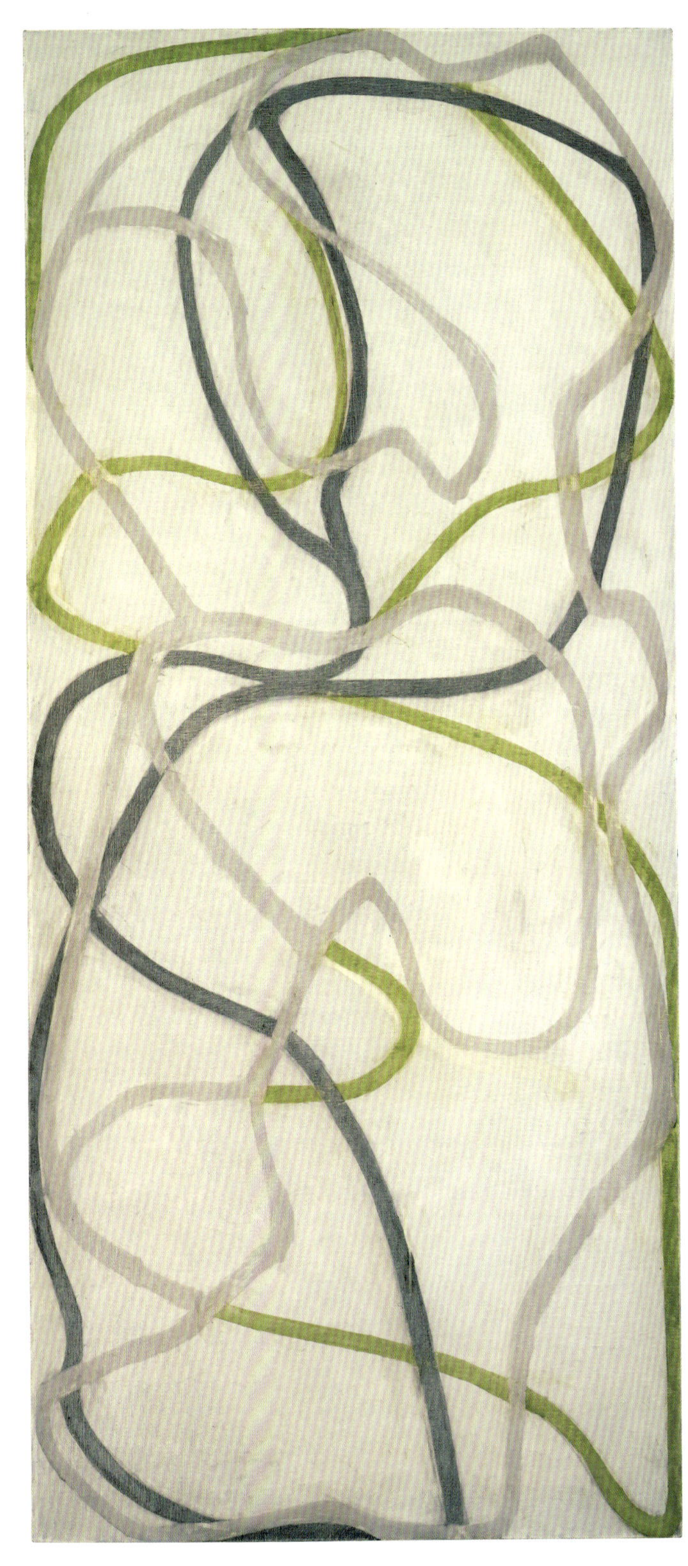

153. *Suzhou.* 1995–96
Oil on linen
72 x 32" (182.9 x 81.3 cm)

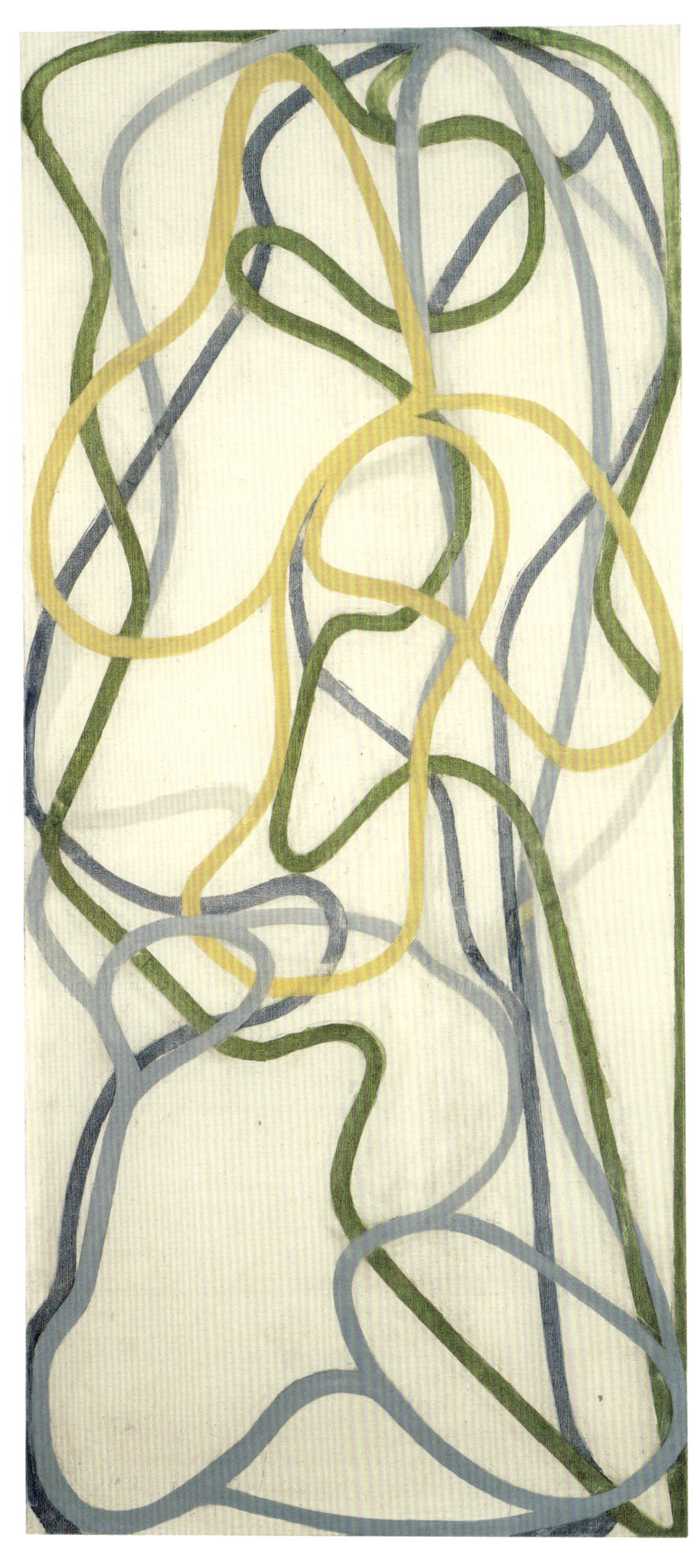

154. *China Painting.* 1995–96
Oil on linen
71 x 32" (180.3 x 81.3 cm)

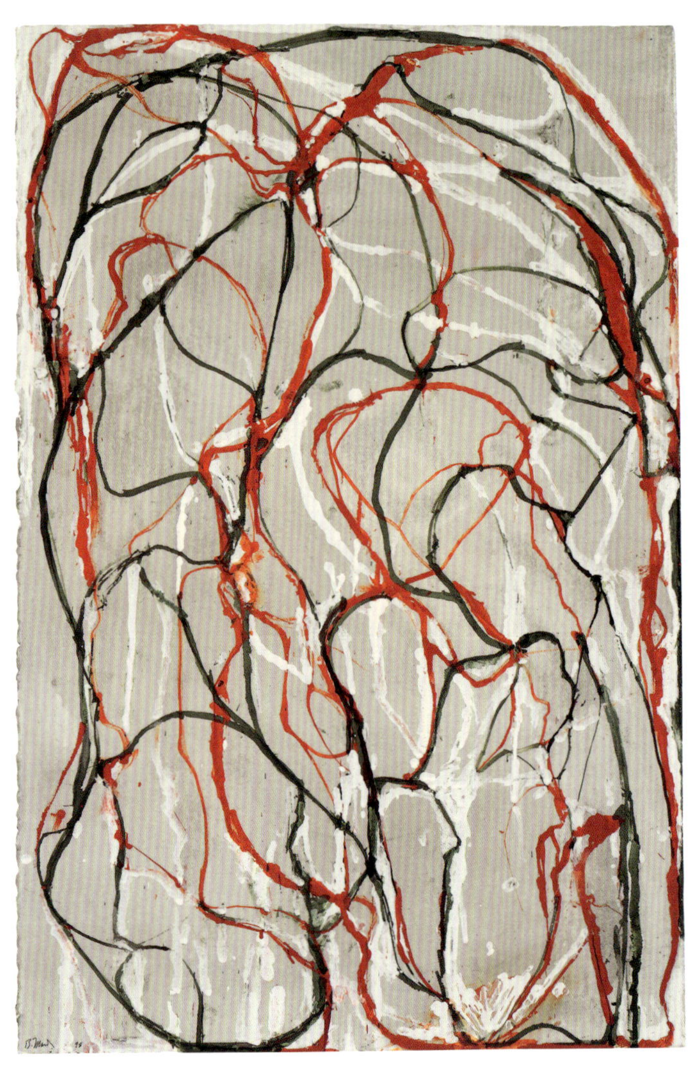

155. *Untitled Red and Green Drawing 1.* 1998
Ink on paper
29 3/4 x 20 1/8" (75.6 x 51.1 cm)

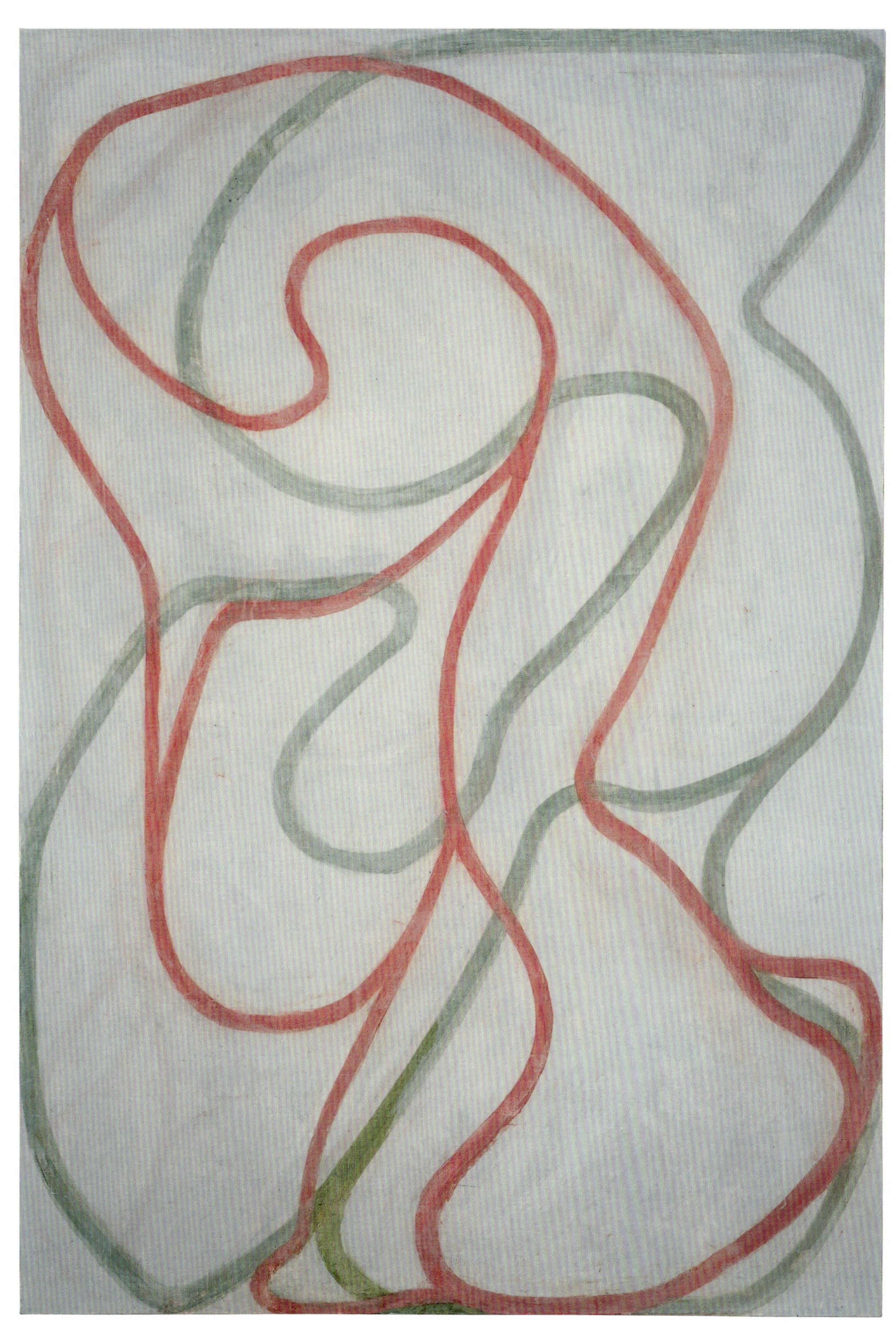

156. *Attendant*. 1996–99
Oil on linen
6' 10" x 57" (208.3 x 144.8 cm)

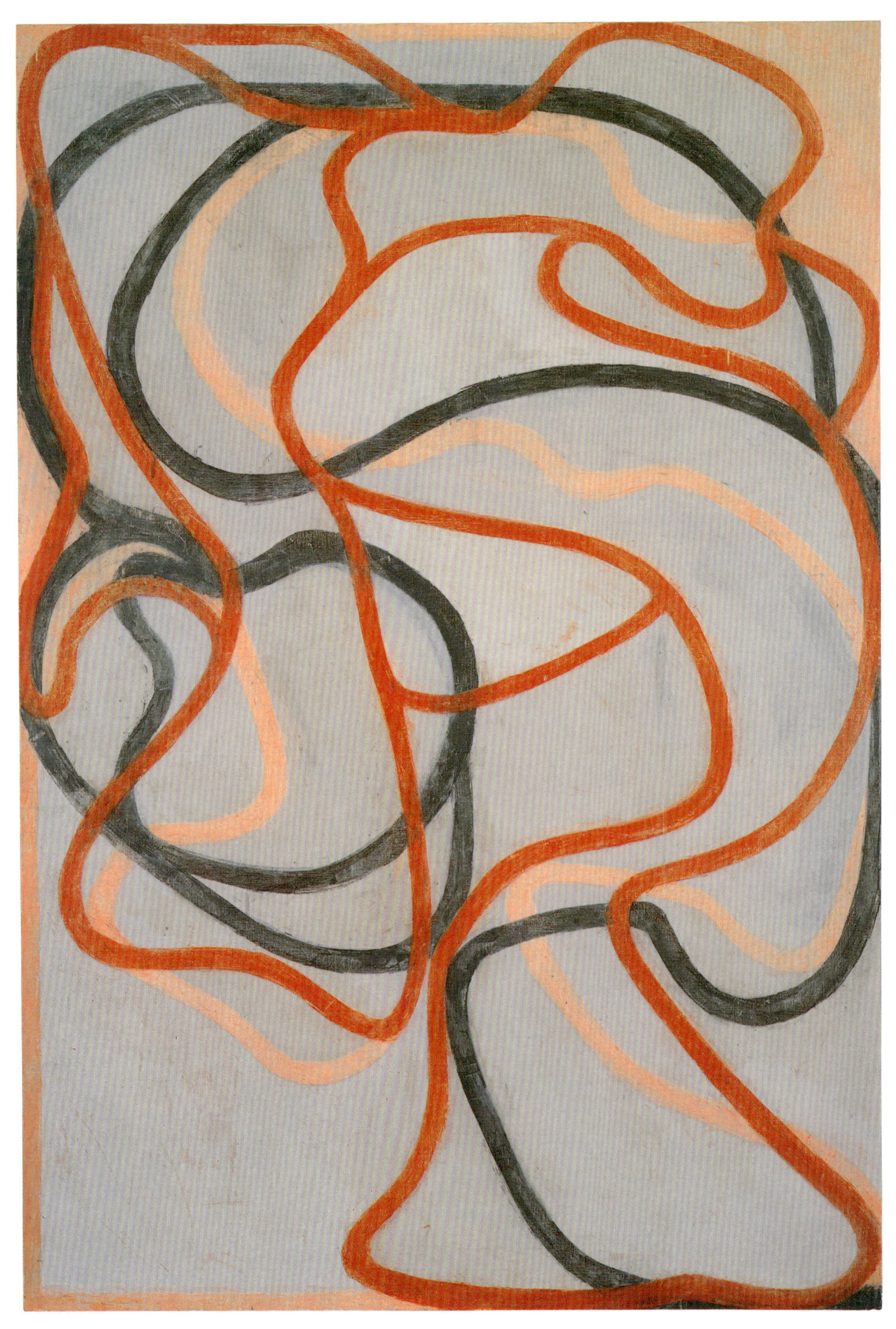

157. *Attendant 2.* 1996–99
Oil on linen
6' 10" x 57" (208.3 x 144.8 cm)

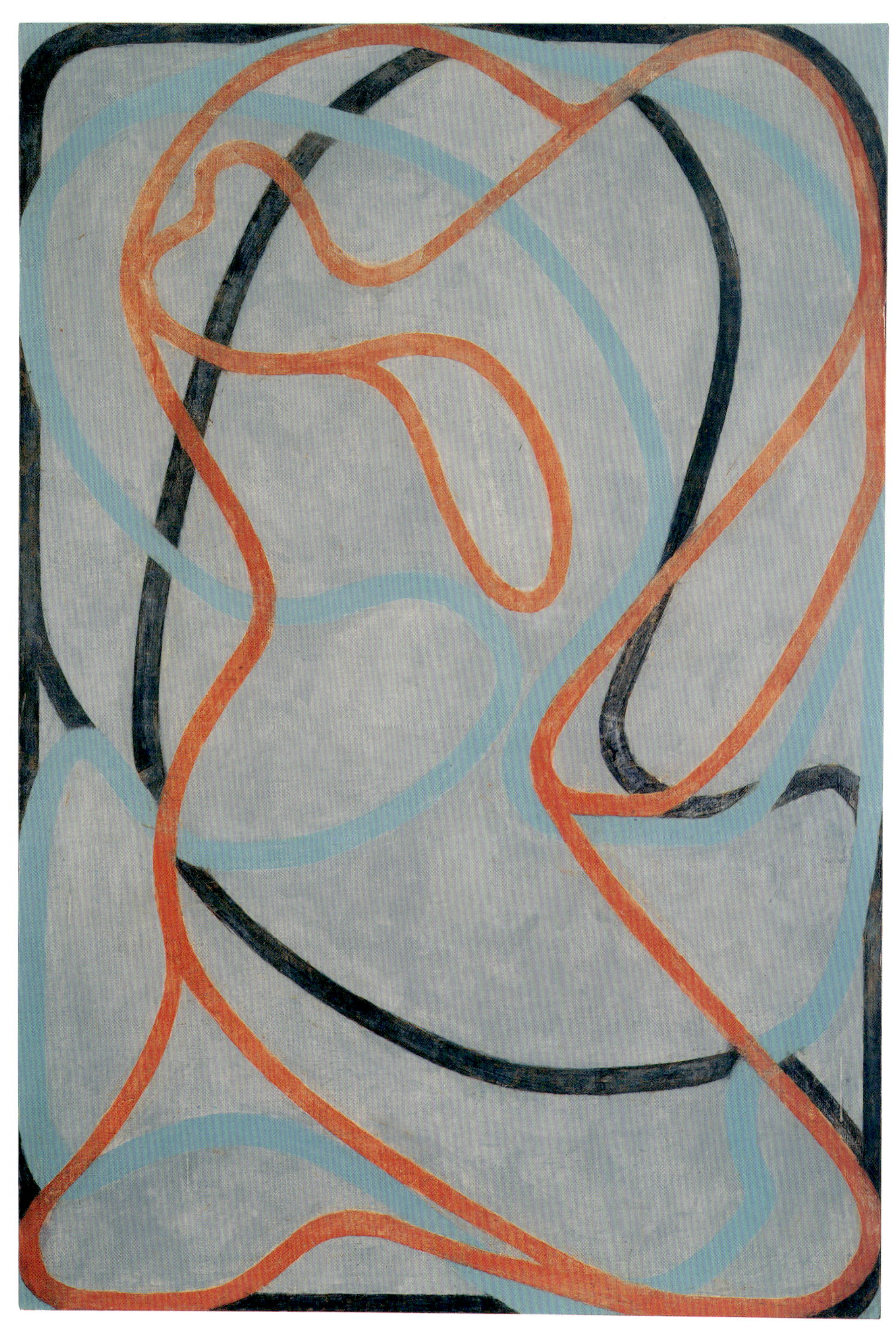

158. *Attendant 3.* 1996–99
Oil on linen
6' 10" x 57" (208.3 x 144.8 cm)

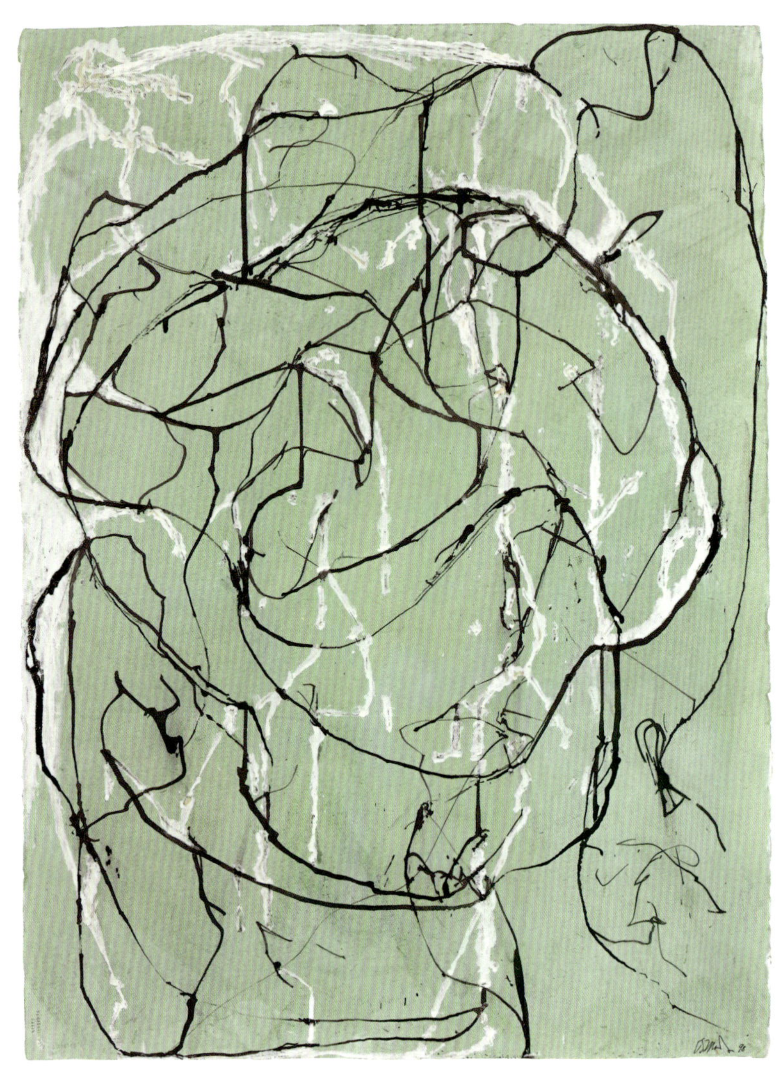

159. *Post Calligraphic Drawing.* 1998
Ink on paper
30 x 22½" (76.2 x 57.2 cm)

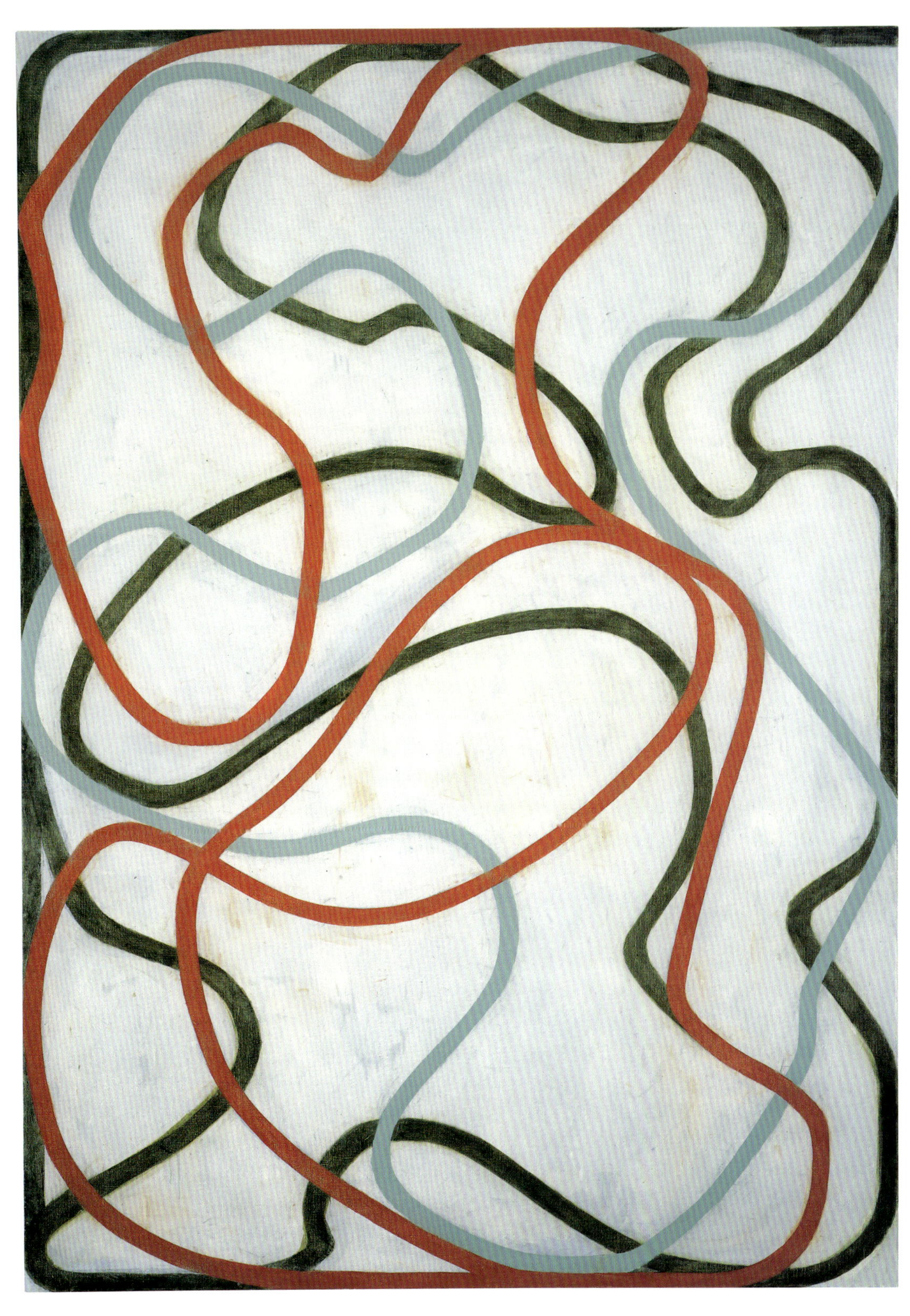

160. *Bear Print*. 1997–98/2000
Oil on linen
7' x 60" (213.4 x 152.4 cm)

161. *Epitaph Painting 1*. 1996–97
Oil on linen
8' 1/2" x 7' 11" (245.1 x 241.3 cm)

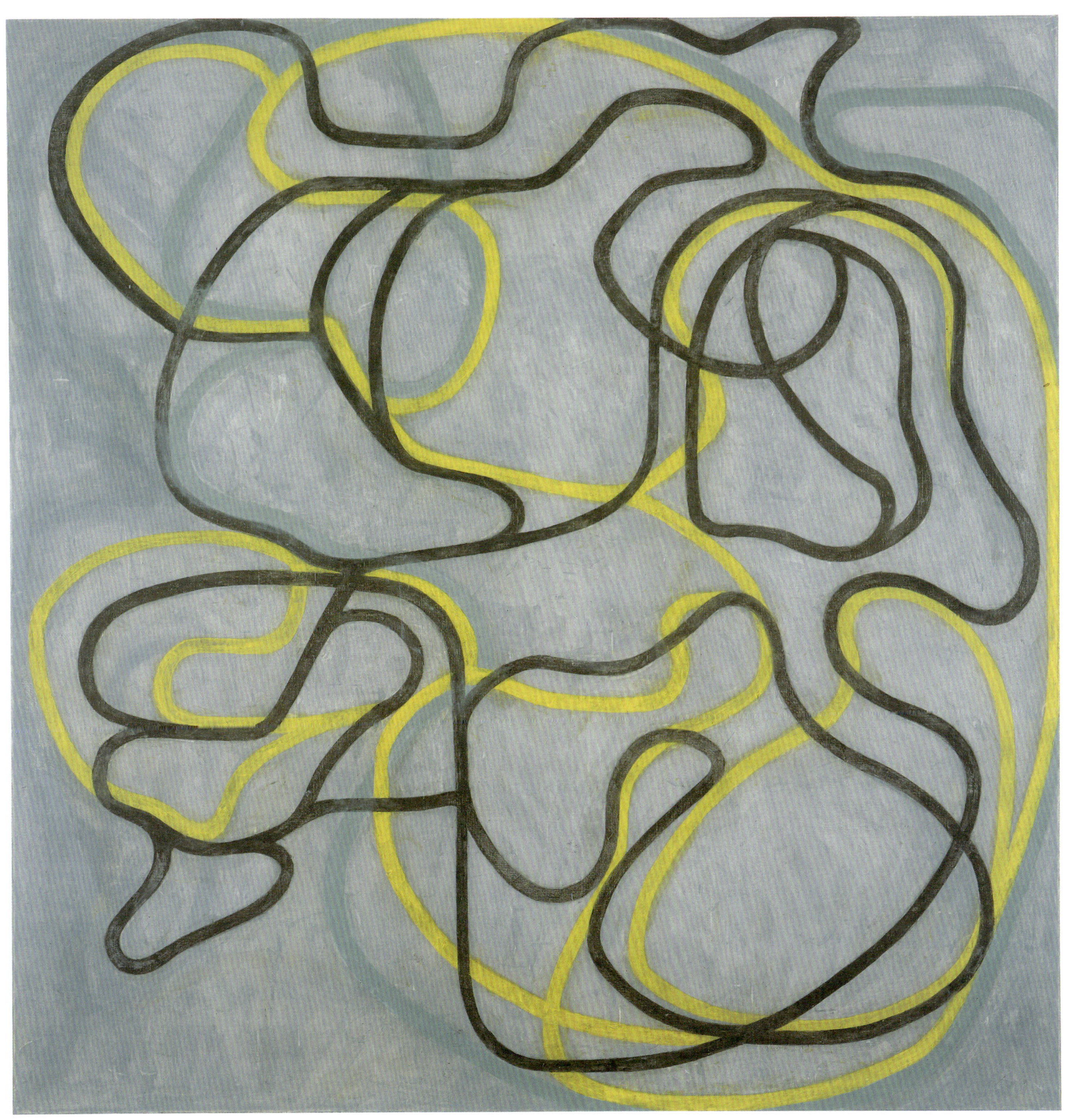

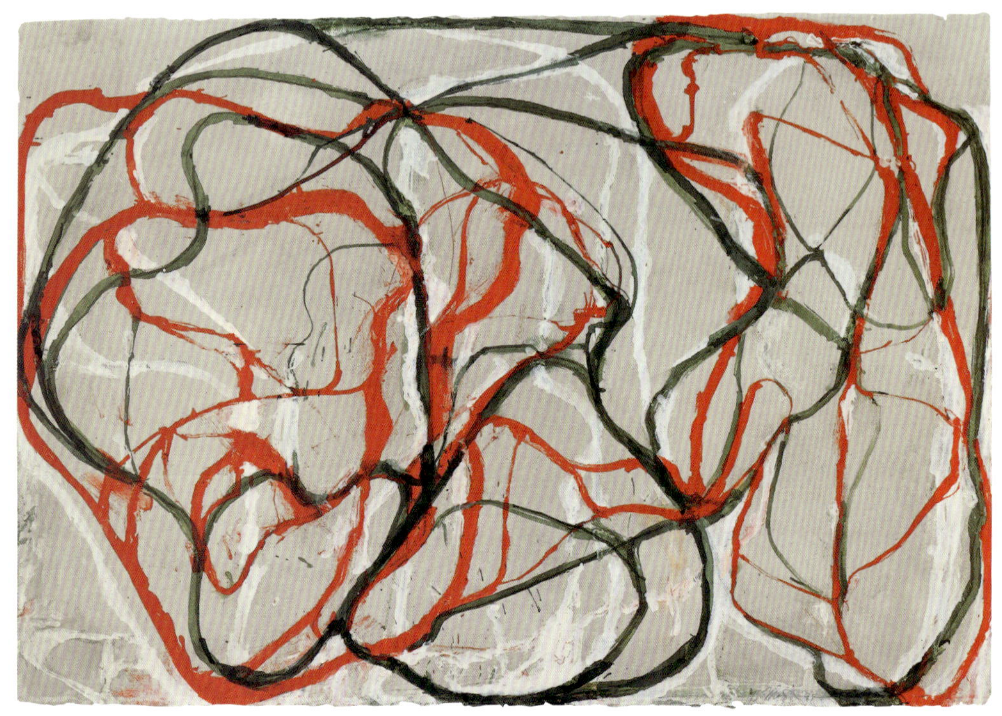

162. *Untitled Red and Green Drawing 5.* 1998
Ink on paper
$20\frac{3}{8}$ x $29\frac{9}{16}$" (51.8 x 75.1 cm)

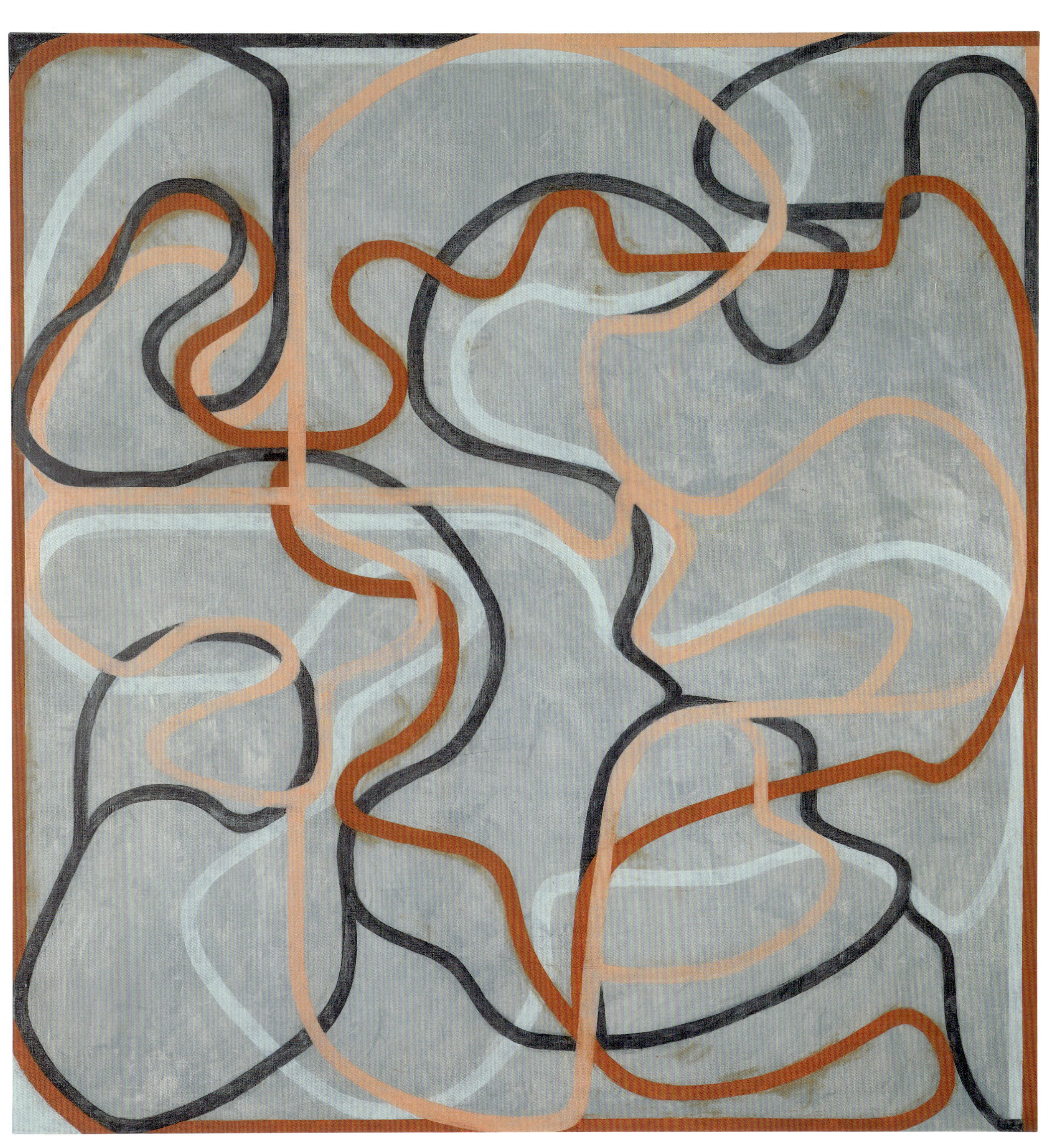

163. *Epitaph Painting 5.* 1997–2001
Oil on linen
9' ½" x 8' 8" (275.6 x 264.2 cm)

164. *Dragons.* 2000–2004.
Ink on paper
40½ x 29¾" (102.9 x 75.6 cm)

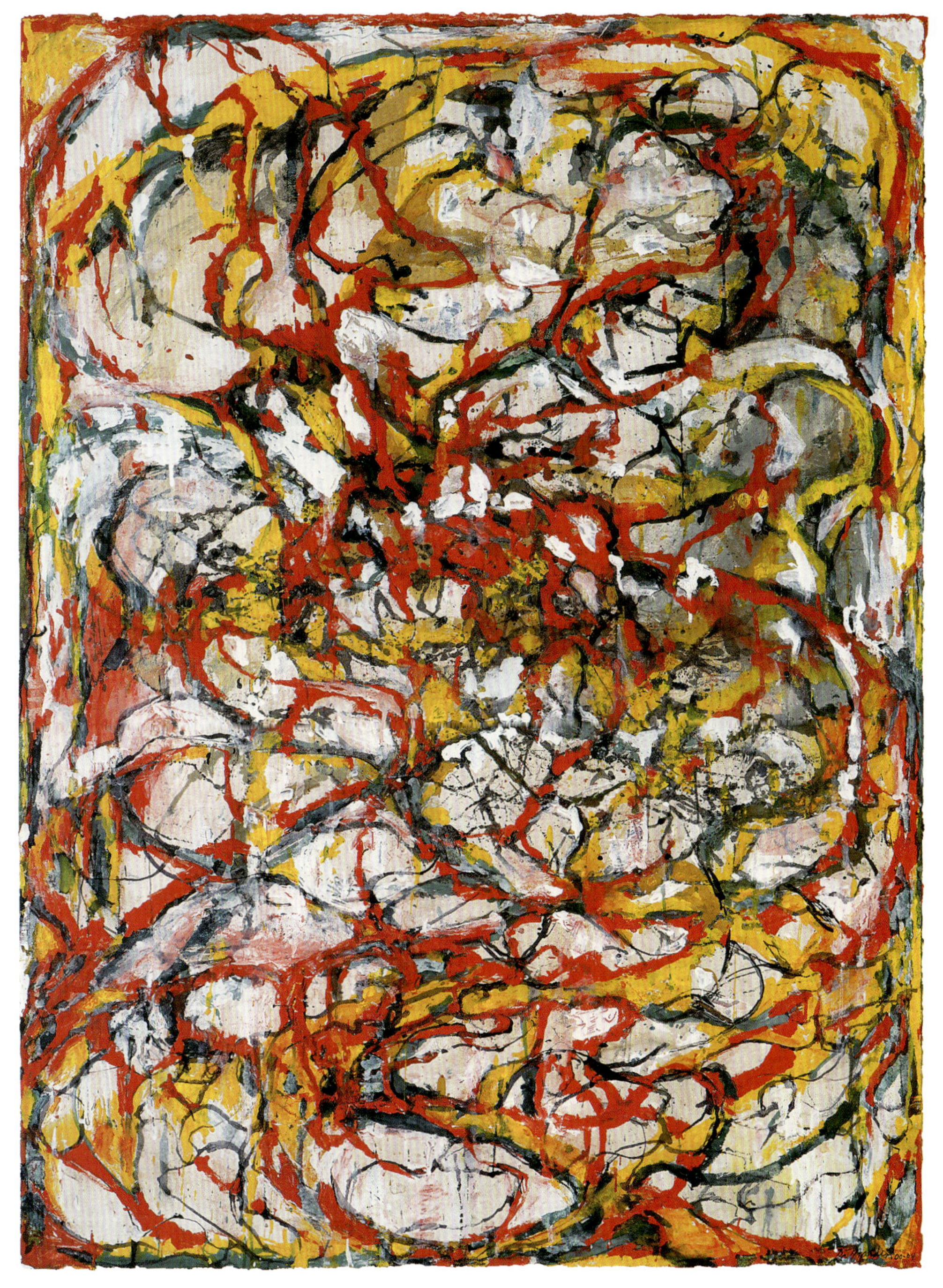

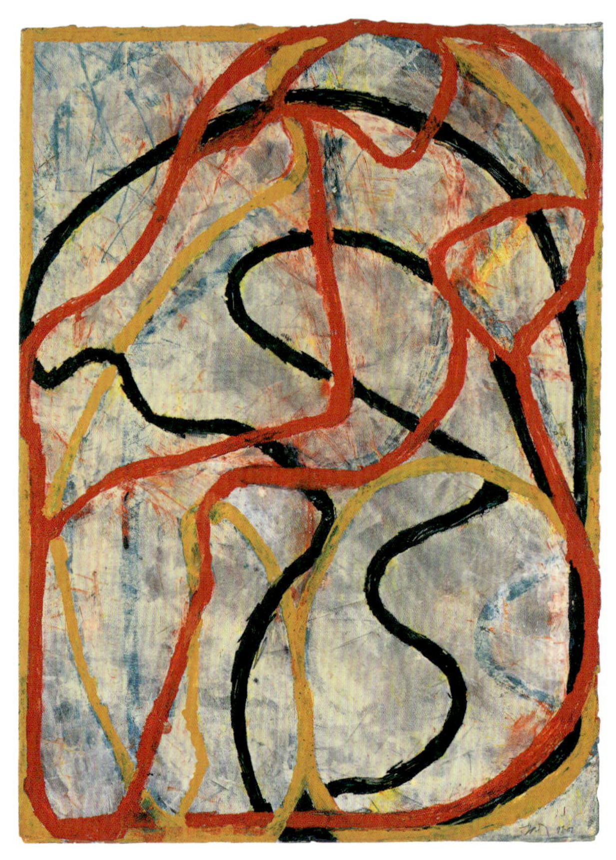

165. *St. Barts 4.* 1999–2001
Ink on paper
20¼" x 15" (51.4 x 38.1 cm)

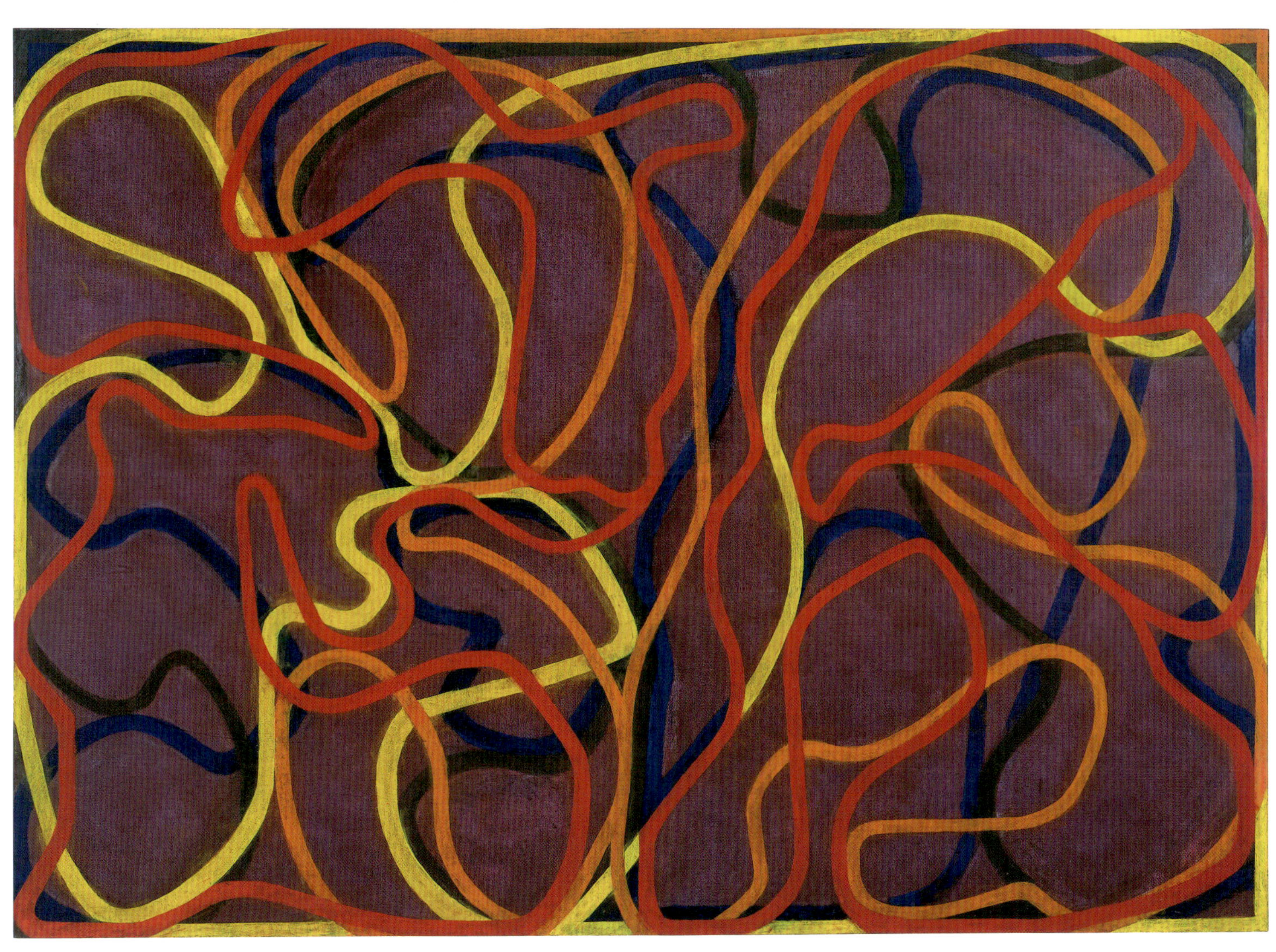

166. *Red Rocks (1).* 2000–2002
Oil on linen
6' 3" x 8' 11" (190.5 x 271.8 cm)

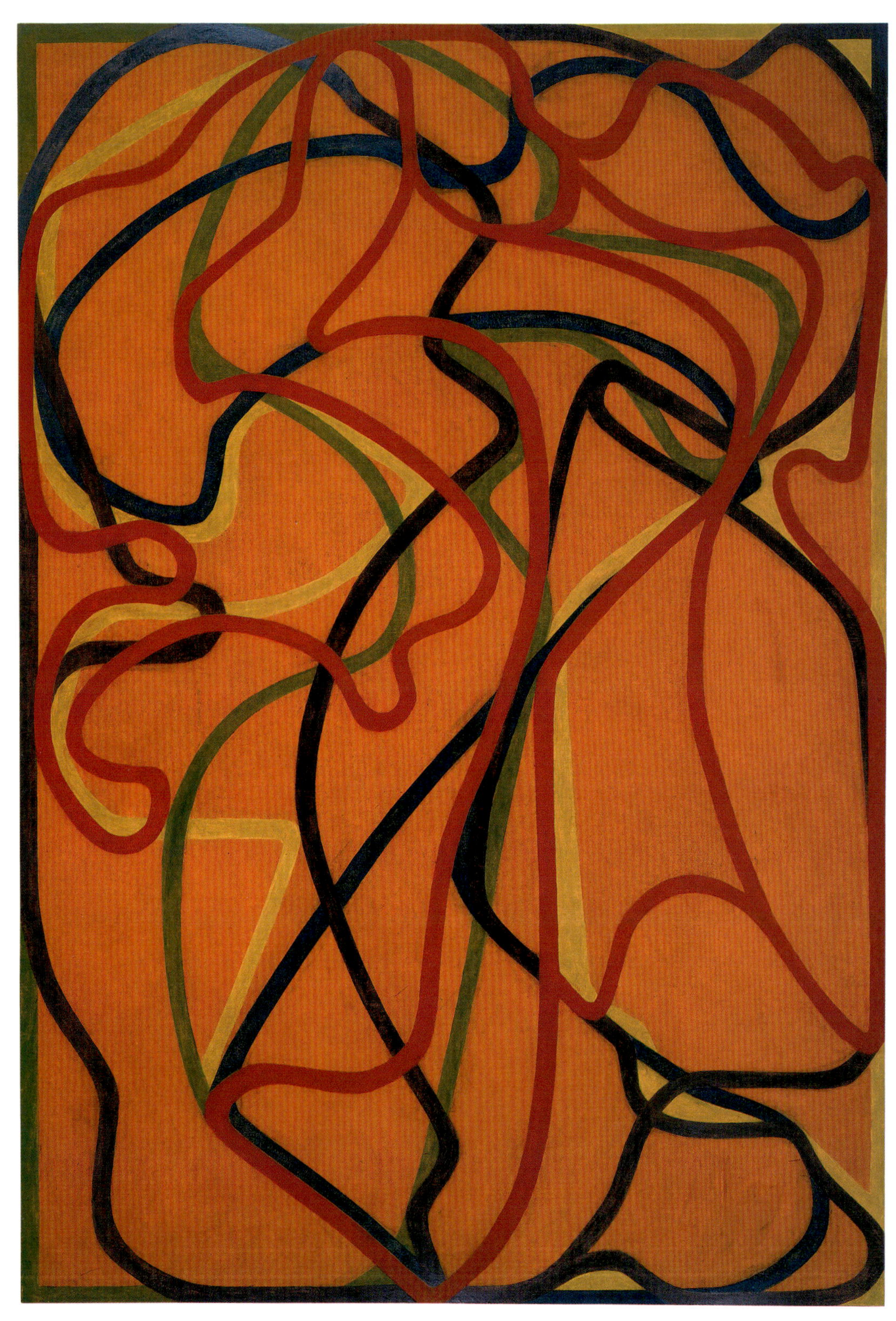

167. *6 Red Rock 1*. 2000–2002
Oil on linen
8' 11" x 6' 3" (271.8 x 190.5 cm)

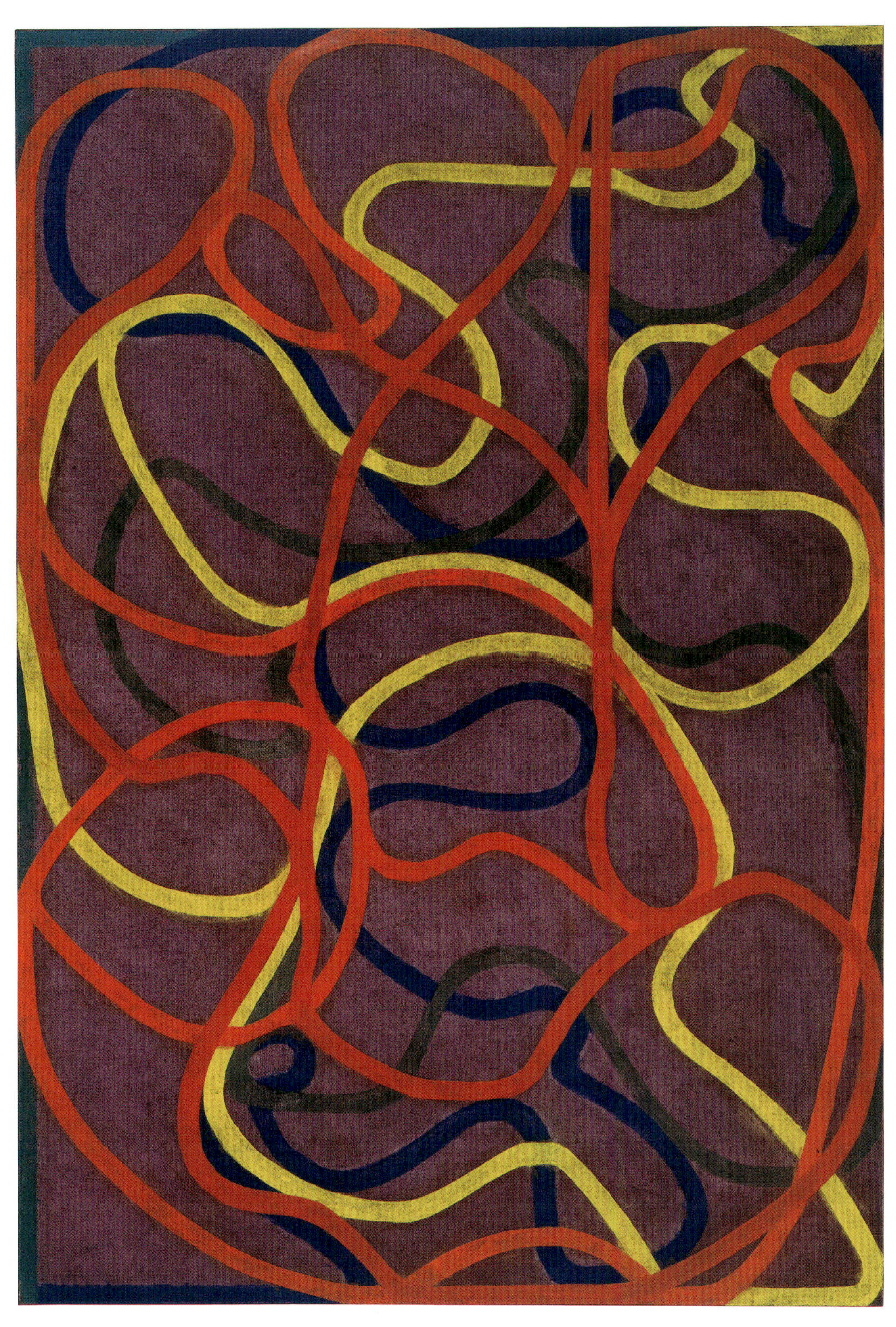

168. *7 Red Rock 2*. 2000–2002
Oil on linen
8' 11" x 6' 3" (271.8 x 190.5 cm)

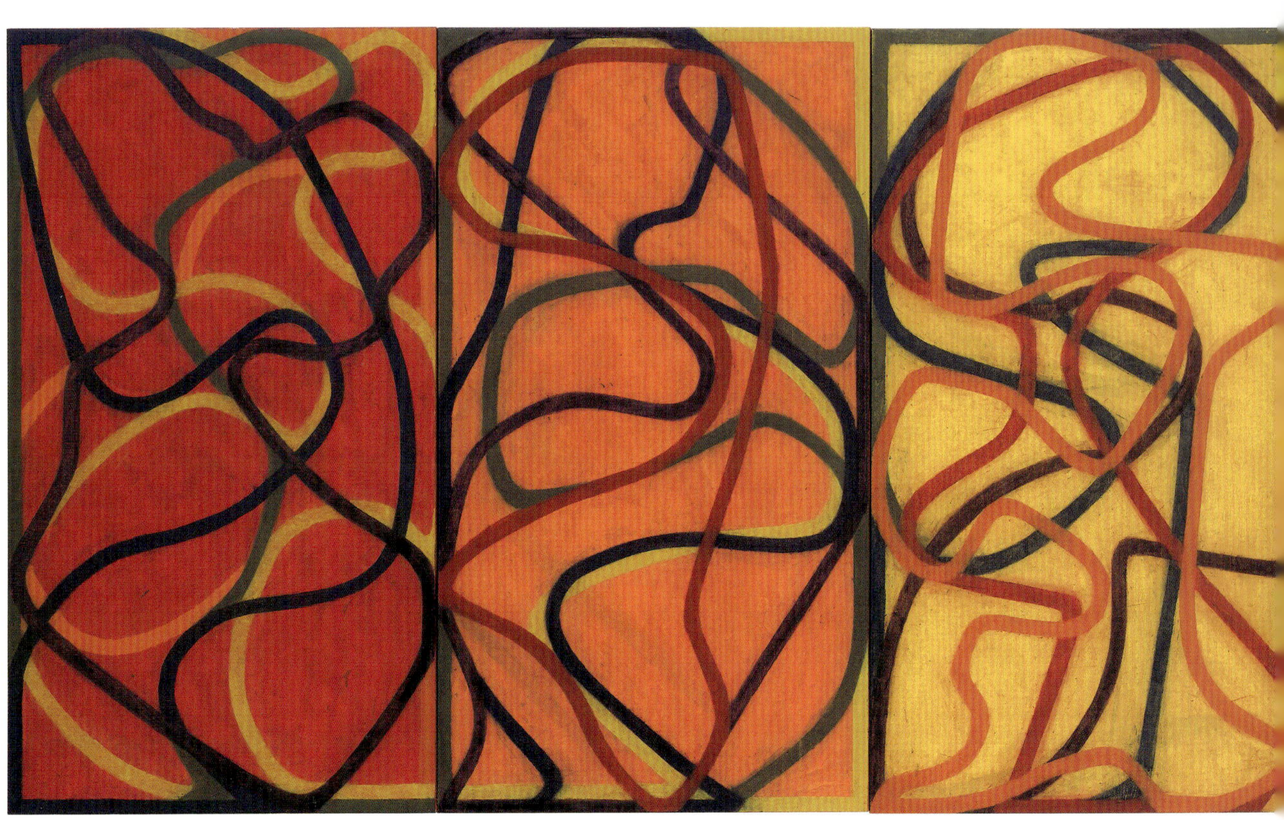

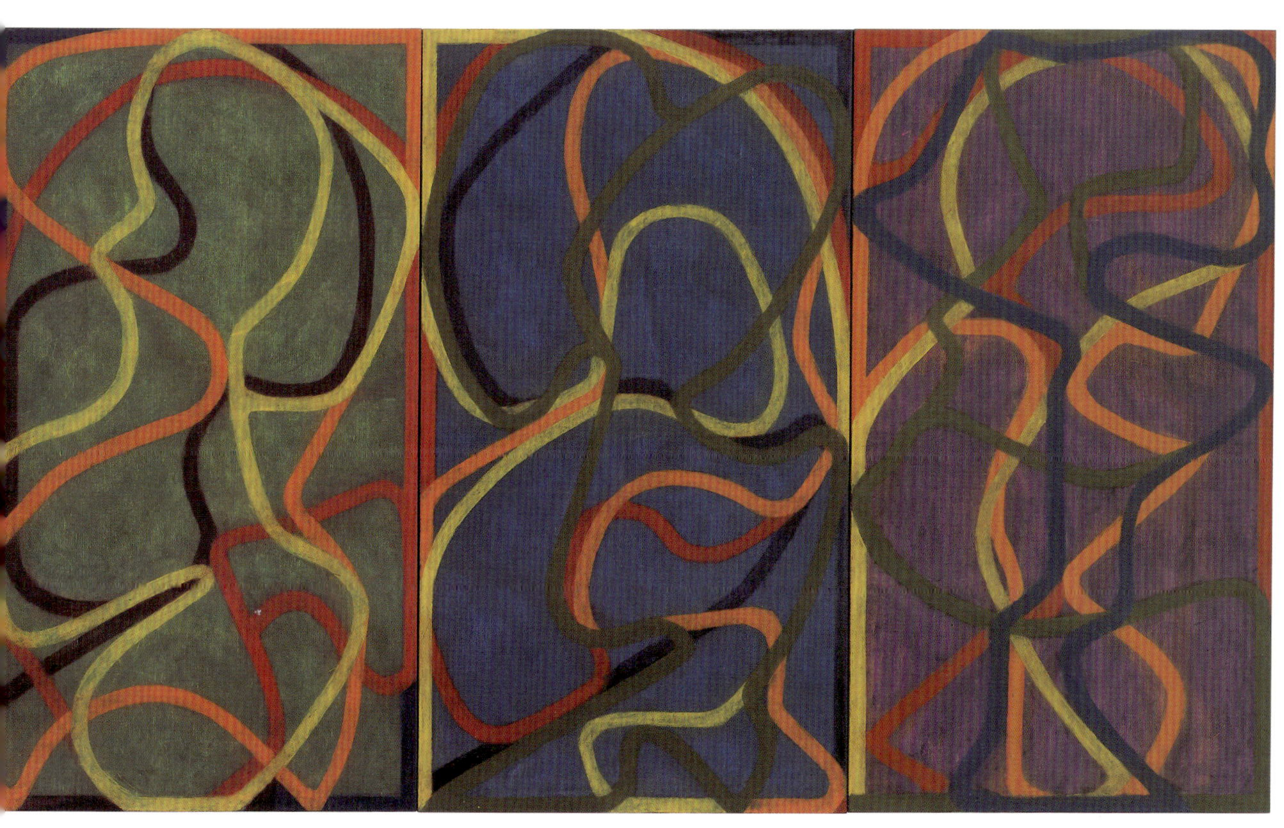

169. *The Propitious Garden of Plane Image, First Version.* 2000–2005
Oil on linen
Six panels, overall: 42" x 12' (106.7 x 365.8 cm)

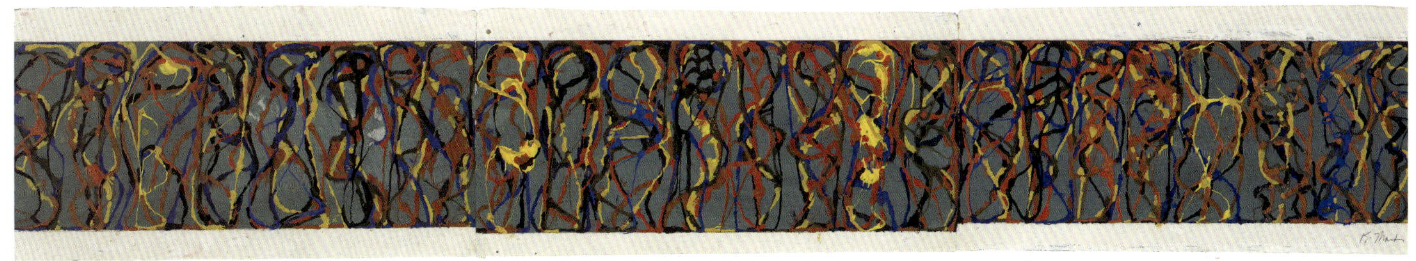

170. *Drawing for the Propitious Garden, St. Barts.* 2003
Ink on paper
$11^1/_4$ x $66^1/_2$" (28.6 x 168.9 cm)

Francesca Pietropaolo

Chronology

1938

October 15: Birth of Nicholas Brice Marden, Jr., in Bronxville, a suburb of New York City. The son of Nicholas Brice Marden, a mortgage servicer, and Kathryn Fox Marden, he is the second of three children.

1943–56

Attends public schools in Briarcliff Manor, a middle-class town in Westchester County, New York, where the family lives.

> *[Briarcliff Manor was] a small town. During the war I guess there were about 1500 people there. It's suburban. It had been farm country . . . early in the century, then mostly residential. I was brought up in a house that was one of the old farms. . . . There's the beautiful Hudson River there. We used to go over and look at it.*[1]

> *There were always reproductions of paintings on the wall and a couple of original paintings. There was one thing that I remember very distinctly. It was a Bellini portrait . . . always hanging by the stairway. This was a little reproduction out of the* National Geographic *and he was just always called "Joe" for years. . . . Then later . . . in studying art history . . . I came across Joe and finally got to see it in London.*[2]

> *[Fred Serginian] (the father of my best friend when I was a kid) was a big influence. . . . He still painted. . . . He was like head of the art department at Young & Rubicam for a long time. And he would tell stories about when he was a student and studying with the Ashcan School people. [George] Luks was a big teacher of his. . . . He was always very encouraging, especially when I started out in art school. My parents were just totally perplexed, you know, coming from a town where everybody goes to college, a very Ivy League kind of place. . . . And I had come from this Princeton family, my grandfather taught there, and my father . . . and my brother went there and I always wanted to go there. But then I decided I didn't want to go.*[3]

In his early teens, Marden starts to visit museums in New York:

> *Mrs. [Marjorie] Serginian, [Fred's] wife . . . used to take us to museums. I can remember going to [The Metropolitan Museum of Art]. And the first time I was at The Museum of Modern Art was a very, very distinct impression. . . . I really dug it, but I can't remember anything specifically about it, [except] vaguely Brancusi.*[4]

1956

Fall: Enrolls at Florida Southern College, Lakeland, where he will spend one academic year. "I went down there and just immediately hated it the second I saw it. The idea was to . . . take liberal arts for a year and take art courses to see if I was interested." Takes a drawing class and a design class with Dean Eckert: "On vacations he would give me . . . these passes to go to the Whitney [Museum of American Art, New York] and to the Modern."[5]

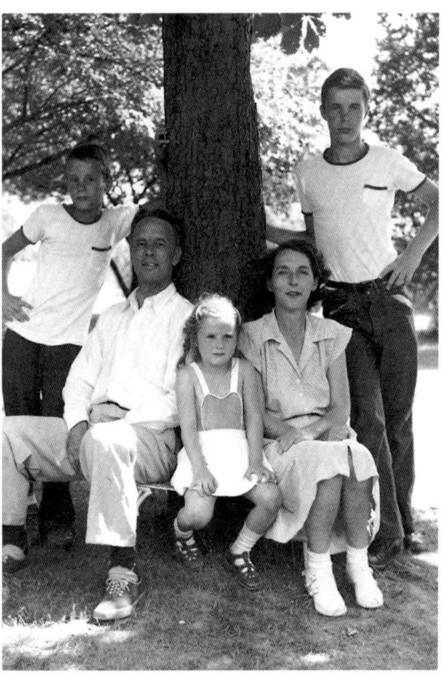

The Marden family, Briarcliff Manor, June 1949. Left to right: Brice Marden (the artist), Nicholas Brice Marden, Mary Carroll Marden, Kathryn Fox Marden, and Michael Marden

December 19, 1956–February 3, 1957: *Jackson Pollock*, a posthumous retrospective at The Museum of Modern Art, New York. Marden visits it: "That show really excited me."[6] He had learned about Pollock through *Life* and *Time* magazines.[7]

1958

November: Sets out to visit an exhibition of Pollock drawings at the Sidney Janis Gallery, New York, but finds it closed. Then,

> *I wandered into Betty Parsons's gallery and said, "Do you have any Pollocks?" And a guy sitting there . . . just pulled out about ten Pollocks. And some really big ones. I found out later it was [the artist] Sven Lukin, who was just covering for somebody on their lunch hour . . . it was an incredible experience.*[8]

1958–61

Attends Boston University School of Fine and Applied Arts, graduating with a BFA in 1961. Studies sculpture with Hugh Townley, painting with Reed Kay, and color and design with Arthur Hoener, who had studied with Josef Albers at Yale. The painter Pat Steir is among his classmates. While in Boston, regularly visits the Museum of Fine Arts, as well as the Busch-Reisinger Museum and the Fogg Art Museum in nearby Cambridge.

> *Boston was fantastic. That was my first city. . . . A college town . . . full of young people. . . . Really lively. . . . The first year in Florida I really wasn't learning that much about art or how to make it. . . . But Boston was just right from the beginning. . . . Everything I did out of school had to do with art, like going to museums, going to galleries. . . . My friend Fred Serginian and his wife had been giving me a subscription to* Artnews *for years and I just thought Abstract Expressionism was great; I loved it. But Boston University was very academically oriented. . . . [Oskar] Kokoscha and [Max] Beckmann were like the big heroes. It was a big Expressionist school and it was a whole school of that kind of painting, you know, Hyman Bloom. . . . We had to do a lot of drawing. . . . And I can remember taking a color course and just not understanding anything, this was Albers's color course [taught by Hoener].*[9]

Studies first-year drawing with Conger Metcalf and second-year drawing with Murray Reich. Paints portraits and still lifes: "I painted still lifes all the time. And I got very much involved with Cézanne. I started beginning to understand a lot of the things about Cézanne and . . . early Matisse."[10] At school, he will later write, "Constant painting and drawing from nature developed a sense of the real, that which was correct and had form."[11] Meanwhile, "At home I was working more on problems that had grown out of design classes . . . abstract problems, really trying to figure out how to paint, abstract, and what it was about."[12] He had a "surreptitious involvement with non-objective painting."[13]

On weekends, visits New York. "We'd go to like fifteen galleries on Saturday and . . . three museums on Sunday, and then I'd go back to Boston." Looks at the work of Franz Kline and Willem de Kooning.

> *I used to love Kline. . . . After this damn Albers color course . . . I just thought I didn't know anything about color, so I just worked in black and white all the time and then I really got into Kline and de Kooning.*
>
> *[In Boston] there were other painters, Alan Cote, and there was a co-op gallery there called the Nova Gallery and Murray Reich was in that and Harvey Quaytman and people like that and they'd get discussions going like the Club in New York. . . . It never would quite work, but I'd go there and just listen.*[14]

1960

March 6–27: *The Second Competitive Drawing Exhibition*, Marden's first group show, at the Lyman Allyn Art Museum, New London, Connecticut.

August 20: Marries Pauline Baez, sister of the singer Joan Baez.

1961

March 23: Birth of Marden's son, Nicholas Brice Marden II.

Summer: Attends Yale Summer School of Music and Art, in Norfolk, Connecticut. "That was a fantastic summer; I did a lot of painting and I painted a lot of landscapes and . . . a lot of abstract paintings."[15] Bernard Chaet and Jon Schueler are on the painting faculty, and other instructors include Richard Zieman, Al Blaustein, and Richard Lytle. Among Marden's fellow students,

> *Chuck Close was there. He was fantastic. And he was just this brassy dude from Seattle, made these big wide-open West Coast abstract paintings. He was great. Then . . . Bill Hochhausen was there. He was from Cooper [Union, New York] and he knew the whole New York thing, so we all listened to him. And then . . . Jim Olsen from Texas, who . . . was doing very slick art-magazine paintings, abstract painting. . . . David [Novros] was like my best friend and he was from [the University of Southern California]. He was doing really good paintings then, very complicated.*[16]

Marden devotes the summer "to extending my painting vocabulary: I painted whatever I wanted and felt no restrictions."[17] At the end of the summer semester he is invited to go to Yale.[18]

1961–63

Attends the School of Art and Architecture at Yale University, studying with Esteban Vicente, Alex Katz, Jon Schueler, Jack Tworkov, Reginald Pollack, Philip Pearlstein, and Gabor Peterdi. Among his fellow students are Richard Serra, Chuck Close, Nancy Graves, and Robert Mangold. He graduates with an MFA in 1963.

They had this building and it had this big long alley that was like these stalls, but in the four corners you got a big studio. And I got one of those corners the first year there. I didn't know anybody, and I was very shy and was married with the baby and we were living in another part of town . . . and I was up there just working all the time.[19]

While at school, definitively embraces abstraction. "Eventually I just gave up painting the figure; I think I started one self-portrait and then I just stopped."[20] Also, after painting primarily in black and white as an undergraduate, he begins to use color, though in the subdued tones of the Spanish painters Velázquez, Goya, and Zurbarán as well as of Manet, whose *Street Singer* (c. 1862) and *Execution of the Emperor Maximilian* (1867) he had closely observed at Boston's Museum of Fine Arts. This predominantly gray palette will last in his work into the early 1970s. His paintings, he writes, "are blatantly simple color shape statements, but then go very confusing . . . and the object becomes a playground of contents, mysteries, and questions." They are "highly emotional" and "to be felt"; "emotional participation (sympathy) is desired on the part of the viewer as is physical participation (empathy)."[21] The paint in these mostly small works is applied in short, rapid strokes moving in varying directions, with gestures limited by the size and the shape of the canvas.

I became aware of an underlying rectilinear structure which constantly reappeared in my work. I began to concentrate on this idea of rectangles. . . . I consider: 1) color [as] tonality; 2) edge [as] interpretations and meetings of shapes; 3) space [as] the lack of it in naturalistic terms; 4) technicalities [as] permanence; 5) paint [as] surface; 6) light; 7) atmosphere; 8) form [as] poetry, mystery, that unexplainable thing that a good painting has.[22]

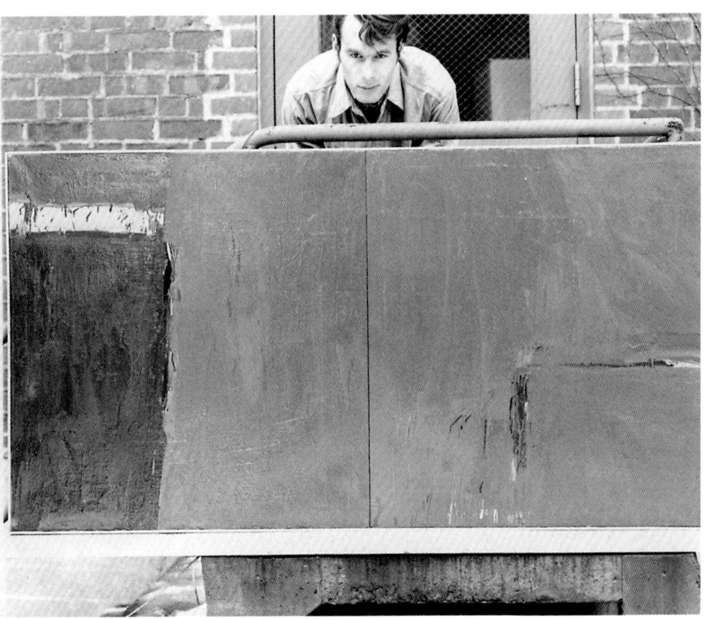

Marden with *California Painting* (1962), Yale University, 1962

1963

April 6–20: Is represented in *7 Yale Painters: Paul Covington, Kent Floeter, Brice Marden, Paul Tschinkel, Oscar Watters, Paul Zavorskas, Charles Close*, at the Munson Gallery, New Haven.

Graduates from Yale in late June. In the summer, visits Carmel, California, where he stays with his sister-in-law, Joan Baez. Then, having moved with his family to New York—into a railroad apartment at 153 Avenue C, on the Lower East Side—he supports himself by working part-time as a guard at The Jewish Museum, which during these years, under the direction of Alan R. Solomon, is an important museum of contemporary art.

December 6, 1963–January 6, 1964: Harriet Korman organizes his first solo exhibition, at the Wilcox Gallery, Swarthmore College, Pennsylvania.

1964

February 13–April 12: The first Jasper Johns retrospective, organized by Solomon at The Jewish Museum. Johns's art, especially *Gray Rectangles* (1957) and the number paintings of 1958 and 1959, provides an important stimulus for Marden, and his use of gray encourages Marden's own commitment to that color.

Spring and summer: Marden and his family spend four months in Paris, where he makes charcoal-and-graphite drawings in which the work's surface divides into an overall grid. "In Paris I did drawings because I had no place to paint."[23] He also makes frottage rubbings in his notebooks, as well as scratching tracks in paper with a comb. In the spring, sees a retrospective of Jean Fautrier's work at the Musée d'Art Moderne de la Ville de Paris, and is impressed by the paintings' physicality.[24] Also sees paintings by Alberto Giacometti and becomes interested in their space, gray palette, and linear strokes.[25]

September: Marden and Pauline separate. Marden returns to the apartment on the Lower East Side.

In Paris. . . de Gaulle was doing this cleanup. . . . They were replastering or stuccoing a lot of the walls. And I would just spend an afternoon watching them work down these walls. And then when I got back to New York—there were paintings that I had started at Yale, and then I just sort of reworked them, and they became . . . much more fieldlike.[26]

In the work of this period the surfaces of Marden's paintings thicken and become more homogenous. Individual brushstrokes give way to a more uniform skin of paint achieved with a knife. He continues either to divide the canvas into two rectangles of differing grays or to place a rectangle next to a grid of equal shape. He also starts to make one-panel monochrome paintings, beginning with *Return I* (1964–65; plate 13) and *Portrait* (1964–65), that he describes as "having grown out of the involvement with those walls in Paris, and thinking about Giacometti."[27]

1965

Works for Chiron Press, a silkscreen shop used by many contemporary artists. Moves into the loft above Chiron Press at 76 Jefferson Street, on the fringes of Chinatown. This year and next, makes a series of drawings over a screenprint by John Goodyear. Frequents artists' hangouts such as Max's Kansas City, a restaurant and bar opened in December 1965 by Mickey Ruskin and frequented by artists, writers, models, photographers, and musicians such as Robert Smithson, William Burroughs, Joseph Kosuth, Carl Andre, John Chamberlain, Mick Jagger, and many others. Here Marden meets artist Helen Harrington, his future wife.

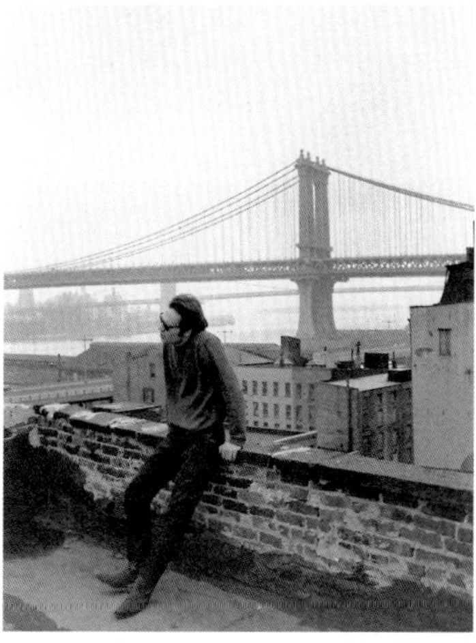

1966

Completes *Wax I*, his first painting made with a blend of oil paint, turpentine, and beeswax. This medium, suggested to him by the painter Harvey Quaytman, reduces the oil's shine and increases the tactility of the surface. (Marden had begun to experiment with wax in 1964, in charcoal-and-graphite drawings.) Unlike the harder and more transparent encaustic used by Jasper Johns, Marden's mixture is bound by oil instead of wax. He keeps it warm on a hot plate, mixing it constantly and initially using a refrigerator door as a palette. Brushing on the hot mixture, he smoothes it with a spatula and a knife, building up layers of the medium to create a dense surface that both absorbs and reflects light. On some of his one-panel monochromes, such as *Nebraska* (1966; plate 15), he marks off an inch-wide strip at the bottom of the canvas below which he does not paint; instead, he allows drips from the surface above to accumulate here, pointing out the process used to make the painting and reminding viewers of the nature of the canvas as a physical object.

> *With encaustic, after you put the stroke on, you reheat it so it binds with the surface. And I was using oil paint with a mixture of wax and turpentine, used as the painting medium, to thin out the paint. And I just put it on and then worked it. And it was never reheated. . . . You put it on . . . and you had about an hour to get the first general working—but then as it started hardening, the next strokes that went on with the knife become matte-er . . . So you really didn't have a lot of time you could work it. So that's why they were so layered. And if you'd miss, you'd just have to scrape it off.*[28]

April 27–June 12: *Primary Structures*, an exhibition at The Jewish Museum. At the opening, Marden meets Klaus Kertess, who, with his partner Jeff Byers, is preparing to open the Bykert Gallery, New York.

Late Spring–Summer: Visits northern California, traveling by road to get there and passing on the way through Nebraska, which particularly impresses him. A notebook records that he returns from the trip in June–July, and that on the way west he is in Funk, Nebraska, at 4:30 p.m. on June 3.

Fall: Leaves his job with Chiron Press.

November 15–December 7: Marden's first New York exhibition, a solo show at the Bykert Gallery. A reviewer writes, "These paintings are very unaggressive and slow but they have distinct, sensuous appeal."[29] The show includes *Nebraska*, which Marden explains is a painting not of Nebraska's landscape but of the memory of its experience. "One of the things I was trying to do in making a one-color painting was to make a painting that read possibly in a number of ways. So you could have a gray painting or a green painting. There were very beautiful greens in Nebraska."[30]

After the Bykert exhibition closes, the artist Dorothea Rockburne, who at the time is working as Robert Rauschenberg's secretary, helps Marden get a job in Rauschenberg's studio, where he will work for four years. Rauschenberg, he will later say, "is very generous with his thinking. . . . We would sit around and talk about what we did. It was a great experience."[31]

> *I still really felt much more of an Abstract Expressionist than Minimalist. I mean, I wasn't rejecting Abstract Expressionism, and I was very conscious of the fact that these things were being made by hand; I wanted it . . . seen that they were made by hand. So that was . . . a definite part of it.*[32]

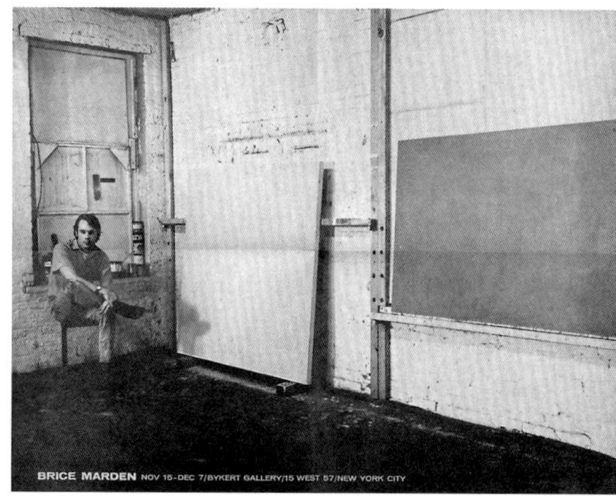

Marden on the roof of 76 Jefferson Street, Manhattan, where he lived and worked, 1966

Announcement for Marden's first New York exhibition, at the Bykert Gallery, November 15–December 7, 1966

1967

SEPTEMBER 13–OCTOBER 11: Is represented in *A Romantic Minimalism*, at the Institute of Contemporary Art, University of Pennsylvania, Philadelphia.

1968

JANUARY 6–31: Paintings from Marden's Back Series (1967–68) are shown at the Bykert Gallery. In a play on the tension between abstraction and representation, the canvases' height is derived from that of Helen Harrington's body.

> *Working on a painting is very physical . . . the shapes of the paintings are so closely related to the human scale, you work with them, and after a while it gets to be a dance.*[33]

Begins to make diptychs and then triptychs of abutting panels and varied tones.

NOVEMBER 7: Marries Helen Harrington.

1969

Starts teaching at the School of Visual Arts, New York, where he will work through 1974.

APRIL 26–MAY 17: *Brice Marden: New Paintings* at the Bykert Gallery. In a review of the show in *Artnews* a critic writes, "There is a dynamic captured in these surprising equilibriums that draws you into a heightened awareness of, even excitement about, colors that are sometimes barely determinate. Marden is a master of the low-key."[34]

SEPTEMBER 25–OCTOBER 25: Marden's first European solo show, at the Galerie Yvon Lambert, Paris. With Helen, Marden stays in Paris in the fall, working on *Au Centre*, *Paris Painting*, and *D'après la Marquise de la Solana* (plate 30), a response to Goya's portrait of the *marquise* in the Louvre.

SEPTEMBER 30–OCTOBER 12: Is represented in *Prospect '69*, at the Stadtische Kunsthalle, Düsseldorf.

1970

JANUARY 30–FEBRUARY 15: *Brice Marden*, an exhibition at Françoise Lambert, Milan.

APRIL 21–MAY 24: Is represented in *Modular Painting*, at the Albright-Knox Art Gallery, Buffalo.

OCTOBER 31–NOVEMBER 26: Solo show at Bykert Gallery.

1971

Works in etching at the invitation of Robert Feldman, director of Parasol Press, New York. His first portfolio, *Ten Days*, is published by Parasol Press and printed by Kathan Brown in Oakland, California.

The Mardens visit Hydra, a Greek island some eighty miles south of Athens. They will return here annually.

Marden's arrival in Hydra coincides with a move in his work toward a deeper dialogue with nature and with the art of the past, as well as a search for more complex ranges of color, structure, and space. He also moves toward brighter colors. The specificity of a place and its light bears strongly on the work.

> *If I make a painting in Greece, it looks like it was made in Greece. . . . the characteristics of the place just somehow get into the painting, or get into my painting, because I want it there. . . . if I'm in that place, I'm responding to that place. But also, if you're painting in Greece . . . there's this light out there that you sort of have to bring the color up to it.*[35]

> *Manhattan is an island of stone. Hydra is an island of stone. . . . Living on islands leads you to think certain ways. . . . I identify very strongly with the landscape in both of those places. I'm sure that if I wasn't living in a city, I wouldn't be using . . . so much . . . verticals and horizontals. But then . . . living in Greece it's the whole light. There's a kind of clarity, plus it has also pulled me much closer to older art.*[36]

FEBRUARY 25–APRIL 18: Is represented in *Structure of Color*, at the Whitney Museum of American Art.

DECEMBER 18, 1971–JANUARY 30, 1972: Is represented in *White on White: The White Monochrome in the 20th Century*, at the Museum of Contemporary Art, Chicago.

1972

Visits the Rothko Chapel in Houston, inaugurated the previous year. The triptychs and single-panel paintings in this "environment where your whole spirit becomes isolated" make a strong impression on Marden.[37] He has seen Mark Rothko's work at the Sidney Janis Gallery in the late 1950s and early '60s, and Rothko himself on the artist's occasional visits to the Bykert Gallery: "He was really foreboding, not the kind who you'd walk up and start chatting with. . . . I really liked it when the work started to become harder and harder; there was a combination of atmosphere and hard edge."[38]

> *I have always felt more related to the Abstract Expressionists than any other group. I think that's what I came out of. . . . I started with Franz Kline, because I was coming from Spanish paintings. . . . You always admired de Kooning. . . . But then it was Rothko to whom I would respond, especially in his later paintings. . . . The whole idea of beauty was not embarrassing to me, as it was for a lot of people. It's one of the things that was encouraging about Rothko, that he didn't seem to be embarrassed about it, either.*[39]

Begins the Grove Group series (1972–76; plates 46–49), which conveys his impressions of Greek olive groves. The five paintings are all six feet by nine feet and run from one to three panels. Within a seemingly narrow range of blue grays and blue-green grays, Marden achieves remarkable variations of color, light, and scale.

Paints *Hydra I.*

In 1972 and 1974 respectively, begins two series of drawings incorporating postcards, as well as graphite and wax or pen and ink. In Homage to Art (plates 52, 53), the postcards show paintings such as Zurbarán's *Crucifixion* and Piet Mondrian's *Broadway Boogie Woogie*; in Souvenir de Grèce (plates 149, 150) they show Greek sculpture and architecture.

February: Visits Rauschenberg on Captiva Island, Florida.

April 23–June 4: Is represented in *Painting: New Options*, at the Walker Art Center, Minneapolis.

June 30–October 8: Documenta V, in Kassel, West Germany, includes the paintings *D'après la Marquise de la Solana* (1969), *Tropezienne (Thinking Blue)* (1969–70), and *Avrutun* (1971).

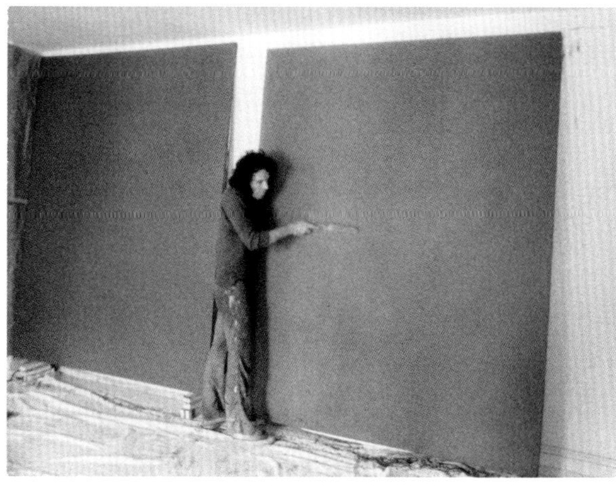

Marden painting *Mur Chez Lambert*, in the apartment of Yvon Lambert, Paris, 1973

1973

First purchase of property on Hydra. Here, having no studio, Marden works in the garden and on the terrace, making drawings on paper.

Begins to draw with a new tool: sticks cut from an ailanthus tree near his studio, on Bond Street, Manhattan. With unrefined points and of varying lengths and thicknesses, these twigs dipped in ink force Marden to work more slowly and deliberately. The drawings begin with grids but later develop more fluid lines. "Touch replaces gesture," the critic Roberta Smith writes of them.[40]

It made a very beautiful fine line . . . and you had a certain distance from the paper. . . . There were a lot of accidents that would happen; the ink would spill. . . . And then you can start . . . working out of the accidents into a more controlled situation. . . . I was really just trying to loosen up the drawing and loosen up the image.[41]

By getting farther away, with a delicate instrument . . . in a way it becomes closer: the slightest move is reflected. There's also accident, and I use it. That's the Abstract Expressionist thing. That's really part of . . . my whole vocabulary. I think that's a very important point. What one is physically . . . I am 5' 8½", and I weigh this much, and I am left-handed, and I'm a certain age. That has a big effect on what the thing looks like. The kind of mark I can make physically. If everybody tried to draw the same line, they just couldn't do it. I keep finding I want to work with longer and longer sticks, to get further and further away, and to get a different swing into the drawing. Instead of using fingers and wrists, I want to have a little bit more arm and shoulder. But I find that painting doesn't have the fluidity that the drawing has. And that's always, to me, the battle, to get fluidity into the painting.[42]

Begins the Figure paintings (1973–74). Of these, *Fourth Figure (Red Yellow Blue)* (1973–74; plate 62) is his first investigation of the primary colors, to be followed by four paintings titled *Red, Yellow, Blue.*

January 10–March 18: Is represented in the Whitney Biennial, at the Whitney Museum of American Art.

February 24–March 22: *Brice Marden New Paintings: Grove Group*, at the Bykert Gallery, New York. A critic writes, "Instead of eliminating surface involvement, he has centered on the sensuous particularity of surface through the unification of color and texture so that the work often seems to be about smoothness and tactility in themselves rather than as aspects of other qualities."[43]

September 28–October 7: Is represented in *Prospect 73: Maler, Painters, Peintres*, at the Stadtische Kunsthalle, Düsseldorf.

November 1973–February 1974: Is represented in *Contemporanea*, at the Parcheggio di Villa Borghese, Rome.

1974

January 24–March 10: *Brice Marden Drawings, 1963–1973*, at the Contemporary Arts Museum, Houston, and at subsequent American venues through March 1975. In conjunction with the retrospective, a *cahier* of seventy drawings titled *Suicide Notes* (1972–73) and inscribed "I don't know what my mind means!?" is published, by Paul Bianchini.

[Drawing] is an intimate medium. It's very direct, it's very close. There's less between the artist and the art. There is real closeness, direct contact. A painting is about refinement of image. And drawing isn't. I don't think drawing is less than painting. . . . The less you have between you and what you're making the better. The best drawing instruments are the ones where you are what your hand is. When the hand moves with the least resistance. In a way, pencil is much less resistant than a brush.[44]

October 9, 1974–January 5, 1975: Is represented in *Eight Contemporary Artists*, at The Museum of Modern Art, New York.

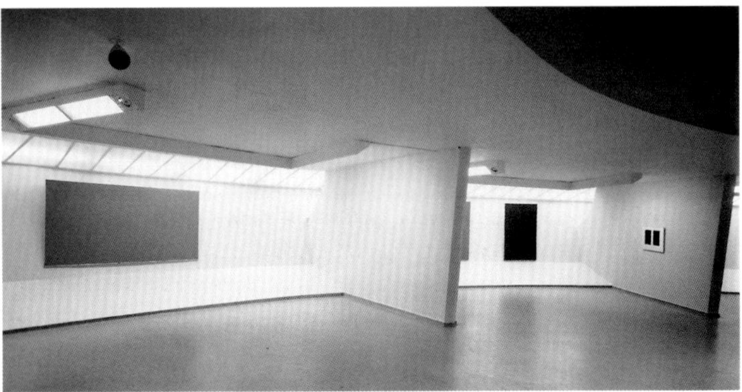

1975
March 7–May 4: *Brice Marden*, a retrospective at the Solomon R. Guggenheim Museum, New York.

April 18–June 15: *Brice Marden, David Novros, Mark Rothko*, at the Rice Museum and Sewall Art Gallery, Institute for the Arts, Rice University, Houston. The show includes Marden's *The Seasons* (1974–75: plate 64), painted in response to the Rothko Chapel—a work of four panels, each in a different color and light, and hung three inches apart.

April 25–June 22: Is represented in *Fundamentele Schilderkunst*, at the Stedelijk Museum, Amsterdam.

1976
January 19–March 7: Is represented in *Drawing Now*, at The Museum of Modern Art, New York.

Returns to Oakland and works on *Five Threes*, to be published by Parasol Press and printed by Crown Point Press.

1977
February 19–April 3: Is represented in the Whitney Biennial.

December: Travels to Rome for a solo show at the Gian Enzo Sperone gallery, then visits Pompeii.

1978
Begins work on a proposal he has been invited to submit for stained-glass windows to replace an earlier set, removed in 1950, in the Late Gothic chevet of the Basel Cathedral. The proposal—for five large choir windows, four sets of circular arch windows, and six rose windows—will occupy much of Marden's time between 1978 and 1985, as he works on studies incorporating the alchemic colors red, yellow, green, and blue. The project encourages his spiritual interests, and he combines the literal transparency of glass with an imagined transparency of the plane, an issue he has been exploring in drawings since 1972. In his multiple single-color studies for the windows, he also explores the use of the diagonal.

Helen Marden becomes pregnant and Marden creates a series of five paintings on the Annunciation, with each work embodying one of the conditions of the Virgin outlined in a fifteenth-century Italian sermon: *conturbatio* (disquiet; plate 70), *cogitatio* (reflection), *interrogatio* (inquiry), *humiliatio* (submission), and *meritatio* (merit; plate 71). Marden will later describe the group as being about "taking light through."[45] The paintings implicitly refer to earlier attempts to combine the abstract with the spiritual by artists such as Mondrian, Kazimir Malevich, Vasily Kandinsky, Barnett Newman, and Rothko in the Rothko Chapel.

September 23–October 21: First exhibition with The Pace Gallery, New York.

November 15: Birth of the Mardens' first daughter, Maya Mirabelle Zahara Marden.

1979
Begins the painting *Thira* (plate 83), which will be completed the following year. The work's colors and post-and-lintel structure relate to classical Roman painting, as well as to the work of Marden's friend Novros. *Thira* is the Greek word for "door," and the T shape might also refer to the three-armed cross of the Old Testament as well as to the first letter of "god" ("theos") in Greek.

Most of my shapes or canvases tend to be human-sized, six foot, or then get small. But lately they've become much larger. . . . You identify with them on a different level. They are not the size of a human being any more. They are more the size of a kind of space that a human being could be in.[46]

February 6–April 1: Is represented in the Whitney Biennial.

1980
First visit to St. Barts, in the French West Indies. Later visits will take place in 1986, 1995, 2000, 2001, 2003, 2004, and 2005.
June 24: Birth of the Mardens' second daughter, Melia Io Bricia Marden.

1981
Replaces the wax in his paint with terpineol, an oil medium that dries flat.

Brice Marden, Solomon R. Guggenheim Museum, New York, March 7–May 4, 1975, installation view. Left to right: *The Dylan Painting* (plate 17), *For Me (Back Series)* (plate 22), and *Two Studies, Back Series* (plate 21)

Begins a group of paintings titled Elements (plates 103, 105).

In Hydra, still working outdoors, begins to paint on marble fragments, remnants from the construction of a bench commissioned by Helen for the terrace of their house (plates 99–101).

March 12–April 26: *Brice Marden: Paintings, Drawings, and Etchings, 1975–1980*, at the Stedelijk Museum, Amsterdam.

May 8–June 21: *Brice Marden: Paintings, Drawings, and Prints, 1975–1980*, at the Whitechapel Art Gallery, London.

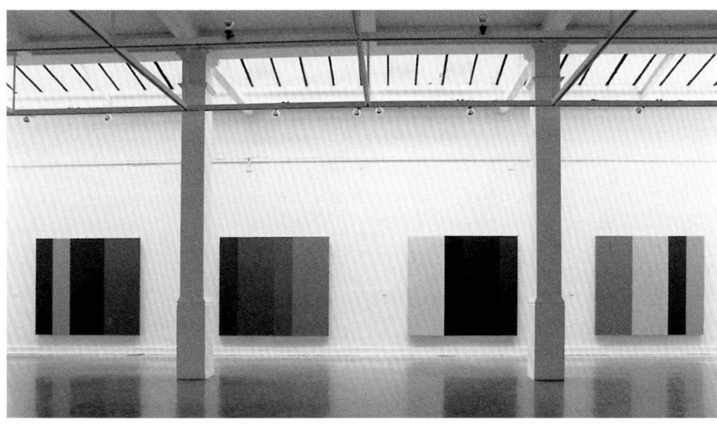

Brice Marden: Paintings, Drawings, and Prints, 1975–1980, Whitechapel Art Gallery, London, May 8–June 21, 1981, installation view. Left to right: *Conturbatio* (plate 70), *Cogitatio* (1978), *Humiliatio* (1978), and *Meritatio* (plate 71)

1982

October 29–November 27: *Brice Marden: Marbles, Paintings, and Drawings*, at The Pace Gallery.

Early 1980s

Although Marden is critically acclaimed, he searches for a new artistic direction and suffers a crisis. Withdrawing from his family, he moves to his studio on Bond Street and begins to wean himself from alcohol and drugs. Family ties will be gradually restored. Meanwhile makes fewer large paintings, becoming more occupied with drawing and with his window designs for Basel Cathedral.

1983

Begins the Sketch series, small paintings in which the plane image both mirrors and modifies the measure and shape of the support, especially when the diagonal is introduced as in *Sketch III* (1983). The random drips that formerly appeared along the bottom edge of the canvas are now drawn into the interior.

Begins *Coda* (1983–84), in which the paint is thin enough to reveal the weave of the canvas and an underlying pencil grid. This transparency marks a departure from the densely layered skin of earlier works.

June: Travels with his family to Tangier, Morocco, where he teaches painting. Spends a month exploring and viewing Islamic architecture in Fez and Marrakesh.

August: Drives through Spain and France, visiting museums and friends.

December–January: Helen, Mirabelle, and Melia visit Bangkok, Thailand, and Pedang, Malaysia, while Marden is in Europe working on the Basel commission. Marden meets them in Phuket, Thailand, for Christmas. They stay in Thailand through January 1984. Here Marden starts collecting seashells, particularly volutes.

> *I did a trip in Thailand. And I would draw the landscape one night, and the next day we'd be someplace else, so I would draw a different landscape right on the same drawing. So it was this kind of layering. But using a much looser hand, you know. Which was inspired somewhat by the calligraphy.*[47]

1984

February: The family spends three weeks in Sri Lanka, where the temple of Gal Vihara, in Polonnaruwa, strongly impresses Marden. At the end of the month they travel to Madras, India, to visit the artist Francesco Clemente and his family. They return to New York via Hydra in mid-March.

Marden likes to keep favorite objects in his studio for inspiration. These come to include a collection of Asian art, as well as seashells and Neolithic jade carvings.

April 1–May 16: Is represented in *The Meditative Surface*, at The Renaissance Society at the University of Chicago.

September 28–October 27: *Brice Marden: Recent Work*, at The Pace Gallery.

October 4, 1984–January 6, 1985: *Masters of Japanese Calligraphy, 8th–19th Century*, at New York's Japan House Gallery and Asia Society. Marden visits the show and is struck by the beauty of Japanese calligraphy: "It was so exciting, and I just started doing a lot of drawing somewhat in relation to it. Then just reworked my painting to incorporate a lot of the drawings."[48] He acquires several copies of the exhibition catalogue to keep it at hand: "I keep one copy in Greece, one in Pennsylvania, and one in New York, so I have it wherever I am."[49] Chinese calligraphy too will become an important source.

December 15, 1984–April 15, 1985: Is represented in *La Grande Parade: Highlights in Painting after 1940*, at the Stedelijk Museum, Amsterdam.

1985

The Basel Cathedral project is abandoned because of disagreements among its organizers in the city of Basel.

Moves his studio to 276 Bowery.

November 9, 1985–January 5, 1986: The Carnegie International, at the

Carnegie Museum of Art, Pittsburgh, includes *Number One* (1983–84), *Elements III* (1983–84), *Green (Earth)* (1983–84; plate 104), and *Elements IV* (1983–84; plate 105).

1986

JANUARY–JUNE: Works on *Etchings to Rexroth*, a portfolio of twenty-five etchings to be published by Peter Blum Editions and printed by Jennifer Melby, New York. Accompanying the prints are poems by the eighth-century Chinese master Tu Fu, in translations by Kenneth Rexroth.

> *Etching, you know, has a more physical resistance to it than drawing. For me etching becomes something between drawing and painting. I like to work etchings along with the paintings. Things have happened in the etchings that have gone back into the paintings.*[50]

NOVEMBER 23, 1986–MARCH 8, 1987: Is represented in *The Spiritual in Art: Abstract Painting, 1890–1985*, at the Los Angeles County Museum of Art, and at subsequent American and European venues through November 1987.

1987

Moves from The Pace Gallery to the Mary Boone Gallery, New York, which runs an exhibition of paintings showing his new direction from March 7 to 28. A reviewer writes, "Marden's recent change is more than what used to be called 'taking a risk.' It's an act of faith: one that is made without such safety nets as historical precedent, logical development, or formalism to fall back on."[51]

1988

Begins the Cold Mountain paintings, inspired by the writing of the ninth-century Chinese poet Cold Mountain (Han Shan). Another, visual influence is Jackson Pollock: "I sort of came back to Pollock. . . . He doesn't apply the image; he lets the image evolve out of the activity. And for me, this is very important, and it's basically what I'm exploring in my own work."[52] Becomes interested in Dao and Zen.

> *I was . . . looking at a lot of Chinese calligraphy. Getting poems by chance, I found the Red Pine translation [of Cold Mountain] at a bookstore. It has the Chinese characters and the translations in it. It was that form that I picked up on—four couplets, and five or ten characters per couplet. In the beginning I did drawings using the form that the poems take in the Chinese, then I started joining image and calligraphy, using the shape of the poem as a skeleton. . . . I use the form of calligraphy, then it disappears, but, it's always there. . . . It's about joining things up, making relationships, but at the same time letting the drawing itself do the work.*[53]

One force in the making of Cold Mountain is the need for a new emotional register: "By using the monochromatic palette in the past basically all I could get were chords. I wanted to be able to make something more like fugues, more complicated, back-and-forth renderings of feelings."[54]

FALL: Sees the Anselm Kiefer exhibition at The Museum of Modern Art (October 17, 1988–January 3, 1989). Will later say that this gave him the ambition to "paint big that *won't* go dead."[55]

NOVEMBER 5, 1988–JANUARY 22, 1989: The Carnegie International includes *4 (Bone)* (1987–88; plate 115), *12 (Gray)* (1987–88), *Untitled #1* (1986; plate 111), and *Untitled #2* (1986).

1989

Acquires further property on Hydra, the DeGaigneron house, allowing space for a painting studio.

APRIL 26–JULY 16: The Whitney Biennial includes *Diagramed Couplet #1*, *Diagramed Couplet #2*, and *Diagramed Couplet #3* (all 1988–89).

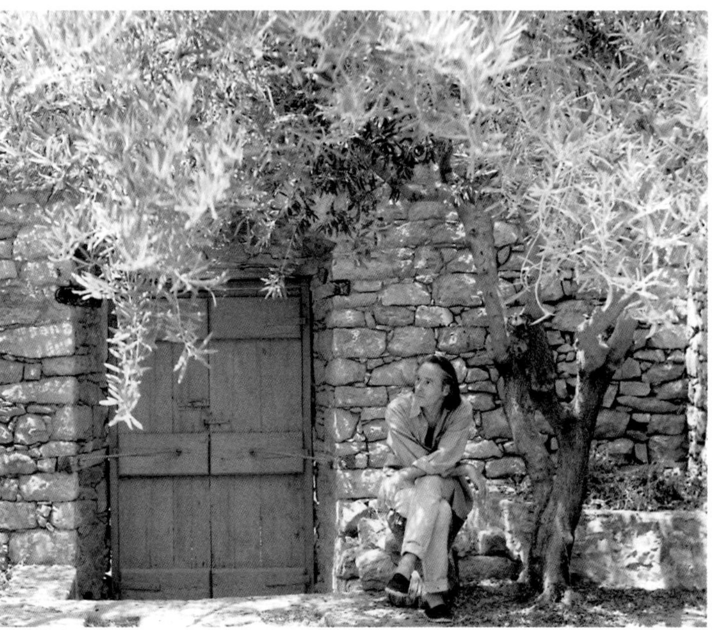

1990

MARCH 27–JULY 23: Is represented in *Polyptiques*, at the Musée du Louvre, Paris.

MAY 16–JULY 1: Is represented in *Amerikanische Zeichnungen in den achtziger Jahren*, at the Graphische Sammlung Albertina, Vienna.

1991

Acquires property in Eagles Mere, Pennsylvania, and sets up a studio there.

Starts work on *The Muses* (1991–93; plate 137). In Greek mythology, the Muses represent the arts of lyric, sacred, and epic poetry, as well as dance, music, history, and astronomy.

Marden in Hydra, Greece, 1990

I remember reading [Robert] Graves and he talked about these bands of reveling, orgiastic maenads that conducted these wild, primal dances in the forest. Later they became the Muses. I was more interested in their early stages.[56]

January 15–March 15: *Brice Marden: The Grove Group*, at the Gagosian Gallery, New York.

May 8–June 28: *Brice Marden: Recent Drawings and Etchings*, at the Matthew Marks Gallery, Marden's new dealer in New York.

October 17, 1991–May 31, 1992: *Brice Marden: Cold Mountain*, at the Dia Center for the Arts, New York, and at subsequent American and European venues through June 1993. *New York Times* critic Roberta Smith writes of the show, "The paintings reveal what used to be hidden. The colors—the palest of greens, grays or yellows—recall the moody, withdrawn feelings of Marden's early canvases, except that they now share the stage with the tensile, outgoing networks of line, which explain their genesis to the viewer at every turn."[57]

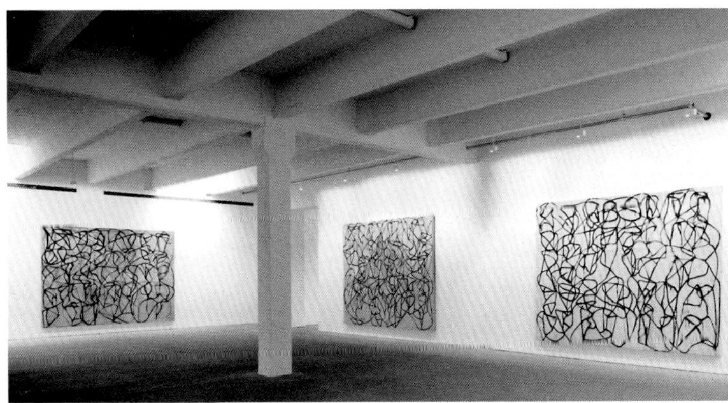

1992

February 16–May 5: *Allegories of Modernism: Contemporary Drawing*, at The Museum of Modern Art, includes *Basel Drawing* (1983; plate 107), *Drawing for Conjunctions* (1988–89; plate 119), and other works.

February 26–June 21: *Brice Marden: Prints, 1961–1991*, at the Tate Gallery, London, and at subsequent European and American venues through January 1993.

April 26–June 21: Is represented in *Slow Art: Painting in New York Now*, at P.S. 1/Institute for Art and Urban Resources, Long Island City, New York.

June 13–September 20: Documenta IX, in Kassel, includes the paintings *The Studio* (plate 132) and *Kalo Keri* (plate 133; both 1990).

1995

Begins to use a flatter, thicker line than in earlier paintings.

Brice Marden: Cold Mountain, Dia Center for the Arts, New York, October 17 1991–May 31, 1992, installation view. Left to right: *Cold Mountain 2* (plate 123), *Cold Mountain 3*, and *Cold Mountain 4* (all 1989–91)

David Seidner. *Brice Marden in His Studio, New York City, 1993.* Chromogenic print

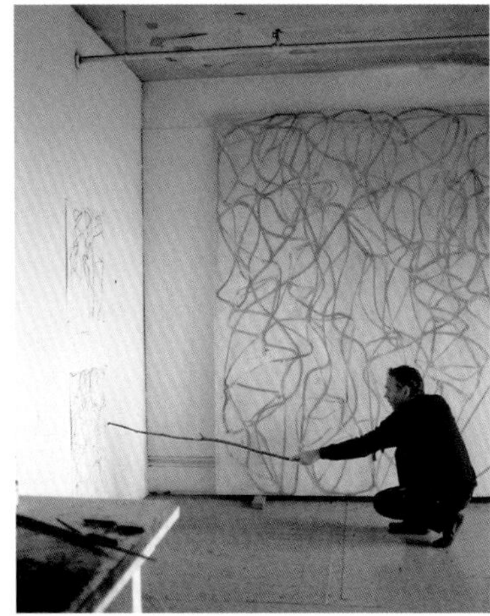

March 23–June 4: The Whitney Biennial includes *February in Hydra* (1991–94), which Marden will later rework as a horizontal painting and rename *Study for the Muses (Eaglesmere Version)* (1991–94/1997–99), and *Muses (Hydra Version)* (1991–94), which he will rework and rename *Study for the Muses (Hydra Version)* (1991–95/1997; plate 145).

November: Travels to China, Japan, and Hong Kong.

1996

February 9–May 12: Is represented in *Abstraction in the Twentieth Century: Total Risk, Freedom, Discipline*, at the Solomon R. Guggenheim Museum, New York.

Sees *Mark Rothko: The Chapel Commission*, an exhibition of the artist's late work at the Menil Collection, Houston, commemorating the twenty-fifth anniversary of the chapel's dedication.

At certain times of the day you can see a striation and a vertical stroking on the chapel paintings. . . . you had a plane and at the same time there was another kind of energy because of the striations. Toward the end of the period when I was doing my own monochromatic panels, I was very carefully painting vertical strokes, which you can't really see unless you get down on the floor or take the work out in a little different lighting situation. That technique came out of Rothko's paintings.[58]

1997

June 15–November 9: The Venice Biennale includes the Souvenir de Grèce series of works on paper and the painting *The Muses*.

July 2–August 24: *Brice Marden: Work Books, 1964–1995*, at the Staatliche Graphische Sammlung, Munich, and at subsequent European and American venues through September 1998.

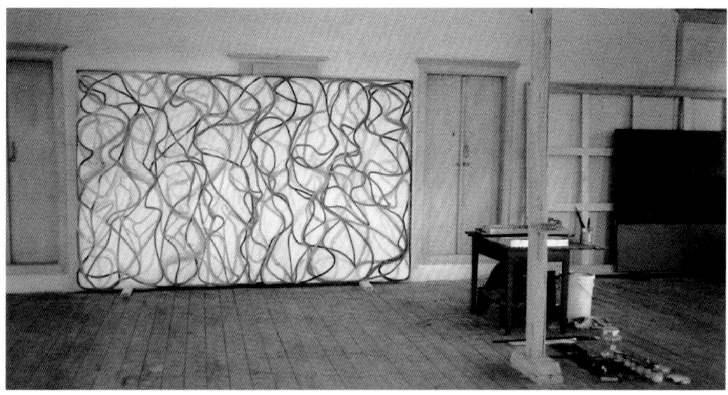

1998
Becomes a member of the American Academy of Arts and Letters.

NOVEMBER 20, 1998–MARCH 28, 1999: *Brice Marden Drawings: The Whitney Museum of American Art Collection*, at the Whitney Museum of American Art.

1999
FEBRUARY 14–APRIL 25: *Brice Marden: Work of the 1990s. Paintings, Drawings, and Prints*, at the Dallas Museum of Art, and at subsequent American venues through August 2000.

2000
Starts work on the group of paintings to be called The Propitious Garden of Plane Image, still ongoing in the summer of 2006.

NOVEMBER 17, 2000–JANUARY 7, 2001: *Brice Marden*, at the Serpentine Gallery, London.

2001
Takes a studio on West Street, New York.

> *When I start a painting now, I use a long brush, so I have a distance from it, and it's somewhat loosely done. And it's all intuitive, there's no plan. . . . But then I keep going over it and over it, so it loses its sense of gesture, or a look of gesture, like flying whites, you know, and stuff like that.*[59]

DECEMBER 12, 2001–FEBRUARY 24, 2002: *Brice Marden: Works on Paper, 1964–2001*, at the Istituto Nazionale per la Grafica, Rome, and at subsequent European venues through August 2002.

2002
Acquires Rose Hill property in Tivoli, New York.

MAY 3–JUNE 21: *Brice Marden: Attendants, Bears, and Rocks*, at the Matthew Marks Gallery.

2003
Sets up a studio at Rose Hill.

Creates four set designs for the opera *Orfeo ed Euridice*, directed and choreographed by Karole Armitage and performed in the fall at Teatro San Carlo, Naples.

APRIL 5–MAY 31: Is represented in *The Stage of Drawing: Gesture and Act*, at The Drawing Center, New York, and at subsequent Australian and European venues through March 2004.

JUNE 14, 2003–JANUARY 4, 2004: *Brice Marden*, at Daros Exhibitions, Zurich.

2004
MARCH 5–MAY 19: Is represented in *Singular Forms (Sometimes Repeated): Art from 1951 to the Present*, at the Solomon R. Guggenheim Museum.

MARCH 14–AUGUST 2: Is represented in *A Minimal Future? Art as Object, 1958–1968*, at the Museum of Contemporary Art, Los Angeles.

MAY 8–JUNE 27: *Brice Marden: Paintings on Marble*, at the Matthew Marks Gallery.

2005
FEBRUARY 4–APRIL 25: Is represented in *Contemporary Voices: Works from The UBS Art Collection*, at The Museum of Modern Art.

MARCH 30–AUGUST 29: Is represented in *Drawing from the Modern, 1945–1975*, at The Museum of Modern Art.

SEPTEMBER 1, 2005–JANUARY 8, 2006: Is represented in *Building and Breaking the Grid*, at the Whitney Museum of American Art.

2006
JANUARY 26–APRIL 24: Is represented in *Transforming Chronologies: An Atlas of Drawings, Part One*, at The Museum of Modern Art.

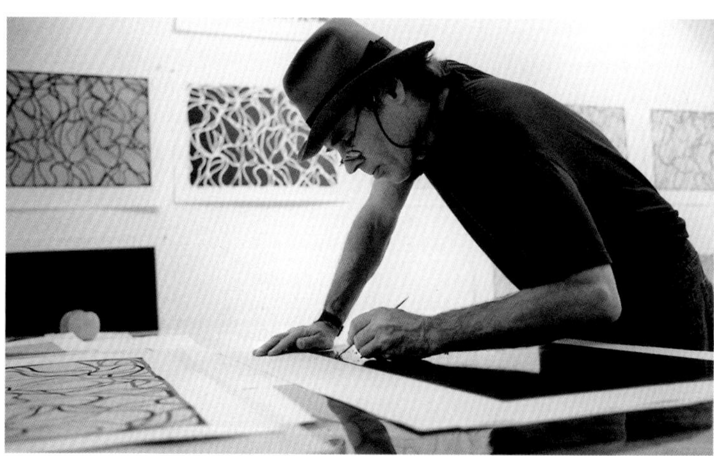

Marden's studio in Hydra, 1996, with *Study for the Muses (Hydra Version)* (plate 145)

Marden working on the Muses print series at Gemini G.E.L., Los Angeles, 1999

1. Brice Marden, in "Interview with Brice Marden conducted by Paul Cummings, October 3, 1972," transcript, Archives of American Art, Smithsonian Institution.
2.Ibid.
3. Ibid.
4. Ibid.
5. Ibid.
6. Ibid.
7. Marden, on a panel with Richard Serra, Jessica Stockholder, and Terry Winters, moderated by Kirk Varnedoe, The Museum of Modern Art, New York, December 8, 1998, in conjunction with the exhibition *Jackson Pollock*. Sound Recordings of Museum-Related Events #99.8. The Museum of Modern Art Archives, New York.
8. Marden, on the panel moderated by Varnedoe.
9. Marden, in "Interview by Paul Cummings."
10. Ibid.
11. Marden, "Statements and Photographs submitted in partial fulfillment of the requirements for Master of Fine Arts degree," Yale University, May 1, 1963, p. 1.
12. Marden, in "Interview by Paul Cummings."
13. Marden, "Statements and Photographs," p. 1.
14. Marden, in "Interview by Paul Cummings."
15. Ibid.
16. Ibid.
17. Marden, "Statements and Photographs," p. 1.
18. Marden, in "Interview by Paul Cummings."
19. Ibid.
20. Ibid.
21. Marden, "Statements and Photographs," p. 3.
22. Ibid., pp. 1, 5–6.
23. Marden, quoted in Eva Keller and Regula Malin, eds. *Brice Marden: Drawings and Paintings, 1964–2002* (Zurich: Daros Collection and Scalo Publishers, 2003), p. 45.
24. Jean Fautrier died on July 21 of that year.
25. Marden, in conversation with Gary Garrels, April 3, 2004, Museum of Contemporary Art, Los Angeles. Transcript from tape provided by the Museum of Contemporary Art.
26. Ibid.
27. Marden, quoted in Jeremy Lewison, *Brice Marden Prints, 1961–1991: A Catalogue Raisonné* (London: Tate Gallery Publications, 1992), p. 19.
28. Marden, in the unpublished conversation with Garrels.
29. Amy Goldin, "Brice Marden," *57th Street Review* 1, no. 1 (November 15, 1966): 7.
30. Marden, in Robert Storr and Marden, "In The Studio," public panel, Japan Society, New York, April 26, 2004. Transcript from tape provided by the Japan Society.
31. Marden, in the film *Brice Marden*, produced and directed by Edgar B. Howard and Theodore R. Haimes (New York: Tuckernuck Productions, 1977) and available through the Checkerboard Film Foundation, New York.
32. Marden, in Storr, "In The Studio."
33. Ibid.
34. Harris Rosenstein, "Brice Marden (Bykert)," *Artnews* 68, no. 3 (May 1969): 69.
35. Marden, in the unpublished conversation with Garrels.
36. Marden, on the sound track to Howard and Haimes, *Brice Marden.*
37. Marden, in Mark Rosenthal, "Brice Marden. Interview by Mark Rosenthal, 19 September 1997," in Jeffrey Weiss, *Mark Rothko* (Washington, D.C.: National Gallery of Art, 1998), p. 362.
38. Ibid., pp. 360–61.
39. Ibid, p. 361.
40. Roberta Smith, "Brice Marden's Painting," *Arts Magazine* 47, no. 7 (May–June 1973): 36-41.
41. Marden, in Storr, "In The Studio."
42. Marden, in Pat Steir, "Brice Marden: An Interview," *Brice Marden: Recent Drawings and Etchings* (New York: Matthew Marks Gallery, 1991), n.p. Quoted here as adapted by Lynne Cooke at http://www.diacenter.org/exhibs/marden/coldmountain/interview.html.
43. Lizzie Borden, "Reviews: Brice Marden, Bykert Gallery," *Artforum* 11, no. 9 (May 1973): 76–77.
44. Marden, in Steir, "Brice Marden: An Interview," n.p.
45. Marden, in Klaus Kertess, *Brice Marden Paintings and Drawings*, (New York: Harry N. Abrams, 1992), p. 28.
46. Marden, on the sound track to Howard and Haimes, *Brice Marden.*
47. Marden, in Storr, "In The Studio."
48. Ibid.
49. Marden, quoted in Brenda Richardson, *Brice Marden Cold Mountain* (Houston: Houston Fine Art Press, 1992), p. 51.
50. Marden, in Steir, "Brice Marden: An Interview," n.p.
51. John Yau, "Reviews: Brice Marden," *Artforum* 25, no. 10 (Summer 1987): 118.
52. Marden, on the panel moderated by Varnedoe.
53. Marden, in Steir, "Brice Marden: An Interview," n.p.
54. Ibid.
55. Marden, quoted in Richardson, *Brice Marden Cold Mountain*, p. 55.
56. Marden, in conversation with Charles Wylie, in *Brice Marden: Work of the 1990s. Paintings, Drawings, and Prints* (Dallas: Dallas Museum of Art, 1999), p. 25. See also Robert Graves, *The Greek Myths* (London and Baltimore: Penguin Books, 1955).
57. Smith, "Brice Marden Moves Ahead by Turning Back," *New York Times*, October 20, 1991, sec. H, p. 37.
58. Marden, in Rosenthal, "Brice Marden. Interview by Mark Rosenthal," p. 359.
59. Marden, in Storr, "In The Studio."

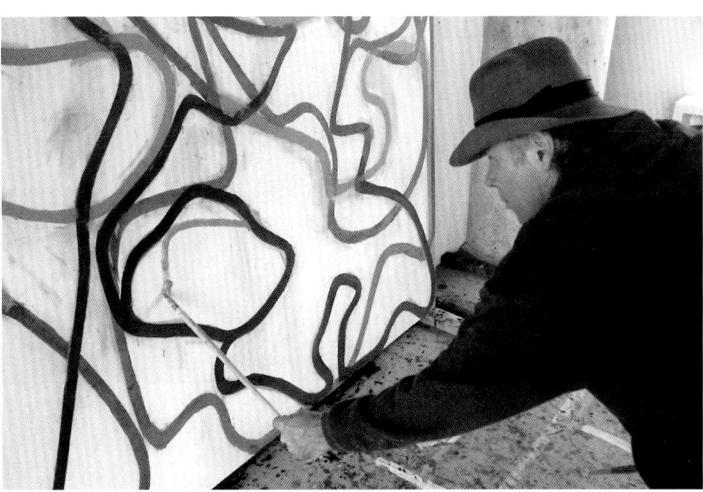

Marden painting in his Manhattan studio, 2001

CATALOGUE OF THE EXHIBITION

The catalogue that follows is ordered chronologically, with a division into paintings and drawings. In dates, dashes indicate a continuous period of work on a piece; slashes indicate a stop in work and a resumption at a later date. In dimensions, height precedes width precedes depth.

Brice Marden: A Retrospective of Paintings and Drawings travels to three venues: The Museum of Modern Art, New York; the San Francisco Museum of Modern Art; and the Hamburger Bahnhof, Museum für Gegenwart, Berlin. The exhibition is changing slightly at each venue to accommodate the different gallery spaces in the three museums and to reflect the richness of Marden holdings in different regions of the United States and in Europe. (The Berlin exhibition, too, includes no drawings.) The catalogue below indicates those works that are appearing in only one or two of the three venues. When no such notation is made, the work appears in all three venues. The catalogue also indicates a few works that were important to illustrate in the plate section but that are not included in the exhibition.

Paintings

Untitled. 1963 (plate 1)
Oil on paper mounted on canvas, 20¾ x 27¾" (52.7 x 70.5 cm)
Collection the artist
New York and San Francisco only

Untitled. 1963 (p. 30, fig. 1)
Oil on canvas, 20 x 24" (50.8 x 61 cm)
Private collection, Los Angeles
San Francisco only

Dark. 1963 (plate 5)
Oil on canvas, 48 x 46" (121.9 x 116.8 cm)
Private collection, Los Angeles
San Francisco only

Decorative Painting. 1964 (plate 8)
Oil on canvas, 41½ x 17¾" (105.4 x 45.1 cm)
Collection François Pinault
Not in exhibition

Untitled. 1964–65 (plate 7)
Oil on canvas, 20 x 39" (50.8 x 99.1 cm)
Stenn Family Collection, Chicago
San Francisco and Berlin only

Return I. 1964–65 (plate 13)
Oil on canvas, 50¼ x 68¼" (127.6 x 173.4 cm)
The Museum of Modern Art, New York. Fractional and promised gift of Kathy and Richard S. Fuld, Jr.

Nebraska. 1966 (plate 15)
Oil and beeswax on canvas, 58 x 72" (147.3 x 182.9 cm)
Collection the artist

Nico. 1966 (plate 16)
Oil and beeswax on canvas, 68" x 8' 4" (172.7 x 254 cm)
Private collection

Two Part Study. 1966 (plate 18)
Oil and beeswax on canvas, two panels, overall: 26 x 30" (66 x 76 cm)
Private collection
San Francisco and Berlin only

The Dylan Painting. 1966/1986 (plate 17)
Oil and beeswax on canvas, 60" x 10' (152.4 x 304.8 cm)
San Francisco Museum of Modern Art. Helen Crocker Russell Fund purchase and gift of Mrs. Helen Portugal

For Helen. 1967 (plate 19)
Oil and beeswax on canvas, two panels, overall: 69 x 36" (175 x 91 cm)
Collection Helen Harrington Marden

For Me (Back Series). 1967–68 (plate 22)
Oil and beeswax on canvas, 69 x 45" (175.3 x 114.3 cm)
Collection Robert Rauschenberg
New York and San Francisco only

For Otis (Back Series). 1967–68 (plate 23)
Oil and beeswax on canvas, 69 x 45" (175.3 x 114.3 cm)
Private collection. Courtesy Thomas Ammann Fine Art, Zurich
Berlin only

Untitled. 1968 (p. 36, fig. 3)
Oil and beeswax on canvas, two panels, overall: 69" x 7' 6" (175.3 x 228.6 cm)
Private collection, San Francisco
San Francisco only

Fave. 1968–69 (plate 28)
Oil and beeswax on canvas, two panels, overall: 72 x 66" (182.8 x 167.6 cm)
The Blanton Museum of Art, The University of Texas at Austin. Gift of Mari and James A. Michener

Point. 1969 (plate 29)
Oil and beeswax on canvas, three panels, overall: 53" x 8' 9" (134.5 x 267 cm)
Collection Linda and Harry Macklowe

D'après la Marquise de la Solana. 1969 (plate 30)
Oil and beeswax on canvas, three panels, overall: 6' 5⅝" x 9' 9⅜" (196 x 297 cm)
Solomon R. Guggenheim Museum, New York. Panza Collection, 1991
New York and Berlin only

Three Deliberate Greys for Jasper Johns. 1970 (plate 31)
Oil and beeswax on canvas, three panels, overall: 72" x 12' 6" (183 x 381 cm)
National Gallery of Canada, Ottawa. Purchase

For Pearl. 1970 (plate 34)
Oil and beeswax on canvas, three panels, overall: 8' x 8' 2¼" (243.8 x 249.6 cm)
Private collection

Pumpkin Plumb. 1970/1973 (plate 38)
Oil and beeswax on canvas, three panels, overall: 69 x 51¼" (175 x 130 cm)
Collection Helen Harrington Marden

Rodeo. 1971 (plate 35)
Oil and beeswax on canvas, two panels, overall: 8 x 8' (243.8 x 243.8 cm)
The Art Institute of Chicago. Ada S. Garrett Prize Fund; estate of Katharine Kuh; through prior gift of Mrs. Henry C. Woods; gift of Lannan Foundation
San Francisco only

Toward Brindisi. 1972 (plate 33)
Oil and beeswax on canvas, two panels, overall: 72 x 72" (182.9 x 182.9 cm)
Courtesy Barbara Annis Fine Art
New York only

Star (for Patti Smith). 1972/1974 (plate 37)
Oil and beeswax on canvas, three panels, overall: 68 x 45" (173 x 114 cm)
Donald L. Bryant Jr. Family Trust

Summer Table. 1972–73 (plate 36)
Oil and beeswax on canvas, three panels, overall: 60" x 8' 9¼" (152.4 x 267.3 cm)
Whitney Museum of American Art, New York. Purchase, with funds from the National Endowment for the Arts

Adriatic. 1972–73 (plate 40)
Oil and beeswax on canvas, two panels, overall: 6' 1/16 x 9' 7/16" (183 x 275.4 cm)
Solomon R. Guggenheim Museum, New York. Panza Collection
San Francisco and Berlin only

Grove Group I. 1972–73 (plate 46)
Oil and beeswax on canvas, 72" x 9' (182.9 x 274.3 cm)
The Museum of Modern Art, New York. Treadwell Corporation Fund

Grove Group II. 1972–73 (plate 47)
Oil and beeswax on canvas, two panels, overall: 72" x 9' (182.9 x 274.3 cm)
Private collection. Fractional gift to the San Francisco Museum of Modern Art

First Figure (Homage to Courbet). 1973–74 (plate 61)
Oil and beeswax on canvas, three panels, overall: 6' 3" x 30" (190.5 x 76.2 cm)
Private collection, Atherton, California
San Francisco only

Fourth Figure (Red Yellow Blue). 1973–74 (plate 62)
Oil and beeswax on canvas, three panels, overall: 6' 3" x 30" (190.5 x 76.2 cm)
Private collection

Winter Painting. 1973–75 (plate 65)
Oil and beeswax on canvas, three panels, each (left to right): 72 x 60" (183 x 152 cm), 72 x 30" (183 x 76 cm), 72 x 30" (183 x 76 cm), overall: 72" x 10' (183 x 305 cm)
Stedelijk Museum, Amsterdam
Not in exhibition

Red Yellow Blue II. 1974 (plate 63)
Oil and beeswax on canvas, three panels, overall: 6' 2" x 72" (188 x 182.9 cm)
The Museum of Contemporary Art, Los Angeles. The Barry Lowen Collection
San Francisco only

The Seasons. 1974–75 (plate 64)
Oil and beeswax on canvas, four panels, overall: 8' x 20' 9" (243.8 x 632.5 cm)
The Menil Collection, Houston
New York and San Francisco only

Grove Group IV. 1976 (plate 48)
Oil and beeswax on canvas, two panels, overall: 72" x 9' (182.9 x 274.3 cm)
Solomon R. Guggenheim Museum, New York. Purchased with funds contributed by the National Endowment for the Arts, in Washington, D.C., a Federal agency; matching funds contributed by Sidney Singer
New York only

Grove Group V. 1976 (plate 49)
Oil and beeswax on canvas, three panels, overall: 72" x 9' (182.9 x 274.3 cm)
Museum of Contemporary Art, Chicago. Gerald S. Elliott Collection
San Francisco and Berlin only

Lethykos (for Tonto). 1976 (plate 66)
Oil and beeswax on canvas, four panels, each (left to right): 7' x 24" (213.4 x 61 cm), 7' x 12" (213.4 x 30.5 cm), 7' x 12" (213.4 x 30.5 cm), 7' x 24" (213.4 x 61 cm), overall: 7' x 72" (213.4 x 182.9 cm)
The Museum of Modern Art, New York. Fractional and promised gift of Marie-Josée and Henry R. Kravis

Morada. 1976 (plate 67)
Oil and beeswax on canvas, four panels, each (left to right): 7' x 24" (213 x 61 cm), 7' x 12" (213 x 30.5 cm), 7' x 12" (213 x 30.5 cm), 7' x 24" (213 x 61 cm), overall: 7' x 72" (213.4 x 182.9 cm)
Stedelijk Museum, Amsterdam
Berlin only

For Hera. 1977 (plate 68)
Oil and beeswax on canvas, three panels, overall: 7 x 10' (213.4 x 304.8 cm)
Daros Collection, Switzerland
Berlin only

Moon III. 1977 (plate 69)
Oil and beeswax on canvas, three panels, overall: 7 x 10' (213.4 x 304.8 cm)
Daros Collection, Switzerland

Conturbatio. 1978 (plate 70)
Oil and beeswax on canvas, four panels, each: two panels 7' x 16" (213.4 x 40.6 cm), two panels 7' x 32" (213.4 x 81.3 cm), overall: 7 x 8' (213.4 x 243.8 cm)
Private collection. Courtesy PaceWildenstein
New York and San Francisco only

Meritatio. 1978 (plate 71)
Oil and beeswax on canvas, four panels, each: two panels 7' x 32" (213.4 x 81.3 cm), two panels 7' x 16" (213.4 x 40.6 cm), overall: 7 x 8' (213.4 x 243.8 cm)
Virginia Museum of Fine Arts, Richmond. Gift of The Sydney and Frances Lewis Foundation
Not in exhibition

Thira. 1979–80 (plate 83)
Oil and beeswax on canvas, eighteen panels assembled in three parts, overall: 8 x 15' (243.8 x 457.2 cm)
Centre Pompidou, Paris. Musée national d'art moderne/Centre de Création Industrielle. Donation of the Georges Pompidou Art and Culture Foundation (in honor of Pontus Hulten)
New York only

Marble #6 (Papastratos Table). 1981 (plate 101)
Oil on marble, 29¼ x 19¾ x ⅞" (74.3 x 50.2 x 2.2 cm)
Collection Matthew Marks, New York
New York and San Francisco only

Marble #4. 1981 (plate 99)
Oil on marble, 9⅜ x 32¾ x ¾" (23.8 x 83.2 x 1.9 cm)
Private collection
New York and San Francisco only

Marble #12. 1981 (plate 100)
Oil on marble, 16⅝ x 45¾" x ⅞" (42.2 x 116.2 x 2.2 cm)
Private collection
New York and San Francisco only

Elements I. 1981–82 (plate 103)
Oil on canvas, four panels, overall: 7' x 51" (213.4 x 129.5 cm)
Daros Collection, Switzerland

Black and White Painting. 1982 (plate 102)
Oil on canvas, 24 x 18" (61 x 45.7 cm)
Private collection. Courtesy Thomas Ammann Fine Art, Zurich
San Francisco only

Green (Earth). 1983–84 (plate 104)
Oil on canvas, twelve panels, overall: 7' x 9' 1" (213.4 x 276.9 cm)
Collection Frances F. Bowes
New York only

Elements IV. 1983–84 (plate 105)
Oil on canvas, eight panels, overall: 7' x 6' $\frac{1}{2}$" (213.4 x 184.2 cm)
Collection Linda and Harry Macklowe
San Francisco and Berlin only

Window Study #3. 1983–85 (plate 109)
Oil on linen, 24 x 18" (61 x 45.7 cm)
Collection John and Mary Pappajohn
San Francisco only

#13 Helen's Valentine. 1986 (plate 110)
Oil on paper, $30\frac{1}{8}$ x $22\frac{1}{2}$" (76.5 x 57.2 cm)
Collection Helen Harrington Marden
San Francisco and Berlin only

Untitled #1. 1986 (plate 111)
Oil on linen, 72 x 58" (183 x 147 cm)
Daros Collection, Switzerland
Berlin only

Untitled #3. 1986–87 (plate 112)
Oil on linen, 72 x 58" (182.9 x 147.3 cm)
Agnes Gund Collection

Diptych. 1986–87 (plate 113)
Oil on linen, two panels, overall: 6' 3" x 12' (190.5 x 366 cm)
Private collection

2 (Dialog). 1987–88 (plate 114)
Oil on linen, 7' x 60" (213.4 x 152.4 cm)
Private collection

4 (Bone). 1987–88 (plate 115)
Oil on linen, 7' x 60" (213.4 x 152.4 cm)
Collection Helen Harrington Marden

11 (To Léger). 1987–88 (plate 116)
Oil on linen, 7' x 60" (213.4 x 152.4 cm)
Collection Linda and Harry Macklowe
New York and San Francisco only

Couplet I. 1988–89 (plate 121)
Oil on linen, 9' x 60" (274.3 x 152.4 cm)
Collection Uli Knecht, Stuttgart
Berlin only

Couplet IV. 1988–89 (plate 122)
Oil on linen, 9' x 60" (274.3 x 152.4 cm)
The Museum of Modern Art, New York. Fractional and promised gift of Kathy and Richard S. Fuld, Jr.

Cold Mountain 2. 1989–91 (plate 123)
Oil on linen, 9 x 12' (274.3 x 365.8 cm)
Hirshhorn Museum and Sculpture Garden, Smithsonian Institution, Washington, D.C. Holenia Purchase Fund, in Memory of Joseph H. Hirshhorn

Cold Mountain 5 (Open). 1989–91 (plate 124)
Oil on linen, 9 x 12' (274.3 x 365.8 cm)
Robert and Jane Meyerhoff Collection, Phoenix, Maryland
New York only

Cold Mountain 6 (Bridge). 1989–91 (plate 125)
Oil on linen, 9 x 12' (274.3 x 365.8 cm)
San Francisco Museum of Modern Art. Purchased through a gift of Phyllis Wattis

Small Corpus. 1989–94 (plate 142)
Oil on parchment stretched over birch panel, $26\frac{1}{2}$ x $19\frac{3}{8}$" (67.3 x 49.2 cm)
Collection Sarah-Ann and Werner H. Kramarsky
Not in exhibition

The Studio. 1990 (plate 132)
Oil on linen, 7' $8\frac{5}{8}$" x 59" (235.3 x 149.9 cm)
Private collection

Kalo Keri. 1990 (plate 133)
Oil on linen, 7' $8\frac{5}{8}$" x 59" (235.3 x 149.9 cm)
Kunstmuseum Winterthur. Presented anonymously
Not in exhibition

Presentation. 1990–92 (plate 134)
Oil on linen, 7' $8\frac{3}{8}$" x 59" (234.6 x 149.9 cm)
Colección Patricia Phelps de Cisneros, Caracas

The Muses. 1991–93 (plate 137)
Oil on linen, 9 x 15' (274.3 x 457.2 cm)
Daros Collection, Switzerland

Virgins. 1991–93 (plate 139)
Oil on linen, 8' x 8' 6" (243.8 x 259.1 cm)
Private collection
New York only

The Sisters. 1991–93 (plate 136)
Oil on linen, 7' x 59" (213.4 x 149.9 cm)
Private collection, San Francisco

Corpus. 1991–93 (plate 140)
Oil on linen, 6' 7" x 57" (200.7 x 144.8 cm)
Froehlich Collection, Stuttgart
Berlin only

Aphrodite. 1991–93 (plate 143)
Oil on linen, 8' 4" x 70" (254 x 177.8 cm)
Private collection
Not in exhibition

Study for the Muses (Hydra Version). 1991–95/1997 (plate 145)
Oil on linen, 6' 11" x 11' 3" (210.8 x 342.9 cm)
Private collection, New York

Vine. 1992–93 (plate 141)
Oil on linen, 8' x 8' 6" (243.8 x 259.1 cm)
The Museum of Modern Art, New York. Gift of Werner and Elaine Dannheisser

Light in the Forest. 1993–95 (plate 147)
Oil on linen, 71 x 57" (180.3 x 144.8 cm)
Private collection. Courtesy Matthew Marks Gallery, New York
New York and Berlin only

Skull with Thought. 1993–95 (plate 148)
Oil on linen, 71 x 57" (180.3 x 144.8 cm)
Collection Keith and Kathy Sachs
New York only

Suzhou. 1995–96 (plate 153)
Oil on linen, 72 x 32" (182.9 x 81.3 cm)
Collection Uli Knecht, Stuttgart
Berlin only

China Painting. 1995–96 (plate 154)
Oil on linen, 71 x 32" (180.3 x 81.3 cm)
Private collection

Tang Dancer. 1995–96 (plate 152)
Oil on linen, 72 x 33" (182.9 x 83.8 cm)
Private collection
New York only

Epitaph Painting 1. 1996–97 (plate 161)
Oil on linen, 8' 1/2" x 7' 11" (245.1 x 241.3 cm)
Private collection, San Francisco
San Francisco and Berlin only

Attendant. 1996–99 (plate 156)
Oil on linen, 6' 10" x 57" (208.3 x 144.8 cm)
Collection Helen Harrington Marden
Berlin only

Attendant 2. 1996–99 (plate 157)
Oil on linen, 6' 10" x 57" (208.3 x 144.8 cm)
Collection Dr. Paul and Dorie Sternberg, and partial and promised gift to The Art Institute of Chicago

Attendant 3. 1996–99 (plate 158)
Oil on linen, 6' 10" x 57" (208.3 x 144.8 cm)
Collection Åke Skeppner, Courtesy Thomas Ammann Fine Art, Zurich
Berlin only

Bear Print. 1997–98/2000 (plate 160)
Oil on linen, 7' x 60" (213.4 x 152.4 cm)
Collection Peter Morton, Los Angeles
New York and San Francisco only

Epitaph Painting 5. 1997–2001 (plate 163)
Oil on linen, 9' 1/2" x 8' 8" (275.6 x 264.2 cm)
Collection Richard and Betty Hedreen

Red Rocks (1). 2000–2002 (plate 166)
Oil on linen, 6' 3" x 8' 11" (190.5 x 271.8 cm)
Collection the artist
Berlin only

6 Red Rock 1. 2000–2002 (plate 167)
Oil on linen, 8' 11" x 6' 3" (271.8 x 190.5 cm)
Robert and Jane Meyerhoff Collection, Phoenix, Maryland

7 Red Rock 2. 2000–2002 (plate 168)
Oil on linen, 8' 11" x 6' 3" (271.8 x 190.5 cm)
Private collection, Atherton, California

The Propitious Garden of Plane Image, First Version. 2000–2005 (plate 169)
Oil on linen, six panels, overall: 42" x 12' (106.7 x 365.8 cm)
Private collection, Atherton, California
San Francisco only

The Propitious Garden of Plane Image, Second Version. 2000–2006 (plate 171, photographed unfinished in May 2006)
Oil on linen, six panels, overall: 72" x 24' (182.9 x 731.5 cm)
Collection the artist. Courtesy Matthew Marks Gallery, New York

The Propitious Garden of Plane Image, Third Version. 2000–2006 (plate 172, photographed unfinished in May 2006)
Oil on linen, six panels, overall: 72" x 24' (182.9 x 731.5 cm)
Collection the artist. Courtesy Matthew Marks Gallery, New York
New York and Berlin only

Drawings

Untitled. 1962 (p. 39, fig. 4)
Charcoal on paper, 14 3/8 x 17 1/2" (36.5 x 44.5 cm)
Collection the artist
New York only

Untitled. 1962–63 (plate 2)
Charcoal and graphite on paper, 14 1/2 x 18 1/4" (36.8 x 46.4 cm)
Collection the artist
New York only

Untitled. 1963 (plate 4)
Charcoal on paper, 14 1/2 x 18 1/8" (36.8 x 46 cm)
Private collection
New York only

Untitled. 1963 (plate 3)
Charcoal and graphite on paper, 14 1/4 x 18 1/4" (36.2 x 46.4 cm)
Private collection, Chicago
New York only

Untitled. 1964 (plate 6)
Charcoal on paper, 22 1/4 x 30 3/8" (56.5 x 77.2 cm)
Private collection
San Francisco only

Untitled. 1964 (plate 9)
Graphite and charcoal on paper, 26 x 40" (66 x 101.6 cm)
Private collection
New York only

Untitled. 1964 (plate 10)
Charcoal and graphite on paper, 21 3/4 x 29 1/2" (55.2 x 74.9 cm)
Private collection, Houston, Texas

Untitled. 1964–65 (plate 11)
Graphite and beeswax on paper, 22 x 30" (55.9 x 76.2 cm)
Private collection

Untitled. 1964–65 (plate 12)
Charcoal on paper, 19 3/4 x 22 1/4" (50.2 x 56.5 cm)
Collection the artist
New York only

Teddy's Drawing. 1964–65 (plate 14)
Graphite and beeswax over silkscreen on paper, 40 x 26" (101.6 x 66 cm)
Private collection

Untitled. 1964–67 (plate 24)
Graphite, ink, and beeswax on paper, 26 x 40" (66 x 101.6 cm)
Private collection

Two Studies, Back Series. 1967 (plate 21)
Graphite over pastel on paper, 23 x 31" (58.4 x 78.7 cm)
Whitney Museum of American Art, New York. Purchase, with funds from The Lauder Foundation, Evelyn and Leonard Lauder Fund for the Acquisition of Master Drawings and the Drawing Committee
San Francisco only

Patent Leather Valentine. 1967 (plate 20)
Graphite and beeswax over pastel on paper, 16 1/2 x 14 3/4" (41.9 x 37.5 cm)
Collection Helen Harrington Marden

Untitled. 1968 (plate 25)
Graphite and oil pastel on paper, 26 x 40" (66 x 101.6 cm)
Private collection

Untitled. 1968 (plate 26)
Graphite and beeswax on paper, 22 x 30" (55.9 x 76.2 cm)
Collection Dorothea Rockburne
San Francisco only

Untitled. 1968
Beeswax, graphite, and crayon on paper, 22 x 30½" (55.9 x 77.5 cm)
Whitney Museum of American Art, New York. Given in memory of Herman More by four of his friends
New York only

Untitled. 1968 (plate 27)
Oil crayon, pastel, and graphite on paper, 22½ x 30½" (57.2 x 77.5 cm)
The Art Institute of Chicago. Restricted gift of Jack and Sandra Guthman, and Mr. and Mrs. Thomas Dittmer
New York only

Untitled. 1970 (p. 53, fig. 20)
Graphite and beeswax on paper, 26 x 40" (66 x 101.6 cm)
Collection Robert Mangold and Sylvia Plimack Mangold
San Francisco only

Untitled. 1970 (plate 32)
Graphite and beeswax on paper, two sheets, overall: 40 x 50" (101.6 x 127 cm)
Collection Paul F. Walter

Untitled. 1972 (plate 39)
Graphite and beeswax on paper, 22 x 30" (55.9 x 76.2 cm)
Collection Susan and Larry Marx, Aspen. Courtesy Neal Meltzer Fine Art
New York only

Adriatic Study. 1972 (p. 41, fig. 6)
Graphite and beeswax on paper, 21¾ x 30" (55.2 x 76.2 cm)
Private collection, St. Louis
New York only

Grove Group 1. 1972 (plate 41)
Graphite and beeswax on paper, 22 x 30" (55.9 x 76.2 cm)
The Museum of Modern Art, New York. Fractional and promised gift of Kathy and Richard S. Fuld, Jr. in honor of Gary Garrels

Grove Group 2. 1972 (plate 42)
Graphite and beeswax on paper, 22 x 30" (55.9 x 76.2 cm)
The Museum of Modern Art, New York. Fractional and promised gift of Kathy and Richard S. Fuld, Jr. in honor of Gary Garrels

Grove Group 3. 1972 (plate 43)
Graphite and beeswax on paper, 22 x 30" (55.9 x 76.2 cm)
The Museum of Modern Art, New York. Fractional and promised gift of Kathy and Richard S. Fuld, Jr. in honor of Gary Garrels

Grove Group 4. 1972 (plate 44)
Graphite and beeswax on paper, 22 x 30" (55.9 x 76.2 cm)
The Museum of Modern Art, New York. Fractional and promised gift of Kathy and Richard S. Fuld, Jr. in honor of Gary Garrels

Grove Group 5. 1972 (plate 45)
Graphite and beeswax on paper, 22 x 30" (55.9 x 76.2 cm)
The Museum of Modern Art, New York. Fractional and promised gift of Kathy and Richard S. Fuld, Jr. in honor of Gary Garrels

Suicide Notes. February 1972–July 1973 (plate 54)
Brown-paper-covered notebook, twenty-eight sheets, 12¼ x 8¾" (31.1 x 22.2 cm)
The Museum of Modern Art, New York. The Judith Rothschild Foundation Contemporary Drawings Collection

Suicide Notes. February 1972–July 1973 (plates 55–60)
Sheets from notebook, ink on paper, 11¾ x 7¾" (29.8 x 19.7 cm)
Plates 55, 56, 59: bound in notebook. The Museum of Modern Art, New York. The Judith Rothschild Foundation Contemporary Drawings Collection
Plate 58 and eleven others: separated from notebook. Collection the artist
Plates 57, 60, and one other: separated from notebook. Private collection

Grove Addenda II. 1973 (plate 50)
Collage, graphite, and beeswax on paper, 30 x 22" (76.2 x 55.9 cm)
Collection Roselyne Chroman Swig

Homage to Art 2 (Goya). 1973 (plate 52)
Graphite, beeswax, and collage on paper, 30¼ x 22¾" (76.8 x 57.8 cm)
Private collection, Houston, Texas

Grove Addenda III. 1973–74 (plate 51)
Collage, graphite, and beeswax on paper, 30 x 22¾" (76.2 x 57.8 cm)
Collection Anne Anka, Los Angeles
New York only

Homage to Art 14 (Fra Angelico). 1974 (plate 53)
Graphite, beeswax, and collage on paper, 30¾ x 20¾" (76.8 x 52.7 cm)
Private collection

Souvenir de Grèce 4. 1974/1994 (plate 150)
Graphite, beeswax, and collage on paper, 29¾ x 22½" (75.6 x 57.2 cm)
Collection Douglas S. Cramer
San Francisco only

Souvenir de Grèce 11. 1974/1996 (plate 149)
Graphite, beeswax, and collage on paper, 29¾ x 22½" (75.6 x 57.2 cm)
Private collection

Souvenir de Grèce 16. 1974/1996 (plate p. 19, fig. 8)
Graphite, beeswax, and collage on paper, 29¾ x 22½" (75.6 x 57.2 cm)
Courtesy Locksley Shea Gallery

Study for the N Drawing. 1975 (plate 72)
Graphite and beeswax on paper, 30⅜ x 22¼" (77.2 x 56.5 cm)
Private collection
New York only

Inside Outside. 1977 (plate 73)
Graphite and beeswax on paper, two sheets, overall: 30 x 44½" (76.2 x 113 cm)
Private collection

Mosaic Study #3. 1978 (plate 74)
Graphite, oil, and beeswax on paper, 30¼ x 22¼" (76.8 x 56.5 cm)
Collection Judith Neisser

Mosaic Study #4. 1978 (plate 75)
Graphite, oil, and beeswax on paper, 30¼ x 22¼" (76.8 x 56.5 cm)
Private collection. Courtesy Matthew Marks Gallery, New York

Mosaic Study #5. 1978 (plate 76)
Graphite and beeswax on paper, 30¾ x 22¼" (78.1 x 56.5 cm)
Collection the artist

Mirabelle Addenda 1–9. 1979 (plates 77–82)
Nine sheets, all ink on paper, ranging from 9 3/16" to 9 1/4" (23.3 x 23.5 cm) vertically and from 6 3/4" to 7 1/4" (17.1 to 18.4 cm) horizontally
Nos. 1, 4, 7, 8: Collection the artist
Nos. 2, 3, 6, 9: Whitney Museum of American Art, New York. Gift of the artist
No. 5: Collection Klaus Kertess
San Francisco only

Hydra Group II. 1979–81 (plate 84)
Oil on paper, 19 1/2 x 18 3/4" (49.5 x 47.6 cm)
Collection Helen Harrington Marden
San Francisco only

Hydra Group X. 1979–81 (plate 85)
Oil on paper, 19 1/2 x 18 1/4" (49.5 x 47.6 cm)
Whitney Museum of American Art, New York. Purchase, with funds from The Lauder Foundation, Evelyn and Leonard Lauder Fund for the Acquisition of Master Drawings
San Francisco only

4 and 3 Drawing. 1979–81 (plate 89)
Ink on paper, 30 1/2 x 40 1/2" (77.5 x 102.9 cm)
Collection Phil Schrager, Omaha

Painting Study II. 1980 (plate 88)
Ink over screenprint on paper, 20 x 24" (50.8 x 61 cm)
Collection Mirabelle Marden
San Francisco only

Melia Group. 1980–81 (plates 90–98)
Nine sheets, all ink and gouache on paper, ranging from 11 1/4" to 11 3/4" (28.6 to 29.8 cm) vertically and from 7 3/4" to 8 1/2" (19.7 x 21.6 cm) horizontally
Private collection. Courtesy Matthew Marks Gallery, New York
San Francisco only

Study #1. 1981–82 (plate 86)
Oil and graphite on paper, 18 1/2 x 39 1/2" (47 x 100.3 cm)
Collection Susan and Larry Marx, Aspen. Courtesy Neal Meltzer Fine Art
San Francisco only

Untitled (Window Study No. 1). 1983 (plate 106)
Ink on paper, 23 1/4 x 18" (59.1 x 45.7 cm)
Collection Ed Cohen
San Francisco only

Basel Drawing. 1983 (plate 107)
Ink and gouache on paper, 25 1/2 x 19 3/4" (64.8 x 50.2 cm)
Collection the artist
San Francisco only

Masking Drawing Five (Red Drawing Five). 1984 (plate 108)
Gouache, graphite, ink, and oil on paper, 14 7/8 x 13 1/2" (37.8 x 34.3 cm)
Private collection
San Francisco only

2. 1986 (plate 87)
Oil and graphite on paper, 18 1/4 x 39 1/2" (46.4 x 100.3 cm)
Private collection
San Francisco only

Summer Scroll #8 (Five Kinds of Hydra Trees). 1986 (plate 117)
Ink on paper, 10 3/4 x 29 1/4" (27.3 x 74.3 cm)
Collection Melia Marden
San Francisco only

In the Summer Garden II. 1987–88 (plate 118)
Ink on paper, 15 x 22 1/2" (38.1 x 57.2 cm)
Collection Jasper Johns
San Francisco only

Drawing for Conjunctions. 1988–89 (plate 119)
Ink and gouache on paper, 16 x 11 3/4" (40.6 x 29.8 cm)
Agnes Gund Collection
San Francisco only

St. Barts 10. 1989/1991 (plate 127)
Ink on paper, 10 3/4 x 16" (27.3 x 40.6 cm)
The Museum of Modern Art, New York. Gift of the Elaine Dannheisser Foundation
San Francisco only

Muses Drawing 2. 1989–91 (plate 138)
Ink, ink wash, and gouache on paper, 26 x 40 5/8" (66 x 103.2 cm)
Kunstmuseum Basel, Kupferstichkabinett
New York only

Muses Drawing 4. 1989–91 (plate 135)
Ink and gouache on paper, 26 x 40 5/8" (66 x 103.2 cm)
Private collection

Muses Drawing 5 (Mnemosyne). 1989–91 (plate 131)
Ink and ink wash on paper, 26 x 40 5/8" (66 x 103.2 cm)
The Museum of Modern Art, New York. Fractional and promised gift of Sarah-Ann and Werner H. Kramarsky

Hydra Summer 1990 III. 1990 (plate 120)
Ink and gouache on paper, 14 x 8 1/2" (35.6 x 21.6 cm)
Collection Mr. and Mrs. Michael Wilsey
San Francisco only

St. Barts 1. 1990
Ink on paper, 10 3/4 x 16" (27.3 x 40.6 cm)
Collection the artist
San Francisco only

St. Barts 2. 1990 (plate 126)
Ink on paper, 10 3/4 x 16" (27.3 x 40.6 cm)
Private collection, Chicago
San Francisco only

Venus. 1990–91 (plate 144)
Ink and gouache on paper, 40 x 25 1/2" (101.6 x 64.8 cm)
Private collection, Houston, Texas

Cold Mountain Addendum 2. 1990–92 (plate 130)
Ink, ink wash, and gouache on paper, 25 3/4 x 34 1/4" (65.4 x 87 cm)
Private collection

Han Shan Goes to the Tropics. 1991 (plate 128)
Ink and ink wash on paper, 25 7/8 x 34 3/8" (65.7 x 87.3 cm)
Private collection, New York

Rain. 1991
Ink and ink wash on paper, 25 7/8 x 34 3/8" (65.7 x 87.3 cm)
The Museum of Modern Art, New York. Gift of The Edward John Noble Foundation Inc. and Jo Carole and Ronald S. Lauder

Cold Mountain Addendum 1. 1991–92 (plate 129)
Ink, ink wash, and gouache on paper, 26 x $34\frac{1}{4}$" (66 x 87 cm)
Private collection

Aphrodite (Negril) with Green. 1991–94
Ink and gouache on paper, $40\frac{1}{4}$ x 26" (103.5 x 66 cm)
The Art Institute of Chicago. Restricted gift of Mr. and Mrs. Lewis Manilow in memory of B.C. Holland; Adelaide C. Brown, Mr. and Mrs. Philip B. Heller, and William H. Tuthill funds; Margaret Fisher Endowment

Daoist Conclusion. 1991–95 (plate 151)
Ink and gouache on paper, $40\frac{1}{2}$ x $25\frac{7}{8}$" (102.9 x 65.7 cm)
Private collection

Aphrodite (Negril). 1992–93 (plate 146)
Ink on paper, $40\frac{1}{2}$ x $25\frac{7}{8}$" (102.9 x 65.7 cm)
Private collection, St. Louis
New York only

Untitled Red and Green Drawing 1. 1998 (plate 155)
Ink on paper, $29\frac{3}{4}$ x $20\frac{1}{8}$" (75.6 x 51.1 cm)
Collection Jennifer and David Stockman
New York only

Untitled Red and Green Drawing 5. 1998 (plate 162)
Ink on paper, $20\frac{3}{8}$ x $29\frac{9}{16}$" (51.8 x 75.1 cm)
Donald L. Bryant Jr. Family Trust
New York only

Post Calligraphic Drawing. 1998 (plate 159)
Ink on paper, 30 x $22\frac{1}{2}$" (76.2 x 57.2 cm)
Private collection, New York

St. Barts 4. 1999–2001 (plate 165)
Ink on paper, $20\frac{1}{4}$ x 15" (51.4 x 38.1 cm)
Private collection
New York only

Dragons. 2000–2004 (plate 164)
Ink on paper, $40\frac{1}{2}$ x $29\frac{3}{4}$" (102.9 x 75.6 cm)
Private collection

Drawing for the Propitious Garden, St. Barts. 2003 (plate 170)
Ink on paper, $11\frac{1}{4}$ x $66\frac{1}{2}$" (28.6 x 168.9 cm)
Private collection, New York

BIBLIOGRAPHY

Compiled by Francesca Pietropaolo

Books and Other Writings by Marden

In chronological order.

"Statements and Photographs submitted in partial fulfillment of the requirements for Master of Fine Arts degree." Yale University, 1963.

"Three Deliberate Greys for Jasper Johns." *Art Now: New York*, March 1971, n.p.

Suicide Notes. Lausanne, Switzerland: Editions des Massons, 1974.

Reporter's Notebook: Drawings Made in Greece, Summer 1981. New York: The Pace Gallery, 1984.

Thirty-six Poems by Tu Fu. The poems trans. Kenneth Rexroth. New York: Peter Blum Editions, 1987. With an introduction by John Yau.

Cold Mountain Studies. Munich: Schirmer/Mosel, 1991. With an essay by Heiner Bastian.

Interviews

In alphabetical order by interviewer.

Bell, Tiffany. "Responses to Neo-Expressionism." *Flash Art* (international edition) 17, no. 112 (May 1983): 40–46.

Brown, Mick. "Driven to Abstraction." *The Daily Telegraph* (London), October 28, 2000, sec. A, pp. 1, 11.

Cummings, Paul. "Interview with Brice Marden." Unpublished interview with the artist, October 3, 1972. Archives of American Art, Smithsonian Institution, Washington D.C.

D'Arcy, David. "Artist's Interview: Brice Marden, Heir Presumptive to Pollock." *The Art Newspaper*, April 1999, p. 17.

de Smecchia, Muni. "Artisti: Brice Marden." *Vogue Italia*, April 1988, pp. 136–39.

Enright, Robert. "The Sensuous Puritan: The Art of Brice Marden." *Border Crossings* (Canada) 18, no. 2 (May 1999): 14–27.

Fricke, Marion, and Roswitha Fricke. "Brice Marden (Interview)." *Art Press Spécial* (Paris) 17 (1996): 84–86.

Furlong, William. "Brice Marden in Conversation with William Furlong." *Art Monthly* (London) 117 (June 1988): 3–5.

Garrels, Gary. Unpublished conversation with Brice Marden, April 3, 2004, at the Museum of Contemporary Art, Los Angeles, in conjunction with the 2004 exhibition *A Minimal Future? Art as Object 1958–1968*.

Garrels, Gary, Matthew Marks, Dana Cranmer, and Carol Mancusi-Ungaro. Unpublished interview with Brice Marden, March 30, 2004, at the Museum of Contemporary Art, Los Angeles. Transcript in the Archives of The Museum of Modern Art, New York.

Hay, Jonathan. "An Interview with Brice Marden." In *Chinese Work*, exh. cat., pp. 19–31. New York: Matthew Marks Gallery, 1997.

Howard, Edgar B. Unpublished interview with Brice Marden, December 11, 1976. Checkerboard Film Foundation, New York.

Katz, Vincent. "Curiously Determined Objects." *Art on Paper* (New York) 2, no. 3 (January–February 1998): 27–31.

Lee, Janie C. "Interview with Brice Marden." In *Brice Marden Drawings: The Whitney Museum of American Art Collection*, exh. cat., pp. 13–23. New York: Whitney Museum of American Art and Harry N. Abrams, 1998.

Mahoney, Robert. "Brice Marden: This Is What Things Are About." *Flash Art* (international edition) 23, no. 155 (November–December 1990): 116–20.

Martin, Chris. "In Conversation: Brice Marden." *The Brooklyn Rail*, August–September 2002, pp. 12–13.

McCann, Cecile N. "An Interview with Brice Marden." *Artweek* (Oakland, Calif.) 7, no. 42 (December 4, 1976): 15–16.

Moore, Alan, Edit deAk, and Mike Robinson. "Conversation with Brice Marden." *Art-Rite* (New York) no. 9, special issue on painting (Spring 1975): 39–42.

Ostrow, Sol. "Brice Marden." *BOMB* no. 22 (Winter 1988): 30–37. Reprinted in *Speak Art! The Best of BOMB Magazine's Interviews with Artists*, ed. Betsy Sussler, pp. 14–25. Amsterdam: G + B Arts International, 1997.

Price, Aimée Brown. "Artist's Dialogue: A Conversation with Brice Marden." *Architectural Digest* 40, no. 5 (May 1983): 50, 54, 58–59

Rosenthal, Mark. "Brice Marden: Interview by Mark Rosenthal, 19 September 1997."In Jeffrey Weiss et al., *Mark Rothko*, pp. 358–62. Washington, D.C.: National Gallery of Art, 1998.

Sharp, Willoughby, ed. "Points of View: A Taped Conversation with Four Painters." *Arts* 45, no. 3 (December 1970–January 1971): 41–42.

Steir, Pat. "Brice Marden, An Interview." In *Brice Marden: Recent Drawings and Etchings*, exh. cat. New York: Matthew Marks Gallery, 1991.

Storr, Robert. "Brice Marden: Laisser à l'abstraction son mystère." *Art Press* (Paris), no. 12 (March 1987): 13–18.

———. "Interview mit Robert Storr am 24 Oktober 1986." In Rosemarie Schwarzwälder, ed. *Abstrakte Malerei aus Amerika und Europa/Abstract Painting of America and Europe*, pp. 53–83. Vienna: Galerie nächst St. Stephan, Rosemarie Schwarzwälder, and Klagenfurt: Ritter Verlag, 1988.

———. "In the Studio." Public panel, Japan Society, New York, April 26, 2004. Tape in archives of the Japan Society.

Varnedoe, Kirk, Francesco Clemente, Brice Marden, and Richard Serra. "Cy Twombly: An Artist's Artist." *Res* (Cambridge, Mass.) 28 (Autumn 1995): 163–80. A conversation among artists moderated by Varnedoe and held on October 14, 1994 at The Museum of Modern Art, New York, in conjunction with the exhibition *Cy Twombly: A Retrospective*.

Varnedoe, Kirk, Brice Marden, Richard Serra, Jessica Stockholder, and Terry Winters. Panel moderated by Varnedoe on December 8, 1998, at The Museum of Modern Art, New York, in conjunction with the exhibition *Jackson Pollock*. Sound-Recordings of Museum-Related Events #99.8. The Museum of Modern Art Archives.

Vogell, Sabine B. "'Ich wurde meine Malerei als konservativ bezeichnen . . . ': Ein Interview mit Brice Marden von Sabine B. Vogell." *Artis* (Bern), November 1989, pp. 36–39.

Wei, Lilly. "Talking Abstract, Part One." *Art in America* 75, no. 7 (July 1987): 82–83.

White, Robin. "Brice Marden: Interview by Robin White at Crown Point Press, Oakland, California, 1980." *View* (Oakland, Calif.) 3, no. 2 (June 1980): 1–24. Reprinted in Japanese in *Bijutsu Techô* (Tokyo), February 1988, pp. 166–78.

Yau, John. "An Interview with Brice Marden." In *Brice Marden: Drawings and Paintings, 1964–2002*, eds. Eva Keller and Regula Malln, exh. cat., pp. 44–60. Zurich: Scalo and Daros Services, 2003.

Zaya, Octavio. "El proceso creativo: Entrevista con Brice Marden." *Atlantica* (Las Palmas de Gran Canaria, Spain), no. 7 (Spring 1994): 34–39.

Zhang, Yiguo. "Brice Marden and Chinese Calligraphy: An Interview." In *Brushed Voices: Calligraphy in Contemporary China*, exh. cat., pp. 125–32. New York: Miriam and Ira D. Wallach Art Gallery, Columbia University, 1998.

Articles and Reviews

In alphabetical order by author.

Adams, Brooks. "Un Léger pour les années 80." *Art Press* no. 127 (July–August 1988): 4–9.

Aletti, Vince. "Best of 2002." *Artforum* 41, no. 4 (December 2002): 112–13.

Anderson, Alexandra C. "Brice Marden at Bykert." *Art in America* 61, no. 3 (May–June 1973): 99–101.

Andre, Carl. "Brice Marden Paintings, Bykert Gallery: Two Part Review." *57th Street Review* 1, no. 1 (November 15, 1966): n.p.

Andre, Carl, ed. "New in New York: Line Work." *Arts* 41, no. 7 (May 1967): 49–50.

Anfam, David. "New York and Boston: Motherwell, Francis, Noland, Truitt, and Marden." *The Burlington Magazine* 133, no. 1061 (August 1991): 569–71.

"Art & Language I: Brice Marden, over J. Gilbert-Rolfe's 'Brice Marden's Schilderkunst' (*Artforum*, Oktober 1974)." *Museumjournaal*, August 1980, pp. 200–209.

Ashbery, John. "Grey Eminence." *Artnews* 71, no. 1 (March 1972): 26–27, 64–66.

———. "A Few Choice Openings: Brice Marden at Pace." *New York*, October 2, 1978, p. 130.

———. "Coups de Grace." *New York* 13, no. 40 (October 13, 1980): 59–60.

Ashton, Dore. "New York Commentary: Brice Marden." *Studio International* 171, no. 908 (February 1969): 95.

———. "New York Commentary: Brice Marden." *Studio International* 178, no. 193 (July–August 1969): 29.

———. "Young Abstract Painters: Right On!" *Arts* 44, no. 4 (February 1970): 31–35.

Ashton. Dore. "The Fort Worth Art Museum: Brice Marden: Drawings, 1963–1973." *Fort Worth Star-Telegram*, November 10, 1974, sec. A, p. 25.

Baird, Daniel. "Attendants, Bears, and Rocks: Brice Marden at the Matthew Marks Gallery." *The Brooklyn Rail*, August–September 2002, pp. 10–11.

Baker, Kenneth. "The Elective 'Affinities': Taking Stock of Anti-Expressionism." *Boston Phoenix*, June 21, 1983, sec. 3, p. 5.

———. "Method to His Monochromes." *San Francisco Chronicle*, February 2, 2000, sec. C, pp. 1, 3.

Bankowsky, Jack. "The Art of the Matter: Curating the Whitney Biennial." *Artforum* 33, no. 5 (January 1995): 66–71, 104, 109.

Bann, Stephen. "Adriatico—à propos of Brice Marden." *20th Century Studies* (University of Kent at Canterbury) nos. 15–16 (December 1976): 116–29.

———. "Brice Marden: Vom Materiellen zum Immateriellen." *Kunstforum International* no. 88 (March–April 1987): 170–76. Reprinted from *Brice Marden: Paintings, Drawings, Etchings, 1975–1980*. Amsterdam: The Stedelijk Museum, 1981.

Barringer, Felicity. "Matisse: 'He's Kind of Cast a Spell on Me.'" *Artnews* 92 (April 1993): 150.

Bass, Ruth. "Reviews: Brice Marden, Matthew Marks Gallery." *Artnews* 92, no. 7 (September 1993): 169.

Batchelor, David. "Brice Marden." *Artscribe* no. 72 (November–December 1988): 74–75.

Battaglia, Carlo. "Tre artisti: Ryman, Marden, Bell." *Qui Arte Contemporanea* no. 11 (June 1973): 24–26.

Battcock, Gregory. "The Moral Integrity of Smudges." *New York Free Press*, January 25, 1968, p. 10.

———. "Brice Marden." *Arts* 42, no. 4 (February 1968): 66.

———. "Art in America: Confusione." *Domus* no. 544 (March 1975): 55.

Bell, Jane. "Arts Reviews: Ten Painters in New York, Michael Walls." *Arts* 49, no. 2 (October 1974): 62.

———. "Brice Marden (The Pace Gallery)." *Artnews* 77, no. 9 (November 1978): 183–84.

Bell, Tiffany. "Drawing with Respect to Painting." *Arts* 60, no. 10 (June 1986): 123–24.

———. "Les Peintures monochromes de Robert Mangold et Brice Marden." *Artstudio* no. 6 (Spring 1990): 98–107.

Betz, Margaret. "New Editions." *Artnews* 76, no. 7 (September 1977): 104.

Blanc, Dominique. "Quand les artistes collectionnent." *L'Oeil* no. 528 (July–August 2001): 60–67.

Blok, Cor. "Holland: The Fundamental Painting." *Studio International* 190, no. 976 (July–August 1975): 74–75.

Boice, Bruce. "The Quality Problem." *Artforum* 11, no. 2 (October 1972): 68–70.

Borden, Lizzie. "Group Drawing Show, Bykert Gallery." *Artforum* 10, no. 6 (February 1972): 88–90.

———. "Cosmologies." *Artforum* 11, no. 2 (October 1972): 45–50.

———. "Brice Marden, Bykert Gallery." *Artforum* 11, no. 9 (May 1973): 76–77.

Bourdon, David. "The Mini-Conceptual Age." *The Village Voice*, October 17, 1974, pp. 40, 43.

———. "You Can't Tell a Painter by His Colors." *The Village Voice*, March 24, 1975, pp. 94, 96.

———. "Art: It's Happening Again." *The Village Voice*, April 19, 1976, p. 104.

Bremer, Nina. "The Solomon Guggenheim Museum Exhibition: Brice Marden." *Pantheon* (Munich) 33, no. 3 (July–September 1975): 276.

Brenson, Michael. "They Seek Spiritual Meaning in an Age of Skepticism." *New York Times*, May 11, 1986, sec. H, pp. 37, 41.

———. "Brice Marden's Webs in Action over a Void." *New York Times*, April 15, 1988, sec. C, p. 29.

"Brice Marden (Kunstverein, München)." *Architectural Digest* (Germany), June–July 1997, n.p.

"Brice Marden, 'Cold Mountain Series Zen Studies 1–6.'" *Print Collector's Newsletter* 22, no. 6 (January–February 1992): 213.

"Brice Marden, 'Five Threes.'" *Print Collector's Newsletter* 8, no. 5 (November–December 1977): 145.

"Brice Marden, 'Untitled.'" *Print Collector's Newsletter* 1, no. 4 (September–October 1983): 144.

"Brice Marden, Works of the 1990s: Paintings, Drawings, and Prints (Hirshhorn Museum and Sculpture Garden)." *Journal of the Print World* 22, no. 3 (Summer 1999): 21.

"Brice Marden." *Art: Das Kunstmagazin*, December 2000, p. 2.

Brunelle, Al. "Brice Marden (Bykert)." *Artnews* 67, no. 9 (January 1969): 24.

Bruschi, Valentina. "Marden: Tra classicità e filosofia Zen." *Il Messaggero* (Rome), December 23, 2001, p. 18.

Bryson, Norman, and Jeremy Gilbert-Rolfe. "XLVII Venice Biennale." *Art/Text* no. 59 (November 1997–January 1998): 32–35.

Bumpus, Judith. "Brice Marden: Paintings, Drawings, and Prints, 1974–80." *Connoisseur*, May 1981, p. 14.

Buonagurio, Edgar. "Arts Reviews: Brice Marden." *Arts* 53, no. 6 (February 1979): 32.

Burn, Guy. "Brice Marden." *Arts Review* 44 (April 1992): 106.

Burton, Johanna. "Brice Marden: Attendants, Bears, and Rocks." *Time Out* (New York), June 13–20, 2002, p. 56.

Burton, Scott. "Reviews and Previews: Brice Marden." *Artnews* 66, no. 10 (February 1968): 14–15.

Bussagli, Marco. "In vetrina le carte espressive di Marden." *Avvenire*, January 20, 2002.

Busse, Klaus-Peter. "'I am Nature,' Erfahrungsformen von Natur III: Brice Marden." *Kunst + Unterricht* no. 193 (June 1995): 10–11.

Caley, Shaun. "Spotlight: Brice Marden." *Flash Art* (international edition) no. 135 (Summer 1987): 92.

Cameron, Dan. "Seven Types of Criticality." *Arts* 61, no. 9 (May 1987): 14–17.

Cane, Louis. "Brice Marden." *Peinture: Cahiers Théoriques* nos. 8–9 (February 1974): 46–49.

Cappellazzo, Amy. "A Modern Master Comes to Miami." *Ocean Drive* (Miami), January 2000, pp. 280–81.

Carroll, Sandi. "Marden Finds Life of Art a Joy." *New Smyrna Beach Observer*, January 26, 2000, sec. 1, pp. 1, 3A.

Castle, Ted. "A Bouquet of Mistakes: Eight of Today's Most Successful Artists Talk about Their Work at a Special Gathering." *Flash Art* 176, no. 108 (Summer 1982): 54–55.

Cavaliere, Barbara. "Arts Reviews: Brice Marden." *Arts* 53, no. 4 (December 1978): 21–24.

———. "Arts Reviews: Brice Marden." *Arts* 55, no. 4 (December 1980): 54–55.

Christoph, Horst. "Die Leibe zur Geometrie." *Profil* (Vienna), November 10, 1986, pp. 88–89.

Civello, Renato. "L'opera grafica di Brice Marden." *Secolo d'Italia*, December 30, 2001.

Clark, Vicky A. "Post-Modernism in the 1988 International." *Carnegie Magazine* (Pittsburgh) 109, no. 10 (July–August 1989): 12–16.

Clerici, Dedi Ferrari. "Un artista moderno nell'Antica Stamperia." *Esperienza* (Rome), February 2002.

Coen, Ester. "Marden: Alla ricerca della purezza con l'energia emotiva del segno." *La Repubblica*, January 21, 2002.

Cohen, David. "New York and Washington: Brice Marden." *The Burlington Magazine* 144, no. 1157 (August 1999): 504–6.

Cohen, Ronny. "Minimal Prints." *Print Collector's Newsletter* 21, no. 2 (May–June 1990): 42–46.

Constable, Rosalind. "The Gallery of the Year." *New York*, May 20, 1968, pp. 39–42.

Corbett, William. "From Boston University, a Look East." *ArtsMedia*, February 15–March 15, 2002, pp. 10–13.

Cork, Richard. "Cutting a Cool Contour." *New Standard* (London), June 11, 1981, p. 18.

———. "Richard Cork's Choice: Brice Marden." *The Times* (London), November 18, 2000, *Play* magazine, p. 27.

Cotter, Holland. "In Boston, All Roads Lead to Museums." *New York Times*, August 7, 1998, sec. E, p. 31, 33.

———. "Monumental Pleasure in a Capital of Art Treasures." *New York Times*, August 6, 1999, sec. E, pp. 37, 39.

Crichton, Fenella. "London: Brice Marden at Hester van Royen." *Art International* 19, no. 4 (April 1975): 39–40, 37–41, 63.

Crimp, Douglas. "New York Letter." *Art International* 17, no. 6 (Summer 1973): 89–90.

Criqui, Jean-Pierre. "International Shorts Preview: Handmade's Tale." *Artforum* 39, no. 1 (September 2000): 77.

Cumming, Laura. "The Brice is Right." *The Observer*, November 19, 2000, arts section, p. 10.

Curto, Guido. "Marden: Astrattista lirico che guarda alla Grecia classica." *Torino Sette (La Stampa)*, March 8–14, 2002.

Darwent, Charles. "Shy, Assertive, Even Lonely, His Wiggly Lines Are Moody Trails." *The Independent on Sunday* (London), November 26, 2000, p. 5.

Davis, Douglas. "Keeping the Eye Busy." *Newsweek* 85, no. 13 (March 31, 1975): 68–69.

———. "'This is the Loose-Paint Generation': The New Painting Harks Back to Abstract Expressionism." *National Observer* (Washington, D.C.), August 4, 1969, p. 20.

de Candia, Mario. "Astrazione minimale: Una vetrina su Marden." *Trovaroma*, December 7, 2001.

DeLynn, Jane. "Traditional Life, Non-traditional Art: Helen and Brice Marden." *Avenue* 14, no. 7 (February 1990): 72–73.

Desai, Vishakha N. "Reorienting Ourselves to Asian Art." *Artnews* 95, no. 10 (November 1996): 152.

Dietsch, Deborah K. "Forward Motion." *South Florida Sun-Sentinel*, December 19, 1999, sec. D, pp. 1, 10.

Dippel, Rini. "Fundamental Schilderkunst: Aspekten van Recente Ontwikkelingen in de Abstrakte Kunst." *Museumjournaal* 20, no. 2 (April 1975): 57–62.

Domingo, Willis. "Brice Marden (Bykert)." *Arts* 45, no. 3 (December 1970–January 1971): 58.

———. "Color Abstraction: A Survey of Recent American Painting." *Arts* 45, no. 3 (December 1970–January 1971): 34–40.

Dorment, Richard. "One Look and You Feel You Could Look Forever." *The Daily Telegraph,* November 15, 2000, p. 26.

Draxler, Helmut. "Vienna: 'Abstrakte Malerie.'" *Artforum* 25, no. 9 (May 1987): 163.

Dreiss, Joseph. "Brice Marden." *Arts* 48, no. 9 (June 1974): 58–59.

Drolet, Owen. "Reviews: Brice Marden, Matthew Marks." *Flash Art* (international edition) 26, no. 172 (October 1993): 86.

Ellenzweig, Allen. "Brice Marden, Knoedler Contemporary Prints." *Arts* 49, no. 7 (March 1975). 12.

Ellis, Stephen. "Brice Marden at Mary Boone." *Art in America* 76, no. 6 (June 1988): 157–58.

Endres, Ulla. "Brice Marden." *Das Kunstwerk* 42, no. 3 (September 1989): 93.

Evett, Kenneth. "Kenneth Evett on Art: Death Wish." *New Republic* 172, no. 20 (May 17, 1975): 30–32.

Faxon, Alicia. "Looking East: Brice Marden, Michael Mazur, Pat Steir." *Art New England*, June–July 2002, pp. 31–32.

Findley, Elizabeth. "All Life's Stages Intriguing to Him." *Providence Sunday Journal*, November 27, 1977, sec. H, p. 9.

Flam, Jack. "Old Artists, New Styles." *Wall Street Journal*, March 25, 1987, p. 28.

Foster, Hal. "Brice Marden, Pace Gallery." *Artforum* 19, no. 4 (December 1980): 72–74.

Franceschetti, Gianni. "I calligrammi di Brice Marden." *Rinascita*, January 4, 2002.

Francis, Richard. "London, Tate Gallery: Brice Marden: Prints, 1961–1991." *The Burlington Magazine* 134, no. 1,070 (May 1992): 321–22.

Ffrench-Frazier, Nina. "New York's Winterset: Brice Marden." *Art International* 24, nos. 5–6 (January–February 1981): 140–42.

Frank, Elizabeth. "Review of Exhibitions: Brice Marden at Pace." *Art in America* 69, no. 1 (January 1981): 123–24.

"Galleries: Brice Marden." *The New Yorker* 73, no. 15 (June 9, 1997): 24.

Gardner, Paul. "Call It a Mid-life Crisis." *Artnews* 93, no. 4 (April 1994): 140–43.

Gibson, Eric. "New York Letter." *Art International* 22, no. 7 (November–December 1978): 66–71.

Gilbert-Rolfe, Jeremy. "Reviews and Previews: Brice Marden, David Novros." *Artforum* 12, no. 9 (May 1974): 64.

———. "Brice Marden, Bykert Gallery." *Artforum* 12, no. 10 (June 1974): 68–69.

———. "Brice Marden's Painting." *Artforum* 13, no. 2 (October 1974): 30–38.

———. "Editor's Choice: Brice Marden's 'The Muses' at the Venice Biennale." *BOMB* no. 61 (Fall 1997): 18.

Gilmour, Pat. "Brice Marden, Whitechapel Art Gallery." *Arts Review* (London) 33, no. 10 (May 22, 1981): 215.

———. "The Prints of Brice Marden." *Print Collector's Newsletter* 23, no. 2 (May–June 1992): 49–52.

Glover, Michael. "Abstraction's Rich Possibilities." *The Independent*, November 21, 2000, p. 10.

Glueck, Grace. "Art: Sparkling Early Gems of Winslow Homer." *New York Times,* December 3, 1966, p. 35.

———. "Art: Drawings by All-Star Cast." *New York Times*, March 21, 1970, p. 24.

———. "From Master to Modular." *Art in America* 58, no. 6 (November–December 1970): 164–69.

Godfrey, Tony. "The Human Presence in Recent Abstract Painting." *Aspects* (Newcastle Upon Tyne) no. 8 (Autumn 1979): n.p.

———. "Brice Marden at the Whitechapel." *Artscribe* no. 29 (June 1981): 57.

Goedhuis, Michael. "Michael Goedhuis Talks to Brice Marden." *Asian Art News* 10, no. 2 (March 2000): 16–18.

"Goings on About Town: Art." *The New Yorker* 66, no. 51 (February 4, 1991): 9.

Goldberg, Lenore, et al. "The Whitney Biennial: Four Views." *Arts* 47, no. 5 (March 1973): 63–66.

Goldin, Amy. "Brice Marden." *57th Street Review* 1, no. 1 (November 15, 1966): 7.

———. "Reviews and Previews: Brice Marden." *Artnews* 65, no. 8 (December 1966): 14.

Gollin, Jane. "Brice Marden." *Artnews* 65, no. 7 (November 1966): 15.

Goodman, Wendy. "A Lofty Marriage." *New York* 34, no. 14 (April 9, 2001): 48–53.

Gookin, Kirby. "Brice Marden, Gagosian Gallery." *Artforum* 29, no. 8 (April 1991): 119–20.

Gopnik, Adam. "The Art World: What Comes Naturally." *The New Yorker* 68, no. 22 (July 20, 1992): 66–69.

———. "The Repressionists: A New Group of European Painters Haunts the Biennale." *The New Yorker* 73, no. 19 (July 14, 1997): 86–88.

Green, Hope. "Bringing the East to the West Where the Twain Meet in Art." *Boston University Bridge* 5, no. 21 (February 1, 2002): 12.

Gregg, Gail. "An Offhand Sublime." *Artnews* 99, no. 3 (March 2000): 130–33.

Gruen, John. "Brice Marden (Bykert)." *New York Times*, November 30, 1970, p. 57.

Gruterich, Marlis. "Brüssel: Brice Marden." *Heute Kunst* no. 3 (October 1973): 29.

Hackworth, Nick. "Toeing a New Line: Brice Marden, Serpentine Gallery." *Evening Standard*, November 23, 2000.

Hale, Nike. "Of a Classic Order: Brice Marden's 'Thira.'" *Arts* 55, no. 2 (October 1980): 152–53.

———. "Marden's Greek Landscape: Minimalist Lay of the Land." *Art/World* 5, no. 2 (October 17—November 14, 1980): 1, 13.

Handy, Ellen. "New York in Review: Brice Marden." *Arts* 66, no. 2 (October 1991): 91–93.

Harris, Susan A. "Brice Marden." *Arts* 59, no. 5 (January 1985): 40.

Hase, Bettina von. "Full Beam." *Art Review* 2, no. 3 (March 2004): 66–71.

Hay, David. "The Scene Heats Up under the Miami Sun." *New York Times*, February 27, 2000, sec. 2, pp. 1, 51–52.

Hayt, Elizabeth. "Brash American Intruders amid l'Élégance." *New York Times*, January 25, 1998, pp. 41, 46.

Helfer, Judith. "Abstrakte Kunst-Reduziert: Brice Marden, Guggenheim Museum." *Aufbau*, March 28, 1975, p. 10.

Hemming, Sarah. "Brice Marden, Serpentine Gallery." *Daily Express*, November 17, 2000.

Henry, Gerrit. "New York Reviews: Brice Marden." *Artnews* 28, no. 1 (January 1983): 141.

Herrera, Hayden. "Reviews and Previews: David Novros, Brice Marden." *Artnews* 73, no. 4 (April 1974): 97–98.

———. "Reviews and Previews: Brice Marden." *Artnews* 73, no. 6 (Summer 1974): 110–11.

Hess, Thomas B. "Holder: The Saga of a Detour." *New York* 6, no. 12 (March 19 1973): 74–75.

———. "On the Sunny Side of the Street." *New York* 7, no. 10 (March 11, 1974): 74–75.

———. "Hello, Old Paint." *New York* 7, no. 16 (April 22, 1974): 72–74.

———. "Rules of the Game, Part II: Marden and Rockburne." *New York* 7, no. 45 (November 11, 1974): 101–2.

———. "The Convertible Oyster." *New York* 8, no. 14 (April 7, 1975): 68–70.

Hindry, Ann. "Marden: L'Orée du tableau." *Artstudio* no. 1 (Summer 1986): 48–55.

Hindry, Ann. "Brice Marden: Les Rigueurs de la couleur." *Beaux-Arts* no. 113 (June 1993): 44–49.
Hirsch, Faye. "Brice Marden, Gagosian Gallery." *Arts* 65, no. 8 (April 1991): 76.
Hoesterey, Ingeborg. "Brice Marden (Guggenheim Museum)." *Art International* 19, no. 6 (June 15, 1975): 72–79.
Hofleitner, Johanna. "Reviews, Vienna: Brice Marden, Weiner Secession." *Flash Art* (international edition) 27, no. 177 (Summer 1994): 134.
Hughes, Robert. "Eight Cool Contemporaries." *Time* 104, no. 20 (November 11, 1974): 98, 100.
———. "Careerism and Hype amidst the Image Haze: American Painters of the '80s Are Buffered by Cultural Inflation." *Time* 125, no. 24 (June 17, 1985): 78–83.
———. "Lines That Go for a Walk." *Time* 138, no. 18 (November 4, 1991): 96–97.
"Huit jeunes artistes au MoMA." *Art Press* no. 15 (December 1974–January 1975): 22–23.
Imhoff, Paul. "Neue Glasfenster für Basler Münster: Welcher Kunstler bekommt den Auftrag?" *Basler Zeitung*, July 24, 1985, p. 17.
Januszczak, Waldemar. "Whitechapel Art Gallery: Brice Marden." *The Guardian*, May 20, 1981, p. 10.
Jones, Ronald. "Brice Marden." *Frieze* no. 26 (January–February 1996): 73–74.
Karlins, N. F. "Snail Trails across Flagstones: The Latest Work of Brice Marden." *The Westsider* (New York), December 28, 1995–January 3, 1996, p. 13.
Karmel, Pepe. "Alternative Visions II." *New York Times*, February 17, 1995, sec. C, p. 30.
Kasher, Steven. "The Substance of Paper." *Artforum* 16, no. 7 (March 1978): 26–28.
Keeffe, Jeffrey. "'Generation': Susan Caldwell Gallery," *Artforum* 17, no. 9 (May 1979): 60–63.
Kent, Sarah. "Line Dancing: A Decade of Brice Marden's Spiky Abstracts." *Time Out* (London), November 29–December 6, 2000, p. 57.
Kernan, Nathan. "New York: Recent and Contemporary Art." *The Burlington Magazine* 144, no. 1,193 (August 2002): 519–20.
Kertess, Klaus. "Painting Hot Staying Cool." *Elle* 7, no. 3 (November 1991): 118–22.
Kimmelman, Michael. "Brice Marden Reveals His Connections." *New York Times*, April 14, 1991, sec. H, p. 35.
———. "Brice Marden." *New York Times*, May 24, 1991, sec. C, p. 26.
———. "A Tour That Moves from Calligraphy to Pollock." *New York Times*, June 24, 1994, sec. C, pp. 1, 28.
"Knoedler Contemporary Prints Gallery, New York: Exhibit." *Arts* 49, no. 7 (March 1975): 12.
Koepplin, Dieter. "Zu Ende gezeichnet." *Basler Magazin*, July 8, 1995, p. 9.
Koldehoff, Stefan. "Georg Baselitz, Cy Twombly, Brice Marden, Sigmar Polke." *Art: Das Kunstmagazin* no. 12 (December 1999): 22–27.
Kosuth, Joseph. "Bykert Group." *Arts* 41, no. 8 (Summer 1967): 58–59.
Kozloff, Max. "Traversing the Field. 'Eight Contemporary Artists' at MoMA." *Artforum* 13, no. 4 (December 1974): 44–49.
Kramer, Hilton. "Art: German Documenta." *New York Times*, July 1, 1972, p. 11.
———. "Documenta 5; The Bayreuth of the Neo-Dadaists." *New York Times*, July 9, 1972, sec. D, p. 15.
———. "Marden Art at the Guggenheim: Painter Points Way for Color-Field Abstraction." *New York Times*, March 15, 1975, p. 15.
———. "Art: Stuart Davis in His Pictorial Period." *New York Times*, October 10, 1980, sec. C, p. 24.
Kritzwiser, Kay. "Picasso Power at Dunkelman Gallery: Other Galleries." *Toronto Globe and Mail*, November 29, 1969, p. 26.
Kurtz, Bruce, ed. "Documenta 5: A Critical Preview." *Arts* 46, no. 8 (Summer 1972): 30–37.
"Kurze Wege." *Kreiszeitung Syker Zeitung*, August 9, 2002.
Kuspit, Donald. "Brice Marden, Dia Center for the Arts." *Artforum* 30, no. 5 (January 1992): 97–98.
Kutner, Janet. "Scene in Art: Three-Artist Show Spans Forty Years." *Dallas Morning News*, May 4, 1975, sec. C, p. 8.
———. "Brice Marden, David Novros, Mark Rothko: The Urge to Communicate through Non-Imagistic Painting." *Arts* 50, no. 1 (September 1975): 61–63.
———. "The Visceral Aesthetic of a New Decade's Art." *Arts* 51, no. 4 (December 1976): 100–3.
———. "Strokes of Genius." *Dallas Morning News*, February 12, 1999, guide, p. 57.
———. "Marden Explores Brushes with Freedom." *Dallas Morning News*, February 14, 1999, sec. C, pp. 1, 10.
———. "Marden Show Gives DMA a Welcome Jolt of the Current." *Dallas Morning News*, February 21, 1999, sec. C, p. 7.
Lambertini, Luigi. "Guardando all'Oriente." *Corriere della Sera*, January 7, 2002.
Lambirth, Andrew. "Weaving Like a Serpent." *Royal Academy Magazine*, Winter 2000, n.p.
Larson, Kay. "Avant to Be in Style." *The Village Voice*, October 8–14, 1980, pp. 85, 93.
———. "Far Out." *New York* 24, no. 8 (February 25, 1991): 111–12.
———. "French Provincial." *New York* 24, no. 23 (June 10, 1991): 65–66.
———. "Six Threads." *Atelier* (Tokyo), October 1991, pp. 39–44.
———. "Different Strokes: Brice Marden's Bold New Direction Has Made Him the Art World's Cult Hero." *New York* 24, no. 41 (October 21, 1991): 74–83 . Reprinted in Japanese in *Atelier* (Tokyo), February 1992, pp. 46–56.
Larson, Philip. "Minneapolis: Brice Marden at Locksley/Shea." *Arts* 49, no. 5 (January 1975): 23.
———. "Aquatints Again." *Print Collector's Newsletter* 8, no. 3 (July–August 1977): 61–65.
Lawson, Thomas. "Painting in New York: An Illustrated Guide." *Flash Art* (international edition) 13, no. 92–93 (October–November 1979): 4–11.
Lazzarino, Silvana. "Brice Marden: Disegni e incisioni al confine tra realtà e fantasia." *Il Giornale*, January 28, 2002.
Lebensztejn, Jean-Claude. "Eight Statements (on Matisse)." *Art in America* 63, no. 4 (July–August 1975): 72–73.
———. "Mumû: Autour de cinq 'Annonciations' de Marden." *Avant-Guerre sur l'art, etc.* (Saint-Etienne) no. 1 (1980): 9–20.
Leder, Dennis. "Five Annunciations." *America* (New York), February 3, 1979, pp. 74–75.
Levin, Kim. "Galleries: Downtown." *The Village Voice*, January 16, 1996, p. 8.
Lewis, Jim. "Maximum Marden." *Harper's Bazaar* no. 3407 (October 1995): 270–72, 290, 294.
Lippard, Lucy R. "Rejective Art." *Art International* 10, no. 8 (October 20, 1966): 33–36.
———. "The Silent Art." *Art in America* 55, no. 1 (January–February 1967): 58–64.
———. "Rebelliously Romantic?" *New York Times*, June 4, 1967, sec. D, p. 25.
Loock, Ulrich. "Brice Marden: Plane Image." *Artis* (Bern), November 1989, pp. 30–35.
Lorent, Claude. "Dématérialisation spatialiste de Marden à Meyer." *Art & Culture* (Belgium), April 1994, pp. 22–23.
Loyaute, Benjamin. "Avignon: Collections d'artistes." *Connaissance des Arts*, July–August 2001, p. 17.
Lucie-Smith, Edward. "Brice Marden." *Art International* 24, nos. 9–10 (August–September 1981): 70, 72.
Lüddemann, Stefan. "Schaltplan der Weltkultur." *Neue Osnabrücker Zeitung*, July 4, 2002.
Madoff, Steven Henry. "The Return of Abstraction." *Artnews* 85, no. 1 (January 1986): 80–85.
Mahoney, Robert. "Reviews. New York: Brice Marden, DIA Center for the Arts." *Flash Art* (international edition) 25, no. 162 (January–February 1992): 129.
Mahr, Peter. "European and American Abstract Painting, Nachst St. Stephan." *Artscribe* no. 62 (March–April 1987): 89–90.
Marchand-Kiss, Christophe. "Brice Marden, Portrait." *Beaux-Arts*, July–August 1992, pp. 91–93.
Masheck, Joseph. "New York." *Artforum* 9, no. 5 (January 1971): 69–74.
Mason, Brook S. "Marden's Momentum." *Artnews* 98, no. 6 (June 1999): 66.
Masschke, Kathy L. "The Revelation of Brice Marden: Designs for the Stained Glass Windows of the Basel Cathedral." *Glass Magazine* no. 44 (Summer 1991): 28–35.
Matuszczyk, Franz. "Brice Marden: Das bewusste Werden des Ganzen." *Die Glocke* (Gütersloh), June 6, 2002.
Mayer, Rosemary. "Group Show, Bykert." *Arts* 47, no. 5 (March 1973): 72–73.
———. "Attitudes Toward Materials, Content, and the Personal." *Arts* 47, no. 7 (May–June 1973): 63–66.
McCann, Cecile N. "Brice Marden's Classic Rectangles." *Artweek* (Oakland, Calif.) 4, no. 8 (February 24, 1973): 3.
McEwen, John. "Par Excellence." *The Spectator*, June 13, 1981, p. 26.

———. "Londres: Brice Marden, Galerie Anthony d'Offay." *Art Press* 10, no. 127 (July–August 1988): 78.
———. "Nature Makes the Abstract Seem Almost Natural." *Sunday Telegraph Review*, December 3, 2000, p. 8.
McQuaid, Cate. "Capturing Eastern Spirit in a Spectacle of Paint." *Boston Globe*, January 24, 2002, sec. D, pp. 1, 8.
Mead, Andrew. "A Full Emptiness." *Modern Painters* 6, no. 1 (Spring 1993): 107–9.
Meyer, Franz. "Brice Marden's Design for Stained Glass." *Parkett* no. 7 (January 1986): 44–49.
Migayrou, Frédéric. "Brice Marden: Les Tonalités du contact." *Artistes* no. 22–23 (October 1984): 4–15.
Millberg, Steve. "What's an Art Gallery Doing in This Factory?" *Omaha-World Herald*, December 12, 1982, magazine section, pp. 4, 6–7, 11.
Mitchell, Deborah. "The Brice of Fame." *Vanity Fair* 58, no. 424 (December 1995): 221.
Morris, Lynda. "Strata: Paintings, Drawings, and Prints." *Studio International* 187, no. 963 (February 1974): 92–93.
Müller, Grégoire. "After the Ultimate." *Arts* 44, no. 5 (March 1970): 28–31.
Naves, Mario. "Five Painters." *New Criterion* 17, no. 6 (February 1999): 49–52.
———. "Currently Hanging: An Excess of Refinement." *New York Observer*, June 3, 2002, p. 20.
Nemser, Cindy. "Marden and Duran at Bykert." *Arts* 44, no. 5 (March 1970): 62.
Nemy, Enid. "Artists' Families Needing Aid Get It from Rauschenberg's Group." *New York Times*, September 25, 1974, p. 46.
Newhall, Edith. "Body Painting." *New York* 35, no. 15 (May 6, 2002): 91.
O'Sullivan, Michael. "What You Make of It—and More." *Washington Post*, June 1999, p. 51.
Packer, William. "Loop the Loop." *Financial Times* (London), November 28, 2000, p. 22.
Paglieri, Marina. "L'arte di due metropoli per un omaggio a Marden." *La Repubblica*, March 13, 2001.
Perl, Jed. "Mostly Marden." *The New Criterion* 12, no. 1 (September 1993): 60–64.
Peppiatt, Michel. "Paris." *Art International* 13, no. 9 (November 1969): 53–57.
Perreault, John. "Art: Word Works." *The Village Voice*, January 18, 1968, p. 36.
———. "Art." *The Village Voice*, June 13, 1968, pp. 15, 28.
———. "Color: Problems and Solutions." *SoHo Weekly News* (New York), March 13, 1975, p. 15.
Perrone, Jeff. "Reviews: Brice Marden, Sperone Westwater Fischer." *Artforum* 14, no. 10 (June 1976): 65–66.
Petzal, Monica. "Exhibitions: Brice Marden, Robert Mangold." *Art Monthly* (London) no. 177 (June 1981): 10–11.
Phillips, Antonia. "Squares for the Spirit: Brice Marden, Whitechapel Art Gallery." *The Times Literary Supplement* (London), June 12, 1981, p. 670.
Picard, Lil. "Brief aus New York." *Das Kunstwerk* (Stuttgart) 21, no. 5–6 (February–March 1968): 47–48, 77.
Pincus-Witten, Robert. "Ryman, Marden, Manzoni: Theory, Sensibility, Mediation." *Artforum* 10, no. 10 (June 1972): 50–53.
Plagens, Peter. "The Impossible Exhibition." *Newsweek* 125, no. 14 (April 3, 1995): 68.
Pleynet, Marcelin. "De Pictura." *Peinture, Cahiers Théoriques* (Paris), no. 10–11 (December 1975): 13–53.
Poirer, Maurice. "Color-Coded Mysteries." *Artnews* 84, no. 1 (January 1985): 52–61.
———. "New York Reviews: Brice Marden." *Artnews* 86, no. 6 (Summer 1987): 201–2.
Poirier, Maurice, and Jane Necol. "The '60s in Abstract: 13 Statements and an Essay." *Art in America* 71, no. 9 (October 1983): 122–23.
Positano, Anna Maria. "Brice Marden: Works on Paper, 1964–2001, Istituto Nazionale per la Grafica." *Art on Paper* 7, no. 1 (September–October 2002): 99.
Pozzi, Lucio. "Colore e superficie." *DATA* (Milan) 3, no. 10 (Winter 1973): 86–91.
Pratesi, Ludovico. "Brice Marden: 40 anni d'arte USA in settanta disegni." *La Repubblica*, December 14, 2001.
"Prints and Photographs Published: Brice Marden." *Print Collector's Newsletter* 10, no. 5 (November 1979): 162.
"Prints and Photographs Published: Brice Marden." *Print Collector's Newsletter* 13, no. 4 (September–October 1983): 144.
Prokopoff, Stephen. "A Logic of Vision." *Arts* 49, no. 1 (September 1974): 45–47.
Ramsden, Mel. "Jeremy Gilbert-Rolfe's As-Silly-As-You-Can-Get 'Brice Marden's Painting,' (*Artforum*, October 1974)." *The Fox* (New York), no. 2 (April 1975): 8–14.
Ratcliff, Carter. "Reviews and Previews: Brice Marden, Robert Duran." *Artnews* 69, no. 1 (March 1970): 63.
———. "New York Letter." *Art International* 14, no. 5 (May 20, 1970): 76.
———. "Reviews and Previews: Brice Marden (Bykert)." *Artnews* 69, no. 8 (December 1970): 58.
———. "New York Letter." *Art International* 15, no. 2 (February 20, 1971): 64–73.
———. "Adversary Spaces." *Artforum* 11, no. 2 (October 1972): 40–44.
———. "New York Letter." *Art International* 16, no. 4 (April 20, 1972): 26–36.
———. "Once More, with Feeling." *Artnews* 71, no. 4 (Summer 1972): 35–37, 67–69.
———. "Abstract Painting, Specific Space: Novros and Marden in Houston." *Art in America* 63, no. 5 (September–October 1975): 84–88.
———. "Mostly Monochrome." *Art in America* 69, no. 4 (April 1981): 111–31.
———. "Manet et l'Amérique." *Art Press* (Paris), no. 72 (July–August 1983): 20–22.
———. "How to Study the Paintings of Brice Marden." *Parkett* no. 7 (January 1986): 22–36.
Ratcliff, Carter, et al. "Collaboration: Brice Marden." *Parkett* no. 7 (January 1986): 22–54.
Raynor, Vivien. "Japanese Fold Works on Display at Brooklyn Museum: An Invitational (Condeso/Lawler Gallery)." *New York Times*, July 26, 1985, sec. C, p. 22.
Reginato, James. "Marden's Retreat." *W* 26, no. 11 (November 1997): 246–53, 264, 266–67.
Ricard, Rene. "An Art of Regret." *Artforum* 23, no. 10 (Summer 1985): 86–91.
Richard, Paul. "Putting It All on the Lines." *Washington Post*, May 30, 1999, sec. G, pp. 1, 10.
Richardson, Brenda. "Reports: Bay Area Survey." *Arts* 45, no. 1 (September–October 1970): 52–53.
———. "Heart Print: Brice Marden's 'Cold Mountain' Paintings." *Tricycle: The Buddhist Review* 2, no. 1 (Fall 1992): 58–65. Excerpted from Richardson, *Brice Marden Cold Mountain*, exh. cat.
———. "Throwing a Curve." *Vogue* 189, no. 2 (February 1999): 154, 156.
Richardson, John. "Brice Marden's Abstract Heart." *Vanity Fair*, May 1999, pp. 168–77, 201–3.
Robins, Corinne. "Empty Paintings." *SoHo Weekly News*, April 22, 1976, pp. 19, 20.
Rose, Andrea. "Die Liebe des Künstlers zum Detail." *Westfälische Nachrichten*, June 6, 2002.
Rose, Barbara. "New York: Group Show, Bykert." *Artforum* 6, no. 3 (November 1967): 57–60.
Rosenbloom, Paul A. "Paris: Group Show." *Studio International* 186, no. 958 (September 1973): 103–4.
Rosenblum, Robert. "Painters' Drawings." *Architectural Digest* 53, no. 10 (October 1996): 164–69.
Rosenstein, Harris. "Total and Complex." *Artnews* 66, no. 3 (May 1967): 52–54, 67–68.
———. "Group Shows: Bykert." *Artnews* 66, no. 4 (Summer 1967): 66.
———. "Brice Marden (Bykert)." *Artnews* 68, no. 3 (May 1969): 69.
Rubenstein, Meyer Raphael. "New York: Brice Marden, Matthew Marks." *Artnews* 90, no. 7 (September 1991): 123.
Russell, John. "Eight of Today's Artists Exhibit at the Modern." *New York Times*, October 9, 1974, p. 52.
———. "Art: Chinese Landscape Paintings at the Met." *New York Times*, April 10, 1976, p. 13.
———. "Art: Marden on Marble, on Canvas and on Paper." *New York Times*, November 12, 1982, sec. C, p. 20.
———. "Art: Brice Marden's Building Blocks of Color." *New York Times*, October 12, 1984, sec. C, p. 22.
———. "Modern Art Museums: The Surprise Is Gone." *New York Times*, August 4, 1985, sec. H, pp. 1, 25.
———. "No, the Louvre Wasn't Broke, but Fixing It Is a Fine Idea." *New York Times*, August 5, 1990, sec. H, pp. 29, 31.
Sable, Jared. "Objects of Contemplation." *Toronto Telegram*, November 29, 1969, p. 4.
Saltz, Jerry. "Circuit Party." *The Village Voice*, June 4, 2002, p. 65.
Salustri, Marco. "Vetrine alla Calcografia: Arriva Marden." *Il Tempo*, December 14, 2001, p. 35.

Sargent-Wooster, Ann. "New York Reviews: Brice Marden (Sperone Westwater Fischer Gallery)." *Artnews* 75, no. 6 (Summer 1976): 177.
Sassi, Edoardo. "Il lato lugubre di Marden." *Corriere della Sera*, December 29, 2001.
Schiess, Robert. "Glasscheiben fur das Basler Munster: Ein Sterben auf Amtswegen."*Kunst-Bulletin des Schweizerischen Kunstvereins*, December 1987, pp. 16–19.
Schjeldahl, Peter. "New Abstract Painting: A Variety of Feelings." *New York Times*, October 13, 1974, sec. D, p. 29.
———. "98A Boundary Road." *House and Garden* 157, no. 6 (June 1985): 136–39, 210.
———. "The Documenta of the Dog." *Art in America* 80, no. 9 (September 1992): 88–97.
———. "Into the Rainbow: Brice Marden's Abstractions." *The New Yorker* 78, no. 14 (June 3, 2002): 96–97.
Schwabsky, Barry "Reviews: Brice Marden." *Artscribe* no. 65 (September–October 1987): 77–79.
———. "Reviews: Brice Marden." *Artforum* 34, no. 5 (January 1996): 80.
———. "Brice Marden: Work of the 1990s." *Artforum* 37, no. 5 (January 1999): 47.
Searle, Adrian. "Give Us a Swirl." *The Guardian*, November 21, 2000, p. 12.
Shiff, Richard. "Brice Marden, Dallas Museum of Art." *Artforum* 37, no. 5 (May 1999): 173.
Shone, Richard. "Venice Biennale and Other Exhibitions." *The Burlington Magazine* 139, no. 1,134 (September 1997): 651–53.
Shorr, Harriet. "Brice Marden at Bykert." *Art in America* 62, no. 3 (May–June 1974): 104–5.
Siegel, Jeanne. "Reviews and Previews." *Artnews* 72, no. 4 (April 1973): 78–80.
———. "Brice Marden: Art and Place." *Arti* (Athens) 26 (September–October 1995): 47–85.
Siegel, Katy. "Brice Marden." *Artforum* 41, no. 1 (September 2002): 204–5.
Smith, Roberta. "Brice Marden's Painting." *Arts* 47, no. 7 (May–June 1973): 36–41.
———. "Brice Marden, Bykert Gallery." *Artforum* 13, no. 5 (January 1975): 63–64.
———. "Drawing Now (and Then)." *Artforum* 14, no. 8 (April 1976): 52–59.
———. "Reductivism Redux." *The Village Voice*, February 22, 1983, p. 89.
———. "Art: New Oil Paintings by Brice Marden at Boone." *New York Times*, March 20, 1987, sec. C, p. 23.
———. "Brice Marden Moves Ahead by Turning Back." *New York Times*, October 20, 1991, sec. H, p. 37.
———. "Abstraction: Simple and Complex." *The Village Voice*, November 23, 1982, p. 106.
———. "Revisiting the '70s in Brice Marden's 'Grove Group.'" *New York Times*, January 18, 1991, sec. C, p. 28.
———. "Heading West, with Canvas." *New York Times*, November 17, 1995, sec. C, p. 28.
———. "A Profusion of Painting, Very Much Alive." *New York Times*, May 10, 2002, sec. E, p. 31.
Spagnesi, Licia. "Marden: La mia danza con le muse." *Arte*, April 1999, pp. 106–9.
Spears, Dorothy. "Brice Marden." *Arts* 66, no. 5 (January 1992): 63.
Spitz, Bob. "Different Strokes." *Mirabella* 3, no. 11 (November 1991): 94–96.
Staniszewski, Mary Anne. "New York Reviews: Brice Marden." *Artnews* 96, no. 10 (December 1980): 190.
"Statements by Alex Katz, Frank Stella, Brice Marden, Elizabeth Murray, and Bill Jensen on Willem de Kooning." *Art Journal* 48, no. 3 (Fall 1989): 234–36.
Stein, Karen. "Brice Marden." *New York* 28, no. 36 (September 11, 1995): 60–61.
Steir, Pat. In Paul Gardner, ed. "What Artists Like about the Art They Like When They Don't Know Why." *Artnews* 90, no. 8 (October 1991): 119.
Stevens, Mark. "Skin Deep." *New York* 35, no. 18 (May 27, 2002): 48–49.
Storr, Robert. "Brice Marden at Pace." *Art in America* 71, no. 1 (January 1983): 120–21.
———. "Brice Marden: Double Vision." *Art in America* 73, no. 3 (March 1985): 118–25.
Sullivan, James, and Jesse Hamlin. "Artists, Art-Lovers Paint the Town: It's Party Time at Yerba Buena and SFMoMA." *San Francisco Chronicle*, January 31, 2000, sec. D, p. 3.
Taylor, Paul. "Marden's Metamorphosis." *Connoisseur* 221, no. 957 (October 1991): 20–25, 108–11.
Taylor, Tanis. "Art: Brice Marden (Serpentine Gallery)." *Metro* (London), November 17, 2000.
Thomas, Mary. "Marden's Meditative Side Shines in Vibrant Exhibit at Carnegie." *Pittsburgh Post-Gazette*, May 13, 2000, sec. B, p. 10.
Trepp, Judith. "Winterthur: Brice Marden, Kunstmuseum." *Artnews* 96, no. 10 (November 1997): 241.
Tuchman, Phyllis. "Marden's Latest Abstracts Achieve Unusual Animation." *New York Newsday*, June 14, 1991, p. 80.
———. "Behind the Lines: The Art and Spirit of Brice Marden." *Bostonia* (The Alumni Quarterly of Boston University), Spring 1998, pp. 15–19.
Turner, Elisa. "Accomplished Abstract Career Comes into Focus." *Miami Herald*, December 19, 1999, sec. M, p. 5.
Tyson, Janet. "Poetry in Paint." *Fort Worth Star-Telegram*, February 23, 1999, sec. E, pp. 1, 2.
"Vier Mal Landesmuseum." *Westfälische Nachrichten*, July 12, 2002.
Wasserman, Emily. "Brice Marden, Bykert Gallery." *Artforum* 6, no. 7 (March 1968): 56–58.
———. "Robert Duran, Brice Marden, Bykert Gallery." *Artforum* 8, no. 8 (April 1970): 78–79.
Wei, Lilly. "Review of Exhibitions: Brice Marden at PaceWildenstein and Matthew Marks." *Art in America* 84, no. 3 (March 1996): 95.
Weil, Rex. "Brice Marden, Hirshhorn Museum and Sculpture Garden." *Artnews* 98, no. 10 (November 1999): 197.
Weiss, Matthias. "Papiergesten." *Westfälischer Anzeiger*, June 27, 2002.
Westfall, Stephen. "Marden's Web." *Art in America* 80, no. 3 (March 1992): 95–99.
"Whitney Biennial." *Atelier* (Tokyo), July 1995, pp. 2–18.
Wilson, Ellen S. "An Artist Reinvents Himself: Brice Marden, Work of the 1990s." *Inside Carnegie* (Pittsburgh), May–June 2000, p. 16.
Wilson, William. "A MoCA Show to Hold Your Breath By." *Los Angeles Times*, June 22, 1986, calendar, p. 110.
Winter, Peter. "Cologne-Düsseldorf: Corrective Measures." *Art International* no. 8 (Autumn 1989): 59–62.
Wolmer, Denise. "In the Galleries: Brice Marden." *Arts* 46, no. 6 (April 1972): 65.
Wood, Tony. "A Twist Away From the Edge." *Times Literary Supplement*, December 8, 2000, p. 20.
Wortz, Melinda. "Fourteen Abstract Painters." *Artweek* (Oakland, Calif.) 6, no. 18 (May 3, 1975): 1, 20.
Wylie, Charles. "Brice Marden: 'Uxmal,' 1992–1993." *St. Louis Art Museum Bulletin* 21, no. 3 (Winter 1995): 32–33.
Yablonsky, Linda. "Brice Marden (at Matthew Marks Gallery)." *Time Out (*New York), October 25–November 1, 1995.
Yarrow, Andrew L. "Minimalism and the Guggenheim." *New York Times*, February 17, 1990, Arts sec., p. 15.
Yau, John. "Reviews: Brice Marden." *Artforum* 25, no. 10 (Summer 1987): 118.
———. "Brice Marden: The Desire to Undo the Self until It Enters the Realm of the Modest and Private." *Flash Art* (international edition) 21, no. 142 (October 1988): 92–95.
———. "Making His Mark." *Vogue* (New York), July 1989, pp. 190–95.
———. "Brice Marden: Shell Drawings, Venus." *Grand Street* 10, no. 40 (1991): 65–81.
———. "Brice Marden's Cold Mountain: Drawing from Jackson Pollock." *Artspace* 16, nos. 1–2 (January–April 1992): 48–51.
———. "Drawing a New Line." *Art on Paper* 8, no. 3 (January–February 2004): 56–61.
Zimmer, William. "Vehicles for Rare Color." *SoHo Weekly News*, October 5, 1978, pp. 96, 98.
———. "Brice Marden, Pace Gallery." *SoHo Weekly News*, October 15–21, 1980, p. 78.
Zutter, Jörg. "*Kunst als Resultat Kultureller und Politischer Energien*." *Kunstforum International* (May–August 1981): 341–45.

Among the articles above, the following contain statements by Marden: Andre, Carl, ed., "New in New York: Line Work"; Barringer, "Matisse: 'He's Kind of Cast a Spell on Me'"; Castle, "A Bouquet of Mistakes"; "Huit jeunes artistes au MoMA"; Kurtz, ed., "Documenta 5: A Critical Preview"; Lebensztejn, "Eight Statements (on Matisse)"; Poirier and Necol, "The '60s in Abstract: 13 Statements and an Essay"; and "Statements by Alex Katz, Frank Stella, Brice Marden, Elizabeth Murray, and Bill Jensen on Willem de Kooning."

Books

Alexander, Brooke, et al. *Selected Prints and Multiples IV*. New York: Brooke Alexander Editions, 1987.

Baker, Kenneth. *Minimalism: Art of Circumstance.* New York: Abbeville Press, 1988.

Bann, Stephen. "A Cold Coming: Brice Marden's Wager with Tradition." In Lynne Cooke and Karen Kelly, eds. *Robert Lehman Lectures on Contemporary Art No. 1*. New York: Dia Center for the Arts, 1996.

Battcock, Gregory, ed. *Minimal Art: A Critical Anthology.* New York: E. P. Dutton & Company, 1968.

Beudert, Monique. "Brice Marden." In Jack Flam, Beudert, and Jennifer Wells. *The PaineWebber Art Collection*. New York: Rizzoli, 1995.

Daval, Jean-Luc, et al. *Art Actuel: Skira Annuel*. Geneva: Editions Skira and Cosmopress, 1976.

Dickhoff, Wilfried. "Brice Marden: Ensouled Form." In *After Nihilism: Essays on Contemporary Art*. Cambridge: at the University Press, 2000.

Hergott, Fabrice. "Brice Marden." In *La Collection du Musée national d'art moderne*. Paris: Editions du Centre Pompidou, 1986.

Kertess, Klaus. *Brice Marden Paintings and Drawings*. New York: Harry N. Abrams, 1992.

Kimmelman, Michael. *Portraits: Talking with Artists at the Met, the Modern, the Louvre, and Elsewhere*. New York: Random House, 1998.

Kobayashi, Yotaro. *Fuji Xerox Print Collection, 1988–2002*. Tokyo: Fuji Xerox Co., 2002.

Koella, Rudolf, and Dieter Schwartz, eds. *Kunstmuseum Winterthur: Modern Art from the Collection of the Kunstverein.* Frankfurt: Insel Verlag, 1992.

Lebensztejn, Jean-Claude. *Ecrits sur l'art récent: Brice Marden, Malcolm Morley, Paul Sharits*. Paris: Editions Aldines, 1995.

Lewison, Jeremy. *Brice Marden Prints, 1961–1991: A Catalogue Raisonné*. London: Tate Gallery Publications, 1992.

Moritz, Charles, ed. *Current Biography Yearbook*. New York: The H. W. Wilson Company, 1990.

Orfeo ed Euridice. Naples: Teatro di San Carlo, 2003. With essays by Fiamma Arditi and Achille Bonito Oliva.

Richardson, Brenda. "Brice Marden: Lifelines." In Peter Fischer et al. *Abstraction, Gesture, Ecriture: Paintings from the Daros Collection*. Zurich: Scalo, 1999.

Seidner, David. *Artists at Work: Inside the Studios of Today's Most Celebrated Artists*. New York: Rizzoli, 1999.

Siegel, Jeanne. *Painting after Pollock*. Amsterdam: Gordon and Breach Publishing, 1999.

Sims, Patterson. *Whitney Museum of American Art: Selected Works from the Permanent Collection*. New York: Whitney Museum of American Art and W. W. Norton, 1985.

Stiles, Kristine, and Peter Selz, eds. *Theories and Documents of Contemporary Art: A Sourcebook of Artists' Writings*. Berkeley: University of California Press, 1996.

Yau, John. *Skowhegan School of Painting and Sculpture, 43rd Anniversary Awards Dinner*. Skowhegan: Skowhegan School of Painting and Sculpture, 1989.

Among the books above, the following contain statements by Marden: Daval et al., *Art Actuel: Skira Annuel*; Stiles and Selz, eds., *Theories and Documents of Contemporary Art*; and Siegel, *Painting after Pollock*.

Exhibition Catalogues

Alloway, Lawrence, and Mary Delahoyd. *Concept*. Poughkeepsie: Vassar College Art Gallery, 1969.

American Works, 1945–1975. New York: C & M Arts, 1997.

American Works on Paper, 1945–1975. New York: Knoedler, 1975.

Andre, Carl, et al. *Abstract Painting, 1960–69*. Long Island City, N.Y.: P.S. 1, The Institute for Art and Urban Resources, 1983.

Arenas, Amelia. *From the Collection: Abstraction Pure and Impure*. Exh. brochure. New York: The Museum of Modern Art, 1995.

Armstrong, Richard, Richard Marshall, and Lisa Phillips. *1989 Biennial Exhibition*. New York: Whitney Museum of American Art and W. W. Norton, 1989.

Armstrong, Tom. *Amerikanische Malerei, 1930–1980.* Munich: Haus der Kunst, 1981.

Armstrong, Tom, and Susan C. Larsen. *Art in Place: Fifteen Years of Acquisitions*. New York: Whitney Museum of American Art, 1989.

Art américain: Collection du Musée. Grenoble: Musée de Peinture et de Sculpture, 1976.

Artists for Amnesty. New York: Blum Helman Gallery and Germans van Eck Gallery, 1990.

Ashton, Dore. *Drawings by New York Artists*. Salt Lake City: Utah Museum of Fine Arts, 1970.

———. *L'Art vivant aux États-Unis.* Paris: Fondation Maeght, 1970.

Auping, Michael. *Abstraction, Geometry, Painting: Selected Geometric Abstract Painting in America since 1945.* Buffalo: Albright-Knox Art Gallery, and New York: Harry N. Abrams, 1989.

Auras and Epitaphs. Hydra, Greece: First Public School of Hydra, 2001.

Baro, Gene. *American Drawing in Black and White, 1970–1980*. Brooklyn: Brooklyn Museum of Art, 1980.

Bastian, Heiner. *7000 Eichen*. Bern: Benteli Verlag, 1985.

Baur, Andreas. *Holländisches Bad: Radierungen; Zur Renaissance einer Technik.* Hamburg: Kunsthaus, 1996.

Beaud, Marie-Claude, et al. *L'Avant-garde, 1960–1976: Trois villes, trois collections.* Marseilles: Musée Cantini, 1977.

Bernadac, Marie-Lure, ed. *Dessins: Acquisitions, 1992–1996.* Paris: Editions du Centre George Pompidou, 1996.

Besset, Maurice, et al. *La Couleur seule: L'Experience du monochrome*. Lyons: Musée d'Art Contemporain, 1988.

Bishop, Robert, et al. *New York: The State of Art*. Albany: New York State Museum, 1977.

Blum, Peter, and Erich Franz. *In Quest of the Absolute*. New York: Peter Blum Editions, 1996.

Bourel, Michel, and Sylvie Couderc. *Art minimal II: De la surface au plan*. Bordeaux: CAPC Musée d'art contemporain de Bordeaux, 1986.

Brandt, Frederick R., and Susan L. Butler. *Late 20th-Century Art: Selections from the Sydney and Frances Lewis Collection in the Virginia Museum of Fine Arts*. Richmond: Virginia Museum of Fine Arts, 1981.

Breuer, Karin, Ruth E. Fine, and Steven A. Nash. *Thirty-five Years at Crown Point Press: Making Prints, Doing Art*. Los Angeles: University of California Press, and San Francisco: Fine Arts Museums of San Francisco, 1997.

Brice Marden. Zurich: Thomas Ammann Fine Art, 1996.

Brice Marden: Drawings, 1964–1994. New York: Pace Wildenstein, 1995.

Brice Marden: Paintings and Drawings. Nagoya: Galerie Valuer, 1980.

Brice Marden: *Paintings, Drawings, Etchings.* New York: Matthew Marks Gallery, 1993.

Brice Marden: Recent Drawings and Etchings. New York: Matthew Marks Gallery, 1991.

Brice Marden: Recent Work. New York: The Pace Gallery, 1984.

Brodie, Judith, and Andrew Robinson, eds. *A Century of Drawing: Works on Paper from Degas to LeWitt*. Washington, D.C.: National Gallery of Art, 2001.

Brown, Julia, and Bridget Johnson, eds. *The First Show: Painting and Sculpture from Eight Collections, 1940–1980*. Los Angeles: Museum of Contemporary Art, and New York: The Arts Publisher, 1983.

Brown, Kathan. *Crown Point Press*. San Francisco: San Francisco Art Institute, 1972.

Brüderlin, Markus, et al. *Ornament and Abstraction.* Cologne: DuMont Literatur und Kunst Verlag, 2002.

Bürgi, Bernhard Mendes, et al. *Painting on the Move*. Basel: Schwabe, 2002.

Cathcart, Linda L. *American Painting of the 1970s*. Buffalo: Albright-Knox Art Gallery, 1978.

———. *The Americans: The Collage*. Houston: Contemporary Arts Museum, 1982.

Celant, Germano. *Das Bild einer Geschichte, 1956/1976: Die Sammlung Panza di Biumo*. Milan: Electa, 1980.

———. *La Biennale di Venezia XLVII Esposizione Internazionale d'Arte: Future, Present, Past.* Milan: Electa, 1997.

Celant, Germano, and Giuseppe Panza di Biumo. *Changing Perceptions: The Panza Collection at the Guggenheim Museum*. Bilbao: Guggenheim Museum, 2000.

Cheim, John, Diego Cortez, Carmen Gimenez, and Klaus Kertess. *Drawing the Line against AIDS*. New York: AMFAR International, 1993.

Claura, Michel, and René Denizot. *Une Exposition de peinture reunissant certains peintres qui mettraient la peinture en question.* Paris: s.n., 1973.

Codognato, Mario. *Brice Marden: Works on Paper, 1964–2001*. London: Trolley Books, 2002.

Continuing Abstraction in American Art. New York: Whitney Museum of American Art, 1974.
Cooper, Harry, Lisa Corrin, and Julia Peyton-Jones. *Brice Marden*. London: Serpentine Gallery, 2000.
Craig-Martin, Michael. *Drawing the Line: Reappraising Drawing Past and Present*. London: South Bank Centre, 1995.
Criqui, Jean-Pierre. *Brice Marden: Attendants, Bears, and Rocks*. New York: Matthew Marks Gallery, 2002.
Crimp, Douglas. "Opaque Surfaces." In Germano Celant, Crimp, and Cornello Brandini. *Arte come arte*. Milan: Centro Comunitario di Brera, 1973.
Cummings, Paul. *Abstract Drawings, 1911–1981*. New York: Whitney Museum of American Art, 1982.
Danoff, I. Michael. *Art and Things: Painting in the Sixties from the Michener Collection*. Austin: University of Texas at Austin, 1973.
Davenport, Guy. *Artists' Sketchbooks*. New York: Matthew Marks Gallery, 1991.
de Wilde, Edy. *63/73*. Amsterdam: Stedelijk Museum, 1974.
———. *La Grande Parade: Highlights in Painting after 1940*. Amsterdam: Stedelijk Museum, 1984.
de Wilde, Edy, et al. *'60–'80: Attitudes/Concepts/Images*. Amsterdam: Stedelijk Museum, 1982.
de Wilde, Edy, and Rini Dippel. *Fundamentele Schilderkunst*. Amsterdam: Stedelijk Museum, 1975.
de Wilde, Edy, Stephen Bann, and Roberta Smith. *Brice Marden: Schilderijen, tekeningen, etsen, 1975–1980/Brice Marden: Paintings, Drawings, Etchings, 1975–1980*. Amsterdam: Stedelijk Museum, 1981. In Dutch and English. Published in English, with a foreword by Nicholas Serota, as *Brice Marden: Paintings, Drawings, and Prints, 1975–1980*. London: Whitechapel Art Gallery, 1981.
Deecke, Thomas. *Avantgarden retrospektiv*. Münster: Westfalischer Kunstverein, 1981.
Delahoyd, Mary, et al. *Painting '75 '76 '77*. Bronxville, N.Y.: Sarah Lawrence Gallery, 1977.
Dickhoff, Wilfried. *Brice Marden*. Cologne: Galerie Michael Werner, 1989.
Diederichs, Joachim, et al. *Documenta 6*. Kassel: Paul Dierichs, 1977.
Drawings USA/71. St. Paul: Minnesota Museum of Art, 1971.
Dreishpoon, Douglas, and Joann Moser. *Highlights from the Dillard Collection of Art on Paper*. Greensboro: Weatherspoon Art Gallery, University of North Carolina, 1999.
Duncan, Michael, and James Reid. *Brice Marden at Gemini*. Los Angeles: Gemini, 2002.
Encrevé, Lucile, and Laurence des Cars. *Brice Marden/Gustave Courbet*. Paris: Musée d'Orsay in association with Argol Editions, 2006.
Erdheim, Mario, et al. *Kulturen-Verwandtschaften in Geist und Form*. Vienna: Galerie nächst St. Stephan, Rosemarie Schwarzwalder, 1991.
Fairbrother, Trevor, et al. *Brice Marden: Boston*. Boston: Museum of Fine Arts, 1992.
Field, Richard S. *Recent American Etching*. Middletown, Conn.: Davison Art Center, Wesleyan University, 1975.
Fischer, Peter, and Iris Müller-Westermann. *In the Power of Painting: A Selection from the Daros Collection*. Zurich: Alesco, and New York; Scalo, 2000.
Flam, Jack D. *Artists Choose Artists II*. New York: CDS Gallery, 1983.
Fuchs, R. H. *Funkties van Tekenen*. Otterlo: Rijksmuseum Kroller-Muller, 1975.
Fuchs, Rudi, Gianfranco Zappettini, and Filiberto Menna. *1.2.3.n.* Milan: Edizioni Studio Enesse, 1978.
Garrels, Gary. *Drawing from the Modern, 1945–1975*. New York: The Museum of Modern Art, 2005.
Gilbert-Rolfe, Jeremy. *Jasper Johns, Brice Marden, Terry Winters: Drawings*. Los Angeles: Margo Leavin Gallery, 1992.
Gohr, Siegfried, Johannes Gachnang, and Walter Nikkels. *Bilderstreit: Widerspruch, Einheit, und Fragment in der Kunst seit 1960*. Cologne: DuMont Literatur und Kunst Verlag, 1989.
Goldstein, Ann, and Lisa Mark, eds. *A Minimal Future? Art as Object 1958–1968*. Los Angeles: The Museum of Contemporary Art, and Cambridge, Mass.: The MIT Press, 2004.
Goodrich, Lloyd, Bernarda B. Shahn, and Ellen Ellenzweig. *A Selection of American Art: The Skowhegan School, 1946–1976*. Boston: The Institute of Contemporary Art, 1976.
Gorski, Daniel. *Drawings, 1967*. Ithaca, N.Y.: Ithaca College Museum of Art, 1967.
Grynsztejn, Madeleine, and Dave Hickey. *About Place: Recent Art from the Americas*. Chicago: The Art Institute of Chicago, 1995.
Grynsztejn, Madeleine, et al. *Sacred Images in Secular Art*. New York: Whitney Museum of American Art, 1986.
Halbreich, Kathy. *Affinities: Myron Stout, Bill Jensen, Brice Marden, Terry Winters*. Cambridge, Mass.: Hayden Gallery, Massachusetts Institute of Technology, 1983.
Hanson, Anne Coffin, et al. *Options and Alternatives: Some Directions in Recent Art*. New Haven, Conn.: Yale University Art Gallery, 1973.
Haskell, Barbara. *Three Decades of American Art Selected by the Whitney Museum*. Tokyo: Seibu Museum of Art, 1976.
Haskell, Barbara, Marcia Tucker, and Patterson Sims. *1977 Biennial Exhibition: Contemporary American Art*. New York: Whitney Museum of American Art, 1977.
Hay, Jonathan. *Brice Marden: Chinese Work*. New York: Matthew Marks Gallery, 1997.
Hedberg, Gregory, and Robert Rosenblum. *The Tremaine Collection: Twentieth-Century Masters. The Spirit of Modernism*. Hartford, Conn.: Wadsworth Atheneum, 1984.
Herkenhoff, Paulo, et al. *XI Mostra da gravura Cidade de Curitiba*. Curitiba, Brazil: Museu da gravura, 1995.
Hinson, Tom E. *Contemporary Artists*. Cleveland: The Cleveland Museum of Art, 1981.
Hollenstein, Roman. "Brice Marden." In Jean Christophe Ammann. *Von Twombly bis Clemente: Ausgewählte Werke einer Privatsammlung*. Basel: Kunsthalle Basel, 1985.
Honnef, Klaus, et al. *Bilder ohne Bilder*. Bonn: Rheinisches Landesmuseum, and Cologne: Rheinland-Verlag, 1977.
———. *Geplante Malerei*. Münster: Westfälischer Kunstverein, 1974.
Hopkins, Henry T., and Peter Plagens. *Drawings*. Fort Worth: Fort Worth Art Center Museum, 1969.
Hopps, Walter. *Cinquante ans de dessins américains, 1930–1980*. Houston: The Menil Foundation, and Paris: Editions de l'École Nationale des Beaux-Arts, 1985.
Hopps, Walter, et al. *La Rime et la raison: Les Collections Menil*. Paris: Editions de la Réunion des musées nationaux, 1984.
———. *The Menil Collection: A Selection from the Paleolithic to the Modern Era*. New York: Harry N. Abrams, 1987.
Hurwitz, Sidney. *21 Alumni*. Boston: Boston University, School of Fine and Applied Arts, 1969.
In Honor of de Kooning. New York: Xavier Fourcade, 1983.
Janis, Sidney. *Less Is More*. New York: Sidney Janis Gallery, 1977.
Jaukkuri, Maaretta, ed. *Private/Public: ARS '95 Helsinki*. Helsinki: Museum of Contemporary Art, 1995.
Joachimides, Christos M., and Norman Rosenthal. *American Art in the 20th Century: Painting and Sculpture, 1913–1993*. Munich: Prestel Verlag, 1993. Accompanying an exhibition at the Martin Gropius Bau, Berlin, and the Royal Academy of Arts, London.
Joachimides, Christos M., Norman Rosenthal, and Nicholas Serota. *A New Spirit in Painting*. London: Royal Academy of Arts, 1981.
Johnson, James Douglas. *Nineteen Americans—1970/1975*. Rome: American Embassy, 1975.
Judd, Donald, Agnes Martin, and Ad Reinhardt. *Imageless Icons: Abstract Thoughts*. London: Gagosian Gallery, 2005.
Kardon, Janet. *Private Notations: Artists' Sketchbooks II*. Philadelphia: Philadelphia College of Art, 1976.
Keller, Eva, and Regula Malin, eds. *Brice Marden: Drawings and Paintings, 1964–2002*. Zurich: Scalo and Daros Services, 2003.
Kern, Hermann, and Klaus Kertess. *Brice Marden: Zeichnungen, 1964–1978*. Munich: Kunstraum, 1979.
Kertess, Klaus. *New Painting: Stressing Surface*. Katonah: Katonah Gallery, 1974.
———. *Painting as Landscape: Views of American Modernism, 1920–1984*. Pasadena, Calif.: Baxter Art Gallery, and Southampton, N.Y.: The Parrish Art Museum, 1985.
———. *Lead*. New York: Hirschl & Adler Modern, 1987.
———. *The Shaman as Artist, The Artist as Shaman*. Aspen, Colo.: Aspen Art Museum, 1994.

Kertess, Klaus. *00*. New York: Barbara Gladstone Gallery, 2000.
Kertess, Klaus, et al. *1995 Biennial Exhibition*. New York: Whitney Museum of American Art, 1995.
Knight, Christopher. *The Barry Lowen Collection*. Los Angeles: Museum of Contemporary Art, 1986.
Koepplin, Dieter, and Marie-Lure Bernadac. *De Beuys à Trockel: Dessins contemporains du Kunstmuseum de Bâle*. Paris: Editions du Centre Pompidou, 1996.
Koepplin, Dieter. *Brice Marden*. Basel: Offentliche Kunstsammlung Basel and Museum für Gegenwartskunst, 1993.
Krauss, Rosalind. *Grids: Format and Image in 20th Century Art*. New York: The Pace Gallery, 1978.
———. *Works on Paper: American Art, 1945–1975*. Seattle: Washington Art Consortium, 1977.
La Collection Yvon Lambert. Yokohama: Yokohama Museum of Art, 1998.
Laclotte, Michel, et al. *Polyptyques: Le Tableau multiple du Moyen Âge au vingtième siècle*. Paris: Éditions de la Réunion des musées nationaux, 1990.
Lambert, Yvon, and Michel Claura. *Actualité d'un bilan*. Paris: Galerie Yvon Lambert, 1972.
Lane, John R., et al. *1985 Carnegie International Exhibition*. Pittsburgh: Carnegie Museum of Art, 1985.
Larson, Philip, and Dean Swanson. *Painting: New Options*. Minneapolis: Walker Art Center, 1972.
Laursen, Steingrim. *Yngre amerikansk kunst: Tegninger og grafik*. Charlottelund: Gentofte Radhus, 1973.
Leavin, Margo. *20th Century Collage*. Los Angeles: Margo Leavin Gallery, 1991.
Lebensztejn, Jean-Claude. *Brice Marden: Recent Paintings and Drawings*. New York: The Pace Gallery, 1978.
Lebensztejn, Jean-Claude, and Klaus Kertess. *Brice Marden*. Paris: Galerie Montenay, 1987.
Lee, Janie C. *Brice Marden Drawings: The Whitney Museum of American Art Collection*. New York: Whitney Museum of American Art and Harry N. Abrams, 1998.
Licht, Jennifer. *Eight Contemporary Artists*. New York: The Museum of Modern Art, 1974.
———. *Some Recent American Art*. Melbourne: National Gallery of Victoria, 1973.
Linker, Kate. "Abstraction: Form as Meaning." In Howard Singerman, ed. *Individuals: A Selected History of Contemporary Art, 1945–1986*. Los Angeles: Museum of Contemporary Art, and New York: Abbeville Press, 1986.
Lipman, Jean, and Richard Marshall. *Art about Art*. New York: Whitney Museum of American Art, 1978.
Lippard, Lucy R. *Invitational*. Amherst, Mass.: University Art Gallery, University of Massachusetts, 1971.
Loock, Ulrich, and Yve-Alain Bois. *Brice Marden: Paintings, 1985–1993*. Bern: Kunsthalle Bern, 1993.
Loock, Ulrich, and Daniel Kurjacovic, eds. *Mixing Memory and Desire*. Lucerne: Kunstmuseum Luzern, 2001.
Lynton, Norbert, Kathan Brown, and Nancy Tousley. *Minimal Art: Druckgraphik*. Hannover: Kestner-Gesellschaft, 1976.
Mantura, Bruno, ed. *Contemporanea*. Rome: Incontri internazionali d'arte, and Florence: Centro Di, 1973.
Marandel, J. Patrick, et al. *Master Drawings, 1520–1990*. New York: Janie C. Lee Gallery, and London: Kate Ganz, 1991.
Marck, Jan van der. *American Art: Third Quarter Century*. Seattle: Seattle Art Museum, 1973.
Marino, Pietro. *20 artisti americani*. Bari: Dedalo, 1971.
Marshall, Richard. *American Art since 1970: Painting, Sculpture, and Drawings from the Collection of the Whitney Museum of American Art, New York*. New York: Whitney Museum of American Art, 1984.
Margo Leavin Gallery: 25 Years. Los Angeles: Margo Leavin Gallery, 1995.
Master Drawings of the Twentieth Century. New York: Mitchell-Innes & Nash, 1998.
Mayhall, Dorothy. *The Minimal Tradition*. Ridgefield, Conn.: The Aldrich Museum of Contemporary Art, 1979.
McFadden, Sarah, Joan Simon, and John Caldwell. *1988 Carnegie International Exhibition*. Pittsburgh: The Carnegie Museum of Art, 1988.
McKinney, Donald. *Yves Klein, Brice Marden, Sigmar Polke*. New York: Hirschl & Adler Modern, 1989.
Mehring, Christine, and Pamela Lee. *Drawing Is Another Kind of Language: Recent American Drawings from a New York Private Collection*. Cambridge, Mass.: Harvard University Art Museums, and Stuttgart: Daco-Verlag Günter Bläse, 1997.
Menna, Filiberto, Italo Mussa, and Tommaso Trini. *La riflessione sulla pittura*. Acireale: Palazzo Comunale, 1973.
Messer, Thomas M. *Fifty Years of Collecting: An Anniversary Selection. Painting since World War II*. New York: Solomon R. Guggenheim Foundation, 1987.
Messerli, Niggi, and Philip Ursprung. *Brice Marden, Samuel Buri, Ernst Messerli: Projekte für das Basler Münster*. Liestal: Kunsthalle Palazzo, 1990.
Mézil, Eric, et al. *Artists' Collections*. Paris: Collection Lambert, and Arles: Actes Sud, 2001.
Miller, Jo. *Eighteenth National Print Exhibition*. Brooklyn: Brooklyn Museum of Art, 1972.
Molon, Dominic. "Brice Marden." In *Collective Vision: Creating a Contemporary Art Museum*. Chicago: Museum of Contemporary Art, 1996.
Morgan, Robert C. "Color Field Painting, Reductivist Painting, and Minimal Art." In Sam Hunter, ed. *An American Renaissance: Painting and Sculpture since 1940*. Fort Lauderdale: Museum of Art, and New York; Abbeville Press, 1986.
Motherwell, Robert. *The Drawing Society of New York Regional Exhibition, 1970*. New York: Cooper-Hewitt Museum of Decorative Arts and Design, 1970.
Murata, Keinosuke, et al. *Minimal Art*. Osaka: National Museum of Art, 1990.
Murdock, Robert M. *Modular Painting*. Buffalo: Albright-Knox Art Gallery, 1970.
Nachtigaller, Roland, and Nicola von Velsen, eds. *Documenta IX*. Stuttgart: Edition Cantz, and New York: Harry N. Abrams, 1992.
Nakabayashi, Kazuo, and Kunio Motoe. *Painting-Singular Object: A Perspective on Contemporary Art*. Tokyo: National Museum of Modern Art, 1995.
Neff, Terry Ann R., ed. *Selections from the William J. Hokin Collection*. Chicago: Museum of Contemporary Art, 1985.
Newman, Sasha M., and Lesley K. Baier, eds. *Yale Collects Yale, 1950–1993*. New Haven: Yale University Art Gallery, 1993.
1969 Annual Exhibition: Contemporary American Painting. New York: Whitney Museum of American Art, 1969.
1973 Biennial Exhibition: Contemporary American Art. New York: Whitney Museum of American Art, 1973.
1979 Biennial Exhibition. New York: Whitney Museum of American Art, 1979.
Nodelman, Sheldon. *Marden, Novros, Rothko: Painting in the Age of Actuality*. Houston: Institute for the Arts, Rice University, 1978.
Nordland, Gerald. *Fourteen Abstract Painters*. Los Angeles: Frederick S. Wight Art Gallery, University of California, 1975.
Orchier, Poppy Gandler. *Minimalist Prints*. New York: Susan Sheehan Gallery, 1990.
Orlandini, Marisa Volpi. *Glossario*. Rome: Qui Arte Contemporanea, 1973.
Painting, Drawing, and Sculpture of the '60s and the '70s from the Dorothy and Herbert Vogel Collection. Philadelphia: Institute of Contemporary Art, 1975.
Paoletti, John, and Ruth E. Fine. *From Minimal to Conceptual Art: Works from the Dorothy and Herbert Vogel Collection*. Washington, D.C.: National Gallery of Art, 1994.
Pavie, Yann. *1900–1976: 100 dessins du Musée de Grenoble*. Grenoble: Maison de la Culture de Grenoble, 1976.
Perry-Lehmann, Meira, ed. *Modern Masterworks on Paper from The Israel Museum, Jerusalem*. Jerusalem: The Israel Museum, 1999.
Phillips, Lisa. *Surveying the Seventies: Selections from the Permanent Collection of the Whitney Museum of American Art*. Stamford, Conn.: Whitney Museum of American Art, 1982.
———. *The American Century: Art & Culture, 1950–2000*. New York: Whitney Museum of American Art and W. W Norton, 1999.
Pincus-Witten, Robert. *White on White: The White Monochrome in the 20th Century*. Chicago: Museum of Contemporary Art, 1971.
———. *Brice Marden: The Grove Group*. New York: Gagosian Gallery, 1991.
———. *Brice Marden: Classic Paintings*. New York: C & M Arts, 1999.
Pissarro, Joachim. *Then and Now: Art since 1945 at Yale*. New Haven: Yale University Art Gallery, 1998.
Pleynet, Marcelin. *Tendances actuelles de la nouvelle peinture américaine*. Paris: ARC, Musée d'art moderne de la ville de Paris, 1975.
Plous, Phyllis. *Contemporary Drawing/New York*. Santa Barbara: UCSB Art Museum, University of California, 1978.

Poling, Clark V. *Contemporary Art in Atlanta Collections: Paintings and Drawings.* Atlanta: High Museum of Art, 1976.
Powell, Earl A., III. *The James A. Michener Collection: Twentieth Century American Painting*. Austin: University Art Museum, University of Texas at Austin, 1977.
Prat, Jean-Louis. *Dessins de la Fondation Maeght.* St. Paul: Fondation Maeght, 1980.
Prather, Marla. "Brice Marden." In Mark Rosenthal, ed. *The Robert and Jane Meyerhoff Collection, 1945 to 1995.* Washington, D.C.: National Gallery of Art, 1996.
Prokopoff, Stephen. *A Romantic Minimalism*. Philadelphia: Institute of Contemporary Art, 1967.
———. *Five Artists: A Logic of Vision*. Chicago: Museum of Contemporary Art, 1974.
———. *The Reductive Object: A Survey of the Minimalist Aesthetic in the 1960s.* Boston: The Institute of Contemporary Art, 1979.
Prospect '69. Düsseldorf: Stadtische Kunsthalle, 1969.
Quargnal, Elettra, and Marisa Volpi Orlandini. *Arte americana contemporanea*. Udine: Istituto per L'Enciclopedia del Friuli Venezia Giulia, 1980.
Ratcliff, Carter. *The Meditative Surface*. Chicago: The Renaissance Society at the University of Chicago, 1984.
Ravenal, John B. "Brice Marden." In John T. Paoletti, ed. *No Title: The Collection of Sol LeWitt*. Middletown: Wesleyan University in association with the Wadsworth Atheneum, Hartford, 1981.
Reynolds, Jock. *American Abstraction at the Addison*. Andover: Addison Gallery of American Art, 1991.
Richardson, Brenda. *The Bay Area Collects: Sandra and Breck Caldwell.* Berkeley: University of California at Berkeley, 1974.
———. *Brice Marden Cold Mountain*. Houston: Houston Fine Art Press, 1993.
Rimanelli, David. *Brice Marden.* New York: Matthew Marks Gallery, 1995.
Rohatyn, F. *American Artists in the American Ambassador's Residence in Paris.* Paris: Jeanne Greenberg Art Advisory, 1998.
Rorimer, Anne, and James A. Speyer. *Seventy-second American Exhibition.* Chicago: The Art Institute of Chicago, 1976.
Rose, Bernice. *Drawing Now.* New York: The Museum of Modern Art, 1976.
———. *Allegories of Modernism: Contemporary Drawing.* New York: The Museum of Modern Art, 1992.
Rosenthal, Mark. *Contemporary Drawing: Exploring the Territory.* Aspen: Aspen Art Museum, 1995.
———. *Abstraction in the Twentieth Century: Total Risk, Freedom, Discipline.* New York: Guggenheim Museum, 1996.
Rubin, David S. *Contemporary Triptychs*. Claremont, Calif.: Trustees of Pomona College, 1982.
Russell, Emily, ed. *Art at Work: Forty Years of the Chase Manhattan Collection*. New York: Chase Manhattan Corporation, 2000.
Sandler, Irving. *20 Artists: Yale School of Art, 1950–1970*. New Haven: Yale University Art Gallery, 1981.
Schenker, Christoph. "Brice Marden." In *InK—Dokumentation 5*. Zurich: Halle für Internationale Neue Kunst, 1980.
Schjeldahl, Peter. *Brice Marden: New Paintings.* New York: Mary Boone/Michael Werner Gallery, 1987.
———. "Contemporary American Art." In Timo Vuorikoski, ed. *Amerikkalaista Nykytaidetta*. Tampere, Finland: Sara Hildén Art Museum, 1988.
———. "Minimalism." In Alistair Hicks, ed. *Art of Our Time: The Saatchi Collection*, vol. 1. London: Lund Humphries, 1984, and New York: Rizzoli, 1985.
Schwartz, Ellen, and Corinne Robins. *Beauties & Beasts*. New York: Pratt Manhattan Center Gallery, Pratt Institute, 1984.
Schwartzman, Allan, and Kathleen Thomas. *The 1970s: New American Painting*. New York: The New Museum of Contemporary Art, 1979.
Schwarz, Dieter, ed. *Von Edgar Degas bis Gerhard Richter: Arbeiten auf Papier aus der Sammlung des Kunstmuseums Winterthur*. Winterthur: Kunstmuseum Winterthur, 2000.
Schwarz, Dieter, and Michael Semff. *Brice Marden: Work Books, 1964–1995.* Munich: Staatliche Graphische Sammlung, 1997.
Schwarzwälder, Rosemarie, ed. *Abstrakte Malerei aus Amerika und Europa/Abstract Painting of America and Europe*. Vienna: Galerie nächst St. Stephan, Rosemarie Schwarzwälder, and Klagenfurt: Ritter Verlag, 1988.
Shearer, Linda. *Brice Marden*. New York: Solomon R. Guggenheim Museum, 1975.
Sims, Patterson. *Minimalism to Expressionism: Painting and Sculpture since 1965.* New York: Whitney Museum of American Art, 1983.
Sims, Patterson, and Suzanne Stroh. *1976–1986: Ten Years of Collecting Contemporary American Art. Selections from the Edward R. Downe, Jr. Collection*. Wellesley: Wellesley College Museum, 1986.
Smith, Elizabeth A. T., et al. *Life, Death, Love, Hate, Pleasure, Pain: Selected Works from the Museum of Contemporary Art, Chicago, Collection*. Chicago: Museum of Contemporary Art, 2002.
Smith, Roberta. "Drawing from Within." In Rolf Wedewer, ed. *Amerikanische Zeichnungen in den achtziger Jahren*. Munich: Verlag Fred Jahn, 1990.
Smolik, Noemi, et al. *Abstrakte Malerei zwischen Analyse und Synthese.* Vienna: Galerie nächst St. Stephan, Rosemarie Schwarzwälder, and Klagenfurt: Ritter Verlag, 1992.
Solomon, Elke M. *American Drawings, 1963–1973.* New York: Whitney Museum of American Art, 1973.
———. *Recent Drawings: William Allan, James Bishop, Vija Celmins, Brice Marden, Jim Nutt, Alan Saret, Pat Steir, Richard Tuttle.* New York: American Federation of Arts, 1975.
Source and Inspiration: A Continuing Tradition. New York: Hirschl & Adler Folk, 1988.
Spector, Nancy, et al. *Singular Forms (Sometimes Repeated): Art from 1951 to the Present.* New York: Solomon R. Guggenheim Museum, 2004.
Speyer, A. James. *Seventy-second American Exhibition*. Chicago: The Art Institute of Chicago, 1976.
Speyer, A. James, and C. C. Cunningham. *Seventieth American Exhibition*. Chicago: The Art Institute of Chicago, 1972.
Stavitsky, Gail, ed. *Waxing Poetic: Encaustic Art in America*. Piscataway, N.J.: Rutgers University Press, 2000.
Steininger, Florian, et al. *Willem de Kooning*. Wolfratshausen: Edition Minerva, 2005.
Steir, Pat. *Brice Marden: Recent Drawings and Etchings.* New York: Matthew Marks Gallery, 1991.
Stomberg, John, and Catherine L. Blais. *Looking East: Brice Marden, Michael Mazur, Pat Steir*. Seattle: University of Washington Press, 2002.
Storr, Robert. *On the Edge: Contemporary Art from the Werner and Elaine Dannheisser Collection*. New York: The Museum of Modern Art, 1997.
Storr, Robert, et al. *Drawn from Artists' Collections*. New York: The Drawing Center, 1999.
Storsve, Jonas, and Guy Tosatto, eds. *Au fil du trait: De Matisse à Basquiat.* Paris: Editions du Centre Pompidou, 1998.
Strelow, Hans. *Prospect '73: Maler, Painters, Peintres.* Düsseldorf: Stadtische Kunsthalle, 1973.
Sundell, Nina C. "Brice Marden." In *The Robert and Jane Meyerhoff Collection, 1958–1979*. Baltimore: Jane B. Meyerhoff, 1980.
Szeemann, Harald, ed. *Documenta 5*. Kassel: Documenta and Bertelsmann Verlag, 1972.
Taguchi, Hiroshi, Yasuaki Ishizaka, and Nobuyuki Hiromoto. *Innovation: American Art of Today from the Misumi Art Collection.* Chiba: Kawamura Memorial Museum of Art, 1996.
Temkin, Ann. *Contemporary Voices: Works from the UBS Art Collection*. New York: The Museum of Modern Art, 2005.
Ten Americans from Pace. London: Wildenstein & Co, 1980.
Tenth Anniversary Exhibition: 100 Drawings and Photographs. New York: Matthew Marks Gallery, 2001.
Tousley, Nancy. *Prints: Bochner, LeWitt, Mangold, Marden, Martin, Renouf, Rockburne, Ryman.* Toronto: Art Gallery of Ontario, 1975.
Tuchman, Maurice, et al. *The Spiritual in Art: Abstract Painting, 1890–1985.* Los Angeles: Los Angeles County Museum of Art, and New York: Abbeville Press, 1986.
Tucker, James. *Art on Paper Invitational.* Greensboro, N.C.: Weatherspoon Art Gallery, 1967.
Tucker, Marcia. *The Structure of Color*. New York: Whitney Museum of American Art, 1971.
20th-Century American Art from Friends' Collections. New York: Whitney Museum of American Art, 1977.
XXV Years. San Francisco: John Berggruen Gallery, 1995.
25 Years: An Exhibition of Selected Works. Los Angeles: Margo Leavin Gallery, 1995.
Watanabe, Yohko, et al. *Revolution: Art of the Sixties from Warhol to Beuys.* Tokyo: Museum of Contemporary Art, 1995.

Weber, Dawson. "Brice Marden." In Jonathan Fineberg and Josef Helfenstein, eds. *Drawings of Choice from a New York Collection*. Champaign: Krannert Art Museum, University of Illinois, 2002.

Wedewer, Rolf, and Rolf Ricke. *USA: Zeichnungen 3*. Leverkusen: Städtisches Museum Leverkusen Schloss Morsbroich, 1975.

Weller, Allen S. *Contemporary American Painting and Sculpture, 1967*. Urbana: University of Illinois Press, 1967.

Wye, Deborah. *Thinking Print: Books to Billboards, 1980–95*. New York: The Museum of Modern Art, 1996.

Wye, Deborah, Wendy Weitman, and David Elliott. *Modern Means: Continuity and Change in Art, 1880 to the Present. Highlights from The Museum of Modern Art*. New York: The Museum of Modern Art, in association with the Mori Art Museum, Tokyo, 2004.

Wylie, Charles. *Brice Marden: Work of the 1990s. Paintings, Drawings, and Prints*. Dallas: Dallas Museum of Art, 1999.

Yau, John. *Brice Marden: Recent Paintings & Drawings*. London: Anthony d'Offay Gallery. 1988.

———. *Repetition*. New York: Hirschl & Adler Modern, 1989.

de Zegher, Catherine, ed. *The Stage of Drawing: Gesture and Act*. London: Tate Publishing, and New York: The Drawing Center, 2003.

Zeichnungen amerikanischer Künstler. Cologne: Galerie Ricke, 1970.

Zimmer, William. *Brice Marden: Marbles, Paintings, and Drawings*. New York: The Pace Gallery, 1982.

Among the exhibition catalogues above, the following contain statements and other writings by Marden: de Wilde, *La Grande Parade*; Duncan and Reid, *Brice Marden at Gemini*; Honnef, *Geplante Malerei*; Keller and Malin, eds., *Brice Marden: Drawings and Paintings*; Lebensztejn, *Brice Marden: Recent Paintings and Drawings*, Lebensztejn and Kertess, *Brice Marden*; Licht, *Some Recent American Art*; Lynton, Brown, and Tousley, *Minimal Art*; *Master Drawings of the Twentieth Century*; Mehring and Lee, *Drawing Is Another Kind of Language*; Tousley, *Prints*; "Notes: A Mediterranean Painting," in Tucker, *The Structure of Color*; Lippard, *Invitational*; "Selected from Notes, 1971–72," in Lambert and Claura, *Actualité d'un bilan*; "Statement and Proposal: 'Star (for Patti Smith)," in Hanson et al., *Options and Alternatives* (this statement is partially reprinted in Licht, *Eight Contemporary Artists*); "Technical Statement," in Shearer, *Brice Marden*; de Wilde and Dippel, *Fundamentele Schilderkunst*; Kardon, *Private Notations*; "5 Lines for Klaus, 4/30/79," in Kern and Kertess, *Brice Marden: Zeichnungen/Drawings*; de Wilde, Bann, and Smith, *Brice Marden: Schilderijen, tekeningen, etsen*, and *Brice Marden: Paintings, Drawings, and Prints*; Marshall, *American Art since 1970*; "Notes, 1979–82/84," in *Brice Marden: Recent Work*; "The Grove Group Notebook," in Pincus-Witten, *Brice Marden: The Grove Group*; "Past Recent Now," in Fairbrother, *Brice Marden: Boston*; "Jackson Pollock," in Richardson, *Brice Marden Cold Mountain* (audiotaped talk given by Marden at The Museum of Modern Art, New York, on November 16, 1989, transcribed by Richardson); *Brice Marden* (Zurich: Thomas Ammann, 1996);.

Films and Sound Recordings

Howard, Edgar B., director, and Theodore R. Haimes, director and producer. *Brice Marden*, 16-mm film, color, 22 minutes. New York: Tuckernuck Productions, 1977. Available through the Checkerboard Film Foundation, New York.

Vision 4: Word of Mouth. Oakland: Crown Point Press, and San Francisco: The Museum of Conceptual Art, 1980. Set of three LP's of talks by twelve artists including Marden, recorded in Ponape, Micronesia. With illustrated booklet.

EXHIBITION HISTORY

Compiled by Francesca Pietropaolo

An asterisk indicates that the exhibition had a catalogue. For full information on exhibition catalogues see the Bibliography.

Solo Exhibitions

1963

Swarthmore, Pa.: Wilcox Gallery, Swarthmore College. *Brice Marden.* December 6, 1963–January 6, 1964.

1966

New York: Bykert Gallery. *Brice Marden.* November 15–December 7.

1968

New York: Bykert Gallery. *Brice Marden: Back Series.* January 6–31.

New York: Bykert Gallery. *Drawings by Brice Marden.* November 30, 1968–January 2, 1969.

1969

New York: Bykert Gallery. *Brice Marden: New Paintings.* April 26–May 17.

Paris: Galerie Yvon Lambert. *Brice Marden.* September 25–October 25.

1970

Milan: Françoise Lambert. *Brice Marden.* January 30–February 15.

New York: Bykert Gallery. *Brice Marden.* October 31–November 26.

1971

Düsseldorf: Konrad Fischer. *Brice Marden: Bilder und Zeichnungen.* May 18–June 7.

Turin: Gian Enzo Sperone. *Brice Marden.* June 11– .

1972

New York: Bykert Gallery. *Brice Marden.* February 5–March 1.

Minneapolis: Locksley-Shea Gallery. *Brice Marden: New Paintings.* April 21–May 12.

Düsseldorf: Konrad Fischer. *Brice Marden.* June.

San Francisco: John Berggruen Gallery. *Ten Days: A Portfolio of 8 Etchings.* June 7–July 8.

1973

Corona del Mar, Calif.: Jack Glenn Gallery. *Brice Marden.* February 3–March 2.

New York: Bykert Gallery. *Brice Marden New Paintings: Grove Group.* February 24–March 22.

Düsseldorf: Konrad Fischer. *Brice Marden.* July.

Paris: Galerie Yvon Lambert. *Brice Marden: 25 Ink Drawings, 5 Homages to Art, 1 Painting.* September 18–October 18.

Milan: Galleria Françoise Lambert. *Brice Marden: Disegni.* October 19–November 19.

1974

Houston: Contemporary Arts Museum. *Brice Marden Drawings, 1963–1973.* January 24–March 10. Traveled: Loretto-Hilton Gallery, Webster College, St. Louis, March 31–April 27; Bykert Gallery, New York, October 19–November 1 (as *Brice Marden Drawings, 1964–1974*); Fort Worth Art Museum, November 10, 1974–January 5, 1975; Minneapolis Institute of Arts, January 15–March 1, 1975.

New York: Bykert Gallery. *New Paintings, Brice Marden.* March 23–April 17.

Los Angeles: Cirrus Gallery. *12 Etchings by Brice Marden.* May 7–31.

Toronto: Jared Sable Gallery. *Brice Marden.* September 14–28.

New York: Bykert Gallery. *Brice Marden: Drawings, 1964–1974.* October 19–November 1.

Minneapolis: Locksley Shea Gallery. *Brice Marden: Paintings, Drawings, Etchings.* October 25–November 15.

1975

New York: Solomon R. Guggenheim Museum. *Brice Marden.* March 7–May 4.*

London: Hester van Royen. *Brice Marden Prints.* April.

Rome: D'Alessandro/Ferranti. *Brice Marden.* April 22–May 6.

Düsseldorf: Konrad Fischer. *Brice Marden: Shape Book.* September 2–23.

1976

Paris: Galerie Yvon Lambert. *Brice Marden.* January 8–February 4.

New York: Sperone Westwater Fischer. *Paintings and Drawings Made by Brice Marden.* April 3–22.

1977

Washington, D.C.: Max Protetch Gallery. *Brice Marden: Drawings–Lithographs.* April 16– .

Providence: Bell Gallery, Brown University. *Brice Marden: Works on Paper.* November 19–December 11.

Athens, Greece: Jean and Karen Bernier. *Brice Marden: Etchings and Recent Drawings.* November 22–December 3.

Rome: Gian Enzo Sperone. *Brice Marden.* December 17– .

1978

New York: The Pace Gallery. *Brice Marden: Recent Paintings and Drawings.* September 23–October 21.*

1979

Munich: Kunstraum München. *Brice Marden: Zeichnungen, 1964–1978.* September 19–October 27. Traveled: Institut für Moderne Kunst, Nuremberg, November 22, 1979–January 11, 1980.*

1980

Nagoya: Galerie Valuer. *Brice Marden: Paintings and Drawings.* February 1–23.*

Zurich: InK, Halle für Internationale Neue Kunst. *Brice Marden.* February 21–April 3.*

Düsseldorf: Konrad Fischer. *Brice Marden: New Paintings.* April 12–May 8.

New York: The Pace Gallery. *Brice Marden.* September 26–October 25.

1981

Amsterdam: Stedelijk Museum. *Brice Marden: Schilderijen, tekeningen, etsen, 1975–1980/Brice Marden: Paintings, Drawings, and Etchings, 1975–1980.* March 12–April 26.* Traveled: Whitechapel Art Gallery, London, as *Brice Marden: Paintings, Drawings, Prints, 1975–1980.* May 8–June 21.*

Athens, Greece: Jean Bernier Gallery. *Brice Marden (Marbles).* November–December.

1982

New York: The Pace Gallery. *Brice Marden: Marbles, Paintings, and Drawings.* October 29–November 27.*

1983

Lund: Galleriet. *Brice Marden, ätta Serigrafier.* October 29–November 23.

1984

Cologne: Raum für Malerei. *Brice Marden: Three Paintings, 1964–1966.* May 2–June 16.

New York: The Pace Gallery. *Brice Marden: Recent Work.* September 28–October 27.*

Los Angeles: Daniel Weinberg Gallery. *Brice Marden: Paintings and Drawings.* December 8, 1984–January 12, 1985.

1985

Krefeld: Galerie Hock. *Brice Marden: Arbeiten auf Papier.* April 27–May 25.

1987

New York: Mary Boone/Michael Werner Gallery. *Brice Marden: New Paintings.* March 7–28.*

Paris: Galerie Montenay. *Brice Marden.* June 9–July 4.*

1988

New York: Mary Boone/Michael Werner Gallery. *Brice Marden.* April 9–May 7.

London: Anthony d'Offay Gallery. *Brice Marden: Recent Paintings and Drawings.* April 22–May 24.*

1989

Cologne: Galerie Michael Werner. *Brice Marden.* May 12–June 6.*

1991

New York: Gagosian Gallery. *Brice Marden: The Grove Group.* January 15–March 15.*

Boston: Museum of Fine Arts. *Connections: Brice Marden.* March 23–July 21.*

New York: Matthew Marks Gallery. *Brice Marden, Recent Drawings and Etchings.* May 8–June 28.*

New York: Dia Center for the Arts. *Brice Marden: Cold Mountain.* October 17, 1991–May 31, 1992. Traveled: Walker Art Center Minneapolis, June 28–September 13, 1992; The Menil Collection, Houston, October 2–November 29, 1992; Museo Nacional Centro de Arte Reina Sofía, Madrid, January 12–March 15, 1993; Städtisches Kunstmuseum, Bonn, April 30–June 20, 1993.*

1992

London: Curwen Gallery. *Brice Marden: Prints from the Early Seventies.* February 19–March 14.

London: Tate Gallery. *Brice Marden: Prints, 1961–1991.* February 26–June 21. Traveled: Musée d'Art Moderne de la Ville de Paris, July 6–October 4; Baltimore Museum of Art, October 25, 1992–January 3, 1993.

1993
New York: Matthew Marks Gallery. *Brice Marden: Paintings, Drawings, Etchings.* May 1–June 26.*
Basel: Museum für Gegenwartskunst. *Brice Marden.* May 16–August 1. Traveled: Museum Fridericianum, Kassel, March 13–May 24, 1994.
Los Angeles: Margo Leavin Gallery, *Brice Marden: New Etchings.* July 10–August 21.*
Frankfurt: Galerie Meyer-Ellinger. *Originalgrafik und Mappenwerke aus den Jahren 1969–1993.* September 14–October 23.
Bern: Kunsthalle Bern. *Brice Marden: Painting, 1985–1993.* October 9–November 28. Traveled: Wiener Secession, Vienna, February 2–March 13, 1994.*
Saint Louis: The Saint Louis Art Museum. *Brice Marden: A Painting, Drawings, and Prints.* November 23, 1993–February 20, 1994.
1994
Zurich: Annemarie Verna Galerie. *Brice Marden: Etchings.* February 5–April 7.
Berlin: Galerie Pels-Leusden. *Brice Marden Prints.* February 7–April 7.
Amsterdam: Stedelijk Museum. *Couplet 2: Brice Marden, Paintings, 1985–1993.* April 29–June 30.
Melbourne: Niagara Galleries. *Brice Marden Prints.* May 17–June 4.
1995
New York: Matthew Marks Gallery. *Brice Marden.* October 13, 1995–January 14, 1996.*
New York: Pace Wildenstein. *Brice Marden: Drawings, 1964–1994.* November 3–December 2.*
1996
Zurich: Thomas Ammann Fine Art. *Brice Marden.* June 10–September 28.*
1997
New York: Matthew Marks Gallery. *Chinese Work.* May 3–June 27.*
Munich: Staatliche Graphische Sammlung. *Brice Marden: Work Books, 1964–1995.* July 2–August 24. Traveled: Kunstmuseum Winterthur, September 6–November 23; Wexner Center for the Arts, Ohio State University, Columbus, January 31–April 2, 1998; Fogg Art Museum, Harvard University, Cambridge, Mass., July 18–September 27, 1998.*
1998
New York: Whitney Museum of American Art. *Brice Marden Drawings: The Whitney Museum of American Art Collection.* November 20, 1998–March 28, 1999.*
1999
Dallas: Dallas Museum of Art. *Brice Marden: Work of the 1990s. Paintings, Drawings, and Prints.* February 14–April 25. Traveled: Hirshhorn Museum and Sculpture Garden, Smithsonian Institution, Washington, D.C., May 27–September 6; Miami Art Museum, December 17, 1999–March 5, 2000; Carnegie Museum of Art, Pittsburgh, May 20–August 13, 2000.*
New York: C & M Arts. *Brice Marden: Classic Paintings.* March 30–May 29.*
Houston: The Museum of Fine Arts. *Brice Marden: Work Books and Series.* October 3, 1999–January 2, 2000.
2000
Los Angeles: Margo Leavin Gallery. *Brice Marden Etchings: Five Threes, 1976–77; 12 Views for Caroline Tatyana, 1977–89; Focus I–V, 1979.* April 8–29.
London: Serpentine Gallery. *Brice Marden.* November 17, 2000–January 7, 2001.*
2001
San Francisco: John Berggruen Gallery. *Brice Marden: "For Caroline, 1989"; Twelve Etchings and Aquatints and Seven Recent Color Lithographs.* February 1–March 3.
Lynchburg, Va.: The Maier Museum of Art, Randolph-Macon Woman's College. *Drawing the Line: A Retrospective of Drawings by Brice Marden.* October 27–December 22.
Melbourne: Niagara Galleries. *Brice Marden.* November 27–December 21.
Rome: Istituto Nazionale per la Grafica. *Brice Marden: Works on Paper, 1964–2001.* December 12, 2001–February 24, 2002. Traveled: Archivio di Stato, Turin, March 12–April 28, 2002; Westfälisches Landesmuseum für Kunst und Kulturgeschichte, Münster, June 6–August 25, 2002.*
2002
Boston: Sherman Gallery, Boston University. *Brice Marden: Prints.* January 18–March 1.
New York: Matthew Marks Gallery. *Brice Marden: Attendants, Bears, and Rocks.* May 3–June 21.*
Los Angeles: Gemini. *Brice Marden at Gemini.*
2003
Zurich: Daros. *Brice Marden.* June 14, 2003–January 4, 2004.*
2004
New York: Matthew Marks Gallery. *Brice Marden: Paintings on Marble.* May 8–June 27.
2005
New York: Akira Ikeda Gallery. *An Empty Space: Brice Marden.* January–June.
Wellesley, Mass.: Davis Museum and Cultural Center, Wellesley College. *Brice Marden: Etchings to Rexroth.* September 14–December 18.

Group Exhibitions

1960
New London, Conn.: Lyman Allyn Art Museum. *The Second Competitive Drawing Exhibition.* March 6–27.
1963
New Haven: Munson Gallery. *7 Yale Painters: Paul Covington, Kent Floeter, Brice Marden, Paul Tschinkel, Oscar Watters, Paul Zavorskas, Charles Close.* April 6–20.
1965
New York: Leo Castelli Gallery. *Drawing Show.* December 14, 1965–January 5, 1966. Benefit for the Foundation for Contemporary Performance Arts.
1966
New York: Park Place Gallery. *Park Place Invitational.* June 12–July.
1967
Ithaca, N.Y.: Ithaca College Museum of Art. *Drawings, 1967.* January 17–February 25.*
Champaign: Krannert Art Museum, University of Illinois at Urbana-Champaign. *Contemporary American Painting and Sculpture, 1967.* March 5–April 9.*
New York: Bykert Gallery. *Gallery Group Show.* May 16–June 12.
Philadelphia: Institute of Contemporary Art, University of Pennsylvania. *A Romantic Minimalism.* September 13–October 11.*
Greensboro: Weatherspoon Art Gallery, University of North Carolina. *Art on Paper Invitational.* October 15–November 22.*
Omaha, Nebr.: University of Omaha. *Rejective Art.* November 9–30. Traveled: The Museum of Fine Arts, Houston, December 14, 1967–January 4, 1968; School of Architecture, Clemson University, Clemson, S.C., January 19–February 9, 1968. Organized by the American Federation of Arts, New York.
New York: Bykert Gallery. *Gallery Group Show.* November 15–December 7.
1968
New York: Bykert Gallery. *Painting and Sculpture.* May 25–June 22.
Toronto: Carmen Lamanna Gallery. *New York Now.* December 20, 1968–January 7, 1969.
1969
Boston: School of Fine and Applied Arts, Boston University. *21 Alumni.* January 17–February 7.*
Poughkeepsie, N.Y.: Vassar College Art Gallery. *Concept.* April 30–June 11.*
Düsseldorf: Stadtische Kunsthalle. *Prospect '69.* September 30–October 12.*
Fort Worth: Fort Worth Art Center Museum. *Drawings.* October 28–November 30.*
Toronto: Carmen Lamanna Gallery. *Scenic Landmarks of New York Presents a Scenic Landmark for Toronto.* November 21–December 9.
New York: Whitney Museum of American Art. *1969 Annual Exhibition: Contemporary American Painting.* December 16, 1969–February 1, 1970.*
1970
New York: Bykert Gallery. *Brice Marden/Bob Duran.* February 3–26.
New York: Cooper-Hewitt Museum of Decorative Arts and Design, Smithsonian Institution. *The Drawing Society of New York Regional Exhibition: 1970.* March 9–May 9. Organized by the American Federation of Arts, New York.*
Minneapolis: Locksley Shea Gallery. *Brice Marden/Jo Baer: Major Works.* March 20–April 11.
Buffalo: Albright-Knox Art Gallery. *Modular Painting.* April 21–May 24.*
Cologne: Galerie Ricke. *Drawings by American Artists.* May.*
New York: Bykert Gallery. *Gallery Group Show.* May 19–June 20.
San Francisco: Michael Walls Gallery. *Uses of Structure in Recent American Painting.* July 15–August 22.
St. Paul-de-Vence: Fondation Maeght. *L'Art vivant aux États-Unis.* July 16–September 30.*

Paris: Galerie Yvon Lambert. *American Drawings*. September.
Salt Lake City: Utah Museum of Fine Arts, University of Utah. *Drawings by New York Artists*. November 28, 1970–January 12, 1971. Traveled: Henry Art Gallery, University of Washington, Seattle, March 3–26, 1971; University Art Collection, Arizona State University, Tempe, Az., May 10, 1972–June 12, 1972; Georgia Museum of Art, Athens, Ga., July 2–August 6, 1972.*
Houston: Janie C. Lee Gallery. *Drawing Show*. December 12, 1970–January 31, 1971.

1971

New York: Whitney Museum of American Art. *The Structure of Color*. February 25–April 18.*
Saint Paul: Minnesota Museum of Art. *Drawings USA/71*. April 15–June 27.*
New York: Bykert Gallery. *Lynda Benglis/Porfirio di Donna/Sol LeWitt/Brice Marden/Dorothea Rockburne/Robert Ryman/Richard Tuttle*. May 18–June 22.
Milan: Françoise Lambert. *Gallery Group Show*. June.
Bari, Italy: Chase Manhattan Bank. *20 artisti americani: The Collection of Angelo Raffaele Baldassarre*. October 21–November 7.*
New York: Bykert Gallery. *Drawings and Prints*. November 6–December 2.
Amherst: University Art Gallery, University of Massachusetts. *Invitational*. December 3–24.*
Rochester, N.Y.: Memorial Art Gallery, University of Rochester. *Aspects of Current Painting: New York*. December 6–30.
Chicago: Museum of Contemporary Art. *White on White: The White Monochrome in the 20th Century*. December 18, 1971–January 30, 1972.*

1972

Minneapolis: Walker Art Center. *Painting: New Options*. April 23–June 4.*
Indianapolis: Indianapolis Museum of Art. *Painting and Sculpture Today, 1972*. April 26–June 4.
Berkeley: University Art Museum, University of California, Berkeley. *Eight New York Painters*. May 10–June 25.
Houston: Janie C. Lee Gallery. *Drawings/72*. May 20–June 30.
Chicago: The Art Institute of Chicago. *Seventieth American Exhibition*. June 24–August 20.*
Kassel: Museum Fridericianum and Neue Galerie. Documenta 5. June 30–October 8.*
San Francisco: San Francisco Art Institute. *Crown Point Press*. September 1–October 1.
Paris: Galerie Yvon Lambert. *Actualité d'un bilan*. October 29–December 15.*
Austin: Michener Galleries, University of Texas at Austin. *The Michener Collection: American Paintings of the Twentieth Century*. November 22, 1972–March 1, 1973.
Brooklyn, N.Y.: Brooklyn Museum of Art. Eighteenth National Print Exhibition. November 22, 1972–February 4, 1973. Traveled: California Palace of the Legion of Honor, San Francisco, March 24–June 17, 1973.

1973

New York: Bykert Gallery. *Group Show*. January 6–24.
New York: Whitney Museum of American Art. Whitney Biennial. January 10–March 18.*
Charlottelund, Denmark: Gentofte Radhus. *Yngre amerikansk kunst: Tegninger og grafik*. January 24–February 11. Traveled: Aarhus Kunstmuseum, Aarhus, Denmark, February 18–March 4; Henie-Onstad Kunstsenter, Oslo, March 18–April 15; Hamburger Kunsthalle, Hamburg, April 28–June 11; Moderna Museet, Stockholm, September 15–October 21.*
Milan: Centro Comunitario di Brera. *Arte come arte*. April–May.*
New Haven: Yale University Art Gallery. *Options and Alternatives: Some Directions in Recent Art*. April 4–May 16.*
New York: Whitney Museum of American Art. *American Drawings, 1963–1973*. May 25–July 22.*
Paris: 16 Place Vendome. *Une exposition de peinture reunissant certains peintres qui mettraient la peinture en question*. May 29–June 23. Traveled: International Cultural Center, Antwerp; Städtisches Museum, Mönchengladbach, November 15–December 23.*
Rome: QUI arte contemporanea–Galleria Editalia. *Glossario*. June– July.*
Seattle: Seattle Art Museum Pavilion. *American Art: Third Quarter Century*. August 22–October 14.*
Düsseldorf: Stadtische Kunsthalle. *Prospect 73: Maler, Painters, Peintres*. September 28–October 7.*
Acireale, Italy: Palazzo Comunale. *La riflessione sulla pittura*. September 29–October 15.*
Austin: Michener Galleries, University of Texas at Austin. *Art and Things: Painting in the Sixties from the Michener Collection*. October 7, 1973–February 10, 1974.*
Rome: Parcheggio di Villa Borghese. *Contemporanea*. November 1973–February 1974.*
Venice, Calif.: Ace Gallery. *Selected Paintings: Johns, Kelly, Lichtenstein, Marden, Rauschenberg, Stella, Twombly, Warhol*. December.
New York: Paula Cooper Gallery. *Drawings and Other Work*. December 15, 1973–January 9, 1974.

1974

London: Royal College of Art Galleries. *Strata: Paintings, Drawings, and Prints by Ellsworth Kelly, Brice Marden, Agnes Martin, Robert Ryman, and Cy Twombly*. January 14–February.
Houston: Texas Gallery. *Various Paintings*. January 19–February 8.
New York: Bykert Gallery Downtown. *Etchings and Drawings: Brice Marden/Paintings: David Novros*. February 9–March 2.
Melbourne: National Gallery of Victoria. *Some Recent American Art*. February 12–March 10. Organized and circulated under the auspices of The International Council of The Museum of Modern Art, New York. Traveled: Art Gallery of New South Wales, Sydney, April 5–May 5; Art Gallery of South Australia, Adelaide, May 3–June 30; West Australian Art Gallery, Perth, July 26–August 21; City of Auckland Art Gallery, New Zealand, October 14–November 17.*
New York: Susan Caldwell Gallery. *Berthot, Bishop, Longo, Marden, Novros, Ohlson, Swain, Wurmfield*. February 23–March 20.
Münster: Westfälischer Kunstverein. *Geplante Malerei*. March 30–April 28.*
Amsterdam: Stedelijk Museum. *63/73*. April 1–30.*
Chicago: Museum of Contemporary Art. *Five Artists: A Logic of Vision*. May 4–June 23.*
Katonah, N.Y.: Katonah Gallery. *New Painting: Stressing Surface*. June 1–July 14.
New York: Michael Walls Gallery. *Ten Painters in New York*. June 15–July 6.
Berkeley: University Art Museum, University of California, Berkeley. *The Bay Area Collects: Sandra and Breck Caldwell*. July 3–August 11.*
New York: Whitney Museum of American Art. *Continuing Abstraction in American Art*. September 19–November 1.*
New York: The Museum of Modern Art. *Works from Change Inc*. September 25–October 20.
New York: The Museum of Modern Art. *Eight Contemporary Artists*. October 9, 1974–January 5, 1975.*
Edinburgh: Scottish Arts Council Gallery. *Painting Exhibition*. October 26–November 17.
Poughkeepsie, N.Y.: Vassar College Art Gallery. November 18–December 21.

1975

San Francisco: Daniel Weinberg Gallery. *Drawings*. January.
Minneapolis: Dayton's Gallery 12. *Works on Paper*. January 4– .
New York: Susan Caldwell Gallery. *22 Artists*. January 4–25.
New York: M. Knoedler & Co. *Etchings: William Bailey and Brice Marden*. January 7–24.
Bogotá: Museo de Arte Moderno. *Color*. February–March. Organized by The International Council of The Museum of Modern Art.
New York: Gian Enzo Sperone. *Carl Andre, Brice Marden, Bruce Nauman*. March 1– .
Los Angeles: Frederick S. Wight UCLA Art Galleries, University of California, Los Angeles. *Fourteen Abstract Painters*. March 25–May 25.*
Houston: Rice Museum and Sewall Art Gallery, Institute for the Arts, Rice University. *Brice Marden, David Novros, Mark Rothko*. April 18–June 15.*
New York: The Clocktower. *Selections from the Collection of Dorothy and Herbert Vogel*. April 19–May 17.
Amsterdam: Stedelijk Museum. *Fundamentele Schilderkunst*. April 25–June 22.*
Houston: Texas Gallery. *David Novros/Brice Marden*. May.
Kansas City, Mo.: Douglas Drake Gallery. *Less/More*. May 2–June 27.
Los Angeles: Margo Leavin Gallery. *Drawings*. May 12–June 21.
Leverkusen: Städtisches Museum Leverkusen Schloss Morsbroich. *USA Zeichnungen 3*. May 15–June 29.*
Otterlo: Kröller-Müller Museum. *Funkties van Tekenen*. May 25–August 24.*
Huntsville: Gallery of Art, University of Alabama. *Recent Drawings: William Allan, James Bishop, Vija Celmins, Brice Marden, Jim Nutt, Alan Saret, Pat Steir, Richard Tuttle*. June–December 1975. Traveled: The Art Museum, Princeton University, Princeton, N.J.; Cummer Gallery of Art, Jacksonville, Fla.; State University of New York, Stony Brook.* Organized by the American Federation of Arts, New York.
Paris: ARC 2, Musée d'Art Moderne de la Ville de Paris. *Tendances actuelles de la nouvelle peinture américaine*. June 24–August 31.*

Philadelphia: Institute of Contemporary Art, University of Pennsylvania. *Painting, Drawing, and Sculpture of the '60s and the '70s from the Dorothy and Herbert Vogel Collection.* October 7–November 18. Traveled: Contemporary Arts Center, Cincinnati, December 17, 1975–February 15, 1976.*

Middletown, Conn.: Davison Art Center, Wesleyan University. *Recent American Etching.* October 10–November 23.

New York: M. Knoedler & Co. *American Works on Paper, 1945–1975.* November–December.*

St. Louis: Greenberg Gallery. *Works on Paper.* December 1975–January 15, 1976.

New York: Bykert Gallery. *Drawings.* December 6, 1975–January 7, 1976.

Toronto: Art Gallery of Ontario. *Prints: Bochner, LeWitt, Mangold, Marden, Martin, Renouf, Rockburne, Ryman.* December 18, 1975–January 18, 1976.*

Rome: American Embassy. *Nineteen Americans, 1970/1975.*

Ljubljana: Moderna Galerija Ljubljana. 11th Biennial of Graphic Art Yugoslavia.

1976

New York: The Museum of Modern Art. *Drawing Now.* January 19–March 7. Traveled: Kunsthaus Zürich, October 10–November 14; Staatliche Kunsthalle, Baden-Baden, November 25, 1976–January 16, 1977; Graphische Sammlung Albertina, Vienna, January 20–February 28, 1977; Tel Aviv Museum, Israel, May 12–June 2, 1977.* Circulated under the auspices of The International Council of The Museum of Modern Art, New York.

Chicago: The Art Institute of Chicago. *American Painting and Sculpture: Seventy-second American Exhibition.* March 13–May 9.*

Atlanta: High Museum of Art. *Contemporary Art in Atlanta Collections: Paintings and Drawings.* April 24–May 30.*

San Francisco: Daniel Weinberg Gallery. *A Selection of Works.* May 3– .

Boston: The Institute of Contemporary Art. *A Selection of American Art: The Skowhegan School, 1946–1976.* June 16–September 5. Traveled: Colby Museum of Art, Waterville, Me., October 1–30.*

Tokyo: Seibu Museum of Art. *Three Decades of American Art Selected by the Whitney Museum.* June 18–July 20.*

Grenoble: Musée de Peinture et de Sculpture. *Art américain: Collection du Musée.* June 24–September 8.*

Detroit: The Detroit Institute of Arts. *American Artists: A New Decade.* July 31–September 19. Traveled: Fort Worth Art Museum, Fort Worth, November 14, 1976–January 2, 1977.*

Philadelphia: Philadelphia College of Art. *Private Notations: Artists' Sketchbooks II.* October 23–November 24.*

New Haven: Yale University Art Gallery. *Choice/Yale Art Students.* October 25–November 26.

Grenoble: Maison de la Culture, Musée de Grenoble. *1900–1976: 100 dessins du Musée de Grenoble.* November–December.*

New York: Rosa Esman Gallery. *Small Masterworks.* December 7, 1976–January 6, 1977.

Hannover: Kestnergesellschaft. *Minimal Art: Druckgraphik.* December 10, 1976–January 23, 1977.*

1977

Marseilles: Musée Cantini. *L'Avant-garde, 1960–1976: Trois villes, trois collections.* February–March. Traveled: Musée du Peinture et de Sculpture, Grenoble, April–May; Musée d'Art et d'Industrie, Saint-Etienne, summer; Centre national d'art et de culture Georges Pompidou, Musée National d'Art Moderne Paris, November.*

New York: Whitney Museum of American Art. Whitney Biennial. February 19–April 3.*

Bronxville, N.Y.: Sarah Lawrence Gallery. *Painting '75 '76 '77, Part I.* February 19–March 10. Traveled: The American Foundation for the Arts, Miami, April–May; Contemporary Arts Center, Cincinnati, August–September.*

Pullman, Wash.: Washington State University. *Works on Paper: American Art, 1945–1975.* February 28–April 11.

Bronxville, N.Y.: Sarah Lawrence Gallery. *Painting '75 '76 '77, Part II.* April 2–20. Traveled: The American Foundation for the Arts, Miami, June–July; The Contemporary Arts Center, Cincinnati, Ohio, August–September.*

New York: Sidney Janis Gallery. *Less Is More.* April 7–May 7.*

Chicago: Young Hoffman Gallery. *Andre, Flavin, Gastini, Judd, LeWitt, Mangold, Marden, Renouf, Ryman: Sculpture Paintings Drawings.* May 20–June 25.

Kassel: Museum Fridericianum and Neue Galerie. Documenta 6. June 24–October 2.*

New York: Whitney Museum of American Art. *20th-Century American Art from Friends' Collections.* July 27–September 27.*

New York: Solomon R. Guggenheim Museum. *Recent Gifts and Purchases.* September 16–October 16.

Albany: New York State Museum. *New York: The State of Art.* October 8–November 27.* Bonn: Rheinisches Landesmuseum. *Bilder ohne Bilder.* December 8, 1977–January 8, 1978.*

1978

Los Angeles: Margo Leavin Gallery. *Three Generations: Studies in Collage.* January 26–March 4.

Santa Barbara: UCSB Art Museum, University of California, Santa Barbara. *Contemporary Drawing/New York.* February 22–March 26.*

Milan: Studio Enesse. *1.2.3.n.* spring.*

New York: Whitney Museum of American Art. *Art about Art.* July 19–September 24. Traveled: North Carolina Museum of Art, Raleigh, October 15–November 26; Frederick S. Wight UCLA Art Galleries, University of California, Los Angeles, December 17, 1978–February 11, 1979; Portland Art Museum, Portland, Ore., March 6–April 15, 1979.*

Orlando, Fla.: Loch Haven Art Center. *Two Decades of Abstraction.* September 15–October 29. Traveled: University Galleries, University of South Florida, and the Tampa Bay Art Center, Tampa, January 8–February 17, 1979; Miami-Dade Community College and Florida International University, Miami, February 1979–March 1979.

Richmond, Va.: The Anderson Gallery, Virginia Commonwealth University. *Late 20th-Century Art from the Sydney and Frances Lewis Collection.* December 5, 1978–January 8, 1979. Circulated nationally through May 1983.

Buffalo: Albright-Knox Art Gallery. *American Painting of the 1970s.* December 8, 1978–January 14, 1979. Traveled: Newport Harbor Art Museum, Newport Beach, Calif., February 3–March 18, 1979; Oakland Museum, April 10–May 20, 1979; Cincinnati Art Museum, July 6–August 26, 1979; Art Museum of South Texas, Corpus Christi, September 9–October 29, 1979; Krannert Art Museum, University of Illinois at Urbana-Champaign, November 11, 1979–January 2, 1980.*

New York: The Pace Gallery. *Grids: Format and Image in 20th Century Art.* December 16, 1978–January 20, 1979. Traveled: Akron Art Institute, Akron, Ohio, March 24–May 6, 1979.*

1979

New York: Whitney Museum of American Art. Whitney Biennial. February 6–April 1.*

Boston: The Institute of Contemporary Art. *The Reductive Object.* March 6–April 29.*

Ridgefield, Conn.: Aldrich Museum of Contemporary Art. *The Minimal Tradition.* April 29–September 2.*

Houston: Texas Gallery. *From Allan to Zucker.* August 17–September 28.

New York: Susan Caldwell Gallery. *Generation.*

New York: New Museum of Contemporary Art. *The 1970s: New American Painting.* Circulated internationally June 15, 1979–February 10, 1981.*

1980

St. Paul-de-Vence: Fondation Maeght. *Dessins de la Fondation Maeght.* March 29–May 31.*

London: Wildenstein & Co. *Ten Americans from Pace.* June 18–July 18.*

Düsseldorf: Stadtische Kunsthalle. *Die Sammlung Panza di Biumo.* September 19–October 12. Traveled: Museum für Gegenwartskunst, Basel, November 9, 1980–June 28, 1981.*

Udine: Civici Musei e Gallerie di Storia e Arte. *Arte americana contemporanea.* September 20–November 16.*

Brooklyn, N.Y.: Brooklyn Museum of Art. *American Drawing in Black and White, 1970–1980.* November 22, 1980–January 18, 1981.*

New York: Leo Castelli Gallery. *Drawings to Benefit the Foundation for Contemporary Performance Arts.* November 29–December 20.

1981

London: Royal Academy of Arts. *A New Spirit in Painting.* January 15–March 18.*

New Haven: Yale University Art Gallery. *20 Artists: Yale School of Art, 1950–1970.* January 29–March 29.*
Münster: Westfälischer Kunstverein. *Avantgarden retrospektiv.* February 1–March 22.*
Cleveland: The Cleveland Museum of Art. *Contemporary Artists.* October 21–November 29.*
Munich: Haus der Kunst. *Amerikanische Malerei, 1930–1980.* November 14, 1981–January 31, 1982.*
Calais: Musée des Beaux-Arts de Calais. *De Picasso à Sol LeWitt: 80 dessins du Musée de Grenoble.* November 19, 1981–January 31, 1982.

1982

Stamford, Conn.: Whitney Museum of American Art, Fairfield County. *Surveying the Seventies.* February 12–March 31.*
Claremont, Calif.: Montgomery Art Gallery, Pomona College. *Contemporary Triptychs.* February 27–April 9.
Amsterdam: Stedelijk Museum. *'60–'80: Attitudes/Concepts/Images.* April 9–July 11.*
New York: Whitney Museum of American Art. *Abstract Drawings, 1911–1981.* May 5–July 11.*
Houston: Contemporary Arts Museum. *The Americans: The Collage.* July 11–October 3.*

1983

Long Island City, N.Y.: P.S.1/Institute for Art and Urban Resources. *Abstract Painting, 1960–69.* January 16–March 13.*
New York: Paula Cooper Gallery. *A Painting Exhibition.* January 18–February 23.
New York: Max Hutchison Gallery. *Paint as Image.* January 22–February 19.
Cambridge, Mass.: Hayden Gallery, Massachusetts Institute of Technology. *Affinities: Myron Stout, Bill Jensen, Brice Marden, Terry Winters.* May 7–June 26.*
New York: Whitney Museum of American Art. *Minimalism to Expressionism: Painting and Sculpture since 1965.* June 2–December 4.*
New York: CDS Gallery. *Artists Choose Artists.* June 7–July 16.*
New York: Paula Cooper Gallery. *Mangold, Marden, Ryman.* September 13–October 1.
Fort Worth: Fort Worth Art Museum. *Twentieth Century Drawings.* November 1983–March 1984.
Los Angeles: Museum of Contemporary Art (Temporary Contemporary). *The First Show: Painting and Sculpture from Eight Collections, 1940–1980.* November 20, 1983–February 19, 1984.*
New York: Xavier Fourcade. *In Honor of de Kooning.* December 8, 1983–January 21, 1984.*

1984

Los Angeles: Daniel Weinberg Gallery. *Drawing Conclusions: A Survey of American Drawings, 1958–1983.* January 29–February 26.
Hartford: Wadsworth Atheneum. *The Tremaine Collection: Twentieth- Century Masters.* February 26–April 29.*
La Jolla: La Jolla Museum of Contemporary Art. *American Art Since 1970*, March 10–April 22. Traveled to: Museo Tamayo, Mexico City, May 17–July 29; North Carolina Museum of Art, Raleigh, September 29–November 25; Sheldon Memorial Art Gallery, University of Nebraska, Lincoln, January 12–March 3, 1985; Center for the Fine Arts, Miami, March 30–May 26, 1985. Organized by the Whitney Museum of American Art, New York.*
New York: Galerie Maeght Lelong. *Painting: Philip Guston, Robert Mangold, Brice Marden, Malcolm Morley, Cy Twombly.* March 22–April 27.
Chicago: The Renaissance Society at the University of Chicago. *The Meditative Surface.* April 1–May 16.*
New York: Pratt Manhattan Center, Pratt Institute. *Beauties & Beasts.* April 2–28.*
Paris: Galeries Nationales du Grand Palais. *La Rime et la raison: Les Collections Menil.* April 17–July 30.*
Amsterdam: Stedelijk Museum. *La Grande Parade: Highlights in Painting after 1940.* December 15, 1984–April 15, 1985.*

1985

Tübingen: Kunsthalle Tübingen. *7000 Eichen.* March 2–April 14. Traveled: Kunsthalle Bielefeld, June 2– August 11.*
New York: John Weber Gallery. *Minimal Art: A Survey of Early and Recent Work.* March 9–30.
Pasadena: Baxter Art Gallery, California Institute of Technology. *Painting as Landscape: Views of American Modernism, 1920–1984.* March 13–May 5. Traveled: The Parrish Art Museum, Southampton, N.Y., August 4–September 22.*
Chicago: Museum of Contemporary Art. *Selections from the William J. Hokin Collection.* April 20–June 16.*
Paris: Ecole Nationale Supérieure des Beaux-Arts. *Fifty Years of American Drawing 1930–1980.* May 3–July 13. Traveled: Städtische Galerie, Städelsches Kunstinstitut, Frankfurt, November 28, 1985–January 26, 1986. Organized by The Menil Collection, Houston.*
New York: Condeso/Lawler Gallery. *An Invitational.* June 18–July 27.
New York: Solomon R. Guggenheim Museum. *Painterly Visions, 1940– 1984: The Guggenheim Museum Collection and Major Loans.* June 28–September 3.
Basel: Kunsthalle Basel. *Von Twombly bis Clemente: Ausgewählte Werke einer Privatsammlung.* July 14–September 15.*
New York: Mary Boone Gallery. *Joseph Beuys, Georg Baselitz, Brice Marden.* October 5–26.
Pittsburgh: Carnegie Museum of Art. Carnegie International. November 9, 1985–January 5, 1986.*

1986

Fort Lauderdale, Fla.: Fort Lauderdale Museum of Art. *An American Renaissance: Painting and Sculpture since 1940.* January 12–March 30.*
New York: Janie C. Lee Master Drawings. *Master Drawings, 1918–1985.* Spring.*
New York: New York Studio School. *Drawing with Respect to Painting II.* April 8–May 9.
Long Island City, N.Y.: P.S.1/Institute for Art and Urban Resources. *Images of the Unknown.* April 13–June 15.
New York: Whitney Museum of American Art. *Sacred Images in Secular Art.* May 1–July 13.*
New York: Charles Cowles Gallery. *The Heroic Sublime.* May 31–July 11.
Los Angeles: Museum of Contemporary Art. *The Barry Lowen Collection.* June 16–August 10.*
New York: Whitney Museum of American Art. *Major Acquisitions since 1980: Selected Paintings and a Sculpture.* September 18–November 30.
New York: Luhring, Augustine & Hodes. *Landscape.* October 15–November 15.
Vienna: Galerie nächst St. Stephan Rosemarie Schwarzwälder. *Abstrakte Malerei am Beispiel von drei europäischen und drei amerikanischen Malern.* October 31–December 23.
Wellesley, Mass.: Wellesley College Museum. *1976–1986: Ten Years of Collecting Contemporary American Art. Selections from the Edward R. Downe, Jr. Collection.* November 13, 1986–January 18, 1987.
Los Angeles: Los Angeles County Museum of Art. *The Spiritual in Art: Abstract Painting, 1890–1985.* November 23, 1986–March 8, 1987. Traveled: Museum of Contemporary Art, Chicago, April 17–July 19, 1987; Haags Gemeentemuseum, The Hague, September 1–November 23, 1987.*
Los Angeles: Museum of Contemporary Art. *Individuals: A Selected History of Contemporary Art, 1945–1986.* December 10, 1986–January 10, 1987.*
Bordeaux: capc, Musée d'art contemporain. *Art minimal II: De la surface au plan.* December 12, 1986–February 22, 1987.*

1987

Vienna: Galerie nächst St. Stephan Rosemarie Schwarzwälder. *Werkgruppen: Arbeiten auf Papier.* April 28–June 6.
Chicago: Donald Young Gallery. *Artschwager, Federle, Mangold, Marden, Richter, Ryman.* May 5–30.
London: Anthony d'Offay Gallery. *Works on Paper.* May 5–29.
Houston: The Menil Collection. *The Menil Collection: A Selection from the Paleolithic to the Modern Era.* June 7– .*
New York: Solomon R. Guggenheim Museum. *Fifty Years of Collecting: An Anniversary Selection; Painting since World War II.* November 13, 1987–March 13, 1988.*
New York: Hirschl & Adler Modern. *Lead.* December 3, 1987–January 16, 1988.*

1988

New York: Hirschl & Adler Folk. *Source and Inspiration: A Continuing Tradition.* January 16–February 20.*
Tampere, Finland: Sara Hildén Art Museum. *Amerikkalaista Nykytaidetta.* February 6–April 10. Traveled: Kunstnernes Hus, Oslo, April 23–May 29.*

Lyons: Musée d'Art Contemporain. *La Couleur seule: L'Experience du monochrome.* October 7–December 5.*
Pittsburgh: Carnegie Museum of Art. Carnegie International. November 5, 1988–anuary 22, 1989.*
New York: Leo Castelli Gallery. *The 25th Anniversary Exhibition.* December 8–30. Benefit for the Foundation for Contemporary Performance Arts.

1989

New York: Hirschl & Adler Modern. *Repetition.* February 25–March 25.*
Cologne: Museum Ludwig. *Bilderstreit: Widerspruch, Einheit, und Fragment in der Kunst seit 1960.* April 8–June 28.*
New York: Whitney Museum of American Art. Whitney Biennial. April 26–July 16.*
New York: Hirschl & Adler Modern. *Yves Klein, Brice Marden, Sigmar Polke.* April 29–May 26.*
New York: Tony Shafrazi Gallery. *Don't Bungle the Jungle.* June 3–30. Benefit exhibition.
New York: Lennon, Weinberg. *Works on Paper.* June 13–August 11.
Los Angeles: Daniel Weinberg Gallery. *A Decade of American Drawing, 1980–1989.* July 15–August 26.*
New York: Whitney Museum of American Art. *Art in Place: Fifteen Years of Acquisitions.* July 27–October 22.*
Buffalo: Albright-Knox Art Gallery. *Abstraction, Geometry, Painting: Selected Geometric Abstract Painting in America since 1945.* September 17–November 5. Traveled: Center for the Fine Arts, Miami, December 15, 1989–February 25, 1990; Milwaukee Art Museum, April 1–June 1, 1990; Yale University Art Gallery, New Haven, July 1–August 30, 1990.*
New York: Luhring Augustine Gallery. *Jasper Johns, Brice Marden, Bruce Nauman: Prints from the Seventies.* September 19–October 14.
Brooklyn, N.Y.: Brooklyn Museum of Art. *Projects and Portfolios.* October 6–December 31.

1990

New York: Blum Helman Gallery. *Minimal Art.* January 10–February 10.
New York: Vivian Horan Fine Art. *Seven American Artists.* February 21–March 21.
Paris: Musée du Louvre. *Polyptiques: Le tableau multiple du Moyen Âge au vingtième siècle.* March 27–July 23.*
Vienna: Galerie nächst St. Stephan Rosemarie Schwarzwälder. *Kulturen-Verwandtschaften in Geist und Form.* March 31–May 26.*
New York: Susan Sheehan Gallery. *Minimalist Prints.* May 1–June 29.*
New York: Tony Shafrazi Gallery. *American Masters of the '60s.* May 9–June 23.
New York: Blum Helman Gallery and Germans van Eck Gallery. *Artists for Amnesty.* June 6–16.*
Vienna: Graphische Sammlung Albertina. *Amerikanische Zeichnungen in den achtziger Jahren.* May 16–July 1. Traveled: Städtisches Museum Leverkusen Schloss Morsbroich, Leverkusen, September 12–November 4.*
Osaka: National Museum of Art. *Minimal Art.* October 6–November 25.*
Tourcoing, France: Musée des Beaux-Arts. *La Diaphane: Une Reflection, une collection, une exposition, un lieu.* November 24, 1990–February 2, 1991.
New York: David Nolan Gallery. *An Overview of Drawing.* December 15, 1990–January 26, 1991.
Liestal, Switzerland: Kunsthalle Palazzo. *Brice Marden, Samuel Buri, Ernst Messerli: Projekte für das Basler Münster.* December 15, 1990–February 9, 1991.*

1991

New York: Wolff Gallery. *Strategies for the Next Painting.* January 8–February 9. Traveled: Feigen Gallery, Chicago, February 23–March 30.
New York: Lorence-Monk Gallery. *Dead Heroes, Disfigured Love.* February 2–23.
Vienna: Museum Moderner Kunst Stiftung Ludwig. *Die Sammlung Marzona: Arte Povera, Minimal Art, Concept Art, Land Art.* February 18–April 8.
New York: Matthew Marks Gallery. *Artists' Sketchbooks.* March 20–May 4.*
New York: Janie C. Lee Gallery/Kate Ganz Limited. *Master Drawings, 1520–1990.* April 13–May 11.*
Andover, Mass.: Addison Gallery of American Art. *American Abstraction at the Addison.* April 18–July 31.*
Vienna: Museum des 20. Jahrhunderts. *Bildlicht: Malerei zwischen Material und Immaterialitat.* May 2–July 7.
Mexico City: Centro Cultural de Arte Contemporáneo. *20th Century Collage.* June 13–August 31. Traveled: Musée d'art contemporain, Nice, September 27–November 11.*
New York: Paula Cooper Gallery and Matthew Marks Gallery. *Benefit Exhibition for ACT-UP.* December 5–21.

1992

Vienna: Galerie nächst St. Stephan Rosemarie Schwarzwälder. *Abstrakte Malerei zwischen Analyse und Synthese.* January 24–March 18.*
New York: The Museum of Modern Art. *Allegories of Modernism: Contemporary Drawing.* February 16–May 5.*
Baltimore: Baltimore Museum of Art. *Marking the Decades: Prints, 1960–1990.* February 23–April 20.
Los Angeles: Margo Leavin Gallery. *Jasper Johns, Brice Marden, Terry Winters: Drawings.* April 11–May 16.*
Long Island City, N.Y.: P.S.1/Institute for Art and Urban Resources. *Slow Art: Painting in New York Now.* April 26–June 21.
Kassel: Documenta IX. June 13–September 20.*
Palo Alto, Calif.: Stanford Art Gallery, Stanford University. *The Anderson Print Collection.* August 11–December 13.

1993

Palo Alto, Calif.: Palo Alto Cultural Center. *Directions in Bay Area Printing: Three Decades.* January.
Los Angeles: Daniel Weinberg Gallery. *Twenty Years: A Series of Anniversary Exhibitions, Part I.* April 14–June 12.
New Haven: Yale University Art Gallery. *Yale Collects Yale, 1950–1993.* April 30–July 31.*
Venice: Peggy Guggenheim Collection. *Drawing the Line against AIDS.* June 8–13. An exhibition in conjunction with Art against AIDS Venezia under the aegis of the 45th Venice Biennale.*
Berlin: Martin-Gropius-Bau. *American Art in the 20th Century: Painting and Sculpture, 1913–1993.* May 8–July 25. Traveled: Royal Academy of Arts, London, September 16–December 12.*
New York: John Weber Gallery. *Early Minimalist Masterworks.* September 1–October 9.
Ridgefield, Conn.: Aldrich Museum of Contemporary Art. *Timely and Timeless.* October 10, 1993–January 9, 1994.

1994

New York: Marlborough Graphics. *Metamorphosis: Surrealism to Organic Abstraction.* January 12–March 5.
Aspen, Colo.: Aspen Art Museum. *The Shaman as Artist, the Artist as Shaman.* February 10–April 10.*
Chicago: Museum of Contemporary Art. *Under Development: Dreaming the MCA's Collection.* April 30–August 28.
New York: Solomon R. Guggenheim Museum. *The Tradition of the New: Postwar Masterpieces from the Guggenheim Collection.* May 20–September 11.
Washington, D.C.: National Gallery of Art. *From Minimal to Conceptual Art: Works from the Dorothy and Herbert Vogel Collection.* May 29–November 27.*
New York: Robert Miller Gallery. *Abstract Works on Paper.* July 19–August 24.
New York: Luhring Augustine Gallery. *The Ossuary.* February 19–March 19.

1995

San Francisco: John Berggruen Gallery. *XXV Years.* January 13–February 25.*
Helsinki: Museum of Contemporary Art. *Private/Public: ARS '95 Helsinki.* February 2–May 28.*
Chicago: Art Institute of Chicago. *About Place: Recent Art from the Americas.* March 11–May 21.*
New York: Whitney Museum of American Art. Whitney Biennial. March 23–June 4.*
Paris: Musée national d'art moderne, Centre national d'art et de culture Georges Pompidou. *Du trait à la ligne.* April 26–June 19.
Aspen, Colo.: Aspen Art Museum. *Contemporary Drawing: Exploring the Territory.* July 27–September 24.*
Münster: Westfälisches Landesmuseum für Kunst und Kulturgeschichte. *"Zu Ende gezeichnet": Bildhafte Zeichnungen von der Zeit Dürers und Holbeins bis zur Gegenwart; Meisterwerke aus dem Kupferstichkabinett Basel.* September 10–November 5.
Los Angeles: Margo Leavin Gallery. *25 Years: An Exhibition of Selected Works.* September 22–October 28.*
Tokyo: Museum of Contemporary Art. *Revolution: Art of the Sixties from Warhol to Beuys.* September 30–December 10.*

New York: The Museum of Modern Art. *From the Collection: Abstraction Pure and Impure.* October 20, 1995–May 21, 1996.*

Tokyo: National Museum of Modern Art. *Painting—Singular Object: A Perspective on Contemporary Art.* November 3–December 17. Traveled: National Museum of Modern Art, Kyoto, January 5–February 12, 1996.*

New York: Littlejohn Contemporary. *An Accumulation of Supple Solids. . . .* December 5, 1995–January 20, 1996.

Montreal: Saidye Bronfman Centre for the Arts. *Diary of a Human Hand.* December 7, 1995–January 19, 1996. Traveled: Center for Curatorial Studies, Bard College, Annandale-on-Hudson, N.Y., March 16–31, 1996.

St. Gallen: Kunstmuseum St. Gallen. *Colour and Paint.* December 9, 1995–February 18, 1996.

1996

New York: Solomon R. Guggenheim Museum. *Abstraction in the Twentieth Century: Total Risk, Freedom, Discipline.* February 9–May 12.*

Washington, D.C.: National Gallery of Art. *The Robert and Jane Meyerhoff Collection, 1945 to 1995.* March 31–July 21.*

New York: Peter Blum Gallery. *In Quest of the Absolute.* April 6–June 8.*

New York: The Museum of Modern Art. *Thinking Print: Books to Billboards, 1980–95.* June 20–September 10.*

Chicago: Museum of Contemporary Art. *In the Shadow of Storms: Art in the Postwar Era from the MCA Collection.* July 2, 1996–May 25, 1997.*

Sakura, Japan: Kawamura Memorial Art Museum. *Innovation.* September 14–November 4.*

Paris: Musée national d'art moderne/Centre de création industrielle, Centre national d'art et de culture Georges Pompidou. *Dessins: Acquisitions, 1992–1996.* October 9, 1996–January 6, 1997.*

Hamburg: Kunsthaus Hamburg. *Holländisches Bad: Radierungen. Zur Renaissance einer Technik.* October 15–November 17. Traveled: Brecht-Haus Weissensee, Berlin, March 18–April 20, 1997.*

Paris: Centre national d'art et de culture Georges Pompidou. *De Beuys à Trockel: Dessins contemporains du Kunstmuseum de Bâle.* July 10–September 30.

1997

Basel: Kunstmuseum Basel. *Die Sammlung Anne-Marie und Ernst Vischer-Wadler: Ein Vermachtnis.* January 11–March 9.*

New York: Susan Sheehan Gallery. *Judd, Marden, Ryman: Prints.* March 11–April 19.

Vienna: Galerie nächst St. Stephan Rosemarie Schwarzwälder. *Von Farben und Papieren.* April 8–May 10.

Washington, D.C.: National Gallery of Art. *Thirty-five Years at Crown Point Press: Making Prints, Doing Art.* June 8–September 1. Traveled: Palace of the Legion of Honor, San Francisco, October 4, 1997–January 4, 1998.*

Venice, Italy: Venice Biennale. *Futuro, Presente, Passato.* June 15–November 9.*

New York: Robert Miller Gallery. *Affinities with the East.* June 24–August 1.

Chapel Hill: Ackland Art Museum, University of North Carolina at Chapel Hill. *Geometric Abstraction.* August 6–October 26.

Paris: American Ambassador's Residence. *American Artists in the American Ambassador's Residence in Paris.* September 25–December 17, 1999.*

New York: The Museum of Modern Art. *On the Edge: Contemporary Art From the Werner and Elaine Dannheiser Collection.* September 30, 1997–January 20, 1998.*

New York: C & M Arts. *American Works, 1945–1975.* October 8–December 6.*

San Francisco: Haines Gallery. *Obsession + Devotion.* October 15–November 15.

New York: Gina Fiore Salon of Fine Arts. *State of the Gesture: Bishop, Krasner, Marden, Pollock, Brennan, Kreshtool, Lundsager, Tsao.* October 17–December 29.

Bilbao: Guggenheim Museum. *Los museos Guggenheim y el arte de este Siglo.* October 18, 1997–April 5, 1998.

Cambridge, Mass.: Arthur M. Sackler Museum, Harvard University. *Drawing Is Another Kind of Language: Recent American Drawings from a New York Private Collection.* December 12, 1997–February 22, 1998. Traveled: Kupferstichkabinett der Akademie der bildenden Künste Wien, Vienna, June 17–July 30, 1998; Kunstmuseum Winterthur, September 4–November 15, 1998; Kunstmuseum Ahlen, Germany, December 6, 1998–January 31, 1999; Akademie der Künste, Berlin, February 19–April 25, 1999; Fonds régional d'art contemporain de Picardie and Musée de Picardie, Amiens, May 21–August 15, 1999; The Parrish Art Museum, Southampton, N.Y., September 26–November 13, 1999; Lyman Allyn Art Museum, New London, Conn., January 7–March 12, 2000; Block Museum of Art, Northwestern University, Evanston, Ill., September 23–December 10, 2000; The Contemporary Museum, Honolulu, April 20–June 10, 2001.*

1998

New Haven: Yale University Art Gallery. *Then and Now: Art since 1945 at Yale.* February 10–August 1.*

Yokohama: Yokohama Museum of Art. *La Collection Yvon Lambert.* April 11–June 21.*

New York: Mitchell-Innes & Nash. *Master Drawings of the 20th Century.* May 5–June 5.*

New York: The Museum of Modern Art. *Elements of the Natural, 1950–1992: Selections from the Drawings Collection.* May 7–August 25.

New York: Matthew Marks Gallery. *Painting Now and Forever, Part I.* June 25–July 31.

Nîmes: Musée d'Art Contemporain. *Au fil du trait: De Matisse à Basquiat.* June 26–September 27.*

1999

New York: Matthew Marks Gallery. *January 1999.* January.

Cleveland: The Cleveland Museum of Art. *Modern Masterworks on Paper from the Israel Museum, Jerusalem.* June 13–August 29.*

Houston: The Museum of Fine Arts. *Forty Years of the Chase Manhattan Collection: Art at Work.* March 3–May 2.*

New York: The Drawing Center. *Drawn from Artists' Collections.* April 24–June 12. Traveled: Armand Hammer Museum of Art and Cultural Center, University of California, Los Angeles, July 13–September 26.*

Montclair, N.J.: Montclair Art Museum. *Waxing Poetic: Encaustic Art in America.* May 23–August 15. Traveled: Knoxville Museum of Art, Tenn., September 24, 1999–January 9, 2000.*

New York: Matthew Marks Gallery. *Group Show.* September 25–November 27.

New York: Whitney Museum of American Art. *The American Century: Art & Culture, 1900–2000. Part II.* September 26, 1999–February 13, 2000.*

Los Angeles: Daniel Weinberg Gallery. *One by Four: Drawings by Brice Marden, James Siena, Myron Stout, Terry Winters.* November, 12, 1999–January 8, 2000.

Greensboro: Weatherspoon Art Gallery, University of North Carolina. *Highlights from the Dillard Collection of Art on Paper.* November 14, 1999–January 23, 2000.*

2000

Stockholm: Moderna Museet. *In the Power of Painting: A Selection from the Daros Collection.* February 5–March 26.*

Chicago: Museum of Contemporary Art. *Age of Influence: Reflections in the Mirror of American Culture.* April 8–June 4.

Lucerne: Neues Kunstmuseum. *Mixing Memory and Desire.* June 20–September 24.*

Cambridge, Mass.: Arthur M. Sackler Museum, Harvard University. *A Decade of Collecting: Recent Acquisitions of Prints and Drawings, 1940–2000.* June 3–August 27.

New York: Barbara Gladstone Gallery. *00.* July 8–September 2.*

Bilbao: Guggenheim Museum. *Changing Perceptions: The Panza Collection at the Guggenheim Collection.* November 16, 2000–January 28, 2001.*

Winterthur: Kunstmuseum Winterthur. *Von Edgar Degas bis Gerhard Richter: Arbeiten auf Papier aus der Sammlung des Kunstmuseums Winterthur.* August 8–November 19. Traveled: Národní Galerie, Prague, December 15, 2000–March 25, 2001; Rupertinum, Salzburg, April 5–May 20, 2001; Westfälisches Landesmuseum für Kunst und Kulturgeschichte, Münster, June 3–August 26, 2001.*

2001

San Francisco: John Berggruen Gallery. *Prints by Lucian Freud and Brice Marden.* February 1–March 3.

New York: The Museum of Modern Art. *Collaborations with Parkett, 1984 to Now.* May 4–June 5.

San Francisco: San Francisco Museum of Modern Art. *Points of Departure.* May 23–September 16.

Basel: Fondation Beyeler. *Ornament and Abstraction.* June 10–September 23.*

Avignon: Musée d'art contemporain, Collection Lambert en Avignon. *Artists' Collections.* July 1–October 30.*

Hydra, Greece: First Public School of Hydra. *Auras and Epitaphs.* July 14–September 3.*

Hanover, N.H.: Dartmouth College. *Works on Paper: Richmond Burton, Brice Marden, and Agnes Martin.* September 26–October 22.

New Haven: Holcombe T. Green Jr. Hall, Yale University. *Alumni Choice: An Exhibition of Works on Paper.* October 1–28.

New York: The Painting Center. *Repetition in Discourse*. October 2–27.
New York: Matthew Marks Gallery. *Tenth Anniversary Exhibition: 100 Drawings and Photographs.* November 2–December 22.*
Portland, Ore.: Savage Gallery. *Bryan Hunt, Brice Marden.* November 2–December 22.
Washington, D.C.: National Gallery of Art. *A Century of Drawing: Works on Paper from Degas to LeWitt*. November 18, 2001–April 7, 2002.*

2002

New York: Chambers Fine Art. *Rocks and Art: Nature Found and Made.* January 17–March 9.
Boston: Boston University Art Gallery, Boston University. *Looking East: Brice Marden, Michael Mazur, and Pat Steir.* January 18–February 24.*
Basel: Kunstmuseum Basel. *Painting on the Move: A Century of Contemporary Painting (1900–2000).* May 26–September 8.*
Chicago: Museum of Contemporary Art. *Life, Death, Love, Hate, Pleasure, Pain: Selected Works from the Museum of Contemporary Art, Chicago, Collection.* November 16, 2002–April 20, 2003.*
Champaign: Krannert Art Museum, University of Illinois at Urbana-Champaign. *Drawings of Choice from a New York Collection.* September 4–November 3. Traveled: Arkansas Arts Center, Little Rock, November 14, 2002–February 2, 2003; Georgia Museum of Art, University of Georgia, Athens, Ga., February 11–March 23, 2003; Bowdoin College Museum of Art, Brunswick, Me., April 10–June 8, 2003; Cincinnati Art Museum, August 22–November 16, 2003.*

2003

San Francisco: Fraenkel Gallery. *Not Exactly Photographs.* March 6–April 26.
New York: The Drawing Center. *The Stage of Drawing: Gesture and Act. Selected from the Tate Collection.* April 5–May 31. Traveled: Museum of Contemporary Art, Sydney, June 18–August; Tate Gallery Liverpool, September 26, 2003–March 28, 2004.*
Amsterdam: Van Gogh Museum. *Van Gogh Modern: Vincent van Gogh and Contemporary Art.* June 27–December 10.

2004

New York: Solomon R. Guggenheim Museum. *Singular Forms (Sometimes Repeated): Art from 1951 to the Present.* March 5–May 19.*
Los Angeles: Museum of Contemporary Art. *A Minimalist Future: Art as Object, 1958–1968.* March 14–August 2.*
Tokyo: Mori Art Museum. *Continuity and Change in Art, 1880 to the Present: Highlights from The Museum of Modern Art.* April 28–August 1. Organized by The Museum of Modern Art, New York, in collaboration with the Mori Art Museum.*
London: The British Museum. *Matisse to Freud: A Critic's Choice. The Alexander Walker Bequest.* June 15, 2004–January 9, 2005.

2005

Vienna: BA-CA Kunstforum. *Willem de Kooning.* January 13–March 28. Traveled: Kunsthal Rotterdam, April 16–July 3.
London: Gagosian Gallery. *Imageless Icons: Abstract Thoughts.* February 3–March 26.
New York: The Museum of Modern Art. *Contemporary Voices: Works from The UBS Art Collection*. February 4–April 25.*
New York: The Museum of Modern Art. *Drawings from the Modern, 1945–1975.* March 30–August 29.*
New York: Whitney Museum of American Art. *Building and Breaking the Grid.* September 1, 2005–January 8, 2006.
New York: Senior & Shopmaker Gallery. *Early Prints by Robert Mangold, Brice Marden, Joan Mitchell.* September 22–December 3.
Los Angeles: Daniel Weinberg Gallery. *Drawings.* November 12–December 23.

2006

New York: The Museum of Modern Art. *Transforming Chronologies: An Atlas of Drawings, Part One.* January 26–April 24.*
Paris: Musée d'Orsay. *Correspondance—Brice Marden/Gustave Courbet*. January 31–April 30.

Photograph Credits

All works by Brice Marden © 2006 Brice Marden/Artists Rights Society (ARS), New York.

Unless otherwise noted, all images of works by Brice Marden are courtesy the artist and Matthew Marks Gallery, New York, photographs by Bill Jacobson.

© Roland Aellig: p. 224.

Thomas Ammann Fine Art, Zurich: pp. 151, 214.

Barbara Annis Fine Art, New York: p. 163.

© The Art Institute of Chicago: p. 155. Photograph Tom Vinetz: p. 165.

The Baltimore Museum of Art: p. 77.

Sylvan Barnet and William Burto: p. 89, fig. 13.

Benjamin Blackwell: p. 180, plate 50; pp. 184, 207, 216.

© The Blanton Museum of Art, The University of Texas at Austin. Photograph Rick Hall: p. 157.

CNAC/MNAM/Dist. Réunion des Musées Nationaux/Art Resource, N.Y.: p. 205.

© Copper Canyon Press: p. 87, fig. 9.

Daros Collection, Switzerland: pp. 194, 195, 215, 222, 249.

Stan Dart, Associate Professor of Geography, University of Nebraska at Kearney. Published in *A Prairie Mosaic: An Atlas of Central Nebraska's Land, Culture, and Nature*. Eds. Steven J. Rothenberger and Susanne George-Bloomfield. Kearney: University of Nebraska at Kearney, 2000: p. 64, fig. 28.

Davis Museum and Cultural Center, Wellesley College, Wellesley, Mass. Photograph Steve Briggs: p. 86, fig. 8.

Photo © D. James Dee: pp. 168, 245.

Eskenazi Ltd.: p. 93, fig 17.

David Geffen. © 2006 Jasper Johns/Licensed by VAGA, New York: p. 15, fig. 6. © 2006 Pollock-Krasner Foundation/Artists Rights Society (ARS), New York: p. 59.

Solomon R. Guggenheim Museum, New York: p. 51, fig. 19. Kathryn Carr: pp. 159, 171, 178. © 2006 Pollock-Krasner Foundation/Artists Rights Society (ARS), New York: p. 115, fig. 8.

Mark Gulezian: p. 199.

Christa Haiml: p. 115, fig. 6.

Hirshhorn Museum and Sculpture Garden, Smithsonian Institution, Washington, D.C. Photograph Lee Stalsworth: p. 235.

Kemin Hu: p. 94.

© International Center of Photography, New York. David Seidner Archive: p. 297 right.

Maggie Keswick, from her book *The Chinese Garden: History, Art and Architecture*, Harvard University Press, 3rd ed., 2003: p. 97, fig. 23.

© 2006 The Franz Kline Estate/Artists Rights Society (ARS), New York. Photograph © Christie's Images Ltd. 2003: p. 48, fig. 14.

Sarah-Ann and Werner H. Kramarsky. Photograph Peter Muscato: p. 39, fig. 5.

Krantz Studios, Omaha: p. 209.

Courtesy Brice Marden: p. 14, fig. 5; pp. 127–29, 288, 290, 291, 293, 294, 295, 298 top.

Courtesy Brice Marden. Photograph © 1999 Sidney B. Felsen: p. 298 bottom.

Courtesy Brice Marden. Photograph Bill Jacobson: pp. 296, 297 left.

Courtesy Brice Marden. Photograph Mirabelle Marden: p. 299.

Matthew Marks Gallery, New York. Photograph Bill Jacobson, © 2006 Robert Mangold/Artists Rights Society (ARS), New York: p. 53, fig. 21. Photograph Oren Slor: p. 104.

Neal Meltzer Fine Art: pp. 170, 206.

Menil Archives, The Menil Collection, Houston: p. 114, fig. 4; p. 116.

The Menil Collection, Houston. Photograph Hickey and Robertson, Houston: pp. 188, 189.

Mitchell-Innes & Nash, New York: pp. 172, 73, 174, 175.

Mugrabi Collection: p. 45.

© Museum of Contemporary Art, Chicago. Photograph Joe Ziolkowski: p. 179.

The Museum of Contemporary Art, Los Angeles. Photograph Squidds and Nunns: p. 187.

© 2006 Museum of Fine Arts, Boston: p. 13; p. 42, fig. 8.

The Museum of Modern Art, New York, Digital Imaging Studio. Photograph David Allison: pp. 182; 183, plates 55, 56, 59. Photograph Tom Griesel: pp. 53, fig. 20; 63; 64, fig. 27; 65; 87, fig. 9; 141; 154; 233. Photograph Kate Keller, © 2006 Mondrian/Holtzman Trust c/o HCR International Warrenton, Va.: p. 20, fig. 10. Photograph Kate Keller, © 2006 Pollock-Krasner Foundation/Artists Rights Society (ARS), New York: p. 24. Photograph Paige Knight, © 2006 Artists Rights Society (ARS), New York/ADAGP, Paris: p. 15, fig. 7. Photograph Paige Knight, © Sigmar Polke: p. 22, fig. 12. Photograph Paige Knight: pp. 43, fig. 10; 253. Photograph Jonathan Muzikar, © Helen Dickinson Baldwin: p. 30, fig. 2. Photograph Mali Olatunji, © 2006 The Willem de Kooning Foundation/Artists Rights Society (ARS), New York: p. 60, fig. 23. Photograph John Wronn, © 2006 The Willem de Kooning Foundation/Artists Rights Society (ARS), New York: p. 23. Photograph John Wronn, © 2006 Ellsworth Kelly: p. 100. Photograph John Wronn: pp. 86, fig. 7; 176; 242. Scanning services: pp. 288, 290, 291, 295, 296, 297 left, 298, 299.

The Museum of Modern Art, New York. Photograph Esther Adler: p. 113.

The Museum of Modern Art, New York. Photograph Corey D'Augustine: p. 122.

© National Gallery of Canada, Ottawa: p. 161.

National Palace Museum, Taiwan, Republic of China: p. 89, fig. 14.

© 2006 Barnett Newman Foundation/Artists Rights Society (ARS), New York: p. 19, fig. 9.

Ovitz Family Collection, Los Angeles. Courtesy PaceWildenstein: p. 101.

PaceWildenstein, New York. Photograph Ellen Page Wilson: p. 196.

© Douglas M. Parker, Los Angeles: p. 236.

© 2006 Pollock-Krasner Foundation/Artists Rights Society (ARS), New York: p. 99. Photograph © Tate, London 2006: p. 91.

Pierre Rambach. Photograph Christian Poite: p. 80.

Private collection, Houston: p. 139, plate 10.

Private collection, Los Angeles: p. 30, fig. 1.

Private collection, San Francisco/Matthew Marks Gallery, New York: p. 36, fig. 3.

Ian Reeves: p. 177.

Reproduced as sheet 7 of Untitled Work Book 30 in Dieter Schwarz and Michael Semff, *Brice Marden, Work Books: 1964–1995*, Düsseldorf: Richter, 1997: p. 88, fig. 12.

Réunion des Musées Nationaux/Art Resource, N.Y. Photograph Hervé Lewandowski: p. 44, fig. 11.

© Rijksmuseum Amsterdam: p. 12.

The Rothko Chapel. Photograph Hickey and Robertson, Houston: p. 114, fig. 5.

San Francisco Museum of Modern Art. Photograph Ben Blackwell: p. 145.

State Hermitage Museum, Saint Petersburg. © 2006 Succession H. Matisse, Paris/Artists Rights Society (ARS), New York: p. 22, fig. 13.

Stedelijk Museum, Amsterdam: pp. 191, 193.

Michael Tropea: p. 132, plate 3; p. 238, plate 126.

© 1977 Tuckernuck Productions. *Brice Marden*, directed by Edgar B. Howard and Theodore R. Haimes, available through the Checkerboard Film Foundation, New York, courtesy Edgar B. Howard: p. 43, fig. 9.

Untitled Press, Inc. Photograph Geoffrey Clements: p. 150.

© Virginia Museum of Fine Arts: p. 197.

Walker Art Center, Minneapolis. © 2006 Barnett Newman Foundation/Artists Rights Society (ARS), New York: p. 44, fig. 12.

Joshua M. White: p. 180, plate 51.

© Whitney Museum of American Art, New York. Photograph Robert E. Mates, N.J., © 2006 Jasper Johns/Licensed by VAGA, New York: p. 115, fig. 7. Geoffrey Clements: p. 206, plate 85. Photograph © Steven Sloman, New York, 1990: p. 167.

In reproducing the images contained in this publication, the Museum obtained the permission of the rights holders whenever possible. In those instances where the Museum could not locate the rights holders, notwithstanding good-faith efforts, it requests that any contact information concerning such rights holders be forwarded, so that they may be contacted for future editions.

Index of Plates

Lenders to the Exhibition

Stedelijk Museum, Amsterdam
The Blanton Museum of Art, The University of Texas at Austin
Kunstmuseum Basel, Kupferstichkabinett
The Art Institute of Chicago
Museum of Contemporary Art, Chicago
The Menil Collection, Houston
The Museum of Contemporary Art, Los Angeles
The Museum of Modern Art, New York
Solomon R. Guggenheim Museum, New York
Whitney Museum of American Art, New York
National Gallery of Canada, Ottawa
Musée national d'art moderne, Centre Pompidou, Paris
San Francisco Museum of Modern Art
Hirshhorn Museum and Sculpture Garden, Smithsonian Institution, Washington, D.C.

Anne Anka, Los Angeles
Frances F. Bowes
Donald L. Bryant Jr. Family Trust
Colección Patricia Phelps de Cisneros, Caracas
Ed Cohen
Douglas S. Cramer
Daros Collection, Switzerland
Froehlich Collection, Stuttgart
Kathy and Richard S. Fuld, Jr.
Agnes Gund Collection
Richard and Betty Hedreen
Jasper Johns
Klaus Kertess
Uli Knecht, Stuttgart
Sarah-Ann and Werner H. Kramarsky
Marie-Josée and Henry R. Kravis
Linda and Harry Macklowe
Brice Marden
Helen Harrington Marden
Melia Marden
Mirabelle Marden
Matthew Marks, New York
Robert Mangold and Sylvia Plimack Mangold
Susan and Larry Marx, Aspen. Courtesy Neal Meltzer Fine Art
Robert and Jane Meyerhoff Collection, Phoenix, Maryland
Peter Morton, Los Angeles
Judith Neisser
John and Mary Pappajohn
Robert Rauschenberg
Dorothea Rockburne
Keith and Kathy Sachs
Phil Schrager, Omaha
Georg and Patsy von Segesser
Åke Skeppner. Courtesy Thomas Ammann Fine Art, Zurich
Stenn Family Collection, Chicago
Dorie Sternberg
Jennifer and David Stockman
Roselyne Chroman Swig
Paul F. Walter
Mr. and Mrs. Michael Wilsey

Anonymous lenders

An anonymous lender, courtesy Barbara Annis Fine Art, New York
An anonymous lender, courtesy Thomas Ammann Fine Art, Zurich
An anonymous lender, courtesy Matthew Marks Gallery, New York
An anonymous lender, courtesy PaceWildenstein, New York
Courtesy Locksley Shea Gallery, Minneapolis

Trustees of The Museum of Modern Art